W9-AVO-698

Expert Health Advice

by

MATTHEW LESKO

with

Mary Ann Martello

Publicity: Debbie Samson

Production: Meserve Associates, Inc.

Production Designer: Beth Meserve

Cover Design: Lester Zaiontz

FIRST EDITION

Library of Congress Cataloging-in-Publication Date
    Lesko, Matthew
    Martello, Mary Ann

Expert Health Advice
ISBN #1-878346-42-3 (paperback)

Other books written by Matthew Lesko:

Lesko's Info-Power III

Government Giveaways for Entrepreneurs III

Info-Fobia: How To Survive In An Information Society

Free Legal Help

Free Health Care

Everything You Need To Run A Business At Home

Discounts For Seniors

Free Stuff For Seniors

Free Money to Change Your Life

Seniors' Yellow Pages

For information on any of Matthew Lesko's publications, call 1-800-UNCLE-SAM; or contact his website: www.lesko.com.

Table of Contents

Introduction

Health care practitioners barely have enough time to care for their patients, let alone keep up on the mountains of information, data, and studies that are generated daily by health care researchers. The government alone spends over 10 billion dollars a year to conduct health research. How can you get the latest, up-to-date information on any health topic? You can call the government. You have access to the best information and the top doctors in every health care field in this country. And what is nice is that none of this will cost you a dime. You have already paid for it with your tax dollars, and now it is yours for the asking.

We all have heard that there is no such thing as a dumb question. So why, when the doctor asks us if we have any questions, do most of us just freeze? When the doctor is telling you about your new diagnosis, does it seem that he is using words only other doctors understand? Often doctors have waiting rooms filled with patients, so they may not have the time to fully explain your condition. Here is your chance to read about your health issues, and the best part is that these chapters are written in an easy to understand format. You don't need a medical dictionary or a degree to comprehend them. In many cases, the words your doctor uses that you may have trouble understanding are defined for you. Now when your doctor talks to you, you will know what he is really talking about. Here is your chance to learn more about hundreds of different health conditions and treatment options. Many of the chapters in this book also provide you with a list of questions to ask your doctor, so that you can take a more active role in your ongoing medical treatment.

Studies show that doctors tend to have a certain method in treating different conditions. How do you know what is the best way for you? Remember, this is your body and you make the ultimate decisions. By examining your treatment options and asking your doctor specific questions, you can choose the treatment that is right for you. Also, organizations and associations are included in this book where you can discover the latest research or support groups available so that you need not face your problems alone.

Although this book is loaded with answers to thousands of your health related questions, it can't possibly cover everything. So if you don't get your questions answered from reading a specific chapter, you can contact the organizations listed for further expert advice. If you're not sure how to approach these organizations, don't worry. Just call. You'll see that they are human, real people with the ability to help, just like you and me.

These contacts can also be used to identify any additional remedies or discoveries that have been found since the publication of this book. This is very important in today's world. Our fast changing information society actually makes this book out of date as soon as it is printed. The answers to your health related questions can be changing right now as you read this book. So to find out what's new, you can contact these sources, and they can tell you what new information will be included in books due for publication next year.

Eliminate much of your fear of disease and illness through the power of information. You are on your way to improved health by becoming a more informed health consumer, and in doing so, taking an active role in your individual destiny.

Matthew Lesko

Accident Prevention[*]

Accidents seldom "just happen," and many can be prevented. Because accidental injuries occur more often in later life and result in more serious injuries, attention to safety is especially important for older people.

Older people have more accidents due to poor eyesight and hearing. In addition, arthritis, neurological diseases, and balance problems can make older people unsteady.

Various diseases, medications, and alcohol or preoccupation with personal problems can result in drowsiness or distraction. Mishaps can also be the result of mental depression or poor physical condition.

When accidents occur, older people are often severely injured and tend to heal slowly. Particularly in white women, bones can become thin and brittle with age, causing minor falls that result in broken hips.

Many accidents can be prevented by staying in good mental and physical health and by improving safety habits.

Falls are the most common cause of fatal injury in older people. Here's what you can do to avoid them:

- Light all stairways. Put light switches at both the bottom and top of stairs.
- Use bedside remote-control light switches or night lights.
- Be sure both sides of stairways have sturdy handrails.
- Tack down carpeting on stairs and use nonskid treads.
- Remove throw rugs that tend to slide.
- Arrange furniture and other objects so they are not obstacles.

---

[*] Source: *Age Page*, National Institute on Aging, U.S. Department of Health and Human Services, Public Health Service, National Institutes of Health, Gaithersburg, MD 20898; 800-222-2225.

- Use grab bars on bathroom walls and nonskid mats or strips in the bathtub.
- Keep outdoor steps and walkways in good repair.

Personal health is also important in preventing falls. Because older people tend to become faint or dizzy when standing too quickly, experts recommend rising slowly from a sitting or lying position. Both illness and the side effects of medicines increase the risk of falls.

Burns are especially disabling to older people, and recovery from such injuries is slow. Here's what you can do to prevent burns and fires:

- Never smoke in bed or when drowsy.
- When cooking, don't wear loosely fitting or flammable clothing. Bathrobes, nightgowns, and pajamas catch fire.
- Set water heater thermostats or faucets so that water does not scald the skin.
- Plan which emergency exits to use in case of fire.
- Use caution with all appliances, especially space heaters.

Many older people trap themselves behind door locks that are hard to open during an emergency. Install one good lock that can be opened from the inside quickly, rather than many inexpensive locks.

Motor vehicle accidents are the most common cause of accidental death among the 65 to 74 age group, and the second most common cause among older people in general. Your ability to drive may be impaired by such age-related changes as reduced side vision, poor night vision, and slower reaction time. You can compensate for some of these changes by driving on familiar roads, avoiding driving at night, and planning routes which have no left turns at busy intersections. Use caution when parking and, if possible, park the car so that you rarely have to back it up. Always wear your safety belt when in the car.

As a pedestrian, take plenty of time when crossing the road, especially in bad weather; use crosswalks where they are available; and plan your route to choose the fewest number of road crossings at the safest places. Be especially wary of crossing at traffic lights where right turns against the red are permitted.

Older people are encouraged to use public transportation. If you ride on public transportation:

- Stay alert and brace yourself when a bus is slowing down or turning.
- Watch for slippery pavement and other hazards when entering or leaving any vehicle.
- Have fare ready to prevent losing your balance while fumbling for change.
- Do not carry too many packages and leave one hand free to grasp railings.

People over age 65 make up about 12 percent of the population and suffer 27 percent of all accidental deaths. The National Safety Council reports that each year about 27,000 persons over 65 die from accidental injuries and thousands of others are severely injured. Attention to safety can prevent much disability, especially important in later life, and untimely death.

Resources

For more information on how to reduce the chance of falling, see the *Age Page* "Preventing Falls and Fractures." For this *Age Page* and other information on aging, write to the NIA Information Center, P.O. Box 8057, Gaithersburg, MD 20898-8057; 800-222-2225, 800-222-4225 (TTY).

The National Safety Council offers classes on driving defensively. For information on courses in your area, write to the National Safety Council, 444 North Michigan Avenue, Chicago, IL 60611.

The American Automobile Association has the Mature Operator Program for people 55 years of age and over. Contact your local AAA office and ask if the program is being offered in your area, or write to the AAA Foundation for Traffic Safety, 1730 M Street, NW, Suite 401, Washington, DC 20036.

The American Association of Retired Persons offers the 55 Alive/Mature Driving program. Write to the AARP, Traffic and Driver Safety Program, 1909 K Street, NW, Washington, DC 20049.

AIDS Prevention Guide:
The Facts About HIV Infection And AIDS[*]

What Is HIV Infection?
And What Is AIDS?

Young People Do Get AIDS
Many people think that young people don't get AIDS. That's not true. AIDS can affect anyone of any age, of any ethnic or racial background, who engages in behavior with an infected person that can transmit HIV, the virus that causes AIDS.

As of December 1993, nearly 68,000 people aged 20-29 have been diagnosed with AIDS. Because a person can be infected with the virus that causes AIDS for as long as 10 or more years before the signs of AIDS appear, many of these young people were likely infected when they were teenagers.

People are becoming infected with HIV at younger ages. In fact, in the early 1980s, the average age at infection was over 30. In the four years between 1987 and 1991, the average age at infection decreased to 25. During these four years, it is estimated, one in every four new HIV infections occurred in people under 25 years of age.

Many teens engage in behaviors that increase their risk of becoming infected. Adults sometimes have no idea that the young people they know may be having sexual intercourse or experimenting with injected drugs. These activities can increase their risk of infection with the virus that causes AIDS.

All young people need to know about AIDS and the specific actions they can take to protect themselves and their loved ones from becoming infected. Let's begin with the basics.

---

[*] Source: CDC National AIDS Clearinghouse, P.O. Box 6003, Rockville, MD 20849; 800-458-5231.

What Is AIDS?

AIDS stands for acquired immunodeficiency syndrome, a disease in which the body's immune system breaks down. The immune system fights off infections and certain other diseases. Because the system fails, a person with AIDS develops a variety of life-threatening illnesses.

AIDS Is Caused By HIV Infection

AIDS is caused by the virus called the human immunodeficiency virus, or HIV. A virus is a small germ that can cause disease.

Some Disturbing Facts

Surveys have found that:

- the average age for a girl in the United States to have sexual intercourse for the first time is 16. The average age for a boy is 15.5.

- it is estimated that 3 million teens are infected with sexually transmitted diseases (venereal diseases-VD) each year. The virus that causes AIDS is sexually transmitted.

- 60 percent of all American high school seniors have used illegal drugs. Some of these drugs are injected. The virus that causes AIDS is spread through the sharing of needles or syringes.

If HIV enters your body, you may become infected with HIV. A blood test can detect HIV antibodies if you are infected. Antibodies are substances your body makes to fight an infection.

A person who is infected can infect others, even if no symptoms are present. You cannot tell by looking at someone whether he or she is infected with HIV. An infected person can appear completely healthy.

Even when no symptoms are visible, however, anyone infected with HIV should be under a doctor's care.

People infected with HIV can develop many health problems. These can include extreme weight loss, severe pneumonia, forms of cancer, and damage to the nervous system. These illnesses signal the onset of AIDS. In some people, these illnesses may develop within a year or two. Others may stay healthy for as long as 10 or more years before symptoms appear. Early medical treatment may prolong a person's life.

No one will develop AIDS unless he or she has been infected with HIV. By preventing HIV infection, we can prevent AIDS.

How You Can And Cannot Become Infected With HIV

You can become infected with HIV in two main ways:

- Having sexual intercourse — vaginal, anal, or perhaps oral — with an infected person.

- Sharing needles or syringes with an infected person.

Also, women infected with HIV can pass the virus to their babies during pregnancy or during birth. In some cases they can also pass it on when breastfeeding. Some people have been infected by receiving blood transfusions, especially during the period before 1985, when careful screening and laboratory testing of the blood supply began. You cannot be infected by giving blood at a blood bank.

How Do You Get HIV From Sexual Intercourse?
HIV can be spread through unprotected sexual intercourse, from male to female, female to male, or male to male. Female-to-female sexual transmission is possible, but rare. Unprotected sexual intercourse means sexual intercourse without correct and consistent condom use.

HIV may be in an infected person's blood, semen, or vaginal secretions. It is thought that it can enter the body through cuts or sores — some so small you don't know they're there — on tissue in the vagina, penis, or rectum, and possibly the mouth.

HIV is transmitted by anal, vaginal, or oral intercourse with a person who is infected with HIV.

Since many infected people have no apparent symptoms of the condition, it's hard to be sure who is or is not infected with HIV. So, the more sex partners you have, the greater your chances of encountering one who is infected, and becoming infected yourself.

How Do You Get HIV From Using Needles?
Sharing needles or syringes, even once, is an easy way to be infected with HIV and other germs. Sharing needles to inject drugs is the most dangerous form of needle sharing. Blood from an infected person can remain in or on a needle or syringe and then be transferred directly into the next person who uses it.

Sharing other types of needles also may transmit HIV and other germs. These types of needles include those used to inject steroids and those used for tattooing or ear-piercing.

If you plan to have your ears pierced or get a tattoo, make sure you go to a qualified technician who uses sterile equipment. Don't be shy about asking questions. Reputable technicians will explain the safety measures they follow.

HIV And Babies
A woman infected with HIV can pass the virus on to her baby during pregnancy or during birth. She can also pass it on when breastfeeding. If a woman is infected before or during pregnancy, her child has about one chance in four of being born infected. Taking AZT during pregnancy can reduce this risk.

Any woman who is considering having a baby and who thinks she might have placed herself at risk for HIV infection — even if this occurred years ago — should seek counseling and testing before she gets pregnant. To find out where to go in your area for counseling and testing, call your local health department or the CDC National AIDS Hotline 800-342-AIDS.

For more information about counseling and testing, see the part of this chapter titled "Common Questions, Accurate Answers."

Blood Transfusions And HIV
Although in the past some people became infected with HIV from receiving blood transfusions, this risk has been virtually eliminated. Since 1985, all donated blood has been tested for evidence of HIV. All blood found to contain evidence of HIV is discarded. Currently in the United States, there is almost no chance of infection with HIV through a blood transfusion.

You cannot get HIV from giving blood at a blood bank or other established blood collection center. The needles used for blood donations are sterile. They are used once, then destroyed.

What Are Ways By Which You Cannot Get HIV And AIDS?
HIV infection doesn't just happen. You can't simply "catch" it like a cold or flu. Unlike cold or flu viruses, HIV is not spread by coughs or sneezes.

You won't get HIV through everyday contact with infected people at school, work, home, or anywhere else.

You won't get HIV from clothes, phones, or toilet seats. It can't be passed on by things like spoons, cups, or other objects that someone who is infected with the virus has used. You cannot get it from everyday contact with an infected person. You won't get AIDS from a mosquito bite. The AIDS virus does not live in a mosquito, and it is not transmitted through a mosquito's salivary glands like other diseases such as malaria or yellow fever. You won't get it from bed bugs, lice, flies, or other insects. You won't get HIV from sweat, tears, or sneezes either.

Not All Of The Answers Are In
You won't get HIV from a kiss. Experts are not completely certain about HIV transmission through deep, prolonged, or "French" kissing. While scientists believe it is remotely possible, there has

never been a known case of HIV transfusion, through kissing. Most scientists agree that transmission of HIV through deep or prolonged kissing may be possible, but would be extremely unlikely.

Common Questions, Accurate Answers

An important part of being ready to talk to young people about preventing HIV infection and AIDS is being able to answer questions they may ask.

If someone asks you a question about HIV infection or AIDS and you do not know the answer, it's okay to say you don't know. Don't make up an answer — faking it often does more harm than good.

Treat a tough question as a chance to show the questioner how to get information about HIV infection and AIDS independently. You, or anyone else, can get accurate answers to difficult questions by calling your local AIDS hotline or the CDC National AIDS Hotline (800-342-AIDS). You do not have to give your name, and the call is free.

To help you answer questions that might come up, here are some commonly asked questions with scientifically correct answers:

If somebody in my class at school has AIDS, am I likely to get it too?

- No. HIV is transmitted by unprotected sexual intercourse, needle sharing, or infected blood. It can also be given by an infected mother to her baby during pregnancy, birth, or breastfeeding.

- People infected with HIV cannot pass the virus to others through ordinary activities of young people in school.

- You will not become infected with HIV just by attending school with someone who is infected or who has AIDS.

Can I become infected with HIV from "French" kissing?

- Not likely. HIV occasionally can be found in saliva, but in very low concentrations — so low that scientists believe it is virtually impossible to transmit infection by deep kissing.

- The possibility exists that cuts or sores in the mouth may provide direct access for HIV to enter the bloodstream during prolonged deep kissing.

- There has never been a single case documented in which HIV was transmitted by kissing.

- Scientists, however, cannot absolutely rule out the possibility of transmission during prolonged, deep kissing because of possible blood contact.

Can I become infected with HIV from oral sex?

- It is possible.

- Oral sex often involves semen, vaginal secretions, or blood-fluids that contain HIV.

- HIV is transmitted by the introduction of infected semen, vaginal secretions, or blood into another person's body.

- During oral intercourse, the virus could enter the body through tiny cuts or sores in the mouth.

As long as I use a latex condom during sexual intercourse, I won't get HIV infection, right?

- Latex condoms have been shown to prevent HIV infection and other sexually transmitted diseases.

- You have to use them properly. And you have to use them every time you have sex — vaginal, anal, and oral — with a male.

- The only sure way to avoid infection through sex is to abstain from sexual intercourse, or engage in sexual intercourse only with someone who is not infected.

- For more information about condoms, see the question on how to use a condom.

My friend has anal intercourse with her boyfriend so that she won't get pregnant. She won't get AIDS from doing that, right?
- Wrong. Anal intercourse with an infected partner is one of the ways HIV has been transmitted.

- Whether you are male or female, anal intercourse with an infected person is very risky.

If I have never injected drugs and have had sexual intercourse only with a person of the opposite sex, could I have become infected with HIV?
- Yes. HIV does not discriminate. You do not have to be homosexual or use drugs to become infected.

- Both males and females can become infected and transmit the infection to another person through intercourse.

- If a previous sex partner was infected, you may be infected as well.

Is it possible to become infected with HIV by donating blood?
- No. There is absolutely no risk of HIV infection from donating blood.

- Blood donation centers use a new, sterile needle for each donation.

I had a blood transfusion. Is it likely that I am infected with HIV?
- It is highly unlikely. All donated blood has been tested for HIV since 1985.

- Donors are asked if they have practiced behaviors that place them at increased risk for HIV. If they have, then are not allowed to donate blood.

- Today the American blood supply is extremely safe.

- If you are still concerned about the remote possibility of HIV infection from a transfusion, you should see your doctor or seek counseling about getting an HIV antibody test. Call the CDC National AIDS Hotline (800-342 -AIDS) or your local health department to find out about counseling and testing facilities in your area.

Can I become infected with HIV from a toilet seat or other objects I routinely use?

- No. HIV does not live on toilet seats or other everyday objects, even those on which body fluids may sometimes be found. Other examples of everyday objects are doorknobs, phones, money, and drinking fountains.

Can I become infected with HIV from a mosquito or other insects?

- You won't get HIV from a mosquito bite. The AIDS virus does not live in a mosquito, and it is not transmitted through a mosquito's salivary glands like other diseases such as malaria or yellow fever. You won't get it from bed bugs, lice, flies, or other insects, either.

A friend of mine told me that as long as I am taking birth control pills, I will never get HIV infection. It this true?

- No. Birth control pills do not protect against HIV.

- You can become infected with HIV while you are taking birth control pills.

- The only sure way not to become infected is to:
  - avoid needle sharing

- abstain from unprotected sexual intercourse, or engage in sexual intercourse only with a partner who is not infected.

- Latex condoms, when used consistently and correctly, are highly effective in preventing HIV infection and other STDS. Use them properly every time you have sex.

- Even if you are taking the pill, you should use a latex condom unless you are sure that your partner is not infected.

I think I might have been infected two months ago when I had intercourse without a condom with someone I didn't know. Should I get an HIV test?

- You should seek counseling about the need for HIV testing.

What do I do if I think I am infected with HIV?

- Remember, you must have engaged in behaviors that place you at risk for HIV infection. Those behaviors include:
  - sharing needles with an infected person.
  - having unprotected sexual intercourse with an infected person.

- If you are still concerned, you need to talk to someone about getting an HIV test that will determine if you are infected. That person might be a parent, doctor, or other health care provider, or someone who works at an AIDS counseling and testing center.

- Call the CDC National AIDS Hotline (800-342-AIDS) to find out where you can go in your area to get counseling about an HIV test. You don't have to give your name, and the call is free. You can also call your state or local health department. The number is under "Health Department" in the Government section of your telephone book.

- Your doctor may advise you to be counseled and tested if you have hemophilia or have received a blood transfusion between 1978 and 1985.

What is the proper way to use a condom?
You can significantly decrease your chances of infection with HIV or any other sexually transmitted disease if you follow this list of simple instructions:

- Use a latex condom every time you have sex-anal, oral, or vaginal. Latex serves as a barrier to the virus. "Lambskin" or "natural membrane" condoms may not be as good because of the pores in the material. Look for the word "latex" on the package.

- As soon as the penis becomes erect, put the condom on it.

- Leave a small space in the top of the condom to catch the semen, or use a condom with a reservoir tip. Remove any air that remains in the tip by gently pressing toward the base of the penis.

- When you use a lubricant, check the label to make sure it is water-based. Do not use petroleum-based jelly, cold cream, baby oil, or other lubricants such as cooking oil or shortening. These weaken the latex condom and can cause it to break.

- If you feel the condom break while you are having sex, stop immediately and pull out. Do not continue until you have put on a new condom.

- After climax (ejaculation), withdraw while the penis is still erect, holding on to the rim of the condom while pulling out so that it doesn't come off

- Never use a condom more than once.

- Don't use a condom that is brittle or that has been stored near heat or in your wallet or glove compartment for a long time. Check the package for date of expiration.

- A condom can't do you any good if you don't have one when you need it.

I think my son may be having sexual relations with other males. Is there any information in addition to the materials in this guide that I need to know about before I talk to him about HIV and AIDS?

- The information presented in this guide is pertinent to all youth, regardless of their sexual orientation.

- HIV does not discriminate. It is not who you are, but what you do that determines whether you can become infected with the virus.

- A latex condom should be used when having any type of intercourse.

- For more information on specifically male-to-male HIV transmission, call the CDC National AIDS Hotline at 800-342-AIDS.

Talking With Young People About HIV Infection And AIDS

Young people today often face tough decisions about sex and drugs. Most likely, you will not be with the children you care about when they face these choices. But if you talk to them about decision making and HIV and AIDS prevention now, you can help them resist peer pressure and make informed choices that will help protect their health, now and for the rest of their lives.

Think Of Yourself As A Counselor

When talking with a young person about HIV infection and AIDS, think of your role as that of counselor, advisor, coach, best friend, or guide. Your goal: to help a young person learn how to make smart decisions about how to act in a healthful manner and avoid infection with HIV.

Tips For Starting A Conversation

You can start talking about HIV infection and AIDS at any time and in any way you choose. If you find it awkward to bring the topic up, you can look for cues that will help you. Here are some examples:

The Media. You can find plenty of cues in the media, which give HIV infection and AIDS a lot of attention. Look for stories about AIDS and advertisements about HIV prevention on television, on the radio, in newspapers, and in magazines. Start a conversation by commenting on one of them or asking a young person how he or she feels about it.

School. Ask a young person what he or she is learning in health, science, or any other class about HIV infection and AIDS. Use the answer to launch your conversation.

Deciding What Young People Need To Know

As an adult who knows the young people you will talk with, you are in the best position to decide what they need to know about HIV infection and AIDS.

Think carefully about their knowledge and experience. How old are the children? How much do they already know about HIV infection, AIDS, and other related subjects, such as sex and drug use? Where have they gotten their information? From friends? School? Television? You? Is it likely to be accurate?

Also ask yourself these questions: Is it possible that the young people you will be talking with are sexually active? Have they tried drugs? Do they spend time with people who do these things? In addition, consider your family's religious and cultural values. Do you want to convey these in the conversation? How will you get them across?

These are important questions. Answering them will help you stress the information that the young people in your life most need to know.

Community. Local events, such as AIDS benefits or health fairs, can serve as handy conversation starters. You might even propose going to such an event with a young person as an educational experience.

Children May Ask. Don't be surprised if a young person asks you directly about HIV infection and AIDS. You can also use young people's questions about related topics, such as dating or sex, to lead into a conversation about HIV infection and AIDS.

How To Keep The Conversation Running Smoothly

It Can Be A Challenge. Talking about HIV infection and AIDS can be difficult. You may feel uncomfortable just thinking about it. That's understandable. If you are nervous or embarrassed, don't be afraid to say so. Bringing your feelings into the open can help break the tension. Besides, a young person will sense your uneasiness even if you don't mention it.

Review The Facts. You don't have to be an expert to talk with a young person about HIV infection and AIDS. But you should understand the basic facts so that you will deliver the right information. This guide will help you become familiar with the key facts. Talking about the facts with another adult may help you feel more comfortable as you prepare to talk with young people.

Step into A Young Person's Shoes. What kinds of things did you do when you were the age of the young person with whom you plan to speak? How did you think? The better you understand a young person's point of view, the more effectively you'll be able to communicate. Also, thinking of some important differences between the world a child grows up in today and the one you grew up in can help you make your discussion timely and relevant.

Have A Mutual Conversation. A conversation is an exchange of ideas and information, not a lecture. Encourage the young person with whom you speak to talk and ask questions. Ask about his or her thoughts, feelings, and activities. Show that you want to learn from a young person just as you hope he or she will learn from you.

Listen. Listen to the young person with whom you speak as closely as you hope he or she will listen to you. Stop talking if he or she wants to speak. Give him or her your full attention, and make eye contact.

Be Upbeat. Try to show a positive attitude as you lead the discussion. A critical, disapproving tone can prompt a young person to ignore you.

Don't Get Discouraged. Young people often challenge what they hear from adults. If a young person questions what you say, try not to get into an argument. Encourage the young person to check your information with another source, such as the CDC National AIDS Hotline (800-342-AIDS). You can also show him or her some of the information in this guide, especially the handout for his or her age group. If your first conversation is cut short for any reason, don't give up. It is important to try again.

Smart Decisions:
Young People Can Make Them With Your Help
Even though young people may not ask for it, they often want guidance from adults. You can offer guidance to the young people you care about by helping them develop the skills to make smart decisions about their education, their social life, their health. Just as important, you can help young people to understand that they have the ability and the responsibility to make the key decisions that can prevent the spread of HIV and AIDS.

Young People Do Make Decisions. Young people often feel they have no control over their lives. Adults tell them when to go to school, when to be home, when to go to bed, and when to wake up. It's important to help them see that they make decisions about their lives every day, such as what music they listen to and whom they spend time with. Point out that they also make or will make tough choices with serious consequences about sex and drugs.

Cause And Effect. Many young people do not fully understand the direct relationship between their decisions and the consequences that may result. In your role as a counselor or guide, you can help them see that thoughtful decisions can bring them direct benefits and save them from harsh consequences, such as HIV infection and AIDS.

Recognize Peer Pressures. Young people's decisions are often strongly influenced by pressure to conform with friends and acquaintances. Peer pressure can also cause young people to act on impulses rather than to think through their decisions.

You can help the young people with whom you speak consider the effects of peer pressure. Point out that it is okay to act according to their best judgment, not according to what friends encourage them to do. Suggest that their friends may be testing limits and looking for support in making sound choices. Talk about the difficulties you may have had defying peer pressure. Then talk about the reasons you are glad you did.

Deciding What To Say To Younger Children (Late Elementary And Middle School Aged)

Since most children in this age group are not sexually active or trying drugs, you may decide that the young people you speak with do not need to know the details of how HIV is transmitted through unprotected sexual intercourse and injecting drug use. However, if you think they may be considering or may be doing things that put them at risk of infection, you will need to be sure they know the risks regardless of their age.

Children this age probably have heard about AIDS and may be scared by it. Much of what they have heard may have been incorrect. To reassure them, make sure they know that they cannot become infected through everyday contact, such as going to school with someone who is infected with HIV.

Children also may have heard myths and prejudicial comments about HIV infection and AIDS. Correct any notions that people can be infected by touching a doorknob or being bitten by a mosquito. Urge children to treat people who are infected with HIV or who have AIDS with compassion and understanding, not cruelty and anger. Correcting myths and prejudices early will help children protect themselves and others from HIV infection and AIDS in the future.

Consider including the following points in a conversation about HIV infection and AIDS with children in the late elementary and middle school aged levels:

- AIDS is a disease caused by a tiny germ called a virus.

- Many different types of people have AIDS today-male and female, rich and poor, white, Black, Hispanic, Asian, and Native American.

- As of December 1993, nearly 68,000 people aged 20-29 have been diagnosed with AIDS. Because a person can be infected with HIV for as long as 10 or more years before the signs of AIDS appear, a significant number of these young people would have been infected when they were teenagers.

- There are many myths about AIDS. (Correct some of them if you can.)

- You can become infected with HIV either by having unprotected sexual intercourse with an infected person or by sharing drug needles or syringes with an infected person. Also, women infected with HIV can pass the virus to their babies during pregnancy or during birth.

- A person who is infected can infect others in the ways described above, even if no symptoms are present. You cannot tell by looking at someone whether he or she is infected with HIV. An infected person can appear completely healthy.

- People who have AIDS should be treated with compassion.

Information For Young People
(Late Elementary And Middle School Aged)

You may have heard about a disease called AIDS. A lot of people have been talking about it lately. Many people have gotten AIDS in the past few years. A lot of them have died.

AIDS is a condition that weakens the body's power to fight off sickness. It's a very serious medical problem. That's why people are talking about it. But sometimes people talk without knowing the facts.

AIDS is caused by a tiny germ. Doctors call a germ like this a virus. The virus that causes AIDS is called the human immunodeficiency virus (HIV).

The key thing for you to understand about AIDS is that it is not easy to get through the things you do every day. You cannot "catch" AIDS like you can a cold or the chicken pox. You cannot get AIDS from doing things like going to school, using a bathroom, or riding in a school bus.

It is important to know the facts about AIDS. You can be a leader by knowing the truth. All of the following statements about AIDS are true. Read them. Remember them. When you hear something about AIDS that isn't true, speak up. Say that you know the facts. Tell people the truth.

- You cannot get AIDS from the things you do every day, such as going to school, using a toilet, or drinking from a glass.

- You cannot get AIDS from sitting next to someone in school who has AIDS.

- You cannot get AIDS from a kiss on the cheek, or from touching or hugging someone who is infected.

- You cannot get AIDS from a mosquito or any other kind of insect. The virus that causes AIDS dies inside of bugs, so there is no way they can give it to you.

- You can become infected with HIV either by having unprotected sexual intercourse with an infected person or by sharing drug needles or syringes with an infected person. Also, women infected with HIV can.pass the virus to their babies during pregnancy, during birth, or through breast-feeding.

- A person who is infected can infect others during sexual intercourse, even if no symptoms are present. You cannot tell by looking at someone whether he or she is infected with HIV. An infected person can appear completely healthy.

- You can play with someone who has HIV or AIDS just as you can with any of your other friends. This will not make you sick.

- Many different types of people have AIDS — male and female, rich and poor, white, Black, Hispanic, Asian, and Native American.

- As of December 1993, nearly 68,000 people aged 20-29 have been diagnosed with AIDS. Because a person can be infected with the virus that causes AIDS for as long as 10 or more years before the signs of AIDS appear, scientists believe that a significant number of these young people would have been infected when they were teenagers.

- Being sick isn't fun. Treat people with AIDS the way you want to be treated when you are sick.

See How Much You Know About HIV Infection And AIDS

1. What is the name of the disease that weakens the body's power to fight off illness?

2. What is the name of the virus that causes AIDS?

3. Check all of the things that cannot infect you with HIV:
   [ ]   a toilet
   [ ]   a kiss on the cheek
   [ ]   a drinking glass
   [ ]   a mosquito
   [ ]   going to school with someone who is infected with HIV
   [ ]   helping someone who is infected with HIV or who has AIDS

Answers To Quiz
1. AIDS 2. HIV 3. All of the items should be checked. They can't infect you with HIV.

Deciding What To Say To Teenagers (Junior And Senior High School Aged)

Teens need to know a lot more about HIV infection and AIDS than do younger children. Teens are more likely to face choices about drug and alcohol use, and sex.

Because HIV is spread through unprotected sexual intercourse or sharing drug needles and syringes, teens need to learn how to make decisions that keep themselves and others from being infected with HIV. Because alcohol and drugs can cloud thinking, teens need to learn that using these substances can cause them to make decisions which can put them at risk.

Like younger children, teens also must learn to distinguish myths from facts about HIV infection and AIDS. They need to learn about the issues that the disease poses for society, such as the importance of opposing prejudice and discrimination. Discussing all of these things will help equip teens to make decisions that can prevent the spread of HIV infection and AIDS.

In a conversation with a teen, consider including the following points about making decisions, HIV infection, and AIDS:

- Give a definition of AIDS.

- Give a definition of HIV infection.

- Point out that as of December 1993, more than 361,000 Americans have AIDS and that nearly 68,000 of them are between the ages of 20 and 29. A significant number of these people would have been infected when they were teenagers.

- Explain how HIV is transmitted from one person to another.

- Explain how to reduce the risk for HIV infection from sex.

- Explain how HIV is transmitted through drug use.

- Discuss how to join the community response to AIDS.

- Give your thoughts on the importance of understanding and compassion toward people with AIDS.

- Talk about the importance of eliminating prejudice and discrimination related to AIDS.

Becoming Infected Through Sexual Intercourse
Many teenagers are sexually active. Unprotected sexual intercourse with an infected partner is one way to become infected with HIV.

Avoiding sexual intercourse is one sure way to avoid infection with the virus. In deciding what you want to say to a young person about sex, you may want to consider these ideas:

Delay Sexual Intercourse. You may want to bear in mind that the idea of delaying sexual intercourse conflicts with the many sexual messages young people encounter every day on television, in movies, at school, and from friends. Many young people conclude that "everyone is doing it."

By discussing the benefits of delaying sexual intercourse, you can help a young person make a wise and informed decision about when to become sexually active. You may wish to emphasize the following benefits of delaying sexual intercourse:

- Most religious, cultural, and social traditions and family values favor postponing intercourse until marriage.

- The longer sexual intercourse is delayed, the longer the guarantee of one's safety from all sexually transmitted diseases, including HIV infection. Every 11 seconds a teen in the United States gets a sexually transmitted disease.

- Delaying sexual intercourse gives a person time to be sure he or she is physically and emotionally ready to engage in a sexual relationship.

- Delaying sexual intercourse helps prevent unwanted pregnancy. Every 30 seconds a teen in the United States gets pregnant.

How To Avoid Risky Situations. Even young people who truly intend to delay sexual intercourse can have trouble refusing strong persuasion. You can help them succeed by talking with them about how to anticipate and avoid situations in which they might be pressured to have sex.

For instance, pressure can arise when two people are alone at one of their homes or in a car parked on "lovers' lane." Tell young people that when such a situation occurs, they can refuse verbally, or they can simply leave. If they cannot walk home, they can call a friend or a parent to pick them up. Advise them to have change with them at all times so that they will be able to use a public telephone.

Explain to them that no one has the right to force them to have sexual intercourse, and then tell them some effective ways to refuse. You may want to consider the suggestions in the following section.

How To Say No To Risky Activities. Young people will be more likely to refuse activities that place them at risk for HIV infection if you suggest some effective ways to say no.

For instance, when you talk about sex and HIV infection, discuss ways to say no to sex. You might suggest some of the following examples, or use your own.

- "I am just not ready for it yet."

- "I know it feels right for you and I care about you. But I'm not going to do it until I'm sure it's the right thing for me to do."

- "I care about you but I don't want the responsibility that comes with sex."

- "I think sex outside of marriage is wrong."

- "I feel good about not having sex until I'm married. I've made my decision and I feel comfortable with it."

Ask the young people you talk with to think of some of their own ways to say no and to practice them with you.

What Can They Do Instead? Telling young people only what they shouldn't do can make a parent sound very negative. It will be helpful to discuss some risk-free alternatives. Young people will be better able to choose safe behaviors if you tell them ways to express their romantic feelings without risk of HIV infection.

You can make a list of these activities and review it during your conversation. Ask the young people you talk with to suggest some of their own ideas.

If You Think A Teen Is Sexually Active. Short of abstaining from sex, the best way to protect oneself from sexually transmitted diseases, such as HIV infection, is to have sex only with one faithful, uninfected partner in a long-term relationship. It is crucial that people understand that the more sex partners they have, the greater their risk of getting a sexually transmitted disease, such as HIV.

You can also help young people avoid dangerous sexual decisions by stressing that young people should avoid making decisions about sexual intercourse while under the influence of alcohol or other drugs. These substances cloud judgment and lower inhibitions, and people with clouded judgment are more likely to take sexual risks that will increase their chance of HIV infection.

You may wish to discuss the importance of using a latex condom. Such discussion may help young people make wise decisions that will reduce the risk of HIV infection during sexual intercourse. Latex condoms provide a barrier and, if used correctly and consistently, greatly reduce the risk of infection with sexually transmitted diseases, including HIV. People who decide to be sexually active outside a mutually faithful, long-term relationship with an uninfected partner should understand the importance of using a condom every time they have sexual intercourse.

For more detailed information about how to use a latex condom, read the part in this chapter called "Common Questions, Accurate Answers."

Preventing HIV Transmission Caused By Needle Sharing
HIV often spreads among people who share needles and syringes.
If you know young people who use needles for a medical reason
(such as people with hemophilia or diabetes), make sure they use
and dispose of their needles properly. Needles should be used only
under a doctor's order and should never be shared.

In your role of counselor or guide, it is vital that you urge young
people not to use drugs. Many drug users face a short, bleak future
— jail, hospitalization, or an early grave — and drug use increases
their risk of HIV infection.

If you talk with a young person about drug use and HIV infection,
talk about ways to say no to drugs. You might suggest some of the
following ways, or use examples of your own:

- "I just don't want to take drugs."

- "I don't want to lose my job. Drugs and work don't mix."

- "I want to be a good athlete. Drugs will harm my body."

- "I want to go to college. I can't risk getting hooked on
  drugs."

- "I want to join the Army. Drugs could blow my chances."

- "Drugs are illegal. I won't break the law."

- "When I take drugs, I don't feel in control. I don't like that
  feeling."

- "I love my life. Drugs can kill me."

Ask the young people you talk with to think of their own ways to
say no to drugs and practice them with you.

If you think a young person you know has a drug problem, get professional help now. Contact your doctor, local health department, or social service agency to find out who can help you in your community. Call the 24-hour hotline of the National Institute on Drug Abuse (800-662-HELP) to find out where you can get help in your area.

Information For Young People
(Junior And Senior High School Aged)

As of December 1993, nearly 68,000 people between the ages of 20 and 29 have been diagnosed with AIDS. Many of them probably were infected with the virus that causes AIDS when they were teenagers.

You or your friends may unknowingly be doing things that put you at risk for getting infected with HIV. For instance, the virus that causes AIDS can be passed from one person to another through unprotected sexual intercourse. Today a teen in the United States gets pregnant every 30 seconds. Every 11 seconds a teen in the United States gets a sexually transmitted disease (STD), such as gonorrhea or chlamydia. The same sexual activities that cause pregnancy and give you STDs can infect you with the virus that causes AIDS.

There are other ways besides sexual intercourse that teens can get AIDS. To find out how to protect yourself and your friends, read on.

What is AIDS?
AIDS stands for acquired immunodeficiency syndrome.

AIDS is a condition in which the body's immune system — the system that fights off sickness — breaks down. Because the system fails, a person with AIDS typically develops a variety of life-threatening illnesses.

What is HIV Infection?

AIDS is caused by a virus that scientists call human immunodeficiency virus, or HIV. A virus is a small germ that can cause disease.

If HIV enters your body, you may become infected with HIV. From the time a person is infected, he or she can infect others, even if no symptoms are present. A special blood test can detect HIV.

HIV can hide in a person's body for years without producing any symptoms. Even if no symptoms are present, anyone infected with HIV should be under a doctor's care.

People infected with HIV can develop many health problems. These can include extreme weight loss, severe pneumonia, certain forms of cancer, and damage to the nervous system. These illnesses signal the onset of AIDS. In some people, these illnesses may develop within a year or two. Others may stay healthy for as long as 10 or more years before symptoms appear.

What Is The Difference Between HIV And AIDS?

HIV infection and AIDS are serious health problems. AIDS is the result of a long process that begins with HIV infection.

A person will not develop AIDS unless he or she has been infected with HIV. By preventing HIV infection, we can prevent future cases of AIDS.

How Does Someone Become Infected With HIV?

A person becomes infected when HIV is introduced into his or her body. There are two main ways that people become infected with HIV:

- By engaging in unprotected sexual intercourse — vaginal, anal, or oral — with an infected person.

- By sharing drug needles or syringes with an infected person. Also, women who are infected with HIV can pass it on to their babies during pregnancy, birth, or breastfeeding.

Last, some people have become infected through receiving blood transfusions. Since 1985, the American blood supply has been tested for HIV. Transmission through an infected blood transfusion is extremely rare today.

How Do You Get HIV Through Sex?

HIV is spread through unprotected sexual intercourse, from male to female, female to male, or male to male. Female-to female transmission is also possible.

HIV may be in an infected person's blood, semen, or vaginal secretions. It is thought that it can enter the body through cuts or sores — some so small you don't know they're there — on tissue in the vagina, penis, or rectum, and possibly the mouth.

Since many people infected with HIV have no symptoms, you can't be sure who is infected. Any contact with infected blood, semen, or vaginal secretions may spread the virus. Therefore, the more sex

---

Important Questions

How can you tell if the person you are dating or would like to date has been infected with HIV? The simple answer is, you can't. But as long as sexual intercourse and sharing needles are avoided, it doesn't matter.

If you are thinking about becoming sexually involved with someone, here are some important questions to consider.

Has this person had any sexually transmitted diseases? How many people has he or she had sex with? Has he or she experimented with drugs? All of these are sensitive questions. But they are important, and you have a responsibility to ask.

You should think of it this way: If you know someone well enough to have sex, the two of you should be able to talk about HIV infection and AIDS. If someone is unwilling to talk, you shouldn't have sex.

---

partners you have, the greater your chances of encountering one who is infected, and then becoming infected yourself.

How Do You Get HIV From Sharing Needles?

Sharing needles, even once, is a very easy way to be infected with HIV. Whether you inject drugs or steroids, you risk becoming infected with HIV if you share needles or syringes. Blood from an infected person can stay in a needle or syringe and then be transmitted to the next person who uses it.

How Can I Avoid HIV Infection?

Don't do drugs of any kind. Sharing needles to inject drugs can infect you. And many drugs, especially alcohol, can cloud your judgment and cause you to do things that place you at risk for HIV infection.

Delay sexual intercourse. Don't have sexual intercourse. Abstinence is the only sure protection. If you do have sexual intercourse, wait until you are in a long-term, mutually faithful relationship, such as marriage, with an uninfected partner. By choosing not to have intercourse, you:

- help guarantee your safety from all sexually transmitted diseases, including HIV infection. Remember, every 11 seconds a teen in the U.S. gets a sexually transmitted disease.

- give yourself more time to be sure you are physically and emotionally ready to engage in a sexual relationship.

- give yourself more time to learn and understand more about the physical and emotional aspects of sexual relationships.

- follow religious, cultural, and social traditions that favor postponing intercourse until marriage.

- help guarantee your safety from unwanted pregnancy. Remember, every 30 seconds a teen in the U.S. gets pregnant.

When you decide you are ready to become sexually active, do so only with one uninfected partner in a mutually faithful, long-term relationship, such as marriage.

Avoid sexual intercourse with people who may be infected with HIV. These include people who have:

- injected drugs.
- had multiple or anonymous sex partners.
- had any sexually transmitted diseases.

If you have sexual intercourse outside of a mutually faithful, long-term relationship with an uninfected partner, use a latex condom whenever having any type of sexual intercourse.

Do not make decisions about sexual intercourse while under the influence of alcohol or other drugs. These substances can cloud your judgment and cause you to take risks that could put you in danger of becoming infected with HIV.

How Else Can I Help Stop AIDS?

If you've read this far, you know the facts about HIV infection and AIDS. You'd be surprised at how many people don't know them. A lot of people believe all sorts of myths about AIDS — myths that can be very harmful.

These myths can cause people to unknowingly put themselves, and others, at risk of infection. They can also cause people to treat others unfairly. For instance, some people incorrectly think that AIDS only affects certain groups of people. Because they fear AIDS, they do cruel things to people in those groups.

Do You Know The Facts About HIV Infection And AIDS?

1. HIV can be spread through which of the following?
    A. insect bites
    B. everyday contact
    C. sharing drug needles
    D. sexual intercourse

2. You can tell by looking whether a person is infected with HIV.
    [ ] TRUE   [ ] FALSE

3. From the time a person is infected with HIV, he or she can infect others.
    [ ] TRUE   [ ] FALSE

4. Providing help to people infected with HIV or people with AIDS does not put you at risk of infection.
    [ ] TRUE   [ ] FALSE

5. Babies can be infected by their mothers during pregnancy, birth, or breastfeeding.
    [ ] TRUE   [ ] FALSE

6. If you have sexual intercourse only with members of the opposite sex, you cannot be infected with HIV.
    [ ] TRUE   [ ] FALSE

7. If they are used properly and consistently, latex condoms are an effective way to prevent the spread of HIV.
    [ ] TRUE   [ ] FALSE

8. The more sex partners you have, the greater your chances of becoming infected with HIV.
    [ ] TRUE   [ ] FALSE

9. If you think you've been exposed to HIV, you should seek counseling and be tested.
    [ ] TRUE   [ ] FALSE

Answers To Quiz
1. C and D   2. FALSE   3. TRUE   4. TRUE   5. TRUE
6. FALSE   7.TRUE   8. TRUE   9. TRUE

We should work to make sure that such prejudice and unfair treatment doesn't happen. Now that you know the facts about HIV infection and AIDS, you can tell others the truth and speak out against myths and prejudice.

What's more, people infected with HIV and those with AIDS can use your help. If you know someone who has AIDS, you can give compassion, friendship, or other help without fear of infection from everyday contact.

Even if you don't know anyone who is infected, you can join your community's effort to stop AIDS. You can volunteer your time with a local health organization, youth group, or religious group that has an HIV and AIDS program. Or you can contribute just by informally educating your peers about AIDS. Who knows? You just may save someone's life.

How To Join The Community Response

Everyone Can Help
You are a vital member of the community team that provides HIV and AIDS education, reinforces safe behavior, and promotes healthful attitudes. When parents and other adults join with civic groups, youth groups, educators, and religious groups, communities can convey these messages to young people and prevent the spread of HIV infection and AIDS.

Both adults and young people can join the community's efforts by talking to friends, neighbors, colleagues, and relatives. Remember, you don't have to be an expert to teach people about HIV infection and AIDS. By speaking with peers, people who know the facts about HIV infection and AIDS can help stop the spread of the disease.

Using Community Organizations
Many communities have valuable resources to inform their young people about HIV infection and AIDS. These organizations, such

as the American Red Cross, the March of Dimes, National Urban League, National Council of La Raza, Boys' Clubs and Girls' Clubs, and your local "Y," can tell you how to get involved with public education, volunteer programs, and fund-raising drives. To find out about such resources in your community, look for listings in the telephone book.

You can also invite speakers from these groups to address your group about HIV infection and AIDS prevention, where that focuses on AIDS treatment, counseling, or education can help you find good speakers. To get the name of such an organization in your community, call the CDC National AIDS Hotline (800-342-AIDS). People with AIDS, health educators, or local and state government officials might make good speakers.

You Are The Key
Many community groups involved in the fight against AIDS operate on shoestring budgets and depend heavily on individuals contributions of time and money. Please help them succeed. Your community will appreciate it.

Help A Person With AIDS
One important way you can help is to volunteer your services to people with AIDS. As their condition becomes more disabling, people with AIDS have increasing trouble meeting their daily needs. You can offer help by shopping, cooking meals, or just visiting and talking with people with AIDS on a regular basis. To find out what you can do to help people with AIDS, you can contact an AIDS education or service organization, or an organization of people with AIDS in your community. For more information, call the CDC National AIDS Hotline (800-342-AIDS) or your local health department.

Comprehensive Health Education In Schools
You can talk to your local school board, superintendent, principal, teachers, guidance counselors, or child to find out about the HIV infection and AIDS education programs your local school offers and how you can contribute.

A comprehensive health education curriculum with an HIV infection and AIDS component is an excellent way to provide children with knowledge, skills, and support to lead healthy lives. A comprehensive school health education curriculum is an organized, sequential, school health curriculum that starts at the appropriate ages and continues through senior year. It can teach students at the appropriate ages about sexually transmitted diseases, drug abuse, AIDS, and other health concerns, and help them develop decision-making skills and healthy lifestyles.

Make sure your local educators know that you want young people to learn about HIV infection and AIDS prevention in school. PTA meetings can be excellent settings to discuss this issue.

Using Local Media

Your local media play an important role in your community's response to HIV and AIDS. Call or write to your local television and radio stations and newspapers, urging them to air more AIDS public service announcements that target young people, publish stories related to HIV infection and AIDS, and report prevention facts accurately.

Obtaining And Distributing Educational Materials

You can get a variety of educational materials, including posters, brochures, and additional copies of this guide through the CDC National AIDS Hotline (800-342-AIDS) or by writing to: CDC National AIDS Clearinghouse, P.O. Box 6003, Dept. G, Rockville, MD 20849.

You can hang posters in restaurants, bowling alleys, bus stops, beauty parlors, shops, and pharmacies. Think of the young people you know, and try to reach them in other creative ways.

There is also information available on how businesses can help respond to HIV and AIDS. Call the Business Responds to AIDS Resource Service of the CDC National AIDS Clearinghouse at 800-458-5231.

Where To Go For Further Information And Assistance

National Resources

The Centers for Disease Control and Prevention National AIDS Hotline (800-342-AIDS) offers 24-hour service seven days a week to respond to any questions that you or a young person may have about HIV infection and AIDS. All calls are free, and you need not give your name. The service is available in Spanish (800-344-7432) and for the deaf (800-243-7889).

Hotline information specialists also can refer you to groups in your area that work professionally on HIV infection and AIDS issues. Also, they can direct you to local counseling and testing centers, and tell you where to get additional materials.

For additional copies of this guide and other publications on AIDS and HIV infection, you can call or write: CDC National AIDS Clearinghouse, P.O. Box 6003, Rockville, MD 20849; 800-458-5231.

State And Local Health Departments

If you have questions about AIDS prevention efforts in your community, the CDC National AIDS Hotline can tell you how to reach your state or local health department. Also, you can find the number listed under "Health Department" in the local and state government section of your telephone book.

Community Organizations

Thousands of local organizations, such as the PTA, March of Dimes, National Urban League, National Council of La Raza, the American Red Cross, and Boys' Clubs and Girls' Clubs, are working hard to stop the spread of HIV infection. To find out about such organizations in your community, look for them by name in the telephone book or call your local health department.

Schools

Talk to your local school board, superintendent, principal, teachers, or guidance counselors to find out about the HIV and AIDS education programs that your local school offers, and how you can help to make them work. Make sure they know that you support learning about preventing HIV infection and AIDS as part of comprehensive health education in school.

The Health Care Team

If you have concerns about your health or the health of your child, share them with a doctor, nurse, or another health care provider.

Aging and Alcohol Abuse[*]

Anyone at any age can have a drinking problem. Great Uncle George may have always been a heavy drinker — his family may find that as he gets older the problem gets worse. Grandma Betty may have been a teetotaler all her life, just taking a drink "to help her get to sleep" after her husband died — now she needs a couple of drinks to get through the day. These are common stories. Drinking problems in older people are often neglected by families, doctors, and the public.

Physical Effects of Alcohol

Alcohol slows down brain activity. Because alcohol affects alertness, judgement, coordination, and reaction time — drinking increases the risk of falls and accidents. Some research has shown that it takes less alcohol to affect older people than younger ones. Over time, heavy drinking permanently damages the brain and central nervous system, as well as the liver, heart, kidneys, and stomach. Alcohol's effects can make some medical problems hard to diagnose. For example, alcohol causes changes in the heart and blood vessels that can dull pain that might be a warning sign of a heart attack. It also can cause forgetfulness and confusion, which can seem like Alzheimer's disease.

Mixing Drugs

Alcohol, itself a drug, is often harmful if mixed with prescription or over-the-counter medicines. This is a special problem for people over 65, because they are often heavy users of prescription medicines and over-the-counter drugs.

Mixing alcohol with other drugs such as tranquilizers, sleeping pills, pain killers, and antihistamines can be very dangerous, even

---

[*] Source: *Age Page*, National Institute on Aging, U.S. Department of Health and Human Services, Public Health Service, National Institutes of Health, Gaithersburg, MD 20898; 800-222-2225.

fatal. For example, aspirin can cause bleeding in the stomach and intestines; when it is combined with alcohol, the risk of bleeding is much higher.

As people age, the body's ability to absorb and dispose of alcohol and other drugs changes. Anyone who drinks should check with a doctor or pharmacist about possible problems with drug and alcohol interactions.

Who Becomes a Problem Drinker?

There are two types of problem drinkers — chronic and situational. Chronic abusers have been heavy drinkers for many years. Although many chronic abusers die by middle age, some live well into old age. Most older problem drinkers are in this group.

Other people may develop a drinking problem late in life, often because of "situational" factors such as retirement, lowered income, failing health, loneliness, or the death of friends or loved ones. At first, having a drink brings relief, but later it can turn into a problem.

Getting Help

Older problem drinkers have a very good chance for recovery because once they decide to seek help, they usually stay with

---

How to Recognize a Drinking Problem

Not everyone who drinks regularly has a drinking problem. You might want to get help if you:

* Drink to calm your nerves, forget your worries, or reduce depression
* Lose interest in food
* Gulp your drinks down fast
* Lie or try to hide your drinking habits
* Drink alone more often
* Hurt yourself, or someone else, while drinking
* Were drunk more than three or four times last year
* Need more alcohol to get "high"
* Feel irritable, resentful, or unreasonable when you are not drinking
* Have medical, social, or financial problems caused by drinking

---

treatment programs. you can begin getting help by calling your family doctor or clergy member. Your local health department or social services agencies can also help.

Resources

Alcoholics Anonymous (AA) is a voluntary fellowship of alcoholics who help themselves and each other get and stay sober. Check the phone book for a local chapter or write the national office at: 475 Riverside Drive, 11th Floor, New York, NY 10115; or call 202-870-3400.

The National Institute on Alcohol Abuse and Alcoholism (NIAAA) provides information on alcohol abuse and alcoholism. Contact: NIAAA, 6000 Executive Boulevard, Bethesda, MD 20892-7003; 301-443-3860.

The National Council on Alcoholism and Drug Dependence, Inc. can refer you to treatment services in your area. Contact National Headquarters, 12 West 21st Street, 8th Floor, new York, NY 10010; 800-NCA-CALL (800-622-2255).

The National Institute on Aging offers a variety of resources on health and aging. Contact the NIA Information Center, P.O. Box 8057, Gaithersburg, MD 20898-8057; 800-222-2225, 800-222-4225 (TTY).

Alzheimer's Disease*

Alzheimer's disease is the most common cause of dementia, a major form of mental impairment, in older people. The disease affects the parts of the brain that control thought, memory, and language. Symptoms include confusion and inability to carry out routine, everyday tasks. Initially, the only symptom of Alzheimer's disease may be mild forgetfulness. In later stages, behavioral and personality changes such as aggressive acts or aimless wandering may accompany the marked cognitive decline, and eventually patients may require total care. At present, the cause of the disease is unknown, and there is no cure.

It is estimated that currently 4 million people in the United States may have Alzheimer's disease. The disease usually occurs after age 65, although younger people also may develop Alzheimer's. The risk of Alzheimer's disease increases steadily with age. According to recent estimates, approximately 3 percent of people ages 65 to 74 have Alzheimer's disease and nearly half of those over age 85 could have the disorder. Although the risk of getting the disease increases with age, it is not a normal part of aging.

Alzheimer's disease is named after Dr. Alois Alzheimer, a German psychiatrist. In 1906, Dr. Alzheimer described changes in the brain tissue of a woman who had died of an unusual mental illness. He found abnormal deposits (now called senile or neuritic plaques) and tangled bundles of nerve fibers (now called neurofibrillary tangles). These plaques and tangles in the brain have since come to be recognized as the characteristic abnormal brain changes of Alzheimer's disease.

In addition to plaques and tangles, scientists have found other abnormal changes in the brains of persons with Alzheimer's disease, including a loss of nerve cells in several areas of the brain that are vital to memory and other mental abilities. They have also

---

* Source: Alzheimer's Disease Education and Referral (ADEAR) Center, P.O. Box 8250, Silver Spring, Maryland 20907-8250; 800-438-4380.

noted reduced amounts of neurotransmitter chemicals that serve a key function for relaying complex messages among the billions of nerve cells in the brain, An interruption in the flow of communication between nerve cells caused by Alzheimer's disease may disrupt normal patterns of mental functioning.

Symptoms

The onset of Alzheimer's disease is gradual. Usually the person has trouble remembering recent events or activities or the names of familiar persons or things. Problems in carrying out simple math problems also may be evident. Such difficulties may be annoying, but are not usually dramatic enough to cause alarm. However, as the disease progresses, symptoms become more marked. For example, the person may be confused or disoriented, may be easily frustrated, have trouble making decisions, or have communication problems in speaking, understanding speech, reading, or writing. Personality or behavior changes may develop, such as aggressiveness or wandering. Such changes are serious enough to cause the person or a family member to seek medical help.

Diagnosis

No definitive test to diagnose Alzheimer's disease in living patients exists. The appearance of plaques and tangles can be noted only by examining brain tissue, and this procedure is usually done as part of an autopsy. Therefore, a probable diagnosis of Alzheimer's disease must be based on the patient's medical history, a physical examination, and tests of mental ability. A number of other conditions, some of which are treatable, also may cause memory or other cognitive deficits, and must be ruled out. These conditions include thyroid gland problems, drug reactions, depression, brain tumors, and dementia caused by blood vessel disease in the brain.

A patient history includes a review of present and past medical problems, as well as an examination of current ability to carry out daily activities. The patient or family and friends may contribute relevant information. Clinical tests are used to decide whether a person has Alzheimer's disease or another disease and to detect any other medical problems. These may include blood and urine tests and an examination of spinal fluid, which is obtained by taking a small sample of fluid from the spinal cord.

Brain imaging such as CT (computerized tomography) scan, MRI (magnetic resonance imaging), or PET (positron emission testing) may be used to detect abnormalities in the brain. Neuropsychological tests are used to evaluate a person's mental abilities in many areas including memory, problem solving, attention, calculation, and language. The results of all tests and the patient's medical history help the doctor determine if symptoms are caused by Alzheimer's or by another condition.

Although the early and accurate diagnosis of Alzheimer's disease is difficult, in many specialized centers, it is possible to get a reliable diagnosis with 80 to 90 percent accuracy (when compared with autopsy findings). A goal of current research is to develop an accurate test for Alzheimer's disease in living patients using skin or blood samples.

Treatment

Alzheimer's disease advances in stages, ranging from mild forgetfulness to severe dementia. The course of the disease varies from person to person, as does the rate of decline; the duration of Alzheimer's disease from the beginning of symptoms to death can be from 5 to 20 years.

At this time, there is no effective treatment for Alzheimer's disease that can stop the progression of the disorder. However, experimental drugs have shown promise in easing symptoms in some patients. Moreover, medications can help control various behavioral symptoms, thereby making patients more comfortable and management easier for caregivers. For example, medication to improve sleep patterns, reduce wandering, or ease the anxiety and depression that may develop in some patients is available.

People with Alzheimer's should be checked regularly by a health professional such as a doctor or nurse to monitor the progression of the disease, and to treat any other illnesses and aggravating symptoms that may occur during its course. Health professionals also can offer guidance and support to the family.

Most often, the spouse or another family member provides the day-to-day care of the Alzheimer's patient. As the disease progresses and the patient requires more supervision, the job of caregiving can become overwhelming and affect the caregiver's mental and physical health, family life, career, and finances.

Many Alzheimer's disease patients and their families are assisted by the Alzheimer's Association, a private service organization with local chapters nationwide that provide educational programs and support groups for caregivers and family members of patients with Alzheimer's disease. For contact information, see the Alzheimer's Association listing at the end of this fact sheet.

Research

Scientists at research centers across the country are trying to learn what causes the disease and how to prevent it. The major chemical component of senile plaques in the brains of Alzheimer's disease patients has been identified as a protein called beta-amyloid, which is not normally found in brain tissue. Similarly, scientists recently discovered that an abnormally changed form of a protein called "tau" makes up the basic structure of neurofibrillary tangles. Researchers are now studying how these abnormal proteins lead to the formation of plaques and tangles. They are also looking for better ways to diagnose and treat Alzheimer's disease, to improve patients' ability to function, and to support the caregivers of Alzheimer's patients.

In addition, a number of risk factors are under study. Researchers believe that inherited (genetic) factors may be involved in as many as half of Alzheimer's disease patients. However, genetic factors alone may not be enough to bring on the disorder; other risk factors may combine with a person's genetic makeup to increase the chance of developing the disease. Genetic markers, or indicators, have been found in some patients with the disease and in their relatives who do not yet show signs of impairment. Unfortunately, no blood or urine test currently exists that can detect or predict Alzheimer's disease.

Another possible risk factor-environmental toxins-is also being examined. For example, the detection of aluminum and other trace metals in the brain tissue of Alzheimer's patients is being studied to see whether such deposits influence the disease process or whether they are simply the results of disrupted brain structures. Other research focuses on the possibility that a virus may be involved in Alzheimer's disease.

In their search for treatments for the disease, scientists are investigating drugs that might improve memory and other thought processes, including drugs that increase levels of neurotransmitters. Another approach under investigation is the possibility of transplanting healthy cells into the brain to offset those lost as a result of the disease. In addition, researchers are looking for ways to strengthen already weakened or damaged brain cells.

Other research is aimed at helping both patients and caregivers cope with the patients' loss of abilities associated with the disease and the increased stress this places on caregivers. For example, investigators are examining ways to manage difficult patient behaviors such as wandering, incontinence (loss of bladder and/or bowel control), and agitation. Still other research efforts focus on alternative care programs that provide relief to the caregiver and support for the patient. Some communities are designing and evaluating programs to help patients retain optimal functioning. The National Institute on Aging (NIA), the Federal Government's lead agency for research on Alzheimer's disease, funds Alzheimer's Disease Centers located throughout the United States. The Centers carry out a wide range of research, including studies on the causes of Alzheimer's disease and studies aimed at diagnosing, treating, and managing the symptoms of the disease. To obtain a list of the Centers, contact the Alzheimer's Disease Education and Referral Center listed below.

For More Information

To learn about support groups, services, and publications for people with Alzheimer's disease, contact the following:

Eldercare Locator
800-677-1116

Alzheimer's Association
919 North Michigan Ave.
Suite 1000
Chicago, Illinois 60611
800-272-3900

Alzheimer's Disease Education and Referral (ADEAR) Center
P.O. Box 8250
Silver Spring, MD 20907-8250
800-438-4380

Arthritis Fact Sheet[*]

The human skeleton and muscles help to make possible the graceful gyrations of the dancer and the prowess of the athlete, as well as the many more mundane movements of our everyday lives. We tend to take for granted the normally smooth sliding motion of our joints — until it is hampered. One of the most common ills — arthritis — affects this vital function. Arthritis is a disorder of the joints, the junctions between bones.

About 50 million people in the United States have arthritis. Although many suffer only intermittently, according to the National Institute of Arthritis and Musculoskeletal and Skin Diseases, the condition interferes with day-to-day activities for 4.4 million people, and causes partial disability in 1.5 million and complete disability in another 1.5 million individuals. The Arthritis Foundation estimates that 70 million days of missed work can be chalked up to arthritis in the United States each year, as can 500 million days of restricted activity.

Symptoms of the more than 100 types of arthritis range from minor stiffness to grave disability and deformity. Although arthritis cannot be cured, its course can be slowed and symptoms relieved. And, with increasing understanding of the disease process underlying at least some forms of the illness, the outlook for new, more effective drugs is promising.

The Synovial Joint

Arthritis affects the synovial joint, a liquid-filled capsule built of fibrous bands of connective tissue — the ligaments — that attach adjoining movable bones. The capsule is lined on the inside with a membrane that secretes the cushioning synovial fluid, which is stored in membrane-lined packets called bursae. In healthy joints

---

[*] Source: National Institute of Arthritis and Musculoskeletal and Skin Diseases, U.S. Department of Health and Human Services, 1 AMS Way, Bethesda, MD 20892; 301-495-4484.

What is arthritis?
The term "arthritis" literally means joint inflammation, but it also refers to a family of more than 100 rheumatic diseases. These diseases may affect not only the joints but also other connective tissues of the body, including important supporting structures such as muscles, tendons, and ligaments, as well as the skin and certain internal organs.

What is the cause?
Some forms of arthritis are caused by infections or injuries; for many forms the cause is unknown.

Whom do the types of arthritis affect?
Arthritis and related musculoskeletal diseases can affect people of all ages from the very young to the very old. Some forms of arthritis occur predominantly in women; others are more common in men.

What are the symptoms?
The rheumatic diseases vary greatly from person to person and from one disease to another.

What are the treatments?
A comprehensive treatment program may include medication, exercise, rest, joint protection, and even surgery. Treatments depend on the form of arthritis and the needs of the individual.

What are the most common types?
The most common types of arthritis include osteoarthritis, rheumatoid arthritis, ankylosing spondylitis (arthritis of the spine), gout, lupus, fibromyalgia, and juvenile arthritis. Other important forms are Raynaud's syndrome, scleroderma, and Sjogren's syndrome.*

What is the health impact?
Together forms of arthritis affect an estimated 37 million Americans (1 out of 7), including some 200,000 children.

* NIAMS, through its Information Clearinghouse, can provide additional information on many forms of arthritis.

between movable bones, only a thin film of synovial fluid covers the surfaces. A decrease in synovial fluid is associated with the joint stiffness that we normally feel as we age. In arthritis, the amount of synovial fluid increases, swelling the joint.

Opposing bones facing a joint are capped by cartilage, a flexible, bloodless tissue. In a healthy synovial joint, the slipperiness of the cartilage tips and the fluid in the joint allow the bones to move nearly friction-free.

Joint deterioration can be hereditary or can result from injury, infection, autoimmune disease (attack by the individual's own immune system), or even a drug reaction. Although the physical changes behind some forms of arthritis are well understood, we know relatively little about how those changes begin.

Of the more than 100 types of arthritis, by far the most prevalent are osteoarthritis (with nearly 16 million sufferers) and rheumatoid arthritis (with nearly 3 million sufferers). It is not surprising that the rarer forms of arthritis may initially be misdiagnosed as one of these more prevalent two forms.

This was the case with 10-year old Christopher Green, of Scotia, N.Y., who had fever for two weeks and then rapidly developed near crippling arthritis in his legs and hips. Chris's condition was first diagnosed as juvenile rheumatoid arthritis, but the appearance of other symptoms soon led his physicians to suspect Kawasaki disease, a condition first identified in Japan in 1974, where several epidemics have occurred. Kawasaki disease includes arthritis 15 percent of the time. Chris fully recovered the use of his joints after three weeks, and his doctors do not expect the arthritis to recur — although the condition is so recently identified that they cannot be certain.

Another rare form of arthritis is on the rise. It begins with infection by Streptococcus pyogenes, also known as strep A. The incidence is 4 to 5 cases per 100,000 people, and the death rate is a whopping 20 to 25 percent. From the initial symptoms of a sore throat and pneumonia, the illness can progress to meningitis (inflammation of the membrane covering the brain). If the patient survives, arthritis may develop.

Setting Therapy Goals

Arthritis therapy aims to protect the affected joint, maintain as much mobility as possible, and strengthen neighboring muscles to minimize loss of function. These goals can be approached by lifestyle changes, use of support devices and drugs, and finally, by surgery.

Eating fish (such as salmon and other deep sea fish) rich in the oils eicosapentainoic acid and ocosahexanoic acid improves symptoms of rheumatoid arthritis, says Charles Dinarello, M.D., at the Tufts University School of Medicine. "Our work on the mechanism of fish oil action suggests that its anti-inflammatory properties are at least partly due to lowering tumor necrosis factor," Dinatello says, referring to one of the immune system biochemicals that collects in rheumatoid arthritis joints.

Over the past decade, more and more rheumatologists have suggested that their patients exercise. Regular activity that does not place weight on affected joints, but strengthens surrounding bones, muscles and ligaments, can be valuable for many types of arthritis. With the help of a physical therapist, isometric and isotonic exercises and massaging can be tailored to the specific affected joints. For example, exercise that rotates the neck can relieve stiffness and pain and improve mobility in a person with an arthritic spine.

Devices and Drugs

An "activities of daily living" evaluation can help an arthritic patient identify painful movements, which will assist in the development of devices that can be used at home or in the workplace. A person with arthritic hands might use extensions — long handles — on utensils and pens. Shelves can be rearranged so that the most frequently used items are within easy reach of someone with arthritic shoulders. Crutches and canes can help those with arthritic knees or hips. Special thumb, hand or wrist splints and gloves can temporarily restore hand function. Wearing loose-fitting clothes that avoid putting pressure on sensitive joints and avoiding obesity make life for the arthritic patient a little easier.

In the 1940s, it was discovered that crude extracts from adrenal glands of animals could rapidly relieve the inflammation of arthritis. In the 1950s, drug companies developed the anti-inflammatory agents cortisone and hydrocortisone. These potent drugs resemble the human adrenal hormone cortisol. But their use is limited today.

"Cortisone has adverse effects that were originally discovered in the early 1950s. It is an immune suppressant, weakening the body's defense against infections," says Dottie Pease, consumer safety officer at FDA's pilot drug evaluation department. Cortisone taken by mouth can lead to osteoporosis, and direct injection into joints can damage the cartilage. Further, it can cause cataracts, skin thinning, diabetes, fluid retention, poor wound healing, and increased susceptibility to infection. Still, cortisone can offer great, albeit temporary, relief.

Today, the first pharmaceutical line of defense against arthritis is the NSAIDs (nonsteroidal anti-inflammatory drugs), which include the salicylates, such as aspirin, prescribed at higher than usual doses. Coated and time-release preparations can lessen the risk of gastrointestinal bleeding, the major side effect of these drugs.

The NSAIDs block release of prostaglandins, which trigger inflammation. Some more commonly used NSAIDs include ibuprofen, flurbiprofen, indomethacin, and naproxen. Currently, 15 NSAIDs are available.

Drugs called disease modifiers are used in rheumatoid arthritis patients who have had symptoms for at least six months and for whom NSAIDs no longer control swelling of joints. One such treatment is gold injected into a joint, which helps about 50 percent of patients, but unfortunately remains effective in only 5 to 15 percent of them after five years of use.

"No one knows how it works, but it is not an anti-inflammatory," says Pease. The physical presence of gold in the joint may reduce swelling, or the metal may chemically react with a biochemical in some as yet unknown way.

Another disease modifier is methotrexate, an anti-cancer drug that tempers the runaway cell division in the synovial joint. If these disease modifiers do not work, agents that suppress the immune response, such as cyclophosphamide, may be tried.

Biologics Block Cytokines

Unraveling the immune imbalances that underlie some forms of arthritis, and investigating how drugs alter immune function to quell inflammation are opening up an entirely new avenue to treating arthritis — the use of "biologics," or body chemicals. A prime target for new arthritis drugs is blocking cytokine production, a different approach to halting prostaglandin synthesis, which is the mechanism of most existing arthritis drugs.

Innovative approaches under way include work at Nova Pharmaceuticals in Baltimore with unusual amino acids that, in test animals, block the release of inflammation-provoking cytokines from activated T cells (a specialized type of white blood cell). Laboratory research at Immunex Corporation in Seattle, Synergen Corporation in Boulder, Colo., and Hoffmann La Roche in Nutley, N.J., focuses on using interleukin-1 to prevent inflammation. Interleukin-1 is an immune system chemical that must bind to the lining inside joints to start the inflammatory process.

Joint Replacement

For advance arthritis, joints can be replaced with synthetic materials, usually metals like cobalt-chrome and titanium alloys in the larger joints and polymers (lone-chained molecules) such as silicone in the smaller joints, such as in the fingers. The devices must be durable and must not stimulate attack by the already overactive immune system, interfere with healing, or push surrounding structures out of their normal position.

Before the advent of implants, surgeons would remove joint surfaces, hoping that the scar tissue filling in the area would allow more mobility than the arthritic joint. This type of surgery often failed. Implants proved far more successful. They were pioneered by an army surgeon from Grand Rapids, Mich., Alfred Swanson, M.D. He fashioned the first such devices in the late 1950s out of silicone clastomers, polymers made from the element silicone, which is found in quartz.

Research to fine-tune the implants continued in the 1960s, and in 1969, the first silicone-based joint implants came on the market. These implants provided a flexible hinge for the joints of the fingers, wrists and toes. Since then, more than two dozen models have been developed, several by Swanson, who is now a professor of surgery at Michigan State University. More than a million people have received joint replacements — mostly in the hip — and they are still based on silicone.

During implant surgery, technically called "implant resection arthroplasty," the surgeon first removes the surface of the joint bones as well as excess cartilage. The centers of the tips of abutting bones are hollowed out, and the stems of the implant are inserted here. Between the bones lies the hinge part of the implant, which both aligns the bones and allows them to bend at the joint. The implant is "Fixed," or held in place, with bone cement and, finally, the tendons, muscles and ligaments are repaired. As the site heals, the patient must exercise, but it can take a year of physical therapy to achieve maximum rehabilitation.

A new type of hand surgery replaces joints and realigns fingers at the same time. "All rheumatoid arthritis patients who have a severe deviation of their fingers away from the thumb are candidates for this procedure," says Robert Pearly, M.D., associate professor of plastic surgery at Stanford University Medical Center.

He recently introduced an operation that repositions the tendon at the base of the little finger. He finds that holding the pinky in place forces the other fingers to align properly. Pearl's patients start moving the hand the night after the operation, and wear a splint-like support device for the next three weeks. "By six weeks after the operation, patients are able to do most of their usual activities, especially the simple tasks that most of us take for granted, but were virtually impossible for these individuals," he says.

Newer joint replacements use materials that resemble body components. "Recent hip implants have been coated with calcium phosphate materials, like hydroxylapatite, which interact with bone. The aim is to enhance the attachment of the implant to the bone with a biologically active material," says Tom Callahan, Ph.D., of FDA's Center for Devices and Radiological Health. Rather than filling in the spaces with cement, investigators are testing a variety of porous coatings that allow "biological fixation," in which bone can grow in to the implant area.

Hope, but No Miracles

Arthritis treatment seems to attract charlatans peddling "miracle cures," folk remedies, and superstition. Over the years, people with arthritis have been advised to cover themselves with horse manure, wear copper bracelets, sit in abandoned radium mines, and swallow any number of magic elixirs.

Although we still do not know precisely what causes this collection of disorders, nor in most cases how to halt its course, modern medicine has an arsenal of treatments available that attempt to make life easier. With better understanding of the immune system's role in the spectrum of arthritis, more treatment options may become available.

How To Take Your Medicine:
Beta Blocker Drugs*

How you take a drug can affect how well it works and how safe it will be for you. Sometimes it can be almost as important as what you take. Timing, what you eat and when you eat, proper dose, and many other factors can mean the difference between feeling better, staying the same, or even feeling worse. This drug information chapter is intended to help you make your treatment work as effectively as possible. It is important to note, however, that this is only a guideline. You should talk to your doctor about how and when to take any prescribed drugs. This chapter features a group of drugs called beta blockers.

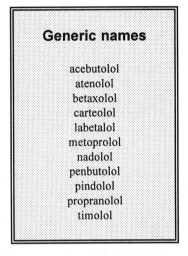

Generic names

acebutolol
atenolol
betaxolol
carteolol
labetalol
metoprolol
nadolol
penbutolol
pindolol
propranolol
timolol

Conditions These Drugs Treat

All beta blockers are used to treat high blood pressure. Many are also used to prevent the heart-related chest pain or pressure associated with angina pectoris (a condition often occurring during exertion where too little blood reaches the heart). Atenolol, metoprolol, timolol, and propranolol are used to improve survival after a heart attack. Propranolol is used to treat heart rhythm problems, other specific heart conditions, migraine headaches, and tremors. Beta blockers can be used for other conditions as determined by your doctor.

Beta blockers cannot cure these conditions. However, by blocking certain receptors in the body, beta blockers lower and regulate the heartbeat and lessen the heart's workload.

---

* Source: Office of Public Affairs, Public Health Service, Food and Drug Administration, 5600 Fishers Lane, Rockville, MD 20857; 301-443-1544.

While taking beta blockers, it is important that you continue any diet and exercise program prescribed by your doctor, as these are often important parts of the therapy for the conditions being treated.

How to Take

Beta blockers can be taken either with food or on an empty stomach.

If you are taking an extended-release product such as Inderal LAR (propranolol), swallow it whole. Don't chew it or crush it in any way.

If you are taking the concentrated solution of propranolol, always use the dropper provided. You can mix the solution with water or any other beverage (or, if you prefer, pudding or applesauce). After taking a dose, rinse the glass with some liquid and drink that liquid as well to be sure that the entire dose is taken.

Be sure to take the right number of tablets or capsules for each dose. Taking your medicine at the same time each day will help you remember to take it regularly.

Missed Doses

Do not suddenly stop taking a beta blocker without first talking to your doctor. Your condition could worsen if you stop taking this medicine or miss many doses.

If you miss a dose, take it as soon as you remember. If you take the beta blocker once a day, you can take it up to eight hours before the next scheduled dose. If you take the medication more often than once a day, you can take it up to four hours before the next scheduled dose. Ask your doctor or pharmacist if you have questions.

Never take two doses at the same time. Always have enough of your beta blocker medicine to last over weekends, holiday periods, and when you travel.

Relief of Symptoms

For conditions such as high blood pressure, angina, heart rhythm disturbances, or tremors, some effects can be

> ## Drug Tips
>
> Don't store drugs in the bathroom medicine cabinet. Heat and humidity may cause the medicine to lose its effectiveness. Keep all medicines, even those with child-resistant caps, out of the reach of children. Remember, the caps are child-resistant, not child-proof. Discard medicines that have reached the expiration date.

seen immediately and usually peak within a week. If treating migraine headaches, it may take up to six weeks before the full effects occur. For any of these conditions, the dosage of the beta blockers may need to be adjusted by your doctor when you first begin taking it. Also, the appropriate dosage can vary greatly among people, depending on individual responses.

Since many of the conditions that beta blockers treat are chronic, you may have to take this medicine for the rest of your life.

Side Effects and Risks

Common side effects include slowed heartbeat, tiredness, nausea, diarrhea, constipation, and decreased sexual ability. Other mild side effects can include difficulty sleeping or nightmares, headache, drowsiness, and numbness or tingling of the fingers, toes, or scalp. Also, if you have diabetes, beta blockers can obscure some of the signs of low blood sugar, such as tremors or rapid heartbeat. Check with your doctor if any of these side effects seem troublesome or if you have any questions.

More serious reactions can sometimes occur with beta blockers. These include the following:

- the beginning or worsening of heart failure. Symptoms of this include shortness of breath (especially on exertion), coughing, weakness, weight gain, and swelling of feet, ankles, or lower legs.
- severe wheezing or difficulty breathing, especially in people who have or have had asthma, chronic bronchitis, emphysema, or other breathing conditions. Because beta blockers can trigger or worsen these conditions, make sure your doctor knows about them.
- an extremely slow heartbeat (less than 50 beats per minute).
- cold hands and feet or blue fingernails, which could mean reduced circulation to these areas.
- confusion, hallucinations or depression. If any of these or other serious reactions occur, call your doctor immediately.

Precautions and Warnings

If you suddenly stop taking a beta blocker you could worsen your condition and experience potentially dangerous side effects, such as chest pain, fast or irregular heartbeat, high blood pressure, and headaches. Always check with your doctor before discontinuing a beta blocker.

Consult with your doctor if you think you could become pregnant or plan to breastfeed while on a beta blocker.

Learn how the medicine affects you. Don't drive or operate machines if this medicine makes you drowsy, dizzy, or lightheaded. If you are taking labetalol, dizziness or lightheadedness can occur when getting up from sitting or lying down. If this happens, sit up slowly, placing your legs over the side of the bed or couch and stay there for a few minutes before trying to stand. Before any surgery, or dental work, tell the physician or dentist that you are taking beta blockers. Tell your physician if you are taking or considering taking any other prescription or nonprescription medication.

Drinking alcohol while on beta blockers can sometimes increase the chance of side effects such as dizziness or tiredness.

What You Need To Know About Breast Cancer[*]

Breast cancer is the most common type of cancer among women in the United States (other than skin cancer). Each year, more than 180,000 women in this country learn they have breast cancer. This chapter is meant to help patients with breast cancer and their families and friends better understand this disease. We hope others will read it as well to learn more about breast cancer.

This chapter discusses screening and early detection, symptoms, diagnosis, treatment, and rehabilitation. It also has information to help patients cope with breast cancer.

Knowledge of breast cancer keeps increasing. For up-to-date information, call the National Cancer Institute's Cancer Information Service (CIS), described at the end of this chapter. The toll-free number is 800-4-CANCER (800-422-6237).

The CIS staff uses a National Cancer Institute cancer information database called PDQ and other NCI resources to answer callers' questions.

Male Breast Cancer

Breast cancer also affects more than 1,000 men in this country each year. Although this chapter was written mainly for women, much of the information on symptoms, diagnosis, treatment, and living with the disease applies to men as well. (The discussion of breast cancer screening does not apply to men. Experts do not recommend routine screening for men.)

The staff can send callers information from PDQ and other NCI materials about cancer, its treatment, and living with the disease.

---

[*] Source: National Cancer Institute (NCI), 31 Center Drive, MSC 2580, Building 31, Bethesda, MD 20892; 800-4-CANCER.

What Is Cancer?

Cancer is a group of diseases that occur when cells become abnormal and divide without control or order.

Every organ in the body is made up of various kinds of cells. Cells normally divide in an orderly way to produce more cells only when they are needed. This process helps keep the body healthy.

If cells divide when new cells are not needed, they form too much tissue. The mass or lump of extra tissue, called a tumor, can be benign or malignant.

- Benign tumors are not cancer. They can usually be removed, and in most cases, they don't come back. Most important, the cells in benign tumors do not invade other tissues and do not spread to other parts of the body. Benign breast tumors are not a threat to life.

- Malignant tumors are cancer. The cancer cells grow and divide out of control. They can invade and damage nearby tissues and organs. Also, cancer cells can break away from a malignant tumor and enter the bloodstream or lymphatic system. That is how breast cancer spreads and forms secondary tumors in other parts of the body. The spread of cancer is called metastasis.

The Breasts

Each breast has 6 to 9 overlapping sections called lobes. Within each lobe are many smaller lobules, which end in dozens of tiny bulbs that can produce milk. The lobes, lobules, and bulbs are all linked by thin tubes called ducts. These ducts lead to the nipple in the center of a dark area of skin called the areola. Fat fills the spaces around the lobules and ducts. There are no muscles in the breast, but muscles lie under each breast and cover the ribs.

Each breast also contains blood vessels and vessels that carry colorless fluid called lymph. The lymph vessels lead to small bean-shaped structures called lymph nodes. Clusters of lymph nodes are found in the axilla (under the arm), above the collarbone, and in the chest. Lymph nodes are also found in many other parts of the body.

Types of Breast Cancer

There are several types of breast cancer. The most common one begins in the lining of the ducts and is called ductal carcinoma. Another type, called lobular carcinoma, arises in the lobules. Other cancers that begin in the breast are rare and are not discussed in this chapter. The Cancer Information Service can supply information about them.

When breast cancer spreads outside the breast, cancer cells are often found in the lymph nodes under the arm (axillary lymph nodes). If the cancer has reached these nodes, it may mean that cancer cells have spread to other parts of the body-other lymph nodes and other organs, such as the bones, liver, or lungs.

Cancer that spreads is the same disease and has the same name as the original (primary) cancer. When breast cancer spreads, it is called metastatic breast cancer, even though the secondary tumor is in another organ. Doctors sometimes call this "distant" disease.

Screening and Early Detection

Women can take an active part in the early M detection of breast cancer. They should talk with their doctor about the symptoms to watch for and an appropriate schedule of checkups. The doctor's advice will be based on the woman's age, medical history, and other factors.

Women should ask the doctor about:

- Mammograms (x-rays of the breast);

- Clinical breast exams (breast exams by a doctor or nurse); and

- Breast self-examination.

A mammogram is a special kind of x-ray. It is different from a chest x-ray or x-rays of other parts of the body.

Mammography performed in women with no symptoms of breast cancer is usually called screening. Although mammography cannot find every breast cancer, it is currently the best early detection tool available. Studies show that having mammograms regularly (not just once) saves lives in women aged 50 and older. Experts disagree about whether women under 50 should have regular mammograms. It is important for each woman to discuss mammography with her doctor so they can decide together what is right for her.

Mammography uses very low levels of radiation. It usually involves two x-rays of each breast, one taken from the side and one from the top. The breast must be squeezed between two plates for the pictures to be clear. While this squeezing may be a bit uncomfortable, it lasts only a few seconds. In many cases (but not all), mammograms can show breast tumors before they cause symptoms or can be felt. A mammogram can also show small deposits of calcium in the breast. Although most calcium deposits are benign, a cluster of very tiny specks of calcium (called microcalcifications) may be an early sign of cancer.

Mammography should be done only by specially trained medical staff using approved machines designed just for taking x-rays of the breast. A qualified doctor, called a radiologist, should read the mammogram. The results should be communicated promptly to the woman by the mammography facility or by her own doctor. The Mammography Quality Standards Act is a Federal law requiring that all mammography facilities be certified. Women should talk with their doctor or call the Cancer Information Service at

800-4-CANCER for help in finding a certified mammography facility.

For women of all ages, a breast exam by a doctor or nurse (called a clinical breast exam) is usually part of the regular medical checkup. Remember, however, that for women over 50, a clinical breast exam is no substitute for regular mammography.

Also, many women choose to examine their own breasts once a month. It's important to remember that every woman's breasts are different. And each woman's breasts change because of aging, the menstrual cycle, pregnancy, menopause, or taking birth control pills or other hormones. It is normal for the breasts to feel a little lumpy and uneven. Also, it is common for a woman's breasts to be swollen and tender right before or during her menstrual period. A woman should contact her doctor about any unusual changes in her breasts, whether she notices them during breast self-exam or at another time. And, again, remember that for women over 50, a breast self-exam is not a substitute for regular screening mammography.

Symptoms

Early breast cancer usually does not cause pain.In fact, when breast cancer first develops, there may be no symptoms at all. But as the cancer grows, it can cause changes that women should watch for:

- A lump or thickening in or near the breast or in the underarm area;

- A change in the size or shape of the breast;

- A discharge from the nipple; or

- A change in the color or feel of the skin of the breast, areola, or nipple (dimpled, puckered, or scaly).

A woman should see her doctor if she notices any of these changes. Most often, they are not cancer, but only a doctor can tell for sure.

Diagnosis

An abnormal area on a mammogram, a lump, or other changes in the breast can be caused by cancer or by other, less serious problems. To find out the cause of any of these signs or symptoms, a woman's doctor does a careful physical exam and asks about her personal and family medical history. In addition to checking general signs of health, the doctor may do one or more of the breast exams described below.

> When a woman needs a biopsy, these are some questions she may want to ask her doctor:
>
> - What type of biopsy will I have? Why?
>
> - How long will the biopsy or aspiration take? Will I be awake? Will it hurt?
>
> - How soon will I know the results?
>
> - If I do have cancer, who will talk with me about treatment? When?

Palpation. The doctor can tell a lot about a lump-its size, its texture, and whether it moves easily-by palpation, carefully feeling the lump and the tissue around it. Benign lumps often feel different from cancerous ones.

Mammography. X-rays of the breast can give the doctor important information about a breast lump. If an area on the mammogram looks suspicious or is not clear, additional x-rays may be needed.

Ultrasonography. Using high-frequency sound waves, ultrasonography can often show whether a lump is solid or filled with fluid. This exam may be used along with mammography.

Based on these exams, the doctor may decide that no further tests are needed and no treatment is necessary. In such cases, the doctor may need to check the woman regularly to watch for any changes.

Often, however, the doctor must remove fluid or tissue from the breast to make a diagnosis.

Aspiration or needle biopsy. The doctor uses a needle to remove fluid or a small amount of tissue from a breast lump. This procedure may show whether a lump is a fluid-filled cyst (not cancer) or a solid mass (which may or may not be cancer). Using special techniques, tissue can be removed with a needle from an area that is suspicious on a mammogram but cannot be felt.

If tissue is removed in a needle biopsy, it goes to a lab to be checked for cancer cells. Clear fluid removed from a cyst may not need to be checked by a lab.

Surgical biopsy. The surgeon cuts out part or all of a lump or suspicious area. A pathologist examines the tissue under a microscope to check for cancer cells.

When Cancer Is Found

When cancer is present, the pathologist can tell what kind of cancer it is (whether it began in a duct of a lobule) and whether it is invasive (has invaded nearby tissues in the breast).

Special laboratory tests of the tissue help the doctor learn more about the cancer. For example, hormone receptor tests (estrogen and progesterone receptor tests) can help predict whether the cancer is sensitive to hormones. Positive test results mean hormones help the cancer

If the diagnosis is cancer, the patient may want to ask these questions:

- What kind of breast cancer do I have? Is it invasive?

- What did the hormone receptor test show? What other lab tests were done on the tumor tissue, and what did they show?

- How will this information help the doctor decide what type of treatment or further tests to recommend?

grow and the cancer is likely to respond to hormonal therapy. Other lab tests are sometimes done to help the doctor predict whether the cancer is likely to grow slowly or quickly.

The patient's doctor may refer her to doctors who specialize in treating cancer, or she may ask for a referral. Treatment generally begins within a few weeks after the diagnosis. There will be time for the woman to talk with the doctor about her treatment choices, to get a second opinion, and to prepare herself and her loved ones.

Treatment

Many treatment methods are used for breast cancer. Treatment depends on the size and location of the tumor in the breast, the results of lab tests (including hormone receptor tests), and the stage (or extent) of the disease. The doctor may order x-rays and blood tests. The doctor may also do special exams of the liver, lungs, or bones because breast cancer may spread to these areas. To develop a treatment plan to fit each patient's needs, the doctor also considers the woman's age and general health as well as her feelings about the treatment options.

Women with breast cancer are likely to have many questions and concerns about their treatment options. They want to learn all they can about their disease and their treatment choices so that they can take an active part in decisions about their medical care.

The doctor is the best person to answer questions about treatment for a particular patient: what her treatment choices are, how successful the treatment is expected to be, and how much it is likely to cost. Most patients also want to know how they will look after treatment and whether they will have to change their normal activities. Also, the patient may want to talk with her doctor about taking part in a study of new treatment methods. Information about such studies, called clinical trials, is discussed later in this chapter.

Calling the National Cancer Institute's Cancer Information Service at 800-4-CANCER is another way to gather up-to-date treatment information, including information about clinical trials. The staff can answer questions and can send free material about breast cancer treatment. They can suggest other sources of information and support. They can also talk with callers about questions to ask the doctor.

Many patients find it helpful to make a list of questions before seeing the doctor. To make it easier to remember what the doctor says, patients may take notes or ask whether they may use a tape recorder. Some patients also find that it helps to have a family member or friend with them when they see the doctor — to take part in the discussion, to take notes, or just to listen.

> Here are some questions a woman may want to ask the doctor before treatment begins:
>
> - What are the treatment choices?
>
> - What are the expected benefits of each kind of treatment?
>
> - What are the risks and possible side effects of each treatment?
>
> - Are new treatments under study in clinical trials? Would a clinical trial be appropriate for me?

There is a lot to learn about breast cancer and its treatment. Patients should not feel that they need to ask all their questions or understand all the answers at once. They will have many other chances to ask the doctor to explain things that are not clear and to ask for more information.

Planning Treatment

Before starting treatment, the patient might want a second opinion about the diagnosis and the treatment plan. Some insurance companies require a second opinion; others may cover a second opinion if the patient requests it. It may take a week or two to arrange to see another doctor. Studies show that a brief delay (up to several weeks) between biopsy and treatment does not make breast cancer treatment less effective. There are a number of ways to find a doctor for a second opinion:

- The patient's doctor may refer her to one or more specialists. Specialists who treat breast cancer include surgeons, medical oncologists, and radiation oncologists. Sometimes these doctors work together at cancer centers or special centers for breast diseases.

- The Cancer Information Service, at 800-4-CANCER, can tell callers about treatment facilities, including cancer centers and other NCI supported programs in their area.

- Patients can get the names of specialists from their local medical society, a nearby hospital, or a medical school.

Methods of Treatment

Methods of treatment for breast cancer are local or systemic. Local treatments are used to remove, destroy, or control the cancer cells in a specific area. Surgery and radiation therapy are local treatments. Systemic treatments are used to destroy or control cancer cells anywhere in the body. Chemotherapy and hormonal therapy are systemic treatments. A patient may have just one form of treatment or a combination. Different forms of treatment may be given at the same time or one after another.

Here are some questions a woman may want to ask her doctor before having surgery:

- What kinds of surgery can I consider? Which operation do you recommend for me?

- How will I feel after the operation? If I have pain, how will you help me?

- Where will the scars be? What will they look like?

- If I decide to have plastic surgery to rebuild my breast, when can that be done?

- Will I have to do special exercises?

- When can I get back to my normal activities?

Surgery is the most common treatment for breast cancer. Several types of surgery may be used. The doctor can explain each of them in detail, can discuss the benefits and risks of each type, and can describe how each will affect the patient's appearance. An operation to remove the breast (or as much of the breast as possible) is a mastectomy. An operation to remove the cancer but not the breast is called breast-sparing surgery. Lumpectomy and segmental mastectomy are types of breast-sparing surgery. They usually are followed by radiation therapy to destroy any cancer cells that may remain in the area. In most cases, the surgeon also removes lymph nodes under the arm to help determine whether cancer cells have entered the lymph system.

In radical mastectomy (also called Halsted radical mastectomy), the surgeon removes the breast, the chest muscles, all of the lymph nodes under the arm, and some additional fat and skin. For many years, this operation was considered the standard one for women with breast cancer, but it is very rarely necessary and is seldom used now.

Radiation therapy (also called radiotherapy) is the use of high-energy x-rays to damage cancer cells and stop them from growing. The rays may come from radioactive material outside the body and directed at the breast by a machine (external radiation). The radiation can also come from radioactive material placed directly in the breast in thin plastic

Before having radiation therapy, a patient may want to ask her doctor these questions:

- Why do I need this treatment?

- What are the risks and side effects of this treatment?

- When will the treatments begin? When will they end?

- How will I feel during therapy?

- What can I do to take care of myself during therapy?

- Can I continue my normal activities?

- How will my breast look afterward?

tubes (implant radiation). Sometimes the patient receives both kinds of radiation therapy.

For external radiation therapy, patients go to the hospital or clinic each day. When this therapy follows breast-sparing surgery, the treatments are given 5 days a week for 5 to 6 weeks. At the end of that time, an extra "boost" of radiation is often given to the place where the tumor was removed. The boost may be either external or internal (using an implant). Patients stay in the hospital for a short time for implant radiation.

Chemotherapy is the use of drugs to kill cancer cells. Chemotherapy for breast cancer is usually a combination of drugs. The drugs may be given by mouth or by injection. Either way, chemotherapy is a systemic therapy because the drugs enter the bloodstream and travel through the body.

Chemotherapy is given in cycles: a treatment period followed by a recovery period, then another treatment, and so on. Most patients have chemotherapy in an outpatient part of the hospital, at the doctor's office, or at home. Depending on which drugs are given and the woman's general health, however, she may need to stay in the hospital during her treatment.

Patients may want to ask these questions about chemotherapy or hormonal therapy:

- Why do I need this treatment?

- If I need hormonal treatment, which would be better for me, drugs or an operation?

- What drugs will I be taking? What will they do?

- Will I have side effects? What can I do about them?

- How long will I be on this treatment?

Hormonal therapy is used to keep cancer cells from getting the hormones they need to grow. This treatment may include the use of drugs that change the way hormones work or surgery to remove the ovaries, which make female hormones. Like chemotherapy, hormonal therapy is a systemic treatment; it can affect cancer cells throughout the body.

Treatment Choices

Treatment decisions are complex. These decisions are often affected by the judgment of the doctor and by the desires of the patient.

A patient's treatment options depend on a number of factors. These factors include her age and menopausal status, her general health, the location of the tumor, and the size of her breasts. Certain features of the tumor cells (such as whether they depend on hormones to grow) are also considered. The most important factor is the stage of the disease. The stage is based on the size of the tumor and whether it has spread. On the following pages are brief descriptions of the stages of breast cancer and the treatments most often used for each stage. (Other treatments may sometimes be appropriate.)

Lobular carcinoma in situ, or LCIS, refers to abnormal cells in the lining of a lobule. Although these abnormal cells seldom become invasive cancer, their presence is a sign that a woman has a higher-than-average risk of developing breast cancer in either breast. Some patients with LCIS may have no treatment, but return to the doctor regularly for checkups. Others may have surgery to remove both breasts to prevent cancer from developing. Underarm lymph nodes are not usually removed.

Ductal carcinoma in situ, also called intraductal carcinoma or DCIS, refers to abnormal cells in the lining of a duct. The cells have not broken through the duct or invaded nearby tissue. Occasionally, however, DCIS becomes invasive cancer, and the cells can spread. Patients with DCIS may have a mastectomy or may have breast-sparing surgery followed by radiation therapy. Underarm lymph nodes are not usually removed.

Stage I and **stage II** are early stages of breast cancer, but the cancer has invaded nearby tissue. Stage I means that cancer cells have not spread beyond the breast and the tumor is no more than about an inch across. Stage II means that cancer has spread to underarm lymph nodes and/or the tumor in the breast is 1 to 2 inches across.

Women with early stage breast cancer may have breast-sparing surgery followed by radiation therapy as their primary local treatment, or they may have a mastectomy. These approaches are equally effective in treating early stage breast cancer. (The main difference is how the woman looks afterward.) The choice of breast-sparing surgery or mastectomy depends mostly on the size and location of the tumor, the size of the woman's breast, certain features of the mammogram, and how the woman feels about preserving her breast. With either approach, lymph nodes under the arm generally are removed.

Some women with stage I and most with stage II breast cancer have chemotherapy and/or hormonal therapy. This added treatment is called adjuvant therapy. It is given to try to prevent the cancer from recurring.

Stage III is also called locally advanced cancer. The tumor in the breast is large (more than 2 inches across), the cancer is extensive in the underarm lymph nodes, or it has spread to other lymph node areas or to other tissues near the breast. Inflammatory breast cancer is a type of locally advanced breast cancer.

Patients with stage III breast cancer usually have both local treatment to remove or destroy the cancer in the breast and systemic treatment to stop the disease from spreading. The local treatment may be surgery and/or radiation therapy to the breast and underarm. The systemic treatment may be chemotherapy, hormonal therapy, or both; it may be given before or after the local treatment.

Stage IV is metastatic cancer. The cancer has spread from the breast to other organs of the body.

Women who have stage IV breast cancer receive chemotherapy and/or hormonal therapy to shrink the tumor or destroy cancer cells. They may have surgery or radiation therapy to control the cancer in the breast. Radiation may also be useful to control tumors in other parts of the body.

Recurrent cancer means the disease has come back in spite of the initial treatment. Even when a tumor in the breast seems to have been completely removed or destroyed, the disease sometimes returns because undetected cancer cells remained in the area after treatment or because the disease had already spread before treatment. Most recurrences appear within the first 2 or 3 years after treatment, but breast cancer can recur many years later.

Cancer that returns only in the area of the surgery is called a local recurrence. If the disease returns in another part of the body, it is called metastatic breast cancer (or distant disease). The patient may have one type of treatment or a combination of treatments.

Side Effects of Treatment

It is hard to limit the effects of cancer treatment so that only cancer cells are removed or destroyed. Because healthy cells and tissues may also be damaged, treatment often causes unpleasant side effects.

The side effects of cancer treatment are different for each person, and they may even be different from one treatment to the next. Doctors try to plan treatment to keep problems to a minimum. They also watch patients carefully so that they can help with any problems that occur. The National Cancer Institute booklets Radiation Therapy and You and Chemotherapy and You have helpful information about these cancer treatments and coping with their side effects.

Surgery

Removal of a breast can cause a woman's weight to shift and be out of balance — especially if she has large breasts. This imbalance can also cause discomfort in a woman's neck and back. Also, the skin in the breast area may be tight, and the muscles of the arm and shoulder may feel stiff. After a mastectomy, a few women have some permanent loss of strength in these muscles, but for most women, reduced strength and limited movement are temporary. The doctor, nurse, or physical therapist can recommend exercises to help a woman regain movement and strength in her arm and shoulder.

Because nerves may be injured or cut during surgery, a woman may have numbness and tingling in the chest, underarm, shoulder, and arm. These feelings usually go away within a few weeks or months, but in some patients some numbness may be permanent.

Removing the lymph nodes under the arm slows the flow of lymph. In some women, lymph builds up in the arm and hand and causes swelling (lymphedema). Women need to protect the arm and hand on the treated side from injury. They should ask the doctor how to handle any cuts, scratches, insect bites, or other injuries that may occur. Also, they should contact the doctor if an infection develops in the arm or hand.

Radiation Therapy

The radiation oncologist will explain the possible side effects of radiation therapy for breast cancer including uncommon side effects that may involve the heart, lungs, and ribs. One of the common side effects is fatigue, especially in the later weeks of treatment. Resting is important, but doctors usually advise their patients to try to stay reasonably active. Women should match their activities to their energy level. Another common side effect is for the skin in the treated area to become red, dry, tender, and itchy. Toward the end of treatment, the skin may become moist and "weepy." This area should be exposed to the air as much as possible. Patients should avoid wearing a bra or clothes that may rub; loose-fitting cotton clothes are usually best. Good skin care is important at this time, but patients should not use any lotions or creams without the doctor's advice, and they should not use any deodorant on the treated side. The effects of radiation therapy on the skin are temporary. The area will heal when the treatment is over.

For most women, the breast will look and feel about the same after radiation therapy. Occasionally, the treated breast may be firmer. Also, it may be larger (due to fluid buildup) or smaller (because of tissue changes) than it was before. For some women, the breast skin is more sensitive after radiation treatment; for others, it is less sensitive.

Chemotherapy
The side effects of chemotherapy depend mainly on the drugs the patient receives. As with other types of treatment, side effects vary from person to person. In general, anticancer drugs affect rapidly dividing cells. These include blood cells, which fight infection, cause the blood to clot, and carry oxygen to all parts of the body. When blood cells are affected by anticancer drugs, patients are more likely to get infections, bruise or bleed easily, and have less energy. Cells in hair follicles and cells that line the digestive tract also divide rapidly. As a result of chemotherapy, patients may lose their hair and may have other side effects, such as loss of appetite, nausea, vomiting, diarrhea, or mouth sores. Many of these side effects can be controlled with medicine, and they generally are short-term problems. They gradually go away during the recovery part of the chemotherapy cycle or after the treatment is over.

With modern chemotherapy, long-term side effects are fortunately quite rare, but there have been cases in which the heart is weakened, and second cancers such as leukemia have occurred. Also, some anticancer drugs can damage the ovaries. If the ovaries fail to produce hormones, the woman may have symptoms of menopause, such as hot flashes and vaginal dryness. Her periods may become irregular or may stop, and she may not be able to become pregnant. In women over the age of 35 or 40, some of these effects, such as infertility, are likely to be permanent.

Hormonal Therapy

Hormonal therapy can cause a number of side effects. They depend largely on the specific drug or type of treatment, and they vary from patient to patient. Tamoxifen is the most common hormonal treatment. This drug blocks the body's use of estrogen but does not stop estrogen production. Tamoxifen may cause hot flashes, vaginal discharge or irritation, and irregular periods, and it sometimes brings on menopause. Any unusual bleeding should be reported to the doctor.

Serious side effects of tamoxifen are rare, but this drug can cause blood clots in the veins, especially in the legs. In a very small number of women, tamoxifen has calved cancer of the lining of the uterus. The doctor may do biopsies or other tests of the lining of the uterus to monitor for this condition. (This does not apply to women who have had a hysterectomy, surgery to remove the uterus.)

Young women whose ovaries are removed to deprive the cancer cells of estrogen experience menopause immediately. The side effects they have are likely to be more severe than the effects of natural menopause.

Nutrition for Cancer Patients

Loss of appetite can be a problem for cancer patients. They may not feel hungry when they are uncomfortable or tired. Also, some of the common side effects of cancer treatment, such as nausea and vomiting, can make it hard to eat. The doctor may suggest medicine to help with these problems because good nutrition is important. Patients who eat well often feel better and have more energy. Eating well means getting enough calories and protein to help prevent weight loss, regain strength, and rebuild normal tissues.

Doctors, nurses, and dietitians can explain the side effects of treatment and can suggest ways to deal with them. Patients and their families also may want to read the National Cancer Institute booklet, *Eating Hints for Cancer Patients*, which contains many useful suggestions.

After Treatment

Rehabilitation is a very important part of breast cancer treatment. The health care team makes every effort to help women return to their normal activities as soon as possible. Recovery will be different for each woman, depending on the extent of the disease, the treatment she had, and other factors.

Exercising after surgery can help a woman regain motion and strength in her arm 'and shoulder. It can also reduce pain and stiffness in her neck and back. Carefully planned exercises should be started as soon as the doctor says the woman is ready, often within a day or so after surgery. Exercising begins slowly and gently and can even be done in bed. Gradually, exercising can be more active, and regular exercise should become part of a woman's normal routine. (Women who have a mastectomy and immediate breast reconstruction — plastic surgery to rebuild the breast — need special exercises, which the doctor or nurse will explain.)

Often, lymphedema after surgery can be prevented or reduced with certain exercises and by resting with the arm propped up on a pillow. If lymphedema occurs later on, the doctor may suggest exercises and other ways to deal with this problem. For example, some women with lymphedema wear an elastic sleeve or use an elastic cuff to improve lymph circulation. The doctor also may suggest other approaches, such as medication, manual lymph drainage (massage), or use of a machine that compresses the arm. If lymphedema continues, the woman may be referred to a specialist.

After a mastectomy, some women decide to wear a breast form (prosthesis). Others prefer to have breast reconstruction, either at the same time as the mastectomy or later on. Each option has its pros and cons, and what is right for one woman may not be right for another. What is important is that nearly every woman treated for breast cancer has choices. It may be helpful to talk with a plastic surgeon before the mastectomy, but reconstruction is still possible later on.

Various procedures are used to reconstruct the breast. Some use implants; others use tissue moved from another part of the woman's body. The woman should ask the plastic surgeon to explain the risks and benefits of each type of reconstruction. The Cancer Information Service can suggest sources of printed information about breast reconstruction and can tell callers how to contact breast cancer support groups. Members of such groups are often willing to share their personal experiences with breast reconstruction.

Followup Care
Regular followup exams are important after breast cancer treatment. The doctor will continue to check the woman closely to be sure that the cancer has not returned. Regular checkups usually include exams of the chest, underarm, and neck. From time to time, the woman has a complete physical exam and a mammogram. The doctor sometimes orders blood tests, a chest x-ray, scans (special x-rays), and other exams. Women who have been treated with chemotherapy or hormonal therapy may need to have further tests and a yearly pelvic exam.

A woman who has had cancer in one breast has a slightly higher-than-average risk of developing cancer in her other breast. She should report any changes in the treated area or in the other breast to her doctor right away.

Also, a woman who has had breast cancer should tell her doctor about other physical problems if they come up, such as pain, loss of appetite or weight, changes in menstrual periods, unusual vaginal bleeding, or blurred vision. She should also report dizziness, coughing or hoarseness, headaches, backaches or digestive problems that seem unusual or that don't go away. These symptoms may be a sign that the cancer has returned, but they can also be signs of many other problems. Only the doctor can tell for sure.

Living With Cancer

The diagnosis of breast cancer can change a woman's life and the lives of those close to her. These changes can be hard to handle. It is common for the woman and her family and friends to have many different and sometimes confusing emotions.

At times, patients and their loved ones may be frightened, angry, or depressed. These are normal reactions when people face a serious health problem. Many people find it helps to share their thoughts and feelings with loved ones. Sharing can help everyone feel more at ease. It can open the way for others to show their concern and offer their support.

Sometimes women who have had breast cancer are afraid that changes to their body will affect not only how they look but how other people feel about them. They may be concerned that breast cancer and its treatment will affect their sexual relationships. Many couples find that talking about these concerns helps them find ways to express their love during and after treatment. Some seek counseling or a couples' support group.

Cancer patients may worry about holding a job, caring for their families, or starting new relationships. Worries about tests, treatments, hospital stays, and medical bills are also common. Doctors, nurses, or other members of the health care team can help calm fears and ease confusion about treatment, working, or daily activities. Also, meeting with a nurse, social worker, counselor, volunteer, or member of the clergy can be helpful to patients who want to talk about their feelings or discuss their concerns about the future or about personal relationships.

Members of the health care team can provide information and suggest other resources. In addition, the public library is a good source of books and articles on living with cancer. Cancer patients and their families can also find helpful suggestions in the National Cancer Institute booklets listed at the end of this chapter.

Support for Breast Cancer Patients

Finding the strength to deal with the changes brought about by breast cancer can be easier for patients and those who love them when they have appropriate support services.

Many patients find it helpful to talk with others who are facing problems like theirs. Cancer patients often get together in self-help and support groups, where they can share what they have learned about cancer and its treatment and about coping with the disease. Often a social worker or nurse meets with the group.

Several organizations offer special programs for breast cancer patients. Trained volunteers, who have had breast cancer themselves, may talk with or visit patients, provide information, and lend emotional support before and after treatment. They often share their experiences with breast cancer treatment and rehabilitation and with breast reconstruction.

Friends and relatives, especially those who have had cancer themselves, can also be very supportive. It is important to keep in mind, however, that each patient is different. Treatments and ways of dealing with cancer that work for one person may not be right for another, even if they both have the same kind of cancer. It is always a good idea to discuss the advice of friends and family members with the doctor.

Often, the doctor's staff or a social worker at the hospital or clinic can suggest local and national groups that can help with emotional support, rehabilitation, financial aid, transportation, or home care. Information about programs and services for breast cancer patients and their families is also available through the Cancer Information Service.

What the Future Holds

Researchers are always looking for better ways to is detect and treat breast cancer, and the chances of recovery keep improving. Still, it is natural for patients to be concerned about their future.

Sometimes patients use statistics they have heard to try to figure out their own chances of being cured. It is important to remember, however, that statistics are averages based on large numbers of patients. They can't be used to predict what will happen to a particular woman because no two cancer patients are alike. The doctor who takes care of the patient and knows her medical history is in the best position to talk with her about the chance of recovery (prognosis). Women should feel free to ask the doctor about their prognosis, but they should keep in mind that not even the doctor knows exactly what will happen. Doctors often talk about surviving cancer, or they may use the term remission. Doctors use these terms because, although many breast cancer patients will be cured, the disease can recur, even many years later.

The Promise of Cancer Research

Doctors and researchers at hospitals and medical centers all across the country are studying breast cancer. They are trying to learn more about what causes this disease and how to prevent it. They are also looking for better ways to diagnose and treat it.

Causes and Prevention
Doctors can seldom explain why one person gets breast cancer and another doesn't. It is clear, however, that breast cancer is not caused by bumping, bruising, or touching the breast. And this disease is not contagious; no one can "catch" breast cancer from another person.

By studying large numbers of women all over the world, researchers have found certain risk factors that increase a woman's chance of developing breast cancer. There may be other risk factors we don't know about. Some known risk factors can be avoided, but many cannot. Having risk factors means having a higher-than-average chance of getting this disease. However, studies show that most women with known risk factors do not get breast cancer. And many women who get breast cancer have none of the risk factors we know about, other than the risk that comes with growing older.

The following are some of the known risk factors for breast cancer:

- **Age**. The risk of breast cancer increases as a woman gets older. Most breast cancers occur in women over the age of 50; the risk is especially high for women over 60. This disease is uncommon in women under the age of 35.

- **Family history**. The risk of getting breast cancer increases for a woman whose mother, sister, or daughter has had the disease. The woman's risk increases more if her relative's cancer developed before menopause or if it affected both breasts. About 5 percent of women with breast cancer have a hereditary form of this disease. These women usually develop breast cancer at a younger age (before menopause) and they have multiple family members with the disease.

- **Personal history**. The risk of breast cancer is greater than average in women who have had lobular carcinoma in situ. About 25 percent of women diagnosed with this condition develop invasive breast cancer. Also, women who have had breast cancer face an increased risk of getting breast cancer again. As many as 10 to 15 percent of women treated for breast cancer (or ductal carcinoma in situ) get a second primary (new) breast cancer later on.

Other risk factors for breast cancer include starting to menstruate at an early age (before 12) or having a late menopause (after 55).

The risk is also greater in women who had their first child after the age of 30 and those who never had children. These factors are all related to a woman's natural hormones. At this time, no one knows whether the risk of breast cancer is affected by taking medicines that contain hormones (either for birth control, to treat infertility, or as estrogen replacement therapy to control symptoms of menopause). Scientists hope to find the answer to this important question by studying a large number of women taking part in hormone-related research.

Many women are concerned about benign breast conditions. For most women, the ordinary "lumpiness" they feel in their breasts does not increase their risk of breast cancer. However, women who have had breast biopsies that show certain benign changes in breast tissues, such as atypical hyperplasia, do have an increased risk of breast cancer.

Scientists are exploring other possible risk factors for breast cancer. For example, research is in progress to determine whether the risk of breast cancer is affected by environmental factors. Pesticides, electromagnetic fields, engine exhausts, and contaminants in water and food are some of the environmental factors under study.

Some aspects of a woman's lifestyle may affect her chances of developing breast cancer. For example, some studies point to a slightly higher risk of breast cancer among women who drink alcohol. The risk appears to go up with the amount of alcohol consumed, so women who drink should do so only in moderation.

Scientists are trying to learn whether having an abortion or a miscarriage increases the risk of breast cancer. Thus far, studies have produced conflicting evidence, and this question is still unresolved.

Older women who are overweight seem to have a greater risk of breast cancer. Although the possible link between diet and breast cancer is still under study, some scientists believe that choosing a low-fat diet, eating well-balanced meals with plenty of fruits and vegetables, and maintaining ideal weight may lower a woman's risk. Also, recent studies suggest that regular exercise may decrease the risk of breast cancer in younger women.

Women who are at high risk for breast cancer can take part in a study of the drug tamoxifen, which is often used to treat breast cancer patients. This nationwide study is designed to help doctors learn whether tamoxifen can prevent breast cancer in these women. The Cancer Information Service can provide information about this study.

Detection

At present, regular mammography is the most effective tool we have to detect breast cancer. However, mammography is not always accurate. (A woman who feels something is wrong with her breasts should not assume a normal mammogram rules out a problem. She should discuss her concerns with her doctor.) Mammography cannot reveal every breast cancer at an early stage, and it sometimes arouses suspicion when no cancer is present. Researchers are looking for ways to make mammography more accurate. They are also exploring other techniques to produce detailed pictures of the tissues in the breast.

In addition, researchers are studying tumor markers, substances that may be present in abnormal amounts in the blood or urine of a woman who has breast cancer. Some of these markers are used to follow women who have already been diagnosed with breast cancer. At this time, however, no blood or urine test is reliable enough to be used routinely to detect breast cancer.

Treatment

Researchers are looking for more effective ways to treat breast cancer. They are also exploring ways to reduce the side effects of treatment and improve the quality of patients' lives. When laboratory research shows that a new treatment method has promise, cancer patients receive the treatment in clinical trials.

These trials are designed to answer important questions and to find out whether the new approach is both safe and effective. Often, clinical trials compare a new treatment with a standard approach. Patients who take part in clinical trials may have the first 14 chance to benefit from improved treatment methods, and they make an important contribution to medical science.

Trials to study new treatments for patients with all stages of breast cancer are under way. Researchers are testing new treatment methods, new chemotherapy doses and treatment schedules, and new ways of combining treatments. They are working with various anticancer drugs and drug combinations as well as with several types of hormonal therapy. They are also exploring new ways to combine chemotherapy with hormonal therapy and radiation therapy. Some trials include biological therapy, treatment with substances that boost the immune system's response to cancer or help the body recover from the side effects of treatment.

In a number of trials, doctors are trying to learn whether very high doses of anticancer drugs are more effective than the usual doses in destroying breast cancer cells. Because these higher doses seriously damage the patient's bone marrow, where blood cells are formed, researchers are testing ways to replace the bone marrow or to help it recover. These new approaches (bone marrow transplantation, peripheral stem cell support, and the use of colony-stimulating factors) are described in the section on medical terms.

Cancer patients may want to read a National Cancer Institute booklet called *What Are Clinical Trials All About?*, which explains some of the possible benefits and risks of treatment studies. Those who are interested in taking part in a trial should discuss this option with their doctor.

One way to learn about clinical trials is through PDQ, a computerized resource developed by the National Cancer Institute. This resource contains information about cancer treatment and about clinical trials in progress all over the country. The Cancer

Information Service can provide PDQ information to patients and the public.

Medical Terms

Adjuvant therapy (AD-ju-vant): Treatment given in addition to the primary treatment.

Areola (a-REE-oe-la): The area of dark-colored skin that surrounds the nipple.

Aspiration (as-per-AY-shun): Removal of fluid from a lump, often a cyst, with a needle.

Atypical hyperplasia (hy-per-PLAY-zha): A benign (noncancerous) condition in which breast tissue has certain abnormal features. Women with this condition have an increased risk of breast cancer.

Axilla (ak-SIL-a): The underarm.

Axillary dissection (AK-sil-air-ee): Surgery to remove lymph nodes under the arm.

Benign (bee-NINE): Not cancerous; does not invade nearby tissue or spread to other parts of the body.

Biological therapy (by-o-LOJ-i-kal): Treatment to stimulate or restore the ability of the immune system to fight infection and disease. Also called immunotherapy.

Biopsy (BY-op-see): The removal of a sample of tissue, which is then examined under a microscope to check for cancer cells. Excisional biopsy is surgery to remove an entire lump and an area of normal tissue around it. In incisional biopsy, the surgeon removes just part of the lump. Removal of tissue with a needle is called a needle biopsy.

Bone marrow: The soft, sponge-like material inside some bones. Blood cells are produced in the bone marrow.

Bone marrow transplantation (tranz-plan-TAY- shun): A procedure in which doctors replace marrow destroyed by high doses of anticancer drugs or radiation. The replacement marrow is taken from the breast cancer patient before treatment, and the procedure is called autologous (aw-TAHL-o-gus) bone marrow transplantation.

Medical Terms (continued)

Cancer: A term for more than 100 diseases in which abnormal cells divide without control. Cancer cells can spread through the bloodstream and lymphatic system to other parts of the body.

Carcinoma (kar-sin-OE-ma): Cancer that begins in the lining or covering of an organ.

Chemotherapy (kee-moe-THER-a-pee): Treatment with anticancer drugs.

Clinical trials: Research studies that involve patients. Each study is designed to answer scientific questions and to find better ways to prevent or treat cancer.

Colony-stimulating factors: Laboratory-made substances similar to substances in the body that stimulate the production of blood cells. Treatment with colony-stimulating factors can help cells in the bone marrow recover from the effects of chemotherapy and radiation therapy.

Cyst (sist): A closed sac or capsule filled with fluid.

Diaphanography (DY-a-fan-OG-ra-fee): An exam that involves shining a bright light through the breast to reveal features of the tissues inside. This technique is under study; its value in detecting breast cancer has not been proven. Also called transillumination.

Duct: A small channel in the breast through which milk passes from the lobules to the nipple. Cancer that begins in a duct is called ductal carcinoma.

Ductal carcinoma in situ (DUK-tal kar-sin-0-ma in SY-too): Abnormal cells that involve only the lining of a duct. The cells have not spread outside the duct to other tissues in the breast. Also called DCIS or intraductal carcinoma.

Estrogen (ES-troe-jin): A female hormone.

Gynecologist (guy-ni-KOL-o-jist): A doctor who specializes in treating diseases of the female reproductive organs.

Hair follicle (FOL-i-kul): A sac from which a hair grows.

Hormonal therapy: Treatment of cancer by removing, blocking, or adding hormones.

Medical Terms (continued)

Hormones: Chemicals produced by glands in the body. Hormones control the actions of certain cells or organs.

Hormone receptor test: A test to measure the amount of certqin proteins, called hormone receptors, in breast cancer tissue. Hormones can attach to these proteins. A high level of hormone receptors means hormones probably help the cancer grow.

Infertility: The inability to have children.

Infiltrating cancer: See invasive cancer.

Inflammatory breast cancer: A rare type of breast cancer in which cancer cells block the lymph vessels in the skin of the breast. The breast becomes red, swollen, and warm, and the skin of the breast may appear pitted or have ridges. Also called stage III breast cancer.

Invasive cancer: Cancer that has spread beyond the layer of tissue in which it developed. Invasive breast cancer is also called infiltrating cancer or infiltrating carcinoma.

Lobe: A part of the breast: each breast contains 6 to 9 lobes.

Lobular carcinoma in situ (LOB-yoo-lar kar-sin-O-ma in SY-too): Abnormal cells in the lobules of the breast. This condition seldom becomes invasive cancer. However, having lobular carcinoma in situ is a sign that the woman has an increased risk of developing breast cancer. Also called LCIS.

Lobule (LOB-yool): A subdivision of the lobes of the breast. Cancer that begins in a lobule is called lobular carcinoma.

Local therapy: Treatment that affects cells in the tumor and the area close to it.

Lumpectomy (lump-EK-toe-mee): Surgery to remove only the cancerous breast lump; usually followed by radiation therapy.

Lymph (limf): The almost colorless fluid that travels through the lymphatic system and carries cells that help fight infection and disease.

Lymph nodes: Small, bean-shaped structures located along the channels of the lymphatic system. Bacteria or cancer cells that enter the lymphatic system may be found in the nodes. Also called lymph glands.

Medical Terms (continued)

Lymphatic system (lim-FAT-ik): The tissues and organs (including the bone marrow, spleen, thymus, and lymph nodes) that produce and store cells that fight infection and disease. The channels that carry lymph also are part of this system.

Lymphedema (lim-fa-DEE-ma): Swelling of the hand and arm caused by extra fluid that may collect in tissues when underarm lymph nodes are removed or blocked; sometimes called "milk arm."

Malignant (ma-LIG-nant): Cancerous; can spread to other parts of the body.

Mammogram (MAM-o-gram): An x-ray of the breast.

Mammography (mam-OG-ra-fee): The use of x-rays to create a picture of the breast.

Mastectomy (mas-TEK-to-mee): Surgery to remove the breast (or as much of the breast as possible). Menopause: The time of a woman's life when menstrual periods stop; also called "change of life."

Menstrual cycle (MEN-stroo-al): The hormone changes that lead up to a woman's having a period. For most women, one cycle takes 28 days.

Metastasis (meh-TAS-ta-sis): The spread of cancer from one part of the body to another. Cells in the metastatic (secondary) tumor are like those in the original (primary) tumor.

Microcalcifications (MY-krow-kal-si-fi-KA-shunz): Tiny deposits of calcium in the breast that cannot be felt but can be detected on a mammogram. A cluster of these very small specks of calcium may indicate that cancer is present.

Oncologist (on-KOL-o-jist): A doctor who specializes in treating cancer.

Ovaries (OH-va-reez): The pair of female reproductive organs that produce eggs and hormones.

Palpation (pal-PAY-shun): A simple technique in which a doctor presses on the surface of the body with his or her fingers to feel the organs or tissues underneath.

Pathologist (pa-THOL-o-jist): A doctor who identifies diseases by studying cells and tissues under a microscope.

Medical Terms (continued)

Peripheral stem cell support (per-IF-er-al): A method for replacing bone marrow destroyed by cancer treatment. Certain cells (stem cells) in the blood that are similar to those in bone marrow are removed from the patient's blood before treatment. The cells are given back to the patient after treatment to help the bone marrow recover and continue producing healthy blood cells.

Progesterone (proe-JES-ter-own): A female hormone.

Prognosis (prog-NOE-sis): The probable outcome or course of a disease; the chance of recovery.

Prosthesis (pros-THEE-sis): An artificial replacement of a part of the body. A breast prosthesis is a breast form worn under clothing.

Radiation therapy (ray-dee-AY-shun): Treatment with high-energy rays to kill cancer cells. Radiation therapy that uses a machine located outside the body to aim high-energy rays at the cancer is called external radiation. When radioactive material is placed in the breast in thin plastic tubes, the treatment is called implant radiation.

Radiologist: A doctor who specializes in creating and interpreting pictures of areas inside the body. The pictures are produced with x-rays, sound waves, or other types of energy.

Remission: Disappearance of the signs and symptoms of cancer. When this happens, the disease is said to be "in remission." A remission can be temporary or permanent.

Risk factor: Something that increases a person's chance of developing a disease.

Screening: Checking for disease when there are no symptoms.

Stage: The extent of the cancer. The stage of breast cancer depends on the size of the cancer and whether it has spread.

Stem cells: The cells from which all blood cells develop.

Surgery: An operation.

Systemic therapy (sis-TEM-ik): Treatment that reaches and affects cells all over the body.

Medical Terms (continued)

Thermography (ther-MOG-ra-fee): A test to measure and display heat patterns of tissues near the surface of the breast. Abnormal tissue generally is warmer than healthy tissue. This technique is under study; its value in detecting breast cancer has not been proven.

Tissue (TISH-oo): A group or layer of cells that performs a specific function.

Tumor: An abnormal mass of tissue.

Ultrasonography (UL-tra-son-OG-ra-fee): A test in which high-frequency sound waves that cannot be heard by humans are bounced off tissues and the echoes are converted into a picture (sonogram). These pictures are shown on a monitor like a TV screen. Tissues of different densities look different in the picture because they reflect sound waves differently. A sonogram can often show whether a breast lump is a fluid-filled cyst or a solid mass.

Xeroradiography (ZEE-roe-ray-dee-OG-ra-fee): A type of mammography in which a picture of the breast is recorded on paper rather than on film.

X-ray: High-energy radiation. It is used in low doses to diagnose diseases and in high doses to treat cancer.

Resources

Information about cancer is available from several sources, including the ones listed below. You may wish to check for additional information at your local library or bookstore or from support groups in your community.

Cancer Information Service (CIS)

The Cancer Information Service, a program of the National Cancer Institute, provides a nationwide telephone service for cancer patients and their families and friends, the public, and health professionals. The staff can answer questions and can send booklets about cancer. They can provide information from the National Cancer Institute's PDQ database. The CIS staff also know about local resources and services. One toll-free number, 800-4-CANCER (800-422-6237), connects callers all over the country to the office that serves their area. Spanish speaking staff members are available.

American Cancer Society (ACS)

The American Cancer Society is a voluntary organization with units all over the country. It supports research, conducts educational programs, and offers many services to patients and their families. It provides free booklets on breast self-examination, breast cancer, and sexuality. To obtain booklets or to learn about Reach to Recovery or other services and activities in local areas, call the Society's toll-free number, 800-ACS-2345 (800-227-2345), or the number listed under American Cancer Society in the white pages of the local telephone book.

National Alliance of Breast Cancer Organizations (NABCO)

Tenth Floor, 9 East 37th Street, New York, NY 10016; 800-719-9154. The National Alliance of Breast Cancer Organizations is a network of organizations that offer detection, treatment, and support to breast cancer patients. NABCO can refer people to such organizations. NABCO also provides information about breast cancer and works for legislation that benefits women treated for this disease.

Booklets

The National Cancer Institute booklets listed below and others are free from the Cancer Information Service at 800-4-CANCER.

Booklets About Cancer Treatment
- *Radiation Therapy and You: A Guide to Self-Help During Treatment*
- *Chemotherapy and You: A Guide to Self-Help During Treatment*
- *Helping Yourself During Chemotherapy*
- *Eating Hints for Cancer Patients*
- *Get Relief From Cancer Pain*
- *Questions and Answers About Pain Control* (also available from the American Cancer Society)
- *What are Clinical Trials All About?*

Booklets About Living With Cancer
- *Taking Time: Support for People With Cancer and the People Who Care About Them*
- *Facing Forward: A Guide for Cancer Survivors*
- *When Cancer Recurs: Meeting the Challenge Again*
- *Advanced Cancer: Living Each Day*

What You Need To Know About Cancer[*]

This chapter is about cancer. If you have questions after reading this, please call the Cancer Information Service to talk with someone. The staff can talk with you in English or Spanish. The number is 800-422-6237 (800-4-CANCER). The call is free.

This information about cancer is from the National Cancer Institute (NCI). It describes some of the warning signs of cancer and stresses the importance of early detection. It also explains how this disease is diagnosed and treated and has information to help you deal with cancer if it affects you or someone you know. This chapter also lists some possible causes of cancer and suggests ways to avoid many of them.

The information cannot answer every question you may have about cancer and cannot take the place of talks with doctors, nurses, and other members of the health care team. We hope our information will help with those talks.

Researchers continue to look for better ways to diagnose and treat cancer, and our knowledge is growing. For up-to-date information about cancer, call the NCI-supported Cancer Information Service (CIS) toll free at 800-4-CANCER (800-422-6237). The CIS is described at the end of this chapter.

What Is Cancer?

Cancer is a group of more than 100 different diseases. Cancer occurs when cells become abnormal and keep dividing and forming more cells without control or order.

All organs of the body are made up of cells. Normally, cells divide to produce more cells only when the body needs them. This orderly process helps keep us healthy.

---

[*] Source: National Cancer Institute (NCI), 31 Center Drive, MSC 2580, Building 31, Bethesda, MD 20892; 800-4-CANCER.

If cells keep dividing when new cells are not needed, a mass of tissue forms. This mass of extra tissue, called a growth or tumor, can be benign or malignant.

- Benign tumors are not cancer. They can usually be removed and, in most cases, they do not come back. Most important, cells from benign tumors do not spread to other parts of the body. Benign tumors are rarely a threat to life.

- Malignant tumors are cancer. Cancer cells can invade and damage nearby tissues and organs. Also, cancer cells can break away from a malignant tumor and enter the bloodstream or the lymphatic system. This is how cancer spreads from the original (primary) tumor to form new tumors in other parts of the body. The spread of cancer is called metastasis.

Most cancers are named for the type of cell or the organ in which they begin. When cancer spreads, the new tumor has the same kind of abnormal cells and the same name as the primary tumor. For example, if lung cancer spreads to the liver, the cancer cells in the liver are lung cancer cells. The disease is called metastatic lung cancer (it is not liver cancer).

Early Detection

In many cases, the sooner cancer is diagnosed and treated, the better a person's chance for a full recovery. If you develop cancer, you can improve the chance that it will be detected early if you have regular medical checkups and do certain self-exams. Often a doctor can find early cancer during a physical exam or with routine tests-even if a person has no symptoms. Some important medical exams, tests, and self-exams are discussed on the next pages. The doctor may suggest other exams for people who are at increased risk for cancer. (Information about risk factors are noted later in this chapter.)

Ask your doctor about your cancer risk, about problems to watch for, and about a schedule of regular checkups. The doctor's advice will be based on your age, medical history, and other risk factors. The doctor also can help you learn about self-exams. (More information and free booklets about self-exams are available from the Cancer Information Service.)

Many local health departments have information about cancer screening or early detection programs. The Cancer Information Service also can tell you about such programs.

Exams for Both Men and Women

Skin - The doctor should examine your skin during regular checkups for signs of skin cancer. You should also check regularly for new growths, sores that do not heal, changes in the size, shape, or color of any moles, or any other changes on the skin. Warning signs like these should be reported to the doctor right away.

Colon and Rectum - Beginning at age 50, you should have a yearly fecal occult blood test. This test is a check for hidden (occult) blood in the stool. A small amount of stool is placed on a plastic slide or on special paper. It may be tested in the doctor's office or sent to a lab. This test is done because cancer of the colon and rectum may cause bleeding. However, noncancerous conditions may also cause bleeding, so having blood in the stool does not necessarily mean a person has cancer. If blood is found, the doctor orders more tests to help make a diagnosis.

To check for cancer of the rectum, the doctor inserts a gloved finger into the rectum and feels for any bumps or abnormal areas. A digital rectal exam should be done during regular checkups.

Every 3 to 5 years after age 50, you should have sigmoidoscopy. In this exam, the doctor uses a thin, flexible tube with a light to look inside the rectum and colon for abnormal areas.

Mouth - Your doctor and dentist should examine your mouth at regular visits. Also, by looking in a mirror, you can check inside your mouth for changes in the color of the lips, gums, tongue, or inner cheeks, and for scabs, cracks, sores, white patches, swelling, or bleeding. It is often possible to see or feel changes in the mouth that might be cancer or a condition that might lead to cancer. Any symptoms in your mouth should be checked by a doctor or dentist. Oral exams are especially important for people who use alcohol or tobacco products and for anyone over age 50.

Exams for Men
Prostate - Men over age 40 should have a yearly digital rectal exam to check the prostate gland for hard or lumpy areas. The doctor feels the prostate through the wall of the rectum.

Testicles - Testicular cancer occurs most often between ages 15 and 34. Most of these cancers are found by men themselves, often by doing a testicular self-exam. If you find a lump or notice another change, such as heaviness, swelling, unusual tenderness, or pain, you should see your doctor. Also, the doctor should examine the testicles as part of regular medical checkups.

Exams for Women
Breast - When breast cancer is found early, a woman has more treatment choices and a good chance of complete recovery. So it is important that breast cancer be detected as early as possible. The National Cancer Institute encourages women to take an active part in early detection. They should talk to their doctor about this disease, the symptoms to watch for, and an appropriate schedule of checkups. Women should ask their doctor about:

- Mammograms (x-rays of the breast),
- Breast exams by a doctor or nurse, and
- Breast self-examination (BSE).

A mammogram can often show tumors or changes in the breast before they can be felt or cause symptoms. However, we know mammograms cannot find every abnormal area in the breast. This is especially true in the breasts of young women. Another important step in early detection is for women to have their breasts examined regularly by a doctor or a nurse.

Between visits to the doctor, women should examine their breasts every month. By doing BSE, women learn what looks and feels normal for their breasts, and they are more likely to find a change. Any changes should be reported to the doctor. Most breast lumps are not cancer, but only a doctor can make a diagnosis.

Cervix - Regular pelvic exams and Pap tests are important to detect early cancer of the cervix. In a pelvic exam, the doctor feels the uterus, vagina, ovaries, fallopian tubes, bladder, and rectum for any change in size or shape.

For the Pap test, a sample of cells is collected from the upper vagina and cervix with a small brush or a flat wooden stick. The sample is placed on a glass slide and checked under a microscope for cancer or other abnormal cells.

Women should start having a Pap test every year after they turn 18 or become sexually active. If the results are normal for 3 or more years in a row, a woman may have this test less often, based on her doctor's advice.

Symptoms of Cancer

You should see your doctor for regular checkups and not wait for problems to occur. But you should also know that the following symptoms may be associated with cancer: changes in bowel or bladder habits, a sore that does not heal, unusual bleeding or discharge, thickening or lump in the breast or any other part of the body, indigestion or difficulty swallowing, obvious change in a wart or mole, or nagging cough or hoarseness. These symptoms are not always a sign of cancer. They can also be caused by less serious conditions. Only a doctor can make a diagnosis. It is important to see a doctor if you have any of these symptoms. Don't wait to feel pain: Early cancer usually does not cause pain.

Diagnosis

If you have a sign or symptom that might mean cancer, the doctor will do a physical exam and ask about your medical history. In addition, the doctor usually orders various tests and exams. These may include imaging procedures, which produce pictures of areas inside the body; endoscopy, which allows the doctor to look directly inside certain organs; and laboratory tests. In most cases, the doctor also orders a biopsy, a procedure in which a sample of tissue is removed. A pathologist examines the tissue under a microscope to check for cancer cells.

Imaging

Images of areas inside the body help the doctor tell whether a tumor is present. These images can be made in several ways. In many cases, the doctor uses a special dye so that certain organs show up better on film. The dye may be swallowed or put into the body through a needle or a tube.

X-rays are the most common way doctors make pictures of the inside of the body. In a special kind of x-ray imaging, a CT or CAT scan uses a computer linked to an x-ray machine to make a series of detailed pictures.

In radionuclide scanning, the patient swallows or is given an injection of a mildly radioactive substance. A machine (scanner) measures radioactivity levels in certain organs and prints a picture on paper or film. By looking at the amount of radioactivity in the organs, the doctor can find abnormal areas.

Ultrasonography is another procedure for viewing the inside of the body. High-frequency sound waves that cannot be heard by humans enter the body and bounce back. Their echoes produce a picture called a sonogram. These pictures are shown on a monitor like a TV screen and can be printed on paper.

In MRI, a powerful magnet linked to a computer is used to make detailed pictures of areas in the body. These pictures are viewed on a monitor and can also be printed.

Endoscopy
Endoscopy allows the doctor to look into the body through a thin, lighted tube called an endoscope. The exam is named for the organ involved (for example, colonoscopy to look inside the colon). During the exam, the doctor may collect tissue or cells for closer examination.

Laboratory Tests
Although no single test can be used to diagnose cancer, laboratory tests such as blood and urine tests give the doctor important information. If cancer is present, lab work may show the effects of the disease on the body. In some cases, special tests are used to measure the amount of certain substances in the blood, urine, other body fluids, or tumor tissue. The levels of these substances may become abnormal when certain kinds of cancer are present.

Biopsy
The physical exam, imaging, endoscopy, and lab tests can show that something abnormal is present, but a biopsy is the only sure way to know whether the problem is cancer. In a biopsy, the doctor removes a sample of tissue from the abnormal area or may remove the whole tumor. A pathologist examines the tissue under a microscope. If cancer is present, the pathologist can usually tell what kind of cancer it is and may be able to judge whether the cells are likely to grow slowly or quickly.

Staging
When cancer is found, the patient's doctor needs to know the stage, or extent, of the disease to plan the best treatment. The doctor may order various tests and exams to find out whether the cancer has spread and, if so, what parts of the body are affected. In some cases, lymph nodes near the tumor are removed and checked for cancer cells. If cancer cells are found in the lymph nodes, it may mean that the cancer has spread to other organs.

Treatment

Cancer is treated with surgery, radiation therapy, chemotherapy, hormone therapy, or biological therapy. Patients with cancer are often treated by a team of specialists, which may include a medical oncologist (specialist in cancer treatment), a surgeon, a radiation oncologist (specialist in radiation therapy), and others. The doctors may decide to use one treatment method or a combination of methods. The choice of treatment depends on the type and location of the cancer, the stage of the disease, the patient's age and general health, and other factors.

Some cancer patients take part in a clinical trial (research study) using, new treatment methods. Such studies are designed to improve cancer treatment. (See additional information about clinical trials later in this chapter.)

Getting a Second Opinion
Before starting treatment, the patient may want another doctor to review the diagnosis and treatment plan. Some insurance companies require a second opinion; others may pay for a second opinion if the patient requests it. There are a number of ways to find specialists to consult for a second opinion:

- The patient's doctor may suggest a specialist for a second opinion.
- The Cancer Information Service, at 800-4-CANCER, can tell callers about treatment facilities, including cancer centers and other programs in their area supported by the National Cancer Institute.
- Patients can get the names of doctors from their local medical society, a nearby hospital, or a medical school.

Preparing for Treatment
Many people with cancer want to learn all they can about their disease and their treatment choices so they can take an active part in decisions about their medical care. Often, it helps to make a list

of questions to ask the doctor. Patients may take notes or, with the doctor's consent, tape record the discussion. Some patients also find it helps to have a family member or friend with them when they talk with the doctor to take part in the discussion, to take notes, or just to listen.

When a person is diagnosed with cancer, shock and stress are natural reactions. These feelings may make it difficult to think of every question to

Here are some questions a patient may want to ask the doctor:

- What is my diagnosis?
- What is the stage of the disease?
- What are my treatment choices? Which do you recommend for me? Why?
- What are the chances that the treatment will be successful?
- Would a clinical trial be appropriate for me?
- What are the risks and possible side effects of each treatment?
- How long will treatment last?
- Will I have to change my normal activities?
- What is the treatment likely to cost?

ask the doctor. Patients may find it hard to remember everything the doctor says. They should not feel they need to ask all their questions or remember all the answers at one time. They will have other chances for the doctor to explain things that are not clear and to ask for more information.

Methods of Treatment

Surgery - Surgery is local treatment to remove the tumor. Tissue around the tumor and nearby lymph nodes may also be removed during the operation.

Radiation Therapy - In radiation therapy (also called radiotherapy), high-energy rays are used to damage cancer cells and stop them from growing and dividing. Like surgery, radiation therapy is a local treatment; it can affect cancer cells only in the treated area. Radiation may come from a machine (external radiation). It also may come from an implant (a small container of radioactive material) placed directly into or near the tumor (internal radiation). Some patients get both kinds of radiation therapy.

External radiation therapy is usually given on an outpatient basis in a hospital or clinic 5 days a week for several weeks. Patients are not radioactive during or after the treatment.

For internal radiation therapy, the patient stays in the hospital for a few days. The implant may be temporary or permanent. Because the level of radiation is highest during the hospital stay, patients may not be able to have visitors or may have visitors only for a short time. Once an implant is removed, there is no radioactivity in the body. The amount of radiation in a permanent implant goes down to a safe level before the patient leaves the hospital.

Chemotherapy - Treatment with drugs to kill cancer cells is called chemotherapy. Most anticancer drugs are injected into a vein (IV) or a muscle; some are given by mouth. Chemotherapy is systemic treatment, meaning that the drugs flow through the bloodstream to nearly every part of the body.

Often, patients who need many doses of IV chemotherapy receive the drugs through a catheter (a thin flexible tube). One end of the catheter is placed in a large vein in the chest. The other end is outside the body or attached to a small device just under the skin. Anticancer drugs are given through the catheter. This can make chemotherapy more comfortable for the patient. Patients and their families are shown how to care for the catheter and keep it clean. For some types of cancer, doctors are studying whether it helps to put anticancer drugs directly into the affected area.

Chemotherapy is generally given in cycles: A treatment period is followed by a recovery period, then another treatment period, and so on. Usually a patient has chemotherapy as an outpatient-at the hospital, at the doctor's office, or at home. However, depending on which drugs are given and the patient's general health, the patient may need to stay in the hospital for a short time.

Hormone Therapy - Some types of cancer, including most breast and prostate cancers, depend on hormones to grow. For this reason, doctors may recommend therapy that prevents cancer cells from getting or using the hormones they need. Sometimes, the patient has surgery to remove organs (such as the ovaries or testicles) that make the hormones; in other cases, the doctor uses drugs to stop hormone production or change the way hormones work. Like chemotherapy, hormone therapy is a systemic treatment; it affects cells throughout the body.

Biological Therapy - Biological therapy (also called immunotherapy) is a form of treatment that uses the body's natural ability (immune system) to fight infection and disease or to protect the body from some of the side effects of treatment. Monoclonal antibodies, interferon, interleukin-2 (IL-2), and several types of colony-stimulating factors (CSF, GM-CSF, G-CSF) are forms of biological therapy.

Side Effects of Cancer Treatment

It is hard to limit the effects of treatment so that only cancer cells are removed or destroyed. Because treatment also damages healthy cells and tissues, it often causes unpleasant side effects.

The side effects of cancer treatment vary. They depend mainly on the type and extent of the treatment. Also, each person reacts differently. Doctors try to plan the patient's therapy to keep side effects to a minimum and they can help with any problems that occur.

Surgery - The side effects of surgery depend on the location of the tumor, the type of operation, the patient's general health, and other factors. Although patients are often uncomfortable during the first few days after surgery, this pain can be controlled with medicine. Patients should feel free to discuss pain relief with the doctor or nurse. It is also common for patients to feel tired or weak for a while. The length of time it takes to recover from an operation varies for each patient.

Radiation Therapy - With radiation therapy, the side effects depend on the treatment dose and the part of the body that is treated. The most common side effects are tiredness, skin reactions (such as a rash or redness) in the treated area, and loss of appetite. Radiation therapy also may cause a decrease in the number of white blood cells, cells that help protect the body against infection.

Although the side effects of radiation therapy can be unpleasant, the doctor can usually treat or control them. It also helps to know that, in most cases, they are not permanent.

Chemotherapy - The side effects of chemotherapy depend mainly on the drugs and the doses the patient receives. Generally, anticancer drugs affect cells that divide rapidly. These include blood cells, which fight infection, help the blood to clot, or carry oxygen to all parts of the body. When blood cells are affected by anticancer drugs, patients are more likely to get infections, may bruise or bleed easily, and may have less energy. Cells that line the digestive tract also divide rapidly. As a result of chemotherapy, patients may have side effects, such as loss of appetite, nausea and vomiting, hair loss, or mouth sores. For some patients, the doctor may prescribe medicine to help with side effects, especially with nausea and vomiting. Usually, these side effects gradually go away during the recovery period or after treatment stops.

Hair loss, another side effect of chemotherapy, is a major concern for many patients. Some chemotherapy drugs only cause the hair to thin out, while others may result in the loss of all body hair. Patients may feel better if they decide how to handle hair loss before starting treatment.

In some men and women, chemotherapy drugs cause changes that may result in a loss of fertility (the ability to have children). Loss of fertility may be temporary or permanent depending on the drugs used and the patient's age. For men, sperm banking before treatment may be a choice. Women's menstrual periods may stop, and they may have hot flashes and vaginal dryness. Periods are more likely to return in young women.

In some cases, bone marrow transplantation and peripheral stem cell support are used to replace tissue that forms blood cells when that tissue has been destroyed by the effects of chemotherapy or radiation therapy.

Hormone Therapy - Hormone therapy can cause a number of side effects. Patients may have nausea and vomiting, swelling or weight gain, and, in some cases, hot flashes. In women, hormone therapy also may cause interrupted menstrual periods, vaginal dryness, and, sometimes, loss of fertility. Hormone therapy in men may cause impotence, loss of sexual desire, or loss of fertility. These changes may be temporary, long lasting, or permanent.

Biological Therapy - The side effects of biological therapy depend on the type of treatment. Often, these treatments cause flu-like symptoms such as chills, fever, muscle aches, weakness, loss of appetite, nausea, vomiting, and diarrhea. Some patients get a rash, and some bleed or bruise easily. In addition, interleukin therapy can cause swelling. Depending on how severe these problems are, patients may need to stay in the hospital during treatment. These side effects are usually short-term; they gradually go away after treatment stops.

Doctors and nurses can explain the side effects of cancer treatment and help with any problems that occur. The National Cancer Institute booklets *Radiation Therapy and You* and *Chemotherapy and You* also have helpful information about cancer treatment and coping with side effects.

Nutrition for Cancer Patients

Some patients lose their appetite and find it hard to eat well. In addition, the common side effects of treatment, such as nausea, vomiting, or mouth sores, can make it difficult to eat. For some patients, foods taste different. Also, people may not feel like eating when they are uncomfortable or tired.

Eating well means getting enough calories and protein to help prevent weight loss and regain strength. Patients who eat well during cancer treatment often feel better and have more energy. In addition, they may be better able to handle the side effects of treatment.

Doctors, nurses, and dietitians can offer advice for healthy eating during cancer treatment. Patients and their families also may want to read the National Cancer Institute booklet *Eating Hints: Recipes and Tips For Better Nutrition During Cancer Treatment*, which contains many useful suggestions.

Clinical Trials

When laboratory research shows that a new treatment method has promise, cancer patients can receive the treatment in carefully controlled trials. These trials are designed to find out whether the new approach is both safe and effective and to answer scientific questions. Often, clinical trials compare a new treatment with a standard approach so that doctors can learn which is more effective.

Researchers also look for ways to reduce the side effects of treatment and improve the quality of patients lives. Patients who take part in clinical trials make an important contribution to medical science. These patients take certain risks, but they also may have the first chance to benefit from improved treatment methods.

Clinical trials offer important options for many patients. Cancer patients who are interested in taking part in a clinical trial should talk with their doctor. They may want to read *What Are Clinical Trials All About?*, a booklet that explains treatment studies and outlines some of their possible benefits and risks.

One way to learn about clinical trials is through PDQ, a computerized resource developed by the National Cancer Institute. PDQ contains information about cancer treatment and about clinical trials in progress all over the country. The Cancer Information

Service can provide PDQ information to doctors, patients, and the public.

Support for Cancer Patients

Living with a serious disease is difficult. Cancer patients and those who care about them face many problems and challenges. Coping with these problems is often easier when people have helpful information and support services.

Cancer patients may worry about holding their job, caring for their family, or keeping up daily activities. Worries about tests, treatments, hospital stays, and medical bills are also common. Doctors, nurses, and other members of the health care team can answer questions about treatment, working, or daily activities. Meeting with a social worker, counselor, or member of the clergy also can be helpful to patients who want to talk about their feelings or discuss their concerns about the future or about personal relationships.

Friends and relatives, especially those who have had personal experience with cancer, can be very supportive. Also, it helps many patients to meet with others who are facing problems like theirs. Cancer patients often get together in support groups, where they can share what they have learned about cancer and its treatment and about coping with the disease. It is important to keep in mind, however, that each patient is different. Treatments and ways of dealing with cancer that work for one person may not be right for another — even if both have the same kind of cancer. It is always a good idea to discuss the advice of friends and family members with the doctor.

Often, a social worker at the hospital or clinic can suggest groups that help with rehabilitation, emotional support, financial aid, transportation, or home care. The American Cancer Society has many services for patients and families. Local offices of the American Cancer Society are listed in the white pages of the telephone directory. (More information about this organization is available at the end of this chapter.)

In addition, the public library has many books and articles on living with cancer. The Cancer Information Service also has information on local resources.

What the Future Holds

Researchers are finding better ways to detect and treat cancer, and the chance of recovery keeps improving. Still, it is natural for patients to be concerned about their future.

Sometimes patients use statistics to try to figure out their chance of being cured. It is important to remember, however, that statistics are averages based on large numbers of patients. They cannot be used to predict what will happen to a particular patient because no two patients are alike. The doctor who takes care of the patient is in the best position to discuss the chance of recovery (prognosis). Patients should feel free to ask the doctor about their prognosis, but they should keep in mind that not even the doctor knows exactly what will happen. Doctors often talk about surviving cancer, or they may use the term remission rather than cure. Even though many cancer patients are cured, doctors use these terms because the disease may recur.

Causes and Prevention of Cancer

The number of new cases of cancer in the United States is going up each year. People of all ages get cancer, but nearly all types are more common in middle-aged and elderly people than in young people. Skin cancer is the most common type of cancer for both men and women. The next most common type among men is prostate cancer; among women, it is breast cancer. Lung cancer, however, is the leading cause of death from cancer for both men and women in the United States. Brain cancer and leukemia are the most common cancers in children and young adults.

The more we can learn about what causes cancer, the more likely we are to find ways to prevent it. Scientists study patterns of cancer in the population to look for factors that affect the risk of developing this disease. In the laboratory, they explore possible causes of cancer and try to determine what actually happens when normal cells become cancerous.

Our current understanding of the causes of cancer is incomplete, but it is clear that cancer is not caused by an injury, such as a bump or bruise. And although being infected with certain viruses may increase the risk of some types of cancer, cancer is not contagious; no one can "catch" cancer from another person.

Cancer develops gradually as a result of a complex mix of factors related to environment, lifestyle, and heredity. Scientists have identified many risk factors that increase the chance of getting cancer. They estimate that about 80 percent of all cancers are related to the use of tobacco products, to what we eat and drink, or, to a lesser extent, to exposure to radiation or cancer-causing agents (carcinogens) in the environment and the workplace. Some people are more sensitive than others to factors that can cause cancer.

Many risk factors can be avoided. Others, such as inherited risk factors, are unavoidable. It is helpful to be aware of them, but it is also important to keep in mind that not everyone with a particular risk factor for cancer actually gets the disease; in fact, most do not. People at risk can help protect themselves by avoiding risk factors where possible and by getting regular checkups so that, if cancer develops, it is likely to be found early.

These are some of the factors that are known to increase the risk of cancer:

Tobacco. Tobacco causes cancer. In fact, smoking tobacco, using "smokeless" tobacco, and being regularly exposed to environmental tobacco smoke without actually smoking are responsible for one-third of all cancer deaths in the United States each year. Tobacco use is the most preventable cause of death in this country.

Smoking accounts for more than 85 percent of all lung cancer deaths. If you smoke, your risk of getting lung cancer is affected by the number and type of cigarettes you smoke and how long you have been smoking. Overall, for those who smoke one pack a day, the chance of getting lung cancer is about 10 times greater than for nonsmokers. Smokers are also more likely than nonsmokers to develop several other types of cancer (such as oral cancer and cancers of the larynx, esophagus, pancreas, bladder, kidney, and cervix). The risk of cancer begins to decrease when a smoker quits, and the risk continues to decline gradually each year after quitting.

The use of smokeless tobacco (chewing tobacco and snuff) causes cancer of the mouth and throat. Precancerous conditions, or tissue changes that may lead to cancer, begin to go away after a person stops using smokeless tobacco.

Exposure to environmental tobacco smoke, also called involuntary smoking, increases the risk of lung cancer for nonsmokers. The risk goes up 30 percent or more for a nonsmoking spouse of a person who smokes. Involuntary smoking causes about 3,000 lung cancer deaths in this country each year.

If you use tobacco in any form and you need help quitting, talk with your doctor or dentist, or join a smoking cessation group sponsored by a local hospital or voluntary organization. For information on such groups or other programs, call the Cancer Information Service or the American Cancer Society.

Diet. Your choice of foods may affect your chance of developing cancer. Evidence points to a link between a high-fat diet and certain cancers, such as cancer of the breast, colon, uterus, and prostate. Being seriously overweight appears to be linked to increased rates of cancer of the prostate, pancreas, uterus, colon, and ovary, and to breast cancer in older women. On the other hand, studies suggest that foods containing fiber and certain nutrients help protect us against some types of cancer.

You may be able to reduce your cancer risk by making some simple food choices. Try to have a varied, well-balanced diet that includes generous amounts of foods that are high in fiber, vitamins, and minerals. At the same time, try to cut down on fatty foods. You should eat five servings of fruits and vegetables each day, choose more whole-grain breads and cereals, and cut down on eggs, high-fat meat, high-fat dairy products (such as whole milk, butter, and most cheeses), salad dressings, margarine, and cooking oils.

Sunlight. Ultraviolet radiation from the sun and from other sources (such as sunlamps and tanning booths) damages the skin and can cause skin cancer. (Two types of ultraviolet radiation-UVA and UVB-are explained in the section on medical terms at the end of this chapter.) Repeated exposure to ultraviolet radiation increases the risk of skin cancer, especially if you have fair skin or freckle easily. The sun's ultraviolet rays are strongest during the summer from about 11 a.m. to about 3 p.m. (daylight saving time). The risk is greatest at this time, when the sun is high overhead and shadows are short. As a rule, it is best to avoid the sun when your shadow is shorter than you are.

Protective clothing, such as a hat and long sleeves, can help block the sun's harmful rays. You can also use sunscreens to help protect yourself. Sunscreens are rated in strength according to their SPF (sun protection factor), which ranges from 2 to 30 and higher. Those rated 15 to 30 block most of the sun's harmful rays.

Alcohol. Drinking large amounts of alcohol increases the risk of cancer of the mouth, throat, esophagus, and larynx. (People who smoke cigarettes and drink alcohol have an especially high risk of getting these cancers.) Alcohol can damage !he liver and increase the risk of liver cancer. Some studies suggest that drinking alcohol also increases the risk of breast cancer. So if you drink at all, do so in moderation-not more than one or two drinks a day.

Radiation. Exposure to large doses of radiation from medical x-rays can increase the risk of cancer. X-rays used for diagnosis expose you to very little radiation and the benefits nearly always outweigh the risks.

However, repeated exposure can be harmful, so it is a good idea to talk with your doctor or dentist about the need for each x-ray and ask about the use of shields to protect other parts of your body.

Before 1950, x-rays were used to treat noncancerous conditions (such as an enlarged thymus, enlarged tonsils and adenoids, ringworm of the scalp, and acne) in children and young adults. People who have received radiation to the head and neck have a higher-than-average risk of developing thyroid cancer years later. People with a history of such treatments should report it to their doctor and should have a careful exam of the neck every I or 2 years.

Chemicals and other substances in the workplace. Being exposed to substances such as metals, dust, chemicals, or pesticides at work can increase the risk of cancer. Asbestos, nickel, cadmium, uranium, radon, vinyl chloride, benzidene, and benzene are well-known examples of carcinogens in the workplace. These may act alone or along with another carcinogen, such as cigarette smoke. For example, inhaling asbestos fibers increases the risk of lung diseases, including cancer, and the cancer risk is especially high for asbestos workers who smoke. It is important to follow work and safety rules to avoid contact with dangerous materials.

Hormone replacement therapy. Many women use estrogen therapy to control the hot flashes, vaginal dryness, and osteoporosis (thinning of the bones) that may occur during menopause. However, studies show that estrogen use increases the risk of cancer of the uterus. Other studies suggest an increased risk of breast cancer among women who have used high doses of estrogen or have used estrogen for a long time. At the same time, taking estrogen may reduce the risk of heart disease and osteoporosis.

The risk of uterine cancer appears to be less when progesterone is used with estrogen than when estrogen is used alone. But some scientists are concerned that the addition of progesterone may also increase the risk of breast cancer.

Researchers are still studying and finding new information about the risks and benefits of taking replacement hormones. A woman considering hormone replacement therapy should discuss these issues with her doctor.

Diethylstilbestrol (DES). DES is a form of estrogen that doctors prescribed from the early 1940s until 1971 to try to prevent miscarriage. In some daughters of women who were given DES during pregnancy, the uterus, vagina, and cervix do not develop normally. DES-exposed daughters also have an increased chance of developing abnormal cells (dysplasia) in the cervix and vagina. In addition, a rare type of vaginal and cervical cancer has been found in a small number of DES-exposed daughters. Women who took DES during pregnancy may have a slightly increased risk of developing breast cancer. DES-exposed mothers and daughters should tell their doctor about this exposure. DES daughters should have regular special pelvic exams by a doctor familiar with conditions related to DES.

Exposure to DES before birth does not appear to increase the risk of cancer in DES-exposed sons; however, reproductive and urinary system problems may occur. These men should tell the doctor and should have regular medical checkups.

Close relatives with certain types of cancer. A small number of cancers (including melanoma and cancers of the breast, ovary, and colon) tend to occur more often in some families than in the rest of the population. It is not always clear whether a pattern of cancer in a family is due to heredity, factors in the family's environment, or chance. Still, if close relatives have been affected by cancer, it is important to let your doctor know this and then follow the doctor's advice about cancer prevention and checkups to detect problems early.

Medical Terms

Benign (be-NINE): Not cancerous; does not invade nearby tissue or spread to other parts of the body.

Biological therapy (by-o-LOJ-i-kul): Treatment to stimulate or restore the ability of the immune system to fight infection and disease. Also called immunotherapy.

Biopsy (BY-op-see): The removal of a sample of tissue, which is then examined under a microscope to check for cancer cells. When only a sample of tissue is removed, the procedure is called incisional biopsy; when the whole tumor is removed, it is excisional biopsy. Removing tissue or fluid with a needle is called needle biopsy or needle aspiration. Bone marrow transplantation: A procedure in which doctors replace marrow destroyed by treatment with high doses of anticancer drugs or radiation. The replacement marrow may be taken from the patient before treatment or may be donated by another person. When the patient's own marrow is used, the procedure is called autologous (aw-TOL-o-gus) bone marrow transplantation.

Cancer: A term for diseases in which abnormal cells divide without control. Cancer cells can invade nearby tissue and can spread through the bloodstream and lymphatic system to other parts of the body.

Carcinogen (kar-SIN-o-jin): A substance or agent that is known to cause cancer.

Catheter (KATH-e-ter): A thin plastic tube. When a catheter is placed in a vein, it provides a pathway for drugs, nutrients, or blood products. Blood samples also can be removed through the catheter.

Chemotherapy (kee-mo-THER-a-pee): Treatment with anticancer drugs.

Clinical trials: Research studies that involve patients.

Colony-stimulating factors: Substances that stimulate the production of blood cells. Treatment with colony-stimulating factors (CSF) can help the blood-forming tissue recover from the effects of chemotherapy and radiation therapy. These include granulocyte colony-stimulating factors (G-CSF) and granulocyte-macrophage colony-stimulating factors (GM-CSF).

CT or CAT scan: Detailed pictures of areas of the body created by a computer linked to an x-ray machine. Also called computed tomography scan or computed axial tomography scan.

Endoscopy (en-DOS-ko-pee): A procedure in which the doctor looks inside the body through a lighted tube called an endoscope.

Medical Terms (continued)

Estrogen (ES-tro-jin): A female hormone.

Fecal occult blood test (FEE-kul o-KULT): A test to check for hidden blood in stool. (Fecal refers to stool. Occult means hidden.)

Gene therapy: Treatment that alters genes (the basic units of heredity found in all cells in the body). In early studies of gene therapy for cancer, researchers are trying to improve the body's natural ability to fight the disease or to make the tumor more sensitive to other kinds of therapy.

Hormone therapy: Treatment that prevents certain cancer cells from getting the hormones they need to grow.

Hormones: Chemicals produced by glands in the body. Hormones control the actions of certain cells or organs.

Imaging: Procedures that produce pictures of areas inside the body.

Immune system: The complex group of cells and organs that defends the body against infection and disease.

Immunotherapy (IM-yoo-no-THER-a-pee): See Biological therapy.

Impotence (IM-po-tens): Inability to have an erection.

Interferon (in-ter-FEER-on): A type of biological response modifier (a substance that can improve the body's natural response to disease). It slows the rate of growth and division of cancer cells, causing them to become sluggish and die.

Interleukin-2 (in-ter-LOO-kin): A type of biological response modifier (a substance that can improve the body's natural response to disease). It stimulates the growth of certain disease-fighting blood cells in the immune system. Also called IL-2.

Local treatment: Treatment that affects the tumor and the area close to it.

Lymph (limf): An almost colorless fluid that travels through the lymphatic system and carries cells that help fight infection and disease.

Medical Terms (continued)

Lymph nodes: Small, bean-shaped organs located along the channels of the lymphatic system. Bacteria or cancer cells that enter the lymphatic system may be found in the nodes. Also called lymph glands.

Lymphatic system (lim-FAT-ik): The tissues and organs, including the bone marrow, spleen, thymus, and lymph nodes, that produce and store cells that fight infection and disease. This system also has channels that carry lymph.

Malignant (ma-LIG-nant): Cancerous.

Mammogram (MAM-o-gram): An x-ray of the breast.

Melanoma: Cancer of the cells that produce pigment in the skin. Melanoma usually begins in a mole.

Metastasis (meh-TAS-ta-sis): The spread of cancer from one part of the body to another. Cells in the metastatic (secondary) tumor are like those in the original (primary) tumor.

Monoclonal antibodies: Substances that can locate and bind to cancer cells wherever they are in the body. They can be used alone, or they can be used to deliver drugs, toxins, or radioactive material directly to the tumor cells.

MRI: A procedure using a magnet linked to a computer to create pictures of areas inside the body. Also called magnetic resonance imaging.

Oncologist (on-KOL-o-jist): A doctor who specializes in treating cancer.

Pap test: Microscopic examination of cells collected from the cervix. It is used to detect changes that may be cancer or may lead to cancer, and it can show noncancerous conditions, such as infection or inflammation. Also called Pap smear.

Pathologist (path-OL-o-jist): A doctor who identifies diseases by studying cells and tissues under a microscope.

Pelvic: Having to do with the pelvis, the lower part of the abdomen, located between the hip bones.

Medical Terms (continued)

Peripheral stem cell support (per-IF-er-ul): A method of replacing blood-forming cells destroyed by cancer treatment. Certain cells (stem cells) in the blood that are similar to those in bone marrow are removed from the patient's blood before treatment. The cells are given back to the patient after treatment.

Progesterone (pro-JES-ter-own): A female hormone.

Prognosis (prog-NO-sis): The probable outcome or course of a disease; the chance of recovery.

Radiation therapy (ray-dee-AY-shun): Treatment with high-energy rays to kill or damage cancer cells. External radiation therapy is the use of a machine to aim high- energy rays at the cancer. Internal radiation therapy is the placement of radioactive material inside the body as close as possible to the cancer.

Radioactive (RAY-dee-o-AK-tiv): Giving off radiation.

Radionuclide scanning: An exam that produces pictures (scans) of internal parts of the body. The patient is given an injection or swallows a small amount of radioactive material. A machine called a scanner then measures the radioactivity in certain organs.

Remission: Disappearance of the signs and symptoms of cancer. When this happens, the disease is said to be "in remission." Remission can be temporary or permanent.

Risk factor: Something that increases a person's chance of developing a disease.

Screening: Checking for disease when there are no symptoms.

Side effects: Problems that occur when treatment affects healthy cells. Common side effects of cancer treatment are fatigue, nausea, vomiting, decreased blood cell counts, hair loss, and mouth sores.

Sigmoidoscopy (sig-moy-DOS-ko-pee): A procedure in which the doctor looks inside the rectum and the lower part of the colon (sigmoid colon) through a lighted tube. The doctor may collect samples of tissue or cells for closer examination. Also called proctosigmoidoscopy.

Medical Terms (continued)

Sperm banking: Freezing sperm before cancer treatment for use in the future. This procedure can allow men to father children after loss of fertility.

Stage: The extent of a cancer, especially whether the disease has spread from the original site to other parts of the body.

Stool: The waste matter discharged in a bowel movement; feces.

Surgery: An operation.

Systemic treatment (sis-TEM-ik): Treatment that reaches cells all over the body by traveling through the bloodstream.

Tissue (TISH-oo): A group or layer of cells that together perform a specific function.

Toxins: Poisons produced by certain animals, plants, or bacteria.

Tumor: A mass of excess tissue.

Tumor markers: Substances found in abnormal amounts in the blood, in other body fluids, or in tumor tissue of some patients with certain types of cancer.

Ultrasonography (ul-tra-son-OG-ra-fee): An exam in which sound waves are bounced off tissues and the echoes are converted into a picture (sonogram).

Ultraviolet radiation (ul-tra-VI-o-let ray-dee-AY-shun): Invisible rays that are part of the energy that comes from the sun. Ultraviolet radiation can burn the skin and cause skin cancer. It is made up of two types of rays, UVA and UVB. Skin specialists recommend that people use sunscreens that block both kinds of radiation.

White blood cells: Cells that help the body fight infection and disease.

X-rays: High-energy radiation used in low doses to diagnose disease or injury, and in high doses to treat cancer.

Resources

Information about cancer is available from many sources, including the ones listed below. You may wish to check for additional information at your local library or bookstore and from support groups in your community.

Cancer Information Service
The Cancer Information Service, a program of the National Cancer Institute, is a nationwide telephone service for cancer patients and their families and friends, the public, and health care professionals. The staff can answer questions in English or Spanish and can send free printed material on cancer prevention, early detection and self-exams, specific types of cancer, cancer treatment, and living with cancer. They also know about local resources and services. One toll-free number, 800-4-CANCER (800-422-6237), connects callers with the office that serves their area.

American Cancer Society
The American Cancer Society is a voluntary organization with a national office and local units all over the country. It supports research, conducts educational programs, and offers many services to patients and their families. It also provides free booklets about cancer. To obtain information about services and activities in local areas, call the Society's toll-free number, 800-ACS-2345 (800-227-2345), or the number listed under American Cancer Society in the white pages of the telephone book.

Support for People With Cancer and the People Who Care About Them[*]

Introduction

"A diagnosis of cancer... is a powerful stimulus against procrastinating on warm and kindly or beautiful things ... a reminder that many of the material things aren't all that urgent after all ... Take time to watch the sunset with someone you love; there may not be another as lovely for the two of you."

These are the thoughts of a woman with cancer who needed to share her feelings with someone who would care and who could understand.

This chapter is written for those affected by cancer: you, someone in your family or someone very close to you. We wrote this chapter because, as another person described it, we often feel that "we share a common bond that only victims of cancer know, the feelings of anguish and the loneliness no one else can share."

We've used letters, conversations, books and articles from, with, and by cancer patients, families and friends. The observations of professionals who work with cancer patients as expressed in conferences, seminars, and journals also have been explored. Our main emphasis, though, is on what the people who live with cancer in their own lives and their own homes think, feel, and do to cope with the disease.

No two people with cancer are alike as are no two relatives or friends of people with cancer. Although the material in this chapter is intended to be helpful, some sections may not apply to certain circumstances; a few might suggest responses that make you feel uncomfortable. Each person has to cope with cancer in an

---

[*] Source: National Cancer Institute, U.S. Department of Health and Human Services, Public Health Service, National Institutes of Health, Building 31, Room 10A24, Bethesda, MD 20892, 800-4-CANCER.

individual way. What follows is intended as a guide: a brief look at how some people with cancer and their loved ones feel and the ways they found to deal with those feelings.

Perhaps, if we explore together our emotions — a side of cancer that neither surgery, drugs, nor radiation can treat — we can help each other dispel some of those feelings.

People with cancer, dear friends, and family members face intense fears, anxieties, and frustrations that are new to many of us, although others have taken the journey we now begin. We travel a road paved with an awesome mingling of hope and despair, courage and fear, humor and anger, and constant uncertainty. Perhaps, sharing the experiences of those who have walked the road before will help us define our own feelings and find our own ways of coping.

> Look to this day,
> For it is life,
> The very life of life.
> In its brief course lie all
> The realities and verities of existence,
> The bliss of growth,
> The splendor of action,
> The glory of power-
>
> For yesterday is but a dream,
> And tomorrow is only a vision.
> But today, well lived,
> Makes every yesterday a dream of happiness
> And every tomorrow a vision of hope.
>
> Look well, therefore, to this day.
>
> *Sanskrit Proverb*

Our bodies and minds are not completely separate. It will help us keep our bodies strong if we also deal successfully with the emotional turmoil of cancer. We shall talk about some of the emotional problems we might face and some possible adjustments. We'll explore learning to express and share our feelings about cancer, dealing with new responsibilities, coping with rejection by others, finding new meaning in our days, and using each day to its fullest measure.

There is another good reason for learning to define and live with our feelings about cancer. They may be with us for a long time: Cancer is undeniably a major illness; it is not necessarily fatal. Over 7 million Americans alive today have a history of cancer. For them cancer has become a chronic condition, somewhat like hypertension, diabetes, or a mild heart condition. As is true for others with chronic conditions, periodic health checkups will be part of their lifelong routine. They will, undeniably, be more sensitive to, and anxious about, minor signs of illness or discomfort. Unlike others with chronic disease, they most likely will not need lifelong medication or special diets to remind them daily that they once were ill. Many will live for years, grow old and die much as they had expected to do before cancer was diagnosed.

It is hard not to think about dying, but it's important to concentrate on living . Remember, a diagnosis is not a death sentence. Many cancer patients will be treated successfully, and many others will live a long time after the diagnosis before dying with the disease. Indeed, there are sunrises as well as sunsets to be enjoyed. So let us take a look at living — living with cancer and its treatment, but living nonetheless.

Note: Today many of us find ourselves far from family ties. A circle of close and loving friends may act as "substitute family" for our blood relatives. If this is true for you, think of these friends when the chapter refers to family members and think about sharing this chapter with them.

Sharing The Diagnosis

- Cancer can be unutterably lonely. No one should try to bear it alone.

- Patient, family, and friends usually learn the diagnosis sooner or later. Most people find it easier for all if everybody can share their feelings instead of hiding them. This frees people to offer each other support.

- Patients usually agree that hiding the diagnosis from them denies them the right to make important choices about their life and their treatment.

- Families say patients who try to keep the diagnosis secret rob loved ones of the chance to express that love and to offer help and support.

- Family members and intimate friends also bear great emotional burdens and should be able to share them openly with each other and the patient.

- Even children should be told. They sense when something is amiss, and they may imagine a situation worse than it really is.

- The patient might want to tell the children directly, or it may be easier to have a close friend or loving relative do so.

- The children's ages and emotional maturity should be a guide in deciding how much to tell. The goal is to let children express their feelings and ask questions about the cancer.

- By sharing the diagnosis, patient, family, and friends build foundations of mutual understanding and trust.

One question many people ask after diagnosis is, "Should I tell?" Perhaps not. A family member could be too old, too young, or too emotionally fragile to accept the diagnosis, but people are surprisingly resilient. Most find ways to deal with the reality of illness and the possibility of death — even when it involves those they love most. They find the strength to bounce back from situations that seem to cause unbearable grief.

The way in which people differ is in the speed with which they bounce back. The diagnosis of cancer hits most of us with a wave of shock, of fright, of denial. Each person needs a different amount of time to pull himself or herself together and to deal with the reality of cancer. In reading the sections that follow, you should remember that only you really know your emotional timetable. Think about sharing at a time when you are ready to do so.

Usually, family and close friends learn sooner or later that you have cancer. Most people with cancer have found the best choice is to share the diagnosis and to give those closest to them the opportunity to offer their support. They have found it easier, in the long run, to confide their fears and hopes rather than trying to hide them. Of course, you must use the words and timing that you find comfortable to tell family and friends that you have cancer. We will talk more about that in the next chapter.

If you have no family, it is especially true that the road appears less lonely when shared with a few close friends. You might lose one or two. Some people will find it too difficult to talk with you or to be around you, and they will slip away. On the other hand, you may discover hidden strengths and compassion in the least likely of companions.

A woman with cancer wrote, "As for whether or not people should keep their illness a secret, I think they will learn with whom they can talk. Some people make themselves scarce if cancer is mentioned. But, cancer patients soon learn who their trusted friends are."

Another person said, "I don't think a cancer patient should keep it to himself. If it isn't revealed, family and friends are robbed of the opportunity to share the feelings and anxieties that arise from having the disease. At most, life is very short for everyone. Because there are no guarantees, we should make the most of each day."

On a practical level, trying to hide the diagnosis is usually fruitless. As you move from hope to despair and back again, family and close friends will sense something is deeply troubling you, even before they learn the facts. When you feel ready, try to share your news with them.

As you ponder whether you can share the diagnosis of cancer with others, it might help to remember the following. In telling the people you love that you have cancer, you give them the opportunity to express their feelings, to voice their fears and hopes and to offer their hand in support. Then, each can give and take strength as they are able.

Sometimes family members are the first to learn the diagnosis. If, as a family member, the decision falls to you, should you tell the patient? Some might think not, but most people with cancer disagree. "I think a cancer patient should be told the truth," one wrote. "Time is so valuable, and there may be things the person would like to accomplish. There are decisions to be made..."

All of us have important life choices to make. People with cancer often find these choices become crystal clear when they feel their life span could be cut short. They might outlive any one of us, but people with cancer have the right to know and decide how they will spend their remaining days. There are exceptions to any generalization, but most people relate that "Mom took the news much better than we thought she would."

A woman who herself has cancer recalled how things have changed since her mother was diagnosed in 1930. "My relatives never told my mother that she had cancer. Of course, then, they didn't have the treatment they have available now. Looking back I realize no one fooled her. In not telling her, though, she was deprived of a very valuable outlet for her emotions."

Family members also bear great emotional burdens during the period of diagnosis. They, too, need the comfort of sharing their feelings. Yet, it is almost impossible to support the rest of the family if you are hiding the diagnosis from the person with cancer.

He or she inevitably learns the truth. The consequences can be deep anger, hurt, or bitterness. The patient might believe that no one is being honest about the diagnosis because the cancer is terminal. On the other hand, while you are trying to "spare the patient," the person with cancer might be trying to protect family and friends from learning the truth. Then each ends up suffering alone, with thoughts and feelings locked within.

Even children sense the truth. Some parents who tried to "spare" their children from knowing later voiced regret at not discussing the truth during the course of the disease. Children have amazing capabilities when they understand a situation. However, when their normal world is turned upside down and whispered conversations go on behind closed doors, they often imagine situations that are worse than reality. Young children dwell on "terrible" things they have done or said that place responsibility for the upheaval in the household on themselves. This is especially true if the child is going through a period of testing parental authority or in some other way is in disagreement with family members. Children, especially young ones, tend to view themselves as the center of the universe and see many situations only in direct relationship to themselves.

The children's ages and emotional maturity should suggest what and how much to disclose. It might help to realize that including the children, among those who know, comforts them by confirming their belief that something is amiss within the family.

A parent with cancer might want to tell the children directly. "I've been sick a lot lately, haven't I? I have a disease called cancer. The doctors are doing everything they can to make me well. I can't spend as much time with you as I wish to; it's going to be hard on all of us, but I still love you very much."

Perhaps this is too painful. A close and loving aunt or uncle or friend might be able to explain things more comfortably. "Your daddy is ill. The doctors are almost sure they can make him well, but sometimes his treatments make him feel sad or grouchy. It's nothing you children have done, but he needs your patience and understanding."

The goal in telling the children that someone in the family has cancer is to give them opportunities to ask questions about the disease and to express their feelings about it. Of course, all of us want to shield our children from pain, but pain they understand is easier for them to cope with than hurts that they imagine. Some adults tell us that they still remember the feelings of rejection they suffered as children of cancer patients. As children they were aware of great disruption within the family, but at the time they were denied knowledge of the cause. They were hurt and confused by what seemed to be lack of attention and unreasonable demands or expectations.

We begin to see that the most compelling reason for sharing the diagnosis with adults and children alike is that cancer can be so terribly lonely. No one need try to bear it alone. At times you will feel totally without ally or solace, regardless of supports. There is no need to increase these moments with poses meant to convince others close to you that you do not need their help. At a time when each of us who is trying to cope with cancer is in need of mutual support, we should not shut each other out. Through sharing we can build foundations of mutual understanding to sustain us through the long period ahead. We can share anxiety and sorrow, but we also can share love and joy and express our appreciation for each other in ways we ordinarily might find difficult or embarrassing.

Sharing Feelings

- Some in the family are able to absorb the impact of diagnosis sooner than others. This can create clashing needs as some wish to talk and some need to be private and introspective.

- Verbal and nonverbal clues help determine when is a good time to discuss the illness and how each will learn to live with it.

- If family members cannot help each other, other emotional support systems are available in the form of support groups or professional counselors.

- The person with cancer has the primary right to set the timetable for when he or she is ready to talk. Others can encourage that readiness through their love and continued presence.

- Talking may include expressing anger, fear, and inner confusion.

- False cheeriness — the "everything will be all right" routine — denies the person with cancer the opportunity to discuss fears and anxieties.

- Emphasizing the uniqueness of each person, positive test results, or good response to treatment is true support, both valid and valuable.

- The person with cancer needs family or friends as a constant in a changing world. "I'm here," offers great reserves of support.

Sometimes, the whole family suspects the truth before the diagnosis is made. Someone recognizes the symptoms, or the family doctor seems overly concerned. Nonetheless, hearing those words — tumor... cancer... leukemia — we are stunned as we never may have been in our lives. It is often impossible to take in the diagnosis immediately. We hear it, but somehow we don't believe it. This is normal. People's minds have a wonderful capacity for absorbing information only as they are ready to accept it.

All of us may not operate on the same emotional timetable. One of the family might feel the need to talk about the cancer before the others come to grips with it. Each of us has to decide when we are ready to talk; none should feel forced to do so.

This sometimes creates clashing needs — some need to talk; others need to be private and introspective or even to shut the whole subject out of their minds for a while. The desire to respect privacy may be pitted against an equal need to get the whole thing out in the open.

In some families everyone becomes overly considerate of everyone else's needs for time to adjust. Instead of meeting anyone's needs, everyone avoids one another, building walls just when they ought to be opening doors to communication.

It is important to let the person who has cancer call the signals for when it's time to talk. But, it is always helpful to look for clues to determine when might be a good time to discuss the cancer and how to live with it.

Signs such as apparently idle conversation, more time than usual spent with other family members, or even unusual nervousness might indicate that a person wants to talk but doesn't know where to begin. Yet, facing cancer together makes it easier. It eliminates the need for pretense when there are so many important matters to address. As you talk, you should try to be sensitive to what family members or friends say, how they position their bodies, and whether or not they make eye contact. These clues suggest whether the conversation is serving a purpose or driving someone you care about into hiding.

Some people cannot adjust their feelings and cannot help each other. Not all families can be open and sharing, and a crisis is a difficult time to attempt to adjust family patterns. Nonetheless, the situation may not eliminate the need to air feelings. This is the time to turn to one of several sources outside the family for emotional support. These are described in the section "When You Need Assistance."

When cancer is first diagnosed, some patients can absorb only the most basic information, and even that might need to be repeated.

That's normal. We each have the right to digest information at our own pace and determine when we are ready for more, and when we are ready to talk about what we know or want to know.

If others in the family want to talk about cancer before you are ready, try to postpone the discussion without rejecting the person. "I appreciate your concern but not yet. I can't talk yet," for example, suggests that the day will come when you will be ready to talk. Taking care of your own needs, which are great, while trying to recognize the fears and anxieties of those you love is not easy.

The period right after diagnosis is often a time of anger, fear, and inner confusion. You might need to sort out conflicting emotions before you can express them. Or, you might find yourself lashing out, wishing to find a target for anger and frustration. Often it is those closest who bear the brunt of these outbursts. You don't want to hurt them, but you may be angry that they will live and you might die. Perhaps you assume that they will understand and endure the rage.

Family members have feelings, too. They may lash back, expressing their own anger and hurt at your outbursts, at the possibility of losing you, at the burden of new responsibilities or at their powerlessness to change the reality of the disease. As you express your own feelings, try to remember that others need the same release.

The period following diagnosis is a difficult time of adjustment for family members. Each has to deal with individual feelings, while trying to be sensitive to those of the person who has cancer. Being part of the family doesn't mean you can make people talk about their feelings before they are ready, but you need outlets, too. There are ways to encourage openness. Be ready to listen when others are ready to talk, and let your continued presence show your support. But remember, the person with cancer gets to set the timetable.

If the decision is to talk, you may find yourself the target for a lot of anger and frustration. It is easier to tell yourself that you are not the cause of this hostility than it is to accept this. You know you should respond with patience and compassion, but sometimes you answer anger with anger. Even these exchanges can have value if everyone learns through them to share feelings.

The opposite of anger may be false cheer. In trying to bolster the person with cancer, you may actually cut off his or her attempts to express feelings. Remember that lifting the spirit doesn't mean hiding from the truth. Sensing despondency, some people rush in with assurances that "everything will be all right." But everything is not "all right." If you insist it is, you deny the reality of the patient's world. In response, he or she may withdraw, feeling deserted and left to face an uncertain world alone. Without meaning to, you've abandoned the one you hoped to help and set up patterns that can be difficult to change just when support is so important. Although the cancer may be controlled, the gulf between you may endure.

It may help the one with cancer to know that you share the same fears and anxieties about the uncertainty of the future. People who honestly share these feelings find they can hold them to the light, better accept that the future may be questionable, and turn more readily to fulfilling the present. This is a very difficult period, but if you can share the difficulties, you will find there are more good days to enjoy together. And you are less likely to be devastated by truly difficult ones.

There are ways to find hope during periods of despondency or despair. We all need to remember the individuality of each case. We tend to get caught up in statistics and averages, but no two cancers ever behave exactly the same way. Each individual has different genes and an immune system, a distinctive will to live, and an urge to fight. These cannot be measured on charts or graphs. No one can offer any of us "forever," but there are good prognoses; with an increasing number of cancers, the outlook is good for successful treatment. You can look to promising test results and to treatments that previously have been effective in many people. Even if the future is guarded, there may be another remission, good days, comfortable nights, and shared experiences. These are real beyond any statistics. The enjoyment of life's gifts constitutes living, not the number of days we are given in which to enjoy them.

There are safeguards against hopelessness even if there is no real cause for hope. You can still provide reassurance of continuing love and comfort. At times, "I'm here" may be the two most supportive words you can say.

There are different ways in which you can be important as a family member or friend. You can listen to expressions of feeling or act as a sounding board for a discussion of future plans. You can help focus anger or anxiety by helping to explore some of the specific causes, including drug reactions, the job situation, and finances. This may be what is needed-someone to listen, to react and absorb the patient's outpourings, not necessarily to "do" anything. It is a difficult role, but it can be immensely rewarding.

There is a more passive but equally difficult role. Some cancer patients view theirs as a private battle to be fought alone with only their physicians as allies, and they prefer to fight their emotional battles alone as well. But they need family and friends for silent support, as respite, shelter, or an island of normalcy. It can be draining to provide "safe harbor" from a day in the clinic or nights of sleepless panic. It can be a struggle to be forced to plan an evening out, to ask friends in, or simply to stand by with wordless support. However, there may be times when this is what is needed most.

Many people think they don't know "how to act" with people with cancer. The best you can offer is to be natural, to be yourself. Let your intuition guide you. Do what you comfortably can do; don't try to be someone you are not. This in itself is comforting. Dealing with cancer entails enough mystifying changes without having to adapt to a new you.

Coping Within The Family

- Cancer is a blow to every family it touches. How it is handled is determined to a great extent by how the family has functioned as a unit in the past.

- Problems within the family can be the most difficult to handle; you cannot go home to escape them.

- Adjusting to role changes can cause great upheavals in the way family members interact.

- Performing too many roles at once endangers anyone's emotional well-being and ability to cope. Examine what tasks are necessary and let others slide.

- Consider hiring professional nurses or homemakers. Financial costs need to be compared with the physical and emotional cost of shouldering the load alone.

- Children may need special attention. They need comfort, reassurance, affection, guidance, and discipline at times of disruption in their routine.

Although cancer has "come out of the closet," much of what we read in newspapers and magazines is about the disease itself — its probable causes or new methods of treatment. There is little information about how families deal with cancer on a day-to-day basis. This gap reinforces feelings that families coping with cancer are isolated from the rest of the world: that everyone else is managing nicely while you flounder with your feelings, hide from your spouse, and are incapable of talking to the children.

Cancer is a blow to every family it touches. How you handle it is determined to a great extent by how you have functioned as a family in the past. Families who are used to sharing their feelings with each other usually are able to talk about the disease and the changes it brings. Families in which each member solves problems alone or in which one person has played the major role in making decisions might have more difficulty coping.

Problems within the family can be the most difficult to handle simply because you cannot go home to escape them. Some family members deny the reality of cancer or refuse to discuss it.

It is not uncommon to feel deserted or to feel unable to face cancer openly. "My brother-in-law is suffering from cancer," one man confided. "The entire situation is depressing, and my reaction has been one of running and hiding. I have not visited them for I feel I have nothing to offer."

A woman with cancer found none of her family could help her. "My two wonderful sons tolerated their dad's heart surgeries very well, but now I have cancer, and they don't know how to act. Phone calls and letters expressing sympathy are not what I need. I've tried since last November to express my thoughts to my husband, but he shuts out what I'm saying. I know that he's uncertain about our future, but I can't seem to get through to him; I've learned from other patients that it's a common concern."

In these situations individual counseling or cancer patient groups can provide needed support and reinforcement. Moreover, these resources provide an outlet for the frustrations you are facing within the family.

Families may have difficulty adjusting to the role changes that are sometimes necessary. One husband found it overwhelming to come home from work, prepare dinner, oversee the children's homework, change bedding and dressings, and still try to provide companionship and emotional support for his children and ill wife.

In addition to roles as wife, mother, and nurse, a woman might have to add a job outside the home for the first time. A spouse who was sharing the load sometimes becomes the sole breadwinner and homemaker. The usual head of the household might now be its most dependent member.

These changes can cause great upheavals in the ways members of the family interact. The usual patterns are gone. Parents might look to children for emotional support at a time when the children themselves need it most. Teenagers might have to take over major household responsibilities. Young children can revert to infantile behavior as a way of dealing with the impact of cancer on the family as a unit and on themselves as individuals. The sheer weight of responsibility can become insurmountable, destroying normal family associations, devouring time needed for rest and recreation, and depriving family members of wholesome opportunities for expressing anxiety and resentment.

Performing too many roles at once can endanger emotional well-being and the ability to cope. Examining what's important can solve the problem. For example, you can relax housekeeping standards or learn to prepare simpler meals. Perhaps the children can take on a few more household chores than they have been handling.

If a simple solution is not enough, consider getting outside help. Licensed practical nurses can help with the patient; county or private agencies might provide trained homemakers. If outreach is an important part of your church, feel free to ask for help with cooking, shopping, transportation, and other homemaking tasks. One family was adopted by the daughter's Scout troop when the girls learned of the extra responsibility she had assumed. Everyone benefitted from the relationship.

Let someone who can be objective help you sort out necessary tasks from those that can go undone. The financial cost of professional services needs to be compared with the emotional and physical cost of shouldering the load alone. You also may be able to obtain assistance from hospital, community, or self-help groups or from a clergy member. It is important to remember that the family is still a unit. If the family strength is sapped, the patient suffers, too.

The San Diego chapter of Make Today Count, a mutual support group for patients and families, compiled a "Bill of Rights for the Friends and Relatives of Cancer Patients." Several items address the problems of family burdens:

The relative of a cancer patient has the right and obligation to take care of his own needs. Even though he may be accused of being selfish, he must do what he has to do to keep his own peace of mind, so that he can better minister to the needs of the patient.

Each person will have different needs as the relative of a cancer patient. If these needs are satisfied the patient will benefit by having a more cheerful person to care for him.

The relative may need help from outsiders in caring for the patient. Although the patient may object to this, the relative has the right to assess his own limitations of strength and endurance and to obtain assistance when required.

When the relative knows that he is already doing all that can reasonably be expected of anyone in caring for the patient, he can have a clear conscience in maintaining contacts with the rest of the world.

If the patient attempts to use his illness as a weapon, the relative has the right to reject that and to do only what can reasonably be expected of him.

If the cancer patient's relative responds only to the genuine needs of the moment — both his own needs and those of the patient — the stress associated with the illness can be minimized.

Increased burdens and shifting responsibilities can occur whether the patient in the household is a spouse, a child, or an elderly parent. Each family member must take care to meet his or her own needs and those of the other healthy members of the family as well as those of the patient.

Children might have difficulty coping with cancer in a parent. Mother or Dad may be gone from the house — in a hospital that may be hundreds of miles from home — or home in bed, in obvious discomfort, and perhaps visibly altered in appearance.

In the face of this upheaval, children often are asked to behave exceptionally well: to "play quietly," to perform extra tasks or to be understanding of others' moods beyond the maturity of their years. The children may resent lost attention. Some fear the loss of their parent or begin to imagine their own death. Some children, formerly independent, now become anxious about leaving home and parents. Discipline problems can arise if children attempt to command the attention they feel they are missing.

It may help if a favorite relative or family friend can devote extra time and attention to the children, who do need comfort and reassurance, affection, guidance, and discipline. Trips to the zoo are important, but so is regular help with homework and someone to attend the basketball awards banquet. If your efforts to provide support and security fail, professional counseling for a child, or child and parent together, may be necessary and should not be overlooked.

When You Need Assistance

- When cancer develops, many people need to learn to ask for and accept outside help for the first time. These are good ways to begin:

- Take time to ask medical questions of your doctor, nurse specialists, therapists, and technologists.

- Make lists of questions. Write or tape-record the answers. Take someone else along as a second listener.

- Ask your physician to suggest other doctors if you wish a second opinion on your diagnosis before deciding on treatment.

- Ask your physician about alternative treatments if you have questions about them.

- Physicians wait for clues from their patients to determine how much to say. Let your doctor know whether you want to know everything at once or in stages.

- Remember that there is a difference between a physician who does not know that cancer need not be fatal and one who will not promise you a miracle.

- Trust and rapport between patient and physician are important; you must be able to work together to treat the cancer most effectively.

- Your physician, hospital, library, the National Cancer Institute or affiliated Cancer Information Service offices, and local chapters of the American Cancer Society are good sources of facts about cancer. Many also can provide the names of local support and service organizations established to help you cope with the emotional stresses of the disease.

- Emotional assistance takes many forms. Counseling or psychiatric therapy for individuals, for groups of patients, and for families often is available through the hospital or within the community.

- Many groups have been established by patients and their families to share practical tips and coping skills. One may be right for you.

- Your minister or rabbi, a sympathetic member of the congregation, or a specially trained pastoral counselor may be able to help you find spiritual support.

Which one of us did not feel that the world had stopped turning when cancer struck us? But somehow each day goes on. During the period of active treatment a pressing number of decisions need to be made, questions must be answered and arrangements handled.

There are medical questions. There might be confusion or disagreement over the diagnosis — what did the doctor say; what do various terms mean; what is the outlook for recovery?

Financial burdens can be crushing. Transportation to and from treatment can seem a major, frustrating obstacle. Where does one get a hospital bed, a night nurse, a person to look after the children?

The stress of handling such responsibilities can be enormous. A new kind of communication and acceptance becomes necessary: asking for and accepting outside help, which is an entirely new role for some. People who were raised to believe that "going it alone" indicated maturity and strength now might have to overcome their distaste for appearing to be in anything less than total control.

Some simply do not know where to turn. You might feel uncomfortable asking for help, even from those agencies that were designed precisely for emergencies such as the one you now face. So, where do you turn?

Physicians or nurses are good sources of answers to medical questions. It's helpful to write down on a sheet of paper all questions you have about cancer, its treatment, any side effects from it, or any limitations treatment may place on your activities. (Incidentally, there may be surprisingly few limitations other than those caused by changes in physical capability.) Other members of your treatment team, such as physical therapists, nutritionists, or radiation therapists, can explain the "whys" of these aspects of your therapy.

Writing questions down makes them easier to remember at the next doctor's appointment. It's also helpful to call the office beforehand to alert the receptionist that you will need extra time for your appointment. This time around you can be better prepared to retain the answers. Some people take notes; others bring a tape recorder, or a clear-thinking friend or relative. The point is to depend on something more reliable than your own memory at a time when emotions are likely to overwhelm intellect.

Fear of being thought ignorant or pushy has kept many people from asking their doctors about a most important topic-the alternative treatments they read about in the tabloids or hear about from friends. You may be urged by well-meaning people to try methods that will "spare you any pain or discomfort." Yet they are never available through your cancer specialist. If you are being pressured to abandon the care you are now getting, but haven't discussed it with your doctor because you think you will insult "establishment medicine," you might try this approach. "I keep hearing about the bubblegum treatment for cancer. Can you tell me why it isn't accepted by most American doctors? Why do some people think it works, and why do you believe it won't?"

What you have asked for is information. You haven't attacked the treatment you are getting now or the professionals who are giving it to you. And if you are comfortable with the answers you get, it will help you respond when you are urged to try these methods.

Too many fail to ask the medical questions most important to their physical and emotional well-being through a fear of "taking up the doctor's valuable time." Some say, "I'm sure he told me all this once before." Of course, you want to be a "good" patient or a "cooperative" family member! But it's also true: It's your body. It's your life. It's also true that a well-informed patient is better able to understand his or her therapy, its possible side effects, or any unusual signs that should be reported to the doctor.

A good approach can be simply to admit that you are asking for a repeat performance. "I'm pretty sure you told me some of this before, but I couldn't remember anything; I was so shocked. Now, I think I'd feel less anxious if we talked about it."

Some are ready to hold this conversation sooner than others. Some ask a few questions at a time, absorbing each piece of information before they are ready to go on. Some never ask directly. (If so, someone in the family should speak with the doctor to learn the extent of disease and the outlook for the future.) But sooner or later, in whatever way you find comfortable, it's important to let the doctor know that you understand you have cancer and want to talk about it.

In an ideal world, physicians all would be patient, understanding and able to sense your every mood. They would know when to bring out all the X-ray films and lab tests and when to draw only the sketchiest picture of your case. They would have unlimited time to wait until you were ready to ask questions, and then they would gently help you to phrase them in just the right way.

As a matter of fact, books for cancer specialists — physicians, nurses, therapists — and courses in the health professional schools are beginning to emphasize the importance of recognizing the feelings of the person with cancer. Nonetheless, each person is different, and no textbook can describe your unique needs.

In the real world physicians admit that they wait for clues from you, the person with cancer. They need to know what the patient wants to know. Physicians are not mind readers. Whether you like it or not, it is usually up to you to take the first steps toward open communication with your doctor.

Some physicians never have learned to speak comfortably with patients or families who are facing what might be a life-threatening illness. These physicians may appear to be abrupt, aloof and uncaring, although they are not. Nonetheless, if their discomfort creates a barrier, you might be wise to seek referral to someone else. When fighting cancer you have to work as a team. Lack of trust is fair neither to you nor the doctor. It is fair, however, to let the doctor know you wish to see someone else-even to ask him or her for a referral. The physician probably is as aware as you that a relationship based on trust and open communication has not been established.

It is also appropriate to ask your physician to suggest other doctors if you wish a second opinion on the diagnosis before deciding on treatment.

There still might be a physician here or there who believes that all cancer is fatal and that "nothing can be done." In such a case it is only common sense to ask for referral to a cancer specialist.

Most family physicians practicing now, know that nearly half the patients who get cancer today will live out their lives free of further disease, and others can be provided an extended time of reasonable comfort and activity. While continuing as the personal physician, they usually will refer their patients to cancer specialists — surgeons, radiologists, or medical oncologists — for active treatment. (It's something like an orchestra conductor calling on the soloists while keeping the whole orchestra playing together.)

You need to be honest with yourself and recognize the difference between a physician who believes all cancer is fatal and one who believes the outlook for a particular case is not good. Refusing to promise complete cure is not the same as forsaking the patient.

A physician who uses all available methods to treat the disease, to minimize its effects, and to keep you comfortable and functioning as long as possible is doing everything he or she can to care for your physical needs. How frustrating it is, then, when you seek to relieve your emotional aches and pains, to be rebuffed by the same otherwise excellent specialist. As one man put it, "I found it impossible to discuss the nitty-gritty facts with my doctors and the radiation therapist. I felt that if I told the radiologist how fearful I was, I would be considered childish." Nonetheless, a decision to change physicians should be based on reality and not on a quest to find a doctor who will promise a cure and guarantee to relieve all your fears.

It's easier to come to grips with the reality of any crisis if we replace ignorance with information. There is much to learn about each form of cancer, its treatment, the possibility for recovery, and methods of rehabilitation. Well-versed in the facts, you are less likely to fall prey to old wives' tales, to quacks touting worthless "cures," or to depressing stories of what happened to "poor old Harry" when he got cancer. Often, the more you know, the less you have to fear.

Local libraries, local divisions of voluntary agencies such as the American Cancer Society, and major cancer research and treatment institutions are sources of information about cancer and its treatment. Depending on the degree of your desire for information and your ability to understand scientific terms, you can get everything from short, concise pamphlets to scientific papers. It's a good idea to share the fruits of your research with your own doctor. Cancer is a complex set of diseases; the treatment and its side effects may differ slightly for each person.

On a national level, the National Cancer Institute (NCI), which is part of the National Institutes of Health, operates an information office for the public. Its information specialists can answer many general questions about cancer, its diagnosis, and treatment. In addition, the NCI coordinates a network of information offices among the nation's top cancer research and treatment centers, the Cancer Information Service (CIS). CIS counselors can provide the names of facilities that are most appropriate in terms of both geography and specialization. They also have written materials and information about local self-help and service organizations for cancer patients and their families.

The NCI specialists also maintain lists of excellent cancer hospitals outside the CIS network that are conducting federally funded research in new methods of cancer treatment. They can suggest not only institutions but also specialists with whom your own physician might wish to consult. However, information staff members cannot offer medical advice or arrange for referral to a specific physician or institution.

It is said that we cope with cancer much as we cope with other problems that confront us. Many do come to terms with the reality of cancer. After initial treatment, they find somehow they are able to continue their normal working and social relationships. Or, as one psychologist put it, they learn to get up in the morning and pour the coffee, even knowing that they have cancer. They find, sometimes to their amazement, that they can laugh at bad jokes, or become totally absorbed in a good movie, or a hard-fought football game.

At other times, strength deserts them. They feel overwhelmed by this new world of uncertainties. Some lose interest in favorite hobbies or activities, viewing them as painful reminders of what will be lost if treatment is unsuccessful. They want to cope, but they need help, some support systems beyond their own. Where does one look for such support?

It was not very long ago that emotional assistance for the cancer patient or family was impossible to find. Attention to emotional needs is a relatively recent addition to standard cancer treatment. Growing numbers of hospitals routinely include a mental health professional as a member of the cancer treatment team or offer group counseling programs. This is a hopeful sign; it says, "This diagnosis does not mean imminent death. We have a whole person to treat here, one with a future and a life to live. This person should be able to live as normally as possible. We must provide the emotional tools to get the job done."

Counseling also is now available for health professionals to help them face feelings of frustration and uncertainty in their work. They have recognized the awesome degree of stress that cancer can create in those it touches. You should have no feelings of shame or hesitancy, then, if you feel the need to seek professional help.

Some hospitals consider some form of group counseling as part of the standard treatment — as necessary as an exercise class, for example. Programs are organized in a variety of ways. Many begin within days of surgery. Some groups meet only for the length of the hospital stay; others are long-term to enable members to work through problems in the everyday world. Some are composed of people with the same disease site (breast or colon cancer patients); some by type of treatment (in-hospital surgery or outpatient radiation therapy); and some by patient age. Some are just for patients; others include spouses, family, or other special people.

Groups can incorporate music, poetry, or role-playing in attempts to help members explore their feelings. Some are action-oriented with "veteran" patients helping others now facing the same problem. All counseling groups should be run by trained professionals so that the direction of exploration is truly helpful to each participant.

If you want to explore your feelings in individual therapy, you will find a growing number of psychologists, psychiatrists, or licensed clinical social workers specializing in counseling people affected by cancer. Many find it helpful to explore feelings — especially those they don't want to accept, such as guilt, resentment, and intense anger — with a person who, without judging them, will help them understand these feelings and find ways to channel them constructively.

Often the problem is not an individual one. The family is a unit, and each member is affected when any one member is. Family counseling can help absorb the shock and deal with the stresses of cancer.

It can be difficult for persons with cancer and their family members to discuss their emotions. Cancer patients themselves have tagged the absence of open communication within their families as a major problem. People are particularly hesitant to express negative feelings when no one is "at fault." Yet major shifts in responsibilities such as those cancer brings to a family can cause great resentment by those shouldering (or incapable of shouldering) extra burdens. A loss of accustomed responsibility or authority also can cause resentment mingled with anxiety over a loss of power.

Children, especially, find that their usual roles no longer are defined clearly. Parents may not have the emotional energy to provide the usual support, love, and authority. Teenagers can feel torn between expressing independence and a need to remain close to the sick parent.

These problems become less difficult to face if the family can discuss them. Some can do this without outside help. Those who cannot should feel comfortable in seeking professional assistance.

Your physician, a hospital social worker or hospital psychologist are good sources for referrals to psychologists, psychiatrists, or other mental health professionals trained to counsel individuals and families affected by cancer. Many county health departments include psychological services, and neighborhood or community mental health clinics are becoming common in increasing numbers of cities. Community service organizations such as the United Way usually support mental health facilities. County government listings in the telephone book may include an "Information and Referral" listing, one more resource for counseling services.

There are numerous self-help groups organized by people like you and designed to help you overcome both the practical problems of cancer and the feelings these changes cause. Some groups are local chapters of national organizations; others are strictly "grass roots." Some are only for patients; others include family members.

These organizations shun a "pity me" approach. They exist to help you work through your feelings and frustrations. Whether you accept them or change them, you can do so within the framework of a supportive group of people who know your problems firsthand.

Some offer family members an opportunity to share feelings, fears, and anxieties with others bearing similar burdens. Some provide patients a place to express negative feelings that they don't want to unload on their families. Patients without families can speak openly and release their pent-up emotions without fear of taxing existing friendships.

Some support groups provide skills training and helpful tips for special sets of patients such as those who have had a laryngectomy, ostomy, or mastectomy. Organizations designed to offer emotional support nonetheless can provide opportunities to exchange practical information, such as how to control nausea from chemotherapy or how to talk to an employer about cancer.

A self-help group can give those recovered from cancer an opportunity to aid those who have cancer. With training, some become group counselors or discussion leaders. Many former cancer patients have found that helping others gives a marvelous and oft-needed boost to their own self-esteem. (That can be so important after a long stretch of feeling dependent on and at the mercy of physicians and hospital staff.)

Mutual assistance groups sometimes work with health professionals and the clergy to help them understand the special emotional needs of people with cancer.

Religion is a source of strength for some people. Some find new faith in their divine being and new hope from their sacred writings when cancer enters their lives. Others find the ordeal of disease strengthens their faith, or that faith gives them new-found strength. Others never have had strong religious beliefs and feel no urge to turn to religion at such at time.

Members of the clergy in increasing numbers are completing programs to help them minister more effectively to people with cancer and their families.

Individual pastors can provide hope and solace, but they vary, as do physicians and lay people, in their capacity to cope with life-threatening illnesses and the possibility of death. A religious leader untrained in illness counseling may refer you to an associate trained to work with people with cancer. He or she also might introduce you to another member of the congregation who can provide comfort and, perhaps, more time on a regular basis than the leader of a congregation can spare.

Selves and Self-Images

- Cancer treatment can extend over weeks or months; side effects may come and go.

- Side effects can make you feel rotten, even make you think the cancer has returned.

- The known is less frightening than the unknown. Learn about your cancer, its treatment, and how to treat possible side effects.

- Fears and anxieties caused by cancer can affect a sexual relationship. Remember: Cancer is not catching. And cancer or other chronic illnesses are rarely the cause for infidelity in a good relationship.

- Treatment might make you feel uncomfortable about your body and sexually unattractive. Open discussion of these feelings with your mate is very important.

- Intangible personal qualities make up a great part of your attraction for your mate. These have not changed with treatment.

- Spouses sometimes hesitate to initiate physical contact. Support, love, and affection do include hugs and caresses. These may lead the partner with cancer to feel more comfortable about sexual intimacy.

- Physical exercise improves body image and feelings of well-being.

- Taking on new hobbies and learning new skills can bolster your good feelings about yourself.

- Reconstructive surgery and well-made prostheses help some people overcome physical disabilities and emotional distress.

- If you cannot seem to regain good feelings about yourself, do seek professional counseling or therapy.

- If your relationship is endangered by the stress of cancer, get professional help. You need each other at this time.

Cancer treatment is nearly always aggressive. Surgery can be disfiguring. Radiation or drug treatment may be prescribed following surgery to ensure that no hidden, microscopic cancer cells are left to travel to other parts of the body. Treatment can extend over weeks or months, and its side effects can include nausea, hair loss, fatigue, cramps, skin burns or weight changes. It is not unusual for the treatment to cause more illness or discomfort than the initial disease. The cancer patient has to contend with emotional reactions to such treatment and side effects.

It is difficult to convince yourself that you are recovering when you feel absolutely rotten. It is hard to be optimistic when you feel worse now than at the time of diagnosis. The schedule of radiation or drug treatments may seem endless. You are convinced that there never was a day when you didn't feel awful; there never will be one when you will feel normal - if only you could remember how normal feels.

Some even interpret these physical reactions to treatment as signs that the cancer is returning. This is rarely the case, although it may be necessary to remind yourself of this fact again and again. Feel comfortable in sharing such anxieties with your doctor.

A return to the hospital setting for outpatient treatment causes anxiety for some. Researchers studied a group of women undergoing radiation therapy following breast cancer surgery. They found that the women felt better psychologically immediately after leaving the hospital after surgery than they did once followup treatment began. It can be unsettling, indeed, to return again and again to the hospital or physician's office, places which may have come to represent the most frightening aspects of cancer.

You can try to plan special activities for the days when you feel well and brace yourself for the days when you feel awful. It's helpful to others and easier for you if you inform people that treatment may cause shifts in moods. You can let them know matter-of-factly that you will have up days and down days.

The known is usually easier to cope with than the unknown. It is important to be familiar with each treatment's side effects and its causes. Not only does knowledge reduce fear, but some side effects can be eliminated (or at least eased) through treatment changes, medication, or changes in diet. There is no need to be more uncomfortable than is absolutely necessary. Written materials with information on what to expect in the way of side effects from treatment usually are available from your physician or treatment center. However, the best way to obtain accurate information about your own situation is through a frank and thorough discussion with the nurse or physician administering treatment.

This brings us back to the problem of busy, unresponsive health professionals. If your physician has been less than helpful, try one of the information resources or special support groups referred to in the previous chapter. Ask one more nurse, one more oncology resident. As one of our "expert patients" wrote, "Look for assistance wherever you have to when you need it. It's a mistake to give up when rebuffed or disregarded by any one individual. There is always a source of comfort somewhere. One has only to look for it." Comfort and, we might add, information.

The problems and emotional stresses of cancer might follow you into the bedroom. Some couples arrange the financial matters and handle the day-to-day tasks, only to find that sexual problems threaten their relationship. There are a variety of reasons for such problems.

A few people still have the mistaken belief that cancer is contagious. One man complained, "My wife won't kiss me anymore. She thinks cancer is catching." Fact: Cancer is not catching. If your mate believes it is, call your physician. You may feel embarrassed discussing sex, but this is too important a problem to let modesty stand in the way of a solution.

Infidelity, or more likely fear of it, can present a problem. Exploring these fears with your mate is probably the best way to deal with them. If you admit that you are plagued by uncertainty and insecurity, you probably will receive the needed support and affection and can lay your doubts to rest.

Some cancer patients cite disfiguring treatment as a cause of sexual problems. You need to deal not only with discomfort or disability but also with what this change in your body has done to your feelings about yourself. As awkward as it may seem, you need to find ways to communicate those feelings to your partner. An inability to express them may complicate an already difficult period.

Each of us develops over the years an image in our mind about our body. We may not be completely satisfied with that image, but usually we are comfortable with it when we are involved in a relationship with someone we love. This helps us feel sexually attractive to our mate. Disfigurement, hair loss, nausea, radiation burns - even fatigue - can destroy your good feelings about your physical appeal. If you now believe you are unattractive, you might anticipate rejection and avoid physical contact with your partner. It is well to remember that in most cases your partner is more concerned about your well-being than his or her own. The overriding reactions probably begin with, "Will treatment succeed?" "How can I show my love and support?" and, only finally, "What about sex?"

In reality, your partner may be afraid to appear overeager and therefore insensitive. So it may be up to you to show a desire for physical contact and to let it be known whether you are interested in sexual intercourse as well as other expressions of affection - hugging, caressing and kissing.

It might help to keep in mind that it's not only your body that makes you "sexy." There are also intangible qualities that your mate finds attractive. A sense of humor, intellect, a certain sweetness or great common sense, special talents, loving devotion — each of us knows what makes us special; and it's more than anatomy. If you feel you have lost those special qualities along with a breast or leg or prostate gland, counseling may help you change that perspective.

Time, along with demonstrations of love, understanding and affection by your partner and family should help you work through feelings about your changed body image. In addition, some find that physical activities — sports, dancing classes, exercise, or judo — improve their sense of being in touch with their bodies. A ballet teacher who has had a mastectomy is teaching other women the feeling of grace and balance that comes from dance.

"After I took up yoga," another woman exclaimed with some surprise, "I achieved a sense of wholeness about my body — even without one breast — that I had never had before."

People who take on a challenging activity that moves them beyond a disability — skiing for amputees for example — find it can provide a whole new sense of self-worth. "Can you believe, I have more pride in this ragged body than I did when it was all there?" asked a tennis ace, who took up the game after his colostomy.

Poetry, music, painting, furniture building, sewing, and reading provide creative growth of which you can be equally proud. If anything needs strengthening it is our personal self-image. Acquiring new interests and talents can help develop that strength.

Reconstructive surgery or cosmetic and functional prostheses (artificial devices) help some people with cancer overcome both physical disabilities and emotional distress from disfiguring surgery. A small but growing body of skilled craftsmen build prostheses for people who have had radical oral and facial surgery. These lifelike pieces enable people to go out in public again with some degree of emotional comfort. For some, they are the difference between silence and the ability to speak. For others, they put eating solid food back into the realm of possibility.

Women who have had a mastectomy can wear a breast form (prosthesis) or have breast reconstruction.

Most insurance companies cover restorative or cosmetic surgery and various prosthetic devices as a necessary part of the rehabilitation process. This is good news, for it is further recognition that cancer patients are entitled to as close to normal a life as possible. No longer are they asked to be grateful and satisfied just to be alive.

Disfigurement or debilitation caused by treatment can affect reactions to a partner with cancer. You expect to see beyond these physical changes to the person within, the one who more than ever needs your love and physical reassurance of that love. Nonetheless, you might find yourself responding negatively, unable to provide that support. You might feel awkward about physical contact because you think your partner is not ready for it and that you will be judged insensitive.

It helps to remember that touching, holding, hugging, and caressing are ways to express the acceptance and caring that is so important to the person with cancer. More than words, they show love and express your belief in the patient's continued desirability as a physical being.

Admittedly it is a difficult time. Beset by treatment reactions, anxiety, self-doubt, or a mistaken notion of what your feelings are, your spouse might withdraw from you. Together, try to prevent a cycle of misunderstanding from developing. As the well partner, try to feel sure in your love and reach out gently and repeatedly, if necessary, to provide the reassurance that cancer cannot destroy love.

If barriers begin to grow, perhaps a professional counselor can help you work out your reactions toward the patient, the disease or your feelings that too much of the responsibility has been placed upon your shoulders. Make sure you are doing whatever you can to reestablish bonds of closeness and caring.

Essentially, each of us must deal with heartrending problems in ways that are compatible with our relationship. Facing this battle can strengthen everything that is good in it. Sometimes, it shows us how minor are problems once considered so important. However, cancer also can strain a relationship already stressed by other serious problems.

Sometimes the sexual relationship becomes the barometer of a marriage. In a mature relationship, sex is an expression of love, affection, and respect — not the basis for it. As one woman put it, "If a husband and wife had a good relationship before mutilating surgery, there is little basis for new problems. I contend this is an excuse not to have sexual relations or to seek a new, more exciting partner. The real reasons for problems were there before the surgery, just as the cancer was there before the diagnosis."

Most people find ways to face and overcome the stresses cancer places on their relationship. They find strength in each other, and they work together to establish a new and comfortable routine. Sharing their feelings with each other usually has been their first step toward finding effective solutions.

Sometimes a trained counselor can help you understand ways in which you can begin helping each other. Family therapists or licensed clinical social workers sometimes should be included in the personal cancer treatment team. Support groups of other couples dealing with cancer can be helpful, even in dealing with intimate problems. The usual personal barriers often fall when you know you have sympathetic and experienced confidants who may be able to offer practical (and tested) guidance. Those who have found ways to maintain or recapture closeness and intimacy throughout this ordeal might be able to help others in a group setting.

The World Outside

- Some friends will deal well with your illness and provide gratifying support.

- Some will be unable to cope with the possibility of death and will disappear from your life.

- Most will want to help but may be uncomfortable and unsure of how to go about it. Help your friends support you.

- Ask yourself, "Have friends deserted me or have I withdrawn from them?"

- Telephone those who don't call you.

- Ask for simple assistance — to run an errand, prepare a meal, come and visit. These small acts bring friends back into contact and help them feel useful and needed.

- If you are alone, ask your physician, social worker or pastor to "match" you with another patient. Someone else needs friendships, too.

- Groups of other cancer patients can offer new friendships, understanding, support, and companionship.

- When you return to work, coworkers, like others, may shun you, support you or wait for your cues on how to respond.

- There are laws to protect you against job discrimination.

Anyone who has been affected intimately by cancer knows that it can change the pattern of our relationships outside the family as well as those within. Friends react as they do to other difficult situations. Some handle it well; others are unable to maintain any association at all. Casual acquaintances, and even strangers, can cause unintended pain by asking thoughtless questions about visible scars, artificial devices, or other noticeable changes in appearance.

One or two people within your circle may be gratifying in their devotion and in the sensitivity they show toward your needs. One woman said her mother-in-law found one or two close friends with whom she felt truly relaxed. They were not startled when she laughed nor ill at ease when she cried. With others she maintained an outward calm.

"I have three really good friends with whom I can talk about my cancer," explained another. "I have talked about dying with my sister, and she does understand a lot more than I thought a person without cancer could."

Lost friendships are one of the real heartbreaks people with cancer face. Friends do not call for a variety of reasons. They might not know how to respond to a change in your appearance. They might be avoiding you in order to avoid facing the possibility of your death and the eventuality of their own. Their absence does not necessarily mean they no longer care about you. Still, it is little comfort to know that "out there" you have friends if they have so little confidence in their worth as companions that they would rather say nothing than risk saying the wrong thing.

"I see that my friends don't know how to talk to me, and they shy away from me," wrote one person with cancer. "Most people are very ignorant on the subject of cancer."

If you believe discomfort rather than fear is keeping a particular friend from visiting, you might try a phone call to dissolve the barrier. Yet you cannot combat all the reasons why people avoid you; some still believe that cancer is contagious. Certainly, you cannot call them up and say, "Hey, get out of the Dark Ages. It's not catching!"

Knowing that others are ignorant does little to lessen the hurt and frustration of being needlessly isolated. You only can change the attitudes of others if you are among them. Examine carefully whether friends shun you or whether you have withdrawn from your usual social contacts to protect your own feelings. You can neither enlighten nor draw comfort from an empty room. If possible, the best place to be is out in the world with other people.

Most people fall into a middle group, somewhere between the staunch friends and the "avoiders." They are groping for an approach to cancer with which they can be comfortable. These people may say things which sound inane, insincere, or hurtful. You have to keep reminding yourself that they are trying their best. If you are open about cancer, they may relax, too.

A perceptive high school student explained, "I guess what I'm trying to say boils down to this. One of these days people may not feel so uneasy around a disabled person. I'm not bitter with people; I'm really quite at ease with them and strive to make them feel at ease with me. They feel afraid of me, and consequently trip over their tongues. I have learned a lot by living in a disabled person's world and am quite willing to share it. One of these days, I may be given the chance."

A woman who had extensive surgery for oral cancer explained how she tried to lessen the discomfort of others without causing discomfort for herself. She focused on her disability rather than its cause.

"I am determined to put people at ease, so when I speak on the telephone, or to someone for the first time, I immediately say, 'I have a speech defect, so please don't hesitate to tell me if you don't understand me.' I also carry a pencil and paper and offer to write what can't be understood. I find it much more frustrating to have people try to save my feelings by pretending to understand me when they don't."

A man we know startled his fishing buddies, who were paying a group visit to his hospital room. He positively threw open the door to honest communication when he boomed out, "You know, I've learned one hell of a lot about cancer since I became a member of the club."

We can't all be that direct. He had been a straightforward man all his life. But he had let his friends know that he preferred talking about his cancer to pussyfooting around it.

Many times friends are waiting for some clue as to what behavior is appropriate. They might not be sure you want company. They might call to "see how things are going'" then add as they hang up the phone, "Let me know if there's anything I can do to help."

These friends are asking for more than a job to do. They are asking for direction, giving you clues that they will not desert you if only they have some guidance on how to proceed. The next time friends or relatives offer assistance, try to look at the offer in that light. If you can think of one specific errand they can run, one chore they can take off your hands. You have done them and yourself a favor.

"Mother hasn't been out since Dad became ill. I think a Saturday afternoon at the shopping center would do wonders for her."

"We'll be at the hospital all day Thursday for chemotherapy. It would be such a help to me if you could whip up a casserole for our dinner."

"I don't feel much like talking these days, but if you'd bring your needlepoint and come sit with me, it would be pleasant to have your company."

Most people are grateful if there is something concrete they can do to show their continuing friendship. If such tasks bring them into your home, it gives them a chance to see that you are still living and functioning — not a funeral waiting to happen. Their next visit might be easier, and then they may be able to stop by without a "reason."

Choosing to help friends in this way is no easy undertaking. When you feel stretched to breaking just keeping your own life going, it is difficult to extend your energies further to make others feel at ease. It can be a new and difficult experience for some, this reaching out, but the rewards can be exhilarating. We all feel better giving than receiving, so it might be easier if you think of your requests for assistance as letting others feel useful, rather than as petitions for help.

Regardless of what you do, your friends might desert you. Circumstances might have left you alone before cancer struck. This is a special, awful loneliness for any human being to endure. There are no easy answers, no pat solutions. The mutual support of other people with cancer might provide some solace and comfort. There probably are others in your community who need your companionship as much as you need theirs. Being housebound need not deprive you of visits from others who would like to share some quiet moments or some deeply felt sorrow with someone who will understand. A physician, social worker, visiting nurse, or member of the clergy should be able to help you contact another cancer patient or shut-in who could use company.

For many of us, work forms a cornerstone of life. In addition to income, it provides satisfaction and a chance to interact with peers. Returning to work as soon as you are physically able is one way to return stability to your life. If treatment has made it impossible to return to a former line of work, investigate the availability of rehabilitation and retraining programs within the community to prepare you for another occupation.

You might find on returning to your job that relationships with coworkers have changed. One person with cancer found his associates had requested separate restroom facilities for him — that old "cancer is catching" myth again!

"If we pretend Jane never had cancer, it will go away" is the approach of many coworkers toward cancer patients when they return to work. This can be demoralizing. Some have found that if you look well and are able to function, people tend to underestimate the seriousness of your condition. They might mumble something like, "Glad you're back; you look great," and never ask how you really feel. In turn, you might find you resent their good health and nonchalance as you wonder what happened to the companionship you had looked forward to in returning to work.

The best you can do is assume that your coworkers, like so many others, are unsure of what to say or are trying to protect your feelings — or their own.

Others returning to work might be perfectly delighted with a rather cavalier attitude toward their condition. "Glad you're back," might be all you want to hear before plunging into your old routine. If you are being coddled at home, returning to a situation where others do not think of you as sick might be the greatest therapy yet devised.

Some people believe it eases relationships with coworkers if they are quite open about their condition. One young woman described in a speech to other cancer patients why she decided to tell about the cancer.

"Since my bones don't cooperate, it's hard for me to appear graceful, but I have a choice in this situation," she said. "I can either move as though nothing is bothering me (while gritting my teeth and giving my contact lenses a salty bath), or I can move awkwardly in reasonable comfort. I think this is one of the reasons I don't mind people knowing I have multiple myeloma. I keep having this flash of having died and having someone who just found out about the myeloma saying,'So that's why she kept falling over."'

If cancer treatment meant leaving your old job, discrimination may be a hurdle to returning to work. Even the person who is completely recovered may find it difficult to obtain employment. The rationale, one hears from indirect sources, is that people who have had cancer take too many sick days, are a poor insurance risk or will make coworkers uncomfortable.

How can you cope? You might begin with this information: Under federal law (the Federal Rehabilitation Act of 1973 and the Americans with Disabilities Act of 1990), most employers cannot discriminate against handicapped workers, including people with cancer. These laws apply to federal employers, employers that receive federal funds, and private companies with 25 or more employees (15 or more employees after mid-1994). The laws protect cancer patients in hiring practices, promotions, transfers, and layoffs. Every state also forbids discrimination based on handicap; however, only some of these state laws protect all people with cancer.

If you apply for a job with a government agency or a firm with government contracts and believe you did not get the job because of your cancer, you can file a complaint under Section 504 of the Federal Rehabilitation Act of 1973. You should write directly to the federal agency involved. If you do not know the name of the agency that provides federal funds to the employer, contact the Civil Rights Division of the U.S. Department of Justice, Washington, D.C., (202) 724-2235.

If you believe you were discriminated against by a private employer because of your cancer, you should file your complaint with the closest regional office of the Equal Employment Opportunities Commission. To obtain the location of your regional EEOC office and find out exactly what to do, call the EEOC Public Information System at (800 USA-EEOC).

To find out more about your legal rights, check with:

- Your local American Cancer Society. Offices have state-specific information about cancer and employment discrimination.

- Your social worker. He or she may know about laws in your state and can also tell you which state agency is in charge of protecting employment rights.

- Your state's Department of Labor or Office of Civil Rights.

- The National Coalition for Cancer Survivorship. This organization offers information and limited attorney referrals.

- Regional or national offices of the American Civil Liberties Union.

- Your representative or senator. Congressional and senate offices have information about Federal and state laws. If you're not sure who represents your district, call your local library or local chapter of the League of Women Voters.

Living Each Day

- Each person must work through, in his or her own way, feelings of possible death, fear, and isolation. Returning to normal routines as much as possible often helps.

- Give the pleasures and responsibilities of each day the attention they deserve.

- Responsible pursuits keep life meaningful; recreation keeps it zesty. Fill your life with both.

- Remember the difference between "doing" and "overdoing." Rest is important to both physical and emotional strength.

- It's harder to bolster one's will to live if you are alone. Yet many have acted as their own cheering squad and have found ways to lead meaningful lives.

- Family members must not make an invalid of a person with cancer who is fully capable of physical activity and responsible participation in the family.

- Family members should not equate physical incapability with mental failing. It is especially important that an ill patient feel a necessary part of the family.

- Families must guard against "rehearsing" how they will act if the patient dies by excluding him or her from family affairs now.

Whether the outlook for recovery is good or poor, the days go by, one at a time, and patient and family must learn to live each one. It's not always easy. On learning the diagnosis, some decide that death is inevitable, and there is nothing to do but give up and wait. They are not the first to feel that way.

Orville Kelly, a newspaperman, described his initial battle with the specter of death. "I began to isolate myself from the rest of the world. I spent much time in bed, even though I was physically able to walk and drive. I thought about my own impending funeral and it made me very sad."

These feelings continued from his first hospitalization through the first outpatient chemotherapy treatment. On the way home from that treatment, he was haunted by memories of the happy past, when "everything was all right." Then it occurred to Kelly, "I wasn't dead yet. I was able to drive my automobile. Why couldn't I return home to barbecue ribs?"

He did, that very night. He began to talk to his wife and children about his fears and anxieties. And he became so frustrated at the feelings he had kept locked up inside himself that he wrote the newspaper article that led to the founding of Make Today Count, the mutual help organization for cancer patients and their families.

Each person must work through individual feelings of possible death, fear and isolation in his or her own good time. It is hard to overcome these feelings if they are never confronted head on, but it is an ongoing struggle. One day brings feelings of confidence, the next day despair. Many people find it helps considerably if they strive to return, both as individuals and as a family, to their normal lives.

Each day brings pleasures and responsibilities totally outside the realm of cancer. We should try to give each the attention it deserves. These are the threads of the fabric that enfolds our lives. They give it color and meaning.

The days can be more valuable if you can learn to enjoy common moments as well as memorable occasions. This is true whether you have weeks or years left. It is true, in fact, whether you have a life-threatening disease or not. Physical well-being is closely tied to emotional well-being. The time you take out from attending to cancer strengthens you for the time you must devote to it.

When you have cancer, you need responsibilities, diversions, outings, and companionship just as before. As long as you are able, you should go to work, take the kids to the zoo, play cards with friends, go on a trip. Try to remember that responsible pursuits keep life meaningful, and recreation keeps it zesty. You need activities that give you a sense of purpose and those that provide enjoyment.

Some people find cancer is a spur to do the fun, adventurous, or zany things they've always wanted to do but gave put off as being not quite responsible. That's a great idea. It helps ward off two overreactions — one is giving up, and the other is trying to cram a life's worth of responsible accomplishment into a very short time.

A young woman with cancer put it this way: "Too often we patients fill up our lives with meaningful activities and neglect the frivolous outlets that keep us sane. And we tend to forget how important our sense of humor is." She quotes Betty Rollin, author of *First You Cry*, as saying that cancer won't bestow a sense of humor on someone who doesn't have it, but a sense of humor can sure get you through the experience.

There is no scientific or medical proof for it, but cancer patients who have "places to go and things to do" seem to live longer — or at least they feel that life still stretches before them. "I'm in my own real estate business, started a year ago, and serve as an officer in eight civic organizations," a woman wrote. "Life has never been fuller, and for a 47-year-old grandmother, I've never felt stronger or better." Seven years earlier, her family had been told she had six months to live.

Others have combined humor with too much interest in life to let go of it. "Mine has been a long battle, but I'm not ready to call it quits yet," one such person declared. "I'm just too busy to schedule my demise, or maybe I just haven't the good sense to lie down and let it happen!" Many have found they cannot retire from living. It's much like employment — every day you show up, you may as well give it your best!

"Doing," it might be pointed out, is not the same as overdoing. Try to recognize your limitations as well as your capabilities. Fatigue can bring on crushing despair, and many people have found that as simple a safeguard as adequate rest fends off depression. Exhaustion weakens our physical and emotional defenses.

Pain also can make a mockery of attempts to function normally. Physicians have learned much about controlling pain, so all pain, especially if it is prolonged, should be discussed with your physician.

"Putting one's house in order" is a desire that strikes many who learn they have cancer. This is not the same as giving up. In fact, everyone needs to review insurance policies, update wills, and clean out the closets and drawers from time to time — and that gives you something constructive to do.

It is obvious that many of these remarks have been directed toward the person with cancer who is part of a family. Some live alone, however, and some feel they have no one to "live for." This increases loneliness and can make the will to live seem a bitter irony. They may want to pull the covers over their head and "get it over with." If you have no one else to provide encouragement, you have to act as your own cheering squad. It is hard, but it's not impossible.

An amazing gentleman of 73, who had been treated on and off for 8 years for Hodgkin's disease, described how he coped. "I kept on fighting. This is what you must do. Positive thinking and an active life are two things which will do a great deal to relieve the tension." In order to stay involved with life and mentally active, he enrolled in the university where he had received his bachelor of arts degree and began work on his master's degree. "Some people think I'm crazy," he admits. "Maybe I am, but it is a nice crazy anyway. At least, I have achieved happiness."

An elderly woman decided to "start a new life, make what's left of this one count." She started helping a state school for the retarded, and her home became "a depot for people with used clothing and toys. Now I have branched out to helping with nursing homes. I am so busy and happy; I have no worries."

Not everyone can go beyond themselves and give to others to this extent. You might not have the physical or emotional strength. It may not be natural to you, and you are still the same person you were. But many find cancer is easier to live with if they choose constructive ways to fill their time — to make part of each day count for what they can put into it.

The desire to "do something" is common among nearly everyone with a family member or dear friend who has cancer. There is nothing you can do to change the course of cancer, so you do everything you can for the person. Sometimes, doing everything is the worst course to follow.

People with cancer still have the same needs and often the same capabilities as they did before. If they are physically able, they need to participate in their normal range of activities and responsibilities — right down to taking out the garbage. Helplessness, or worse, an unnecessary feeling of helplessness, is one of the great woes of the person with cancer. In the words of one:

"I am deeply angry over the way patients (not only cancer patients but any patient with a life-threatening diagnosis) are automatically treated as if we were mentally incompetent. Our relatives have RIGHTS; we have none. This is by a sort of mutual consent, an unconscious conspiracy which seems to be part of our culture. Let an individual become a patient ... and he is treated, without any 'competency hearing,' as if he had been found in a court of law to be incompetent. Only the relatives are consulted or empowered to make decisions..."

There is great bitterness in this woman's words, and they can stand as a lesson to all. Although bedridden, a patient probably still is able to discuss treatment options, financial arrangements, and the children's school problems. The rest of the family must make every effort to preserve as much as possible the patient's usual role within the family.

The least you can do is to keep the patient informed of necessary decisions. You can help the seriously ill patient ward off feelings of helplessness or abandonment if you continue to share your activities, goals, and dreams as before.

Few of us who are well know what it is like to be placed in a position of dependency. Cancer attacks one's self concept as a whole person as well as threatening one's life. Feelings of helplessness are real enough when one is flat on one's back. Make every effort not to compound them by ignoring the wishes of the patient, or worse, by trying to make an invalid of a person who is up and around. Pulling one's weight is good exercise.

The needs of the family as a unit are important, too. Maintain normal living patterns within the family as well as possible. This is important for long-range as well as day-to-day coping. Sometimes, when the patient is in active treatment, family life becomes totally disrupted. If that happens, it is harder to resume functioning as a unit during periods of extended remission or permanent control.

"My worst emotional problem," one patient said, "was finding that my improved health posed inconveniences and threw my family's plans all out of line."

Understanding such a situation might help prevent it. There are many ways we cope with fear, anxiety and the threat of loss or death. One way is to begin preparing ourselves for an event by thinking about it, without being aware that we are doing so, as if it had already happened. Thus, we "rehearse" life as it will be so that we can assume our new roles more easily when the time comes. People do this throughout their lives, although usually they are unaware of it. For example, teenagers spend increasing amounts of time with friends rather than with family, "rehearsing" for the time when they will go out on their own.

When a family member has cancer, you may be "rehearsing" the future in your own mind. You might begin to "practice" how the family will function if that person dies. Watch for signs that you are excluding the patient and turn the routine back toward normal if you are. Knowing that these things happen, however, try not to feel guilty if you find yourself emotionally out of step with remission or recovery.

The Years After

Cancer is not something anyone forgets. Anxieties remain as active treatment ceases and the waiting stage begins. A cold or a cramp may be cause for panic. As 6-month or annual checkups approach, you swing between hope and anxiety. As you wait for the mystical 5-year or 10-year point, you might feel more anxious rather than more secure.

These are feelings we all share. No one expects you to forget that you have had cancer or that it might recur. Each must seek individual ways of coping with the underlying insecurity of not knowing the true state of his or her health. The best prescription seems to lie in a combination of one part challenging responsibilities that command a full range of skills, a dose of activities that seek to fill the needs of others, and a generous dash of frivolity and laughter.

You still might have moments when you feel as if you live perched on the edge of a cliff. They will sneak up unbidden. But they will be fewer and farther between if you have filled your mind with thoughts other than cancer.

Cancer might rob you of that blissful ignorance that once led you to believe that tomorrow stretched forever. In exchange, you are granted the vision to see each today as precious, a gift to be used wisely and richly. No one can take that away.

Resources

You may want more information for yourself, your family and your doctor. The services explained below will help you obtain what you need.

Cancer Information Service
The National Cancer Institute sponsors a toll-free Cancer Information Service to help you. By dialing 1-800-4-CANCER (1-800-422-6237), you will be connected to a Cancer Information Service office, where a trained staff member can answer your questions and listen to your concerns. Spanish-speaking CIS staff are also available.

PDQ Service
The National Cancer Institute has developed PDQ, a computerized database designed to give doctors quick and easy access to:
- The latest treatment information for most types of cancer.
- Descriptions of clinical trials that are open for patient entry.
- Names of organizations and physicians involved in cancer care.
To get access to PDQ, a doctor can use an office computer with a telephone hookup and a PDQ access code or the services of a medical library with online searching capability. Cancer Information Service offices (800-4-CANCER) provide free PDQ searches and can tell doctors how to get regular access to the database. Patients may ask their doctor to use PDQ or may call 800-4-CANCER themselves. Information specialists at this toll-free number use a variety of sources, including PDQ, to answer questions about cancer prevention, diagnosis and treatment.

For additional written resources about cancer, treatment, and possible side effects, and nutritional information and recipes for the cancer patient, ask the Cancer Information Service to send you information or write Office of Cancer Communications, National Cancer Institute, Building 31, Room 1OA24, Bethesda, Maryland 20892 or American Cancer Society (ACS), 1599 Clifton Road, N.E., Atlanta, GA 30329; 800-ACS-2345, 404-320-3333.

The American Cancer Society is a voluntary organization with a national office (at the above address) and local units all over the country. It supports research, conducts educational programs, and offers many services for patients and their families. It also provides free booklets on cancer. To obtain information about services and activities in local areas, call the Society's toll-free number, 1-800-ACS-2345, or the number listed under American Cancer Society in the white pages of the telephone book.

Cataract Information for Patients[*]

This chapter has been written to help people with cataracts and their families better understand the condition. It describes the symptoms, diagnoses, and treatment of cataracts.

A cataract is a cloudy area in the eye's lens that can cause vision problems. The most common type is related to aging. More than half of all Americans age 65 and older have a cataract.

In the early stages, stronger lighting may lessen the vision problems caused by cataracts. At a certain point, however, surgery may be needed to improve vision. Today, cataract surgery is safe and very effective.

What is the lens?

The lens is the part of the eye that helps focus light onto the retina. The retina is the eye's light-sensitive layer that sends visual signals to the brain. The lens is located just behind the iris, the colored part of the eye. In focusing, the lens changes shape. It becomes rounder when you look at nearby objects and flatter for distant objects.

What is a cataract?

The lens is made mostly of water and protein. The protein is arranged to let light pass through and focus on the retina. Sometimes some of the protein clumps together and starts to cloud a small area of the lens. This is a cataract. Over time, the cataract may grow larger and cloud more of the lens, making it hard to see.

Although researchers are learning more about cataracts, no one knows for sure what causes them. Scientists think there may be several causes, including smoking and diabetes. Or, it may be that the protein in the lens just changes as it ages. There is also some evidence that cataracts are linked to certain vitamins and minerals.

---

* Source: U.S. Food and Drug Administration, Office of Consumer Affairs, Parklawn Building (HFE-88), 5600 Fishers Lane, Rockville, MD 20857; 301-827-4420.

The National Eye Institute (NEI) is doing a study to see whether taking more of these substances prevents or delays cataracts. Scientists do know that a cataract won't spread from one eye to the other, although many people develop cataracts in both eyes.

What are the symptoms?
The most common symptoms of a cataract are:

- Cloudy or blurry vision.
- Problems with light, such as headlights that seem too bright at night, glare from lamps or the sun, or a halo or haze around lights.
- Colors that seem faded.
- Double or multiple vision (this symptom goes away as the cataract grows).
- Frequent changes in your eyeglasses or contact lenses.

These symptoms can also be a sign of other eye problems. If you have any of these symptoms, check with your eye care professional.

When a cataract is small, you may not notice any changes in your vision. Cataracts tend to grow slowly, so vision gets worse gradually. Some people with a cataract find that their close-up vision suddenly improves, but this is temporary. Vision is likely to get worse again as the cataract grows.

What are the different types of cataract?
- *Age-related cataract*: Most cataracts are related to aging.
- *Congenital cataract*: Some babies are born with cataracts or develop them in childhood, often in both eyes. These cataracts may not affect vision. If they do, they may need to be removed.
- *Secondary cataract*: Cataracts are more likely to develop in people who have certain other health problems, such as diabetes. Also, cataracts are sometimes linked to steroid use.
- *Traumatic cataract*: Cataracts can develop soon after an eye injury, or years later.

How is a cataract detected?
To detect a cataract, an eye care professional examines the lens. A comprehensive eye examination usually includes:

- *Visual acuity test*: This eye chart test measures how well you see at various distances.
- *Pupil dilation*: The pupil is widened with eyedrops to allow your eye care professional to see more of the retina and look for other eye problems.
- *Tonometry*: This is a standard test to measure fluid pressure inside the eye. Increased pressure may be a sign of glaucoma.

Your eye care professional may also do other tests to learn more about the structure and health of your eye.

How is it treated?
For an early cataract, different eyeglasses, magnifying lenses, or stronger lighting may improve vision. If these measures don't help, surgery is the only effective treatment. The surgeon removes the cloudy lens and replaces it with a substitute lens.

A cataract needs to be removed only if it affects your vision so much that it interferes with your daily activities. You make that decision. If you decide on surgery, your eye care professional may refer you to another specialist to remove the cataract. If you have cataracts in both eyes, the surgeon will not remove them both at the same time. You will need to have each done separately.

Sometimes, a cataract should be removed even if it doesn't bother you. For example, if it prevents examination or treatment of another eye problem such as age- related macular degeneration or diabetic retinopathy, a cataract should be treated.

Cataract Surgery

If you've chosen to have surgery, it's helpful to know more about it. This section describes the types of cataract surgery, lens substitutes, and what you can expect before and after surgery.

Is cataract surgery effective?

Cataract removal most common operations performed in the U.S. today. It is also one of the safest and most effective. More than 90 percent of people who have cataract surgery have better vision afterward. However, even with the best results, your vision may not be as good as before the cataract.

How is a cataract removed?

The lens is enclosed in a capsule, an outer covering that holds it in place. There are many different techniques for cataract surgery, but all fall into one of two basic categories:

- *Extracapsular surgery*: Your doctor opens the front of the capsule and removes the lens, leaving the back of the capsule in place. Sound waves (ultrasound) may be used to soften and break up the cloudy lens so that it can be removed through a narrow hollow tube. This is called phacoemulsification or phaco.

- *Intracapsular surgery*: The entire lens is removed, including the capsule. Although extracapsular surgery has largely replaced this technique in the United States, it is safe and effective and may be used in some cases, for example, if the lens is too hard for phaco.

Currently, lasers cannot be used to remove a cataract. Although scientists are working on ways to use lasers in cataract surgery, these techniques are still being studied.

What are the choices for a lens substitute?

The lens is important for focusing. When it's removed, it usually needs to be replaced. There are three types of substitute lenses: an intraocular lens (IOL), a contact lens, or cataract glasses. Today, about 90 percent of patients choose an IOL. Of them, about 90 percent achieve 20/40 vision or better.

Intraocular lens
An IOL is a clear, plastic lens that is placed in your eye during

cataract surgery. It requires no care. With an IOL, you'll have better vision and won't feel or see the new lens. A few people cannot have an IOL because they're sensitive to the material the lens is made of, their eye structure isn't suitable, or they have certain other eye diseases.

Contact lens
Most people who do not have an IOL wear soft contact lenses. Extended-wear lenses are helpful if you have trouble putting in and taking out contacts. (Your eye care professional can remove and clean the lenses for you periodically.) With all contact lenses, it's important for you to follow instructions about proper use and care.

Cataract glasses
Some people don't want to use contact lenses or their eyes are too sensitive to wear them. For these people, cataract glasses may be the best choice. Cataract glasses affect vision differently than regular eyeglasses. Their powerful magnification (20-35 percent) may make it harder for you to judge distance and may distort your side vision. Until you've adjusted to these changes, you will need to be careful when you drive or do other activities.

What happens before surgery?
Before surgery, your eye care professional will do some tests. These may include tests to measure the curve of the cornea (the clear, dome-like structure that protects the front of the eye) and the shape of the eye. For patients who will receive an IOL, this information helps the eye care professional choose the right type of IOL. Other tests may help to determine the health of the retina and to guide the surgery. Photographs of your eye may also be taken before or after surgery.

Many people choose to stay awake during surgery, while others may need to be put to sleep for a short time. If you are awake, you'll have drugs to relax you and to numb the nerves and keep the eye from moving.

What happens after surgery?

Most people who have cataract surgery can go home the same day. Others may have some minor problems, such as bleeding, and may need to stay in the hospital overnight or for a few days.

It's normal to feel itching, sticky eyelids, and mild discomfort for a while after cataract surgery. Some fluid discharge is also common. In most cases, healing will take about six weeks.

If you have discomfort, your eye care professional may suggest a non-aspirin pain reliever every 4-6 hours (aspirin can cause bleeding). After 1-2 days, even moderate discomfort should disappear.

After surgery, your eye care professional will schedule exams to check on your progress. You may need to use eyedrops to help healing or to prevent infection or inflammation. For a few days after surgery, you may also take eyedrops or pills to control the pressure inside your eye. Ask your doctor how to use them, when to take them, and what effects they can have.

Problems after surgery are rare, but they can occur. These can include infection, bleeding, higher pressure inside the eye, inflammation (pain, redness, swelling), and detachment of the retina. With prompt medical attention, these problems can be treated.

Certain symptoms could mean that you need prompt treatment. If you have any of the following symptoms, call your eye care professional immediately: unusual pain, loss of vision, or flashing lights.

When will my vision be normal again?

After the surgery, you can read and watch TV almost right away, but your vision may be blurry. The healing eye needs time to adjust so that it can focus properly with the other eye-especially if the other eye has a cataract. This healing period may take many weeks.

Your eye care professional can suggest ways to improve your vision during this time.

How long it will be before you can see normally depends on the vision in your other eye, the lens substitute you choose, and your vision before surgery. With an IOL, for example, you may notice that colors have a blue tinge, and that after you've been in bright sunlight, everything is reddish for a few hours. It doesn't take long to adjust to these changes.

What is an "after-cataract"?
Sometimes people who have extracapsular surgery develop an after-cataract. When this happens, the back part of the lens capsule left in the eye becomes cloudy and keeps light from reaching the retina. Unlike a cataract, an after-cataract is treated with a laser. In a technique called YAG capsulotomy, your doctor uses a laser beam to make a tiny hole in the capsule to let light pass through. This is a painless outpatient procedure.

What research is being done?
The NEI is conducting and supporting a number of studies, such as the Age-Related Eye Disease Study (AREDS). In this nationwide clinical study, scientists are examining how cataracts develop and what factors put people at risk for developing them. Also, they are looking at whether certain vitamins and minerals affect cataract development.

Other research is focusing on new ways to prevent, diagnose, and treat cataracts. In addition, scientists are studying the role of genetics in the development of cataracts.

What can you do to protect your vision?
Although we don't know how to protect against cataracts, people over the age of 60 are at risk for many vision problems. If you are age 60 or older, you should have an eye examination through dilated pupils. This kind of exam allows your eye care professional to check for signs of age-related macular degeneration, glaucoma, cataracts, and other vision disorders.

For More Information

For more information about cataracts contact:
Agency for Health Care Policy and Research
Publications Clearinghouse, P.O. Box 8547, Silver Spring, MD 20907; 800-358-9295.

American Academy of Ophthalmology
655 Beach Street, P.O. Box 7424, San Francisco, CA 94109-7424; 415-561-8500.

American Optometric Association
243 Lindbergh Boulevard, St. Louis, MO 63141; 314-991-4100.

Prevent Blindness America
500 E. Remington Road, Schaumburg, IL 60173; 800-331-2020, 847-843-2020.

National Eye Institute
2020 Vision Place, Bethesda, MD 20892-3655; 301-496-5248.

For more information about IOLs, contact:
U.S. Food and Drug Administration
Office of Consumer Affairs, Parklawn Building (HFE-88), 5600 Fishers Lane, Rockville, MD 20857; 301-827-4420.

How To Take Your Medicine: Cephalosporins[*]

How you take a drug can affect how well it works and how safe it will be for you. Sometimes it can be almost as important as what you take. Timing, what you eat and when you eat, proper dose, and many other factors can mean the difference between feeling better, staying the same, or even feeling worse. This drug

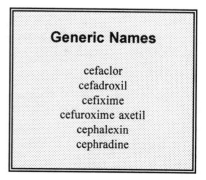

Generic Names

cefaclor
cefadroxil
cefixime
cefuroxime axetil
cephalexin
cephradine

information is intended to help you make your treatment work as effectively as possible. It is important to note, however, that this is only a guideline. You should talk to your doctor about how and when to take any prescribed drugs. There is also a group of drugs called drugs called cephalosporins.

Conditions These Drugs Treat

Cephalosporins are anti-infective agents (as antibiotics are also known) used to treat infections occurring in a variety of places in the body. In general, they are used either after other often less expensive anti-infective agents have been tried or when a certain uncommon type of infection is believed present. All cephalosporins can be used to treat most common urinary tract infections and upper respiratory infections such as pharyngitis (throat inflammation) and tonsillitis. All except cefadroxil may be used to treat otitis media (inflammation of the middle ear). All but cefixime can be used to treat various types of skin infections. Cefuroxime axetil and cefixime can be used to treat bronchitis, while cefaclor can treat lower respiratory infections such as pneumonia. Cephalexin can also be used to treat bone infections.

---

[*] Source: Office of Public Affairs, Food and Drug Administration, Public Health Service, 5600 Fishers Lane, Rockville, MD 20857; 301-827-4420.

Cephalosporins can be used for other infections as determined by your doctor.

Infections in any one area of the body (such as the throat, lung, ear, or urinary tract) can be caused by many types of bacteria. Doctors often try to prescribe the anti-infective that best treats the types of bacteria they judge is causing the infection. To be more certain doctors often culture an area (grow bacteria from an area under laboratory conditions) to determine exactly what types of bacteria are present. This enables them to make a more specific choice of anti-infective. As with other anti-infectives, some cephalosporins can treat certain bacterial infections better than others. This is why doctors sometimes prescribe different cephalosporins for infections that occur in the same area of the body.

How to Take

Cephalosporins can be taken either with food or on an empty stomach. If this medicine upsets your stomach, try taking it with food or milk.

Always store a cephalosporin liquid suspension in the refrigerator (exception: cefixime suspension does not need to be refrigerated). When taking a dose of the suspension, first shake the bottle well. Then use a measuring spoon or other device for administering medicine such as the calibrated medicine dropper included with Keflex pediatric drops. Discard any unused suspension after 14 days.

Be sure to take the right amount of tablets, capsules or suspension for each dose. Taking medicine at the same time each day will help you remember to take it regularly during the period your doctor has prescribed. To make sure your infection goes away completely, always take cephalosporin for the amount of time prescribed even if you feel better sooner. Not taking the cephalosporin for the entire prescribed period can cause your infection to come back. Heart or kidney complications can result if a "strep" (streptococcus) infection is not completely treated.

Missed Doses

To help clear your infection try not to miss any doses. If you do miss a dose, take it as soon as you remember. If it is almost time for your next dose, take two doses separated evenly over the next dosing interval (for example, if you take a dose every eight hours, take your next two doses spaced apart by four hours, then resume taking it every eight hours).

Relief of Symptoms

If your infection is caused by a type of bacteria that the cephalosporin can treat your symptoms should improve within a few days. But, as mentioned before, finish taking the cephalosporin for the full number of days even if you feel better.

Sometimes the symptoms can take longer than a few days to improve or may not go away even after you have taken all of the cephalosporin. This may happen with infections in areas of poor circulation, severe infections, viral infections, or in cases where the infection would be better treated by another anti-infective. If your symptoms have not disappeared after taking all of the cephalosporin or they get worse while taking it call your doctor.

Side Effects and Risks

Common side effects involve mainly the digestive system: mild stomach cramps or upset, nausea, vomiting, and diarrhea. These are usually mild and go away over time. Cephalosporins, as well as other anti-infectives can sometimes cause overgrowth of fungus normally present in the body. This overgrowth can cause mild side effects such as a sore tongue, sores inside the mouth, or vaginal yeast infections.

More serious but infrequent reactions can sometimes occur with cephalosporins, and these include:

- **Allergic reactions**. If you have a penicillin allergy, there is a chance you may also be allergic to a cephalosporin. Be sure to tell doctor if you have had allergic reactions to medications, particularly a penicillin, penicillamine, or a cephalosporin. Allergic reactions to cephalosporins are infrequent, but range from a skin rash that may be itchy, red or swollen to life-threatening reactions such as severe difficulty breathing and shock. Rarely, a specific type of allergic reaction can occur with cefaclor involving a skin rash, joint pains, irritability, and fever.

- **Serious colitis**. This is a rare side effect that includes severe watery diarrhea (sometimes containing blood or mucus), severe stomach cramps, fever, and weakness or faintness. If this happens contact your doctor immediately before you try treating it yourself with any medications.

Precautions and Warnings

Animal studies do not show cephalosporins to be dangerous during pregnancy. Although the effects of cephalosporins during pregnancy have not been studied in humans, they appear to be relatively safe to use during pregnancy. Let your doctor know if you are or intend to become pregnant while on a cephalosporin. Cephalosporins pass into breast milk in small amounts, though this is usually not a problem. Nursing mothers should consult with their doctors before breastfeeding while taking a cephalosporin.

Diabetic patients who test their urine for glucose should be aware that cephalosporins can cause a false-positive reading if copper sulfate urine testing tablets are used.

Cancer of the Colon and Rectum[*]

If you have additional questions after reading this information please contact the Cancer Information Service to talk with someone about cancer. The staff can talk with you in English or Spanish. The number is 800-422-6237 (800-4-CANCER) and the call is free.

Each year, more than 150,000 people in the United States learn that they have cancer of the colon or rectum (also called colorectal or large bowel cancer). This chapter will give you important information about colorectal cancer. It describes symptoms, diagnosis, and treatment, as well as possible causes and prevention. There is also has information to help you deal with colorectal cancer if it affects you or someone you know.

This information cannot take the place of talks with doctors, nurses, and other members of the health care team but we hope it will help with those talks.

Researchers continue to learn more about colorectal cancer and how to treat it. For up-to-date information, call the NCI-supported Cancer Information Service (CIS) toll free at the number listed above.

The Colon and the Rectum

The colon and rectum are part of the digestive system. Together, they form a long, muscular tube called the large intestine (also called the large bowel). The colon is the upper 5 to 6 feet of the large intestine, and the rectum is the last 6 to 8 inches.

After food is digested in the stomach and small intestine, it moves into the colon, where any remaining water is absorbed into the body, leaving solid waste (called stool). Stool moves through the colon and rectum and leaves the body through the anus.

---

[*] Source: Cancer Information Service, National Cancer Institute (NCI), 31 Center Drive, MSC 2580, Building 31, Room 10A16, Bethesda, MD 20892; 800-4-CANCER.

What Is Cancer?

Cancer occurs when cells become abnormal and divide without control or order. Cancer is a group of more than 100 different diseases.

Like all other organs of the body, the colon and the rectum are made of many kinds of cells. Normally, cells divide in an orderly way to produce more cells only when the body needs them. This process helps keep us healthy.

If cells keep dividing when new cells are not needed, a mass of tissue forms. This mass of extra tissue, called a growth or tumor, can be benign or malignant.

- **Benign tumors** are not cancer. They do not invade nearby tissue or spread to other parts of the body. Benign tumors usually can be removed and are seldom a threat to life.

   A polyp is a benign tumor that grows inward from the wall of the colon or rectum. Colorectal polyps should be removed because they can become cancerous. People who have had one colorectal polyp are likely to develop new ones, so they should have regular follow-up exams.

- **Malignant tumors** are cancer. They can invade and damage nearby tissues and organs. Cancer cells can also break away from a malignant tumor and enter the bloodstream and lymphatic system. That is how cancer spreads to form new tumors in other parts of the body. The spread of cancer is called metastasis.

Tumors can develop anywhere in the colon or rectum. If colorectal cancer cells spread outside the colon or rectum, they often travel to nearby lymph nodes (sometimes called lymph glands). Colorectal cancer can also spread to other parts of the body, such as the liver, lungs, brain, kidneys, and bladder.

When cancer spreads to another part of the body, the new tumor has the same kind of abnormal cells and the same name as the original (primary) cancer. For example, if colorectal cancer spreads to the liver, the cancer cells in the liver are colorectal cancer cells. The disease is called metastatic colorectal cancer (it is not liver cancer).

Early Detection

Most health problems respond best to treatment when they are diagnosed and treated as early as possible. This is especially true for colorectal cancer. Treatment is most effective before the disease spreads. People can take an active role in the early detection of colorectal cancer by following these National Cancer Institute guidelines:

- During regular checkups, have a digital rectal exam. For this exam, the doctor inserts a lubricated, gloved finger into the rectum and feels for abnormal areas.

- Beginning at age 50, have an annual fecal occult blood test. This test is a check for hidden (occult) blood in the stool. A small amount of stool is placed on a plastic slide or on special paper. The stool may be tested in the doctor's office or sent to a lab. The test is done because colorectal cancer may cause bleeding that cannot be seen. However, other conditions also may cause bleeding, so having blood in the stool does not necessarily mean a person has cancer.

- Beginning at age 50, have sigmoidoscopy every 3 to 5 years. This is an exam of the rectum and lower colon using a sigmoidoscope. The doctor looks through a thin, lighted tube to check for polyps, tumors, or other abnormalities.

People who may be at a greater than average colon cancer should discuss a schedule for these or other tests with their doctor.

Symptoms

Colorectal cancer can cause many symptoms. Warning signs to watch for include:

- A change in bowel habits;
- Diarrhea or constipation;
- Blood in or on the stool (either bright red or very dark in color);
- Stools that are narrower than usual;
- General stomach discomfort (bloating, fullness, and/or cramps);
- Frequent gas pains;
- A feeling that the bowel does not empty completely;
- Weight loss with no known reason; and
- Constant fatigue.

These symptoms also can be caused by other problems, such as ulcers, an inflamed colon, or hemorrhoids. Only a doctor can determine the cause. People who have any of these symptoms should see their doctor. The doctor may refer them to a doctor who specializes in diagnosing and treating digestive problems (a gastroenterologist).

Diagnosis

To find the cause of symptoms, the doctor asks about the patient's personal and family medical history, does a physical exam, and may order laboratory tests including the following;

- **Lower GI series**: X-rays of the colon and rectum (the lower gastrointestinal tract). The x-rays are taken after the patient is given an enema with a white, chalky solution containing barium. (This test is sometimes called a barium enema.) The barium outlines the colon and rectum on the x-rays, helping the doctor find tumors or other abnormal areas. To make small tumors easier to see, the doctor may expand the colon by carefully pumping in air during the test. This is called an air contrast or double-contrast barium enema.

- **Colonoscopy**: An examination of the inside of the entire colon using a colonoscope, an instrument similar to a flexible sigmoidoscope, but longer.

If a polyp or other abnormal growth is found, the doctor can remove part or all of it through a sigmoidoscope or colonoscope. A pathologist examines the tissue under a microscope to check for cancer cells. This procedure is called a biopsy. Most polyps are benign, but a biopsy is the only way to know for sure.

If the pathologist finds cancer, the patient's doctor needs to learn the stage, or extent, of the disease. Staging exams and tests help the doctor find out whether the cancer has spread and, if so, what parts of the body are affected. Treatment decisions depend on these findings.

Staging may include x-rays, ultrasonography, or CT (or CAT) scans of the lungs and liver because colorectal cancer tends to spread to these organs. The doctor may order blood tests to measure how well the liver is functioning. The doctor also may do a blood test called a CEA assay. This test measures the blood level of carcinoembryonic antigen (CEA), a substance that is sometimes found in higher than normal amounts in people who have colorectal cancer, especially when the disease has spread.

Treatment

The doctor develops a treatment plan to fit each patient's needs. Treatment for colorectal cancer depends on the size and location of the tumor, the stage of the disease, the patient's general health, and other factors. Most people who have cancer want to learn all they can about the disease and their treatment choices so they can take an active part in decisions about their medical care. The doctor is the best person to answer their questions. When talking about treatment choices, the patient may want to ask the doctor about taking part in a research study. Such studies, called clinical trials, are designed to improve cancer treatment. More information about clinical trials is available in this chapter.

Often, it helps to make a list of questions before seeing the doctor. Patients may take notes or, with the doctor's consent, tape record the discussion. Some patients also find that it helps to have a

These are some questions a patient may want ask the doctor before treatment begins:

- What is the stage of the disease?
- What are my treatment choices? Which do you suggest for me? Why?
- Would a clinical trial be appropriate for me?
- What are the expected benefits of each treatment?
- What are the risks and possible side effects of each treatment?
- What can be done about side effects?
- What can I do to take care of myself during therapy?
- What is the treatment likely to cost?

family member or friend with them when they see the doctor-to take part in the discussion, to take notes, or just to listen.

Patients and their loved ones are naturally concerned about the effectiveness of the treatment. Sometimes they use statistics to try to figure out whether the patient will be cured, or how long he or she will live. It is important to remember, however, that statistics are averages based on large numbers of patients. They cannot be used to predict what will happen to a particular person because no two cancer patients are alike. People should feel free to ask the doctor about the chance of recovery (prognosis), but even the doctor does not know for sure what will happen. When doctors talk about surviving cancer, they may use the term remission rather than cure. Even though many patients recover completely, doctors use this term because the disease can come back.

There is a lot to learn about cancer and its treatment. Patients should not feel that they need to understand everything at once.

They will have many other chances to ask the doctor for more information and for an explanation of things that are not clear.

Getting a Second Opinion

Treatment decisions are complex. Sometimes it is helpful for patients to have a second opinion about the diagnosis and the treatment plan. Some insurance companies require a second opinion; others provide coverage for a second opinion at the patient's request. There are several ways to find another doctor to consult:

- The patient's doctor may be able to suggest a doctor who specializes in treating colorectal cancer. Specialists who treat this disease include surgeons, medical oncologists, gastroenterologists, and radiation oncologists.

- The Cancer Information Service, at 800-4-CANCER, can tell callers about treatment facilities, including cancer centers and other National Cancer Institute supported programs.

- Patients can get the names of doctors from their local medical society, a nearby hospital, or a medical school.

Methods of Treatment

Colorectal cancer is generally treated with surgery, chemotherapy, and/or radiation therapy. New treatment approaches such as biological therapy and improved ways of using current methods are being studied in clinical trials. A patient may have one form of treatment or a combination.

Surgery is the most common treatment for colorectal cancer. The type of operation depends on the location and size of the tumor. Most patients have a partial colectomy. In this operation, the surgeon takes out the part of the colon or rectum that contains the cancer and a small amount of surrounding healthy tissue. Surgery is often the only treatment needed for early colorectal cancer.

Usually, lymph nodes near the tumor are removed during surgery to help the doctor be more accurate about the stage of the cancer. A pathologist examines the lymph nodes under a microscope to see whether they contain cancer cells. If the cancer has reached these nodes, the disease may also have spread to other parts of the body, and the patient may need further treatment.

These are some questions a patient may want to ask the doctor before surgery:

- What kind of operation will it be?
- How will I feel afterward? If I have pain, how will you help me?
- Will I need a colostomy? Will it be temporary or permanent?
- How long will I be in the hospital?
- Will I have to be on a special diet? Who will teach me about my diet?
- When can I return to my regular activities:
- Will I need additional treatment?

In most cases, the surgeon reconnects the healthy sections of the colon or rectum. This part of the surgery is called anastomosis. If the healthy sections of the colon or rectum cannot be reconnected, the doctor performs a colostomy, creating an opening (stoma) in the abdomen through which solid waste leaves the body. The patient uses a special bag to cover the stoma and collect waste. A colostomy may be temporary or permanent.

- A temporary colostomy is sometimes needed to allow the lower colon or the rectum to heal after surgery. Later, in a second operation, the surgeon reconnects the healthy sections of the colon or rectum and closes the colostomy. The patient's bowel functions soon return to normal.

- A permanent colostomy may be necessary when the tumor is in the rectum. A few patients who have cancer in the lower colon may also require a permanent colostomy. Overall, however, only about 15 percent of patients with colorectal cancer need a permanent colostomy.

Although it may take some time to adjust to a colostomy, most patients return to their normal lifestyle. A nurse or an enterostomal therapist teaches the patient how to care for a colostomy and suggests ways to continue with normal activities. Support groups, such as those offered through the United Ostomy Association (see end of chapter), may also be helpful.

Chemotherapy is the use of drugs to kill cancer cells. Chemotherapy is sometimes given after surgery for colorectal cancer to try to prevent the disease from spreading. This additional treatment is called adjuvant therapy. Chemotherapy also may be given to relieve symptoms of the disease in patients

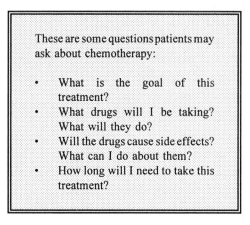

These are some questions patients may ask about chemotherapy:

- What is the goal of this treatment?
- What drugs will I be taking? What will they do?
- Will the drugs cause side effects? What can I do about them?
- How long will I need to take this treatment?

whose primary tumor cannot be completely removed or to control the growth of new tumors. The doctor may use one drug or a combination of drugs.

Chemotherapy is usually given in cycles: a treatment period followed by a recovery period, then another treatment period, and so on. Anticancer drugs may be taken by mouth or given by injection into a blood vessel or body cavity. Chemotherapy is a systemic therapy, meaning that the drugs enter the bloodstream and travel through the body.

In clinical trials, researchers are studying ways of putting chemotherapy drugs directly into the area to be treated. For colorectal cancer that has spread to the liver, drugs can be injected into a blood vessel that leads directly to the liver. (This treatment is called intrahepatic chemotherapy.) Researchers are also investigating a method in which the doctor puts anticancer drugs directly into the abdomen through a thin tube. (This is called intraperitoneal chemotherapy.)

Usually a person has chemotherapy as an outpatient at the hospital, at the doctor's office, or at home. However, depending on which drugs are given, how they are given, and the patient's general health, a short hospital stay may be necessary.

Radiation therapy (also called radiotherapy) is the use of high-energy rays to damage cancer cells and stop them from growing. Like surgery, radiation therapy is local therapy; it can affect cancer only in the treated area. Radiation therapy is sometimes used before surgery to shrink a tumor so that it is easier to remove. More often, radiation therapy is given after surgery to destroy any cancer cells that may remain in the area. It may also be given to relieve pain or other problems in patients whose tumors cannot be surgically removed. Radiation therapy is usually given on an outpatient basis in a hospital or clinic 5 days a week for several weeks.

These are some questions a patient may want to ask the doctor before receiving radiation therapy:

- How will the radiation be given?
- What is the goal of this treatment?
- When will the treatment begin? When will it end?
- What can I do to take care of myself during treatment?

Researchers are conducting clinical trials to look for more effective ways of using radiation therapy. For example, some are studying the benefits of using radiation both before and after surgery ("sandwich" technique), and others are giving radiation during surgery (intraoperative radiation). Doctors are also exploring the use of radiation therapy alone (instead of surgery) for rectal cancer that has not spread.

Biological therapy is a cancer treatment that helps the body's immune (defense) system attack and destroy cancer cells. For some patients, biological therapy may be combined with chemotherapy as adjuvant treatment after surgery. New types of biological therapy are being used to treat patients in clinical trials. Patients may need to stay in the hospital while receiving some types of biological therapy.

Clinical Trials

Many patients with colorectal cancer are treated in clinical trials (treatment studies). Clinical trials help doctors find out whether the new treatment is both safe and effective, and they also help answer scientific questions. Patients who take part in early studies are the first to receive treatments that have shown promise in laboratory research. In later studies, some patients may receive the new treatment while others receive a standard approach. In this way, doctors can compare different therapies. Patients who take part in a trial make an important contribution to medical science and may have the first chance to benefit from improved treatment methods.

Patients who are interested in taking part in a trial should talk with their doctor. They may want to read the National Cancer Institute booklet, *What Are Clinical Trials All About?*, which explains the possible benefits and risks of treatment studies.

One way to learn about clinical trials is through PDQ, a computerized resource developed by the National Cancer Institute. PDQ contains information about cancer treatment and about clinical trials in progress all over the country. The Cancer Information Service can provide PDQ information to doctors, patients, and the public.

Side Effects of Treatment

It is often hard to limit the effects of therapy so that only cancer cells are removed or destroyed. Because healthy tissue also may be damaged, treatment can cause unpleasant side effects.

The side effects of cancer treatment are different for each person, and they may even be different from one treatment to the next. Doctors try to plan treatment in ways that keep side effects to a minimum; they can help with any problems that occur. For this reason, it is very important to let the doctor know about any health problems during or after treatment.

Surgery

Surgery for colorectal cancer (including colostomy) may cause temporary constipation or diarrhea. The doctor can prescribe medicine or suggest a diet to help relieve these problems. Patients who have pain after surgery should tell their doctor so that medicine can be given to relieve their discomfort. For a period of time after the surgery, the person's activity will be limited to allow the operation to heal.

Colostomy patients may have irritation on the skin around the stoma. The doctor, nurse, or enterostomal therapist can teach the patient how to clean the area to prevent irritation and infection.

Chemotherapy

The side effects of chemotherapy depend mainly on the drugs the patient is given. As with any other type of treatment, side effects vary from person to person. In general, anticancer drugs affect rapidly dividing cells. These include blood cells, which fight infection, cause the blood to clot, or carry oxygen throughout the body. When blood cells are affected by anticancer drugs, patients are more likely to get infections, may bruise or bleed easily, and may have less energy. Cells in hair roots and cells that line the digestive tract also divide rapidly. For these reasons, chemotherapy can cause hair loss and problems such as poor appetite, mouth sores, nausea, vomiting, and diarrhea. The doctor can prescribe medicines or suggest other ways to prevent or reduce many of these effects. The side effects of chemotherapy gradually go away during the recovery period or after treatment stops.

Radiation Therapy

Patients who receive radiation therapy to the abdomen may have nausea, vomiting, and diarrhea. The doctor can prescribe medicine or suggest dietary changes to relieve these problems. Radiation therapy for colorectal cancer may cause hair loss in the pelvic area;

the loss may be temporary or permanent, depending on the amount of radiation used. The skin in the treated area also may become red, dry, tender, and itchy. Patients should avoid wearing clothes that rub; loose-fitting cotton clothes are usually best. It is important for patients to take good care of their skin during treatment, but they should not use lotions or creams without the doctor's advice.

During radiation therapy, patients may become very tired, especially in the later weeks of treatment. Although resting is important, doctors usually suggest that patients continue as many of their normal activities as possible.

Biological Therapy
The side effects of biological therapy vary with the type of treatment. Often, these treatments cause flu-like symptoms, such as chills, fever, weakness, nausea, vomiting, and diarrhea. Sometimes patients also get a rash.

Other Side Effects
Cancer can cause loss of appetite. For some patients, the taste of food changes; others may not feel like eating when they are uncomfortable or tired. Also, some of the common side effects of treatment, such as nausea, vomiting, or mouth sores, can make it hard to eat. Yet nutrition is important. Eating well means getting enough calories and protein to help prevent weight loss, regain strength, and rebuild normal tissues. Patients who eat well during cancer treatment often feel better and have more energy. They also may be better able to handle the side effects of treatment. Patients may want to ask their doctor about ways to help provide extra calories and protein.

Sometimes, treatment for colorectal cancer interferes with patients' ability to have sexual intercourse. Depending on the location of the tumor, surgery may damage the nerves that control a man's erection or the arteries that carry blood to the penis, causing temporary or permanent impotence. Also, radiation therapy to the abdomen sometimes causes problems with erection. Women who have had surgery to remove a colorectal tumor may have discomfort during sexual intercourse. Radiation therapy also may cause temporary vaginal dryness or tightness. The doctor or nurse can offer suggestions for dealing with these problems.

Patients who have a colostomy may have special concerns about sexuality. It may take time to adjust to the colostomy before they are ready for sexual intimacy. Many patients find that sharing their thoughts and feelings with a partner, close friend, or therapist helps them deal with these concerns. An enterostomal therapist can help patients adjust to the colostomy and can suggest ways to prevent it from interfering with sexuality.

Doctors, nurses, and dietitians can explain the side effects of cancer treatment and suggest ways to deal with them. The National Cancer Institute booklets *Radiation Therapy and You, Chemotherapy and You*, and *Eating Hints for Cancer Patients* have helpful information about cancer treatment and coping with side effects. Publications about sexuality issues for cancer patients are available from the American Cancer Society and the United Ostomy Association; information about these organizations is at the end of this chapter.

Followup Care

Regular followup exams are very important after treatment for colorectal cancer. The cancer can recur at or near the site of the original tumor or can spread to another area of the body. The doctor will continue to check closely so that, if the cancer comes back, it can be treated again as soon as possible.

Checkups often include a physical exam, a fecal occult blood test, sigmoidoscopy, colonoscopy, chest x-ray, and blood tests, including the CEA assay. Often the CEA level in a patient's blood is high before surgery and returns to normal within several weeks after the tumor has been removed. If the level of CEA begins to rise again, it may mean the cancer has come back. Other tests must also be done, because conditions other than cancer can cause the level to rise.

In addition to follow-up exams to check for a recurrence of colorectal cancer, patients may want to ask their doctor about checking for other types of cancer. Women who have had colorectal cancer have an increased risk of developing cancer of the breast, ovary, or cervix. Men who have had colorectal cancer appear to be at increased risk for developing prostate cancer. In a small number of patients, cancer treatment may cause side effects many years later. Patients may wish to discuss possible effects with their doctor. Patients should continue to have checkups and should report any problem as soon as it appears.

Support for Cancer Patients

Living with a serious disease is not easy. Cancer patients and those who care about them face many problems and challenges. Coping with these difficulties is easier when people have helpful information and support services. Several useful booklets, including *Taking Time: Support for People With Cancer and the People Who Care About Them*, are available from the Cancer Information Service.

Cancer patients may worry about holding their job, caring for their family, or keeping up with daily activities. Worries about tests, treatments, hospital stays, and medical bills are common. Doctors, nurses, and other members of the health care team can answer questions about treatment, working, or other activities. Also, meeting with a social worker, counselor, or member of the clergy can be helpful to patients who want to talk about their feelings or discuss their concerns about the future or about personal relationships.

Friends and relatives can be very supportive. Also, many patients find it helps to discuss their concerns with others who have cancer. Cancer patients often get together in support groups, where they can share what they have learned about coping with cancer and the effects of treatment. It is important to keep in mind, however, that each patient is different. Treatments and ways of dealing with cancer that work for one person may not be right for another-even if they both have the same kind of cancer. It is always a good idea to discuss the advice of friends and family members with the doctor.

Often, a social worker or enterostomal therapist at the hospital or clinic can suggest groups that can help with rehabilitation, emotional support, financial aid, transportation, or home care. For example, the American Cancer Society has many services for cancer patients and their families. Local offices of the American Cancer Society are listed in the white pages of the telephone directory. More information about this group is also at the end of this chapter.

Support groups for patients who have a colostomy are sponsored by the United Ostomy Association. Members of this group have some type of ostomy. They can answer patients' questions about living with a colostomy and can offer advice and emotional support. Information about the United Ostomy Association is at the end of this chapter.

The public library has many books and articles on living with cancer. Cancer patients and their families and friends also can find helpful suggestions in National Cancer Institute booklets. Information about programs and services for cancer patients and their families is available from the Cancer Information Service.

Cause and Prevention

Colorectal cancer is one of the most common types of cancer in the United States. Scientists are trying to learn more about what causes the disease and how it can be prevented.

Although doctors do not yet know why one person gets colorectal cancer and another does not, they do know that no one can catch colorectal cancer from another person. Cancer is not contagious.

Some people are more likely to develop colorectal cancer than others. Studies have found that certain factors increase a person's risk. The following are risk factors for this disease:

- **Polyps.** Most — perhaps all — colorectal cancers develop in polyps. Polyps are benign, but they may become cancerous over time. Removing polyps is an important way to prevent colorectal cancer.

- **Age.** Colorectal cancers occur most often in people who are over the age of 50, and the risk increases as people get older.

- **Family history.** Close relatives of a person who has had colorectal cancer have a higher than average risk of developing the disease. The risk for colon cancer is even higher among members of a family in which many relatives have had it. (In such cases, the disease is called familial colon cancer.)

- **Familial polyposis.** This is an inherited condition in which hundreds of polyps develop in the colon and rectum. Over time, these polyps can become cancerous. Unless the condition is treated, a person who has familial polyposis is almost sure to develop colorectal cancer.

- **Diet.** The risk of developing colon cancer seems to be higher in people whose diet is high in fat, low in fruits and vegetables, and low in high-fiber foods such as whole-grain breads and cereals.

- **Ulcerative colitis.** This disease causes inflammation of the lining of the colon. The risk of colon cancer is much greater than average for people who have this disease, and the risk increases with the length of time they have had it.

Researchers have found some trends in the incidence of colorectal cancer. For example, colorectal cancer occurs most often among people who live in cities. Colon cancer occurs slightly more often among blacks, and rectal cancer is more common among whites. People can lower their risk of getting colorectal cancer. For example, those who have colorectal polyps should talk with the doctor about having them removed. People also can change their eating habits to cut down on fat in their diet. Major sources of fat are meat, eggs, dairy products, and oils used in cooking and salad dressings. People should increase the amount of fiber (roughage) in their diet. Fiber comes from vegetables, fruits, and whole-grain breads and cereals. The National Cancer Institute recommends a low-fat, high-fiber diet that includes at least five servings of fruits and vegetables each day. Additional information about a healthy diet is available from the Cancer Information Service.

People who think they are at risk for developing colorectal cancer should discuss this concern with their doctor. The doctor may suggest ways to decrease the risk and can plan an appropriate schedule for checkups.

Medical Terms

Abdomen (AB-do-men): The part of the body that contains the stomach, small intestine, colon, rectum, liver, spleen, pancreas, kidneys, appendix, gallbladder, and bladder.

Adjuvant therapy (AD-joo-vant): Treatment given in addition to the primary treatment.

Anastomosis (an-as-to-MO-sis): A procedure to connect healthy sections of the colon or rectum after the cancerous portion has been surgically removed.

Anus (AY-nus): The opening of the rectum to the outside of the body.

Benign (be-NINE): Not cancer; does not invade surrounding tissue or spread to other parts of the body.

Biological therapy (by-o-LOJ-i-kul): Treatment to stimulate or restore the ability of the immune (defense) system to fight infection and disease. Also called immunotherapy.

Biopsy (BY-op-see): The removal of a sample of tissue for examination under a microscope to check for cancer cells.

Bowel: Another name for the intestine. There is both a small and a large bowel.

Cancer: A term for the diseases in which abnormal cells divide without control. Cancer cells can invade surrounding tissue and spread to other parts of the body through the bloodstream and lymphatic system.

CEA assay: A laboratory test to measure the level of carcinoembryonic antigen (CEA), a substance that is sometimes found in an increased amount in the blood of colorectal cancer patients.

Chemotherapy (kee-mo-THER-a-pee): Treatment with anticancer drugs.

Clinical trials: Medical research studies conducted with volunteers. Each study is designed to answer scientific questions and to find better ways to prevent, detect, or treat cancer.

Colectomy (ko-LEK-to-mee): An operation to remove all or part of the colon. In a partial colectomy, the surgeon removes only the cancerous part of the colon and a small amount (called a margin) of surrounding healthy tissue.

Medical Terms (continued)

Colon (KO-lun): The long, coiled, tubelike organ that removes water from digested food. The remaining material, solid waste called stool, moves through the colon to the rectum and leaves the body through the anus. The colon is sometimes called the large bowel or the large intestine.

Colonoscope (ko-LON-o-skope): A flexible, lighted instrument used to view the inside of the colon.

Colonoscopy (ko-lun-OS-ko-pee): An examination in which the doctor looks at the colon through a flexible, lighted instrument called a colonoscope.

Colorectal (ko-lo-REK-tul): Related to the colon and/or rectum.

Colostomy (ko-LOS-to-mee): An opening created by a surgeon into the colon from the outside of the body. A colostomy provides a new path for waste material to leave the body after part of the colon has been removed.

CT (or CAT) scan: A series of detailed pictures of areas inside the body created by a computer linked to an x-ray machine. Also called computed tomography (CT) scan or computed axial tomography (CAT) scan.

Digestive system: The organs that are responsible for getting food into and out of the body and for making use of food to keep the body healthy. These include the mouth, esophagus, stomach, liver, gallbladder, pancreas, small intestine, colon, and rectum.

Digital rectal exam: An exam to detect rectal cancer. The doctor inserts a lubricated, gloved finger into the rectum and feels for abnormal areas.

Enterostomal therapist (en-ter-o-STO-mul): A health care specialist trained to help patients care for and adjust to their colostomy.

Familial polyposis (pol-i-PO-sis): An inherited condition in which several hundred polyps develop in the colon and rectum.

Fecal occult blood test (FEE-kul ok-KULT): A test to check for hidden blood in stool. (Fecal refers to stool. Occult means hidden.)

Fiber: The parts of fruits and vegetables that cannot be digested, Also called bulk or roughage.

Gastroenterologist (GAS-tro-en-ter-OL-o-jist): A doctor who specializes in diagnosing and treating diseases of the digestive system.

Medical Terms (continued)

Ileostomy (il-ee-OS-to-mee): An opening created by a surgeon into the ileum, part of the small intestine, from the outside of the body. An ileostomy provides a new path for waste material to leave the body after part of the intestine has been removed.

Immune system (im-YOON): The complex group of organs and cells that defends the body against infection or disease.

Impotence (IM-po-tense): The inability to have or maintain an erection.

Intestine (in-TES-tin): The long, tubelike organ in the abdomen that completes the process of digestion. It consists of the small and large intestines.

Intrahepatic (in-tra-hep-AT-ik): Within the liver.

Intraperitoneal (in-tra-per-i-to-NEE-ul): Within the peritoneal cavity, the area that contains the abdominal organs.

Local therapy: Treatment that affects only a tumor and the area close to it.

Lower GI series: A series of x-rays of the colon and rectum that is taken after the patient is given a barium enema. (Barium is a white, chalky substance that outlines the colon and rectum on the x-ray.)

Lymph (limf): The almost colorless fluid that travels through the lymphatic system and carries cells that help fight infection and disease.

Lymph nodes: Small, bean-shaped organs located throughout the lymphatic system. The lymph nodes store special cells that can trap cancer cells or bacteria that are traveling through the body in lymph. Also called lymph glands.

Lymphatic system (lim-FAT-ik): The tissues and organs, including the bone marrow, spleen, thymus, and lymph nodes, that produce and store cells that fight infection and disease. The channels that carry lymph are also part of this system.

Malignant (ma-LIG-nant): Cancerous; can invade nearby tissues and spread to other parts of the body.

Metastasis (meh-TAS-ta-sis): The spread of cancer from one part of the body to another. Cells that have metastasized are like those in the original (primary) tumor.

Oncologist (on-KOL-o-jist): A doctor who specializes in treating cancer.

Medical Terms (continued)

Ostomy (OS-to-mee): An operation to create an opening from an area inside the body to the outside. See glossary entry for colostomy.

Pathologist (path-OL-o-jist): A doctor who identifies diseases by studying cells and tissues under a microscope.

Polyp (POL-ip): A mass of tissue that develops on the inside wall of a hollow organ such as the colon.

Prognosis (prog-NO-sis): The probable outcome or course of a disease; the patient's chance of recovery.

Radiation therapy: Treatment with high-energy rays from x-rays or other sources to kill cancer cells.

Rectum: The last 6 to 8 inches of the large intestine. The rectum stores solid waste until it leaves the body through the anus.

Remission: Disappearance of the signs and symptoms of cancer. When this happens, the disease is said to be "in remission." A remission can be temporary or permanent.

Risk factor: Something that increases a person's chances of developing a disease.

Side effects: Problems that occur when treatment affects healthy cells. Common side effects of cancer treatment are fatigue, nausea, vomiting, decreased blood cell counts, hair loss, and mouth sores.

Sigmoidoscope (sig-MOY-do-skope): A lighted instrument used to view the inside of the lower colon.

Sigmoidoscopy (sig-moy-DOS-ko-pee): An examination of the rectum and lower colon using a sigmoidoscope. Also called proctosigmoidoscopy or "procto."

Staging: Doing exams and tests to learn the extent of a cancer, especially whether it has spread from its original site to other parts of the body.

Stoma (STO-ma): An opening into the body from the outside created by a surgeon.

Stool: The solid matter discharged in a bowel movement.

Medical Terms (continued)

Surgery: An operation.

Systemic therapy: Treatment that reaches cells throughout the body by traveling through the bloodstream.

Tissue: A group or layer of cells that perform specific functions.

Tumor: An abnormal mass of tissue.

Ulcerative colitis: A disease that causes long-term inflammation of the lining of the colon.

Ultrasonography: A test in which sound waves (ultrasound) are bounced off tissues and the echoes are converted into a picture (sonogram).

X-ray: High-energy radiation. It is used in low doses to diagnose diseases and in high doses to treat cancer.

Booklets

National Cancer Institute printed materials, including the booklets listed below, are available free of charge by calling 800-4-CANCER.

Booklets About Cancer Treatment
- *Chemotherapy and You: A Guide to Self-Help During Treatment*
- *Radiation Therapy and You: A Guide to Self-Help During Treatment*
- *What Are Clinical Trials All About?*
- *Eating Hints for Cancer Patients*
- *Questions and Answers About Pain Control* (also available from the American Cancer Society)

Booklets About Living With Cancer
- *Taking Time: Support for People With Cancer and the People Who Care About Them*
- *Facing Forward: A Guild for Cancer Survivors*
- *When Cancer Recurs: Meeting the Challenge Again*
- *Advanced Cancer: Living Each Day*

Resources

Information about cancer is available from many sources, including the ones listed below. You may want to check for additional information at your local library or bookstore and from support groups in your community.

Cancer Information Service
The Cancer Information Service, a program of the National Cancer Institute, is a nationwide telephone service for cancer patients and their families and friends, the public, and health care professionals. The staff can answer questions in English or Spanish and can send free National Cancer Institute booklets about cancer. They also know about local resources and services. One toll- free number, 800-4-CANCER (800-422-6237), connects callers all over the country with the office that serves their area.

American Cancer Society
The American Cancer Society is a voluntary organization with a national office and local units all over the country. This organization supports research, conducts educational programs, and offers many services to patients and their families. The American Cancer Society also provides free booklets on colorectal cancer and on sexuality. To obtain booklets, or for information about services and activities in local areas, call the Society's toll-free number, 800-ACS-2345, or the number listed under American Cancer Society in the white pages of the telephone book.

United Ostomy Association
36 Executive Park, Suite 126
Irvine, CA 92714
714-660-8624
The United Ostomy Association is a group organized by and for people who have had an ostomy. The organization's goal is to help patients return to a normal life after their surgery. The association sends volunteers to visit with new ostomy patients and sponsors support groups. It also publishes the Ostomy Quarterly and other educational materials. Local chapters of the United Ostomy Association are listed in the white pages of the telephone book.

Constipation*

Constipation is a symptom, not a disease. It is defined as having fewer bowel movements than usual, with a long or hard passing of stools.

Older people are more likely than younger people to have constipation. But experts agree that older people often worry too much about having a bowel movement every day. There is no right number of daily or weekly bowel movements. "Regularity" may mean bowel movements twice a day for some people or just twice a week for others.

What Causes Constipation?

Doctors do not always know what causes this problem. eating a poor diet, drinking too little, or misusing laxatives can be causes. Some medicines can lead to constipation. These include some antidepressants, antacids containing aluminum or calcium, antihistamines, diuretics, and antiparkinsonism drugs.

The role of diet. People may become constipated if they start eating fewer vegetables, fruits, and whole grains. These foods are all high in fiber, and, according to some studies, high-fiber diets can help prevent constipation. Eating more high-fat meats, dairy products, and eggs can be another cause of constipation. So can eating more rich desserts and other sweets high in refined sugars.

People who live alone may lose interest in cooking and eating. As a result they start using a lot of convenience foods. These tend to be low in fiber, so they may help cause constipation. In addition, bad teeth may cause older people to choose soft, processed foods that contain little, if any, fiber.

---

* Source: *Age Page*, National Institute on Aging, U.S. Department of Health and Human Services, Public Health Service, National Institutes of Health, Gaithersburg, MD 20898; 800-222-2225.

People sometimes do not drink enough liquids, especially if they are not eating regular meals. Water and other liquids add bulk to stools, making bowel movements easier.

Misuse of laxatives and enemas. Many people think of laxatives as the cure for constipation. But heavy use of laxatives is usually not necessary and often can be habit-forming. The body begins to rely on the laxatives to bring on bowel movements and, over time, forgets how to work on its own. For the same reason, if you use enemas often you may lose normal bowel function. Another side effect of heavy laxative use is diarrhea.

Overuse of mineral oil — a popular laxative — may reduce the body's ability to use vitamins (A, D, E, and K). Mineral oil may also interact with drugs that prevent blood clots (anticoagulants), causing undesired side effects.

Other causes of constipation. Lack of exercise or lengthy bedrest, such as after an accident or illness, may cause constipation. For people who stay in bed and who suffer from chronic constipation, medications may be the best solution. But simply being more active, when possible, is best.

If people ignore the natural urge to have a bowel movement, they may become constipated. Some people prefer to have their bowel movements only at home, but holding a bowel movement can cause ill effects if the delay is too long.

In some people, constipation may be caused by abnormalities or a blockage of the intestines. These disorders may affect the muscles or nerves responsible for normal bowel movements. A doctor can perform a series of tests to see if a problem like this is the cause of constipation. If so, the problem can often be treated.

Treatment

If you become constipated, first see the doctor to rule out a more serious problem. If the results show that there is no disease or blockage, and if your doctor approves, try these remedies:

- Eat more fresh fruits and vegetables, either cooked or raw, and more whole grain cereals and breads. Dried fruit such as apricots, prunes, and figs are especially high in fiber.

- Drink plenty of liquids (1 to 2 quarts daily), unless you have heart, blood vessel, or kidney problems. But be aware that some people become constipated from drinking large amounts of milk.

- Some doctors recommend adding *small* amounts of unprocessed bran[1] ("miller's bran") to baked goods, cereals, and fruit. Some people suffer from bloating and gas for several weeks after adding bran to their diets. Make diet changes slowly, to allow the digestive system to adapt. Remember, if your diet is well-balanced and contains a variety of foods high in natural fiber, it may not be necessary to add bran to other foods.

- Stay active.

Do not expect to have a bowel movement every day or even every other day. "Regularity" differs from person to person. If your bowel movements are usually painless and occur regularly (whether two

> ### Questions to Ask
>
> Some doctors suggest asking these questions to decide if you are really constipated.
>
> - Do you often have fewer than three bowel movements each week?
> - Do you often have a hard time passing stools?
> - Is there pain?
> - Are there other problems such as bleeding?
>
> If the answers are yes, you probably do have a problem. Otherwise, you probably do not.

---

[1] Unprocessed bran is sold at supermarkets and health food stores. It should not be confused with the packaged cereals that contain large amounts of bran or bran flakes.

movements are usually painless and occur regularly (whether two times a day or three times a week), then you are probably not constipated.

Resources

More information about constipation is available from the National Digestive Diseases Information Clearinghouse, Box NDDIC, Bethesda, MD 20892, 301-654-3810.

For more information about health and aging, call or write NIA Information Center, P.O. Box 8057, Gaithersburg, MD 20898-8057; 800-222-2225, 800-222-4225 (TTY).

Choosing a Contraceptive[*]

Choosing a method of birth control is a highly personal decision, based on individual preferences, medical history, lifestyle, and other factors. Each method carries with it a number of risks and benefits of which the user should be aware.

Each method of birth control has a failure rate-an inability to prevent pregnancy over a one-year period. Sometimes the failure rate is due to the method and sometimes it is due to human error, such as incorrect use or not using it at all. Each method has possible side effects, some minor and some serious. Some methods require lifestyle modifications, such as remembering to use the method with each and every sexual intercourse. Some cannot be used by individuals with certain medical problems.

Spermicides Used Alone

Spermicides, which come in many forms — foams, jellies, gels, and suppositories — work by forming a physical and chemical barrier to sperm. They should be inserted into the vagina within an hour before intercourse. If intercourse is repeated, more spermicide should be inserted. The active ingredient in most spermicides is the chemical nonoxynol-9. The failure rate for spermicides in preventing pregnancy when used alone is from 20 to 30 percent.

Spermicides are available without a prescription. People who experience burning or irritation with these products should not use them.

Barrier Methods

There are five barrier methods of contraception: male condoms, female condoms, diaphragm, sponge, and cervical cap. In each instance, the method works by keeping the sperm and egg apart.

---

[*] Source: Office of Public Affairs, Food and Drug Administration, Public Health Service, 5600 Fishers Lane, HFI-40, Rockville, MD 20857; 301-827-4420.

Expert Health Advice

Usually, these methods have only minor side effects. The main possible side effect is an allergic reaction either to the material of the barrier or the spermicides that should be used with them. Using the methods correctly for each and every sexual intercourse gives the best protection.

Male Condom

A male condom is a sheath that covers the penis during sex. Condoms on the market at press time were made of either latex rubber or natural skin (also called "lambskin" but actually made from sheep intestines). Of these two types, only latex condoms have been shown to be highly effective in helping to prevent STDS. Latex provides a good barrier to even small viruses such as human immunodeficiency virus and hepatitis B. Each condom can only be used once. Condoms have a birth control failure rate of about 15 percent. Most of the failures can be traced to improper use.

Disease Prevention

For many people, the prevention of sexually transmitted diseases (STDs), including HIV (human immunodeficiency virus), which leads to AIDS, is a factor in choosing a contraceptive. Only one form of birth control currently available-the latex condom, worn by the man-is considered highly effective in helping protect against HIV and other STDS. FDA has approved the marketing of male condoms made from polyurethane as also effective in preventing STDS, including HIV. However, at press time, they were not yet being sold in this country. Reality Female Condom, made from polyurethane, may give limited protection against STDs but has not been proven as effective as male latex condoms. People who use another form of birth control but who also want a highly effective way to reduce their STD risks, should also use a latex condom for every sex act, from start to finish.

In April 1993, FDA announced that birth control pills, Norplant, Depo-Provera, IUDs, and natural membrane condoms must carry labeling stating that these products are intended to prevent pregnancy but do not protect against HIV infection and other sexually transmitted diseases. In addition, natural membrane condom labeling must state that consumers should use a latex condom to help reduce the transmission of STDS. The labeling of latex condoms states that, if used properly, they will help reduce transmission of HIV and other diseases.

Some condoms have spermicide added. These may give some additional contraceptive protection. Vaginal spermicides may also be added before sexual intercourse.

Some condoms have lubricants added. These do not improve birth control or STD protection. Non-oil-based lubricant can also be used with condoms. However oil-based lubricants such as petroleum jelly (Vaseline) should not be used because they weaken the latex. Condoms are available without a prescription.

Female Condom

The Reality Female Condom was approved by FDA in April 1993. It consists of a lubricated polyurethane sheath with flexible polyurethane ring on each end. One ring is inserted into the vagina much like a diaphragm, while the other remains outside, partially covering the labia. The female condom may offer some protection against STDS, but for highly effective protection, male latex condoms must be used.(The female condom should not be used at the same time as the male condom because they will not both stay in place.)

FDA Commissioner David A. Kessler, M.D., in announcing the approval, said, "I have to stress that the male latex condom remains the best shield against AIDS and other sexually transmitted diseases. Couples should go on using the male latex condom."

In a six-month trial, the pregnancy rate for the Reality Female Condom was about 13 percent. The estimated yearly failure rate ranges from 21 to 26 percent. This means that about 1 in 4 women who use Reality may become pregnant during a year.

Sponge

The contraceptive sponge, approved by FDA in 1983, is made of white polyurethane foam. The sponge, shaped like a small doughnut, contains the spermicide nonoxynol-9. Like the diaphragm, it is inserted into the vagina to cover the cervix during and after intercourse. It does not require fitting by a health professional and is available without prescription. It is to be used only once and then discarded. The failure rate is between 18 and 28 percent. An extremely rare side effect is toxic shock syndrome (TSS), a potentially fatal infection caused by a strain of the bacterium Staphylococcus aureas and more commonly associated with tampon use.

Diaphragm
The diaphragm is a flexible rubber disk with a rigid rim. Diaphragms range in size from 2 to 4 inches in diameter and are designed to cover the cervix during and after intercourse so that sperm cannot reach the uterus. Spermicidal jelly or cream must be placed inside the diaphragm for it to be effective.

The diaphragm must be fitted by a health professional and the correct size prescribed to ensure a snug seal with the vaginal wall. If intercourse is repeated, additional spermicide should be added with the diaphragm still in place. The diaphragm should be left in place for at least six hours after intercourse. The diaphragm used with spermicide has a failure rate of from 6 to 18 percent.

In addition to the possible allergic reactions or irritation common to all barrier methods, there have been some reports of bladder infections with this method. As with the contraceptive sponge, TSS is an extremely rare side effect.

Cervical Cap
The cervical cap, approved for contraceptive use in the United States in 1988, is a dome-shaped rubber cap in various sizes that fits snugly over the cervix. Like the diaphragm, it is used with a spermicide and must be fitted by a health professional. It is more difficult to insert than the diaphragm, but may be left in place for up to 48 hours.

In addition to the allergic reactions that can occur with any barrier method, 5.2 to 27 percent of users in various studies have reported an unpleasant odor and/or discharge. There also appears to be an increased incidence of irregular Pap tests in the first six months of using the cap, and TSS is an extremely rare side effect. The cap has a failure rate of about 18 percent.

Hormonal Contraception

Hormonal contraception involves ways of delivering forms of two female reproductive hormones-estrogen and proaestocyen-that help regulate ovulation (release of an egg), the condition of the uterine lining, and other parts of the menstrual cycle. Unlike barrier methods, hormones are not inert, do interact with the body, and have the potential for serious side effects, though this is rare. When properly used, hormonal methods are also extremely effective. Hormonal methods are available only by prescription.

Birth Control Pills

There are two types of birth control pills: combination pills, which contain both estrogen and a progestin (a natural or synthetic progesterone), and "mini-pills," which contain only progestin. The combination pill prevents ovulation, while the mini-pill reduces cervical mucus and causes it to thicken. This prevents the sperm from reaching the egg. Also, progestins keep the endometrium (uterine lining) from thickening. This prevents the fertilized egg from implanting in the uterus. The failure rate for the mini-pill is 1 to 3 percent; for the combination pill it is 1 to 2 percent.

Combination oral contraceptives offer significant protection against ovarian cancer, endometrial cancer, iron-deficiency anemia, pelvic inflammatory disease (PID), and fibrocystic breast disease. Women who take combination pills have a lower risk of functional ovarian cysts.

The decision about whether to take an oral contraceptive should be made only after consultation with a health professional. Smokers and women with certain medical conditions should not take the pill. These conditions include: a history of blood clots in the legs, eyes, or deep veins of the legs; heart attacks, strokes, or angina; cancer of the breast, vagina, cervix, or uterus; any undiagnosed, abnormal vaginal bleeding; liver tumors; or jaundice due to pregnancy or use of birth control pills.

Women with the following conditions should discuss with a health professional whether the benefits of the pill outweigh its risks for them:

- high blood pressure
- heart, kidney or gallbladder disease
- a family history of heart attack or stroke
- severe headaches or depression
- elevated cholesterol or triglycerides
- epilepsy
- diabetes

Serious side effects of the pill include blood clots that can lead to stroke, heart attack, pulmonary embolism, or death. A clot may, on rare occasions, occur in the blood vessel of the eye, causing impaired vision or even blindness. The pills may also cause high blood pressure that returns to normal after oral contraceptives are stopped. Minor side effects, which usually subside after a few months' use, include: nausea, headaches, breast swelling, fluid retention, weight gain, irregular bleeding, and depression. Sometimes taking a pill with a lower dose of hormones can reduce these effects.

The effectiveness of birth control pills may be reduced by a few other medications, including some antibiotics, barbiturates, and antifungal medications. On the other hand, birth control pills may prolong the effects of theophylline and caffeine. They also may prolong the effects of benzodiazepines such as Librium (chlordiazepoxide), Valium (diazepam), and Xanax (alprazolam). Because of the variety of these drug interactions, women should always tell their health professionals when they are taking birth control pills.

Norplant

Norplant, the first contraceptive implant was approved by FDA in 1990. In a minor surgical procedure, six matchstick-sized rubber capsules containing procyestin are placed just underneath the skin of the upper arm. The implant is effective within 24 hours and provides progestin for up to five years or until it is removed. Both the insertion and the removal must be performed by a qualified professional.

Because contraception is automatic and does not depend on the user, the failure rate for Norplant is less than 1 percent for women who weigh less than 150 pounds. Women who weigh more have a higher pregnancy rate after the first two years.

Women who cannot take birth control pills for medical reasons should not consider Norplant a contraceptive option. The potential side effects of the implant include: irregular menstrual bleeding, headaches, nervousness, depression, nausea, dizziness, skin rash, acne, change of appetite, breast tenderness, weight gain, enlargement of the ovaries or fallopian tubes, and excessive growth of body and facial hair. These side effects may subside after the first year.

Depo-Provera

Depo-Provera is an injectable form of a progestin. It was approved by FDA in 1992 for contraceptive use. Previously, it was approved for treating endometrial and renal cancers. Depo-Provera has a failure rate of only 1 percent. Each injection provides contraceptive protection for 14 weeks. It is injected every three months into a muscle in the buttocks or arm by a trained professional. The side effects are the same as those for Norplant and progestin only pills. In addition, there may be irregular bleeding and spotting during the first months followed by periods of amenorrhea (no menstrual period). About 50 percent of the women who use Depo-Provera for one year or longer report amenorrhea. Other side effects, such as weight gain and others described for Norplant, may occur.

Intrauterine Devices

IUDs are small, plastic, flexible devices that are inserted into the uterus through the cervix by a trained clinician. Only two IUDs are presently marketed in the United States: ParaGard T380A, a T-shaped device partially covered by copper and effective for eight years; and Progestasert, which is also T-shaped but contains a progestin released over a one-year period. After that time, the IUD should be replaced. Both IUDs have a 4 to 5 percent failure rate.

It is not known exactly how IUDs work. At one time it was thought that the IUD affected the uterus so that it would be inhospitable to implantation. New evidence, however, suggests that uterine and tubal fluids are altered, particularly in the case of copper-bearing IUDs, inhibiting the transport of sperm through the cervical mucus and uterus.

The risk of PID with IUD use is highest in those with multiple sex partners or with a history of previous PID. Therefore, the IUD is recommended primarily for women in mutually monogamous relationships.

In addition to PID, other complications include perforation of the uterus (usually at the time of insertion), septic abortion, or ectopic (tubal) pregnancy. Women may also experience some short-term side effects — cramping and dizziness at the time of insertion; bleeding, cramps and backache that may continue for a few days after the insertion; spotting between periods; and longer and heavier menstruation during the first few periods after insertion.

Periodic Abstinence

Periodic abstinence entails not having sexual intercourse during the woman's fertile period. Sometimes this method is called natural family planning (NFP) or "rhythm." Using periodic abstinence is dependent on the ability to identify the approximately 10 days in each menstrual cycle that a woman is fertile. Methods to help determine this include:

- The basal body temperature method is based on the knowledge that just before ovulation a woman's basal body temperature drops several tenths of a degree and after ovulation it returns to normal. The method requires that the woman take her temperature each morning before she gets out of bed. There are now electronic thermometers with memories and electrical resistance meters that can more accurately pinpoint a woman's fertile period.

- The cervical mucus method, also called the Billings method, depends on a woman recognizing the changes in cervical mucus that indicate ovulation is occurring or has occurred.

Periodic abstinence has a failure rate of 14 to 47 percent. It has none of the side effects of artificial methods of contraception.

Surgical Sterilization

Surgical sterilization must be considered permanent. Tubal ligation seals a woman's fallopian tubes so that an egg cannot travel to the uterus. Vasectomy involves closing off a man's vas deferens so that sperm will not be carried to the penis.

Vasectomy is considered safer than female sterilization. It is a minor surgical procedure, most often performed in a doctor's office under local anesthesia. The procedure usually takes less than 30 minutes. Minor post-surgical complications may occur.

Tubal ligation is an operating room procedure performed under general anesthesia. The fallopian tubes can be reached by a number of surgical techniques, and, depending on the technique, the operation is sometimes an outpatient procedure or requires only an overnight stay. In a minilaparotomy, a 2-inch incision is made in the abdomen. The surgeon, using special instruments, lifts the fallopian tubes and, using clips, a plastic ring, or an electric current, seals the tubes. Another method, laparoscopy, involves making a small incision above the navel, and distending the abdominal cavity so that the intestine separates from the uterus and fallopian tubes. Then a laparoscope — a miniaturized, flexible telescope — is used to visualize the Fallopian tubes while closing them off.

Both of these methods are replacing the traditional laparotomy.

Major complications, which are rare in female sterilization, include: infection, hemorrhage, and problems associated with the use of general anesthesia. It is estimated that major complications occur in 1.7 percent of the cases, while the overall complication rate has been reported to be between 0.1 and 15.3 percent.

The failure rate of laparoscopy and minilaparotomy procedures, as well as vasectomy, is less than 1 percent. Although there has been some success in reopening the Fallopian tubes or the vas deferens, the success rate is low, and sterilization should be considered irreversible.

For More Information

Contact:
Office of Public Affairs
Food and Drug Administration
Public Health Service
5600 Fishers Lane, HFI-40
Rockville, MD 20857
301-443-1544

If You're Over 65 And Feeling Depressed...Treatment Brings New Hope[*]

Depression is a Whole Body Disorder

Most people think of depression only as sadness and low mood, but clinical depression is far more than the ordinary "down" moods everyone experiences now and then, and which pass after a visit with a friend or a good movie.

> Depression.
> The darkest moods.
> Feeling down, empty.
> Difficulty remembering.
> Many things just don't
>   interest you any more.
> Aches and pains that
>   keep coming back.
> Depression that goes on and on
>   and on for weeks and months is
>   called clinical depression.

Depression is also more than a feeling of grief after losing someone you love. Following such a loss, for many people, a depressed mood is a normal reaction to grief. And these people may find it helpful to join a mutual support group, such as widowed-persons, to talk with others experiencing similar feelings.

However, when a depressed mood continues for some time, whether following a particular event or for no apparent reason, the person may be suffering from clinical depression — an illness that can be treated effectively.

Clinical depression is a whole body disorder. It can affect the way you think and the way you feel, both physically and emotionally.

It isn't "normal" to feel depressed all the time when you get older; in fact, most older people feel satisfied with their lives. Nonetheless, among people 65 and over, as many as 3 out of 100 suffer from clinical depression. It can be serious and can even lead to suicide.

---

[*] Source: D/ART Public Inquiries, National Institute of Mental Health, 5600 Fishers Lane, Room 15C-05, Rockville, MD 20857; 301-443-4513.

Expert Health Advice

But there is good news. Nearly 80 percent of people with clinical depression can be treated successfully with medications, psychotherapy, or a combination of both. Even the most serious depressions usually respond rapidly to the right treatment. But first, depression has to be recognized.

Ann's daughter thought her 73-year-old widowed mother was getting senile because she was so confused and forgetful. Ann had seemed to recover well from the death of her husband three years before, but lately she cried about him almost every day. Her daughter arranged for Ann to see a geriatric specialist who diagnosed Ann's condition as depression, not senility. He put her on medication and suggested that she join a widow-to-widow support group. Before long, Ann's memory improved along with her mood.

Types of Clinical Depression

Two serious types of clinical depression are major depression and bipolar disorder.

Major Depression
Major depression makes it almost impossible to carry on usual activities, sleep, eat, or enjoy life. Pleasure seems a thing of the past. This type of depression can occur once in a lifetime or, for many people, it can recur several times. People with a major depression need professional treatment.

Bipolar Disorder (Manic-Depressive Illness)
Another type of depression, bipolar disorder — or manic-depressive illness — leads to severe mood swings, from extreme "lows" to excessive "highs." These states of extreme elation and unbounded energy are called mania. This disorder usually starts when people are in their early twenties. Though unusual for this type of depression to start for the first time in later life, it requires medical treatment, whatever the person's age.

If someone has recently experienced a loss, these feelings may be part of a normal grief reaction. But, if the feelings persist with no lifting mood, the person may need professional treatment.

A Depression Checklist

Check any symptoms (X) experienced for more than two weeks. If four or more of the symptoms for depression or mania have been checked, physical and psychological evaluation by a physician and/or mental health specialist should be sought.

Symptoms of Depression:

   __ A persistent sad, anxious or 'empty" mood
   __ Loss of interest or pleasure in ordinary activities, including sex
   __ Decreased energy, fatigue, feeling "slowed down"
   __ Sleep problems (insomnia, oversleeping, early-morning waking)
   __ Eating problems (loss of appetite or weight, weight gain)
   __ Difficulty concentrating, remembering or making decisions
   __ Feelings of hopelessness or pessimism
   __ Feelings of guilt, worthlessness or helplessness
   __ Thoughts of death or suicide; a suicide attempt
   __ Irritability
   __ Disturbed ability to make decisions
   __ Excessive crying
   __ Recurring aches and pains that don't respond to treatment

Depression and Other Illnesses

Sometimes clinical depression can look like other illnesses with symptoms such as headaches, backaches, joint pain, stomach problems, or other physical discomforts. Older people, when depressed, often speak of these problems rather than of feeling anxious, tired, or sad.

Some signs of depression, such as memory lapses and difficulty concentrating, can mimic Alzheimer's disease or other medical disorders. Similar symptoms may also result from other physical problems or from medications commonly used by older people. Therefore, for a proper diagnosis, it is important to have a thorough medical examination to rule out other disorders.

If the symptoms are caused by depression, they will improve with the right treatment. Sometimes a person can have depression and another illness such as Alzheimer's disease at the same time. Even in such a case, treating the depression can relieve unnecessary suffering.

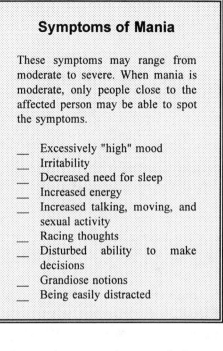

Symptoms of Mania

These symptoms may range from moderate to severe. When mania is moderate, only people close to the affected person may be able to spot the symptoms.

— Excessively "high" mood
— Irritability
— Decreased need for sleep
— Increased energy
— Increased talking, moving, and sexual activity
— Racing thoughts
— Disturbed ability to make decisions
— Grandiose notions
— Being easily distracted

Causes of Depression

There are many causes of depression. Some people become depressed for a combination of reasons. For others, a single cause appears to trigger depression. Some become depressed for no apparent reason. Regardless of the cause, depression needs to be diagnosed and treated.

Some of the causes that are particularly important among older people are:

Other Illnesses
Long-term or sudden illnesses can bring on or aggravate depression. Strokes, certain types of cancer, diabetes, Parkinson's disease, and hormonal disorders are examples of illnesses that may be related to depressive disorders.

Medications
Some medicines cause depressive symptoms as side effects. Certain drugs used to treat high blood pressure and arthritis fall in this category. In addition, different drugs can interact in unforeseen ways when taken together. It is important that each doctor know all

the different types and dosages of medicine being taken and discuss them with the patient.

Genetics and Family History
Depression runs in families. Children of depressed parents have a higher risk of being depressed themselves. Some people probably have a biological makeup that makes them particularly vulnerable.

Personality
Certain personalities — people with low self-esteem or who are very dependent on others — seem to be vulnerable to depression.

Life Events
The death of a loved one, divorce, moving to a new place, money problems, or any sort of loss have all been linked to depression. People without relatives or friends to help may have even more difficulty coping with their losses. Sadness and grief are normal responses to loss, but if many symptoms of depression linger, professional help should be sought.

Help for Depression

One of the biggest obstacles to getting help for clinical depression can be a person's attitude. Many people think that depression will go away by itself, or that they're too old to get help, or that getting help is a sign of weakness or moral failing. Such views are simply wrong.

Depression is a treatable disorder. Even the most seriously depressed person can be treated successfully, often in a matter of weeks, and return to a happier and more fulfilling life. Such outcomes are a common story, even when people feel hopeless and helpless.

There are three major types of treatment for clinical depression: psychotherapy, medication, and, in some cases, other biological treatments. At times, different treatments may be used in combination.

Individuals respond differently to treatments. If after several weeks symptoms have not improved, the treatment plan should be reevaluated. Also, the procedures and possible side effects of all treatments should be fully discussed with the doctor.

People may find that mutual support groups are helpful when combined with other treatments.

Medication

There are many very effective medications, but the three types of drugs most often used to treat depression are tricyclic antidepressants, monoamine oxidase inhibitors (MAOIs), and lithium. Lithium is very effective in the treatment of bipolar disorder and is also sometimes used to treat major depression.

- All medications alter the action of brain chemicals to improve mood, sleep, appetite, energy levels, and concentration.
- Different people may need different medications, and sometimes more than one medication is needed to treat clinical depression.
- Improvement usually occurs within weeks.

Psychotherapy

Talking with a trained therapist can also be effective in treating certain depressions, particularly those that are less severe. Short-term therapies (usually 12-20 sessions) developed to treat depression focus on the specific symptoms of depression.

- Cognitive therapy aims to help the patient recognize and change negative thinking patterns that contribute to depression.
- Interpersonal therapy focuses on dealing more effectively with other people; improved relationships can reduce depressive symptoms.

Biological Treatments

Some depressions may respond best to electroconvulsive therapy. ECT is an effective treatment that is used in extremely severe cases of major depression when very rapid improvement is necessary, or when medications cannot be used or have not worked. Improved procedures make this treatment much safer than in previous years. During treatment, anesthesia and a muscle relaxant protect patients from physical harm and pain.

Research is also being done on the use of light for the treatment of depression.

Where to Get Help

Trained professionals in numerous settings diagnose and treat clinical depression:

Family physicians, clinics, and health maintenance organizations can provide treatment or make referrals to mental health specialists.

Mental health specialists include psychiatrists, psychologists, family therapists, and social

For years, Tom had been looking forward to his retirement-with more time to fish. But after the first few months, not only had he stopped going fishing with his friends, he often did not go out of the house for days. Tom also complained to his wife about not sleeping well and about different aches and pains each day. Fortunately, his wife took him to a doctor who recognized Tom was depressed. After a few weeks of treatment, Tom began to enjoy his retirement as much as he had expected.

workers. Psychiatrists can prescribe antidepressant drugs because they are physicians. Other mental health specialists, however, often work with physicians to ensure that their patients receive the medications they need.

Community mental health centers, which often provide treatment based on the patient's ability to pay, usually have a variety of mental health specialists.

Hospitals and university medical schools may have research centers that study and treat depression.

Advocacy Organizations

National advocacy or consumer organizations provide information about depression, sources of treatment, and local community support groups:

American Association of Retired Persons (AARP)
Widowed Persons Services
Social Outreach and Support
1909 K Street, N.W.
Washington, D.C. 20049
202-728-4370

National Alliance for the Mentally Ill
2101 Wilson Boulevard, Suite 302
Arlington, VA 22201
703-524-7600

National Depressive and Manic Depressive Association
53 W. Jackson Boulevard, Suite 505
Chicago, IL 60604
312-939-2442

National Mental Health Association
1021 Prince Street
Alexandria, VA 22314-2971
703-684-7722

Information on Depression

For more information on depression, diagnosis, and treatments, call or write to the DEPRESSION Awareness, Recognition, and Treatment (D/ART) Program: D/ART Public Inquiries, National Institute of Mental Health, 5600 Fishers Lane, Room 15C-05, Rockville, MD 20857; 301-443-3673.

Diabetes in Adults[*]

Several factors motivated this information on adult-onset diabetes. First, although the illness is a major health problem, striking between 10 and 11 million Americans, diabetes often goes undiagnosed. As many as half the people with the disorder don't know they have it. Second, we now have made major advances in understanding the causes of this disease. Third, and most importantly, these advances have provided new strategies for preventing and treating diabetes.

Background

Diabetes is the seventh leading cause of death in the United States and the single leading cause of kidney disease. More than 250,000 Americans die each year from causes directly related to the illness. The disorder is also the leading cause of blindness and, aside from traumatic injury, the chief cause of amputations in the United States. Diabetics have doubled the risk of the general population for heart attack and stroke. Moreover, diabetics also are less likely to recover from these injuries.

But the good news is that many of the complications of diabetes, as well as the defects underlying the illness, can be controlled and treated — particularly the type of diabetes that develops in adults.

There are actually two forms of diabetes. Type I diabetes affects only about five to 10 percent of the 10 million people with the disease, and it occurs predominantly in children. Type I illness often begins suddenly and can be life-threatening. If medical treatment, including insulin, is not begun very quickly, the child may die. For this reason, Type I diabetes is referred to as insulin-dependent diabetes (IDDM).

---

[*] Source: *Medicine For The Public*, National Diabetes Information Clearinghouse, 1 Information Way, Bethesda, MD 20892; 301-654-3810.

This chapter focuses on Type II diabetes, which affects the other 90 to 95 percent of the diabetic population. In addition to primarily affecting adults, it differs from Type I disease in other significant ways. For example, although some Type II diabetics take insulin, these people do not run the risk of becoming acutely and profoundly ill if they stop using the medication. For this reason, Type II diabetes is also known as noninsulin-dependent diabetes (NIDDM).

Defining the Illness

Whenever one eats a meal, digested sugar, or glucose, leaves the stomach through tiny blood vessels, passing to the liver and pancreas, and from there to the general circulation. The pancreas responds to the influx of glucose by producing the hormone known as insulin. Insulin influences the liver to store excess glucose. It also enables the body's cells to incorporate glucose — a vital source of energy — from the blood. Muscle cells use glucose as fuel, while fat cells store the compound, converting it into lipids or fat particles that can easily be tapped for energy as the body needs it.

People with Type I diabetes do not produce enough insulin for these life-sustaining processes to continue as needed. Researchers have documented that among Type I patients, the pancreatic cells that normally produce the hormone have virtually all been killed — apparently due to a misguided attack by the body's immune system.

Among Type II patients, the underlying problem is different, but the end result is the same: an unhealthy buildup of glucose in the blood and an inability for the body's cells to properly use the compound. Type II individuals have their normal amount of insulin-secreting pancreatic cells — known as the islets — and these cells still produce a reasonable amount and sometimes even greater than normal amount of insulin. But for unknown reasons, the muscle and fat cells in these patients appear insensitive to insulin secretion. Researchers believe the insensitivity results from an apparent defect in the insulin receptors found on the surface of muscle and fat cells. The defect prevents the cells from locking onto insulin in the bloodstream, stopping the cells from properly using blood glucose.

Scientists know that most overweight people have some insulin resistances cellular insensitivity to the action of glucose. In fact, the fatter they are, the more insulin resistance they develop. But the pancreas of most of these and other insulin-resistant individuals can compensate for the insensitivity by producing sufficiently large amounts of insulin. These people do not have Type II diabetes, although they may be at risk for the disorder. But in some people, the pancreas cannot make enough insulin to overcome the resistance problem. These individuals develop Type II disease.

In summary, Type II, or noninsulin-dependent, diabetes occurs due to a combination of two problems: resistance by the body's tissues to insulin activity, and an inability of islet cells to overcome this resistance by producing extra amounts of the hormone.

Symptoms

Diabetes — both Type I and Type II — is an insidious disease. There often are no obvious warning signs that a person either cannot secrete enough insulin or cannot properly use the hormone to break down glucose stored in the blood. Yet once diabetes is suspected, simple and inexpensive blood and urine tests can easily identify the problem. Thus, the ability to identify symptoms that may signal diabetes onset becomes crucial to controlling this disease.

One of the first signs of something wrong is insatiable thirst, often associated with excessive urination. Both symptoms occur because the body attempts to rid itself of unusually high levels of blood sugar through constant excretion of fluids, leaving the individual in constant need of fluid replacement. In turn, massive fluid intake and urination can alternately swell and shrink body tissues, causing other symptoms, such as blurry vision. Such blurriness may prompt people to see a doctor long before other diabetes-related symptoms become apparent. Effective treatment of the diabetes tends to alleviate this visual problem.

As time goes on, diabetic patients — particularly those whose other symptoms have not triggered them to seek medical treatment — may suffer even more serious eye problems. Some may have a progressive, permanent loss of vision before the diagnosis of diabetes is made.

People who develop diabetes often have sensory nerve damage, losing the ability to feel appropriate pain and the sense of touch, especially in the feet. Sometimes, one of the first signs of disease is numbness or tingling in the feet or lower leg. Alternatively, nerve damage may cause unprovoked excruciating pain again usually in the legs and feet that can incapacitate a person, preventing him or her from walking, sleeping or performing other routine functions of daily living.

In those people unable to feel pain, such everyday occurrences as blisters can go unchecked, leading to cuts, bruises, ulcers and other serious injuries of the lower extremities. Ulcers may lead to serious infections that prompt a doctor's visit. Only then is the patient diagnosed as diabetic.

Over time, diabetes can also damage the involuntary nervous system, causing such problems as sexual impotence. Diabetics also have increased atherosclerosis — hardening of the arteries, or the buildup of plaque and fatty material inside blood vessel walls. Often, physicians do not detect this problem — other diabetes symptoms have not tipped them off to look for it — until after a heart attack or stroke.

Some people later found to have diabetes often report feelings of fatigue, malaise and a general lack of energy. Individuals may blame such feelings on aging, depression or their poor physical shape. But when these people do see a doctor, they are found to have diabetes — and are likely to have had it for some years.

Those at Risk

Because the symptoms of Type II diabetes are both varied and elusive, it is imperative to identify those people at highest risk for the disease. These individuals might regularly undergo a thorough medical checkup for diabetes, helping to catch the disorder early on, before extensive damage occurs.

We now know that obese people carry an unusually high risk for developing Type II diabetes. Physicians estimate that 60 to 90 percent of people with this form of diabetes are overweight. Studies show that among the Pima Indians of the southwestern United States, the ethnic group with the highest known incidence of noninsulin-dependent diabetes in the world, obesity is a major health problem.

The risk for Type II diabetes for both sexes also increases with age. As the body ages, its ability to efficiently use insulin for glucose metabolism begins to deteriorate. Heredity is another risk factor. If one or both parents developed noninsulin-dependent diabetes, a person's chances of having the disease is increased. The risk is increased approximately two-fold for each parent with Type II diabetes. If both parents are affected then the risk is four-fold higher. If one of two identical twins develops Type II diabetes, researchers calculate that the second twin has nearly a 90 percent chance of developing the illness within five to 10 years.

In the United States, certain minority populations have a higher-than-normal rate of Type II diabetes. Among blacks, the illness occurs about 1.5 times as frequently as in the general population. Hispanics and Oriental Americans have a rate about twice that of the general population. We've already mentioned the plight of the Pimas. Half of the tribe members over age 35 now develop the disorder. Up until about 40 years ago, the Pimas did not have this high rate. Through about 1940, the Pimas survived mainly on desert foods, dining mostly on vegetables, grains and subsistence crops. As western, high-fat, high-calorie foods became increasingly available to the Pimas, they began to develop widespread obesity. Combined with a possible genetic predisposition for insulin resistance, researchers believe that obesity has triggered the high incidence of Type II diabetes in the Pimas.

Treatment

The chief way to treat or control Type II diabetes is to eat an appropriate calorie diet and begin regular exercise under a doctor's supervision. Both of these lifestyle changes, which can improve cardiovascular fitness, have an added benefit among Type II diabetics. They help people lose weight, which in some cases can reverse or reduce insulin resistance, one of the underlying causes of the disease. Researchers have found that losing weight sometimes increases the body's sensitivity to insulin. In fact, some formerly obese Type II diabetics no longer have the disease after shedding pounds, even if they have not lost enough to attain their ideal body weight. Losing weight, however, does not guarantee elimination of the disease.

Among other lifestyle changes, diabetics should avoid alcohol. Not only is alcohol high in calories and low in nutrients, it can damage the liver and pancreas organs already under stress in diabetes.

Diabetics who smoke should make every effort to stop. Known to raise the risk of heart attack and stroke in the general population, smoking can be particularly dangerous for diabetics, who already have a higher risk for developing cardiovascular problems.

In addition and in conjunction with these behavioral changes, drug therapy may also help the Type II diabetic. About one-third of Type II patients take insulin injections because the drug gives them optimum control of the disease.

Physicians also prescribe other drugs that seem to stimulate the pancreas to make more insulin and to increase the sensitivity of muscle and fat cells to the hormone. The exact action of these medications, available in pill form, is not well understood. There are a variety of such medications but all are in the same basic class of drugs called sulfonylureas. Their generic names include tolbutamide, chlorpropamide, tolazamide, acetohexamide, glipizide and glyburide. Many Type II patients may benefit from these drugs but many do not respond sufficiently and need to take insulin injections for optimal treatment.

Aside from these considerations, patients can help maintain and even improve their condition by becoming active members of the health care team. For example, daily self-inspections of the feet can help spot early signs of infection that might otherwise go unnoticed, given the nerve damage and lack of pain sensation common among diabetics. And individuals also can perform a simple home test to monitor their body's ability to control blood sugar. The test involves pricking a finger with a sterile needle stick and measuring blood levels with a glucose meter now available at drug stores. Such monitoring can supplement, but not replace, more sensitive tests regularly performed by a physician.

While the combination of diet, exercise, drugs and self-monitoring has greatly increased the survival and well being of diabetics, we are far from the end of the journey in controlling, and ultimately preventing, this disease. But with the recent discovery of separate genetic factors that may play a role in Type I and Type II diabetes, it is hopeful that by the year 2000 we will have genetic markers to aid us in improved diagnosis, treatment and prevention of this disease.

Questions and Answers

Q. Can an obese person with Type II diabetes completely eliminate the disease by losing weight through diet and exercise?

A. Yes. For some people, that's exactly the case. In fact, certain individuals don't even have to reach normal weight. It appears that if an obese person who recently developed diabetes begins to lose pounds, their sensitivity to insulin increases even before they attain ideal weight. Unfortunately, this phenomenon does not always occur in the same patients as time goes on. If the disease has persisted for many years, shedding pounds may not be sufficient to overcome it.

Q. Do people of normal weight who have a low-fat, low-calorie diet still have a higher risk for developing diabetes if one of their parents had the disease?

A. Yes. But it is worthwhile for those with a strong family history of diabetes to be extra vigilant about their diet and cardiovascular fitness. It may reduce their elevated risk for developing diabetes, or it may delay onset of the disease.

Q. At what point should a Type II diabetic begin taking insulin supplements?

A. That's a difficult question and there doesn't seem to be a consensus on this. We have no rule that says blood sugar level X means someone requires insulin. Clearly, a patient is a candidate for insulin when other treatment has failed and there's reason to believe the drug may help. But the patient should understand the risks and benefits of insulin therapy, and the decision to go ahead with this treatment should involve all members of the health care team.

Dietary Supplements:
More is Not Always Better[*]

Many people are attracted by ads for vitamins and minerals that imply a supplement will improve appearance, give sex life a boost, prevent or cure diseases, and even lengthen life. But there is, as yet, little scientific evidence to back most of these claims.

Doctors occasionally prescribe dietary supplements to correct nutrient deficiencies diagnosed in their patients. For example, people who are at high risk of developing osteoporosis — a condition causing thin, brittle bones — may be advised by their physicians to take calcium supplements. Dieters, heavy drinkers, and those who are recovering from surgery or an illness may also need certain supplements.

Too often, people take high-dose supplements of various vitamins and minerals without a doctor's advice in the hope of preventing or curing a disease or condition. This can be a waste of money or, worse, a threat to health.

What Do We Know About Supplements?

Scientists still have much to learn about the special nutritional needs of older people. At present, there is no reason to believe that large amounts of vitamins and minerals in supplement form will help prevent or treat health problems or slow aging processes. Multivitamin and mineral pills (often referred to as "one-a-day" type pills) contain either the full recommended dietary allowances (RDAs) established by the National Academy or Sciences National Research Council or, in some cases, less. Many people take these pills as a form of "insurance" that their daily nutritional needs are met. Daily multivitamin tablets may be beneficial for some people,

---

[*] Source: *Age Page*, National Institute on Aging, U.S. Department of Health and Human Services, Public Health Service, National Institutes of Health, Gaithersburg, MD 20898; 800-222-2225.

but the value of any dietary supplement depends on many factors, including eating habits and overall health.

Scientists have identified a large number of nutrients that are vital to health, but supplements contain only some of these. A well-balanced diet — one that contains a wide variety of foods — provides all the necessary nutrients. In addition, there are other substances in foods, such as fiber, that are not essential for life but benefit health. Foods may also contain some essential nutrients that have not yet been identified.

Large amounts of some supplements may upset the natural balance of nutrients that the body normally maintains. Too much of some of them can affect the way other act. Although extra amounts of some nutrients are not absorbed and pass out of the body, others can build up to dangerous levels.

Getting the Nutrients You Need

Most older people can get the nutrients they need by eating a wide range of nutritious foods each day. As a guide, a well-balanced diet should include the following: at least two servings of low-fat milk or dairy products such as cheese, cottage cheese, or yogurt; two servings of protein-rich foods such as poultry, fish, eggs, beans, nuts, or lean meat; four servings of fruit and vegetables, including a citrus fruit or juice and a dark green leafy vegetable; and four servings of breads and cereal products (made with whole grain or enriched flours), rice, or pasta.[2]

Some older people may not get the vitamins and minerals they need from their daily diet. In some cases this is because they find it hard to get or prepare the foods they know they need. Digestive problems, chewing difficulties, and the use of certain drugs can also interfere with good nutrition. People with these problems may benefit from a dietary supplement.

---

[2] These are only general guidelines. Some people may have conditions that restrict their intake of certain foods.

If you are taking a supplement, or thinking about taking one, ask your doctor or a registered dietitian (R.D.) if it's really necessary. He or she can check your health and diet, and decide if any steps should be taken to improve your nutrition. If so, a simple dietary change may be all that is needed. If you have been taking an unprescribed supplement, ask for advice about stopping. It may be better to slowly reduce the amount you take than to stop suddenly.

Some Popular Dietary Practices and Fads

The use of megavitamins and the high-potency formulas are of current concern among scientists. These supplements contain 10 to 100 times the RDA for some vitamins and minerals. People may take them because they think the RDAs are only minimum requirements and that, if a little is good, a lot will be better. The allowances, however, are set high enough to cover the needs of healthy people.

Large doses of some nutrients can act like drugs, often with serious results. Large amounts of either vitamin A or D are particularly dangerous. Too much vitamin A can cause headaches, nausea, diarrhea, and eventually liver and bone damage. High doses of vitamin D can cause kidney damage and even death. When taken in excessive amounts, supplemental iron can build up to harmful levels in the liver and other body organs.

Some supplements are of no value to anyone. One example is vitamin B_{15} or pangamic acid (calcium pangamate). Sold for the treatment of heart disease, diabetes, glaucoma, allergies, and "aging," this substance is not needed in the human diet, and it has no medical usefulness.

Another useless supplement currently sold in pill form is SOD (superoxide dismutase). Scientists have found that animals with long lifespans have more of this enzyme in their bodies than do shorter-lived species. Although this knowledge may lead to a better understanding of aging processes, it is not likely to lead to an "anti-aging" pill. SOD is a protein. When taken by mouth, it breaks down into component parts — called amino acids — which are not reassembled. Therefore, SOD does not enter body cells and has no effect.

Steps You can Take

Consider checking with your doctor before taking any over-the-counter dietary supplement, particularly if you have illnesses such as diabetes, high blood pressure, or arthritis.

Resources

The National Institute on Aging offers a variety of resources on aging. Contact the NIA Information Center, P.O. Box 8057, Gaithersburg, MD 20898-8057.

Digestive Do's and Don'ts[*]

The digestive system performs the amazing task of changing food into the fuel your body needs to carry on. Most of the time this system stays remarkably free of trouble. With age, however, your body may begin to work less efficiently in some ways and your lifestyle may change. Afterward, digestion may be a problem every now and then.

During the chemical process of digestion, food is broken down into pieces tiny enough to be taken into the blood. The blood, in turn, carries these food elements to cells in all parts of the body where they are changed into energy or used to form new structures such as body tissue.

Many body organs are involved in the process of digestion: the esophagus, stomach, pancreas, gallbladder, liver, small intestine, and colon. Many people have few, if any, digestive problems related to aging. Sometimes there are changes affecting the length of time food travels through the system. For example, digestive muscles might move slower or produce less acid.

Lifestyle changes — such as increased use of medicines, reduced exercise, and changes in eating habits — can hamper the digestive system.

Taking Care of the System

To keep your digestive system working at its best:

- Eat a well-balanced diet that includes a variety of fresh fruits, vegetables, and whole grain breads, cereals, and other grain products
- Eat slowly and try to relax for 30 minutes after each meal

---

* Source: *Age Page*, National Institute on Aging, U.S. Department of Health and Human Services, Public Health Service, National Institutes of Health, Gaithersburg, MD 20898; 800-222-2225.

- Exercise regularly
- Drink alcohol in moderation, if at all
- Avoid large amounts of caffeine
- Use caution when taking over-the-counter drugs and always follow your doctor's directions exactly when taking prescribed medications.

When to See a Doctor

No matter how well your digestive system is treated, there are times when things go wrong. Often the problem will take care of itself. Sometimes, symptoms can be a signal that something more serious is wrong. Some important warning signs are:

- Stomach pains that are severe, last a long time, are recurring, or come with shaking, chills, and cold, clammy skin
- Blood in vomit or recurrent vomiting
- A sudden change in bowel habits or consistency of stools lasting more than a few days (for example, diarrhea for more than 3 days or the sudden onset of constipation)
- Blood in stools or coal-black stools
- Jaundice (a yellowing of the skin and the whites of the eyes) or dark, tea-colored urine
- Pain or difficulty in swallowing food
- Loss of appetite or unexpected weight loss
- Diarrhea that wakes you up at night

If you have any of these symptoms, see a doctor at once.

Digestive Diseases

Disorders of the digestive tract cause more hospital admissions than any other group of diseases. They occur most often in people who are middle-age or older.

Stress, infection, diseases, poisons, and defects present at birth can cause digestion problems. But the causes of many digestive diseases are unknown. There is evidence that diet may be involved in a few of them. For example, eating less fiber (the part of the plant that is not digested) may play a role in constipation, cancer of the colon, and diverticulosis, a condition in which small sacs form in the intestinal wall. Alcoholism has been linked to inflammation of the pancreas (pancreatitis).

Progress is being made in diagnosing many digestive diseases. In addition to the upper and lower gastrointestinal series, which uses x-rays and barium to find trouble spots, doctors can use a flexible instrument called the endoscope to see inside the esophagus, stomach, duodenum, and colon. The endoscope is also used to perform biopsies and some forms of surgery. There are also techniques for getting better images of body organs, such as ultrasound and the CT scan (computer tomographic scan), which takes detailed, three-dimensional x-rays.

Treatment advances include new drugs for peptic ulcers, a vaccine to prevent hepatitis B, and microsurgery to remove gallstones.

Some common digestive disorders are listed below.

Constipation. This is a decrease in the number of bowel movements, along with long or hard passing of stools. Older people report this problem much more often than do younger ones. Most cases of constipation can be easily treated. "Regularity" does not necessarily mean one bowel movement every day. Normal bowel habits can range from three movements each day to three each week. Eating a poor diet, drinking too few liquids, changing activities, taking certain prescription medication, or misusing laxatives can lead to constipation. Regularity is usually improved by eating foods high in fiber and staying physically active. (Also see the *Age Page* "Constipation.")

Diarrhea. When body wastes are discharged from the bowel more often then usual in a more or less liquid state, the condition is called diarrhea. There are many possible causes, but many cases are related to infection or improper handling of food. Treatment of the underlying disorder is needed but, most important, replacing lost fluids, even when there is no feeling of thirst, is essential.

Diverticulosis and diverticulitis. In diverticulosis, which is common in older people, small sacs form on the wall of the large intestine. Although they usually cause no symptoms, occasionally there is pain in the lower left side of the abdomen. Treatment includes a diet high in fiber and liquids. Diverticulitis develops after the sacs become inflamed and causes a fever. Treatment consists of bed rest and antibiotics.

Functional disorders. Sometimes symptoms such as pain, diarrhea, constipation, bloating, and gas are caused by a functional disorder such as irritable bowel syndrome. In these disorders there are no signs of disease and yet the intestinal tract still fails to work properly. A functional disorder may cause discomfort, but it is unlikely to lead to a serious disease. A doctor may prescribe medication to relieve symptoms. Because diet and stress are thought to trigger functional disorders, the same guidelines that help to keep your system running smoothly should help control the symptoms.

Gallbladder disease. In this disease, stones (usually composed of cholesterol) form in the gallbladder. These stones are often silent — that is, they cause no symptoms or discomfort, but they sometimes result in problems requiring drug treatment or surgery. Severe pain in the upper abdomen may mean that a gallstone has lodged in one of the tubes leading from the gallbladder.

Gas. Some gas is normally present in the digestive tract. It is usually caused by swallowing air, stress, or eating foods such as cauliflower, brussel sprouts, brown beans, broccoli, bran, and cabbage.[3] The body rids itself of gas by belching or passing gas. However; if gas collects in the digestive tract, it can lead to pain and bloating.

---

[3] Since these foods are good sources of fiber and vitamins, eat smaller amounts rather than removing them from the diet.

Gastritis. An inflammation of the stomach, gastritis can be caused by excess acid production in the stomach, infections, medications, and alcohol. Treatment is aimed at correcting the condition causing the gastritis, such as an infection, too much alcohol, an allergic response, or certain medicines.

Heartburn. A burning pain felt behind the breastbone that occurs after meals and lasts for anywhere from a few minutes to several hours is called heartburn. It is caused by stomach acid washing backward up into the tube connecting the mouth and stomach (esophagus). Heartburn can be brought on by eating spicy or rich foods such as tomato products, chocolate, fried foods, or peppermint, or by smoking cigarettes. It is relieved by changing your diet, taking an antacid, sleeping with the head of the bed raised 6 inches, or stopping cigarette smoking. If pain persists, see a doctor.

Peptic ulcer. This is a sore on the lining of the stomach or the small intestine just below the stomach (duodenum). An ulcer occurs when the lining is unable to resist the damaging effects of acid and pepsin that are produced by the stomach to digest foods. Antacids, which neutralize acid in the stomach, and drugs that decrease the production or acid or coat the ulcer are very useful in treating peptic ulcer. Continued pain should be checked by a doctor.

Indigestion. Known as dyspepsia, this common condition involves painful, difficult, or disturbed digestion. The symptoms include nausea, regurgitation, vomiting, heartburn, abdominal fullness or bloating after a meal, and stomach discomfort or pain. Overeating or eating certain foods can also cause symptoms, but they may also be related to other digestive problems such as peptic ulcer, gallbladder disease, or gastritis. Indigestion usually can be controlled through diet or by treating the specific disorder.

Hemorrhoids. When veins in and around the rectum and anus become weakened and enlarged, they are called hemorrhoids. This condition may be caused by pressure in the rectal veins due to constipation, pregnancy, obesity, or other conditions. The veins may become inflamed, develop blood clots, and bleed. Hemorrhoids are treated with frequent warm baths, creams, or suppositories, and if necessary, by injections or surgery. Eating high-fiber foods and drinking fluids may also help.

Hiatal hernia. In this condition the esophagus breaks through the opening in a thin muscle separating the abdominal cavity from the chest cavity. Hiatal hernias are common after middle-age and usually have no symptoms. But if the lower end of the esophagus becomes weak, stomach acids may flow back to the esophagus and result in a sense of burning. Most problems can be treated without medicines or surgery. For example, a change in eating habits or losing weight may be all that's needed to remove discomfort.

Milk intolerance. Also called lactose intolerance, this is the inability to digest milk and milk products properly due to a lack of lactase, the intestinal enzyme that digests the sugar found in milk. Some people develop this problem as they grow older. The symptoms — which include cramps, gas, bloating, and diarrhea — appear 15 minutes to several hours after consuming milk or a milk product. Most people manage the problem by mixing milk with food or beverages, eating processed cheeses and yogurt, taking smaller servings more frequently, or adding a special nonprescription preparation such as acidophilus to milk that makes it easy to digest. When eating fewer dairy products, help keep bones strong by consuming calcium rich foods such as dark green leafy vegetables, salmon, and bean curd. Since these foods will not provide as much calcium as dairy products, a doctor may suggest supplements.

Ulcerative colitis. This chronic disorder usually develops in young adults, but it also appears in older people. In ulcerative colitis, parts of the large intestine become inflamed causing abdominal cramps and often rectal bleeding. Joint pain and skin rashes may also develop. The symptoms are usually controlled with drugs, but some patients eventually need surgery. Sometimes irritable bowel syndrome (IBS) is incorrectly called "spastic colitis." However, IBS does not cause inflammation and it is not related to ulcerative colitis.

For More Information

For further information about these and other digestive problems, consult your doctor. You can also write to the National Digestive Diseases Information Clearinghouse, P.O. Box NDDIC, 9000 Rockville Pike, Bethesda, MD 20892.

For a free list of NIA publications, call 1-800-222-2225; or write to the NIA Information Center, P.O. Box 8057, Gaithersburg, MD 20898-8057.

Eating Disorders*

Each year millions of people in the United States are affected by serious and sometimes life-threatening eating disorders. The vast majority — more than 90 percent — of those afflicted with eating disorders are adolescent and young adult women. One reason that women in this age group are particularly vulnerable to eating disorders is their tendency to go on strict diets to achieve an "ideal" figure. Researchers have found that such stringent dieting can play a key role in triggering eating disorders.

Approximately 1 percent of adolescent girls develop anorexia nervosa, a dangerous condition in which they can literally starve themselves to death. Another 2 to 3 percent of young women develop bulimia nervosa, a destructive pattern of excessive overeating followed by vomiting or other "purging" behaviors to control their weight. These eating disorders also occur in men and older women, but much less frequently.

The consequences of eating disorders can be severe. For example, one in ten cases of anorexia nervosa leads to death from starvation, cardiac arrest, other medical complications, or suicide. Fortunately, increasing awareness of the dangers of eating disorders — sparked by medical studies and extensive media coverage of the illness — has led many people to seek help. Nevertheless, some people with eating disorders refuse to admit that they have a problem and do not get treatment. Family members and friends can help recognize the problem and encourage the person to seek treatment.

Valuable information is available to individuals suffering from eating disorders, as well as to family members and friends trying to help someone cope with the illness. This chapter describes the symptoms of eating disorders, possible causes, treatment options, and how to take the first steps toward recovery.

---

* Source: Information Resources and Inquiries Branch, National Institute of Mental Health, 5600 Fishers Lane, Room 7C-02, Rockville, MD 20857; 301-443-4513.

Scientists funded by the National Institute of Mental Health (NIMH) are actively studying ways to treat and understand eating disorders. In NIMH-supported research, scientists have found that people with eating disorders who get early treatment have a better chance of full recovery than those who wait years before getting help.

Anorexia Nervosa

People who intentionally starve themselves suffer from an eating disorder called anorexia nervosa. The disorder, which usually begins in young people around the time of puberty, involves extreme weight loss — at least 15 percent below the individual's normal body weight. Many people with the disorder look emaciated but are convinced they are overweight. Sometimes they must be hospitalized to prevent starvation.

Deborah developed anorexia nervosa when she was 16. A rather shy, studious teenager, she tried hard to please everyone. She had an attractive appearance, but was slightly overweight. Like many teenage girls, she was interested in boys but concerned that she wasn't pretty enough to get their attention. When her father jokingly remarked that she would never get a date if she didn't take off some weight, she took him seriously and began to diet relentlessly — never believing she was thin enough even when she became extremely underweight.

Soon after the pounds started dropping off, Deborah's menstrual periods stopped. As anorexia tightened its grip, she became obsessed with dieting and food, and developed strange eating rituals. Every day she weighed all the food she would eat on a kitchen scale, cutting solids into minuscule pieces and precisely measuring liquids. She would then put her daily ration in small containers, lining them up in neat rows. She also exercised compulsively, even after she weakened and became faint. She never took an elevator if she could walk up steps.

No one was able to convince Deborah that she was in danger. Finally, her doctor insisted that she be hospitalized and carefully monitored for treatment of her illness. While in the hospital, she secretly continued her exercise regimen in the bathroom, doing strenuous routines of sit-ups and knee-bends. It took several hospitalizations and a good deal of individual and family outpatient therapy for Deborah to face and solve her problems.

Deborah's case is not unusual. People with anorexia typically starve themselves, even though they suffer terribly from hunger pains. One of the most frightening aspects of the disorder is that people with anorexia continue to think they are overweight even when they are bone-thin. For reasons not yet understood, they become terrified of gaining any weight.

Food and weight become obsessions. For some, the compulsiveness shows up in strange eating rituals or the refusal to eat in front of others. It is not uncommon for people with anorexia to collect recipes and prepare gourmet feasts for family and friends, but not partake in the meals themselves. Like Deborah, they may adhere to strict exercise routines to keep off weight. Loss of monthly menstrual periods is typical in women with the disorder. Men with anorexia often become impotent.

Bulimia Nervosa

People with bulimia nervosa consume large amounts of food and then rid their bodies of the excess calories by vomiting, abusing laxatives or diuretics, taking enemas, or exercising obsessively. Some use a combination of all these forms of purging. Because many individuals with bulimia "binge and purge" in secret and maintain normal or above normal body weight, they can often successfully hide their problem from others for years.

Lisa developed bulimia nervosa at 18. Like Deborah, her strange eating behavior began when she started to diet. She too dieted and exercised to lose weight, but unlike Deborah, she regularly ate huge amounts of food and maintained her normal weight by forcing

*herself to vomit. Lisa often felt like an emotional powder keg —
angry, frightened, and depressed.*

*Unable to understand her own behavior, she thought no one else
would either. She felt isolated and lonely. Typically, when things
were not going well, she would be overcome with an uncontrollable
desire for sweets. She would eat pounds of candy and cake at a
time, and often not stop until she was exhausted or in severe pain.
Then, overwhelmed with guilt and disgust, she would make herself
vomit.*

*Her eating habits so embarrassed her that she kept them secret
until, depressed by her mounting problems, she attempted suicide.
Fortunately, she didn't succeed. While recuperating in the hospital,
she was referred to an eating disorders clinic where she became
involved in group therapy. There she received medications to treat
the illness and the understanding and help she so desperately
needed from others who had the same problem.*

Family, friends, and physicians may have difficulty detecting
bulimia in someone they know. Many individuals with the disorder
remain at normal body weight or above because of their frequent
binges and purges, which can range from once or twice a week to
several times a day. Dieting heavily between episodes of binging
and purging is also common. Eventually, half of those with
anorexia will develop bulimia.

As with anorexia, bulimia typically begins during adolescence. The
condition occurs most often in women but is also found in men.
Many individuals with bulimia, ashamed of their strange habits, do
not seek help until they reach their thirties or forties. By this time,
their eating behavior is deeply ingrained and more difficult to
change.

Binge Eating Disorder

An illness that resembles bulimia nervosa is binge eating disorder.
Like bulimia, the disorder is characterized by episodes of

uncontrolled eating or binging. However, binge eating disorder differs from bulimia because its sufferers do not purge their bodies of excess food.

Individuals with binge eating disorder feel that they lose control of themselves when eating. They eat large quantities of food and do not stop until they are uncomfortably full. Usually, they have more difficulty losing weight and keeping it off than do people with other serious weight problems. Most people with the disorder are obese and have a history of weight fluctuations. Binge eating disorder is found in about 2 percent of the general population — more often in women than men. Recent research shows that binge eating disorder occurs in about 30 percent of people participating in medically supervised weight control programs.

Medical Complications

Medical complications can frequently be a result of eating disorders. Individuals with eating disorders who use drugs to stimulate vomiting, bowel movements, or urination may be in considerable danger, as this practice increases the risk of heart failure.

In patients with anorexia, starvation can damage vital organs such as the heart and brain. To protect itself, the body shifts into "slow gear": monthly menstrual periods stop, breathing, pulse, and blood pressure rates drop, and thyroid function slows. Nails and hair become brittle; the skin dries, yellows, and becomes covered with soft hair called lanugo. Excessive thirst and frequent urination may occur. Dehydration contributes to constipation, and reduced body fat leads to lowered body temperature and the inability to withstand cold.

Mild anemia, swollen joints, reduced muscle mass, and light-headedness also commonly occur in anorexia. If the disorder becomes severe, patients may lose calcium from their bones, making them brittle and prone to breakage. They may also experience irregular heart rhythms and heart failure. In some patients, the brain shrinks, causing personality changes. Fortunately, this condition can be reversed when normal weight is reestablished.

Scientists have found that many patients with anorexia also suffer from other psychiatric illnesses. While the majority have co-occurring clinical depression, others suffer from anxiety, personality or substance abuse disorders, and many are at risk for suicide. Obsessive-compulsive disorder (OCD), an illness characterized by repetitive thoughts and behaviors, can also accompany anorexia. Individuals with anorexia are typically compliant in personality but may have sudden outbursts of hostility and anger or become socially withdrawn.

Bulimia nervosa patients — even those of normal weight — can severely damage their bodies by frequent binge eating and purging. In rare instances, binge eating causes the stomach to rupture; purging may result in heart failure due to loss of vital minerals, such as potassium. Vomiting causes other less deadly, but serious, problems — the acid in vomit wears down the outer layer of the teeth and can cause scarring on the backs of hands when fingers are pushed down the throat to induce vomiting. Further, the esophagus becomes inflamed and the glands near the cheeks become swollen. As in anorexia, bulimia may lead to irregular menstrual periods. Interest in sex may also diminish.

Some individuals with bulimia struggle with addictions, including abuse of drugs and alcohol, and compulsive stealing. Like individuals with anorexia, many people with bulimia suffer from clinical depression, anxiety, OCD, and other psychiatric illnesses. These problems, combined with their impulsive tendencies, place them at increased risk for suicidal behavior.

People with binge eating disorder are usually overweight, so they are prone to the serious medical problems associated with obesity, such as high cholesterol, high blood pressure, and diabetes. Obese individuals also have a higher risk for gallbladder disease, heart disease, and some types of cancer. Research has shown that individuals with binge eating disorder have high rates of co-occurring psychiatric illnesses — especially depression.

Common Symptoms of Eating Disorders

Symptoms:	Anorexia Nervosa*	Bulimia Nervosa*	Binge Eating Disorder
Excessive weight loss in a relatively short period of time	■		
Continuation of dieting although bone-thin	■		
Dissatisfaction with appearance; belief that body is fat, even though severely underweight	■		
Loss of monthly menstrual periods	■	■	
Unusual interest in food and development of strange eating rituals	■	■	
Eating in secret	■	■	■
Obsession with exercise	■	■	
Serious depression	■	■	■
Binging--consumption of large amounts of food		■	■
Vomiting or use of drugs to stimulate vomiting, bowel movements, and urination		■	
Binging but no noticeable weight gain		■	
Disappearance into bathroom for long periods of time to induce vomiting		■	
Abuse of drugs or alcohol		■	■

* Some individuals suffer from anorexia and bulimia and have symptoms of both disorders.

Causes of Eating Disorders

In trying to understand the causes of eating disorders, scientists have studied the personalities, genetics, environments, and biochemistry of people with these illnesses. As is often the case, the more that is learned, the more complex the roots of eating disorders appear.

Personalities

Most people with eating disorders share certain personality traits: low self-esteem, feelings of helplessness, and a fear of becoming fat. In anorexia, bulimia, and binge eating disorder, eating behaviors seem to develop as a way of handling stress and anxieties.

People with anorexia tend to be "too good to be true." They rarely disobey, keep their feelings to themselves, and tend to be perfectionists, good students, and excellent athletes. Some researchers believe that people with anorexia restrict food — particularly carbohydrates — to gain a sense of control in some area of their lives. Having followed the wishes of others for the most part, they have not learned how to cope with the problems typical of adolescence, growing up, and becoming independent. Controlling their weight appears to offer two advantages, at least initially: they can take control of their bodies and gain approval from others. However, it eventually becomes clear to others that they are out-of-control and dangerously thin.

People who develop bulimia and binge eating disorder typically consume huge amounts of food — often junk food — to reduce stress and relieve anxiety. With binge eating, however, comes guilt and depression. Purging can bring relief, but it is only temporary. Individuals with bulimia are also impulsive and more likely to engage in risky behavior such as abuse of alcohol and drugs.

Genetic and Environmental Factors

Eating disorders appear to run in families, with female relatives most often affected. This finding suggests that genetic factors may predispose some people to eating disorders; however, other influences, both behavioral and environmental, may also play a role. One recent study found that mothers who are overly concerned about their daughters' weight and physical attractiveness may put the girls at increased risk of developing an eating disorder. In addition, girls with eating disorders often have fathers and brothers who are overly critical of their weight.

Although most victims of anorexia and bulimia are adolescent and young adult women, these illnesses can also strike men and older women. Anorexia and bulimia are found most often in Caucasians, but these illnesses also affect African Americans and other racial ethnic groups. People pursuing professions or activities that emphasize thinness — like modeling, dancing, gymnastics, wrestling, and long-distance running — are more susceptible to the problem. In contrast to other eating disorders, one-third to one-fourth of all patients with binge eating disorder are men. Preliminary studies also show that the condition occurs equally among African Americans and Caucasians.

Biochemistry
In an attempt to understand eating disorders, scientists have studied the biochemical functions of people with the illnesses. They have focused recently on the neuroendocrine system — a combination of the central nervous and hormonal systems. Through complex but carefully balanced feedback mechanisms, the neuroendocrine system regulates sexual function, physical growth and development, appetite and digestion, sleep, heart and kidney function, emotions, thinking, and memory — in other words, multiple functions of the mind and body. Many of these regulatory mechanisms are seriously disturbed in people with eating disorders.

In the central nervous system — particularly the brain — key chemical messengers known as neurotransmitters control hormone production. Scientists have found that the neurotransmitters serotonin and norepinephrine function abnormally in people affected by depression. Recently, researchers funded by NIMH have learned that these neurotransmitters are also decreased in acutely ill anorexia and bulimia patients and long-term recovered anorexia patients. Because many people with eating disorders also appear to suffer from depression, some scientists believe that there may be a link between these two disorders. This link is supported by studies showing that antidepressants can be used successfully to treat some people with eating disorders. In fact, new research has suggested that some patients with anorexia may respond well to the antidepressant medication fluoxetine, which affects serotonin function in the body.

People with either anorexia or certain forms of depression also tend to have higher than normal levels of cortisol, a brain hormone released in response to stress. Scientists have been able to show that the excess levels of cortisol in both anorexia and depression are caused by a problem that occurs in or near a region of the brain called the hypothalamus.

In addition to connections between depression and eating disorders, scientists have found biochemical similarities between people with eating disorders and obsessive-compulsive disorder (OCD). Just as serotonin levels are known to be abnormal in people with depression and eating disorders, they are also abnormal in patients with OCD. Recently, NIMH researchers have found that many patients with bulimia have obsessive-compulsive behavior as severe as that seen in patients actually diagnosed with OCD. Conversely, patients with OCD frequently have abnormal eating behaviors.

The hormone vasopressin is another brain chemical found to be abnormal in people with eating disorders and OCD. NIMH researchers have shown that levels of this hormone are elevated in patients with OCD, anorexia, and bulimia. Normally released in response to physical and possibly emotional stress, vasopressin may contribute to the obsessive behavior seen in some patients with eating disorders.

NIMH-supported investigators are also exploring the role of other brain chemicals in eating behavior. Many are conducting studies in animals to shed some light on human disorders. For example, scientists have found that levels of neuropeptide Y and peptide YY, recently shown to be elevated in patients with anorexia and bulimia, stimulate eating behavior in laboratory animals. Other investigators have found that cholecystokinin (CCK), a hormone known to be low in some women with bulimia, causes laboratory animals to feel full and stop eating. This finding may possibly explain why women with bulimia do not feel satisfied after eating and continue to binge.

Treatment

Eating disorders are most successfully treated when diagnosed early. Unfortunately, even when family members confront the ill person about his or her behavior, or physicians make a diagnosis, individuals with eating disorders may deny that they have a problem. Thus, people with anorexia may not receive medical or psychological attention until they have already become dangerously thin and malnourished. People with bulimia are often normal weight and are able to hide their illness from others for years. Eating disorders in males may be overlooked because anorexia and bulimia are relatively rare in boys and men. Consequently, getting and keeping people with these disorders into treatment can be extremely difficult.

In any case, it cannot be overemphasized how important treatment is — the sooner, the better. The longer abnormal eating behaviors persist, the more difficult it is to overcome the disorder and its effects on the body. In some cases, long-term treatment may be required. Families and friends offering support and encouragement can play an important role in the success of the treatment program.

If an eating disorder is suspected, particularly if it involves weight loss, the first step is a complete physical examination to rule out any other illnesses. Once an eating disorder is diagnosed, the clinician must determine whether the patient is in immediate medical danger and requires hospitalization. While most patients can be treated as outpatients, some need hospital care.

Conditions warranting hospitalization include excessive and rapid weight loss, serious metabolic disturbances, clinical depression or risk of suicide, severe binge eating and purging, or psychosis.

The complex interaction of emotional and physiological problems in eating disorders calls for a comprehensive treatment plan, involving a variety of experts and approaches. Ideally, the treatment team includes an internist, a nutritionist, an individual psychotherapist, a group and family psychotherapist, and a psychopharmacologist — someone who is knowledgeable about psychoactive medications useful in treating these disorders.

To help those with eating disorders deal with their illness and underlying emotional issues, some form of psychotherapy is usually needed. A psychiatrist, psychologist, or other mental health professional meets with the patient individually and provides ongoing emotional support, while the patient begins to understand and cope with the illness. Group therapy, in which people share their experiences with others who have similar problems, has been especially effective for individuals with bulimia.

Use of individual psychotherapy, family therapy, and cognitive-behavioral therapy — a form of psychotherapy that teaches patients how to change abnormal thoughts and behavior — is often the most productive. Cognitive-behavior therapists focus on changing eating behaviors, usually by rewarding or modeling wanted behavior. These therapists also help patients work to change the distorted and rigid thinking patterns associated with eating disorders.

NIMH-supported scientists have examined the effectiveness of combining psychotherapy and medications. In a recent study of bulimia, researchers found that both intensive group therapy and antidepressant medications, combined or alone, benefited patients.

In another study of bulimia, the combined use of cognitive-behavioral therapy and antidepressant medications was most beneficial. The combination treatment was particularly effective in preventing relapse once medications were discontinued. For patients with binge eating disorder, cognitive-behavioral therapy and antidepressant medications may also prove to be useful.

Antidepressant medications commonly used to treat bulimia include desipramine, imipramine, and fluoxetine. For anorexia, preliminary evidence shows that some antidepressant medications may be effective when combined with other forms of treatment. Fluoxetine has also been useful in treating some patients with binge eating disorder. These antidepressants may also treat any co-occurring depression.

The efforts of mental health professionals need to be combined with those of other health professionals to obtain the best treatment. Physicians treat any medical complications, and nutritionists advise on diet and eating regimens. The challenge of treating eating disorders is made more difficult by the metabolic changes associated with them. Just to maintain a stable weight, individuals with anorexia may actually have to consume more calories than someone of similar weight and age without an eating disorder.

This information is important for patients and the clinicians who treat them. Consuming calories is exactly what the person with anorexia wishes to avoid, yet must do to regain the weight necessary for recovery. In contrast, some normal weight people with bulimia may gain excess weight if they consume the number of calories required to maintain normal weight in others of similar size and age.

Helping the Person With an Eating Disorder

Treatment can save the life of someone with an eating disorder. Friends, relatives, teachers, and physicians all play an important role in helping the ill person start and stay with a treatment program. Encouragement, caring, and persistence, as well as information about eating disorders and their dangers, may be needed to convince the ill person to get help, stick with treatment, or try again.

Family members and friends can call local hospitals or university medical centers to find out about eating disorder clinics and clinicians experienced in treating these illnesses. For college students, treatment programs may be available in school counseling centers.

Family members and friends should read as much as possible about eating disorders, so they can help the person with the illness understand his or her problem. Many local mental health organizations and the self-help groups listed at the end of this brochure provide free literature on eating disorders. Some of these groups also provide treatment program referrals and information on local self-help groups. Once the person gets help, he or she will continue to need lots of understanding and encouragement to stay in treatment.

NIMH continues its search for new and better treatments for eating disorders. Congress has designated the 1990s as the Decade of the Brain, making the prevention, diagnosis, and treatment of all brain and mental disorders a national research priority. This research promises to yield even more hope for patients and their families by providing a greater understanding of the causes and complexities of eating disorders.

For Further Information

For additional information on eating disorders, check local hospitals or university medical centers for an eating disorders clinic, or contact:

National Association of Anorexia Nervosa and Associated Disorders (ANAD), P.O. Box 7, Highland Park, IL 60035; 708-831-3438

Anorexia Nervosa and Related Eating Disorders, Inc. (ANRED), P.O. Box 5102, Eugene, OR 97405; 503-344-1144

American Anorexia/Bulimia Association, Inc. (AABA), 425 East 61st Street, 6th Floor, New York, NY 10021; 212-891-8686

Center for the Study of Anorexia and Bulimia, 1 West 91st Street, New York, NY 10024; 212-595-3449

National Eating Disorder Organization, 445 East Grandille Road, Worthington, OH 43085; 614-436-1112

Foundation for Education about Eating Disorders (FEED), P.O. Box 16375, Baltimore, MD 21210; 410-467-0603

For information on Eating Disorders Awareness Week, contact:
Eating Disorders Awareness & Prevention Inc.
603 Stewart Street, Suite 803
Seattle, WA 98101
206-382-3587

For information on other mental disorders, contact:
Information Resources and Inquiries Branch
National Institute of Mental Health
5600 Fishers Lane, Room 7C-02
Rockville, MD 20857
301-443-4513

How To Take Your Medicine: Erythromycin*

How you take a drug can affect how well it works and how safe it will be for you. Sometimes it can be almost as important as what you take. Timing, what you eat and when you eat, proper dose, and many other factors can mean the difference between feeling better, staying the same, or even feeling worse. This drug information is intended to help you make your treatment work as effectively as possible. It is important to note, however, that this is only a guideline. You should talk to your doctor about how and when to take any prescribed drugs.

This chapter is about a commonly prescribed medication called erythromycin, an antibiotic used alone or in combination with other chemicals or drugs to treat various infections. Erythro-

For eyes:
  erythromycin (Ilotycin)

For skin:
  erythromycin (EryDerm, Erygel, Erymax, T-STAT)

  erythromycin and benzoyl peroxide (Benzamycin)

Oral:
  erythromycin base (E-Base, ERYC, Ery-Tab, PCE)

  erythromycin estolate (Ilosone)

  erythromycin ethylsuccinate (E.E.S., EryPed)

  erythromycin stearate (Erythrocin, Wyamycin S)

  erythromycin and sulfisoxazole (Pediazole)

Intravenous:
  erythromycin gluceptate (Ilotycin)

  erythromycin lactobionate (Erythrocin)

mycins also are used as part of a preoperative bowel preparation that suppresses the normal bacterial flora, thus reducing the chances of infection following bowel surgery.

---

* Source: Office of Public Affairs, Food and Drug Administration, Public Health Service, 5600 Fishers Lane, Rockville, MD 20857; 301-827-4420.

Conditions These Drugs Treat

Erythromycin was first isolated in 1952. Like other antibiotics, it is produced by a microorganism — in this case, Streptomyces erythraeus — and has the capacity to inhibit the growth of or to kill other microorganisms. It is effective against a number of common bacteria, including Chlamydia trachomatis, Corynebacterium diphtheriae, Neisseria gonorrhoeae, Listeria monocytogenes, Streptococcus pneumoniae, Bordetella pertussis, Legionella pneumophilia, and Mycoplasma pneumoniae.

It is used to treat conditions caused by those organisms, such as diphtheria, gonorrhea, Legionnaires' disease, pneumonia, sinusitis caused by S. pneumoniae, pertussis (whooping cough), rheumatic fever, and chlamydial infections of the eyes and genitourinary tract and, in infants, lungs. It also is used for penicillin-allergic patients who have syphilis.

The skin preparations are prescribed for acne.

Erythromycin will not cure or combat colds, flu, or other viral infections.

How to Take

Erythromycin may be applied to the eyes (eye ointment) or to the skin (topical gels, ointments, swabs or liquids), swallowed (liquid, tablet or capsule), or administered intravenously (fluid). The doctor determines the dosage, including the dose and treatment period, depending on the type and severity of the infection.

The medication should be taken for the full time prescribed, even if symptoms are no longer present, to ensure that the infection does not recur. The exception might be if side effects occur, in which case the doctor should be consulted. For patients with "strep" infection, it is important that the medicine be taken for at least 10 days, or as prescribed by the doctor. Serious heart problems, such as rheumatic fever, could develop later if the infection isn't cleared up completely.

In general, the eye ointment is applied at least twice daily, the skin preparations twice daily (in the morning and at night), and erythromycin taken by mouth is taken daily at 6- or 12-hour intervals. Intravenous erythromycin is given continuously.

Most oral forms of erythromycin are absorbed best on an empty stomach and therefore should be taken at least one half hour before or two hours after a meal. They may be taken with food, however, if they upset the stomach.

Of special note:
- Chewable tablets, such as Ilosone and EryPed chewable tablets, must be chewed or crushed before they are swallowed.
- Delayed-release capsules or tablets, such as Ery-Tab and E-Base delayed-release tablets, should be swallowed whole; they should not be broken or crushed.
- Specially marked spoons or other measuring devices that come with liquid oral forms should be used to ensure accurate doses. Household teaspoons should not be used because they may not hold the right amount of liquid.

Missed Doses

Erythromycin taken by mouth works best if it circulates in the blood at a constant level. Therefore, it is important that doses not be missed and that they be taken at regular intervals.

If a dose is missed and just a short time has passed, it should be taken as soon as possible. However, if it is time for the next dose, a physician should be consulted before making up the dose.

Relief of Symptoms

Erythromycin usually clears infections within days. However, because it does not relieve symptoms immediately, the doctor may prescribe other medicines, such as aspirin or acetaminophen, to ease pain and fever until the erythromycin takes effect.

Side Effects and Risks

Erythromycin taken by mouth may cause mild stomach cramps, diarrhea, nausea and vomiting, and sore mouth or tongue. These problems are usually minor and may go away as the body adjusts to the medicine. If they persist, however, the doctor should be consulted.

Although relatively rare, other side effects that may occur are:
- with eye ointment: eye irritation not present before therapy,
- with skin preparations: dry or scaly skin; itching, stinging, peeling, or redness of the skin
- with medications taken by mouth: skin rash, hives, or itching; dark or amber urine; pale stools; severe stomach pain; unusual tiredness or weakness; or yellow eyes or skin (jaundice)
- with intravenous administration: pain, swelling or redness at the injection site.

The doctor should be consulted if any of these side effects occurs.

Precautions and Warnings

Because various adverse drug interactions between erythromycin and other medications can occur, patients should inform their doctors of all prescription and nonprescription drugs they are taking before starting this medicine.

Patients also should tell their doctors:

- if they have ever had an unusual reaction to erythromycin.
- if they are pregnant or could possibly become pregnant. Although erythromycin has not been shown to cause birth defects or other problems in humans, it does cross the placenta.
- if they are breast-feeding, because erythromycin passes into breast milk, a nursing mother should consult her doctor before taking the drug.

- if they are on a low-sodium, low-sugar, or other special diet, or if they are allergic to any foods, sulfites, or other preservatives or dyes that also may be present in an erythromycin-based drug.
- if they have ever had liver disease or hearing loss. Although very rare, patients with kidney problems who take erythromycin may suffer hearing loss, which is reversible after the drug is stopped.

Exercise and Weight Control*

Just about everybody seems to be interested in weight control. Some of us weigh just the right amount, others need to gain a few pounds. Most of us "battle the bulge" at some time in our life. Whatever our goals, we should understand and take advantage of the important role of exercise in keeping our weight under control.

Carrying around too much body fat is a major nuisance. Yet excess body fat is common in modern-day living. Few of today's occupations require vigorous physical activity, and much of our leisure time is spent in sedentary pursuits.

Recent estimates indicate that 34 million adults are considered obese (20 percent above desirable weight). Also, there has been an increase in body fat levels in children and youth over the past 20 years. After infancy and early childhood, the earlier the onset of obesity, the greater the likelihood of remaining obese.

Excess body fat has been linked to such health problems as coronary heart disease, high blood pressure, osteoporosis, diabetes, arthritis and certain forms of cancer. Some evidence now exists showing that obesity has a negative effect on both health and longevity.

Exercise is associated with the loss of body fat in both obese and normal weight persons. A regular program of exercise is an important component of any plan to help individuals lose, gain or maintain their weight.

Overweight or Overfat?

Overweight and "over fat" do not always mean the same thing. Some people are quite muscular and weigh more than the average for their age and height. However, their body composition, the amount of fat versus lean body mass (muscle, bone, organs and

---

* Source: President's Council on Physical Fitness and Sports, 701 Pennsylvania Avenue, Suite 250, Washington, DC 20004; 202-272-3421.

tissue), is within a desirable range. This is true for many athletes. Others weigh an average amount yet carry around too much fat. In our society, however, overweight often implies over fat because excess weight is commonly distributed as excess fat. The addition of exercise to a weight control program helps control both body weight and body fat levels.

A certain amount of body fat is necessary for everyone. Experts say that percent body fat for women should be about 20 percent, 15 percent for men. Women with more than 30 percent fat and men with more than 25 percent fat are considered obese.

How much of your weight is fat can be assessed by a variety of methods including underwater (hydrostatic) weighing, skinfold thickness measurements and circumference measurements. Each requires a specially trained person to administer the test and perform the correct calculations. From the numbers obtained, a body fat percentage is determined. Assessing body composition has an advantage over the standard height-weight tables because it can help distinguish between 11 overweight" and "overfat."

An easy self-test you can do is to pinch the thickness of the fat folds at your waist and abdomen. If you can pinch an inch or more of fat (make sure no muscle is included) chances are you have too much body fat.

People who exercise appropriately increase lean body mass while decreasing their overall fat level. Depending on the amount of fat loss, this can result in a loss of inches without a loss of weight, since muscle weighs more than fat. However, with the proper combination of diet and exercise, both body fat and overall weight can be reduced.

Energy Balance: A Weighty Concept

Losing weight, gaining weight or maintaining your weight depends on the amount of calories you take in and use up during the day, otherwise referred to as energy balance. Learning how to balance energy intake (calories in food) with energy output (calories expended through physical activity) will help you achieve your desired weight.

Although the underlying causes and the treatments of obesity are complex, the concept of energy balance is relatively simple. If you eat more calories than your body needs to perform your day's activities, the extra calories are stored as fat. If you do not take in enough calories to meet your body's energy needs, your body will go to the stored fat to make up the difference. (Exercise helps ensure that stored fat, rather than muscle tissue, is used to meet your energy needs.) If you eat just about the same amount of calories to meet your body's energy needs, your weight will stay the same.

On the average, a person consumes between 800,000 and 900,000 calories each year! An active person needs more calories than a sedentary person, as physically active people require energy above and beyond the day's basic needs. All too often, people who want to lose weight concentrate on counting calorie intake while neglecting calorie output. The most powerful formula is the combination of dietary modification with exercise. By increasing your daily physical activity and decreasing your caloric input you can lose excess weight in the most efficient and healthful way.

Each pound of fat your body stores represents 3,500 calories of unused energy. In order to lose one pound, you would have to create a calorie deficit of 3,500 calories by either taking in 3,500 less calories over a period of time than you need or doing 3,500 calories worth of exercise. It is recommended that no more than two pounds (7,000 calories) be lost per week for lasting weight loss.

Adding 15 minutes of moderate exercise, say walking one mile, to your daily schedule will use up 100 extra calories per day. (Your body uses approximately 100 calories of energy to walk one mile, depending on your body weight.) Maintaining this schedule would result in an extra 700 calories per week used up, or a loss of about 10 pounds in one year, assuming your food intake stays the same.

To look at energy balance another way, just one extra slice of bread or one extra soft drink a day — or any other food that contains approximately 100 calories — can add up to ten extra pounds in a year if the amount of physical activity you do does not increase.

If you already have a lean figure and want to keep it you should exercise regularly and eat a balanced diet that provides enough calories to make up for the energy you expend. If you wish to gain weight you should exercise regularly and increase the number of calories you consume until you reach your desired weight. Exercise will help ensure that the weight you gain will be lean muscle mass, not extra fat.

The Diet Connection

A balanced diet should be part of any weight control plan. A diet high in complex carbohydrates and moderate in protein and fat will complement an exercise program. It should include enough calories to satisfy your daily nutrient requirements and include the proper number of servings per day from the "basic four food groups": vegetables and fruits (4 servings), breads and cereals (4 servings), milk and milk products (2-4 depending on age) and meats and fish (2).

Experts recommend that your daily intake not fall below 1200 calories unless you are under a doctor's supervision. Also, weekly weight loss should not exceed two pounds.

Remarkable claims have been made for a variety of "crash" diets and diet pills. And some of these very restricted diets do result in noticeable weight loss in a short time. Much of this loss is water and such a loss is quickly regained when normal food and liquid intake is resumed. These diet plans are often expensive and may be dangerous. Moreover, they do not emphasize lifestyle changes that will help you maintain your desired weight. Dieting alone will result in a loss of valuable body tissue such as muscle mass in addition to a loss in fat.

How Many Calories?

The estimates for number of calories (energy) used during a physical activity are based on experiments that measure the amount of oxygen consumed during a specific bout of exercise for a certain body weight.

The energy costs of activities that require you to move your own body weight, such as walking or jogging, are greater for heavier people since they have more weight to move. For example, a person weighing 150 pounds would use more calories jogging one mile than a person jogging alongside who weighs 115 pounds. Always check to see what body weight is referred to in caloric expenditure charts you use.

Exercise and Modern Living

One thing is certain. Most people do not get enough exercise in their ordinary routines. All of the advances of modern technology from electric can openers to power steering have made life easier, more comfortable and much less physically demanding. Yet our bodies need activity, especially if they are carrying around too much fat. Satisfying this need requires a definite plan, and a commitment. There are two main ways to increase the number of calories you expend:
1. Start a regular exercise program if you do not have one already.
2. Increase the amount of physical activity in your daily routine.

The best way to control your weight is a combination of the above. The sum total of calories used over time will help regulate your weight as well as keep you physically fit.

Energy Expenditure Chart

		Energy Costs Cals/Hour*
A.	**Sedentary Activities**	
	Lying down or sleeping	90
	Sitting quietly	84
	Sitting and writing, card playing, etc.	114
B.	**Moderate Activities**	**(150-350)**
	Bicycling (5 mph)	174
	Canoeing (2.5 mph)	174
	Dancing (Ballroom)	210
	Golf (2-some, carrying clubs)	324
	Horseback riding (sitting to trot)	246
	Light housework, cleaning, etc.	246
	Swimming (crawl, 20 yards/min)	288
	Tennis (recreational doubles)	312
	Volleyball (recreational)	264
	Walking (2 mph)	198
C.	**Vigorous Activities**	**More than 350**
	Aerobic Dancing	546
	Basketball (recreational)	450
	Bicycling (13 mph)	612
	Circuit weight training	756
	Football (touch, vigorous)	498
	Ice Skating (9 mph)	384
	Racquetball	588
	Roller Skating (9 mph)	384
	Jogging (10 minute mile, 6 mph)	654
	Scrubbing Floors	440
	Swimming (crawl, 45 yards/min)	522
	Tennis (recreational singles)	450
	X-country Skiing (5 mph)	690

* Hourly estimates based on values calculated for calories burned per minute for a 150 pound (68 kg) person.

Active Lifestyles

Before looking at what kind of regular exercise program is best, let's look at how you can increase the amount of physical activity in your daily routine to supplement your exercise program.

- Recreational pursuits such as gardening on weekends, bowling in the office league, family outings, an evening of social dancing, and many other activities provide added exercise. They are fun and can be considered an extra bonus in your weight control campaign.
- Add more "action" to your day. Walk to the neighborhood grocery store instead of using the car. Park several blocks from the office and walk the rest of the way. Walk up the stairs instead of using the elevator; start with one flight of steps and gradually increase.
- Change your attitude toward movement. Instead of considering an extra little walk or trip to the files an annoyance, look upon it as an added fitness boost. Look for opportunities to use your body. Bend, stretch, reach, move, lift and carry. Time-saving devices and gadgets eliminate drudgery and are a bonus to mankind, but when they substitute too often for physical activity they can demand a high cost in health, vigor and fitness.

These little bits of action are cumulative in their effects. Alone, each does not burn a huge amount of calories. But when added together they can result in a sizable amount of energy used over the course of the day. And they will help improve your muscle tone and flexibility at the same time.

What Kind of Exercise?

Although any kind of physical movement requires energy (calories), the type of exercise that uses the most energy is "aerobic" exercise. The term "aerobic" is derived from the Greek word meaning "with oxygen." Jogging, brisk walking, swimming, biking, cross-country skiing and aerobic dancing are some popular forms of aerobic exercise.

Aerobic exercises use the body's large muscle groups in continuous, rhythmic, sustained movement and require oxygen for the production of energy. When oxygen is combined with food (which can come from stored fat) energy is produced to power the body's musculature. The longer you move aerobically, the more energy needed and the more calories used. Regular aerobic exercise will improve your cardiorespiratory endurance, the ability of your heart, lungs, blood vessels and associated tissues to use oxygen to produce energy needed for activity. You'll build a healthier body while getting rid of excess body fat.

In addition to the aerobic exercise, supplement your program with muscle strengthening and stretching exercises. The stronger your muscles, the longer you will be able to keep going during aerobic activity, and the less chance of injury.

How Much? How Often?

Experts recommend that you do some form of aerobic exercise at least three times a week for a minimum of 20 continuous minutes. Of course, if that is too much, start with a shorter time span and gradually build up to the minimum. Then gradually progress until you are able to work aerobically for 20-40 minutes. If you need to lose a large amount of weight, you may want to do your aerobic workout five times a week.

It is important to exercise at an intensity vigorous enough to cause your heart rate and breathing to increase. How hard you should exercise depends to a certain degree on your age, and is determined by measuring your heart rate in beats per minute.

The heart rate you should maintain is called your target heart rate, and there are several ways you can arrive at this figure. The simplest is to subtract your age from 220 and then calculate 60 to 80 percent of that figure. Beginners should maintain the 60 percent level, more advanced can work up to the 80 percent level. This is just a guide however, and people with any medical limitations should discuss this formula with their physician.

You can do different types of aerobic activities, say walking one day, riding a bike the next. Make sure you choose an activity that can be done regularly, and is enjoyable for you. The important thing to remember is not to skip too many days between workouts or fitness benefits will be lost. If you must lose a few days, gradually work back into your routine.

The Benefits of Exercise in a Weight Control Program

The benefits of exercise are many, from producing physically fit bodies to providing an outlet for fun and socialization. When added to a weight control program these benefits take on increased significance.

We already have noted that proper exercise can help control weight by burning excess body fat. It also has two other body-trimming advantages: 1) exercise builds muscle tissue and muscle uses calories up at a faster rate than body fat; and 2) exercise helps reduce inches and a firm, lean body looks slimmer even if your weight remains the same.

Remember, fat does not "turn into" muscle, as is often believed. Fat and muscle are two entirely different substances and one cannot become the other. However, muscle does use calories at a faster rate than fat which directly affects your body's metabolic rate or energy requirement. Your basal metabolic rate (BMR) is the amount of energy required to sustain the body's functions at rest and it depends on your age, sex, body size, genes and body composition. People with high levels of muscle tend to have higher BMRs and use more calories in the resting stage.

Some studies have even shown that your metabolic rate stays elevated for some time after vigorous exercise, causing you to use even more calories throughout your day.

Additional benefits may be seen in how exercise affects appetite. A lean person in good shape may eat more following increased activity, but the regular exercise will burn up the extra calories consumed. On the other hand, vigorous exercise has been reported to suppress appetite. And, physical activity can be used as a positive substitute for between meal snacking.

Better Mental Health

The psychological benefits of exercise are equally important to the weight conscious person. Exercise decreases stress and relieves tensions that might otherwise lead to overeating. Exercise builds physical fitness which in turn builds self-confidence, enhanced self-image, and a positive outlook. When you start to feel good about yourself, you are more likely to want to make other positive changes in your lifestyle that will help keep your weight under control.

In addition, exercise can be fun, provide recreation and offer opportunities for companionship. The exhilaration and emotional release of participating in sports or other activities are a boost to mental and physical health. Pent-up anxieties and frustrations seem to disappear when you're concentrating on returning a serve, sinking a putt or going that extra mile.

Tips to Get You Started

Hopefully, you are now convinced that in order to successfully manage your weight you must include exercise in your daily routine. Here are some tips to get you started:

1. Check with your doctor first. Since you are carrying around some extra "baggage," it is wise to get your doctor's "OK" before embarking on an exercise program.
2. Choose activities that you think you'll enjoy. Most people will stick to their exercise program if they are having fun, even though they are working hard.
3. Set aside a regular exercise time. Whether this means joining an exercise class or getting up a little earlier every day, make time for this addition to your routine and don't let anything get in your way. Planning ahead will help you

get around interruptions in your workout schedule, such as bad weather and vacations.

4. Set short term goals. Don't expect to lose 20 pounds in two weeks. It's taken awhile for you to gain the weight, it will take time to lose it. Keep a record of your progress and tell your friends and family about your achievements.

5. Vary your exercise program. Change exercises or invite friends to join you to make your workout more enjoyable. There is no "best" exercise - just the one that works best for you.

It won't be easy, especially at the start. But as you begin to feel better, look better and enjoy a new zest for life, you will be rewarded many times over for your efforts.

Tips to Keep You Going

1. Adopt a specific plan and write it down.
2. Keep setting realistic goals as you go along, and remind yourself of them often.
3. Keep a log to record your progress and make sure to keep it up-to-date.
4. Include weight and/or percent body fat measures in your log. Extra pounds can easily creep back.
5. Upgrade your fitness program as you progress.
6. Enlist the support and company of your family and friends.
7. Update others on your successes.
8. Avoid injuries by pacing yourself and including a warmup and cool down period as part of every workout.
9. Reward yourself periodically for a job well done!

For More Information

Contact the President's Council on Physical Fitness and Sports, 701 Pennsylvania Avenue, Suite 250, Washington, DC 20004; 202-272-3421.

Aging and Your Eyes[*]

Did you know that many older people have good eyesight into their 80's and beyond? Growing older does not always mean you see poorly. But age brings changes that can weaken your eyes.

There are some easy things to try when these changes occur. You might add brighter lights in more places around the house — like at work counters, stairways, and favorite reading places. This may help you see better and can sometimes prevent accidents caused by weak eyesight.

While older people have more eye problems and eye diseases than younger people, you can prevent or correct many of them by:

- Seeing your doctor regularly to check for diseases like diabetes, which could cause eye problems if not treated.
- Having a complete eye exam with an eye specialist every 1 to 2 years. Most eye diseases can be treated when they are found early. The eye doctor should enlarge (dilate) your pupils by putting drops in your eyes. This is the only way to find some eye diseases that have no early signs or symptoms. The eye doctor should test your eyesight, your glasses, and your eye muscles. You should also have a test for glaucoma.
- Taking extra care if you have diabetes or a family history of eye disease. Have an eye exam through dilated pupils every year. See an eye doctor at once if you have any loss or dimness of eyesight, eye pain, fluids coming from the eye, double vision, redness, or swelling of your eye or eyelid.

---

[*] Source: *Age Page*, National Institute on Aging, U.S. Department of Health and Human Services, Public Health Service, National Institutes of Health, Gaithersburg, MD 20898; 800-222-2225.

Common Eye Complaints

Presbyopia (prez-bee-OH-pee-uh) is a slow loss of ability to see close objects or small print. It is a normal process that happens over a lifetime. You may not notice any change until after the age of 40. People with presbyopia often hold reading materials at arm's length. Some get headaches or "tired eyes" while reading or doing other close work. Presbyopia is often corrected with reading glasses.

Floaters are tiny spots or specks that float across the field of vision. Most people notice them in well-lit rooms or outdoors on a bright day. Floaters often are normal, but sometimes they warn of eye problems such as retinal detachment, especially if they happen with light flashes. If you notice a sudden change in the type or number of spots or flashes, see your eye doctor.

Dry eyes happen when tear glands don't make enough tears or make poor quality tears. Dry eyes can be uncomfortable, causing itching, burning, or even some loss of vision. Your eye doctor may suggest using a humidifier in the home or special eye drops ("artificial tears"). Surgery may be needed for more serious cases of dry eyes.

Tearing, or having too many tears, can come from being sensitive to light, wind, or temperature changes. Protecting your eyes (by wearing sunglasses, for instance) sometimes solves the problem. Tearing may also mean that you have a more serious problem, such as an eye infection or a blocked tear duct. Your eye doctor can treat or correct both of these conditions.

Eye Diseases and Disorders
Common in Older People

Cataracts are cloudy areas in part or all of the eye lens. The lens is usually clear and lets light through. Cataracts keep light from easily passing through the lens, and this causes loss of eyesight. Cataracts often form slowly and cause no pain, redness, or tearing in the eye. Some stay small and don't change eyesight very much. If a cataract becomes large or thick, it usually can be removed by surgery. During surgery, the doctor takes off the clouded lens and, in most cases, puts in a clear, plastic lens. Cataract surgery is very safe. It is one of the most common surgeries done in the United States.

Glaucoma results from too much fluid pressure inside the eye. It can lead to vision loss and blindness. The cause of glaucoma is unknown. If treated early, glaucoma often can be controlled and blindness prevented. To find glaucoma, the eye doctor will look at your eyes through dilated pupils. Treatment may be prescription eye drops, oral medications, or surgery. Most people with glaucoma have no early symptoms or pain from increased pressure.

Retinal disorders are a leading cause of blindness in the United States. The retina is a thin lining on the back of the eye. It is made up of cells that get visual images and pass them on to the brain. Retinal disorders include **age-related macular degeneration, diabetic retinopathy,** and **retinal detachment.**

- *Age-related macular degeneration.* The macula is part of the eye with millions of cells that are sensitive to light. The macula makes vision possible from the center part of the eye. Over time, age-related macular degeneration can ruin sharp vision needed to see objects clearly and to do common tasks like driving and reading. In some cases, it can be treated with lasers.
- *Diabetic retinopathy.* This disorder can result from diabetes. It happens when small blood vessels stop feeding the retina properly. In the early stages, the blood vessels may leak fluid, which distorts sight. In the later stages, new vessels may grow and send blood into the center of the eye, causing serious vision loss. In most cases, laser treatment can prevent blindness. It is very important that people with diabetes have an eye exam through dilated pupils every year.

- *Retinal detachment.* This happens when the inner and outer layers of the retina become separated. With surgery or laser treatment, doctors often can reattach the retina and bring back all or part of your eyesight.

Conjunctivitis happens when the tissue that lines the eyelids and covers the cornea becomes inflamed. It can cause itching, burning, tearing, or a feeling of something in the eye. Conjunctivitis can be caused by infection or allergies.

Corneal diseases and conditions can cause redness, watery eyes, pain, reduced vision, or a halo effect. The cornea is the clear, dome-shaped "window" at the front of the eye. It helps to focus light that enters the eye. Disease, infection, injury, toxic agents, and other things can damage the cornea. Treatments include changing the eyeglass prescription, eye drops, or surgery.

Corneal transplantation is used to restore eyesight when the cornea has been hurt by injury or disease. An eye surgeon replaces the scarred cornea with a healthy cornea donated from another person. Corneal transplantation is a common treatment that is safe and successful. The doctor may prescribe eyeglasses or contact lenses after surgery.

Eyelid problems can come from different diseases or condition. The eyelids protect the eye, distribute tears, and limit the amount of light entering the eye. Pain, itching, tearing, and sensitivity to light are common eyelid symptoms. Other problem may include drooping eyelids (ptosis), blinking spasms (blepharospasm), or inflamed outer edges of the eyelids near the eyelashes (blepharitis). Eyelid problems often can be treated with medication or surgery.

Temporal arteritis causes the arteries in the temple area of the forehead to become swollen. It can begin with a severe headache, pain when chewing, and tenderness in the temple area. It may be followed in a few weeks by sudden vision loss. Other symptoms can include shaking, weight loss, and low-grade fever. Scientists don't know the cause of temporal arteritis, but they think it may be a disorder of the immune system. early treatment with medication can help prevent vision loss in one or both eyes.

Low Vision Aids

Many people with eyesight problems find low vision aids helpful. These are special devices that are stronger than regular eyeglasses. Low vision aids include telescopic glasses, lenses that filter light, and magnifying glasses. Also, there are some useful electronic devices that you can either hold in your hand or put directly on your reading material. People with only partial sight often make surprising improvements using these aids.

Resources

A number of organizations can send you more information:

The National Eye Institute (NEI), part of the National Institutes of Health (NIH), supports research on eye disease and the visual system. NEI can send you free brochures on eye disorders. Write to the NEI, 2020 Vision Place, Bethesda, MD 20892-3655; or call 301-496-5248.

The American Foundation for the Blind can send a list of their free publications on vision. Contact the Foundation at 11 Penn Plaza, Suite 300, New York, NY 10001; or call 1-800-232-5463.

The American Optometric Association provides free information to the public about vision and eye care. Contact the Association at 243 North Lindbergh Boulevard, St. Louis, MO 63141; or call 314-991-4100.

The Lighthouse National Center for Vision and Aging serves as a national clearinghouse for information on vision and aging. Contact the Center at 11 East 59th Street, New York, NY 10022; or call 800-334-5497.

The National Association for the Visually Handicapped is a voluntary health agency that works with people who can partially see. Contact the Association at 22 West 21st Street, New York, NY 10010; or call 212-889-3141.

Resources (continued)

The National Eye Care Project of the American Academy of Ophthalmology (AAO) has a helpline number to refer callers to local ophthalmologists who will volunteer to provide needed medical care. This public service program brings eye care and information to disadvantaged older people. Contact the AAO at P.O. Box 6988, San Francisco, CA 94120-6988; or call 800-222-EYES.

The National Library Service for the Blind and Visually Handicapped provides free library services to people with vision problems and offers braille and large-print materials, recorded books, and other periodicals. Contact the Service at 1291 Taylor Street, NW, Washington, DC 20542; or call 800-424-8567.

The National Society to Prevent Blindness has several free pamphlets on specific diseases affecting the eyes. They also have *Home Eye Test for Adults*, which is available for $1.25 (to cover the cost of postage and handling). Contact the Society at 500 East Remington Road, Schaumburg, IL 60173-5611; or call 800-331-2020.

The Vision Foundation publishes the *Vision Resource List*, which includes information on special products and service for people with visual impairments. Contact the Foundation at 818 Mt. Auburn Street, Watertown, MA 02172; or call 617-926-4232.

The National Institute on Aging (NIA), part of the NIH, distributes *Age Pages* and other materials on a wide range of topics related to health and aging. For a list of free publications, contact the NIA Information Center, P.O. Box 8057, Gaithersburg, MD 20898-8057; 800-222-2225, 800-222-4225 (TTY).

Preventing Falls and Fractures[*]

An injury from falling can limit a person's ability to lead an active, independent life. This is especially true for older people. Each year thousands of older men and women are disabled, sometimes permanently, by falls that result in broken bones. Yet many of these injuries could be prevented by making simple changes in the home.

As people age, changes in their vision, hearing, muscle strength, coordination, and reflexes may make them more likely to fall. Older persons also are more likely to have treatable disorders that may affect their balance — such as diabetes or conditions of the heart, nervous system, and thyroid. In addition, compared with younger people, older persons often take more medications that may cause dizziness or lightheadedness.

Preventing falls is especially important for people who have osteoporosis, a condition in which bone mass decreases so that bones are more fragile and break easily. Osteoporosis is a major cause of bone fractures in women after menopause and older people in general. For people with severe osteoporosis, even a minor fall may cause one or more bones to break.

Steps to Take

Falls and accidents seldom "just happen," and many can be prevented. Each of us can take steps to make our homes safer and reduce the likelihood of falling. Here are some guidelines to help prevent falls and fractures.

- Have your vision and hearing tested regularly and properly corrected.
- Talk to your doctor or pharmacist about the side effects of

---

* Source: *Age Page*, National Institute on Aging, U.S. Department of Health and Human Services, Public Health Service, National Institutes of Health, Gaithersburg, MD 20898; 800-222-2225.

the medicines you are taking and whether they affect your coordination or balance. Ask for suggestions to reduce the possibility of falling.

- Limit your intake of alcohol. Even a small amount of alcohol can disturb already impaired balance and reflexes.
- Use caution in getting up too quickly after eating, lying down, or resting. Low blood pressure may cause dizziness at these times.
- Make sure that the nighttime temperature in your home is at least 65°F. Prolonged exposure to cold temperatures may cause a drop in body temperature, which in turn may lead to dizziness and falling. Many older people cannot tolerate cold as well as younger people can.
- Use a cane, walking stick, or walker to help maintain balance on uneven or unfamiliar ground or if you sometimes feel dizzy. Use special caution in walking outdoors on wet and icy pavement
- Wear supportive rubber-soled or low-heeled shoes. Avoid wearing smooth-soled slippers or only socks on stairs and waxed floors. They make it very easy to slip.
- Maintain a regular program of exercise to improve strength and muscle tone, and keep your joints, tendons, and ligaments more flexible. Many older people enjoy walking and swimming. Mild weight-bearing activities, such as walking or climbing stairs, may even reduce the loss of bone due to osteoporosis. Check with your doctor or physical therapist to plan a suitable exercise program.

Make Your Home Safe

Many older people fall because of hazardous conditions at home. Use this checklist to help you safeguard against some likely hazards.

Stairways, hallways, and pathways should have:
- good lighting and be free of clutter,
- firmly attached carpet, rough texture, or abrasive strips to

secure footing,
- tightly fastened handrails running the whole length and along both sides of all stairs, with light switches at the top and bottom.

Bathrooms should have:
- grab bars located in and out of tubs and showers and near toilets,
- nonskid mats, abrasive strips, or carpet on all surfaces that may get wet,
- nightlights.

Bedrooms should have:
- nightlights or light switches within reach of bed(s).
- telephones (easy to reach), near the bed(s).

Living areas should have:
- electrical cords and telephone wires placed away from walking paths,
- rugs well secured to the floor,
- furniture (especially low coffee tables) and other objects arranged so they are not in the way,
- couches and chairs at proper height to get into and out of easily.

For More Information

For more complete information on simple, relatively inexpensive repairs and safety recommendations for your home, write to the U.S. Consumer Product Safety Commission, Washington, DC 20207; or call 800-638-2772. The Commission also can send you a free copy of the booklet *Home Safety Checklist for Older Consumers.*

The National Institute on Aging offers information on health and aging. For a complete list of publications, write to the NIA Information Center, P.O. Box 8057, Gaithersburg, MD 20898-8057.

What To Do About Flu[*]

Each winter, millions of people suffer from the "flu." For most people, the best treatment is a few days of bed rest, aspirin for fever, and plenty of water, fruit juice, soft drinks, and other liquids.

Flu — the short name for influenza — is a viral infection of the nose, throat, and lungs. It is usually a mild disease in healthy children, young adults, and middle-age people. However, flu can be life-threatening in older people and in people of any age who have chronic illnesses such as heart disease, emphysema, asthma, bronchitis, kidney disease, or diabetes.

When you have the flu your body's ability to fight off other infections is lowered and other more serious infections can occur, especially pneumonia. It is very important for older people to prevent flu, because treating it can be harder as people age. You can prevent flu with a shot. People age 50 and older need to get a flu shot every year.

It is easy to confuse a common cold with the flu. But, a cold usually doesn't cause a fever — the flu does. Also, a cold causes a stuffy nose more often than flu does. Overall, cold symptoms are milder and don't last as long as the flu.

People used to think the flu was caused by the "influence of the stars and planets." In the 1500's, the Italians called the disease "influenza," their word for influence.

Symptoms

Flu symptoms can differ from person to person. Some people have no obvious symptoms. Often, however, people with the flu feel weak, develop a cough, a headache, and a sudden rise in

---

[*] Source: *Age Page*, National Institute on Aging, U.S. Department of Health and Human Services, Public Health Service, National Institutes of Health, Gaithersburg, MD 20898; 800-222-2225.

temperature. The fever can last from one to six days. Other symptoms include aching muscles, chills, and red, watery eyes.

Complications of Flu

The flu is rarely fatal. But while your body is busy fighting off the flu, you may be less able to resist a second infection. Older people and people with chronic diseases have the greatest risk of developing these secondary infections. If this second infection is in the lungs — such as pneumonia — it can be life-threatening. Pneumonia is one of the five leading causes of death among people 65 and older.

The symptoms of pneumonia are similar to the flu but are much more severe. Shaking chills are very common. Coughing becomes more frequent and may produce a colored discharge. The fever will continue during pneumonia and will stay high. Pain in the chest may occur as the lungs become more inflamed.

Sometimes pneumonia — an inflammation of the lungs — is caused by flu virus. More often it is the result of bacteria. Bacterial pneumonia is usually treated with antibiotics, such as penicillin. Antibiotic drugs, which kill bacteria, are very effective if given when you first get pneumonia.

One of the most dangerous complications of pneumonia is the body's loss of fluids. Your doctor will prescribe extra fluids to prevent shock, a serious condition caused by inadequate blood flow.

What Causes Flu?

Scientists discovered in the late 1930's and early 1940's that flu is caused by viruses that enter your system and begin to multiply rapidly. When there are too many viruses for the body to fight off, you get the flu.

The flu can be passed easily from one person to another. When someone infected with the flu coughs or sneezes, droplets with the virus may reach another person, entering their body through the nose or mouth. There, the viruses can multiply and cause flu.

Prevention

Vaccination is the most common form of prevention. The vaccine available today is very effective.

Because older people may have complications from flu, many doctors suggest they get a flu shot each fall. A low fever or redness at the injection site are possible side effects of the shot. For most people the danger from getting flu and possibly pneumonia is greater than the danger from the side effects of the shot. One exception is people who are allergic to eggs; flu vaccines are made in egg products and may cause serious reactions in people who have such allergies.

Preventing flu is hard because the virus changes all the time and in unpredictable ways. The virus this year is usually slightly different from the virus last year. That's why flu shots are good for only one year.

You also can get a shot to prevent pneumococcal pneumonia. This is the type of pneumonia that most older people get. The shot has few side effects and you only need to get it once. It is covered by Medicare. If you haven't had the pneumonia shot (or if you aren't sure), ask your doctor.

Treatment

The usual treatment for the aches and pains of the flu is to take aspirin, drink plenty of liquids, and stay in bed until the fever has been gone for one or two days. Call your doctor if the fever lasts; this may mean a more serious infection is present. An antiviral drug, amantadine, also is recommended to prevent and treat many types of influenza, particularly in high-risk people.

Scientists continue to look for ways to prevent and treat the flu. In the meantime, the Public Health Service's Advisory Committee on Immunization Practices encourages people 65 and older and others with chronic illnesses to get a yearly flu shot.

Resources

The National Institute of Allergy and Infectious Diseases has prepared the brochure *Flu*. For single copies, write to the NIAID, Building 31, Room 7A50, Bethesda, MD 20892.

For more information about health and aging, contact the National Institute on Aging (NIA) Information Center, P.O. Box 8057, Gaithersburg, MD 20898-8057; 800-222-2225, 800-222-4225 (TTY). The NIA distributes free *Age Pages* on a number of topics, including "Shots for Safety" and "Pneumonia Prevention: It's Worth a Shot."

Foot Care[*]

Disease, years of wear and tear, ill-fitting or poorly designed shoes, poor circulation to the feet, or improperly trimmed toenails cause many common foot problems.

To prevent foot problems, check your feet regularly — or, have them checked by a member of the family — and practice good foot hygiene. Podiatrists and primary care physicians (internists and family practitioners) are qualified to treat most feet problems; sometimes the special skills of an orthopedic surgeon or dermatologist are needed.

Preventing Foot Trouble

Improving the circulation of blood to the feet can help prevent problems. Exposure to cold temperatures or water, pressure from shoes, long periods of sitting, or smoking can reduce blood flow to the feet. Even sitting with your legs crossed or wearing tight, elastic garters or socks can affect circulation. On the other hand, raising the feet, standing up and stretching, walking, and other forms of exercise promote good circulation. Gentle massage and warm foot baths can also help increase circulation to the feet.

Wearing comfortable shoes that fit well can prevent many foot ailments. Foot width may increase with age. Always have your feet measured before buying shoes. The upper part of the shoes should be made of a soft, flexible material to match the shape of your foot. Shoes made of leather can reduce the possibility of skin irritations. Soles should provide solid footing and not be slippery. Thick soles lessen pressure when walking on hard surfaces. Low-heeled shoes are more comfortable, safer, and less damaging to the feet than high-heeled shoes.

---

[*] Source: *Age Page*, National Institute on Aging, U.S. Department of Health and Human Services, Public Health Service, National Institutes of Health, Gaithersburg, MD 20898; 800-222-2225.

Common Foot Problems

Fungal and bacterial conditions — including athlete's foot — occur because the feet are usually enclosed in a dark, damp, warm environment. These infections cause redness, blisters, peeling, and itching. If not treated promptly, an infection may become chronic and difficult to cure. To prevent these conditions, keep the feet — especially the area between the toes — clean and dry and expose the feet to air whenever possible. If you are prone to fungal infections, you may want to dust you feet daily with a fungicidal powder.

Dry skin can cause itching and burning feet. Use mild soap sparingly and a body lotion on your legs and feet every day. The best moisturizers contain petroleum jelly or lanolin. Be cautious about adding oils to bath water since they can make the feet and bathtub very slippery.

Corns and calluses are caused by the friction and pressure of bony areas rubbing against shoes. A podiatrist or a physician can determine the cause of this condition and can suggest treatment, which may include getting better-fitting shoes or special pads. Over-the-counter medicines, contain acids that destroy the tissue but do not treat the cause. These medicines can sometimes reduce the need for surgery. Treating corns or calluses yourself may be harmful, especially if you have diabetes or poor circulation.

Warts are skin growths caused by viruses. They are sometimes painful and if untreated, may spread. Since over-the-counter preparations rarely cure warts, get professional care. A doctor can apply medicines, burn or freeze the wart off, or remove it surgically.

Bunions develop when big toe joints are out of line and become swollen and tender. Bunions may be caused by poor-fitting shoes that press on a deformity or an inherited weakness in the foot. If a bunion is not severe, wearing shoes cut wide at the instep and toes may provide relief. Protective pads can also cushion the painful area. Bunions can be treated by applying or injecting certain drugs, using whirlpool baths, or sometimes having surgery.

Ingrown toenails occur when a piece of the nail breaks the skin. This is usually caused by improperly trimmed nails. Ingrown toenails are especially common in the large toes. A podiatrist or doctor can remove the part of the nail that is cutting into the skin. This allows the area to heal. Ingrown toenails can usually be avoided by cutting the toenail straight across and level with the top of the toe.

Hammertoe is caused by shortening the tendons that control toe movement. The toe knuckle is usually enlarged, drawing the toe back. Over time, the joint enlarges and stiffens as it rubs against shoes. your balance may be affected. Hammertoe is treated by wearing shoes and stockings with plenty of toe room. In advanced cases, surgery may be recommended.

Spurs are calcium growths that develop on the bones of the feet. They are caused by muscle strain in the feet and are irritated by standing for long periods of time, wearing badly fitting shoes, or being overweight. Sometimes they are completely painless, but at other times the pain can be severe. Treatment for spurs include using proper foot support, heel pads, heel cups, or other recommendations by a podiatrist or surgeon.

Resources

For more information on foot care, write to either of the following:

American Podiatric Medical Association, 9312 Old Georgetown Rd., Bethesda, MD 20814.

American Orthopedic Foot and Ankle Society, 222 South Prospect, Park Ridge, IL 60068.

The National Institute on Aging offers a variety of information about health and aging. For a list of publications, contact: NIA Information Center, P.O. Box 8057, Gaithersburg, MD 20898-8057; 800-222-2225, 800-222-4225 (TTY).

Hearing and Older People[*]

About one-third of Americans between age 65 and 74 and one-half of those age 85 and older have hearing problems. They may mistake words in a conversation, miss musical notes at a concert, or leave a ringing doorbell unanswered. Hearing problems can be small (missing certain sounds) or large (involving total deafness).

Some people may not admit they are having trouble hearing. But, if ignored or untreated, these problems can get worse. Older people who can't hear well may become depressed or withdraw from others to avoid the frustration or embarrassment of not understanding what is being said. They may become suspicious of relatives or friends who they believe "mumble" or "don't speak up" on purpose. It's easy to mistakenly call older people confused, unresponsive, or uncooperative just because they don't hear well. If you have a hearing problem, you can get help. See your doctor. Special training, hearing aids, certain medicines, and surgery are some of the choices that could help people with hearing problems.

Diagnosis of Hearing Problems

Hearing loss can be caused by exposure to very loud noises over a long period of time, viral or bacterial infections, heart conditions or stroke, head injuries, tumors, certain medicines, heredity, or changes in the ear that happen with aging.

If you have trouble with your hearing, see your family doctor. In some cases, the diagnosis and treatment can take place in his or her office. Or you may be referred to an **otolaryngologist (oto-larin-GOL-o-jist)**. This doctor has special training in the ear, nose, and throat and other areas related to the head and neck. He or she will take a medical history, ask if other family members have hearing problems, do a thorough exam, and order any needed tests.

---

[*] Source: *Age Page*, National Institute on Aging, U.S. Department of Health and Human Services, Public Health Service, National Institutes of Health, Gaithersburg, MD 20898; 800-222-2225.

An **audiologist (aw-dee-OL-i-jist)** is a health professional who can identify and measure hearing loss. He or she may work with the otolaryngologist. The audiologist will use a device called an audiometer to test your ability to hear sounds at different pitches and loudness. The tests are painless. Audiologists do not prescribe drugs or perform surgery.

Common Signs of Hearing Problems

See your doctor if:

* words are hard to understand,
* another person's speech sounds slurred or mumbled, especially if it gets worse when there is background noise,
* certain sounds are overly annoying or loud,
* a hissing or ringing in the background is heard,
* TV shows, concerts, or parties are less enjoyable because you have a hard time hearing.

Types of Hearing Loss

Presbycusis (prez-bee-KU-sis) is the most common hearing problem in older people. In fact, people over age 50 are likely to lose some hearing each year. Presbycusis is an ongoing loss of hearing linked to changes in the inner ear. People with this kind of hearing loss may have a hard time hearing what others are saying or may be unable to stand loud sounds. The decline is slow. Just as hair turns gray at different rates, presbycusis develops at different rates.

Tinnitus (ti-NI-tus) is also common in older people. Tinnitus is a symptom associated with a variety of hearing diseases and disorders. People with tinnitus have a ringing, roaring, or hear other sounds inside the ears. It may be caused by ear wax, an ear infection, the use of too much aspirin or certain antibiotics, or a nerve disorder. Often, the reason for the ringing cannot be found. Tinnitus can come and go; or it can stop altogether.

Conductive hearing loss happens in some older people when the sounds that are carried from the ear drums (tympanic membrane) to the inner ear are blocked. Ear wax in the ear canal, fluid in the middle ear, abnormal bone growth, or a middle ear infection can cause this loss.

Sensorineural (sen-so-ree-NU-ral) hearing loss happens when there is damage to parts of the inner ear or auditory nerve. The degree of hearing loss can vary from person to person. Sensorineural hearing loss may be caused by birth defects, head injury, tumors, illness, certain prescription drugs, poor blood circulation, high blood pressure, or stroke.

If Someone You Know Has a Hearing Problem:

- Face the person and talk clearly.
- Stand where there is good lighting and low background noise.
- Speak clearly and at a reasonable speed; do not hide your mouth, eat, or chew gum.
- Use facial expressions or gestures to give useful clues.
- Reword your statement if needed.
- Be patient, stay positive and relaxed.
- Ask how you can help the listener.
- Set up meetings so that all speakers can be seen or can use a microphone.
- Include the hearing-impaired person in all discussions about him or her to prevent feelings or isolation.

If You Have a Hearing Problem

- Tell others that you have trouble hearing,
- Ask others to face you, speak more slowly and clearly, and not to shout.
- Pay attention to what is being said and to facial expressions or gestures.
- Let the person talking know if you do not understand what is being said; ask for the statement to be repeated or reworded.

Hearing Aids

If you are having trouble hearing, the doctor may suggest using a hearing aid. This is a small device that you put in your ear to make sounds louder. Before buying a hearing aid, you must get a written medical evaluation or sign a waiver saying that you do not want a medical evaluation.

There are many kinds or hearing aids. An audiologist will consider your hearing level, ability to understand speech, comfort in using the controls, and concern for how it looks. He or she will then suggest the specific design, model, and brand of hearing aid that best suits your needs.

> ### Tips to Recognize Hearing Loss
>
> See your doctor if you have:
>
> - difficulty hearing over the telephone,
> - trouble following a conversation when two or more people are talking at the same time,
> - others complaining that you make the TV too loud,
> - to strain to understand conversations,
> - problems hearing because of background noise,
> - the sense that others seem to mumble,
> - difficulty understanding women and children talking.

When you buy a hearing aid, remember you are buying a product and a service. You will need fitting adjustments, directions to use the aid, and repairs during the warranty period.

Be sure to buy a hearing aid that has only the features you need. The most costly product may not be the best model for you, while the one selling for less may be just right. Be aware that the controls for many hearing aids are tiny and can be hard to adjust. This often gets easier with practice. Find a hearing aid dealer (called a dispenser) who has the patience and skill to help you during the month or so it takes you to get used to the new hearing aid.

For More Information

More information about hearing loss is available from the following groups.

American Academy of Otolaryngology — Head and Neck Surgery, Inc. (AAO-HNS), One Prince Street, Alexandria, VA 22314; 703-836-4444, 703-519-1585 (TTY).
AAO-HNS is an organization of medical doctors who specialize in care of the ear, nose, throat, head, and neck. Contact AAO-HNS for physician referrals. Send a stamped, self-addressed business envelope to receive single copies of AAO-HNS publications.

American Speech-Language-Hearing Association (ASHA), 10801 Rockville Pike, Rockville, MD 20852; ASHA Helpline: 800-638-8255 (Voice/TTY).
ASHA is a nonprofit organization of professionals concerned with communication sciences and disorders. ASHA offers information about hearing aids or hearing loss and communication problems in older people. They can provide a list of certified audiologists and speech-language pathologists.

American Tinnitus Association (ATA), P.O. Box 5, Portland, OR 97207-0005; 800-634-8978.
ATA provides information about tinnitus and makes professional referrals. ATA supports a nationwide network of self-help groups for people with tinnitus and their families. Public information includes materials about prevention and treatment.

Self Help for Hard of Hearing People, Inc. (SHHH), 7910 Woodmont Avenue, Suite 1200, Bethesda, MD 20814; 301-657-2248, 301-657-2249 (TTY).
SHHH is an international volunteer organization composed of people who are hard of hearing, their relatives, and friends. SHHH provides self-help programs and referrals to local chapters. Contact them for a list of available publications.

National Information Center on Deafness (NICD), Gallaudet University, 800 Florida Avenue, NE, Washington, DC 20002; 202-651-5051, 202-651-5052 (TTY).
NICD provides fact sheets, resource listings, and reading lists on all aspects of deafness and hearing loss including educational programs, vocational training, sign language programs, legal issues, technology, and barrier-free design.

For More Information (continued)

National Institute on Deafness and Other Communication Disorders (NIDCD), National Institutes of Health, 31 Center Dr., MSC 2320, Bethesda, MD 20892-2320; NIDCD Information Clearinghouse: 800-241-1044, 800-241-1055 (TTY).
NIDCD conducts and supports biomedical and behavioral research and training and the dissemination of information on disorders of hearing, balance, smell, taste, voice, speech, and language. The NIDCD Clearinghouse offers information to health professionals, patients, industry representatives, and the public.

For more information about health and aging contact the **National Institute on Aging Information Center**, P.O. Box 8057, Gaithersburg, MD 20898-8057; 800-222-2225, 800-222-4225 (TTY).

Expert Health Advice

Check Your Weight and
Heart Disease I.Q.*

The following statements are either true or false. The statements test your knowledge of overweight and heart disease. The correct answers can be found at the end of this chapter.

T F 1. Being overweight puts you at risk for heart disease.

T F 2   If you are overweight, losing weight helps lower your high blood cholesterol and high blood pressure.

T F 3   Quitting smoking is healthy, but it commonly leads to excessive weight gain which increases your risk for heart disease.

T F 4   An overweight person with high blood pressure should pay more attention to a low-sodium diet than to weight reduction.

T F 5   A reduced intake of sodium or salt does not always lower high blood pressure to normal.

T F 6   The best way to lose weight is to eat fewer calories and exercise.

T F 7   Skipping meals is a good way to cut down on calories.

T F 8   Foods high in complex carbohydrates (starch and fiber) are good choices when you are trying to lose weight.

T F 9   The since most important change most people can make to lose weight is to avoid sugar.

---

* Source: National Heart, Lung, and Blood Institute, National Institutes of Health, Gaithersburg, MD 20898; 301-251-1222.

T F 10 Polyunsaturated fat has the same number of calories as saturated fat.

T F 11 Overweight children are very likely to become overweight adults.

YOUR SCORE: How many correct answers did you make?

10-11 correct = Congratulations! You know a lot about weight and heart disease. Share this information with your family and friends.

8-9 correct = Very good.

Fewer than 8 = Go over the answers and try to learn more about weight and heart disease.

Answers to Your Weight and Heart Disease I.Q. Test

1 True. Being overweight increases your risk for high blood cholesterol and high blood pressure, two of the major risk factors for coronary heart disease. Even if you do not have high blood cholesterol or high blood pressure, being overweight may increase your risk for heart disease. Where you carry your extra weight may affect your risk too. Weight carried at your waist or above seems to be associated with an increased risk for heart disease in many people. In addition, being overweight increases your risk for diabetes, gallbladder disease, and some types of cancer.

2 True. If you are overweight, even moderate reductions in weight, such as 5 to 10 percent, can produce substantial reductions in blood pressure. You may also be able to reduce your LDL-cholesterol ("bad" cholesterol) and triglycerides and increase your HDL-cholesterol ("good" cholesterol).

3 False. The average weight gain after quitting smoking is 5 pounds. The proportion of ex-smokers who gain large amounts

of weight (greater than 20 pounds) is relatively small. Even if you gain weight when you stop smoking, change your eating and exercise habits to lose weight rather than starting to smoke again. Smokers who quit smoking decrease their risk for heart disease by about 50 percent compared to those people who do not quit.

4   False. Weight loss, if you are overweight, may reduce your blood pressure even if you don't reduce the amount of sodium you eat. Weight loss is recommended for all overweight people who have high blood pressure. Even if weight loss does not reduce your blood pressure to normal, it may help you cut back on your blood pressure medications. Also, losing weight if you are overweight may help you reduce your risk for or control other health problems.

5   True. Even though a high sodium or salt intake plays a key role in maintaining high blood pressure in some people, there is no easy way to determine who will benefit from eating less sodium and salt. Also, a high intake may limit how well certain high blood pressure medications work. Eating a diet with less sodium may help some people reduce their risk of developing high blood pressure. Most Americans eat more salt and other sources of sodium than they need. Therefore, it is prudent for most people to reduce their sodium intake.

6   True. Eating fewer calories and exercising more is the best way to lose weight and keep it off. Weight control is a question of balance. You get calories from the food you eat. You burn off calories by exercising. Cutting down on calories, especially calories from fat, is key to losing weight. Combining this with a regular exercise program, like walking, bicycling, jogging, or swimming, not only can help in losing weight but also in maintaining the weight loss. A steady weight loss of 1 to 2 pounds a week is safe for most adults, and the weight is more likely to stay off over the long run. Losing weight, if you are overweight, may also help reduce your blood pressure and raise your HDL cholesterol, the "good" cholesterol.

7 False. To cut calories, some people regularly skip meals and have no snacks or caloric drinks in between. If you do this, your body thinks that it is starving even if your intake of calories is not reduced to a very low amount. Your body will try to save energy by slowing its metabolism, that is decreasing the rate at which it burns calories. This makes losing weight even harder and may even add body fat. Try to avoid long periods without eating. Five or six small meals are often preferred to the usual three meals a day for some individuals trying to lose weight.

8 True. Contrary to popular belief, foods high in complex carbohydrates (like pasta, rice, potatoes, breads, cereals, grains, dried beans and peas) are lower in calories than foods high in fat. In addition, they are good sources of vitamins, minerals, and fiber. What adds calories to these foods is the addition of butter, rich sauces, whole milk, cheese, or cream, which are high in fat.

9 False. Sugar has not been found to cause obesity; however, many foods high in sugar are also high in fat. Fat has more than twice the calories as the same amount of protein or carbohydrates (sugar and starch). Thus, foods that are high in fat are high in calories. High-sugar foods, like cakes, cookies, candies, and ice cream, are high in fat and calories and low in vitamins, minerals, and protein.

10 True. All fats — polyunsaturated, monounsaturated, and saturated — have the same number of calories. All calories count whether they come from saturated or unsaturated fats. Because fats are the richest sources of calories, eating less total fat win help reduce the number of calories you eat every day. It will also help you reduce your intake of saturated fat. Particular attention to reducing saturated fat is important in lowering your blood cholesterol level.

11 False. Obesity in childhood does increase the likelihood of adult obesity, but most overweight children will not become obese. Several factors influence whether or not an overweight child becomes an overweight adult: (1) the age the child becomes overweight; (2) how overweight the child is; (3) the family history of overweight; and (4) dietary and activity habits. Getting to the right weight is desirable, but children's needs for calories and other nutrients are different from the needs of adults. Dietary plans for weight control must allow for this. Eating habits, like so many other habits, are often formed during childhood, so it is important to develop good ones.

For More Information

For more information, write: NHLBI Obesity Education Initiative, P.O. Box 30105, Bethesda, MD 20824-0105.

Heat, Cold, and Being Old[*]

As you get older, your body becomes less able to respond to long exposure to heat or cold. In cold weather, some older people may develop accidental hypothermia (hi-po-thur-mee-uh), a drop in internal body temperature that can be fatal if not detected and treated promptly. During hot and humid weather, a buildup in body heat can cause heat stroke or heat exhaustion in the elderly. This is especially true of those with heart and circulatory disease, stroke, or diabetes.

Accidental Hypothermia

Hypothermia is a condition of below-normal body temperature — typically 95°F (35°C) or under. *Accidental* hypothermia may occur in anyone who is exposed to severe cold without enough protection. However, some older people can develop accidental hypothermia after exposure to relatively mild cold.

Those elderly most likely to develop accidental hypothermia are: the chronically ill, the poor who are unable to afford enough heating fuel, and those who do not take the normal steps to keep warm. The small number of aged persons whose temperature regulation is defective face the greatest danger. For unknown reasons, these people do not feel cold or shiver, and thus cannot produce body heat when they need it. It is interesting to note that many people who have "felt cold" for years may actually have a lower risk of accidental hypothermia.

The only sure way to detect hypothermia is to use a special low-reading thermometer, available in most hospitals. A regular thermometer will do as long as you shake it down well. If the temperature is below 95°F (35°C) or does not register, get emergency medical help. Other signs to look for include: an

---

[*] Source: *Age Page*, National Institute on Aging, U.S. Department of Health and Human Services, Public Health Service, National Institutes of Health, Gaithersburg, MD 20898; 800-222-2225.

Expert Health Advice

unusual change in appearance or behavior during cold weather; slow, and sometimes irregular, heartbeat; slurred speech; shallow, very slow breathing; sluggishness; and confusion. Treatment consists of rewarming the person under a doctor's supervision, preferably in a hospital.

Heat-Related Illnesses

Heat stroke is a medical emergency requiring immediate attention and treatment by a doctor. Among the symptoms are: faintness, dizziness, headache, nausea, loss of consciousness, body temperature of 104°F (40°C) or higher, measured rectally, rapid pulse, and flushed skin.

Heat exhaustion takes longer to develop than other heat-related illnesses. It results from a loss of body water and salt. The symptoms include: weakness, heavy sweating, nausea, and giddiness. Heat exhaustion is treated by resting in bed away from the heat and drinking cool liquids.

Protective Measures

In Cold Weather: There is no strong scientific basis for recommending specific room temperatures for older people. However, setting the heat at 65°F (18.3°C) in living and sleeping areas should be adequate in most cases, although sick people may need more heat.

Measures you can take to prevent accidental hypothermia include:

- Dress warmly even when indoors, eat enough food, and stay as active as possible.
- Because hypothermia may start during sleep, keep warm in bed by wearing enough clothing and using blankets.
- If you take medicine to treat anxiety, depression, nervousness, or nausea, ask your doctor whether the medication might affect the control of body temperature.
- Ask friends or neighbors to look in on you once or twice a

day, particularly during a cold spell. See if your community has a telephone check-in or personal visit service for the elderly or homebound.

In Hot Weather: The best precaution is to remain indoors in an air-conditioned room. If your home is not air-conditioned, you might go to a cool public place (like a library, movie theater, or store) during the hottest hours.

Other good ways to cool off include taking baths or showers, placing icebags or wet towels on the body, and using electric fans (being careful to avoid getting an electrical shock). In addition, it is wise to:

- Stay out of direct sunlight and avoid strenuous activity.
- Wear lightweight, light-colored, loose-fitting clothing that permits sweat to evaporate.
- Drink plenty of liquids such as water, fruit and vegetable juices, and iced tea to replace the fluids lost by sweating. Try not to drink alcoholic beverages or fluids that have too much salt, since salt can complicate existing medical problems, such as high blood pressure. Use salt tablets only with your doctor's approval.
- Above all, take the heat seriously, and don't ignore danger signs like nausea, dizziness, and fatigue.

Contact for Assistance

Anyone trying to save on fuel costs can protect against hypothermia by dressing warmly and heating only one or two rooms of the home. There are government-funded programs to help low-income families pay high energy bills, weatherize (insulate) their homes, or even get emergency repairs of heating/cooling units. Your local community action agency or area agency on aging should be able to direct you to the proper source of assistance.

Caution, common sense, and prompt medical attention can help older people avoid illnesses due to heat and cold. For the brochure *A Winter Hazard for the Old: Accidental Hypothermia*, write to the National Institute on Aging, Box HYPO, Building 31, Room 5C35, Bethesda, MD 20892.

Eat Right to Lower
Your High Blood Cholesterol[*]

240 Is Too High

He said: "My doctor told me I have high blood cholesterol."

She said: "What is high blood cholesterol?"

He said: "240 and over. That means I have a greater chance for heart disease."

She said: "Does that mean you could have a heart attack?"

He said: "Yes. But, if I lower my high blood cholesterol, I will reduce my chance for heart disease and heart attack. I will try to lower my cholesterol to under 200. That is a desirable level."

"You should know your cholesterol level too."

She said: "That is a good idea. The next time I go to the doctor I will get my level checked."

You Can Lower It

She said: "If it is high, can I really lower it?"

He said: "Yes. That is the good news. The doctor told me to:

- eat fewer foods high in saturated fat and cholesterol, and
- lose weight, since I weigh too much.

The doctor explained the diet to me. He also gave me a booklet. This will remind me what to do."

---

* Source: National Cholesterol Education Program, National Heart Lung and Blood, Institute, P.O. Box 30105, Bethesda, MD 20824-0105; 301-251-1222.

Expert Health Advice

She said: "I feel better knowing that we can lower our blood cholesterol levels."

He said: "Me too. It's a good feeling. Eating less saturated fat and cholesterol is good for almost everyone."

She said: "That is true. We should change the way we eat."

Make Some Changes

He said: "Let's decide what to change first. We can change how we fix our meals. We can also change what foods we buy. We can buy foods low in saturated fat more often."

She said: "I plan to shop soon. Let's decide now what I should buy."

Food High In Saturated Fat

Animal fats (like butter, lard, beef and pork fat, fat back, salt pork, bacon and sausage grease)

Foods fried in animal fats

Gravy

Fatty meat (like corned beef, regular ground beef, ribs, sausage, hot dogs, bacon, bologna, salami)

Whole milk, cream, ice cream

Most cheeses (like cream cheese, cheddar, American, Swiss)

Cheese Danish

Many cakes, cookies, and pies

Food High In Cholesterol

Egg yolks

liver

kidney

Fix Foods The Low Fat Way

He said: "Looks like we have lots of food to choose from. Even before we shop, we can start fixing foods the low fat way."

She said: "Listen to these tips on how to fix foods the low fat way."

- Trim the fat from meat before cooking.

- Bake or broil meat. Do not fry.
- Cook meat on a rack so the fat will drip off.
- When we use fat or oil, use less of it.
- Take the skin off chicken and turkey.

She said: "Tonight I will take the skin off the chicken and then roll it in bread crumbs. Instead of frying it, I will bake it. It will stir be crunchy so we won't miss the skin.

Choosing the right foods and fixing them the low fat way seems easy enough. I bet we can have some pretty good meals."

He said: "We could start packing our lunches and snacks for work. It is cheaper than buying out and we get what is good for us."

She said: "Fruits and low fat cookies are easy to pack for snacks. These are lower in saturated fat than doughnuts or popcorn with butter."

He said: "What about breakfast? I know sausage and bacon are high in saturated fat."

Buy More Often...

Lean cuts of meat, poultry, fish
Skim or 1% milk
Low fat cottage cheese, low fat yogurt
Part-skim milk cheeses (like part-skim mozzarella)
Vegetable oils
Margarine (plain), fresh, frozen, or canned vegetables and fruit
Baking potatoes, rice, pasta
English muffins, bagels, loaf breads, tortillas, pita bread
Cold and hot cereals

Buy Less Often...

Fatty cuts of meat, breaded poultry or fish
Whole milk, cream
Cheese spreads and cheeses (like cheddar, American, Swiss)
Lard, butter, fat back, salt pork, shortening
Toppings (like butter, cheese sauces, gravy, sour cream)
Vegetables in cream or cheese sauces
French fries or hash browns
Doughnuts, Danish pastry
Desserts (like many cakes, cookies, and pies)

She said: "We can have cereals, breads, and fruits more often for breakfast. They are quick to fix and easy to clean up. We could even have sand- wiches or leftovers for breakfast or toast frozen pancakes."

He said: "I like those ideas. Let's start tomorrow."

Menu Ideas

Using these tips, the menus show two days of low fat eating.

Snack On:

Air-popped popcorn with no butter, pretzels
Hard candy, jelly beans
Bagels, raisin toast, or English muffins with margarine or jelly
Low fat cookies (like fig newtons vanilla wafers, gingersnaps)
Fruits, vegetables
Fruit juices and drinks
Frozen yogurt, sherbet, popsicles

Instead Of:

Popcorn with butter
Chocolate bars
Doughnuts, Danish pastry Cake, cookies, brownies
Milkshakes, eggnogs, floats Ice cream

Day 1

Breakfast
Peanut butter sandwich on raisin toast
Apple juice, coffee with skim or 1 % milk

Snack
Low fat yogurt

Lunch
Tuna salad with lettuce and tomato (easy on the mayonnaise)
Bean soup
Low fat crackers
Orange
Skim or 1% milk

Dinner
Barbecued chicken (no skin)

Baked potato with margarine
Coleslaw (easy on the mayonnaise)
Roll with margarine
Skim or 1% milk
Sherbet

Snack
Air-popped popcorn with no butter

Day 2

Breakfast
Shredded wheat with banana
Skim or 1% milk
Toast with margarine and jelly
Coffee with skim or 1% milk

Lunch
Lean ham with slice of part-skim cheese on a hard roll with lettuce
(easy on mayonnaise)
Fig newtons
Apple
Skim or 1% milk

Snack
Grapes

Dinner
Spaghetti with tomato sauce and meatballs made with lean ground
beef, steamed green beans with margarine
Green salad with cucumber, tomato, and a small amount of Italian
dressing
Skim or 1% milk
Frozen yogurt

Snack
English muffin with margarine and jelly

Expect Your Blood Cholesterol Level To Be Lower

She said: "All the changes we make in what we eat should help you lower your high blood cholesterol."

He said: "The doctor will measure my blood cholesterol again to see how I am doing. If it is not low enough, I may have to make more changes in what I eat. I think I am well on my way to lowering my blood cholesterol level."

Get More Help

Ask your doctor, dietitian, or nurse for more help in choosing foods and fixing meals.

To get more information contact:
National Cholesterol Education Program
National Heart Lung and Blood Institute
P.O. Box 30105
Bethesda, MD 20824-0105
301-251-1222

Foods To Choose When You Shop

Choose these foods more often. They are lower in saturated fat and cholesterol.

Meat, Poultry, Fish, and Shellfish
Chicken or turkey
Fish and lean cuts of meat
- Beef: round, sirloin, chuck arm, loin
- Pork: leg, shoulder, tenderloin, lean ham and extra lean ground beef

Dairy Products
Skim or 1% milk
Low fat or nonfat yogurt
Low fat cottage cheese
Cheeses labeled "low fat", "light", or "Part-skim"

Fats and Oils
Margarine (liquid, tub, stick. or diet) Oils (like corn, safflower, olive, peanut, or sesame oil)
Peanut Butter

Sweets and Snacks
(Don't choose these too often, if you are watching your weight. Some may be high in calories)
Popsicles, frozen yogurt, sherbet
Angel food cake
Fig bar cookies, gingersnaps, animal crackers, vanilla wafers, jelly beans, hard candy
Plain popcorn, unsalted pretzels

Fruits and Vegetables
Fresh, frozen, canned, or dried fruits (like oranges, apples, bananas, grapes, berries, peaches, melon, fruit cocktail, prunes)
Plain fresh, frozen or canned vegetables (like green beans, carrots, greens, zucchini, cabbage, tomatoes, broccoli, squash) Fresh, frozen, or canned juices

Breads, Cereals, Pasta, Rice, and Dry Peas and Beans
Sliced breads (like wheat, rye, pumpernickel, or white)
Sandwich buns, dinner rolls, pita breads, English muffins, bagels
Taco shells, plain tortillas, low fat crackers (like graham crackers, bread sticks, or saltines)
Hot cereals
Cold cereals except granola
Rice
Pasta (like plain noodles, spaghetti, macaroni)
Dry peas and beans (like split peas, black-eyed peas, chick peas, kidney beans, navy beans, lentils, soybeans)
Refried beans made with vegetable oil instead of lard
Tofu

How to Prevent High Blood Pressure[*]

It's Important To Know About High Blood Pressure

High Blood Pressure, also called hypertension, is a risk factor for heart and kidney diseases and stroke. This means that having high blood pressure increases your chance (or risk) of getting heart or kidney disease, or of having a stroke. This is serious business: Heart disease is the number one killer in the United States, and stroke is the third most common cause of death.

About one in every four American adults has high blood pressure. High blood pressure is especially dangerous because it often gives no warning signs or symptoms. Fortunately, though, you can find out if you have high blood pressure by having your blood pressure checked regularly. If it is high, you can take steps to lower it. Just as important, if your blood pressure is normal, you can learn how to keep it from becoming high. This chapter will tell you how.

What Is Blood Pressure and What Happens When It Is High?

Since blood is carried from the heart to all of your body's tissues and organs in vessels called arteries, blood pressure is the force of the blood pushing against the walls of those arteries. In fact, each time the heart beats (about 60-70 times a minute at rest), it pumps out blood into the arteries. Your blood pressure is at its greatest when the heart contracts and is pumping the blood. This is called systolic pressure. When the heart is at rest, in between beats, your blood pressure falls. This is the diastolic pressure.

Blood pressure is always given as these two numbers, "systolic and diastolic pressures." Both are important. Usually they are written one above or before the other, such as 120/80 mm Hg, with the top number the systolic, and the bottom the diastolic.

---

[*] Source: National Institute on Aging, 9000 Rockville Pike, Bethesda, MD 20892; 800-222-2225.

Different actions make your blood pressure go up or down. For example, if you run for a bus, your blood pressure goes up. When you sleep at night, your blood pressure goes down. These changes in blood pressure are normal.

Some people have blood pressure that stays up all or most of the time. Their blood pushes against the walls of their arteries with higher-than-normal force. If untreated this can lead to serious medical problems such as:

- **Arteriosclerosis ("hardening of the arteries").** High blood pressure harms the arteries by making them thick and stiff. This speeds the build up of cholesterol and fats in the blood vessels like rust in a pipe, which prevents the blood from flowing through the body, and in time can lead to a heart attack or stroke.

- **Heart attack.** Blood carries oxygen to the body. When the arteries that bring blood to the heart muscle become blocked, the heart cannot get enough oxygen. Reduced blood flow can cause chest pain (angina). Eventually, the flow may be stopped completely, causing a heart attack.

- **Enlarged heart.** High blood pressure causes the heart to work harder. Over time, this causes the heart to thicken and stretch. Eventually the heart fails to function normally causing fluids to back up into the lungs. Controlling high blood pressure can prevent this from happening.

- **Kidney damage.** The kidney acts as a filter to rid the body of wastes. Over a number of years, high blood pressure can narrow and thicken the blood vessels of the kidney. The kidney filters less fluid and waste builds up in the blood. The kidneys may fail altogether. When this happens, medical treatment (dialysis) or a kidney transplant may be needed.

- **Stroke.** High blood pressure can harm the arteries, causing them to narrow faster. So, less blood can get to the brain. If a blood clot blocks one of the narrowed arteries, a stroke (thrombotic stroke) may occur. A stroke can also occur when very high pressure causes a break in a weakened blood vessel in the brain (hemorrhagic stroke).

Who's Likely To Develop High Blood Pressure?

Anyone can develop high blood pressure, but some people are more likely to develop it than others. For example, high blood pressure is more common — it develops earlier and is more severe — in African-Americans than in Caucasians.

In the early and middle adult years, men have high blood pressure more often than women. But as men and women age, the reverse is true. More women after menopause have high blood pressure than men of the same age. And the number of both men and women with high blood pressure increases rapidly in older age groups. More than half of all Americans over age 65 have high blood pressure. And older African-American women who live in the Southeast are more likely to have high blood pressure than those in other regions of the United States.

In fact, the southeastern states have some of the highest rates of death from stroke. High blood pressure is the key risk factor for stroke. Other risk factors include cigarette smoking and overweight. These 11 states — Alabama, Arkansas, Georgia, Indiana, Kentucky, Louisiana, Mississippi, North Carolina, South Carolina, Tennessee, and Virginia — have such high rates of stroke among persons of all races and in both sexes that they are called the "Stroke Belt States."

Finally, heredity can make some families more likely than others to get high blood pressure. If your parents or grandparents had high blood pressure, your risk may be increased. While it is mainly a disease of adults, high blood pressure can occur in children as well.

Even if everyone is healthy, be sure you and your family get your blood pressure checked. Remember high blood pressure has no signs or symptoms.

How Is Blood Pressure Checked?

Having your blood pressure checked is quick, easy, and painless. Your blood pressure is measured with an instrument called a sphygmomanometer (sfig'-mo-ma-nom-e-ter).

It works like this: A blood pressure cuff is wrapped around your upper arm and inflated to stop the blood flow in your artery for a few seconds. A valve is opened and air is then released from the cuff and the sounds of your blood rushing through an artery are heard through a stethoscope. The first sound heard and registered on the gauge or mercury column is called the systolic blood pressure. It represents the maximum pressure in the artery produced as the heart contracts and the blood begins to flow. The last sound heard as more air is released from the cuff is the diastolic blood pressure. It represents the lowest pressure that remains within the artery when the heart is at rest.

What Do the Numbers Mean?

Blood pressure is always expressed in two numbers that represent the systolic and diastolic pressures. These numbers are measurements of millimeters (mm) of mercury (Hg). The measurement is written one above or before the other, with the systolic number on the top and the diastolic number on the bottom. For example, a blood pressure measurement of 120/80 mm Hg is expressed verbally as "120 over 80." See the chart below which shows categories for blood pressure levels in adults.

If your blood pressure is less than 140/90 mm Hg, it is considered normal. However, a blood pressure below 120/80 mm Hg is even better for your heart and blood vessels. People used to think that low blood pressure (for example, 105/65 mm Hg in an adult) was unhealthy. Except for rare cases, this is not true. High blood pressure or "hypertension" is classified by stages and is more serious as the numbers get higher.

What Causes High Blood Pressure?

For most people, there is no single known cause of high blood pressure. This type of high blood pressure is called "primary' or "essential" hypertension. This type of blood pressure can't be cured, although in most cases it can be controlled. That's why it's so important for everyone to take steps to reduce their chances of developing high blood pressure.

Categories for Blood Pressure Levels in Adults

(Age 18 years and older)

	Blood Pressure Level (mm Ng)	
Category	Systolic	Diastolic
Normal	< 130	<85
High normal	130-139	85-89
Hypertension*		
Stage 1	140-159	90-99
Stage 2	160-179	100-109
Stage 3	180-209	110-119
Stage 4	>210	> 120

* Note: Hypertension is the medical term for high blood pressure. These categories are from the National High Blood Pressure Education Program, JNCV Report.

<= less than
>=greater than or equal to

In a few people, high blood pressure can be traced to a known cause like tumors of the adrenal gland, chronic kidney disease, hormone abnormalities, use of birth control pills, or pregnancy. This is called "secondary hypertension." Secondary hypertension is usually cured if its cause passes or is corrected.

How Can You Prevent High Blood Pressure?

Everyone — regardless of race, age, sex, or heredity — can help lower their chance of developing high blood pressure. Here's how:

1) Maintain a healthy weight, lose weight if you are overweight,
2) Be more physically active,
3) Choose foods lower in salt and sodium, and
4) If you drink alcoholic beverages, do so in moderation.

These rules are also recommended for treating high blood pressure, although medicine is often added as part of the treatment. It is far better to keep your blood pressure from getting high in the first place.

Another important measure for your health is to not smoke: While cigarette smoking is not directly related to high blood pressure, it increases your risk of heart attack and stroke.

Let's look more closely at the four rules to prevent high blood pressure and for keeping a healthy heart:

1) Maintain a healthy weight, lose weight if you are overweight

As your body weight increases, your blood pressure rises. In fact, being overweight can make you two to six times more likely to develop high blood pressure than if you are at your desirable weight. Keeping your weight in the desirable range is not only important to prevent high blood pressure but also for your overall health and well being.

It's not just how much you weigh that's important: It also matters where your body stores extra fat. Your shape is inherited from your parents just like the color of your eyes or hair. Some people tend to gain weight around their belly; others, around the hips and thighs. "Apple-shaped" people who have a pot belly (that is, extra fat at the waist) appear to have higher health risks than "pear-shaped" people with heavy hips and thighs.

No matter where the extra weight is, you can reduce your risk of high blood pressure by losing weight. Even small amounts of weight loss can make a big difference in helping to prevent high blood pressure. Losing weight, if you are overweight and already have high blood pressure, can also help lower your pressure.

To lose weight, you need to eat fewer calories than you burn. But don't go on a crash diet to see how quickly you can lose those pounds. The healthiest and longest-lasting weight loss happens when you do it slowly, losing 1/2 to 1 pound a week. By cutting back by 500 calories a day by eating less and being more physically active, you can lose about 1 pound (which equals 3,500 calories) in a week.

Losing weight and keeping it off involves a new way of eating and increasing physical activity for life. Here's how to eat and get on your way to a lower weight:

- *Choose foods low in calories and fat.* Naturally, choosing low-calorie foods cuts calories. But did you know that choosing

> ## Try These Low Fat Foods
>
> Baked, broiled or poached chicken and turkey (without the skin)
>
> Fish, Lean cuts of meat (like round or sirloin)
>
> Skim or 1% milk, evaporated skim milk
>
> Lower-fat, low-sodium cheeses
>
> Fresh, frozen, or canned fruit
>
> Fresh, frozen, or canned (no salt added) vegetables (without cream or cheese sauces)
>
> Plain rice and pasta
>
> English muffins, bagels, sandwich breads and rolls, soft tortillas
>
> Cold (ready-to-eat) cereals lower in sodium
>
> Cooked hot cereals (not instant since it is higher in sodium)
>
> Note: When choosing cheeses, breads, and cereals, use the food label to choose those lower in fat and sodium.

foods low in fat also cuts calories? Fat is a concentrated source of calories, so eating fewer fatty foods will reduce calorie intake. Some examples of fatty foods to cut down on are:

butter, margarine, regular salad dressings, fatty meats, skin of poultry, whole-milk dairy foods like cheese, fried foods, and many cookies, cakes, pastries and snacks. See the box to the left for low fat foods that you can enjoy instead.

- *Choose foods high in starch and fiber.* Foods high in starch and fiber, like those shown in the circle, are excellent substitutes for foods high in fat. They are lower in calories than foods high in fat. These foods are also good sources of vitamins and minerals.

- *Limit serving sizes.* To lose weight, it's not just the type of foods you eat that's important, but also the amount. To take in fewer calories, you need to limit your portion sizes. Try especially to take smaller helpings of high calorie foods like high fat meats and cheeses. And try not to go back for seconds.

Here's a good tip to help you control or change your eating habits: Keep track of what you eat, when you eat, and why, by writing it down. Note whether you snack on high fat foods in front of the television, or if you skip breakfast and then eat a large lunch. Once you see your habits, you can set goals for yourself. Cut back on TV snacks and, when you do snack, have fresh fruit, unsalted air-popped popcorn, or unsalted pretzels. If there's no time for breakfast at home, take a low fat muffin, bagel (skip the cream cheese), or cereal with you to eat at work. Changing your behavior will help you change your weight for the better.

- *Increase physical activity.* There's more to weight loss than just eating less. Another important ingredient is increasing physical activity, which burns calories. Cutting down on fat and calories combined with regular physical activity can help you lose more weight and keep it off longer than either way by itself. Check to see how many calories you can burn during different activities.

2) Be More Physically Active

Besides losing weight, there are other reasons to be more active: Being physically active can reduce your risk for heart disease, help lower your total choles-terol level and raise HDL cholesterol (the "good" choles-terol that does not build up in the arteries), and help lower high blood pressure. And people who are physically active have a lower risk of getting high blood pressure — 20 to 50 percent lower — than people who are not active.

You don't have to be a marathon runner to benefit from physical activity. Even light activities, if done daily, can help lower your risk of heart disease. So

Calories Burned During Physical Activities

Activity	Calories Burned Up Per Hour*	
	Man**	Woman**
Light activity:	300	240
Cleaning house		
Playing baseball		
Playing golf		
Moderate activity:	460	370
Walking briskly (3.5 mph)		
Gardening		
Cycling (5.5 mph)		
Dancing		
Playing basketball		
Strenuous activity:	730	580
Jogging (9 min./mile)		
Playing football		
Swimming		
Very strenuous activity:	920	740
Running (7 min./mile)		
Racquetball		
Skiing		

* May vary depending on a variety of factors including environmental conditions.

** Healthy man 175 pounds; healthy woman, 140 pounds.

Source: Dietary Guidelines for Americans, U.S. Department of Agriculture, U.S. Department of Health and Human Services, Third edition, 1990 (adapted from McArdle, et al., "Exercise Physiology," 1986.

you can fit physical activity into your daily routine in small but important ways such as:

- take a walk at lunch or after dinner
- use the stairs instead of the elevator
- get off the bus one or two stops early and walk the rest of the way
- park farther away from the store or office
- ride a bike
- work in the yard or garden
- go dancing

More vigorous exercise has added benefits. It helps improve the fitness of the heart and lungs. And that in turn protects you more against heart disease. Activities like swimming, brisk walking, running, and jumping rope are called "aerobic." This means that the body uses oxygen to make the energy it needs for the activity. Aerobic activities can condition your heart and lungs if done at the right intensity for at least 30 minutes, three to four times a week. But if you don't have 30 minutes for a break, try to find two 15-minute periods or even three 10-minute periods. Try to do some type of aerobic activity in the course of a week.

Most people don't need to see a doctor before they start exercising, since a gradual, sensible exercise program has few health risks. But if you have a health problem like high blood pressure; if you have pains or pressure in the chest or shoulder area; if you tend to feel dizzy or faint; if you get very breathless after a mild workout; or are middle-age or older and have not been active, and you are planning a vigorous exercise program, you should check with your doctor first. Otherwise, get out, get active, and get fit, and help prevent high blood pressure. The sample walking program at the end of this chapter should help you get started.

3) Choose Foods Lower In Salt and Sodium

Americans eat more salt (sodium chloride) and other forms of sodium than they need. And guess what? They also have higher rates of high blood pressure than people in other countries who eat less salt.

Often, if people with high blood pressure cut back on salt and sodium, their blood pressure falls. Cutting back on salt and sodium also prevents blood pressure from rising. Some people like African-Americans and the elderly are more affected by sodium than others. Since there's really no practical way to predict exactly who will be affected by sodium, it makes sense to limit intake of salt and sodium to help prevent high blood pressure.

All Americans, especially people with high blood pressure, should eat no more than about 6 grams of salt a day, which equals about 2,400 milligrams of sodium. That's about one teaspoon of table salt. But remember to keep track of ALL salt eaten-including that in processed foods and added during cooking or at the table. Americans eat 4,000 to 6,000 milligrams of sodium a day, so most people need to cut back on salt and sodium. See below for the range of sodium in some types of foods.

You can teach your taste buds to enjoy less salty foods. Here are a few tips:

- Check food labels for the amount of sodium in foods. Choose those lower in sodium most of the time. Look for products that say "sodium free," "very low sodium," "low sodium," "light in sodium," "reduced or less sodium," or "unsalted," especially on cans, boxes, bottles, and bags.

- Buy fresh, plain frozen, or canned with "no salt added' vegetables. Use fresh poultry, fish and lean meat, rather than canned or processed types.

Spice It Up

It's easy to make foods tasty without using salt. Try these foods with the suggested flavorings, spices, and herbs:

Meat, Poultry, and Fish
Beef: Bay leaf, marjoram, nutmeg, onion, pepper, sage, thyme

Lamb: Curry powder, garlic, rosemary, mint

Pork: Garlic, onion, sage, pepper, oregano

Veal: Bay leaf, curry powder, ginger, marjoram, oregano

Chicken: Ginger, marjoram, oregano, paprika, poultry seasoning, rosemary, sage, tarragon, thyme

Fish: Curry powder, dill, dry mustard, lemon juice, marjoram, paprika, pepper

Vegetables

Carrots: Cinnamon, cloves, marjoram, nutmeg, rosemary, sage

Corn: Cumin, curry powder, onion, paprika, parsley

Green Beans: Dill, curry powder, lemon juice, marjoram, oregano, tarragon, thyme

Greens: Onion, pepper

Peas: Ginger, marjoram, onion, parsley, sage

Potatoes: Dill, garlic, onion, paprika, parsley, sage

Summer Squash: Cloves, curry powder, marjoram, nutmeg, rosemary, sage

Winter Squash: Cinnamon, ginger, nutmeg, onion

Tomatoes: Basil, bay leaf, dill, marjoram, onion, oregano, parsley, pepper

---

- Use herbs, spices, and salt-free seasoning blends in cooking and at the table instead of salt. See the chart on ways to spice up your foods.

• Cook rice, pasta, and hot cereals without salt. Cut back on instant or flavored rice, pasta, and cereal mixes because they usually have added salt.

• Choose "convenience' foods that are lower in sodium. Cut back on frozen dinners, mixed dishes like pizza, packaged mixes, canned soups or broths, and salad dressings which often have a lot of sodium.

   • When available, buy low-or reduced-sodium, or "no-salt-added" versions of foods like these:
     - Canned soup, dried soup mixes, bouillon
     - Canned vegetables and vegetable juices
     - Cheeses, lower in fat
     - Margarine
     - Condiments like catsup, soy sauce
     - Crackers and baked goods
     - Processed lean meats
     - Snack foods like chips, pretzels, nuts

• Rinse canned foods like tuna to remove some sodium.

4) If You Drink Alcoholic Beverages, Do So in Moderation

Drinking too much alcohol can raise your blood pressure. It may also lead to the development of high blood pressure. So to help prevent high blood pressure, if you drink alcohol, limit how much you drink to no more than two drinks a day. The "Dietary Guidelines for Americans" recommend that for overall health women should limit their alcohol to no more than one drink a day.

This is what counts as a drink:

• 1-1/2 ounces of 80-proof or 1 ounce of 100-proof whiskey,
• 5 ounces of wine, or
• 12 ounces of beer (regular or light).

You may have heard that some alcohol is good for your heart health. Some news reports suggest that people who consume a drink or two a day have lower blood pressure and have longer than those who consume no alcohol or those who consume excessive amounts of alcohol. Others note that wine raises the "good" blood cholesterol that prevents the build up of fats in the arteries. While these news stories may be correct they don't tell the whole story: Too much alcohol contributes to a host of other health problems, such as motor vehicle accidents, diseases of the liver and pancreas, damage to the brain and heart, an increased risk of many cancers, and fetal alcohol syndrome. Alcohol is also high in calories. So you should limit how much you drink.

What Else Might Prevent High Blood Pressure?

Other things also may help prevent blood pressure. Here's a roundup of what's being said about them and whether it's true or false.

Dietary Supplements —
Potassium, Calcium, Magnesium, Fish Oils

- **Potassium.** Eating foods rich in potassium seems to protect some people from developing high blood pressure. You probably can get enough potassium from your diet, so a supplement isn't necessary. Many fruits, vegetables, dairy foods, and fish are good sources of potassium (see circle for examples).

- **Calcium.** Populations with low calcium intakes have high rates of high blood pressure. However, it has not been proven that taking calcium tablets will prevent high blood pressure. But it is important to be sure to get at least the recommended amount of calcium — 800 milligrams per day for adults (pregnant and breastfeeding women need more) — from the foods you eat. Dairy foods like, low fat selections of milk, yogurt, and cheese are good sources of calcium. Low fat and nonfat dairy products have even more calcium than the high fat types.

- **Magnesium.** A diet low in magnesium may make your blood pressure rise. But doctors don't recommend taking extra magnesium to help prevent high blood pressure — the amount you get in a healthy diet is enough. Magnesium is found in whole grains, green leafy vegetables, nuts, seeds, and dry peas and beans.

- **Fish oils.** A type of fat called "omega-3 fatty acids" is found in fatty fish like mackerel and salmon. Large amounts of fish oils may help reduce high blood pressure, but their role in prevention is unclear. But taking fish oil pills is not recommended because high doses can cause unpleasant side effects. The pills are also high in fat and calories. Of course, most fish if not fried or made with added fat are low in saturated fat and calories and can be eaten often.

Other Factors

- **Fats, Carbohydrates, and Protein.** Varying the amount and type of fats, carbohydrates, and protein in the diet has little, if any, effect on blood pressure. But for overall heart health, it is crucial to limit the amount of fat in your diet, especially the saturated fat found in foods like fatty meats and whole milk dairy foods. Saturated fats raise your blood cholesterol level, and a high blood cholesterol level is another risk factor for heart disease. Foods high in fat are also high in calories. Remember, foods high in complex carbohydrate (starch and fiber) are low in fat and calories-so eating these foods in moderate amounts instead of high fat foods can help you to lose weight if you are overweight or to prevent you from gaining weight.

- **Caffeine.** The caffeine in drinks like coffee, tea, and sodas may cause blood pressure to go up, but only temporarily. In a short time your blood pressure will go back down. Unless you are sensitive to caffeine and your blood pressure does not go down, you do not have to limit caffeine to prevent developing high blood pressure.

- **Garlic or Onions.** Increased amounts of garlic and onions have not been found to affect blood pressure. Of course, they are tasty substitutes for salty seasonings and can be used often.

- **Stress Management.** Stress can make blood pressure go up for a while and over time, may contribute to the cause of high blood pressure. So it's natural to think that stress management techniques like biofeedback, meditation, and relaxation would help prevent high blood pressure. But this doesn't seem to be the case: the few studies that have looked at this have not shown that stress management helps to prevent high blood pressure. Of course, stress management techniques are helpful if they help you feel better or stick to a weight-loss and/or exercise program.

Here's a Recap

After going through all the things that may affect blood pressure, it's worth noting again the things that are sure to help you prevent high blood pressure:

1) Maintaining a healthy weight — losing weight if you are overweight,
2) Being more physically active,
3) Choosing foods low in salt and sodium, and
4) If you drink alcoholic beverages, doing so in moderation.

By following these guidelines, you can help reduce or prevent high blood pressure for life — and, in turn, lower your risk for heart disease and stroke.

Want To Know More?

For more information on either high blood pressure or weight and physical activity, contact:
National Heart, Lung, and Blood Institute Information Center
P.O. Box 30105
Bethesda, MD 20824-0105
301-251-1222

Sodium In Foods (In Milligrams)

Meat, Poultry, Fish, and Shellfish
Fresh meat (including lean cuts of beef,
   pork, lamb and veal, poultry, finfish)
   cooked, 3 oz   Less than 90
Shellfish, 3 oz   100-325
Tuna, canned, 3 oz   300
*Sausage, 2 oz   515
*Bologna, 2 oz   535
*Frankfurter, 1-1/2 oz   560
Boiled ham, 2 oz   750
Lean ham, 3 oz   1,025

Eggs
Egg white, 1   55
*Whole egg, 1   65
Egg substitute,
   1/4 cup =1 egg   80-120

Dairy Products
Milk
  *Whole milk, 1 cup   120
  Skim or 1 % milk, I cup   125
  Buttermilk (salt added), 1 cup 260

Cheese
*Natural cheese:
  *Swiss cheese, 1 oz   75
  *Cheddar cheese, 1 oz   175
  *Blue cheese, 1 oz   395
Low fat cheese, 1 oz   150
*Process cheese and cheese
  spreads, 1 oz   340-450
  Lower sodium and fat
  versions   Read the label
*Cottage cheese (regular), 1/2 cup 455
Cottage cheese (low fat), 1/2 cup 460

Yogurt
*Yogurt, whole milk, plain, 8 oz   105
Yogurt, fruited or flavored, low fat
  or nonfat, 8 oz   120-150
Yogurt, nonfat or low fat,
  plain, 8 oz   160-175

Vegetables
Fresh or frozen vegetables, or no salt added
  canned (cooked without salt),
  1/2 cup   less than 70
Vegetables, canned, no sauce,
  1/2 cup   55-470

*Vegetables, canned or frozen with sauce,
  1/2 cup   Read the label
Tomato juice, canned, 3/4 cup   660

**Breads, Cereals, Rice, Pasta, Dry Peas
and Beans**
Breads and Crackers
Bread 1 slice   110-175
English muffin, 1/2   130
Bagel, 1/2   190
Cracker, saltine type, 5 squares   195
*Baking powder biscuit, 1   305

Cereals
Ready-to-eat
Shredded wheat, 3/4 cup Less than 5
Puffed wheat and rice cereals,
  1-1/2 to 1-2/3 cup Less than 5
Granola-type goals, 1/2 cup 5-25
Ring and nugget cereals, 1 cup 170-310
Flaked cereals, 2/3 to 1 cup 170-360

Cooked
Cooked cereal (unsalted),
  1/2 cup   Less than 5
Instant cooked cereal,
  1 packet = 3/4 cup   180

Pasta and rice
Cooked rice and pasta, (unsalted),
  1/2 cup   Less than 10
*Flavored rice mix, cooked,
  1/2 Cup   250-390

Peas and beans
Peanut butter, unsalted,
  2 tbsp   Less than 5
Peanut butter, 2 tbsp   150
Dry beans, home cooked, (unsalted),
  or no salt added canned,
  1/2 cup   Less than 5
Dry beans, plain, canned,
  1/2 cup   350-590
*Dry beans, canned with added fat
  or meat, 1/2 cup   425-630

Fruits
Fruits (fresh, frozen, canned),
  1/2 cup   Less than 10

Sodium In Foods (In Milligrams) (continued)

Fats and Oils

Oil, 1 tbsp	0
*Butter, unsalted, 1 tsp	1
*Butter, salted, 1 tsp	25
Margarine, unsalted, 1 tsp	Less than 5
Margarine, salted, 1 tsp	50
Imitation mayonnaise, 1 tbsp	75
Mayonnaise, 1 tbsp	80
Prepared salad dressings, low calorie, 2 tbsp	50-310
Prepared salad dressings, 2 tbsp	210-440

Snacks

Popcorn, chips, and nuts

Unsalted nuts, 1/4 cup	Less than 5
Salted nuts, 1/4 cup	185
*Unsalted potato chips and corn chips, 1 cup	Less than 5
*Salted potato chips and corn chips, 1 cup	170-285
Unsalted popcorn, 2-1/2 cups	Less than 10
Salted popcorn, 2-1/2 cups	330

Candy

Jelly beans, 10 large	5
*Milk chocolate bar, 1 oz. bar	25

Frozen desserts

*Ice cream, 1/2 cup	35-50
Frozen Yogurt, low fat or nonfat, 1/2 cup	40-55

Ice milk, 1/2 cup	55-60

Condiments

Mustard, chili sauce, hot sauce, 1 tsp	35-65
Catsup, steak sauce, 1 tbsp	100-230
Salsa, tartar sauce, 2 tbsp	200-315
Salt, 1/6 tsp	390
Pickles, 5 slices	280-460
Soy sauce, low sodium, 1 tbsp	600
Soy Sauce, 1 tbsp	1030

Convenience Foods

**Canned and dehydrated soups, 1 cup	600-1,300
**Lower sodium versions	Read label
***Canned and frozen main dishes, 8 oz	500-1,570
***Lower sodium versions	Read label

* Choices are higher in saturated fat, cholesterol, or both.
** Creamy soups are higher in saturated fat and cholesterol.
*** Limit main dishes that have ingredients higher in saturated fat, cholesterol, or both.

Source: Adapted from Home and Garden Bulletin 253-7, U.S. Department of Agriculture, July 1993.

A Sample Walking Program

	Warm-up	Target zone exercising	Cool down time	Total
Week I Session A	Walk normally 5 min.	Then walk briskly 5 min.	Then walk normally 5 min.	15 min.
Session B	Repeat above pattern			
Session C	Repeat above pattern			

Continue with at least three exercise sessions during each week of the program. If you find a particular week's pattern tiring, repeat it before going on to the next pattern. You do not have to complete the walking program in 12 weeks.

Week 2	Walk 5 min.	Walk briskly 7 min.	Walk 5 min.	17 min.
Week 3	Walk 5 min.	Walk briskly 9 min.	Walk 5 min.	19 min.
Week 4	Walk 5 min.	Walk briskly 11 min.	Walk 5 min.	21 min.
Week 5	Walk 5 min.	Walk briskly 13 min.	Walk 5 min.	23 min.
Week 6	Walk 5 min.	Walk briskly 15 min.	Walk 5 min.	25 min.
Week 7	Walk 5 min.	Walk briskly 18 min.	Walk 5 min.	28 min.
Week 8	Walk 5 min.	Walk briskly 20 min.	Walk 5 min.	30 min.
Week 9	Walk 5 min.	Walk briskly 23 min.	Walk 5 min.	33 min.
Week 10	Walk 5 min.	Walk briskly 26 min.	Walk 5 min.	36 min.
Week 11	Walk 5 min.	Walk briskly 28 min.	Walk 5 min.	38 min.
Week 12	Walk 5 min.	Walk briskly 30 min.	Walk 5 min.	40 min.

Week 13 on:
Check your pulse periodically to see if you are exercising within your target zone. As you get more in shape, try exercising within the upper range of your tome zone. Gradually increase your brisk walking time to 30 to 60 minutes, three or four times a week. Remember that your goal is to got the benefits you are seeking and enjoy your activity.

A Sample Walking Program (continued)

Here's how to check if you are within your target heart rate zone:

1) Right after you stop exercising, take your pulse: Place the tips of your first two fingers lightly over one of the blood vessels on your neck, just to the left or right of your Adam's apple. Or try the pulse spot inside your wrist just below the base of your thumb.

2) Count your pulse for 10 seconds and multiply the number by 6.

3) Compare the number to the right grouping below- Look for the age grouping that is closest to your age and read the line across. For example, if you are 43, the closest age on the chart is 45; the target zone is 88-131 beats per minute.

Age	Target HR Zone
20 years	100-150 beats per minute
25 years	98-146 beats per minute
30 years	95-142 beats per minute
35 years	93-138 beats per minute
40 years	90-135 beats per minute
45 years	88-131 beats per minute
50 years	85-127 beats per minute
55 years	83-123 beats per minute
60 years	80-120 beats per minute
65 years	78-116 beats per minute
70 years	75-113 beats per minute

Source: *Exercise and Your Heart*, National Heart, Lung, and Blood Institute and the American Heart Association, NIH Publication No. 93-1677.

HIV, AIDS, and Older Adults[*]

Everyone talks about AIDS (Acquired Immunodeficiency Syndrome), but few talk about how AIDS affects older people. No wonder so many older adults think they are not at risk.

The truth is that 11 percent of all new AIDS cases are now in people age 50 and over. And in the last few years, new AIDS cases rose faster in middle-age and older people than in people under 40.

What is AIDS?

AIDS is a disease caused by a virus called HIV (short for human immunodeficiency virus). HIV attacks the body's immune system. When the immune system is hurt, it can no longer fight diseases the way it used to.

People with HIV seem to be healthy at first. But after several years, they begin to get sick. Often they get serious infections or cancers. When this happens, they are diagnosed with AIDS. The most common cause of death in people with AIDS is a type of pneumonia called pneumocystis carinii pneumonia or PCP.

How Do People Get AIDS?

HIV is spread when body fluids, such as semen and blood, pass from a person who has the infection to another person. For the most part, the virus is spread by sexual contact or by sharing drug needles and syringes.

In older people sexual activity is the most common cause of HIV infection. Second is blood transfusions received before 1985. Since 1985, blood banks have been testing all blood for HIV, so there is now little danger of contracting HIV from transfusions.

---

[*] Source: *Age Page*, National Institute on Aging, U.S. Department of Health and Human Services, Public Health Service, National Institutes of Health, Gaithersburg, MD 20898; 800-222-2225.

Otherwise, HIV is not easy to catch. It is *not* spread by mosquito bites, using a public telephone or restroom, being coughed or sneezed on by an infected person, or touching someone with the disease.

Is AIDS Different in Older People?

The immune system normally gets weaker with age, but this decline is faster in older AIDS patients. They usually become sick and die sooner than younger patients.

It may be harder to recognize AIDS symptoms in older people. Early symptoms of AIDS — feeling tired, confused, having a loss of appetite, and swollen glands — are like other illnesses common in older people. Health professionals may assume these are signs of minor problems.

Prevention

Medical experts predict that a cure or vaccine to prevent AIDS will not be found in the near future. So stopping HIV depends on each person's actions. You can prevent AIDS by thinking about the risk of infection before sexual contact. Use condoms if sexually involved with someone other than a mutually faithful, uninfected partner.

Treatment and Help

Treatment for AIDS usually involved medicine, such as AZT (azidothymidine). AZT does not cure AIDS but many patients use it to keep them healthier longer. Other promising drugs are being tested. Doctors are also learning how to treat the diseases, like PCP, that strike people with AIDS.

People with HIV infection should stay in touch with a doctor who knows about the latest research. For help finding the name of an expert, call a local medical school's department of infectious diseases or the National AIDS Hotline (800-342-AIDS).

Older AIDS patients often may not have anyone to take care of them. Help is available from local groups in some cases and from the Social Security Administration (800-SSA-1213).

Resources

In most cities, health agencies or centers offer HIV testing, counseling, and other services. In addition, the following national organizations offer information:

National AIDS Hotline, 800-342-AIDS, 800-344-SIDA for Spanish, 800-AIDS-889 (TTY). The hotline operates 24 hours a day, 7 days a week. It offers general information and local referrals.

National AIDS Clearinghouse, P.O. Box 6003, Rockville, MD 20850; 800-458-5231. The clearinghouse offers free government publications and information about resources.

National Institute of Allergy and Infectious Diseases (NIAID), Office of Communications, Building 31, Room 7A32, Bethesda, MD 20892. One of the National Institutes of Health, the NIAID will respond to written requests for information on AIDS research and clinical trials of promising therapies.

Seniors in a Gay Environment (SAGE), 208 West 13th Street, New York, NY 10011; 212-741-2247. SAGE provides HIV/AIDS information and referrals for people age 50 and over.

Social Security Administration, contact local office or call 800-SSA-1213. Social Security has two disability benefit programs that provide financial assistance to eligible AIDS patients.

American Association of Retired Persons (AARP), Social Outreach and Support (SOS), 601 E Street, NW, Washington, DC 20049; 202-434-2260. The AARP/SOS program has information on HIV and AIDS and their impact on midlife and older adults.

Hormone Replacement Therapy: Should You Take It?[*]

Menopause is the stage in a woman's life when menstruation stops and she can no longer bear children. During menopause, the body makes less of the female hormones, estrogen and progesterone. After menopause, the lower hormone levels free a woman from concerns about monthly menstrual periods and getting pregnant. But they can also cause troublesome symptoms, such as hot flashes (a sudden flush or warmth, often followed by sweating) and sleep problems.

Sometimes women have other physical problems, such as vaginal dryness. While many women have little or no trouble with menopause, others have moderate to severe discomfort. Estrogen loss also raises a woman's risk for other serious health problems. They include heart disease and stroke, leading causes of death for women over the age of 50. Estrogen loss also can lead to bone loss.

Some bone loss is normal as people age. However, a more serious condition called osteoporosis weakens bones and lets them break easily. It affects 24 million people in this country. Women have a higher risk than men.

Doctors sometimes prescribe hormones to replace those lost during menopause. This treatment, called **hormone replacement therapy** (HRT), can ease symptoms of menopause and protect against risks of heart disease, stroke, and osteoporosis. Although millions of women take HRT, this may not be the right choice for everyone.

What Can You Do?

Doctors usually prescribe HRT combining estrogen and another female hormone, progestin. They usually prescribe estrogen without

---

[*] Source: *Age Page*, National Institute on Aging, U.S. Department of Health and Human Services, Public Health Service, National Institutes of Health, Gaithersburg, MD 20898; 800-222-2225.

progestin for women who have had their uterus removed (hysterectomy). Estrogen can be used in pill or tablet form, vaginal creams, or shots. There are also patches that attach to the skin and release estrogen through the skin. The form of estrogen your doctor chooses may depend on your symptoms. For instance, creams are used for vaginal dryness, while pills or patches are used to ease different menopause symptoms, such as hot flashes, or to prevent bone loss. Progestin usually is taken in pill form.

Doctors may prescribe different schedules for taking HRT. Some women take estrogen for a set number of days, add progestin for a set number of days, and then stop taking one or both for a specific period of time. They repeat the same pattern every month. This pattern often causes regular monthly bleeding like a menstrual period. Some women take HRT every day of the month without any break. This pattern usually stops regular monthly bleeding. Talk with your doctors about the system that is best for you.

Who Should Take HRT?

Many experts believe that the benefits of HRT may be greater than the risks. But scientists do not yet fully know the risks of long-term HRT. Before you decide about HRT, discuss the possible benefits, risks, and side effects with your doctor.

Your doctor may warn against HRT if you have high blood pressure, diabetes, liver disease, blood clots, seizures, migraine headaches, gallbladder disease, or a history of cancer. Also, daughters of mothers who took DES (diethylstilbestrol) during pregnancy may have changes to their reproductive system that make HRT dangerous.

Side Effects and Risks of HRT

Some women may have side effects from HRT, such as unwanted vaginal bleeding, headaches, nausea, vaginal discharge, fluid retention, swollen breasts, or weight gain. Other health concerns for women taking HRT include:

Cancer of the uterus (endometrial cancer). Research shows that women who have their uterus and use estrogen alone are at risk for endometrial cancer. But today, most doctors prescribe the combination of estrogen and progestin. Progestin protects against endometrial cancer. If a woman who still has a uterus takes estrogen alone, her doctor should take sample tissue from her uterus (endometrial biopsy) to check for cancer every year. Women without a uterus have no risk of endometrial cancer.

Risk Factors for Osteoporosis

Women who are at high risk of getting osteoporosis may want to think about taking HRT to prevent it. Risk factors include:

- Having early menopause (natural or due to surgery)
- Being Caucasian or Asian
- Being physically inactive
- Taking corticosteroid medicines (prescribed for arthritis or other inflammatory diseases)
- Having a slight build
- Getting too little calcium from diet
- Smoking cigarettes
- Drinking more than a moderate amount of alcohol
- Having thyroid or kidney disease

Breast cancer. Today, many scientists are studying the possible link between HRT and breast cancer. Some studies have shown that HRT increases the risk of breast cancer.

Heart disease. Estrogen alone or combined with progestin reduces the risk of heart disease. Scientists recently have shown that estrogen lowers risks of heart disease and stroke in women over the age of 50, when they are most at risk for heart disease and stroke.

Abnormal vaginal bleeding. Women taking HRT are more likely than other women to have abnormal vaginal bleeding. When this happens, the doctor may perform a "D and C" (dilation and curettage) to find the cause of bleeding. In more serious cases, the doctor may suggest removing the uterus.

Scientists are still studying the risks of taking estrogen alone or in combination with progestin over a long period of time. Women who have their uterus, are at low risk for stroke, heart disease, or serious bone disease, and have no major menopause symptoms may choose to avoid HRT.

Medical Checkups

If you are taking hormones, you should have regular medical checkups. The American College of Obstetricians and Gynecologists recommends that all women taking HRT get a medical checkup every year. At that time, the doctor or nurse should read your blood pressure, give you pelvic and breast exams, and take an x-ray picture of your breasts (mammogram) to check for breast cancer.

If You Don't Take HRT

If you decide against HRT, there are other ways to deal with the symptoms of menopause. There are drugs that can reduce hot flashes and you can apply water soluble surgical jelly (**not** petroleum jelly) to the vagina to reduce dryness. Simply lowering the room temperature may help you sleep better and ease uncomfortable hot flashes.

To strengthen your bones, good health habits can help, even if you don't start until later in life. Experts suggest that all adult women have 1,000 mg of calcium each day; after menopause, women not using HRT should have 1,500 mg each day. Low-fat milk and dairy foods such as cheese and yogurt are good sources for calcium. If you find it hard to get that amount from your diet, you can take calcium supplements.

Your body also needs vitamin D to absorb calcium. Most people get enough vitamin D just by being out in the sun for at least a short time every day. Supplements or milk fortified with vitamin D are also good sources for this vitamin.

Weight-bearing exercises, which make your muscles work against gravity, help strengthen bones and prevent osteoporosis. Walking, jogging, and playing tennis are all good weight-bearing exercises.

You may also want to ask your doctor about a new drug to treat osteoporosis in women past menopause. The new treatment is safe and effective in increasing bone mass.

Resources

You can get more information on this topic by contacting the organizations listed below:

The American College of Obstetricians and Gynecologists (ACOG) offers the following pamphlets, *Hormone Replacement Therapy, Preventing Osteoporosis,* and *The Menopause Years.* To obtain copies, send a self-addressed envelope to ACOG, 409 12th Street, SW, Washington, DC 20024-2188.

The American Association of Retired Persons (AARP) Women's Initiative has a fact sheet, *Hormone Replacement Therapy: Facts to Help You Decide.* To obtain a copy, write AARP, 601 E Street, NW, Washington, DC 20049; 800-424-3410.

The National Osteoporosis Foundation (NOF) has information for health professionals and the public. Contact NOF, 1150 17th Street, NW, Suite 500, Washington, DC 20036-4603; 800-223-9994.

The National Resource Center on Osteoporosis and Related Bone Diseases is a national clearinghouse with information on the risks, prevention, and treatment of osteoporosis. For more information, call 800-624-BONE.

The North American Menopause Society (NAMS) answers written requests for information. Write NAMS, 11100 Euclid Avenue, 7th Avenue, McDonald Hospital, Cleveland, OH 44105.

The National Women's Health Network distributes educational materials on a variety of women's health topics. Contact National Women's Health Network, 514 10th Street, NW, Washington, DC 20004; 202-347-1140.

Resources (continued)

The Older Women's League (OWL) educates the public about problems and issues of concern to middle age and older women. Contact OWL, 666 11th Street, NW, Suite 700, Washington, DC 20001; 202-783-6686.

The National Cancer Institute (NCI), part of NIH, funds cancer research and offers information for health professionals and the public. For more information about cancer risks and other related issues, call 800-4-CANCER.

The National Heart, Lung, and Blood Institute, part of NIH, carries out research and provides educational information on heart disease, stroke, and other related topics. For more information, call 301-251-1222.

The National Institute on Aging Information Center has information on menopause, osteoporosis, and a variety of other topics related to health and aging. Contact NIA Information Center, P.O. Box 8057, Gaithersburg, MD 20898-8057; 800-222-2225, 800-222-4225 (TTY).

Hospital Hints[*]

Going to the hospital is somewhat like traveling to a foreign country — the sights are not familiar, the language sounds strange, and the people are all new. No matter what the reason for the trip — whether it's an overnight visit for a few tests or a longer stay for medical treatment or major surgery — nearly everyone worries about entering the hospital. Learning more about hospitals and the people who work there may help make the journey less stressful.

The following hints are meant for people who plan to enter the hospital by choice rather than for those who go to the hospital because of an emergency. Relatives and friends of patients who enter the hospital because of an emergency also may find this information useful.

What to Bring

It's best to pack as little as you can. However, be sure to bring the following items:

- a few nightclothes, a bathrobe, and sturdy slippers (put your name on all personal items);
- comfortable clothes to wear home;
- a toothbrush, toothpaste, shampoo, comb and brush, deodorant, and razor;
- a list of all the medicines you take, including prescription and nonprescription drugs;
- details of past illnesses, surgeries, and any allergies;
- your health insurance card;
- a list of the names and telephone numbers (home and business) of family members to contact in case of an emergency; and
- $10 or less for newspapers, magazines, or any other items you may wish to buy in the hospital gift shop.

---

[*] Source: *Age Page*, National Institute on Aging, U.S. Department of Health and Human Services, Public Health Service, National Institutes of Health, Gaithersburg, MD 20898; 800-222-2225.

What Not to Bring

Leave cash, jewelry (including wedding rings, earrings, and watches), credit cards, and checkbooks at home or have a family member or friend keep them. If you must bring valuables, ask if they can be kept in the hospital safe during your stay. In addition, leave electric razors, hair dryers, and curling irons at home since they may not be grounded properly and could be unsafe.

Admission

The first stop in the hospital is the admitting office. Here, the patient or a family member signs forms allowing the hospital staff to provide treatment and to release medical information to the insurance company. Those who don't have private health insurance can talk with an admissions counselor about other payment methods and sources of financial aid such as Medicaid and Medicare.

Hospital Staff [4]

After getting settled in your room, you will begin to meet the members of your health care team.

- Doctors — Each patient has an attending physician, who is in charge of that person's overall care while in the hospital. The attending physician may be the patient's regular doctor, a member of the hospital staff to whom the patient has been referred, or a specialist. In a teaching hospital (where doctors train), a number of physicians care for each patient. The attending physician directs the house staff, which includes medical students, residents (doctors who have just graduated from medical school), and fellows (doctors who receive training in a special area of medicine after their residency training). together, these doctors "round," or see patients, about once a day. Patients gain from the knowledge of senior staff members but may undergo many

---

[4] More detailed information about some members of the hospital staff is found in the NIA *Age Page* "Who's Who in Health Care."

exams by doctors who are in training. In a non-teaching hospital, patients are treated by attending physicians only.

- Nurses — Registered nurses, nurse practitioners, licensed practical nurses, nurse's aides, and nursing students provide many patient-care services. For example, nurses give medicines, check vital signs (blood pressure, temperature, and pulse), provide treatments, and teach patients to care for themselves. The head nurse coordinates nursing care for each patient on the unit (the floor or section of the hospital where your room is located).

- Physical therapists teach patients to build muscles and improve coordination. They may use exercise, heat, cold, or water therapy to help patients whose ability to move is limited.

- Occupational therapists work with patients to restore, maintain, or increase their ability to perform daily tasks such as cooking, eating, bathing, and dressing.

- Respiratory therapists prevent and treat breathing problems. For example, they teach patients exercises to prevent lung infections after surgery.

- Technicians conduct a variety of laboratory tests such as blood and urine tests and x-rays.

- Dietitians teach patients how to plan a well-balanced diet.

- Pharmacists know the chemical makeup and correct use of drugs. They prepare the medicines used in the hospital.

- Social workers offer support to patients and their families. They can provide details about how to obtain health care and social services after leaving the hospital; for example, they know about financial aid programs, support groups, and home-care services.

Geriatric Assessment

Some older people have many complex problems which may threaten their ability to live independently after they go home from the hospital. In some hospitals, a team that includes a doctor, nurse, and social worker looks at the special needs of older patients. This team also may include other specialists and therapists. The team performs a thorough exam, called a geriatric assessment, to learn about the patient's physical and mental health, family life, income, living arrangements, access to community services, and ability to perform daily tasks. The team diagnoses health problems and develops a plan to help older patients get the health care and social services they need.

Hospital Geography

Hospitals have many patient-care areas. For example, patients may be in a private (one bed) or semiprivate (two bed) room. The intensive care unit (also called the ICU) has special equipment and staff to care for very ill patients. Coronary care units (CCU's) give intensive medical care to patients with severe heart disease. In both the ICU and CCU, visiting hours are strictly limited and only family members are allowed to see patients. Surgery is done in the operating room (OR). After an operation, patients spend time in the recovery room before going back to their own room.

In the emergency room (ER), trained staff treat life-threatening injuries or illnesses. Patients who are badly hurt or very sick are seen first. Because the ER is so busy, some patients may have to wait before they are seen by an emergency medical technician (paramedic), nurse, or doctor.

Safety Tips

Because medical equipment is not familiar and medications can make you feel tired or weak, it's good to take a few extra safety steps while in the hospital:

- Use the call bell when you need help.
- Use the controls to lower the bed before getting in or out.
- Be careful not to trip over the many wires and tubes that may be around the bed.
- Try to keep the things you need within easy reach.
- Take only prescribed medicines.
- If you brought your own medicines with you, tell your nurse or doctor, and take them only with your doctor's permission.
- Be careful getting in and out of the bathtub or shower. Hold on to grab bars for support.
- Use handrails on stairways and in hallways.
- If you must smoke, do so only where allowed, and never smoke around oxygen.

Questions

During your hospital stay, you may have many questions about your care. Always feel free to ask your doctor these questions. Your doctor is there to provide the care you need and to discuss your concerns. Your nurse or social worker also may be able to answer many of your questions or help you get the information you need.

You may find it useful to write down your questions as you think of them. For example, you may want to ask your doctor or nurse some or all of the following questions:

- What will this test tell you? Why is it needed, and when will you know the results?
- What treatment is needed, and how long will it last?
- What are the benefits and risks of treatment?
- When can I go home?
- When I go home, will I have to change my regular activities?
- How often will I need checkups?
- Is any other followup care needed?

Discharge

Before going home, you must have discharge orders from your doctor and a release form from the hospital's business office. Discharge planning before leaving the hospital can help you prepare for your health and home-care needs after you go home. This service is often provided by a registered nurse, social worker, or the hospital's discharge planner. Discharge planning is offered in the hospital so that, if needed, a visiting nurse, hospital equipment, meals-on-wheels, or other services will be there when you get home. The discharge planner also knows about senior centers, nursing homes, and other long-term care services. If you, your family, or a close friend have questions about your followup care or living

In Case of Emergency

In the event of a serious illness or accident, it's vital to seek medical help right away. In many areas, you can reach emergency help by calling 911 or the telephone operator. Be sure to tell the operator the type of emergency and your location.

If you have a minor injury or your symptoms aren't severe, call your family doctor or a nearby clinic before going to the emergency room (ER) or a hospital. Sometimes a visit to the ER isn't needed.

If your doctor thinks you should go to the ER, he or she can make things easier for you by calling the hospital to let them know you are coming. Your doctor also may arrange to meet you there.

If there is time, try to take the following items with you to the ER:

- your health insurance card or policy number;
- your doctor's name and telephone number;
- a list of the medicines you take, including prescription and nonprescription drugs;
- details of other medical problems; and
- the names and telephone numbers of close family members.

You may want to write all of this information on a note card that you can carry in your wallet or purse. Persons with some medical problems (such as diabetes, epilepsy, and allergies) should wear or carry identification (for example, an ID bracelet or ID card) to let rescue workers and hospital personnel know about these hidden conditions.

If possible, ask a relative or friend to go to the hospital with you for support.

arrangements after you leave the hospital, the discharge planner may be able to help.

For More Information

Hill-Burton hospitals give free hospital care to qualified people who cannot afford to pay. For a list of these hospitals in your area, call the Hill-Burton Program hotline at 800-638-0742 (toll free) or 800-492-0359 (toll free to residents of Maryland).

The American Hospital Association provides information about hospitals and patients' rights. Their address is 840 North Lake Shore Drive, Chicago, IL 60611; 312-280-6000.

To learn more about health and aging, contact the National Institute on Aging (NIA) Information Center, P.O. Box 8057, Gaithersburg, MD 20898-8057. The NIA distributes free *Age Pages* on a number of topics, including medical care, nutrition, and safety. A list of these publications is available on request.

Impotence[*]

The term "impotence" has traditionally been used to signify the inability of the male to attain and maintain erection of the penis sufficient to permit satisfactory sexual intercourse. However, this use has often led to confusing and uninterpretable results in both clinical and basic science investigations. This, together with its pejorative implications, suggests that the more precise term "erectile dysfunction" be used instead to signify an inability of the male to achieve an erect penis as part of the overall multifaceted process of male sexual function.

This process comprises a variety of physical aspects with important psychological and behavioral overtones. It should be recognized that desire, orgasmic capability, and ejaculatory capacity may be intact even in the presence of erectile dysfunction or may be deficient to some extent and contribute to the sense of inadequate sexual function.

Erectile dysfunction affects millions of men. Although for some men erectile function may not be the best or most important measure of sexual satisfaction, for many men erectile dysfunction creates mental stress that affects their interactions with family and associates. Many advances have occurred in both diagnosis and treatment of erectile dysfunction. However, its various aspects remain poorly understood by the general population and by most health care professionals. Lack of a simple definition, failure to delineate precisely the problem being assessed, and the absence of guidelines and parameters to determine assessment and treatment outcome and long-term results, have contributed to this state of affairs by producing misunderstanding, confusion, and ongoing concern. The fact that results have not been communicated effectively to the public has compounded this situation.

---

[*] Source: National Kidney and Urological Diseases Information Clearinghouse, 3 Information Way, Bethesda, MD 20892; 301-654-4415.

Cause-specific assessment and treatment of male sexual dysfunction will require recognition by the public and the medical community that erectile dysfunction is a part of overall male sexual dysfunction. The multifactorial nature of erectile dysfunction, comprising both organic and psychologic aspects, may often require a multi disciplinary approach to its assessment and treatment. This consensus report addresses these issues, not only as isolated health problems but also in the context of societal and individual perceptions and expectations.

Erectile dysfunction is often assumed to be a natural concomitant of the aging process, to be tolerated along with other conditions associated with aging. This assumption may not be entirely correct. For the elderly and for others, erectile dysfunction may occur as a consequence of specific illnesses or of medical treatment for certain illnesses, resulting in fear, loss of image and self-confidence, and depression.

For example, many men with diabetes mellitus may develop erectile dysfunction during their young and middle adult years. Physicians, diabetes educators, and patients and their families are sometimes unaware of this potential complication. Whatever the causal factors, discomfort of patients and health care providers in discussing sexual issues becomes a barrier to pursuing treatment.

Erectile dysfunction can be effectively treated with a variety of methods. Many patients and health care providers are unaware of these treatments, and the dysfunction thus often remains untreated, compounded by its psychological impact. Concurrent with the increase in the availability of effective treatment methods has been increased availability of new diagnostic procedures that may help in the selection of an effective, cause-specific treatment.

To examine what is known about the demographics, etiology, risk factors, pathophysiology, diagnostic assessment, treatments (both generic and cause-specific), and the understanding of their consequences by the public and the medical community, the National Institute of Diabetes and Digestive and Kidney Diseases and the Office of Medical Applications of Research of the National Institutes of Health, in conjunction with the National Institute of Neurological Disorders and Stroke and the National Institute on Aging, convened a consensus development conference on male impotence on December 7-9, 1992. After 1½ days of presentations by experts in the relevant fields involved with male sexual dysfunction and erectile impotence or dysfunction, a consensus panel comprised of representatives from urology, geriatrics, medicine, endocrinology, psychiatry, psychology, nursing, epidemiology, biostatistics, basic sciences, and the public considered the evidence and developed answers to the questions that follow.

What Are the Prevalence and Clinical, Psychological, and Social Impact of Impotence (Cultural, Geographical, National, Ethnic, Racial, Male/Female Perceptions and Influences)?

Prevalence and Association with Age

Estimates of the prevalence of impotence depend on the definition employed for this condition. For the purposes of this consensus development conference statement, impotence is defined as male erectile dysfunction, that is, the inability to achieve or maintain an erection sufficient for satisfactory sexual performance. Erectile performance has been characterized by the degree of dysfunction, and estimates of prevalence (the number of men with the condition) vary depending on the definition of erectile dysfunction used.

Appallingly little is known about the prevalence of erectile dysfunction in the United States and how this prevalence varies according to individual characteristics (age, race, ethnicity@y, socioeconomic status, and concomitant diseases and conditions). Data on erectile dysfunction available from the 1940's applied to the present U.S. male population produce an estimate of erectile dysfunction prevalence of 7 million.

More recent estimates suggest that the number of U.S. men with erectile dysfunction may more likely be near 10-20 million. Inclusion of individuals with partial erectile dysfunction increases the estimate to about 30 million. The majority of these individuals will be older than 65 years of age. The prevalence of erectile dysfunction has been found to be associated with age. A prevalence of about 5 percent is observed at age 40, increasing to 15-25 percent at age 65 and older. One-third of older men receiving medical care at a Department of Veterans' Affairs ambulatory clinic admitted to problems with erectile function.

Causes contributing to erectile dysfunction can be broadly classified into two categories: organic and psychologic. In reality, while the majority of patients with erectile dysfunction are thought to demonstrate an organic component, psychopsychological aspects of self-confidence, anxiety, and partner communication and conflict are often important contributing factors.

The 1985 National Ambulatory Medical Care Survey indicated that there were about 525,000 visits for erectile dysfunction, accounting for 0.2 percent of all male ambulatory care visits. Estimates of visits per 1,000 population increased from about 1.5 for the age group 25-34 to 15.0 for those age 65 and above. The 1985 National Hospital Discharge Survey estimated that more than 30,000 hospital admissions were for erectile dysfunction.

Clinical, Psychological, and Social Impact
Geographic, Racial, Ethnic, Socioeconomic, and Cultural Variation in Erectile Dysfunction
Very little is known about variations in prevalence of erectile dysfunction across geographic, racial, ethnic, socioeconomic, and cultural groups. Anecdotal evidence points to the existence of racial, ethnic, and other cultural diversity in the perceptions and expectation levels for satisfactory sexual functioning. These differences would be expected to be reflected in these groups' reaction to erectile dysfunction, although few data on this issue appear to exist.

One report from a recent community survey concluded that erectile failure was the leading complaint of males attending sex therapy clinics. Other studies have shown that erectile disorders are the primary concern of sex therapy patients in treatment. This is consistent with the view that erectile dysfunction may be associated with depression, loss of self-esteem, poor self-image, increased anxiety or tension with one's sexual partner, and/or fear and anxiety associated with contracting sexually transmitted diseases, including AIDS.

Male/Female Perceptions and Influences
The diagnosis of erectile dysfunction may be understood as the presence of a condition limiting choices for sexual interaction and possibly limiting opportunity for sexual satisfaction. The impact of this condition depends very much on the dynamics of the relationship of the individual and his sexual partner and their expectation of performance. When changes in sexual function are perceived by the individual and his partner as a natural consequence of the aging process, they may modify their sexual behavior to accommodate the condition and maintain sexual satisfaction, Increasingly, men do not perceive erectile dysfunction as a normal part of aging and seek to identify means by which they may return to their previous level and range of sexual activities. Such levels and expectations and desires for future sexual interactions are important aspects of the evaluation of patients presenting with a chief complaint of erectile dysfunction.

In men of all ages, erectile failure may diminish willingness to initiate sexual relationships because of fear of inadequate sexual performance or rejection. Because males, especially older males, are particularly sensitive to the social support of intimate relationships, withdrawal from these relationships because of such fears may have a negative effect on their overall health.

What Are the Risk Factors Contributing to Impotence? Can These Be Utilized in Preventing Development of Impotence?

Physiology of Erection

The male erectile response is a vascular event initiated by neuronal action and maintained by a complex interplay between vascular and neurological events. In its most common form, it is initiated by a central nervous system event that integrates psychogenic stimuli (perception, desire, etc.) and controls the sympathetic and parasympathetic innervation of the penis. Sensory stimuli from the penis are important in continuing this process and in initiating a reflex arc that may cause erection under proper circumstances and may help to maintain erection during sexual activity.

Parasympathetic input allows erection by relaxation of trabecular smooth muscle and dilation of the helicine arteries of the penis. This leads to expansion of the lacunar spaces and entrapment of blood by compressing venules against the tunica albuginea, a process referred to as the corporal veno-occlusive mechanism. The tunica albuginea must have sufficient stiffness to compress the venules penetrating it so that venous outflow is blocked and sufficient tumescence and rigidity can occur.

Acetylcholine released by the parasympathetic nerves is thought to act primarily on endothelial cells to release a second nonadrenergic-noncholinergic carrier of the signal that relaxes the trabecular smooth muscle. Nitric oxide released by the endothelial cells, and possibly also of neural origin, is currently thought to be the leading of several candidates as this nonadrenergic-noncholinergic transmitter; but this has not yet been conclusively demonstrated to the exclusion of other potentially important substances (e.g., vasoactive intestinal polypeptide). The relaxing effect of nitric oxide on the trabecular smooth muscle may be mediated through its stimulation of guanylate cyclase and the production of cyclic guanosine monophosphate (cGMP), which would then function as a second messenger in this system.

Constriction of the trabecular smooth muscle and helicine arteries induced by sympathetic innervation makes the penis flaccid, with blood pressure in the cavernosal sinuses of the penis near venous pressure. Acetylcholine is thought to decrease sympathetic tone. This may be important in a permissive sense for adequate trabecular smooth muscle relaxation and consequent effective action of other mediators in achieving sufficient inflow of blood into the lacunar spaces. When the trabecular smooth muscle relaxes and helicine arteries dilate in response to parasympathetic stimulation and decreased sympathetic tone, increased blood flow fills the cavernous spaces, increasing the pressure within these spaces so that the penis becomes erect. As the venules are compressed against the tunica albuginea, penile pressure approaches arterial pressure, causing rigidity. Once this state is achieved, arterial inflow is reduced to a level that matches venous outflow.

Erectile Dysfunction
Because adequate arterial supply is critical for erection, any disorder that impairs blood flow may be implicated in the etiology of erectile failure. Most of the medical disorders associated with erectile dysfunction appear to affect the arterial system. Some disorders may interfere with the corporal veno-occlusive mechanism and result in failure to trap blood within the penis, or produce leakage such that an erection cannot be maintained or is easily lost.

Damage to the autonomic pathways innervating the penis may eliminate "psychogenic" erection initiated by the central nervous system. Lesions of the somatic nervous pathways may impair reflexogenic erections and may interrupt tactile sensation needed to maintain psychogenic erections. Spinal cord lesions may produce varying degrees of erectile failure depending on the location and completeness of the lesions. Not only do traumatic lesions affect erectile ability, but disorders leading to peripheral neuropathy may impair neuronal innervation of the penis or of the sensory afferents. The endocrine system itself, particularly the production of androgens, appears to play a role in regulating sexual interest, and may also play a role in erectile function.

Psychological processes such as depression, anxiety, and relationship problems can impair erectile functioning by reducing erotic focus or otherwise reducing awareness of sensory experience. This may lead to inability to initiate or maintain an erection. Etiologic factors for erectile disorders may be categorized as neurogenic, vasculogenic, or psychogenic, but they most commonly appear to derive from problems in all three areas acting in concert.

Risk Factors

Little is known about the natural history of erectile dysfunction. This includes information on the age of onset, incidence rates stratified by age, progression of the condition, and frequency of spontaneous recovery. There also are very limited data on associated morbidity and functional impairment. To date, the data are predominantly available for whites, with other racial and ethnic populations represented only in smaller numbers that do not permit analysis of these issues as a function of race or ethnicity.

Erectile dysfunction is clearly a symptom of many conditions, and certain risk factors have been identified, some of which may be amenable to prevention strategies. Diabetes mellitus, hypogonadism in association with a number of endocrinologic conditions, hypertension, vascular disease, high levels of blood cholesterol, low levels of high density lipoprotein, drugs, neurogenic disorders, Peyronie's disease, priapism, depression, alcohol ingestion, lack of sexual knowledge, poor sexual techniques, inadequate interpersonal relationships or their deterioration, and many chronic diseases, especially renal failure and dialysis, have been demonstrated as risk factors. Vascular surgery is also often a risk factor. Age appears to be a strong indirect risk factor in that it is associated with an increased likelihood of direct risk factors. Other factors require more extensive study. Smoking has an adverse effect on erectile function by accentuating the effects of other risk factors such as vascular disease or hypertension. To date, vasectomy has not been associated with an increased risk of erectile dysfunction other than causing an occasional psychological reaction that could then have a psychogenic influence. Accurate risk factor identification and characterization are essential for concerted efforts at prevention of erectile dysfunction.

Prevention
Although erectile dysfunction increases progressively with age, it is not an inevitable consequence of aging. Knowledge of the risk factors can guide prevention strategies. Specific antihypertensive, antidepressant, and antipsychotic drugs can be chosen to lessen the risk of erectile failure. Published lists of prescription drugs that may impair erectile functioning often are based on reports implicating a drug without systematic study. Such studies are needed to confirm the validity of these suggested associations. In the individual patient, the physician can modify the regimen in an effort to resolve the erectile problem.

It is important that physicians and other health care providers treating patients for chronic conditions periodically inquire into the sexual functioning of their patients and be prepared to offer counsel for those who experience erectile difficulties. Lack of sexual knowledge and anxiety about sexual performance are common contributing factors to erectile dysfunction. Education and reassurance may be helpful in preventing the cascade into serious erectile failure in individuals who experience minor erectile difficulty due to medications or common changes in erectile functioning associated with chronic illnesses or with aging.

What Diagnostic Information Should Be Obtained in Assessment of the Impotent Patient? What Criteria Should Be Employed To Determine Which Tests are Indicated for a Particular Patient?

The appropriate evaluation of all men with erectile dysfunction should include a medical and detailed sexual history (including practices and techniques), a physical examination, a psycho-social evaluation, and basic laboratory studies. When available, a multidisciplinary approach to this evaluation may be desirable. In selected patients, further physiologic or invasive studies may be indicated. A sensitive sexual history, including expectations and motivations, should be obtained from the patient (and sexual partner whenever possible) in an interview conducted by an interested physician or another specially trained professional. A written patient questionnaire may be helpful but is not a substitute for the interview. The sexual history is needed to accurately define the patient's specific complaint and to distinguish between true erectile dysfunction, changes in sexual desire, and orgasmic or ejaculatory disturbances. The patient should be asked specifically about perceptions of his erectile dysfunction, including the nature of onset, frequency, quality, and duration of erections; the presence of nocturnal or morning erections; and his ability to achieve sexual satisfaction. Psychosocial factors related to erectile dysfunction should be probed, including specific situational circumstances, performance anxiety, the nature of sexual relationships, details of current sexual techniques, expectations, motivation for treatment, and the presence of specific discord in the patient's relationship with his sexual partner. The sexual partner's own expectations and perceptions should also be sought since they may have important bearing on diagnosis and treatment recommendations.

The general medical history is important in identifying specific risk factors that may account for or contribute to the patient's erectile dysfunction. These include vascular risk factors such as hypertension, diabetes, smoking, coronary artery disease, peripheral vascular disorders, pelvic trauma or surgery, and blood lipid abnormalities. Decreased sexual desire or history suggesting a hypogonadal state could indicate a primary endocrine disorder. Neurologic causes may include a history of diabetes mellitus or alcoholism with associated peripheral neuropathy. Neurologic disorders such as multiple sclerosis, spinal injury, or cerebrovascular accidents are often obvious or well defined prior to presentation. It is essential to obtain a detailed medication and illicit drug history since an estimated 25 percent of cases of erectile dysfunction may be attributable to medications for other conditions. Past medical history can reveal important causes of erectile dysfunction, including radical pelvic surgery, radiation therapy, Peyronie's disease, penile or pelvic trauma, prostatitis, priapism, or voiding dysfunction. Information regarding prior evaluation or treatment for "impotence" should be obtained. A detailed sexual history, including current sexual techniques, is important in the general history obtained. It is also important to determine if there have been previous psychiatric illnesses such as depression or neuroses.

Physical examination should include the assessment of male secondary sex characteristics, femoral and lower extremity pulses and a focused neurologic examination including perianal sensation, anal sphincter tone, and bulbocavernosus reflex. More extensive neurologic tests, including dorsal nerve conduction latencies, evoked potential measurements, and corpora cavernosal electromyography lack normative (control) data and appear at this time to be of limited clinical value. Examination of the genitalia includes evaluation of testis size and consistency, palpation of the shaft of the penis to determine the presence of Peyronie's plaques, and a digital rectal examination of the prostate with assessment of anal sphincter tone.

Endocrine evaluation consisting of a morning serum testosterone is generally indicated. Measurement of serum prolactin may be indicated. A low testosterone level merits repeat measurement together with assessment of luteinizing hormone (LH), follicle-stimulating hormone (FSH), and prolactin levels. Other tests may be helpful in excluding unrecognized systemic disease and include a complete blood count, urinalysis, creatinine, lipid profile, fasting blood sugar, and thyroid function studies.

Although not indicated for routine use, nocturnal penile tumescence (NPT) testing may be useful in the patient who reports a complete absence of erections (exclusive of nocturnal "sleep" erections) or when a primary psychogenic etiology is suspected. Such testing should be performed by those with expertise and knowledge of its interpretation, pitfalls, and usefulness. Various methods and devices are available for the evaluation of nocturnal penile tumescence, but their clinical usefulness is restricted by limitations of diagnostic accuracy and availability of normative data. Further study regarding standardization of NPT testing and its general applicability is indicated.

After the history, physical examination, and laboratory testing, a clinical impression can be obtained of a primarily psychogenic, organic, or mixed etiology for erectile dysfunction. Patients with primary or associated psychogenic factors may be offered further psychologic evaluation, and patients with endocrine abnormalities may be referred to an endocrinologist to evaluate the possibility of a pituitary lesion or hypogonadism. Unless previously diagnosed, suspicion of neurologic deficit may be further assessed by complete neurologic evaluation. No further diagnostic tests appear necessary for those patients who favor noninvasive treatment (e.g., vacuum constrictive devices or pharmacologic injection therapy). Patients who do not respond satisfactorily to these noninvasive treatments may be candidates for penile implant surgery or further diagnostic testing for possible additional invasive therapies.

A rigid or nearly rigid erectile response to intracavernous injection of pharmacologic test doses of a vasodilating agent (see below) indicates adequate arterial and veno-occlusive function. This suggests that the patient may be a suitable candidate for a trial of penile injection therapy. Genital stimulation may be of use in increasing the erectile response in this setting. This diagnostic technique also may be used to differentiate a vascular from a primarily neuropathic or psychogenic etiology. Patients who have an inadequate response to intracavernous pharmacologic injection may be candidates for further vascular testing. It should be recognized, however, that failure to respond adequately may not indicate vascular insufficiency but can be caused by patient anxiety or discomfort. The number of patients who may benefit from more extensive vascular testing is small, but includes young men with a history of significant perineal or pelvic trauma, who may have anatomic arterial blockage (either alone or with neurologic deficit) to account for erectile dysfunction.

Studies to further define vasculogenic disorders include pharmacologic duplex grey scale/color ultrasonography, pharmacologic dynamic infusion cavernosometry/cavernosography, and pharmacologic pelvic/penile angiography. Cavernosometry, duplex ultrasonography, and angiography performed either alone or in conjunction with intracavernous pharmacologic injection of vasodilator agents rely on complete arterial and cavernosal smooth muscle relaxation to evaluate arterial and veno-occlusive function. The clinical effectiveness of these invasive studies is severely limited by several factors, including the lack of normative data, operator dependence, variable interpretation of results, and poor predictability of therapeutic outcomes of arterial and venous surgery. At the present time these studies might best be done in referral centers with specific expertise and interest in investigation of the vascular aspects of erectile dysfunction. Further clinical research is necessary to standardize methodology and interpretation, to obtain control data on normals (as stratified according to age), and to define what constitutes normality in order to assess the value of these tests in their diagnostic accuracy and in their ability to predict treatment outcome in men with erectile dysfunction.

What Are the Efficacies and Risks of Behavioral, Pharmacological, Surgical, and Other Treatments for Impotence? What Sequences and/or Combination of These Interventions Are Appropriate? What Management Techniques Are Appropriate When Treatment Is Not Effective or Indicated?

General Considerations

Because of the difficulty in defining the clinical entity of erectile dysfunction, there have been a variety of entry criteria for patients in therapeutic trials. Similarly, the ability to assess efficacy of therapeutic interventions is impaired by the lack of clear and quantifiable criteria of erectile dysfunction. General considerations for treatment follow:

- Psychotherapy and/or behavioral therapy may be useful for some patients with erectile dysfunction without obvious organic cause, and for their partners. These may also be used as an adjunct to other therapies directed at the treatment of organic erectile dysfunction. Outcome data from such therapy, however, have not been well-documented or quantified, and additional studies along these lines are indicated.

- Efficacy of therapy may be best achieved by inclusion of both partners in treatment plains.

- Treatment should be individualized to the patient's desires and expectations.

- Even though there are several effective treatments currently available, long-term efficacy is in general relatively low. Moreover, there is a high rate of voluntary cessation of treatment for all currently popular forms of therapy for erectile dysfunction. Better understanding of the reasons for each of these phenomena is needed.

Psychotherapy and Behavioral Therapy

Psychosocial factors are important in all forms of erectile dysfunction. Careful attention to these issues and attempts to relieve sexual anxieties should be a part of the therapeutic intervention for all patients with erectile dysfunction. Psychotherapy and/or behavioral therapy alone may be helpful for some patients in whom no organic cause of erectile dysfunction is detected. Patients who refuse medical and surgical interventions also may be helped by such counseling. After appropriate evaluation to detect and treat coexistent problems such as issues related to the loss of a partner, dysfunctional relationships, psychotic disorders, or alcohol and drug abuse, psychological treatment focuses on decreasing performance anxiety and distractions and on increasing a couple's intimacy and ability to communicate about sex. Education concerning the factors that create normal sexual response and erectile dysfunction can help a couple cope with sexual difficulties. Working with the sexual partner is useful in improving the outcome of therapy. Psychotherapy and behavioral therapy have been reported to relieve depression and anxiety as well as to improve sexual function. However, outcome data of psychological and behavioral therapy have not been quantified, and evaluation of the success of specific techniques used in these treatments is poorly documented. Studies to validate their efficacy are therefore strongly indicated.

Medical Therapy

An initial approach to medical therapy should consider reversible medical problems that may contribute to erectile dysfunction. Included in this should be assessment of the possibility of medication-induced erectile dysfunction with consideration for reduction of polypharmacy and/or substitution of medications with lower probability of inducing erectile dysfunction.

For some patients with an established diagnosis of testicular failure (hypogonadism), androgen replacement therapy may sometimes be effective in improving erectile function. A trial of androgen replacement may be worthwhile in men with low serum testosterone levels if there are no other contraindications. In contrast, for men who have normal testosterone levels, androgen therapy is inappropriate and may carry significant health risks, especially in the situation of unrecognized prostate cancer. If androgen therapy is indicated, it should be given in the form of intramuscular injections of testosterone enanthate or cypionate. Oral androgens, as currently available, are not indicated. For men with hyperprolactinemia, bromocriptine therapy often is effective in normalizing the prolactin level and improving sexual function. A wide variety of other substances taken either orally or topically have been suggested to be effective in treating erectile dysfunction. Most of these have not been subjected to rigorous clinical studies and are not approved for this use by the Food and Drug Administration (FDA). Their use should therefore be discouraged until further evidence in support of their efficacy and indicative of their safety is available.

Intracavernosal Injection Therapy

Injection of vasodilator substances into the corpora of the penis has provided a new therapeutic technique for a variety of causes of erectile dysfunction. The most effective and well-studied agents are papaverine, phentolamine, and prostaglandin E_1. These have been used either singly or in combination. Use of these agents occasionally causes priapism (inappropriately persistent erections). This appears to have been seen most commonly with papaverine. Priapism is treated with adrenergic agents, which can cause life-threatening hypertension in patients receiving monoamine oxidase inhibitors. Use of the penile vasodilators also can be problematic in patients who cannot tolerate transient hypotension, those with severe psychiatric disease, those with poor manual dexterity, those with poor vision, and those receiving anticoagulant therapy. Liver function tests should be obtained in those being treated with papaverine alone. Prostaglandin E_1 can be used together with papaverine and phentolamine to decrease the incidence of side effects such as pain, penile corporal fibrosis, fibrotic nodules, hypotension, and priapism. Further study of the efficacy of multitherapy versus monotherapy and of the relative complications and safety of each approach is indicated. Although these agents have not received FDA approval for this indication, they are in widespread clinical use. Patients treated with these agents should give full informed consent. There is a high rate of patient dropout, often early in the treatment.

Whether this is related to side effects, lack of spontaneity in sexual relations, or general loss of interest is unclear. Patient education and follow up support might improve compliance and lessen the dropout rate. However, the reasons for the high dropout rate need to be determined and quantified.

Vacuum Constrictive Devices

Vacuum constriction devices may be effective at generating and maintaining erections in many patients with erectile dysfunction and these appear to have a low incidence of side effects. As with Intracavernosal injection therapy, there is a significant rate of patient dropout with these devices, and the reasons for this phenomenon are unclear. The devices are difficult for some patients to use, and this is especially so in those with impaired manual dexterity. Also, these devices may impair ejaculation, which can then cause some discomfort. Patients and their partners sometimes are bothered by the lack of spontaneity in sexual relations that may occur with this procedure. The patient is sometimes also bothered by the general discomfort that can occur while using these devices. Partner involvement in training with these devices may be important for successful outcome, especially in regard to establishing a mutually satisfying level of sexual activity.

Vascular Surgery
Surgery of the penile venous system, generally involving venous ligation, has been reported to be effective in patients who have been demonstrated to have venous leakage. However, the tests necessary to establish this diagnosis have been incompletely validated; therefore, it is difficult to select patients who will have a predictably good outcome. Moreover, decreased effectiveness of this approach has been reported as longer term follow-ups have been obtained. This has tempered enthusiasm for these procedures, which are probably therefore best done in an investigational setting in medical centers by surgeons experienced in these procedures and their evaluation.

Arterial revascularization procedures have a very limited role (e.g., in congenital or traumatic vascular abnormality) and probably should be restricted to the clinical investigation setting in medical centers with experienced personnel. All patients who are considered for vascular surgical therapy need to have appropriate preoperative evaluation, which may include dynamic infusion pharmaco-cavernosometry and cavernosography (DICC), duplex ultrasonography, and possibly arteriography. The indications for and interpretations of these diagnostic procedures are incompletely standardized; therefore, difficulties persist with using these techniques to predict and assess the success of surgical therapy, and further investigation to clarify their value and role in this regard is indicated.

Penile Prostheses

Three forms of penile prostheses are available for patients who fail with or refuse other forms of therapy: semirigid, malleable, and inflatable. The effectiveness, complications, and acceptability vary among the three types of prostheses, with the main problems being mechanical failure, infection, and erosions. Silicone particle shedding has been reported, including migration to regional lymph nodes; however, no clinically identifiable problems have been reported as a result of the silicone particles. There is a risk of the need for re-operation with all devices. Although the inflatable prostheses may yield a more physiologically natural appearance, they have had a higher rate of failure requiring re-operation. Men with diabetes mellitus, spinal cord injuries, or urinary tract infections have an increased risk of prosthesis-associated infections This form of treatment may not be appropriate in patients with severe penile corporal fibrosis, or severe medical illness. Circumcision may be required for patients with phimosis and balanitis.

Staging of Treatment

The patient and partner must be well informed about all therapeutic options including their effectiveness, possible complications, and costs. As a general rule, the least invasive or dangerous procedures should be tried first. Psychotherapy and behavioral treatments and sexual counseling alone or in conjunction with other treatments may be used in all patients with erectile dysfunction who are willing to use this form of treatment. In patients in whom psychogenic erectile dysfunction is suspected, sexual counseling should be offered first. Invasive therapy should not be the primary treatment of choice. If history, physical, and screening endocrine evaluations are normal and nonpsychogenic erectile dysfunction is suspected, either vacuum devices or intracavernosal injection therapy can be offered after discussion with the patient and his partner. These latter two therapies may also be useful when combined with psychotherapy in those with psychogenic erectile dysfunction in whom psychotherapy alone has failed. Since further diagnostic testing does not reliably establish specific diagnoses or predict outcomes of therapy, vacuum devices or intracavernosal injections often are applied to a broad spectrum of etiologies of male erectile dysfunction.

The motivation and expectations of the patient and his partner and education of both are critical in determining which therapy is chosen and in optimizing its outcome. If single therapy is ineffective, combining two or more forms of therapy may be useful. Penile prostheses should be placed only after patients have been carefully screened and informed. Vascular surgery should be undertaken only in the setting of clinical investigation and extensive clinical experience. With any form of therapy for erectile dysfunction, long-term followup by health professionals is required to assist the patient and his partner with adjustment to the therapeutic intervention. This is particularly true for intracavernosal injection and vacuum constriction therapies. Followup should include continued patient education and support in therapy, careful determination of reasons for cessation of therapy if this occurs, and provision of other options if earlier therapies are unsuccessful.

What Strategies Are Effective in Improving Public and Professional Knowledge About Impotence?

Despite the accumulation of a substantial body of scientific information about erectile dysfunction, large segments of the public, as well as the health professions, remain relatively uninformed, or, even worse, misinformed, about much of what is known. This lack of information, added to a pervasive reluctance of physicians to deal candidly with sexual matters, has resulted in patients being denied the benefits of treatment for their sexual concerns. Although they might wish doctors would ask them questions about their sexual lives, patients, for their part, are too often inhibited from initiating such discussions themselves. Improving both public and professional knowledge about erectile dysfunction will serve to remove those barriers and will foster more open communication and more effective treatment of this condition.

Strategies for Improving Public Knowledge

To a significant degree, the public, particularly older men, is conditioned to accept erectile dysfunction as a condition of progressive aging for which little can be done. In addition, there is considerable inaccurate public information regarding sexual function and dysfunction. Often, this is in the form of advertisements in which enticing promises are made, and patients then become even more demoralized when promised benefits fail to materialize. Accurate information on sexual function and the management of dysfunction must be provided to affected men and their partners. They also must be encouraged to seek professional help, and providers must be aware of the embarrassment and/or discouragement that may often be reasons why men with erectile dysfunction avoid seeking appropriate treatment.

To reach the largest audience, communications strategies should include informative and accurate newspaper and magazine articles, radio and television programs, as well as special educational programs in senior centers. Resources for accurate information regarding diagnosis and treatment options also should include doctors' offices, unions, fraternal and service groups, voluntary health organizations, State and local health departments, and appropriate advocacy groups. Additionally, since sex education courses in schools uniformly address erectile function, the concept of erectile dysfunction can easily be communicated in these forums as well.

Strategies for Improving Professional Knowledge

- Provide wide distribution of this statement to physicians and other health professionals whose work involves patient contact.

- Define a balance between what specific information is needed by the medical and general public and what is available, and identify what treatments are available.

- Promote the introduction of courses in human sexuality into the curricula of graduate schools for all health care professionals. Because sexual well-being is an integral part of general health, emphasis should be placed on the importance of obtaining a detailed sexual history as part of every medical history.

- Encourage the inclusion of sessions on diagnosis and management of erectile dysfunction in continuing medical education courses.

- Emphasize the desirability for an interdisciplinary approach to the diagnosis and treatment of erectile dysfunction. An integrated medical and psychosocial effort with continuing contact with the patient and partner may enhance their motivation and compliance with treatment during the period of sexual rehabilitation.

- Encourage the inclusion of presentations on erectile dysfunction at scientific meetings of appropriate medical specialty associations, state and local medical societies, and similar organizations of other health professions.

- Distribute scientific information on erectile dysfunction to the news media (print, radio, and television) to support their efforts to disseminate accurate information on this subject and to counteract misleading news reports and false advertising claims.

- Promote public service announcements, lectures, and panel discussions on both commercial and public radio and television on the subject of erectile dysfunction.

What Are the Needs for Future Research?

This consensus on male erectile dysfunction has provided an overview of current knowledge of the prevalence, etiology, pathophysiology, diagnosis, and management of this condition. The growing individual and societal awareness and open acknowledgment of the problem have led to increased interest and resultant explosion of knowledge in each of these areas. Research on this condition has produced many controversies. Numerous questions have been identified that may serve as foci for future research directions. These will depend on the development of precise agreement among investigators and clinicians in this field on the definition of what constitutes erectile dysfunction, and what factors in its multi-faceted nature contribute to its expression. In addition, further investigation of these issues will require collaborative efforts of basic science investigators and clinicians from the spectrum of relevant disciplines and the rigorous application of appropriate research principles in designing studies to obtain further knowledge and to promote understanding of the various aspects of this condition. The needs and directions for future research can be considered as follows:

- Development of a symptom score sheet to aid in the standardization of patient assessment and treatment outcome.

- Development of a staging system that may permit quantitative and qualitative classification of erectile dysfunction.

- Studies on perceptions and expectations associated with racial, cultural, ethnic, and societal influences on what constitutes normal male erectile function and how these same factors may be responsible for the development and/ or perception of male erectile dysfunction.

- Studies to define and characterize what is normal erectile function, possibly as stratified by age.

- Additional basic research on the physiological and biochemical mechanisms that may underlie the etiology, pathogenesis, and response to treatment of the various forms of erectile dysfunction.

- Epidemiological studies directed at the prevalence of mal erectile dysfunction and its medical and psychological correlates, particularly in the context of possible racial, ethnic, socioeconomic, and cultural variability.

- Additional studies of the mechanisms by which risk factors may produce erectile dysfunction.

- Studies of strategies to prevent male erectile dysfunction.

- Randomized clinical trials assessing the effectiveness of specific behavioral, mechanical, pharmacologic, and surgical treatments, either alone or in combination.

- Studies on the specific effects of hormones (especially androgens) on male sexual function; determination of the frequency of endocrine causes of erectile dysfunction (e.g., hypogonadism and hyperprolactinemia) and the rates of success of appropriate hormonal therapy.

- Longitudinal studies in well-specified populations; evaluation of alternative approaches for the systematic assessment of men with erectile dysfunction; cost-effectiveness studies of diagnostic and therapeutic approaches; formal outcomes research of the various approaches to the assessment and treatment of this condition.

- Social/psychological studies of the impact of erectile dysfunction on subjects, their partners, and their interactions, and factors associated with seeking care.

- Development of new therapies, including pharmacologic agents, and with emphasis on oral agents, that may address the cause of male erectile dysfunction with greater specificity.

- Long-term followup studies to assess treatment effects, patient compliance, and late adverse effects. Studies to characterize the significance of erectile function and dysfunction in women.

Conclusions

- The term "erectile dysfunction" should replace the term "impotence" to characterize the inability to attain and/or maintain penile erection sufficient for satisfactory sexual performance.

- The likelihood of erectile dysfunction increases progressively with age but is not an inevitable consequence of aging. Other age-related conditions increase the likelihood of its occurrence.

- Erectile dysfunction may be a consequence of medications taken for other problems or a result of drug abuse.

- Embarrassment of patients and the reluctance of both patients and health care providers to discuss sexual matters candidly contribute to under diagnosis of erectile dysfunction.

- Contrary to present public and professional opinion, many cases of erectile dysfunction can be successfully managed with appropriately selected therapy.

- Men with erectile dysfunction require diagnostic evaluations and treatments specific and responsive to their circumstances. Patient compliance as well as patient and partner desires and expectations are important considerations in the choice of a particular treatment approach. A multi disciplinary approach may be of great benefit in defining the problem and arriving at a solution.

- The development of methods to quantify the degree of erectile dysfunction objectively would be extremely useful in the assessment both of the problem and of treatment outcomes.

- Education of physicians and other health professionals in aspects of human sexuality is currently inadequate, and curriculum development is urgently needed.

- Education of the public on aspects of sexual dysfunction and the availability of successful treatments is essential; media involvement in this effort is an important component This should be combined with information designed to expose "quack remedies" and protect men and their partners from economic and emotional losses.

- Important information on many aspects of erectile dysfunction is lacking; major research efforts are essential to the improvement of our understanding of the appropriate diagnostic assessments and treatments of this condition.

- Erectile dysfunction is an important public health problem deserving of increased support for basic science investigation and applied research.

Life Extension:
Science or Science Fiction?[*]

Explorers once searched for the fountain of youth, and old legends tell of magic potions that keep people young. The ancient questions — Why do people grow old? How can we live longer? — still fascinate people, including the scientists who study aging (gerontologists). But their most important question is this: how can people stay healthy and independent as they grow older?

Recently, researchers have begun to find certain chemicals in our bodies that may someday answer these questions. As a result, some stores and catalogs now sell products that are similar to these chemicals. However, the advertising claims that these products can extend life are very much exaggerated. Here are some of the chemicals being studied and what scientists have learned about them so far.

Antioxidants

These are natural substances that may help prevent disease. Antioxidants fight harmful molecules called oxygen free radicals, which are created by the body as cells go about their normal business of producing energy. Free radicals also come from smoking, radiation, sunlight, and other factors in the environment.

Some antioxidants, such as the enzyme SOD (superoxide dismutase), are produced in the body. Others come from food; these include vitamin C, vitamin E, and beta carotene, which is related to vitamin A.

The body's antioxidant defense system prevents most free-radical damage, but not all. As people grow older, the damage may build

---

[*] Source: *Age Page*, National Institute on Aging, U.S. Department of Health and Human Services, Public Health Service, National Institutes of Health, Gaithersburg, MD 20898; 800-222-2225.

up. According to one theory of aging, this build-up eventually causes cells, tissues, and organs to break down.

There is some evidence to support this theory. For instance, the longer an animal lives, the more antioxidants it has in its body. Also, some studies show that antioxidants may help prevent heart disease, some cancers, cataracts, and other health problems that are common as people get older.

Most experts think that the best way to get these vitamins is by eating fruits and vegetables (five helpings a day) rather than by taking vitamin pills. SOD pills have no effect on the body. They are broken up into different substances during digestion. More research is needed before specific recommendations can be made.

DNA and RNA

DNA (deoxyribonucleic acid) is the material in every cell that holds the genes. Every day some DNA is damaged and most of the time it is repaired. But more and more damage occurs with age,, and it may be that DNA repair, never 100-percent perfect, falls further and further behind. If so, the damage that does not get repaired and builds up could be one of the reasons that people age.

As a result, pills containing DNA and RNA (ribonucleic acid, which works with DNA in the cells to make proteins) are on the market. But DNA and RNA are like SOD tablets. When they are taken by mouth, they are broken down into other substances and cannot get to cells or do any good.

DHEA

Short for dehydroepiandrosterone, DHEA is a hormone that has turned back some signs of aging in animals. When given to mice, it has boosted the immune system and helped prevent some kinds of cancer.

DHEA travels through the body in the blood in a special form, called DHEA sulfate, which turns into DHEA when it enters a cell. Levels of DHEA sulfate are high in younger people but tend to go down with age.

Substances labeled DHEA are being sold as a way to extend life, although no one knows whether they are effective.

Other Hormones

In a recent study with a small number of men, injections of growth hormone boosted the size and strength of the men's muscles and seemed to reverse some signs of aging. Now, larger studies are testing growth hormone and other hormones, such as estrogen and testosterone, to find out whether they can prevent weakness and frailty in older people.

Ten Tips for Healthy Aging

No known substance can extend life, but the chances of staying healthy and living a long time can be improved:

- Eat a balanced diet, including five helpings of fruits and vegetables a day.
- Exercise regularly (check with a doctor before starting an exercise program).
- Get regular health check-ups.
- Don't smoke (it's never too late to quit).
- Practice safety habits at home to prevent falls and fractures. Always wear your seatbelt in a car.
- Stay in contact with family and friends. Stay active through work, play, and community.
- Avoid overexposure to the sun and the cold.
- If you drink, moderation is the key. When you drink, let someone else drive.
- Keep personal and financial records in order to simplify budgeting and investing. Plan long-term housing and money needs.
- Keep a positive attitude toward life. Do things that make you happy.

However, it is much too early to know whether any of these hormones will work. Moreover, the side effects of hormones could be very serious; high amounts of some hormones have been linked to cancer.

The Bottom Line

Currently no treatments, drugs, or pills are known to slow aging or extend life in humans. Check with a doctor before buying pills or anything else that promises to slow aging, extend life, or make a big change in the way you look or feel.

Resources

The National Institute on Aging offers a free booklet on the biology of aging and other information on health and aging. Write or call: NIA Information Center, P.O. Box 8057, Gaithersburg, MD 20898-8057; 800-222-2225, 800-222-4225 (TTY).

Things To Know About
Quality Mammograms*

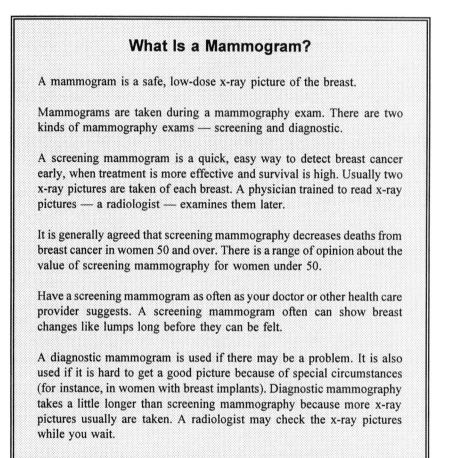

What Is a Mammogram?

A mammogram is a safe, low-dose x-ray picture of the breast.

Mammograms are taken during a mammography exam. There are two kinds of mammography exams — screening and diagnostic.

A screening mammogram is a quick, easy way to detect breast cancer early, when treatment is more effective and survival is high. Usually two x-ray pictures are taken of each breast. A physician trained to read x-ray pictures — a radiologist — examines them later.

It is generally agreed that screening mammography decreases deaths from breast cancer in women 50 and over. There is a range of opinion about the value of screening mammography for women under 50.

Have a screening mammogram as often as your doctor or other health care provider suggests. A screening mammogram often can show breast changes like lumps long before they can be felt.

A diagnostic mammogram is used if there may be a problem. It is also used if it is hard to get a good picture because of special circumstances (for instance, in women with breast implants). Diagnostic mammography takes a little longer than screening mammography because more x-ray pictures usually are taken. A radiologist may check the x-ray pictures while you wait.

This chapter can help you learn more about getting the best possible mammogram. Being informed will help you work with members of your health care team before, during, and after your mammogram to get quality, reliable results.

---

* Source: Agency for Health Care Policy and Research, U.S. Department of Health and Human Services, Public Health Service, P.O. Box 8547, Silver Spring, MD 20907; 800-358-9295.

Many types of health care providers can help you with your breast care. Doctors, nurses, nurse practitioners, and physician assistants can examine your breasts, refer you for mammography when appropriate, and help you get more exams if they are needed. In this booklet, the word "doctor" is used for easier reading, but any of these health care providers can provide good care.

At the mammography facility, the person who takes the x-ray pictures (the radiologic technologist), the radiologist, and the people who keep the equipment in top working order have all had special training in mammography. They work as a team to make sure you get the best mammogram possible.

After your mammogram, your doctor receives your mammography results. Make sure you get your results from either your doctor or the mammography facility.

Make sure you understand the results and any recommendations for followup. And never be afraid to ask questions.

> Call your doctor if you notice:
>
> * A lump or thickening of the breast.
> * A discharge from the nipple that stains your bra or bedclothes.
> * Skin changes in the breast.
>
> These changes may be normal, but you should always have them checked as soon as possible.

Following the seven steps in this chapter can help you maintain your breast health. Stay on top of things every step of the way.

Seven Steps to Breast Health

1. Get regular exams.

This is the most important way you can protect your breast health.

* Get a breast exam from your doctor when you get your regular physical exam.

- Get a mammogram as often as your doctor recommends. Ask your doctor when to schedule your next mammogram.
- Check your breasts each month. Your doctor can show you how.

These three exams can help you and your doctor learn what is normal for your breasts and what may be signs of problems.

2. Choose a quality facility.

Many hospitals, clinics, and imaging or x-ray centers perform mammography. Mobile units (often vans) offer screening at shopping malls, community centers, and offices. All of these facilities must meet the same quality standards.

Your doctor may refer you to a mammography facility. Or you may select the one that is most convenient for you.

> To find a certified mammography facility, ask your doctor or call the National Cancer institute's Cancer Information Service toll free at 800-4-CANCER.
>
> When you go to the mammography facility, look for a certificate as proof that the facility is certified by FDA. It should be displayed some place where it is easy to see and read.

Make sure the mammography facility you choose is certified by the Food and Drug Administration (FDA) unless it is a Veterans Health Administration (VHA) facility.

A new law, called the Mammography Quality Standards Act, requires all mammography facilities except those of VHA to be FDA certified beginning October 1, 1994. To be certified, facilities must meet standards for the equipment they use, the people who work there, and the records they keep. VHA has its own high-quality mammography program, similar to FDA'S.

If the facility is not FDA certified, get your mammogram in a facility that is certified.

3. Schedule the mammogram for when your breasts will be least tender.

During mammography, the breast is pressed between two clear plastic plates for a few seconds. This gives a clear picture of the breast with the least amount of x-rays. But it may be uncomfortable, and a few women complain of some pain.

If you have sensitive breasts, try having your mammogram at a time of month when your breasts will be least tender. Try to avoid the week right before your period. This will help to lessen discomfort.

4. Give and get important information when you schedule the mammogram.

When you call for an appointment, be ready to provide information the mammography facility needs to know. The facility may wait until your appointment to ask some questions, so it's a good idea also to take the information with you when you have your mammogram. The information requested may include:

- Your name, address, and phone number.
- Your age.
- Name, address, and phone number of any facility where you have had a mammogram.
- Any breast disease in your family.
- Any current problems with your breasts, and how long you have had the problems.
- Past problems with your breasts, breast biopsies, or breast surgeries.
- Whether you have breast implants.
- Other personal information:
    - Whether you are pregnant or nursing.

- The timing of your menstrual cycle or when menopause began.
- Anything that might make it harder to do a mammogram (unusually large breasts or inability to stand, for example).
- Name, address, and phone number of your doctor.

Here are some questions for you to ask before your appointment:

- How and when you will find out the results of the exam.
- What you need to do to prepare for the exam.

If you have any other questions before your mammogram, be sure to call your doctor or the mammography facility.

5. Know what to expect.

Understanding what happens during a mammogram will help reduce any anxious feelings you might have. It is important to know that only a small amount of radiation is used in mammography.

When you have a mammogram, you stand in front of a special x-ray machine. The radiologic technologist lifts each breast and places it on a platform that holds the x-ray film. The platform can be raised or lowered to match your height.

The breast is then gradually pressed against the platform by a specially designed clear plastic plate. Some pressure is needed for a few seconds to make sure the x-rays show as much of the breast as possible.

This pressure is not harmful to your breast. In fact, flattening the breast lowers the x-ray dose needed.

Studies show that most women do not find a mammogram painful for the short time needed to take the picture. Try to relax. If the pressure becomes painful, you can tell the radiologic technologist to stop.

If there is an area of your breast that appears to have a problem, the radiologist or radiologic technologist may examine the breast.

6. Come prepared.

- Wear a two-piece outfit so you will have to remove only your top.
- Don't use deodorant, talcum powder, or lotion under your arms or near the breasts that day. These products can show up on the x-ray picture.
- Bring the name, address, and phone number of your doctor or other health care provider.
- Bring a list of the places and dates of mammograms, biopsies, or other breast treatment you have had before.
- Ask the facilities where you had mammograms before to release them to you, and bring them with you if possible. Your new mammogram can be compared with the earlier ones to see if there have been any changes.

It also may be helpful to:

- Bring a list of any questions you may have about mammography and your mammograms.
- If you think you may have trouble hearing or understanding the instructions, consider bringing a friend or family member to help you.
- If you are worried about discomfort, you may want to take a mild over-the-counter pain reliever about an hour before your mammogram. This will not affect the mammogram.

If there is something you do not understand, ask. And keep asking until all your questions are answered.

7. Follow up on your results.

Learning the results of your mammogram is very important. Chances are your mammogram will be normal. But do not assume that your mammogram is normal just because you have not received the results. If you have not received your screening results within 10 days, ask your doctor or call the mammography facility.

If your screening mammogram shows anything unusual, talk to your doctor as soon as possible about what you should do next. Your doctor may schedule a diagnostic mammogram, or you can schedule it yourself, but have it done soon. Discuss the results with your doctor.

When a diagnostic mammogram shows something abnormal, the radiologist may recommend another type of exam. A biopsy is a way to obtain a small piece of breast tissue for study under a microscope. Sometimes a biopsy is needed because of something your doctor found in checking your breast even though the mammogram appears normal.

Whenever a mammogram uncovers a problem or a need to check something further:

- Make sure you understand what you need to do next.
- Always get results of any test that you have.
- Ask questions about your results if something is hard to understand.

If you do not have a doctor or other health care provider, you will need to find one if you have an abnormal mammogram. Ask the mammography facility to help you find a doctor. Then make an appointment right away so you can discuss your results and what should be done next.

Mammography is very effective, but it does not detect all breast problems. If you find something unusual in your breast, see your doctor.

You're in charge of your breast health:

- Schedule screening mammograms as often as your doctor recommends.
- Always find out the results of your mammogram.
- Follow your doctor's recommendations for follow-up and schedule diagnostic mammography, if needed, as soon as possible.
- Have your doctor check your breasts as part of your regular physical exam, and check your breasts yourself each month.
- If you have a breast lump or change at any time, even if your last mammogram was normal, see a doctor as soon as possible.

How Can I learn More About Mammography?

Most mammography facilities have printed information and videotaped instructions on breast care. You can read or watch them when you go for a mammogram.

For More Information

For general information on breast cancer and mammography, contact:

Cancer Information Service (a service of the National Cancer Institute)
800-4-CANCER

Food and Drug Administration (FDA)
MQSA Consumer Inquiries, 1350 Piccard, (HFZ-240), Rockville, MD 20850

American Cancer Society
800-227-2345

Hints for Shopping, Cooking, and Enjoying Meals[*]

Eating provides pleasure and nourishment. People enjoy the taste, smell, color, and texture of foods. Mealtimes also provide an opportunity to relax and talk with others. Even more important, eating a well-balanced diet every day helps you stay healthy and active.

A poor diet can result in lack of energy, malnutrition, and bad health. Some older people (especially men who live alone) lose interest in eating because they have problems buying and preparing food. By developing a few simple habits, grocery shopping, cooking, and mealtime can be easier and more enjoyable.

Plan Ahead

Plan meals in advance and note the ingredients you will need. Before shopping, also check your supply of staples such as flour, sugar, rice, and cereal. Keep some canned or frozen fish, meat, fruits, vegetables, dinners, and soups on hand for days when you don't feel like cooking or can't go out. Bread freezes well but should be used after a week or two of storage. Powdered nonfat milk or canned evaporated milk also can be stored easily.

When planning meals, keep in mind that healthful diets contain a wide variety of foods. Meals should include fresh fruits and vegetables; whole grain or enriched breads and cereals, rice, and pasta; fish, poultry, lean meat, beans, and nuts; and milk, cheese, and other dairy products. Avoid eating too many foods that are high in fat, salt, and sugar.

The grocery list should include both fresh and processed foods. Buy enough fresh fruits and vegetables to last only a few days.

---

[*] Source: *Age Page*, National Institute on Aging, U.S. Department of Health and Human Services, Public Health Service, National Institutes of Health, Gaithersburg, MD 20898; 800-222-2225.

They will lose their freshness and some nutrients if stored too long. Meat will stay fresh in the refrigerator for varying amounts of time. Ground beef, stewed beef, poultry, and fish can be kept safely for only 1 or 2 days and should be frozen if kept longer. Roasts, chops, and steaks can be refrigerated 3 to 5 days before you use them.

Here are some other hints:

- Decide which size item is best for you. A large can or package may be cheaper per unit, but it is not a bargain if most of the contents are thrown away.
- Consider sharing large packages with a friend.
- Frozen vegetables purchased in bags are economical because you can use small amounts at a time.
- If an item at the meat or fresh produce counter is too large, ask an employee to repackage it.
- Read the content labels on packaged and canned foods. The item that is present in the largest amount is listed first, and the ones that follow are present in decreasing amounts. The calories, protein, carbohydrates, fat, and sodium per serving may also be listed.
- Check packages for freshness dates.

How to Save Money

Unit pricing is useful because it lets you know which brand or package size costs less. Plain (generic) labels or store brands are usually cheaper than name brands.

Some stores feature "natural foods," "health foods," and "organic produce." Such foods are no better for you and no "safer" to eat than those found in regular grocery stores, and they are usually more expensive.[5]

---

[5] If a special health claim is made for a particular food, check its reliability with your doctor or the Food and Drug Administration.

The Federal government provides food stamps to help people with low incomes buy groceries. If you think you may be eligible, check with a local food stamps office or agency on aging.

Preparing Food

Here are some things that can make meals healthier and easier:

- Prepare larger amounts of items you enjoy and refrigerate the leftovers to eat in a day or two.
- Divide leftovers into individual servings, write contents (and date) on each package, and freeze for later use.
- Try new recipes from newspapers, magazines, and television shows.
- Include a variety of colors, textures, and temperatures in your meals.
- To avoid excess fat, trim meat before cooking and broil, bake, boil, or pan-fry without added fat. Use low-fat milk and milk products, such as cottage cheese and yogurt.
- To preserve vitamins, don't overcook vegetables to the soft and mushy state. Try eating them raw, steamed, or stir-fry them briefly in a little oil or margarine.
- Most foods such as meat, fish, chicken, vegetables, and fruits should be stored in the refrigerator.

Mealtime

The traditional three meals at set times each day may not be for everyone. Your eating schedule can suit your own needs. For example, you may want to eat the main meal at noon. Or you may prefer small meals throughout the day.

Meals should be enjoyed in a relaxed manner. An attractive table and music can help make mealtime appealing. Here are other ideas:

- Invite a friend for lunch or dinner. (It's more fun to cook for someone else, and the invitation may be returned.)

- Eat in a different place, such as the living room or on the porch.
- Join or start a "pot-luck" club where everyone brings a prepared dish.
- Check with a local agency on aging to find out if your neighborhood provides free or low-cost meals for older people at a community center, church, or school. These meals offer good food and a chance to be with other people.

Nourishing Snacks

Many people enjoy a snack between meals. But some snacks add extra calories or salt to the diet, with few vitamins and minerals. Fruit, vegetable sticks, nuts, yogurt, cheese and crackers, bread, and cereal eaten in moderate amounts are better snack choices than candy, cake, cookies, potato chips, pretzels, and similar items.

Resources

For additional information, write to the Food and Drug Administration Information Office, 5600 Fishers Lane, Parklawn Building, Rockville, MD 20857.

The National Institute on Aging offers information on health and aging. Write to the NIA Information Center, P.O. Box 8057, Gaithersburg, MD 20898-8057; 800-222-2225, 800-222-4225 (TTY).

Know the Right Way to Take Your Medicines[*]

"Swallow capsules whole". . ."Don't chew tablets". . ."Drink plenty of fluids". . ."Take on an empty stomach". . ."Don't miss a dose"

There are so many things to remember when it comes to taking medication, it's not surprising that many people — up to half the population, in fact — don't take their medicines properly. Are these admonitions just a way of harassing the hapless patient who is already confused and upset by illness? Does it really matter if a tablet isn't taken at precisely the right time? Or are these rules the kind that were made to be ignored?

The truth is that directions for taking medications are important. They're specially crafted for each drug to help ensure that it does its job effectively. Basic information on how the drug should be taken is on the label of the container. But if there are any questions about these instructions, the patient, or some family member, should always ask the doctor or pharmacist to clarify them. The doctor also should know what other medications — both prescription and nonprescription — the patient is taking to avoid a drug interaction.

There are few conditions for which only a single dose of a drug is prescribed. Usually medication is taken for a specified period of time (seven to 10 days for an antibiotic, for instance), or perhaps for a lifetime if the patient has a chronic illness (such as high blood pressure). Medicines may also have to be taken at specific intervals during the day. This is necessary to keep the right amount of the drug in the bloodstream all the time. Too much of the drug in the circulation may cause an adverse reaction; too little won't be completely effective.

---

[*] Source: Office of Public Affairs, U.S. Department of Health and Human Services Public Health Service, Food and Drug Administration, 5600 Fishers Lane, Rockville, MD 20857; 301-827-4420.

If the number of doses per day is four, the drug will usually be taken four times during the waking hours, usually once at each meal and once at bedtime. In some cases, however, the precise interval is so important that the patient might have to be awakened during the night to take a dose. The patient should discuss the medication schedule with the doctor to make it as convenient as possible.

Some medications are taken only once a day. If the drug is a diuretic — one that increases urination — it's best to take it in the morning after breakfast. However, when the schedule calls for several doses of the diuretic during the day, the last one should be taken no later than 6 p.m., unless the doctor says otherwise, so that trips to the bathroom won't interfere with sleep.

Similarly, once-a-day drugs that might make the patient nervous or anxious should be taken in the morning to allow uninterrupted sleep at night.

Getting the right amount of a drug sometimes can be tricky if the drug is going in through the nose instead of the mouth. According to the Handbook of Nonprescription Drugs, many asthma patients don't use their inhalers properly, triggering the spray after inhaling. When using an inhaler, patients should breathe out slowly, then activate the inhaler while inhaling slowly and deeply, and hold the breath for at least 10 seconds. Gargling after each use can prevent throat irritation. To prevent clogging, the mouthpiece of the inhaler should be washed daily with warm water.

Topical decongestants — both sprays and drops — can also be tricky. Sprays should be administered while standing or sitting. The patient should spray once into each nostril and blow the nose three to five minutes later to remove mucus. Drops, on the other hand, require the patient to lie down either on the back or side with the head below the shoulders. The drops should be placed deep in each nostril without touching the nasal surface with the dropper (to avoid spreading germs from one user to another. Better still, don't share the drops). Then the patient should remain reclining and breathe through the mouth for about five minutes.

What happens if you miss a dose? It's a good idea to ask the doctor or pharmacist what to do if that happens before starting on a new medication schedule. Sometimes the patient is advised not to take the missed dose, to simply wait until the next dose is due. With some other drugs, the missed dose should be taken as soon as the patient remembers it.

Often a prescription will read "take one hour before or two hours after meals.' The reason is that food in the stomach slows down the absorption of the drug, making it less effective. Most antibiotics are among those drugs that do their job better when taken on an empty stomach. But the reverse is true of one antibiotic, griseofulvin, which is best taken with meals, especially meals with lots of fat. This helps the body absorb this particular medicine better.

If a drug upsets the stomach, it may be taken with milk or small amounts of solid food, such as crackers. Don't use an antacid as a buffer without first checking with your doctor. Some over-the-counter antacids can interfere with the effectiveness of prescription drugs. FDA has recently proposed that the labeling of antacids be changed to call this to consumers' attention.

Whether they are taken with meals or on an empty stomach, its a good idea to take capsules and tablets with a liquid. That means more than just a sip. With all due respect to Mary Poppins, it's a cupful of fluid, not a spoonful of sugar, that helps the medicine go down. Also, a swallow of liquid before taking the tablet or capsule lubricates the esophagus and eases the passage of the medicine to the stomach.

Water is generally the best liquid to use, unless the medicine tastes bad. In that case, ask a pharmacist what other liquid can be taken with that particular medicine, whether it be a tablet, capsule, or liquid. Milk, fruit juice, or soda pop may mask the bad taste, but may also hamper the effectiveness of the drug.

Once you put the medicine in your mouth, don't hesitate. Some coated tablets or capsules get sticky when they come in contact with saliva. Unless you take plenty of fluid, the medicine may stick to the esophagus and not complete its journey to the stomach. Choking, difficulty in swallowing, and blockage of the esophagus may result. The easiest way to take a tablet or capsule is to place it on the center of the tongue. (Don't try to put it way in the back; it will just be more difficult to swallow.) Then drink the liquid normally and the tablet or capsule should go right down. It's advisable to stand or sit erect when swallowing a medicine, allowing gravity to help. The Mayo Clinic Health Letter (June 1986) recommends eating a banana if you think a tablet or capsule is stuck in your esophagus. The banana, partially dissolved in saliva, will provide a smooth coating that will carry the stuck tablet with it as you swallow.

Adequate liquids are also needed to prevent some drugs, such as aspirin and potassium chloride tablets or capsules, from irritating the delicate lining of the esophagus and stomach. Liquids dilute these drugs as they dissolve, decreasing the chance of irritation.

It is extremely important to drink a lot of water — as much as eight or more glasses a day — when taking drugs such as sulfas and lithium. Otherwise, a concentration of these potent substances could cause kidney or bladder damage.

A lot of liquid is also essential when taking bulk-forming laxatives. These drugs won't work at all if there is no liquid to make them expand.

Liquids are also essential if the medication is a powder or a tablet that must be dissolved before it is taken. Never take a powder in its dry form. Be sure the powder is completely dissolved before drinking the liquid. After emptying the glass, swish a little extra water or liquid in it and take one last swallow to get all the medicine.

Certain long-acting or time-release capsules and tablets — designed to do their job over a long period — should always be swallowed whole. If they are crushed or opened, they will release the active ingredients all at once, possibly causing adverse effects from overdose.

On the other hand, chewable tablets need to be thoroughly chewed before being swallowed to help the drug dissolve and enter the bloodstream.

Some drugs work best if they are not swallowed. For example, nitroglycerin, taken for certain heart conditions, is usually administered as a sublingual tablet to be placed under the tongue to dissolve slowly. Because it is absorbed by the lining of the mouth, the medication gets into the bloodstream more quickly than if it were swallowed. The patient taking an under-the-tongue drug should try not to swallow saliva until the tablet is dissolved completely.

Nitroglycerin, as well as a few other drugs, can also be administered through a transdermal patch — a patch applied to the skin that allows the medicine to be absorbed slowly. Transdermal patches must be applied to clean, dry, hairless skin. Areas of extensive scarring, calluses or irritation should be avoided. When patches must be applied regularly, the application site should be varied to avoid causing skin irritation. Also, patients should not try to alter the dosage themselves by cutting or trimming the patches. If the dosage is wrong, the patient should consult with the doctor.

When using eye preparations, it is especially important to remember to wash your hands before applying the ointment or drops. With ointments, pull the lower eyelid away from the eye to form a pouch, and insert a thin strip of the medicine into the pouch. Gently close the eyes for a minute or so, but don't rub them. For eye drops, tilt the head back, apply pressure to the inside corner of the eye with the middle finger, and pull the lower eyelid away from the eye with the index finger of the same hand. Insert the drops without touching the dropper to the eye. Close the eyes gently for a minute or so without blinking. This gives the medicine time to be absorbed into the eye. Do not insert more drops than prescribed, since this may increase the chance for side effects.

When using ear drops, lie down or tilt the head with the ear up and insert the prescribed number of drops without touching the dropper to the ear. Maintain this position for a few minutes to allow the drug to be absorbed. A sterile cotton plug may be placed in the ear to prevent the drops from leaking out. A hint for people who find ear drops uncomfortable because they feel cold: Before using the drops, warm them to approximately body temperature (about 98 degrees Fahrenheit) by placing the dropper bottle in warm water. Don't let the drops get too hot; a higher temperature could cause them to lose potency.

Storage conditions of medicines are very important and must be followed to assure the effectiveness of the medication. Unless instructed otherwise, store medicines away from heat, light, and moisture. This means that the bathroom is not a good place to store medicine. Heat and moisture may cause the medicine ingredients to break down and lose potency, which may reduce its effectiveness. Do not store medicines in the refrigerator or freezer unless instructed to do so. (An exception is suppositories, which generally should be refrigerated, but do not freeze them. A suppository that has softened because it was in a warm place can be chilled in the refrigerator for about 30 minutes before using. After removing the wrapper, moisten the suppository with a little water to lubricate before inserting.) Light, in some cases, may also cause a loss of potency. Amber prescription bottles keep out most light. For this and other reasons, medications should not be transferred from the prescription bottle to different containers. The prescription bottle will carry instructions for use, the expiration date of the medication, and, often, cautions of possible side effects, such as drowsiness, and warnings such as not to use with alcohol or not to take on an empty stomach.

Never take medications that are out of date. The potency of the medicine is only guaranteed until the expiration date, and then only when stored properly. Discard any unused or outdated medicine.

One final word of advice — keep all medicines, whether they are prescription or over-the-counter, out of the reach of children.

What Is Menopause?[*]

I wasn't sure what to expect with menopause, although I certainly looked forward to not having my period anymore. I have to admit, I'm concerned about how my body will change. My mother never talked about menopause. She says her mother never did either, probably because then it was linked to old age and poor health. Now, you hear about it all the time. The "baby boom" generation is making menopause a big issue because of their sheer numbers, and because they'll live with it much longer than their grandmothers did. Back then, menopause did come near the end of life. Now I'm going through it, but I feel like I still have my whole life ahead of me.

More than one third of the women in the United States, about 36 million, have been through menopause. With a life expectancy of about 81 years, a 50-year old woman can expect to live more than one-third of her life after menopause. Scientific research is just beginning to address some of the unanswered questions about these years and about the poorly understood biology of menopause.

Menopause is the point in a woman's life when menstruation stops permanently, signifying the end of her ability to have children. Known as the "change of life," menopause is the last stage of a gradual biological process in which the ovaries reduce their production of female sex hormones — a process which begins about three to five years before the final menstrual period. This transitional phase is called the climacteric, or perimenopause. Menopause is considered complete when a woman has been without periods for one year. On average, this occurs at about age 50. But like the beginning of menstruation in adolescence, timing varies from person to person. Cigarette smokers tend to reach menopause earlier than non-smokers.

---

[*] Source: National Heart, Lung, and Blood Institute Information Center, P.O. Box 30105, Bethesda, MD 20824-0105; 301-251-1222.

How Does It Happen?

The ovaries contain structures called follicles that hold the egg cells. You are born with about 2 million egg cells and by puberty there are about 300,000 left. Only about 400 to 500 ever mature fully to be released during the menstrual cycle. The rest degenerate over the years. During the reproductive years, the pituitary gland in the brain generates hormones that cause a new egg to be released from its follicle each month. The follicle also increases production of the sex hormones estrogen and progesterone, which thicken the lining of the uterus. This enriched lining is prepared to receive and nourish a fertilized egg following conception. If fertilization does not occur, estrogen and progesterone levels drop, the lining of the uterus breaks down, and menstruation occurs.

For unknown reasons, the ovaries begin to decline in hormone production during the mid-thirties. In the late forties, the process accelerates and hormones fluctuate more, causing irregular menstrual cycles and unpredictable episodes of heavy bleeding. By the early to mid fifties, periods finally end altogether. However, estrogen production does not completely stop. The ovaries decrease their output significantly, but still may produce a small amount. Also, another form of estrogen is produced in fat tissue with help from the adrenal glands (near the kidney). Although this form of estrogen is weaker than that produced by the ovaries, it increases with age and with the amount of fat tissue.

Progesterone, the other female hormone, works during the second half of the menstrual cycle to create a lining in the uterus as a viable home for an egg, and to shed the lining if the egg is not fertilized. If you skip a period, your body may not be making enough progesterone to break down the uterine lining. However, your estrogen levels may remain high even though you are not menstruating.

At menopause, hormone levels don't always decline uniformly. They alternately rise and fall again. Changing ovarian hormone levels affect the other glands in the body, which together make up the endocrine system. The endocrine system controls growth, metabolism and reproduction. This system must constantly readjust itself to work effectively. Ovarian hormones also affect all other tissues, including the breasts, vagina, bones, blood vessels, gastrointestinal tract, urinary tract, and skin.

Surgical Menopause

Premenopausal women who have both their ovaries removed surgically experience an abrupt menopause. They may be hit harder by menopausal symptoms than are those who experience it naturally. Their hot flashes may be more severe, more frequent, and last longer. They may have a greater risk of heart disease and osteoporosis, and may be more likely to become depressed. The reasons for this are unknown. When only one ovary is removed, menopause usually occurs naturally. When the uterus is removed (hysterectomy) and the ovaries remain, menstrual periods stop but other menopausal symptoms (if any) usually occur at the same age that they would naturally. However, some women who have a hysterectomy may experience menopausal symptoms at a younger age.

What To Expect

Menopause is an individualized experience. Some women notice little difference in their bodies or moods, while others find the change extremely bothersome and disruptive. Estrogen and progesterone affect virtually all tissues in the body, but everyone is influenced by them differently.

Hot Flashes

Hot flashes, or flushes, are the most common symptom of menopause, affecting more than 60 percent of menopausal women in the U.S. A hot flash is a sudden sensation of intense heat in the upper part or all of the body. The face and neck may become flushed, with red blotches appearing on the chest, back, and arms. This is often followed by profuse sweating and then cold shivering as body temperature readjusts. A hot flash can last a few moments or 30 minutes or longer.

Hot flashes occur sporadically and often start several years before other signs of menopause. They gradually decline in frequency and intensity as you age. Eighty percent of all women with hot flashes have them for two years or less, while a small percentage have them for more than five years. Hot flashes can happen at any time. They can be as mild as a light blush, or severe enough to wake you from a deep sleep. Some women even develop insomnia. Others have experienced that caffeine, alcohol, hot drinks, spicy foods, and stressful or frightening events can sometimes trigger a hot flash. However, avoiding these triggers will not necessarily prevent all episodes.

Hot flashes appear to be a direct result of decreasing estrogen levels. In response to falling estrogen levels, your glands release higher amounts of other hormones that affect the brain's thermostat, causing body temperatures to fluctuate. Hormone therapy relieves the discomfort of hot flashes in most cases. Some women claim that vitamin E offers minor relief, although there has never been a study to confirm it. Aside from hormone therapy, which is not for everyone, here are some suggestions for coping with hot flashes:

- Dress in layers so you can remove them at the first sign of a flash.
- Drink a glass of cold water or juice at the onset of a flash.
- At night keep a thermos of ice water or an ice pack by your bed.
- Use cotton sheets, lingerie and clothing to let your skin "breathe."

Vaginal/Urinary Tract Changes

With advancing age, the walls of the vagina become thinner, dryer, less elastic and more vulnerable to infection. These changes can make sexual intercourse uncomfortable or painful. Most women find it helpful to lubricate the vagina. Water-soluble lubricants are preferable, as they help reduce the chance of infection. Try to avoid petroleum jelly; many women are allergic, and it damages condoms. Be sure to see your gynecologist if problems persist.

Tissues in the urinary tract also change with age, sometimes leaving women more susceptible to involuntary loss of urine (incontinence), particularly if certain chronic illnesses or urinary infections are also present. Exercise, coughing, laughing, lifting heavy objects or similar movements that put pressure on the bladder may cause small amounts of urine to leak. Lack of regular physical exercise may contribute to this condition. It's important to know, however, that incontinence is not a normal part of aging, to be masked by using adult diapers. Rather, it is usually a treatable condition that warrants medical evaluation. Recent research has shown that bladder training is a simple and effective treatment for most cases of incontinence and is less expensive and safer than medication or surgery.

Within four or five years after the final menstrual period, there is an increased chance of vaginal and urinary tract infections. If symptoms such as painful or overly frequent urination occur, consult your doctor. Infections are easily treated with antibiotics, but often tend to recur. To help prevent these infections, urinate before and after intercourse, be sure your bladder is not full for long periods, drink plenty of fluids, and keep your genital area clean. Douching is not thought to be effective in preventing infection.

Menopause and Mental Health
A popular myth pictures the menopausal woman shifting from raging, angry moods into depressive, doleful slumps with no apparent reason or warning. However, a study by psychologists at the University of Pittsburgh suggests that menopause does not cause unpredictable mood swings, depression, or even stress in most women.

In fact, it may even improve mental health for some. This gives further support to the idea that menopause is not necessarily a negative experience. The Pittsburgh study looked at three different groups of women: menstruating, menopausal with no treatment, and menopausal on hormone therapy. The study showed that the menopausal women suffered no more anxiety, depression, anger, nervousness or feelings of stress than the group of menstruating women in the same age range. In addition, although more hot flashes were reported by the menopausal women not taking hormones, surprisingly they had better overall mental health than the other two groups. The women taking hormones worried more about their bodies and were somewhat more depressed.

However, this could be caused by the hormones themselves. It's also possible that women who voluntarily take hormones tend to be more conscious of their bodies in the first place. The researchers caution that their study includes only healthy women, so results may apply only to them. Other studies show that women already taking hormones who are experiencing mood or behavioral problems sometimes respond well to a change in dosage or type of estrogen.

The Pittsburgh findings are supported by a New England Research Institute study which found that menopausal women were no more depressed than the general population: about 10 percent are occasionally depressed and 5 percent are persistently depressed. The exception is women who undergo surgical menopause. Their depression rate is reportedly double that of women who have a natural menopause.

Studies also have indicated that many cases of depression relate more to life stresses or "mid-life crises" than to menopause. Such stresses include: an alteration in family roles, as when your children are grown and move out of the house, no longer "needing" mom; a changing social support network, which may happen after a divorce if you no longer socialize with friends you met through your husband; interpersonal losses, as when a parent, spouse or other close relative dies; and your own aging and the beginning of physical illness. People have very different responses to stress and crisis. Your best friend's response may be negative, leaving her open to emotional distress and depression, while yours is positive, resulting in achievement of your goals. For many women, this stage of life can actually be a period of enormous freedom.

What About Sex?

For some women, but by no means all, menopause brings a decrease in sexual activity. Reduced hormone levels cause subtle changes in the genital tissues and are thought to be linked also to a decline in sexual interest. Lower estrogen levels decrease the blood supply to the vagina and the nerves and glands surrounding it. This makes delicate tissues thinner, drier, and less able to produce secretions to comfortably lubricate before and during intercourse. Avoiding sex is not necessary, however.

Estrogen creams and oral estrogen can restore secretions and tissue elasticity. Water-soluble lubricants can also help.

While changes in hormone production are cited as the major reason for changes in sexual behavior, many other interpersonal, psychological, and cultural factors can come into play. For instance, a Swedish study found that many women use menopause as an excuse to stop sex completely after years of disinterest. Many physicians, however, question if declining interest is the cause or the result of less frequent intercourse.

Some women actually feel liberated after menopause and report an increased interest in sex. They say they feel relieved that pregnancy is no longer a worry.

For women in perimenopause, birth control is a confusing issue. Doctors advise all women who have menstruated, even if irregularly, within the past year to continue using birth control. Unfortunately, contraceptive options are limited. Hormone-based oral and implantable contraceptives are risky in older women who smoke. Only a few brands of IUD are on the market. The other options are barrier methods — diaphragms, condoms, and sponges — or methods requiring surgery such as tubal ligation.

Is My Partner Still Interested?

Some men go through their own set of doubts in middle age. They too, often report a decline in sexual activity after age 50. It may take more time to reach ejaculation, or they may not be able to reach it at all. Many fear they will fail sexually as they get older. Remember, at any age sexual problems can arise if there are doubts about performance. If both partners are well informed about normal genital changes, each can be more understanding and make allowances rather than unmeetable demands. Open, candid communication between partners is important to ensure a successful sex life well into your seventies and eighties.

Long-Term Effects of Menopause

Osteoporosis

One of the most important health issues for middle-aged women is the threat of osteoporosis. It is a condition in which bones become thin, fragile, and highly prone to fracture. Numerous studies over the past 10 years have linked estrogen insufficiency to this gradual, yet debilitating disease. In fact, osteoporosis is more closely related to menopause than to a woman's chronological age.

Bones are not inert. They are made up of healthy, living tissue which continuously performs two processes: break-down and formation of new bone tissue. The two are closely linked. If breakdown exceeds formation, bone tissue is lost and bones become thin and brittle. Gradually and without discomfort, bone loss leads to a weakened skeleton incapable of supporting normal daily activities.

Each year about 500,000 American women will fracture a vertebrae, the bones that make up the spine, and about 300,000 will fracture a hip. Nationwide, treatment for osteoporotic fractures costs up to $10 billion per year, with hip fractures the most expensive. Vertebral fractures lead to curvature of the spine, loss of height, and pain. A severe hip fracture is painful and recovery may involve a long period of bed rest. Between 12 and 20 percent of those who suffer a hip fracture do not survive the six months after the fracture. At least half of those who do survive require help in performing daily living activities, and 15 to 25 percent will need to enter a long-term care facility. Older patients are rarely given the chance for full rehabilitation after a fall. However, with adequate time and care provided in rehabilitation, many people can regain their independence and return to their previous activities.

For osteoporosis, researchers believe that an ounce of prevention is worth a pound of cure. The condition of an older woman's skeleton depends on two things: the peak amount of bone attained before menopause and the rate of the bone loss thereafter. Hereditary factors are important in determining peak bone mass. For instance, studies show that black women attain a greater spinal mass and therefore have fewer osteoporotic fractures than white women. Other factors that help increase bone mass include adequate intake of dietary calcium and vitamin D, particularly in young children prior to puberty; exposure to sunlight; and physical exercise. These elements also help slow the rate of bone loss. Certain other physiological stresses can quicken bone loss, such as pregnancy, nursing, and immobility. The biggest culprit in the process of bone loss is estrogen deficiency. Bone loss quickens during perimenopause, the transitional phase when estrogen levels drop significantly.

Doctors believe the best strategy for osteoporosis is prevention because currently available treatments only halt bone loss - they don't rebuild the bone. However, researchers are hopeful that in the future, bone loss will be reversible. Building up your reserves of bone before you start to lose it during perimenopause helps bank against future losses. The most effective therapy against osteoporosis available today for postmenopausal women is estrogen. Remarkably, estrogen saves more bone tissue than even very large daily doses of calcium. Estrogen is not a panacea, however. While it is a boon for the bones, it also affects all other tissues and organs in the body, and not always positively. Its impact on the other areas of the body must be considered.

Cardiovascular Disease

Most people picture an older, overweight man when they think of a likely candidate for cardiovascular disease (CVD). But men are only half the story. Heart disease is the number one killer of American women and is responsible for half of all the deaths of women over age 50. Ironically, in past years women were rarely included in clinical heart studies, but finally physicians have realized that it is as much a woman's disease as a man's.

CVDs are disorders of the heart and circulatory system. They include thickening of the arteries (atherosclerosis) that serve the heart and limbs, high blood pressure, angina, and stroke. For reasons unknown, estrogen helps protect women against CVD during the childbearing years. This is true even when they have the same risk factors as men, including smoking, high blood cholesterol levels, and a family history of heart disease. But the protection is temporary. After menopause, the incidence of CVD increases, with each passing year posing a greater risk. The good news, though, is that CVD can be prevented or at least reduced by early recognition, lifestyle changes and, many physicians believe, hormone replacement therapy.

Menopause brings changes in the level of fats in a woman's blood. These fats, called lipids, are used as a source of fuel for all cells. The amount of lipids per unit of blood determines a person's cholesterol count. There are two components of cholesterol: high density lipoprotein (HDL) cholesterol, which is associated with a beneficial, cleansing effect in the blood- stream, and low density lipoprotein (LDL) cholesterol, which encourages fat to accumulate on the walls of arteries and eventually clog them. To remember the difference, think of the H in HDL as the healthy cholesterol, and the L in LDL as lethal. LDL cholesterol appears to increase while HDL decreases in postmenopausal women as a direct result of estrogen deficiency. Elevated LDL and total cholesterol can lead to stroke, heart attack, and death.

Managing Menopause

Hormone Replacement Therapy

To combat the symptoms associated with falling estrogen levels, doctors have turned to hormone replacement therapy (HRT). HRT is the administration of the female hormones estrogen and progesterone. Estrogen replacement therapy (ERT) refers to administration of estrogen alone. The hormones are usually given in pill form, though sometimes skin patches and vaginal creams (just estrogen) are used. ERT is thought to help prevent the devastating effects of heart disease and osteoporosis, conditions that are often difficult and expensive to treat once they appear. The cardiovascular effects of progesterone, however, are still unknown. Hormone treatment for menopause is still quite controversial. Its long-term safety and efficacy remain matters of great concern. There is not enough existing data for physicians to suggest that HRT is the right choice for all women. Several large studies are currently attempting to resolve the questions, though it will take several more years to reach any definitive answers.

In the 1940's when estrogen was first offered to menopausal women, it was given alone and in high doses. Today, after 50 years of trial and error, it is well known that estrogen stimulates growth of the inner lining of the uterus (endometrium) that sheds during menstruation. This growth may continue uncontrollably, resulting in cancer. Today, doctors typically prescribe a lower dose of estrogen. However, few doctors still prescribe estrogen alone to women who have a uterus. Most now prefer to add a synthetic form of progesterone called progestin to counteract estrogen's dangerous effect on the uterus. Progestin reduces the risk of cancer by causing monthly shedding of the endometrium. The obvious drawback to this approach is that menopausal women resume monthly bleeding. Once menopause arrives, most women enjoy the freedom of life without a period. Many are reluctant to begin their cycles again. In addition, there are other unpleasant side effects of progestin which often discourage women from continuing HRT. These include breast tenderness, bloating, abdominal cramping, anxiety, irritability, and depression.

The good news is that researchers are evaluating different schedules of low-dose estrogen and progestin to completely eliminate monthly bleeding. Currently most women receive what is called cyclic HRT. They may take estrogen continually and progestin for the first 12 days of each month. The use of a continuous combined dose, where estrogen and smaller amounts of progestin are taken every day is also being studied. In theory, this use of progestin stems endometrial growth so no bleeding will occur. Unfortunately, it may take six months or more until bleeding finally stops. In many cases, monthly bleeding has been replaced by more bothersome irregular bleeding patterns. Obviously, further research is needed to evaluate and perfect this treatment. Various types of progestin in different dosages, preparations, and schedules are being studied in hopes of reducing its other unpleasant side effects while retaining the known advantages of estrogen.

Estrogen and Your Bones

HRT and ERT are successful methods of combatting osteoporosis. As previously discussed, estrogen halts bone loss but cannot necessarily rebuild bone. Long-term estrogen use (10 or more years) may be required to prevent postmenopausal bone loss. Why estrogen helps protect the skeleton is still unclear. We do know that estrogen helps bones absorb the calcium they need to stay strong. It also helps conserve the calcium stored in the bones by encouraging other cells to use dietary calcium more efficiently. For instance, muscles require calcium to contract. If there is not enough calcium circulating in the blood for muscles to use, calcium is "borrowed" froth the bone. Calcium is also needed for blood clotting, sending nerve impulses, and secreting various hormones. Prolonged borrowing from bone calcium for these processes speeds bone loss. That's why it's important to consume adequate amounts of calcium in your diet.

Estrogen's Effect on Your Heart

The majority of past clinical studies have shown that women who use ERT substantially reduce their risk of developing and dying from heart disease. One or two studies demonstrate conflicting evidence, but they are far outnumbered by the positive reports. Results from a 1991 study showed that after 15 years of estrogen replacement, risk of death by CVD was reduced by almost 50 percent and overall deaths were reduced by 40 percent. Some researchers credit this reduction to oral estrogen's ability to maintain HDL and LDL at their healthier, premenopausal levels, through its interaction with proteins in the liver. Others believe it is estrogen's direct effect on the blood vessels themselves (through receptors on the vessel walls) which creates this benefit. In the latter case, both oral estrogen and the skin patch would be effective. Studies are underway to determine which mechanism contributes most to a healthy heart.

Many doctors now believe that estrogen replacement benefits women at risk for heart disease (but not those with blood clots). Risk factors for heart disease include a strong family history of CVD, high blood pressure, obesity, and smoking.

At any time of life, women who smoke are much more likely to develop heart disease or have a stroke than women who do not smoke. But after menopause, a smoker's risk climbs dramatically. Low estrogen levels and smoking are separate risk factors for CVD. When the two are combined, the risk is much higher than either one alone. Smoking also raises your risks for some types of cancer and for chronic lung disease, such as emphysema. Fortunately, quitting smoking — at any age — can cut the risk of disease almost immediately.

Studies have shown that when older people quit, they increase their life expectancy. Their risk of heart disease goes down, their lungs function better, and blood circulation improves. So quitting smoking, whether before, during or after menopause, can have a definite impact on both the length and quality of your life.

Many women who have quit smoking say they found support in group counseling sessions. Local chapters of the American Cancer Society and the American Heart Association are good places to start looking for a smoking cessation group. Nicotine gum and nicotine patches prescribed by a doctor may also help.

While we know that estrogen users have a decreased risk of CVD, women with certain preexisting heart conditions are usually advised not to take HRT or ERT. These conditions include blood clots and recent heart attacks. Researchers hope to further investigate nonhormonal methods of preventing heart disease such as weight reduction or control, exercise, smoking cessation, and dietary modification.

According to a 5-year study reported in 1988, weight gain (a common occurrence among many menopausal women) significantly raises blood pressure, total and LDL cholesterol, and fat levels. Together, these make up a dangerous recipe for heart disease. Several other studies also noted that having about one drink per day had a protective effect on the heart. Physicians advise caution in this area, however, as excess alcohol can increase risks for other serious problems.

While cardiovascular benefits associated with oral estrogen are fairly well-known, there is surprisingly little information on the cardiovascular effects of progestin combined with estrogen. Some studies suggest that progestin counteract the favorable effects of estrogen alone, while other studies show no such effect. This remains just one more gray area where questions outnumber reliable answers.

Drawbacks of HRT: The Cancer Risk

A major issue surrounding HRT and ERT is the influence of estrogen on breast cancer. Researchers believe that the longer your lifetime exposure to naturally occurring estrogen, the greater your risk of breast cancer. It has not been proven, however, that estrogen administered at menopause has the same effect. There is disagreement on the many trials conducted to date because of wide variations in the populations studied and the doses, timing, and types of estrogen used. A recent analysis of previous studies suggests that low-dose estrogen taken on a short-term basis (10 years or less) does not pose an increased risk of breast cancer. Long term use (more than 10 years) at a high dose may significantly increase the risk. By how much is still a matter of heated debate. At the very most, researchers think long-term use could possibly increase the risk of getting breast cancer by 30 percent. This means that incidence would rise from 10 women per 10,000 each year to 13 women per 10,000 each year. To reach any consensus, however, more women need to be monitored for an extended period of time. The fear of cancer is one of the most common reasons that women are unwilling to use HRT. Interestingly, actual death rates for breast cancer have not risen at all. This may be because estrogen users have more frequent medical visits and obtain more preventive care including yearly mammograms.

While no one can determine who will eventually develop breast cancer, there are certain risk factors you should be aware of when considering HRT. A family history of breast cancer (sister or mother) is probably the most important risk factor of all. You may also be at an increased risk if you menstruated before age 12; delayed motherhood until later in life; or have a late menopause (after age 50). Also, the older you are, the higher the risk. Most doctors believe that if you are not in a high risk category for breast or endometrial cancer, the benefits of HRT far outweigh the risks. However, for some women, the side effects of therapy make it impossible to use. This is a personal decision to be made by each woman with help from her doctor.

Other Risks

Physicians usually caution women not to use HRT if they are already at high risk for developing blood clots. Obesity, severe varicose veins, smoking, and a history of blood clots put you in this category. A history of gall bladder disease could also be cause to avoid HRT, as women taking estrogen may have a greater chance of developing gallstones.

Cautions to Estrogen Use		
Serious Risk	*Relative Risk*	*Subjective Complaints*
Stroke	Cigarette smoking	Nausea
Recent heart attack	Hypertension	Headaches
Breast cancer (current or family history)	Benign breast disease	Breakthrough bleeding
Uterine cancer	Benign uterine disease	Depression
Acute liver disease	Endometriosis	Fluid retention
Gall bladder disease	Pancreatitis	
Pancreatic disease	Epilepsy	
Recent blood clot	Migraine headaches	
Undiagnosed vaginal bleeding		
Source: R.I. Young, N.S. Kumar, and J.W. Goldzicher, *Management of Menopause Estrogen Cannot Be Used*, Drugs, 40(2):220-230, 1990		

Hormonal Therapy
Here is what scientists can say so far about the advantages and disadvantages of hormone replacement therapy (HRT-estrogen and progesterone) and estrogen replacement therapy (ERT-estrogen alone). More research is underway.

Pro:	*Con:*
HRT and ERT reduce the risk of osteoporosis.	ERT increases the risk of cancer of the uterus (endometrial cancer).
HRT and ERT relieve hot flashes.	HRT can have unpleasant side effects, such as bloating or irritability.
HRT and ERT reduce the risk of heart disease.	HRT and ERT may increase risk of breast cancer; long-term use may pose the greatest risk.
HRT and ERT may improve mood and psychological well being.	
	In women with blood clots, HRT and ERT may be dangerous.

Keeping Healthy

Good nutrition and regular physical exercise are thought to improve overall health. Some doctors feel these factors can also affect menopause. Although these areas have not been well studied in women, anecdotal evidence is strongly in favor of eating well and exercising to help lower risks for CVD and osteoporosis.

Nutrition

While everyone agrees that a well-balanced diet is important for good health, there is still much to be learned about what constitutes "well-balanced." We do know that variety in the diet helps ensure a better mix of essential nutrients.

Nutritional requirements vary from person to person and change with age. A healthy premenopausal woman should have about 1,000 mgs of calcium per day. A 1994 Consensus Conference at the National Institutes of Health recommended that women after menopause consume 1,500 mgs per day if they are not using hormonal replacement or 1000 mgs per day in conjunction with hormonal replacement. Foods high in calcium include milk, yogurt, cheese and other dairy products; oysters, sardines and canned salmon with bones; and dark-green leafy vegetables like spinach and broccoli. In calcium tablets, calcium carbonate is most easily absorbed by the body. If you are lactose intolerant, acidophilus milk is more digestible. Vitamin D is also very important for calcium absorption and bone formation. A 1992 study showed that women with postmenopausal osteoporosis who took vitamin D for 3 years significantly reduced the occurrence of new spinal fractures. However, the issue is still controversial. High doses of vitamin D can cause kidney stones, constipation, or abdominal pain, particularly in women with existing kidney problems. Other nutritional guidelines by the National Research Council include:

- Choose foods low in fat, saturated fat, and cholesterol. Fats contain more calories (9 calories per gram) than either carbohydrates or protein (each have only 4 calories per gram). Fat intake should be less than 30 percent of daily calories.

- Eat fruits, vegetables, and whole grain cereal products, especially those high in vitamin C and carotene. These include oranges, grapefruit, carrots, winter squash, tomatoes, broccoli, cauliflower, and green leafy vegetables. These foods are good sources of vitamins and minerals and the major sources of dietary fiber. Fiber helps maintain bowel mobility and may reduce the risk of colon cancer. Young and older people alike are encouraged to consume 20 to 30 grams of fiber per day.

- Eat very little salt-cured and smoked foods such as sausages, smoked fish and ham, bacon, bologna, and hot dogs. High blood pressure, which may become more serious with heavy salt intake, is more of a risk as you age.

- Avoid food and drinks containing processed sugar. Sugar contains empty calories which may substitute for nutritious food and can add excess body weight.

For people who can't eat an adequate diet, supplements may be necessary. A dietician should tailor these to meet your individual nutritional needs. Using supplements without supervision can be risky because large doses of some vitamins may have serious side effects. Vitamins A and D in large doses can be particularly dangerous.

As you age, your body requires less energy because of a decline in physical activity and a loss of lean body mass. Raising your activity level will increase your need for energy and help you avoid gaining weight. Weight gain often occurs in menopausal women, possibly due in part to declining estrogen. In animal studies, scientists found that estrogen is important in regulating weight gain. Animals with their ovaries surgically removed gained weight, even if they were fed the same diet as the animals with intact ovaries. They also found that progesterone counteracts the effect of estrogen. The higher their progesterone levels, the more the animals ate.

Exercise
Exercise is extremely important throughout a woman's lifetime and particularly as she gets older. Regular exercise benefits the heart and bones, helps regulate weight, and contributes to a sense of

overall well-being and improvement in mood. If you are physically inactive you are far more prone to coronary heart disease, obesity, high blood pressure, diabetes, and osteoporosis. Sedentary women may also suffer more from chronic back pain, stiffness, insomnia, and irregularity. They often have poor circulation, weak muscles, shortness of breath, and loss of bone mass. Depression can also be a problem. Women who regularly walk, jog, swim, bike, dance, or perform some other aerobic activity can more easily circumvent these problems and also achieve higher HDL cholesterol levels. Studies show that women performing aerobic activity or muscle-strength training reduced mortality from CVD and cancer.

Just like muscles, bones adhere to the "use it or lose it" rule; they diminish in size and strength with disuse. It has been known for more than 100 years that weight-bearing exercise (walking, running) will help increase bone mass. Exercise stimulates the cells responsible for generating new bone to work overtime. In the past 20 years, studies have shown that bone tissue lost from lack of use can be rebuilt with weight-bearing activity. Studies of athletes show they have greater bone mass compared to non athletes at the sites related to their sport. In postmenopausal women, moderate exercise preserves bone mass in the spine helping reduce the risk of fractures.

Exercise is also thought to have a positive effect on mood. During exercise, hormones called endorphins are released in the brain. They are 'feel good' hormones involved in the body's positive response to stress. The mood-heightening effect can last for several hours, according to some endocrinologists. Consult your doctor before starting a rigorous exercise program. He or she will help you decide which types of exercises are best for you. An exercise program should start slowly and build up to more strenuous activities. Women who already have osteoporosis of the spine should be careful about exercise that jolts or puts weight on the back, as it could cause a fracture.

Ongoing/Future Research

To gather more data to help women make a well-informed decision regarding hormone therapy, researchers at the National Institutes of Health (NIH) launched the Post-menopausal Estrogen/Progestin Interventions Trial (PEPI) in 1989. With 127 women enrolled at each of seven medical centers, PEPI will address the short-term safety and efficacy of various methods of HRT. The study will compare women who take estrogen by itself to those who take it with different types of progestin. It will also examine the effects of both cyclical and continuous progestin on cardiovascular risk factors, blood clotting factors, metabolism, uterine changes, bone mass, and general quality of life.

Several new studies are now looking at normal body changes as women move from pre- to postmenopause. Up to now, the lack of such data has been one problem in assessing the value of HRT. Without knowing what "normal" is, scientists have difficulty judging the effect of a particular treatment. Another problem with past studies is the "healthy user effect." In many trials preceding PEPI, the HRT users studied had freely chosen to begin treatment, with advice from their doctors. In general, most physicians discourage women with a preexisting illness or long family history of breast cancer from taking HRT. This factor could skew study results to appear that non-users became ill or died more frequently simply because they failed to take estrogen. Only by randomly assigning study participants to the treatment can this bias be overcome. Until more random trials are completed, the jury is still out on HRT.

Another NIH study is the Women's Health Initiative, a multicenter trial involving 70,000 postmenopausal women ages 50 to 79. The study will assess the long-term benefits and risk of hormone therapy as it relates to cardiovascular disease, osteoporosis, and breast and uterine cancer. It will also help determine the effects of calcium supplementation, dietary changes, and exercise on women in this age group. Some of the specific questions to be addressed by the Women's Health Initiative include:

- How long is estrogen effective for each system of the body (skeletal, cardiovascular, nervous, endocrine)?
- What is the best dose and route of administration of estrogen and progestin to prevent side effects yet maintain efficacy?
- How long is estrogen safe to take?
- Does estrogen act the same way in older women as in younger women?
- Are there effective alternatives to HRT?

Clearly, no one has all the answers about menopause. Medical research is beginning to give us more accurate information, but some myths and negative attitudes persist. Women are challenging old stereotypes, learning about what's happening in their bodies, and taking responsibility for their health. The important thing to remember as you go through menopause is to be good to yourself. Take time to pursue your hobbies, be they gardening, painting or socializing with friends.

Have a positive attitude toward life. Sharing concerns with friends, a spouse, relatives or a support group can help. Don't fight your body — allow the changes that are happening to become a part of you, a part that is natural and that you accept.

Medical Terms

Angina: a disease marked by brief attacks of chest pain

Biopsy: removal and examination of living cells from the body

Cardiovascular disease (CVD): disorders of the heart and circulatory system

ERT: estrogen replacement therapy; the use of estrogen alone for the treatment of menopausal symptoms and the prevention of some long-term effects of menopause.

Endometrium: the tissues lining the uterus

Estrogen: one of the female sex hormones produced primarily by the ovaries before menopause and by fat and other tissues after menopause.

HDL: high density lipoprotein cholesterol, the "good" cholesterol thought to have a cleansing effect in the bloodstream

HRT: hormone replacement therapy; the use of estrogen combined with progestin for the treatment of menopausal symptoms and the prevention of some long-term effects of menopause.

Hysterectomy: surgical removal of the uterus

IUD: Intrauterine birth control device, which prevents implantation of an embryo into the uterus should fertilization occur

LDL: low density lipoprotein cholesterol, the "bad" cholesterol believed to be linked to fat accumulation in the arteries

Menopause: the point when menstruation stops permanently

Oral contraceptives: pills which usually consist of synthetic estrogen and progesterone that are taken for three weeks after the last day of a menstrual period. They inhibit ovulation, thereby preventing pregnancy.

Osteoporosis: a disease in which bones become thin, weak and are easily fractured

Perimenopause: the time around menopause, usually beginning 3 to 5 years before the final period.

Medical Terms (continued)

Progesterone: one of the female sex hormones produced by the ovaries

Progestin: the synthetic form of progesterone

Tubal ligation: a surgical procedure in which the uterine tubes are cut and tied to prevent pregnancy

Urinary incontinence: loss of bladder control

Vasectomy: in males, the surgical removal of part of the sperm duct (vas deferens) to induce infertility

Organizations for Further Study

North American Menopause Society (NAMS)
University Hospitals, Department of OB/GYN, 2074 Abington Road, Cleveland, OH 44106; Fax: 216-844-3348 (written requests)

National Women's Health Network
1325 G Street, NW, Washington, DC 20005; 202-347-1140

American College of Obstetrics and Gynecologists (ACOG)
409 12th Street, SW, Washington, DC 20024; 202-638-5577

Alliance for Aging Research
2021 K Street, NW,, Suite 305, Washington, DC 20006; 202-293-2856

Older Women's League (OWL)
666 11th Street, NW, Suite 700, Washington, DC 20001; 202-783-6686

National Women's Health Resource Center (NVVHRC)
2440 M Street, NW, Suite 201, Washington, DC 20037; 202-293-6045

Wider Opportunities for Women (WOW)
National Commission on Working Women, 1325 G Street, NW, Lower Level, Washington, DC 20005; 202-638-3143

Organizations for Further Study (continued)

American Dietetic Association (ADA)
216 West Jackson Boulevard, Suite 800, Chicago, IL 60606; 312-899-0040

American Heart Association (AHA)
7320 Greenville Avenue, Dallas, TX 75231; 214-373-6300

National Heart, Lung, and Blood Institute (NHLBI)
9000 Rockville Pike, Bethesda, MD 20892; 301-496-4236

National Arthritis and Musculoskeletal and Skin Diseases Information Clearinghouse
Box AMS, 9000 Rockville Pike, Bethesda, MD 20892; 301-495-4484

National Osteoporosis Foundation (NOF)
2100 M Street, NW, Suite 602, Washington, DC 20037; 202-223-2226

Sex Information and Education Council of the U.S. (SIECUS)
130 West 42nd Street, Suite 2500, New York, NY 10036; 212-819-9770

DEPRESSION Awareness, Recognition, and Treatment Program
National Institute of Mental Health, D/ART Public Inquiries, 5600 Fishers Lane, Room 15C-05, Rockville, MD 20857; 301-443-4513

National Mental Health Association (NMHA) Information Center
1021 Prince Street, Alexandria, VA 22314-2971; 703-684-7722, 800-969-6642

National Cancer Institute
Cancer Information Service, 9000 Rockville Pike, Bethesda, MD 20892; 800-4-CANCER, (800-422-6237)

American Cancer Society National Headquarters
1599 Clifton Road, NE, Atlanta, GA 30329; 800-ACS-2345, (800-227-2345)

National Institute on Aging (NIA)
9000 Rockville Pike, Bethesda, MD 20892; 800-222-2225

Resources

The Change: Women, Aging and the Menopause, Germaine Greer, New York: Knopf/ Random House, 1992.

Choice Years, Judith Paige and Pamela Gordon. New York: Villard Books, 1991.

Managing Your Menopause, Wulf H. Utian, M.D., Ph.D., and Ruth S. Jacobowitz. New York: Fireside/Simon & Schuster, 1990.

The Menopause, Hormone Therapy, and Women's Health — Background Paper. Congress of the United States, Office of Technology Assessment, May 1992.

Menopause and Midlife Health, Morris Notelovitz and Diana Tonnesen, New York: St. Martin's Press, 1994.

Menopause News, ed. Judy Askew, 2074 Union St., San Francisco, CA 94123.

The Menopause Self-Help Book, Susan M. Lark, M.D. Berkeley: Celestial Arts, 1990.

The New Ourselves Growing Older, Paula Brown Doress and Diane Laskin Siegal. New York: Simon and Schuster, 1994 (in cooperation with the Boston Women's Health Book Collective).

The Silent Passage; Menopause, Gail Sheehy, New York: Random House, 1991.

Who, What, Where? Resources for Women's Health & Aging, National Institute on Aging, March 1992.

Guide to Choosing a Nursing Home[*]

Selecting a nursing home is one of the most important and difficult decisions that you may be asked to make — either for yourself or for a member of your family. So it's important that you base your decision on the most complete and timely information available.

Ideally, you would have ample time to plan ahead: to examine facilities; to talk to residents of nursing homes and their families; and to find out about the costs of care and make some financial plans to cover the cost of your nursing home care. Planning ahead is one of the best ways to ease the stress that accompanies choosing a nursing home, and it helps assure a good choice of facility and location when the decision is made.

Unfortunately, such a decision often must be made during a time of crisis — frequently when a person is ready to leave the hospital after a serious illness or operation.

However, when an individual can no longer live independently or requires short-term care after a hospital stay, a decision must be made about providing the best alternative arrangement to meet the person's needs for care.

The task of finding the right kind of services in a desirable, nurturing atmosphere requires some preparatory work to gather the many facts needed to help in the decision-making process.

This chapter is a first step to help you choose a nursing home. It is a guide to some of the places to go, people to speak with, and some of the questions you should ask when considering whether a particular nursing home is right for you or someone in your family.

Finding the right facility is all-important to you or your loved one's well-being. The facility selected will be the home and community

---

[*] Source: Health Care Financing Administration, U.S. Department of Health and Human Services, 6325 Security Blvd., Baltimore, MD 21207-5187; 800-638-6833.

for the duration of any stay — often for the remainder of a person's life.

Planning ahead is one of the best ways to ease the stress that accompanies choosing a nursing home.

Consequently, if you are helping a relative find a nursing home, involve him or her as much as possible in the decision-making process. If your relative is mentally alert, it is essential that his or her wishes be respected and that he or she be involved in the process of selecting the home every step of the way.

Many people know very little and don't like to think about life in nursing homes. Therefore, if you or a family member is likely to need nursing home care in the future, discuss the subject well in advance of such a move and educate the family about the realities of nursing home care.

By planning ahead, you will have more control of your life. Even if others must make decisions for you, you will have

> **Notice**
>
> If you are a Medicare or Medicaid beneficiary applying for admission to a nursing facility for care that will be covered by Medicare or Medicaid, it is unlawful for the facility to require you to pay a cash deposit. Federal law prohibits nursing facilities from requiring a deposit or other payment as a condition of admission for care covered under either Medicare or Medicaid. The facility may, however, request that a Medicare beneficiary pay coinsurance amounts and other charges for which a beneficiary is liable. You pay those charges as they become due, not before. A facility may also require a cash deposit before admission if your care will not be covered by either Medicare or Medicaid. If a skilled nursing facility improperly demands a deposit, you should call Medicare's hotline.
>
> The toll-free number is 1-800-638-6833.
>
> You should also be aware that federal law prohibits nursing homes from using physical and chemical restraints on residents for discipline or for the convenience of nursing home personnel. Such restraints may be used only when necessary to treat medical symptoms or to ensure the safety of the person being restrained or other residents. Except in emergencies, physical and chemical restraints may be used only under written orders of physicians.

participated in making your preferences and needs known ahead of time. There are people who can help you, however, as you begin your search.

First Considerations

Do You Need Nursing Home Care?
Nursing homes are only one of a range of long-term, comprehensive medical, personal, and social services designed to meet the needs of chronically ill and disabled persons. Before considering placement in a nursing home, therefore, you should explore the possibility of using home- and community-based care.

What's important is that you discuss your needs and plans with your physician or care giver and your family to decide on the most appropriate place in which you receive care. Your financial ability to pay will also affect your decision (see the section "Payment Considerations" in this chapter).

When a less intensive and less restrictive form of care is called for, a mix of services and/or programs popularly called "alternatives to institutional care" may be most appropriate.

While most long-term care is still provided at home by relatives and friends, an increasing number and variety of community- based health and supportive services and specialized living arrangements are now being created in communities throughout the nation. Among the home- and community-based services available:

- Home Health Care;
- Adult Day Care Centers;
- Foster Care;
- Residential Care in a Board and Care Home;
- Retirement Communities; and
- Hospice Care.

When an individual needs 24-hour nursing care and supervision, however, a nursing home may be the best answer.

Once you decide that nursing home care is needed, you may become anxious, angry, guilty, depressed, or scared at the thought of making such a big decision for yourself or a family member. Such reactions are natural and even to be expected. This chapter can help ease your concerns by assisting you to make informed choices. By planning ahead, you will be better prepared to make the appropriate choice for care. By using this chapter, you will already be familiar with the individuals and organizations to whom you can turn if you need help.

Why Do People Live in Nursing Homes?

The great majority of nursing home residents are elderly. Some are frail and unable to take care of themselves and live safely on their own. Other residents, regardless of age, suffer from chronic illnesses and need some medical attention, but do not require hospital care. Still others have been transferred to the nursing home from a hospital to convalesce after a serious illness, accident or operation.

Approximately 45 percent of everyone turning age 65 this year will stay in a nursing at least once in their lifetime. About one-half of those admitted to nursing homes stay less than six months. However, one in five will stay a year or more, and one in ten will stay three or more years.

Some nursing home residents have no families to care for them at home. In other cases, the families are not able to supply the kind of care the individual needs — there may be no one home during the day, or the care needed may be too specialized or too expensive to provide at home. In still other cases, families may decide that keeping the person at home would be too difficult.

Facts About Long-Term Care And Nursing Homes

During the past two decades, the number of people over age 65 has grown dramatically, more than 55 percent. While people are living longer, the number of people with chronic illnesses or disabilities that will require long-term care services is also increasing. By the year 2000, almost 9 million older Americans will need long-term care services, up from almost 7 million in 1988. Many of these people will require nursing home services. Typically, these people are older women without spouses.

Almost 20,000 nursing homes in the United States now provide care for about 5 percent of older Americans.

Quality-of-Life Issues
When people enter nursing homes, they don't leave their personalities at the door. Nor do they lose their basic human rights and needs for respect, encouragement and friendliness. All individuals need to retain as much control over the events in their daily lives as possible.

Consequently, nursing home residents should have the freedom and privacy to attend to their personal needs. That means several things: from managing their own financial affairs, if they are able, to decorating their rooms with personal belongings. It also means being able to participate in the planning of their treatment and being assured of the confidentiality of their medical records.

In the 1980s, several studies identified some problems with the quality of care that the nation's nursing homes provided to Medicare and Medicaid residents and recommended the implementation of new and higher standards of care in nursing facilities. Congress subsequently enacted legislation to raise these standards. The reforms, which took effect in October of 1990, have served to strengthen both the quality of life and the quality of care for residents. Among other things, they require the provision and enforcement of certain rights of residents to dignity, choice, self-determination, and quality services and activities.

Knowing some of the key details of the law can help you make a better decision about selecting a nursing home. It can also better prepare you to be a resident, to know what to expect, and what to ask for if you are not receiving the care and services to which you are entitled. You will need to ask questions and observe how a nursing home is performing.

Under the law, nursing homes must train their nurse aides. Facilities must also conduct a comprehensive assessment of resident needs within two weeks of admission. The law also requires that nursing home residents have the right to choose activities, schedules and health care that are consistent with their interests and needs. Facilities are expected to provide a safe, clean, comfortable homelike environment.

Residents must receive the necessary care and services that enable them to reach and maintain their highest practicable level of physical, mental and social well-being.

For example, married residents should be assured privacy for visits from spouses. If both husband and wife live in the home, they should be able to share a room, if possible. All residents should have freedom and opportunity to make friends and to socialize.

Residents and their relatives must be able to talk to administrators and staff about questions, problems and complaints without fear of reprisal. Administrators should be courteous, helpful and frank. They should treat residents and their requests with respect. Staff members should respond quickly to calls for assistance and treat residents with courtesy, respect and affection. A long-term care facility may meet every known standard, but that's not enough. Warm, professional relationships between staff and residents are an essential ingredient to quality care.

Residents should not be transferred or discharged arbitrarily and should be given reasonable advance notice if they must be moved.

Many of the specific items you should keep an eye out for are part of the regulations concerning residents' rights — a set of rules that nursing homes certified by Medicaid and Medicare must follow. The law applies to referrals, admissions, accommodations, room assignments and transfers, policies regarding financial matters, care services, physical facilities, residents' privileges, and the assignments of medical staff and volunteers. In addition, a civil rights law ensures equal access regardless of race, color or national origin in all nursing homes.

Beginning The Search

Seek Referrals

Before visiting nursing homes, get information about available options from a variety of different people: professionals in the long-term care field (such as the local ombudsman, see below) to friends or acquaintances who have been in a situation similar to yours. They can help focus your search for a nursing home. In that way, you can save some time and avoid needless frustration.

Once again, it is important to remember that choosing a nursing home will require you to use critical judgment at a variety of levels. That final judgment should also include your "gut feeling." In addition, you should seek information from a broad base of sources and not rely on any one source in making your decision.

Long-Term Ombudsman Program

The ombudsman program is a significant part of the nursing home system. Federal law requires each State Agency on Aging to have an Office of the Long-Term Care Ombudsman. More than 500 local ombudsman programs now exist nationwide. These offices provide help and information to older Americans, their families and friends regarding long-term care facilities.

Ombudsmen visit nursing homes on a regular basis, and they often have knowledge of what goes on in facilities in their communities. In addition, they receive and investigate complaints made by or on behalf of nursing home residents and work to resolve the problems.

If they are unable to resolve problems or if they find serious violations of standards in the facility, ombudsmen refer complaints to State Health Departments for action.

Ombudsmen can also provide information on licensed long-term care facilities in the state or local area, usually including some descriptive information. They cannot advise you on any one particular nursing home, but they will supply current information regarding nursing homes near you. Ask the local ombudsman about:

- Information from the latest survey report on the facility;
- Any complaints against the nursing homes you plan to visit;
- The number and nature of complaints for the past year against the facility;
- The results and conclusions of the investigation into these complaints; and
- What to look for as tell-tale signs of good care in facilities.

If there are local advocacy groups or support groups for the aged and their families, they will also be good sources for recommendations.

Other Community Resources
While the ombudsman program is a good place to begin your search for a nursing home, there are many other valuable community resources that you should consult before deciding which nursing homes to visit. Among these resources:

- Hospital discharge planners or social workers;
- Your family physician;
- Religious organizations;
- Volunteer organizations such as Pets on Wheels;
- State nursing home associations; and
- Close friends or relatives.

In meeting with these resources, ask about the facility's reputation in the community. Does the facility have a list of references - especially family members of current residents?

Other Key Factors to Consider

As you set about deciding on a nursing home, it is also important for you to distinguish between your wants and your needs. To that end, you should ask yourself:

- What kind of care do you need; and
- What is the lifestyle you would like to lead in the facility?

Different kinds of nursing homes provide different types of care; yet all must provide certain basic services. The key is to match the home to the resident — to ensure the nursing home provides the person the kind of care and services needed.

Some people may want a safe and comfortable place to live among pleasant companions. You may want a home that places special emphasis on ethnic factors such as special food or foreign languages, or similarity in religious background.

On the other hand, other residents may require help with grooming and occasional medical treatment. Still others may require constant medical attention, therapy and other skilled nursing care.

Once you identify what you want and need in a home, simply telephoning some of the nursing homes on your list may eliminate the need to visit them. Some of the key questions that you may ask over the phone to facilities are:

- Is the nursing home certified for participation in the Medicare or Medicaid programs?
- What are the facility's admission requirements for residents?
- What is the "typical profile" of a resident in the facility? For example, if you require temporary rehabilitation services and the nursing home specializes in Alzheimer's disease care, it's probably not a good match.
- Does the nursing home require that a resident sign over personal property or real estate in exchange for care?
- Does the facility have vacancies, or is there a waiting list?

Location

As you develop your list of potential nursing homes to visit, you should also consider the location of the facility. For example, how close is it to family members and friends? How easy is it for people to visit? How near is it to other community contacts and resources that you hope to continue to see and use?

Enrollment In A Managed Care Plan

If you or your family member is enrolled in a health maintenance organization (HMO) or competitive medical plan (CMP), ask a representative of the plan about coordination of health care services between the HMO/CMP and the nursing home. Ask which nursing homes the HMO or health plan works with in the area. If you are interested in a nursing home outside of the area served by the HMO, discuss this with the plan representatives.

Public Information

Your State Health Department produces a yearly report on the performance of each nursing home that is certified for Medicare or Medicaid. You should review the latest report. It is required to be made available at the nursing home and is also available through your state health department or from the local ombudsman program.

You should talk to the nursing home administrator and long-term care ombudsman about the results of the survey report. What did the nursing home do to correct problems, if any, that were identified in the report?

Visiting A Nursing Home

Talk to Residents and Staff

It is very important for you or a family member to visit a nursing home before becoming a resident. A visit provides you an opportunity to talk not only with people who work at the facility, but more importantly, with the people who live and receive care at the nursing home and their families.

Ask residents what they like about the home and what they do when they need something to be different. Ask them what they like about the staff. Ask visitors or volunteers the same questions. If you see no volunteers, ask how frequently volunteers come to the home and what they do. Take advantage of this opportunity. You can gain valuable insight into the quality of life in the facility.

When and How Often Should You Visit a Home?
Ideally, you should visit a nursing home more than once and during different times of the day. One visit should be during late morning or midday so you can observe whether people are out of bed, and, if possible, whether the noon meal is being served. You should also plan to visit during the afternoon to observe activities as well as during and after the evening meal and evening hours.

The first time you visit a nursing home, make an appointment to see the administrator or admissions director so that you can fully explain the purpose of your visit. Mention that you would like to watch the daily routine at the nursing home, including staff preparing and serving a meal in the dining room and to residents in their own rooms. Observe as many different resident activities as possible, including therapy sessions.

Most nursing homes will gladly arrange for a guided tour of the facility, and they should be able to direct you to the Residents' Bill of Rights. You may ask for a copy of the statement, which you can then review carefully at home. You may also ask to see the results of the nursing home's most recent Medicare and/or Medicaid survey of the facility and the resulting plan of correction, if there were problems.

The administrator or admissions director can also arrange for you to speak with any of the staff, including the nursing home social worker. In fact, when you visit a nursing home, you should carefully observe staff members at work. Once again, the interactions among staff and between staff and residents should be warm, respectful and professional.

You should also note the physical condition of the nursing home. Is the building clean, free from overwhelming odors, and well-maintained?

Evaluate the quality of the care and concern for residents you see. For example, do nursing assistants speak slowly and clearly so the resident can hear and see them? How does the staff react when a resident's behavior is inappropriate? How does the staff respond to residents with Alzheimer's disease or residents who seem to have some impairments in expressing themselves? Overall, does the staff show an active interest in and affection for individual residents? In addition, ask residents if there is enough staff to meet their needs at all times.

Form Your Own Impressions
Although a formal tour is useful, it is important that you talk to residents and observe conditions in the nursing home by yourself, without facility staff assisting you. Make an unscheduled visit. Ask residents their opinion of the nursing home, and if they will show you around the facility. In either case, be observant. Notice whether the residents are dressed neatly and appropriately for the time of day.

Ask how often residents get a full bath or shower. Do they appear to be contented and enjoying the activities, and do residents interact with one another?

Remember, although some residents may prefer to watch rather than participate in activities at the nursing home, if most residents are passive, it may be a sign that the home has no activity program or that residents are kept on medications.

Are residents eager to discuss their feelings about the nursing home with you, or do they appear apathetic about their surroundings? Ask residents whether the facility has a resident council — a committee of residents that helps advise the facility about resident concerns, needs, wants, likes, and dislikes. The law does not require nursing homes to have such councils.

And, if possible, meet with members of the family council at the nursing home. Family councils, which are similar to resident councils, are composed of family members of the facility's residents. Even if the nursing home does not have a family council, ask to speak with family members of residents of the facility. Also note whether visiting hours are generous and set for the convenience of residents and visitors.

In making these kinds of observations, trust your instincts and perceptions. Be certain to bring a note pad and pen with you to make notes about your impressions soon after you leave the facility. Impressions become blurred with time.

Medical Services
Medical and nursing care are crucial to you or your relative's welfare as a resident of the nursing home. Therefore, you need to spend extra time to ensure your needs will be met in this important area. In most cases, you can choose your own physician, even for emergency care.

Nursing homes also have their own physician. You should understand how often the physician visits the facility and reviews medical records of the residents. Does the physician and nursing staff meet with residents and their families to develop plans for treatment? On average, how many residents is each nurse aide or direct care nurse assigned to care for? Are licensed nurses on duty around the clock? If not, is there 24-hour access by telephone? In addition, will the confidentiality of your medical records be assured? The importance of understanding the answers to these questions in part depends on the needs of the individual resident. Still, you need to know the answers in case you need medical treatment.

Restraints
The law strictly limits circumstances under which facilities can physically restrain residents in beds or chairs. Residents can never be restrained simply for the convenience of staff. All physical or

chemical (medication) restraints must be ordered by a physician. Many nursing homes are making progress in finding other safe ways to care for residents without restraining them. If you see residents with restraints, you should carefully question the staff about the nursing home's philosophy on the use of restraints. Ask what kind of activities and rehabilitation are used to keep residents restraint free.

When a medication is used, facility staff must check the resident to make sure there are no adverse side-effects. When a physical restraint is used, the resident should be monitored frequently to see that all is well, and to take care of any physical needs such as toileting.

Remember that federal law states that nursing home residents have the right to be free from any restraints administered for purposes of discipline or convenience, and not required to treat medical conditions. In addition, the law says you will have the right to be free from neglect and any type of abuse — verbal, sexual, physical, and mental. That includes corporal punishment and involuntary seclusion. Determine the facility's system to protect residents from neglect and abuse.

Food Services

The preparation and serving of meals is one of the most important services provided to nursing home residents each day. On your visit to the nursing homes, take the time to watch servers in action. Ask to sample the food. Are hot foods served hot and cold foods cold?

Ask the dietitian at the facility for a list of menus for the month, and ask how special diets are handled. Among the questions you should get answers to from both the dietitian and residents are:

- Is enough time allowed for eating?
- Is food delivered to residents who are unable or unwilling to eat in the dining room?
- Are snacks available?

- Are those residents in need of special equipment or assistance at meal time provided with such equipment or assistance?

As you watch residents eat their meal, note whether they seem to be enjoying the food. Talk to residents about the quality and variety of their meals.

Fire Safety
Although nursing home fires causing multiple deaths do not occur often, fire safety is very important. It is often difficult to evacuate residents quickly enough should a major fire erupt. Therefore, review the facility's fire safety training program. Do all staff know what to do in the event of an emergency? Are residents provided a supervised place in which to smoke?

Followup Observations
When deciding on which nursing home to enter, one visit is not enough. Ideally, you should plan on a second and, if time permits, a third visit to a facility after reviewing your written notes from the initial visit. Once again, you should make unannounced visits to the nursing home.

On your followup visit, go back at a different time of the day, preferably during the evening and/or weekend. There are usually fewer staff on duty at that time, and the visit will give you an indication of the types of evening or weekend activities, if any, that are available for the residents. These visits will also give you a way to compare the level of attention that staff give to residents and whether the attitude of staff is the same during the night and day and during weekdays and weekends.

Making The Selection

Payment Considerations
For most people, finding ways to finance nursing home care is a major concern. There are four basic ways in which nursing home costs may be financed:

Personal Resources — About one-half of all nursing facility residents pay for costs out of personal resources. When many people enter a nursing home, they first pay for their care out of their own income and savings. Because of the high cost of such care, however, some people use up their resources to the point where they become eligible for Medicaid. You should check with your state Medicaid agency before entering a nursing home to determine the financial eligibility requirements for Medicaid.

Private Insurance — Some Medicare supplementary insurance policies, often referred to as "Medigap" insurance, also can provide a source of payment to supplement Medicare coverage for care in a skilled nursing facility. There is also private, long-term care insurance available.

Medicaid — State and federal coverage is available to eligible low-income individuals who need care at least above the level of room and board. The nursing home must be Medicaid-certified.

Medicare — Under some limited circumstances, Medicare hospital insurance (Part A) will pay for a fixed period of skilled nursing facility care. The nursing home must be Medicare-certified.

Many health maintenance organizations (HMOs) and other managed care plans participate in the Medicare and Medicaid programs. These health care plans often cover certain benefits in addition to those required by Medicare and Medicaid and are experienced in "coordinating" a member's health care. Some HMOs may also offer more medical or supportive services; others may not require a hospital stay before approving a nursing home admission.

What Do Medicare and Medicaid Pay For?
Medicare benefits are payable only if you require daily skilled care which, as a practical matter, can only be provided in a skilled nursing facility on an inpatient basis, and the care is provided in a facility certified by Medicare. Medicare will not pay for your stay if the services you receive are primarily personal care or custodial

services such as assistance in walking, getting in and out of bed, eating, dressing, bathing and taking medicine.

To qualify for Medicare coverage for skilled nursing facility care, you must have been in a hospital at least three consecutive days (not counting the day of discharge) before entering a skilled nursing facility. You must be admitted to the facility for a condition for which you were treated in the hospital and the admission generally must be within 30 days of your discharge from the hospital. A medical professional must certify that you need and receive skilled nursing or skilled rehabilitation services on a daily basis.

Medicare can help pay for up to 100 days of skilled care in a skilled nursing facility during a benefit period. All covered services for the first 20 days of care are fully paid by Medicare. All covered services for the next 80 days are paid by Medicare except for a daily coinsurance amount. The coinsurance amount is calculated each year by Medicare. You are responsible for the coinsurance. If you require more than 100 days of care in a benefit period, you are responsible for all charges beginning with the 101st day.

Many nursing homes have both Medicare and non-Medicare parts. Medicare law does not permit payment for residents in non-Medicare parts of the facility, even if the care needed meets the medical standards for coverage. Therefore, in order for Medicare to pay, the resident must be placed in the section of the nursing home that is certified under Medicare.

To help you avoid such problems, however, SNFs generally work closely with hospital discharge planners and social workers to ensure that only individuals requiring skilled services are admitted to skilled parts of the nursing home. If the SNF determines that the person does not meet skilled standards and then admits the resident to a skilled part, it must provide the individual with a Notice of Non-Coverage. Nursing homes are required to give residents the Notice of Non-Coverage at time of admission, or any time after admission when they believe skilled services are no longer required.

A resident may appeal the nursing home's opinion that the care and services required are not covered by Medicare. The resident should not be charged for services until he or she receives a formal decision on his or her appeal from Medicare. However, if as a result of the appeal, it is determined that Medicare will not cover the stay, the resident is liable for the cost of care since the start of his or her nursing home stay.

When you visit a nursing home, if you are eligible for Medicare coverage, ask to see a copy of the facility's Notice of Non-Coverage. Ask some of the residents in the facility if they have had difficulties or misunderstandings with the facility over payments and whether problems were satisfactorily and quickly resolved.

Medicaid Eligibility

Medicaid pays nursing home expenses for individuals who meet income and resource eligibility requirements. Medicaid can pay for nursing facility care that ranges from skilled nursing care to care that is above the level of room and board, but less intensive than "skilled" care.

It is important to contact the local State Medicaid Agency for eligibility and program information as early in the placement process as possible. Financial guidelines vary from state to state and can be somewhat restrictive, but remember that eligibility is retroactive to the date of application.

Moreover, if either spouse transfers resources, such as real estate or bank accounts, for less than fair market value within 30 months before a spouse goes into a nursing home, this could affect the extent to which the Medicaid program would pay for the cost of care for the spouse in the nursing home and for certain community services.

Changes in Medicaid law — the "spousal impoverishment" provisions — provide some protection for a certain amount of income and resources for a spouse still living at home when the other partner needs nursing home placement.

Long-Term Care Financing and Insurance

Given the increasing likelihood of older Americans having to use long-term care services at some point in their lives, an important part of planning ahead is preparing for your financial future. This is important because most home care and about half of nursing home costs are paid directly by consumers and their families.

There are a variety of financing mechanisms for long-term care services, including continuing care retirement communities and private long-term care insurance.

Medicare supplemental insurance (Medigap) policies generally cover very little long-term care at home or in a nursing home, usually covering only deductibles, coinsurance, and long hospital stays. Medicaid covers nursing home care and some community care benefits such as home health care or adult day care. Coverage varies by state and is generally limited to people with low income and assets.

One option that you might wish to consider is purchasing long-term care insurance. This type of insurance policy covers nursing home care and increasingly includes home care coverage as well.

Because costs for long-term care policies can vary widely, even for similar policies, shopping and price comparison is important. Counseling services may help you select a policy most appropriate to your needs.

People purchase long-term care insurance for several reasons. If you are deciding whether and when to buy long-term care insurance, you should consider the following questions:

- Will your income cover long-term care expenses, along with other ongoing expenses?
- If you purchase such insurance, can you pay for the deductible period and coinsurance?
- Can you pay the premiums now? Can you pay if the premiums rise?
- Will you be able to pay the premiums if your spouse dies?
- Will you be able to pay for upgrading benefits to meet inflation?
- Would you become eligible for Medicaid if you had large medical bills, or entered a nursing home where average yearly costs run almost $30,000?

Before signing a long-term care insurance policy, you should also ask if you have a period during which to cancel the policy and receive a refund for the first premium. As you shop around:

- Be sure that the policy does not base coverage on medical necessity, or require prior hospitalization before entering a nursing home, or prior nursing home stays for home health care.
- Be sure that the insurer can cancel your policy only for reason of nonpayment of premiums.
- Make certain you have realistic inflation protection.
- Check the length of time that preexisting conditions are excluded.
- Check for permanent exclusions on certain conditions, such as Alzheimer's disease.

Finally, if you decide to purchase long-term care insurance, do some checking into the reputation and financial stability of the company offering the insurance. Your state health insurance commissioner and consumer affairs offices should be helpful in identifying reliable companies.

Reviewing the Contract
Before an individual is admitted to a nursing home, the resident, or

the person sponsoring the resident, will have to sign a contract. Before you sign any contract with a nursing home, stop, and carefully review the document.

Remember: the admissions contract is a legally binding document that spells out the conditions under which the resident is accepted.

A comprehensive contract should:

- State your rights and obligations as a resident of the facility, including safeguards for residents rights and grievance procedures;
- Specify how much money you must pay each day or month to live in the nursing home;
- Detail the prices for items not included in the basic monthly or daily charge;
- State the facility's policy on holding a bed if you temporarily leave the home for reasons such as hospitalization or vacation; and
- State whether the facility is Medicaid and/or Medicare certified. If so, and if you desire, the facility must accept Medicaid payments when your own funds run out, or accept Medicare payments if you qualify for Medicare coverage. For Medicare and Medicaid beneficiaries, private pay admissions contracts are illegal and cannot be enforced.

Remember: discrimination against Medicaid nursing home patients is illegal.

Additional Tips Before Signing a Contract

- Ask the nursing home for a copy of a contract. In this way, you will be able to review the document at your own pace, get additional advice from a variety of outside sources, and compile a list of questions that you might have about provisions in the contract.
- Have the nursing home administrator, the home's social worker, or the local ombudsman answer your questions.

- Because the admissions contract is a legally binding document, you should talk to a lawyer, if possible, about the terms of the contract.
- Remember that you can change terms of the contract. But if you make changes, each of them must be initialed by both you and the nursing home representative.
- Be sure that the contract is complete and correct before you sign it. There should be no blank spaces.

Nursing Home Checklist

When you visit a nursing home, you should carry this checklist with you. It will help you to compare one facility with another, but remember to compare facilities certified in the same category; for example, a skilled nursing facility with another skilled nursing home. Because nursing homes may be licensed in more than one category, always compare similar types of service among facilities.

Look at Daily Life:

1. Do residents seem to enjoy being with staff?
2. Are most residents dressed for the season and time of day?
3. Does staff know the residents by name?
4. Does staff respond quickly to resident calls for assistance?
5. Are activities tailored to residents' individual needs and interests?
6. Are residents involved in a variety of activities?
7. Does the home serve food attractively?
8. Does the home consider personal food likes and dislikes in planning meals?
9. Does the home use care in selecting roommates?
10. Does the nursing home have a resident's council? If it does, does the council influence decisions about resident life?
11. Does the nursing home have a family council? If it does, does the council influence decisions about resident life?
12. Does the facility have contact with community groups, such as pet therapy programs and Scouts?

Look at Care Residents Receive:

1. Do various staff and professional experts participate in evaluating each resident's needs and interests?
2. Does the resident or his or her family participate in developing the resident's care plan?
3. Does the home offer programs to restore lost physical functioning (for example, physical therapy, occupational therapy, speech and language therapy)?
4. Does the home have any special services that meet your needs? For example, special care units for residents with dementia or with respiratory problems?
5. Does the nursing home have a program to restrict the use of physical restraints?
6. Is a registered nurse available for nursing staff
7. Does the nursing home have an arrangement with a nearby hospital?

Look at How the Nursing Home Handles Payment:

1. Is the facility certified for Medicare?
2. Is the facility certified for Medicaid?
3. Is the resident or the resident's family informed when charges are increased?

Look at the Environment:

1. Is the outside of the nursing home clean and in good repair?
2. Are there outdoor areas accessible for residents to use?
3. Is the inside of the nursing home clean and in good repair?
4. Does the nursing home have handrails in hallways and grab bars in bathrooms?
5. When floors are being cleaned, are warning signs displayed or are areas blocked off to prevent accidents?
6. Is the nursing home free from unpleasant odors?
7. Are toilets convenient to bedrooms?
8. Do noise levels fit the activities that are going on?

9.   Is it easy for residents in wheelchairs to move around the home?

10.   Is the lighting appropriate for what residents are doing?

11.   Are there private areas for residents to visit with family, visitors, or physicians?

12.   Are residents' bedrooms furnished in a pleasant manner?

13.   Do the residents have some personal items in their bedrooms (for example, family pictures, souvenirs, a chair)?

14.   Do the residents' rooms have accessible storage areas for residents' personal items?

Other Things to Look For:

1.   Does the nursing home have a good reputation in the community?

2.   Does the nursing home have a list of references?

3.   Is the nursing home convenient for family or friends to visit?

4.   Does the local ombudsman visit the facility regularly?

Nutrition: A Lifelong Concern[*]

The basic guidelines for a nutritious diet are the same for most healthy adults. Older people, however, need to pay special attention to the quality of the foods they eat.

An older person's requirement for nutrients — such as proteins, carbohydrates, vitamins, and minerals — is not very different from that of younger adults. But because of changes in the body and decreasing physical activity, older people usually need fewer calories. This is also why many people gain weight more easily as they age.

A nutritious (well-balanced) diet provides vitamins, minerals, and calories from protein, carbohydrate, and some fat. Such a diet must include a variety of foods from each of the major food groups: fruit and vegetables; whole grain and enriched breads, cereals, and grain products such as rice and pasta; fish, poultry, meat, eggs, and dry peas and beans; and milk, cheese, and other dairy products.

Limiting the amount of fat in the diet may help prevent weight gain. Excess weight is a factor in some disorders that occur in older people such as diabetes, heart disease, and high blood pressure. Limiting fat in the diet may also help protect against some cancers. Decreasing excessive salt intake is another good health measure.

Some older people do not eat enough food to supply the necessary nutrients. As a result, they may not get the vitamins, minerals, and calories they need to stay healthy and active.

Following a doctor's advice about eating is best, especially if an illness requires changes in what or how much is eaten or if taking medicines. Some drugs interact with certain foods; others can affect appetite or change the body's nutritional requirements.

---

* Source: *Age Page*, National Institute on Aging, U.S. Department of Health and Human Services, Public Health Service, National Institutes of Health, Gaithersburg, MD 20898; 800-222-2225.

The Major Nutrients

Protein is the basic material in all body cells including those that make up muscles, organs, skin, bones, blood, hormones, and hair. It enables growth and repair of body cells and helps the body resist disease by forming antibodies.

During ingestion, food proteins are broken down into simple nutrients called amino acids, which are the basic building blocks of body tissue. The body can then reassemble these amino acids into other required proteins.

Many foods contain protein. The proteins in meat, fish, dairy products, and eggs contain the eight essential amino acids in proper amounts for adults. These foods are called complete protein foods. The easiest way to get all the essential amino acids is to eat some of these foods every day.[6] Plant foods such as dry peas and beans, grains, nuts, and seeds contain "incomplete" proteins because not all of the essential amino acids are present. However, when one of these foods is combined with an animal protein (milk and cereal, for example) or when certain plant proteins are combined (such as rice with beans), they form complete proteins. Foods high in protein also usually provide essential vitamins and minerals.

Carbohydrates come in two forms. Starches are present in grains, cereals, legumes, potatoes, and other vegetables, and sugars are found mainly in fruit and milk. These foods are good sources of vitamins, minerals, fiber, and calories. Sweet desserts, candy, honey, syrup, and other sugary foods should be limited since they provide calories but few other nutrients.

Breads and cereals are more nutritious if they are made from whole grains. Whole grain products include whole wheat and rye breads and crackers, whole wheat cereals, bran, oatmeal, barley, brown rice, and cornmeal. However, white breads made with enriched

---

[6] People who have high blood cholesterol levels should limit their use of eggs and organ meats such as liver.

flour supply extra amounts of some nutrients such as iron, thiamin, and niacin and can be eaten on occasion to increase variety in the diet.

Fats are concentrated sources of calories. Some fat is needed in the diet because it provides essential fatty acids and gives flavor to foods. However, many American diets are probably too high in fat. Low-fat foods include fish, poultry, lean meat, dry beans and peas, skim milk, yogurt, buttermilk, fruit, vegetables, and grains. Eggs and organ meat should be limited, as well as butter, cream, mayonnaise, margarine, oils, lard, salad dressings, gravies, sauces, certain prepared foods, and snack foods such as potato chips.

Vitamins and minerals are needed by the body in relatively small amounts. The fat-soluble vitamins A, D, E, and K are absorbed from various foods and are stored in the body. The water-soluble vitamins, the B's and C, generally are not stored. Minerals such as calcium, phosphorus, iron, iodine, magnesium, and zinc are also required for building body tissues and regulating their functions.

Vitamins and minerals are abundant in fruit, vegetables, meat, dairy products, and whole grain or enriched breads and cereals.

Older people should pay particular attention to their need for calcium. Women past menopause may develop a disorder called osteoporosis, which thins out the bones and often leads to painful and disabling fractures. Including foods that are high in calcium in the daily diet helps to make sure the body has enough calcium to build and maintain bones. Primary sources of calcium include milk, yogurt, cheese, and other dairy products. The low-fat forms of these foods contain as much calcium as those with fat. Legumes — such as beans and peas — are also a good source of calcium.

Fiber

Another important part of the diet is fiber, which is present in foods that come from plants. The role of fiber is not fully known but it can help prevent constipation. It may also help protect against certain intestinal disorders, and possibly some cancers and chronic diseases.

The best way to include fiber in the diet is to eat whole grain breads and cereals with oats and plenty of vegetables and fruit.

The keys to a good diet are variety and moderation. The greater the variety, the less likely you are to develop either a deficiency or an excess of any single nutrient and the more likely you are to stay healthy or even improve your health.

For More Information

The National Institute on Aging has available a variety of information on health and aging. Write to the NIA Information Center, P.O. Box 8057, Gaithersburg, MD 20898-8057; 800-222-2225, 800-222-4225 (TTY).

Osteoporosis: The Bone Thinner[*]

One in four women over age 60 and nearly half of all people over 75 suffer from osteoporosis, the bone thinner. Osteoporosis is a major cause of fractures in the spine, hip, wrist, and other bones. To help prevent this condition, steps can be taken early in life and during the middle years. Also, treatment is available that may help older people who already have the disorder.

Osteoporosis develops over a period of many years. Gradually and without discomfort, the bones thin out until some of them break, causing pain and disability.

Bones maintain themselves through a process known as remodeling in which small amounts of old bone are removed and new bone is formed in its place. Beginning in the thirties, however, a little more bone is lost than is gained. This bone loss continues throughout life. In women, bone loss speeds-up around menopause — so that an early menopause, particularly when caused by the surgical removal of the ovaries, results in a greater risk of osteoporosis.

The cause of osteoporosis is not fully known. Falling hormone levels, too little calcium in the diet, and a lifetime of inactivity all play a role.

Who Gets It?

White and Asian women most often develop osteoporosis. Among this group, women who have had an early menopause or who have a family history of osteoporosis are at highest risk. Women with fair skin or small frames are also at greater risk than other people. Men are less likely than women to get osteoporosis for a variety of reasons such as their greater bone mass, and because they have no biological counterpart to menopause. However, men may face osteoporosis in their later years.

---

[*] Source: *Age Page*, National Institute on Aging, U.S. Department of Health and Human Services, Public Health Service, National Institutes of Health, Gaithersburg, MD 20898; 800-222-2225.

Diagnosis

An early sign of osteoporosis is loss of height. This happens when weakened bones of the spine (called vertebrae) collapse. Later, as these fractures mount up, a curving of the spine (often called "dowager's hump") may occur.

Osteoporosis may go unnoticed until there is a loss of height, the spine curves, or a fall results in a hip, wrist, or other fracture. Even a minor fall can result in a broken bone.

Tests are available to diagnose osteoporosis. The most common are single and dual-photon absorptiometry and dual-energy x-ray absorptiometry. Before an osteoporosis screening, consider factors such as insurance coverage and available equipment. Talk with your doctor if you are interested in a diagnostic test.

Prevention

Diet and exercise can help prevent osteoporosis. Foods that are high in calcium — such as lowfat cheese, yogurt, and milk — should be a regular part of the diet.

Although the current recommended dietary allowance (RDA) for calcium is 800 mg daily, women who are nearing or have past menopause may need 1,000 to 1,500 mg. If the diet alone does not provide enough calcium, use a supplement. Keep in mind that some people — those who form kidney stones, for example — need to be careful about suddenly increasing their calcium intake.

It is also important to get enough vitamin D every day because it is needed by the body to absorb calcium. The RDA for vitamin D is 200 IU daily for people over 25. Vitamin-fortified milk and cereals, egg yolk, saltwater fish, and liver are high in vitamin D. Fifteen minutes of midday sunshine may also meet the daily need for vitamin D.

Regular exercise is another important preventive measure. Walking, jogging, dancing, and bicycle riding are helpful because they place stress on the spine and the long bones of the body.

Women with osteoporosis risk factors (who have an early menopause or family members with this condition) should ask their doctor about tests to measure bone mass when nearing menopause. They should also discuss using an estrogen supplement.

Treatment

The goal in treating osteoporosis is to stop further bone loss and prevent falls, which are common in older people. Such falls often result in a fractured hip that causes hospitalization, both temporary and long-term disability, and dependence. prevention and treatment for osteoporosis are based on similar goals. For example, exercise helps stimulate formation of new bone.[7] If you already have had a fracture, a doctor should explain the type and amount of activity to be done.

Many doctors prescribe hormones, such as estrogen, which slow the rate of bone loss. Scientists are studying other drugs and combinations of calcium, vitamin D, and estrogen in the hope of finding a way to stop bone loss.

Research

Scientists are conducting studies on osteoporosis at universities, medical centers, and other research institutions around the country. In 1991 the National Institute on Aging (NIA) began a series of clinical trials, called STOP/IT (Sites Testing Osteoporosis Prevention/Intervention Treatments), to test promising ways to lessen, prevent, or reverse osteoporosis in older people. This is one of the first osteoporosis studies to include large numbers of people over age 65.

---

[7] Exercise may also strengthen muscles and help prevent falls.

Resources

More information on osteoporosis is available from NIA. Part of the National Institutes of Health (NIH), NIA supports research on osteoporosis and offers information on a range of health issues that concern older people, including *Age Pages* on estrogen therapy and preventing fractures. For a free list of publications, call 800-222-2225; or write to the NIA Information Center, P.O. Box 8057, Gaithersburg, MD 20898-8057.

The National Institute of Arthritis and Musculoskeletal and Skin Diseases, part of NIH, also supports osteoporosis research. Contact the NIAMS Clearinghouse at Box AMS, Bethesda, MD 20892; or call 301-495-4484.

The National Institute of Diabetes and Digestive and Kidney Diseases is part of NIH. Contact the National Digestive Diseases Information Clearinghouse, Box NDDIC, Bethesda, MD 20892.

The National Osteoporosis Foundation offers nationwide programs to educate the public and health professionals about osteoporosis and related research. Contact NOF at 2100 M Street, NW, Suite 602, Washington, DC 20037; or call 202-223-2226.

How To Take Your Medicine: Penicillins[*]

How you take a drug makes a big difference in how well it works and how safe it will be for you. Sometimes it can be almost as important as what you take. Timing, what you eat and when you eat, proper dose, and many other factors can mean the difference between getting better, staying the same, or even getting worse. This drug information page is intended to help you make your treatment work as well as possible. It is important to note, however, that this is only a guideline. You should talk to your doctor or pharmacist about how and when to take any prescribed drug.

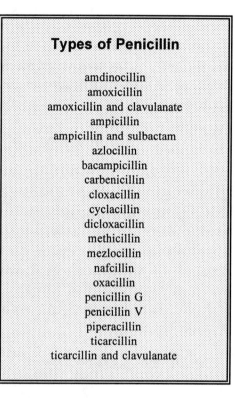

Types of Penicillin

amdinocillin
amoxicillin
amoxicillin and clavulanate
ampicillin
ampicillin and sulbactam
azlocillin
bacampicillin
carbenicillin
cloxacillin
cyclacillin
dicloxacillin
methicillin
mezlocillin
nafcillin
oxacillin
penicillin G
penicillin V
piperacillin
ticarcillin
ticarcillin and clavulanate

Penicillin, the world's first antibiotic, was discovered by British scientist Alexander Fleming in 1928. But it was not used until World War 11, when the need for a treatment for injuries and infectious disease became desperate and penicillin was speeded into production in the United States.

---

[*] Source: *FDA Consumer Magazine*, Office of Public Affairs, Food and Drug Administration, U.S. Department of Health and Human Services, Public Health Service, 5600 Fishers Land, Rockville, MD 20857; 301-827-4420.

By 1945 penicillin was in widespread use. In the years that followed, together with other antibiotics, it decreased the incidence and severity of many infectious diseases, such as pneumonia, tuberculosis and diphtheria.

In addition to their ability to treat infectious diseases, the ability of antibiotics to control infection made possible cardiac surgery, organ transplants, and treatment of severe burns.

Conditions Penicillins Treat

Penicillins work by killing bacteria or preventing their growth. Today there are at least 20 kinds of penicillin. Penicillins are used to treat many different kinds of infection. For example, they are used to treat ear, nose and throat infections, respiratory and urinary tract infections, prostate infections, and certain sexually transmitted diseases. Penicillins are used to prevent bacteria infection before, during and after surgery and to prevent Group A streptococcus ("strep") infections in people with a history of rheumatic heart disease.

None of the penicillins work for colds, flu, or other virus infections.

How to Take

Penicillins come in liquid, tablet and injectable forms. When taking the liquid form, be sure to measure the amount accurately. Liquid doses are best measured in special spoons available from your pharmacist. Teaspoons or tablespoons from the kitchen drawer are rarely the correct dosage size. Chewable tablets should be chewed or crushed before swallowing to insure rapid absorption into the blood.

Most penicillins work best when taken on an empty stomach (either one hour before meals or two hours after) with an 8-ounce glass of water. The water helps prevent the medicine from irritating the delicate lining of the esophagus and stomach.

However, some types of penicillin can be taken on either a full or empty stomach. These include amoxicillin, amoxicillin combined with clavulanate, penicillin V, and the tablet form of bacampicillin.

Liquid amoxicillin can be taken straight or mixed with other liquids such as infant formulas, fruit juice, milk, water, ginger ale, or other cold drinks. But if you mix amoxicillin with another liquid, be sure to drink it immediately and finish the entire drink to get the full dose of medicine.

Penicillins work best when there is a constant amount circulating in the body. So it's important not to miss a dose. Also, it's best to take doses at evenly spaced intervals, both day and night. For example, if you are supposed to take four doses, they should be spaced about six hours apart. If this presents a problem, such as interrupting sleep or other activities, check with your doctor, nurse or pharmacist before modifying the dosage.

Of special note:

- Bottles of carbenicillin tablets usually contain a small packet of a drying agent that keeps the tablets from getting damp and breaking down. The drying agent is not a medicine and should not be swallowed. It should be kept in the bottle until the tablets are gone and then thrown away.
- When taking penicillin G, don't drink orange or grapefruit juice or other acidic beverages (such as soft drinks and carbonated water) within an hour of taking the medicine, or the medicine may not work as well.
- Don't use any penicillins — or any other medicine — after the expiration date on the label because they may not work properly.

Missed Doses

What should you do if you miss a dose of penicillin?

If it's only been a short time, take it as soon as possible. However, if it's almost time for your next dose and you're supposed to take two doses a day, space the missed dose and the next dose five to six hours apart.

If it's almost time for your next dose and you're supposed to take three or more doses a day, double the next dose or space the missed dose and the next dose two to four hours apart.

Then resume your regular medicine schedule.

Relief of Symptoms

Penicillins usually stop infections within days. Because they do not relieve symptoms immediately, your doctor may prescribe other medicines, such as aspirin or acetaminophen, to ease pain and fever until the penicillin takes effect. It is important to finish the entire amount of penicillin prescribed — even if you begin to feel better after a few days — to prevent a recurrence of the infection.

If you have a "strep" infection, it is especially important to keep taking the medicine for at least 10 days, or as prescribed by your doctor. Serious heart problems, such as rheumatic fever, could develop later if the infection isn't cleared up completely.

Side Effects and Risks

Although most penicillins are safe for the majority of people, some people may experience side effects.

The most serious of these is anaphylaxis, a severe allergic reaction that can cause skin rash, hives, itching, difficulty breathing, shock, and unconsciousness. An early sign of anaphylaxis is a feeling of warmth and flushing. If any of these occurs, the medicine should be stopped and emergency help sought immediately. In some cases, these symptoms can progress to death.

Also, if you notice blood in your urine, have large amounts of light-colored urine, or experience swelling of the face or ankles, difficulty breathing, or unusual tiredness or weakness, consult your doctor immediately.

Certain penicillins — amoxicillin and clavulanate, azlocillin, mezlocillin, oxacillin, or piperacillin — may occasionally cause dark or amber urine, pale stools, stomach pain, or yellow eyes or skin. If you experience any of these symptoms, check with your doctor immediately.

On rare occasions some types of penicillin may cause severe abdominal or stomach cramps, pain, or bloating or severe or bloody diarrhea. If diarrhea is severe and watery, or if it has blood in it, check with your doctor immediately.

Other rare side effects include fever, increased thirst, severe nausea or vomiting, unusual tiredness or weakness, weight loss, seizures, or unusual bleeding or bruising. If any of these occur (and they may not occur until several weeks after you stop taking the medicine), check with your doctor immediately.

Common, less serious, side effects that some people experience include mild diarrhea and mild nausea or vomiting. These usually don't require medication, and a doctor need not be consulted unless they continue or are bothersome.

Diarrhea medicine containing kaolin (such as Kaopectate or Donnagel) or attapulgite (such as Diasorb) may be taken to relieve mild diarrhea without checking with your doctor. However, some ingredients in diarrhea medicine, such as lactose, may make diarrhea worse, so read labels carefully.

Occasionally, certain types of penicillin may cause the tongue to darken or discolor. This condition is temporary and will go away when the medicine is stopped.

Because penicillin can change the results of some medical tests, tell lab personnel if you are taking penicillin. Some types of penicillin may cause false test results on some urine sugar tests. Persons with diabetes taking penicillin should not change their diets or the dose of their diabetes medicine based on these tests before checking with their doctors.

Before Taking This Medicine

If you have ever had an allergic reaction to penicillin, be sure to let your doctor know, preferably at your first visit, even if you do not then have an infection.

Your doctor should also be told if you have a general history of allergy, such as asthma, eczema, hay fever or hives; if you have ever had a reaction to Novocain (procaine) or other medicines that cause numbing; or if you are on a special diet or are allergic to any substances such as foods, preservatives or dyes.

Also, before taking penicillin, be sure to let your doctor know:

- if you are pregnant or plan to become pregnant. Although penicillins have not been shown to cause birth defects or other problems in animals, studies have not been done in humans. Penicillin should be used during pregnancy only if clearly needed.
- if you are breast-feeding. Most penicillins pass into the breast milk in small amounts and may cause allergic reactions, diarrhea, fungal infections, and skin rash in babies.
- if you have a history of bleeding problems, kidney disease, liver disease, infectious mononucleosis, or stomach or intestinal disease, especially colitis or enteritis.
- if you are taking any other prescription or nonprescription medicine.

Women on birth control pills containing estrogen should use an additional type of birth control when taking ampicillin, bacampicillin, or penicillin V because the effect of birth control pills may be diminished.

Resources

FDA Consumer, the magazine of the U.S. Food and Drug Administration, provides a wealth of information on FDA-related health issues: food safety, nutrition, drugs, medical devices, cosmetics, radiation protection, vaccines, blood products, and veterinary medicine. For a sample copy of *FDA Consumer* and a subscription order form, write to: Food and Drug Administration, HF140, Rockville, MD 20857.

Pneumonia Prevention:
It's Worth a Shot[*]

Pneumococcal (pronounced new-mo-KOK-al) disease is an infection caused by bacteria. These bacteria can attack different parts of the body. When they invade the lungs, they cause the most common kind of bacterial pneumonia. When the same bacteria attack blood cells, they cause an infection called bacteremia (bak-ter-E-me-ah). And in the brain, they cause meningitis.

Pneumococcal pneumonia is a serious illness that kills thousands of older people in the United States each year.

Can Pneumonia Be Prevented?

Yes. The pneumococcal vaccine is safe, it works, and one shot lasts most people a lifetime. People who get the vaccine are protected against almost all of the bacteria that cause pneumococcal pneumonia and other pneumococcal diseases as well. The shot, which is covered by Medicare, can be a lifesaver.

Some experts say it may be best to get the shot before age 65 — anytime after age 50 — since the younger you are, the better the results. They also say people should have this shot even if they have had pneumonia before. There are many different kinds of pneumonia, and having one kind does not protect against the others. The vaccine, however, does protect against 88 percent of the pneumococcal bacteria that cause pneumonia. It does not guarantee that you will never get pneumonia. It does not protect against viral pneumonia. Most people need to get the shot only once. However some older people may need a booster; check with your doctor to find out if this is necessary.

---

* Source: *Age Page*, National Institute on Aging, U.S. Department of Health and Human Services, Public Health Service, National Institutes of Health, Gaithersburg, MD 20898; 800-222-2225.

Are There Side Effects?

Some people have mild side effects from the shot, but these usually are minor and last only a very short time. In studies, about half of the people getting the vaccine had mild side effects — swelling and soreness at the spot where the shot was given, usually on the arm. A few people (less than 1 percent) had fever and muscle pain as well as more serious swelling and pain on the arm. The pneumonia shot cannot cause pneumonia because it is not made from the bacteria itself, but from an extract that is not infectious. The same is true of the flu shot; it cannot cause flu. In fact, people can get the pneumonia vaccine and a flu shot at the same time.

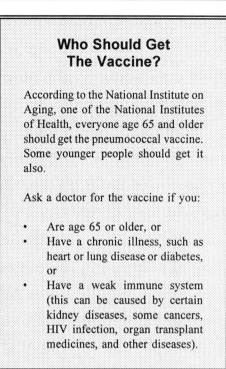

Who Should Get The Vaccine?

According to the National Institute on Aging, one of the National Institutes of Health, everyone age 65 and older should get the pneumococcal vaccine. Some younger people should get it also.

Ask a doctor for the vaccine if you:

- Are age 65 or older, or
- Have a chronic illness, such as heart or lung disease or diabetes, or
- Have a weak immune system (this can be caused by certain kidney diseases, some cancers, HIV infection, organ transplant medicines, and other diseases).

About the Disease and the Vaccine

- There are two main kinds of pneumonia — viral pneumonia and bacterial pneumonia. Bacterial pneumonia is the most serious. One kind of bacteria causes pneumococcal pneumonia. In older people, this type of pneumonia is a common cause of hospitalization and death.

- About 20 to 30 percent of people over age 65 who have pneumococcal pneumonia develop bacteremia. At least 20 percent of those with bacteremia die from it, even though they get antibiotics.

- People age 65 and older are at high risk. They are two to three times more likely than people in general to get pneumococcal infections.

- A recent, large study by the National Institutes of Health shows that the vaccine prevents most cases of pneumococcal pneumonia.

> **Key Facts**
>
> - Everyone age 65 and older should get the pneumococcal vaccine.
> - Anyone with a chronic disease or a weak immune system should also get the vaccine.
> - Most people need to get it only once.
> - Most people have mild or no side effects.
> - It is covered by Medicare.

The U.S. Public Health Service, the National Foundation for Infectious Diseases, and the American Lung Association now recommend that all people age 65 and older get this vaccine.

Resources

More information about adult immunizations is available from the following groups:

National Institute on Aging Information Center, P.O. Box 8057, Gaithersburg, MD 20898-8057; 800-222-2225, 800-222-4225 (TTY).

National Institute of Allergy and Infectious Diseases, 9000 Rockville Pike, Room 7A50, Bethesda, MD 20892; 301-496-5717.

Centers for Disease Control and Prevention, National Immunization Program, 1600 Clifton Road, Atlanta, GA 30333; 404-639-1819.

American Lung Association, 1740 Broadway, New York, NY 10019-4374; 800-LUNG-USA (800-586-4872).

National Foundation for Infectious Diseases, Suite 750, 4733 Bethesda Avenue, Bethesda, MD 20814; 301-656-0003.

Prostate Cancer*

Each year, more than 165,000 men in the United States find out they have prostate cancer. This chapter has been written to help patients and their families and friends understand this type of cancer. We also hope others will read it to learn more about this disease.

The Prostate

The prostate is a male sex gland. It produces a thick fluid that forms part of semen. The prostate is about the size of a walnut. It is located below the bladder and in front of the rectum. The prostate surrounds the upper part of the urethra, the tube that empties urine from the bladder.

The prostate needs male hormones to function. The main male hormone is testosterone, which is made by the testicles. Other male hormones are produced in small amounts by the adrenal glands.

The prostate, like all other organs of the body, is made up of many types of cells. Normally, cells divide to produce more cells only when they are needed. This orderly process helps keep the body healthy.

What Is Cancer

Cancer is a group of diseases that have one thing in common: cells become abnormal, dividing too often and without control or order.

When cells divide without control, they form too much tissue. This tissue can be benign or malignant.

- Benign tissue is not cancer. The cells do not spread to other parts of the body. The abnormal growth of benign tissue in

---

* Source: National Cancer Institute, National Institutes of Health, U.S. Department of Health and Human Services, Public Health Service; 800-4-CANCER.

the prostate is called benign prostatic hyperplasia (BPH). In BPH, the prostate grows larger and pushes against the urethra and bladder, blocking the normal flow of urine. More than half of men in the United States between the ages of 60 and 70 and as many as 90 percent between the ages of 70 and 90 have symptoms of BPH. Although this condition may not be a threat to life, it may require treatment to relieve symptoms.

- Malignant tissue is cancer. The cancer cells form a tumor that can invade and destroy nearby healthy tissue. Cancer cells can also break away from the tumor, spread through the bloodstream and lymphatic system, and form tumors in other parts of the body.

The spread of cancer is called metastasis. When cancer spreads outside the prostate, it often shows up in nearby lymph nodes (also called lymph glands). Prostate cancer can also spread to the bones, liver, bladder, rectum, and other organs.

Cancer that spreads is the same disease and has the same name as the original (primary) cancer. When cancer spreads from the prostate to other parts of the body, the disease is called metastatic prostate cancer rather than bone cancer, liver cancer, or any other name.

Symptoms

Early prostate cancer often does not cause symptoms. When symptoms of prostate cancer do occur, they may include any of the following problems:

- A need to urinate frequently, especially at night.
- Difficulty starting urination or holding back urine.
- Inability to urinate.
- Weak or interrupted flow of urine.
- Painful or burning urination.

- Painful ejaculation.
- Blood in urine or semen.
- Frequent pain or stiffness in the lower back, hips, or upper thighs.

A man who has symptoms like these should see his family doctor or a urologist (a doctor who specializes in treating diseases of the genitourinary system). Only a doctor can determine whether such symptoms are caused by prostate cancer, BPH, or some other condition, such as an infection or stones in the prostate.

Diagnosis

To find the cause of a man's symptoms, the doctor asks about his medical history and does a complete physical exam. The rectal exam is an important procedure. The doctor inserts a gloved, lubricated finger into the rectum and feels the prostate to check for hard or lumpy areas.

Often, the doctor also orders blood tests to measure substances called prostate-specific antigen (PSA) and prostatic acid phosphatase (PAP). The level of PSA in the blood may rise in men who have prostate cancer or benign prostatic hypertrophy. The level of PAP rises above normal in many prostate cancer patients, especially if the cancer has spread beyond the prostate. The doctor cannot diagnose prostate cancer with these tests alone. However, the doctor will take the results of the tests into account when deciding whether to check the patient further for signs of cancer.

The doctor may order other tests to help distinguish benign and malignant conditions of the prostate. In one procedure, transrectal ultrasonography, sound waves that cannot be heard by humans (ultrasound) are sent out by a probe inserted into the rectum. The waves bounce off the prostate, and a computer uses the echoes to create a picture called a sonogram. The patient also may have an intravenous pyelogram, a series of x-rays of the organs of the urinary tract. In addition, the doctor may order urine tests and may look into the urethra and bladder through a thin, lighted tube called a cystoscope.

If test results show that cancer may be present, the patient will need to have a biopsy. In a biopsy, the doctor removes a small amount of prostate tissue, usually with a needle. A pathologist looks at the tissue under a microscope to check for cancer cells. If the diagnosis is cancer, the pathologist can often tell whether the cells are likely to grow slowly or quickly.

Even if the physical exam and test results do not suggest cancer, the doctor may recommend surgery to relieve problems with urination. The surgery used in such cases is transurethral resection of the prostate (TURP or TUR). In TURP, an instrument is inserted through the penis to remove prostate tissue that is pressing against the upper part of the urethra. Sometimes, a small cancer is found when a pathologist examines the tissue under a microscope.

Staging

If cancer is found in the prostate, the doctor needs to know the stage, or extent, of the disease. Staging is a careful attempt to find out whether the cancer has spread and what parts of the body are affected. Treatment decisions depend on these findings. The doctor may use various tests, including the following, to learn the stage of the disease:

- Laboratory tests to check the levels of PSA and PAP in the blood may be repeated.

- If transrectal ultrasonography was not done earlier, this procedure may be part of the staging process.

- The doctor may order a CT or CAT scan, a series of detailed pictures of areas inside the body. The pictures are created by a computer linked to an x-ray machine. The doctor can check the CT scan for swollen lymph nodes, which might mean the cancer has spread. In another procedure, MRI, a computer produces pictures of the prostate and nearby lymph nodes using a powerful magnet instead of x-rays.

- A bone scan shows areas of rapid growth in bones. Radioactive material injected into the bloodstream collects in these areas. A scanner pinpoints the areas and records them on film. Rapid growth in bones may be a sign of cancer that has spread, or it may be the result of other problems in the bones.

- A chest x-ray can show whether cancer has spread to the lungs.

The results of these tests help the doctor decide which of the following stages best describes a patient's disease:

- Stage A-Cancer could not be detected by rectal exam but was found during surgery to relieve problems with urination. Stage A tumors have not spread beyond the prostate.

- Stage B-The tumor can be felt in a rectal exam, but the cancer has not spread beyond the prostate.

- Stage C-The cancer has extended outside the prostate to nearby tissues.

- Stage D-Cancer cells have spread to nearby lymph nodes or to other parts of the body, most commonly to the bones.

Treatment Options

Treatment for prostate cancer depends on many factors. To develop a treatment plan to fit each patient's needs, the doctor considers the stage of the disease and the patient's age, general health, and feelings about the treatments and their possible side effects.

The patient's doctor may want to discuss the case with other doctors who treat prostate cancer. Also, the patient may want to talk with his doctor about taking part in a research study of new treatment methods. More information about such studies, called clinical trials, can be found later in this chapter.

Many patients want to learn all they can about their disease and their treatment choices so they can take an active part in decisions about their medical care. The patient and the doctor should discuss treatment choices thoroughly because treatment for prostate cancer sometimes affects sexual activity and body functions, such as urination. Patients may find helpful information in the sections entitled "Side Effects of Treatment" and "Living With Cancer" later in this chapter.

Men with prostate cancer have many important questions and concerns. The doctor is the best person to answer questions about the extent of the cancer, how it can be treated, how successful the treatment is expected to be, and how much it is likely to cost. People often find it helpful to make a list of questions before they see the doctor. Here are some questions patients may want to ask the doctor:

- What are my treatment choices?
- Would a clinical trial be appropriate for me?
- What are the expected benefits of each kind of treatment?
- What are the risks and possible side effects of each treatment?
- How will treatment affect my sex life?
- If I have pain, how will you help me?
- Will I need to change my normal activities? For how long?
- How often will I need to have checkups?

Taking notes can make it easier to remember what the doctor says. Some patients find it also helps to have a family member or friend with them when they talk with the doctor — to take part in the discussion, to take notes, or just to listen.

There's a lot to learn about prostate cancer and its treatment. Patients should not feel that they need to understand everything the first time they hear it. They will have many chances to ask the doctor to explain things that are not clear.

Planning Treatment

Decisions about prostate cancer treatment are complex. Sometimes it's helpful to have the advice of more than one doctor. Before starting treatment, the patient might want to have a second doctor review the diagnosis and the treatment plan. A short delay will not reduce the chance that treatment will be successful. There are a number of ways to find another doctor to consult:

- The patient's doctor may be able to suggest a doctor who has a particular interest in prostate cancer. Doctors who specialize in treating this disease are oncologists, radiation oncologists, and urologists.

- The Cancer Information Service, at 1-800-4-CANCER, can tell callers about cancer centers and other National Cancer Institute-supported programs in their area.

- Patients can get the names of doctors from their local medical society, a nearby hospital, or a medical school.

Treatment Methods

As mentioned earlier in this chapter, a small (stage A) prostate cancer may be found as a result of surgery done to relieve problems with urination. Many men whose cancer is found in this way do not need treatment but are followed closely with tests and exams.

Prostate cancer patients who do require treatment have surgery, radiation therapy, or hormone therapy. Sometimes, patients receive a combination of these treatments. In addition, doctors are studying other methods of treatment to find out whether they are effective against this disease.

Surgery to remove the entire prostate is called radical prostatectomy. It is done in one of two ways. In retropubic prostatectomy, the prostate and nearby lymph nodes are removed through an incision in the abdomen. In perineal prostatectomy, an incision is made between the scrotum and the anus to remove the prostate. Nearby lymph nodes sometimes art removed through a separate incision in the abdomen.

In radiation therapy (also called radiotherapy), high-energy rays are used to damage cancer cells and stop them from growing. Like surgery, radiation therapy is local therapy; it affects only the cells in the treated area. Most often, the radiation comes from a machine. This treatment is called external radiation therapy. The rays are aimed at the tumor and the area around it. At a few cancer centers, doctors are exploring the use of internal radiation therapy for certain patients. In this form of treatment, doctors use needles to place radioactive materials in or near the tumor. Sometimes, both external and internal radiation therapy are used.

For external radiation therapy for prostate cancer, the patient goes to an outpatient department of a hospital or clinic. Treatment generally is given 5 days a week for 5 to 7 weeks. This schedule helps protect healthy tissues by spreading out the total dose of radiation. The rays are aimed at the pelvic area. At the end of treatment, an extra "boost" of radiation is often given to a smaller area of the pelvis, where most of the tumor was found.

For internal radiation therapy, the patient goes to the hospital to have the radioactive materials implanted and stays in the hospital for a few days. The implant may be temporary or permanent. Because the radiation is most active during his hospital stay, the patient may not be able to have visitors or may have visitors for only a short time.

Surgery and radiation therapy appear to be equally effective for men who require treatment for early stage prostate cancer (some stage A and most stage B patients). Decisions about which treatment to use are made on an individual basis; doctors and patients may prefer one approach over the other. For example, radical prostatectomy is a major operation that a doctor may not recommend for an older man, especially one who has other health problems.

Men with stage C prostate cancer usually receive radiation therapy. Sometimes, surgery alone or a combination of surgery and radiation therapy is used.

The main form of treatment for men with stage D prostate cancer is hormone therapy. It prevents the prostate cancer cells from getting the male hormones they need to grow. Hormone therapy is used to treat prostate cancer that has spread because it is systemic therapy; it can affect cancer cells throughout the body. Decisions about when to use hormone therapy may depend on whether a patient's cancer has spread only to nearby lymph nodes or to other parts of the body. Some doctors do not recommend hormone therapy unless the man has symptoms, such as bone pain, that are caused by the spread of the cancer.

One form of hormone therapy is surgery to remove the testicles. This operation, called orchiectomy, eliminates the main source of male hormones. Without these hormones, the growth of prostate cancer cells slows down. In another form of hormone therapy, patients take the female hormone estrogen to stop the testicles from producing testosterone.

The use of a luteinizing hormone-releasing hormone (LHRH) agonist is another type of hormone therapy. The body produces the hormone LHRH, which normally controls the production of sex hormones. An LHRH agonist is made in the laboratory; it is like LHRH but has a different effect on the body's functions. LHRH agonists, which are given by daily or monthly injection, prevent the testicles from producing testosterone.

After orchiectomy or treatment with estrogen or an LHRH agonist, the body no longer gets testosterone from the testicles. However, the adrenal glands still produce small amounts of male hormones. Sometimes the patient is given pills that contain an antiandrogen, a drug that blocks the effect of any remaining male hormones.

Patients whose prostate cancer has spread to the bones may have a week or two of external radiation therapy. The radiation is aimed at the tumors in the bones. This treatment can help relieve pain caused by these tumors.

Prostate cancer that has spread to other parts of the body usually can be controlled with hormone therapy for a period of time, often several years. Eventually, however, prostate cancer cells are able to grow with very little or no male hormones. When this happens, hormone therapy is no longer effective, and doctors may suggest other forms of treatment that are under study.

Clinical Trials

Researchers are looking for treatment methods that are more effective and have fewer side effects. When laboratory research shows that a new treatment has promise, doctors test the new method by using it to treat cancer patients in clinical trials. These trials are designed to answer scientific questions and to find out whether the new approach is both safe and effective. Patients who take part in clinical trials make an important contribution to medical science and may have the first chance to benefit from improved treatment methods.

Many clinical trials of treatments for prostate cancer are under way. Doctors are studying new ways of using radiation therapy and hormone therapy. They also are testing the effectiveness of chemotherapy and biological therapy for patients whose cancer does not respond to hormone therapy. In addition, scientists are looking for new ways of combining various types of treatment.

Men with prostate cancer who are interested in taking part in a trial should discuss this option with their doctor. *What Are Clinical Trials All About?* is an NCI booklet that explains the possible benefits and risks of treatment studies.

One way to learn about clinical trials is through PDQ, a computerized resource of cancer treatment information. Developed by NCI, PDQ contains an up-to-date list of clinical trials in progress all over the country. Doctors can use a personal computer or the services of a medical library to get PDQ information. The Cancer Information Service, at 1-800-4-CANCER, is another source of PDQ information for doctors, patients, and the public.

Side Effects of Treatment

Although doctors plan treatment very carefully, it is hard to limit the effects of treatment so that only cancer cells are damaged. Because healthy tissue also may be injured, treatment often causes unpleasant side effects.

The side effects of cancer treatment vary. They depend mainly on the type and extent of the treatment. Also, each person reacts differently. Doctors try to plan the patient's therapy to keep problems to a minimum. They watch patients very closely so they can help with any problems that occur.

In the past, surgery to remove the prostate often caused permanent impotence and sometimes caused urinary incontinence. Today, these side effects do not occur as often as in the past. Many surgeons use new techniques, especially when operating on men with fairly small tumors. These techniques may allow surgeons to avoid permanent injury to the nerves that control erection and damage to the opening of the bladder. Men may regain potency and total urinary control within several months to a year after surgery. However, men who have a prostatectomy no longer produce semen, so they have dry orgasms. Although some men find this upsetting, it need not affect sexual pleasure.

Radiation therapy also causes impotence in some men. This does not occur as often with internal radiation therapy as with external radiation therapy; internal radiation therapy is not as likely to damage the nerves that control erection. However, this form of treatment is suitable only for certain patients with early stage cancer; it is used only at a few cancer centers.

Radiation therapy may cause patients to become very tired as treatment continues. Resting as much as possible is important. Patients also may have diarrhea or frequent and uncomfortable urination. Often, the doctor or nurse can suggest ways to ease these problems. In addition, when patients receive external radiation therapy, it is common for the skin in the treated area to become red or dry. The skin should be exposed to the air when possible, and patients should avoid wearing clothes that rub. Patients will be shown how to keep the treated area clean. They should not use any lotion or cream on this area without the doctor's advice.

Orchiectomy, LHRH agonists, and estrogen often cause side effects such as loss of sexual desire, impotence, and hot flashes. When first taken, an LHRH agonist tends to increase tumor growth and make the patient's symptoms worse. Gradually, however, the drug causes a man's testosterone level to fall. Without testosterone, tumor growth slows down and the patient's condition improves. Prostate cancer patients who receive estrogen or an antiandrogen may have nausea, vomiting, or tenderness and swelling of the breasts. (Estrogen is used less now than in the past because it increases a man's risk of heart problems. This form of treatment is not appropriate for men who have a history of heart disease.)

Men who receive chemotherapy or biological therapy for advanced prostate cancer may have other side effects, depending mainly on the drugs or treatment methods used. In general, chemotherapy affects rapidly growing cells, such as blood cells that fight infection, cells that line the digestive tract, and cells in hair follicles. As a result, patients may have side effects such as lower resistance to infection, loss of appetite, nausea, vomiting, or mouth sores. They may also have less energy and may lose their hair. Biological therapy tends to cause flulike symptoms such as chills, fever, muscle aches, weakness, loss of appetite, nausea, vomiting, or diarrhea.

Loss of appetite can be a problem during therapy. Patients may not feel hungry when they are uncomfortable or tired. Also, some of the common side effects of cancer treatment, such as nausea and vomiting, can make it hard to eat. Yet good nutrition is important because patients who eat well generally feel better and have more energy. In addition, they often are better able to tolerate the side effects of treatment. Eating well means getting enough calories and protein to prevent weight loss, regain strength, and rebuild normal tissues. Many patients find that eating several small meals and snacks during the day works better than trying to have three large meals.

Doctors, nurses, and dietitians can explain the side effects of treatment and can suggest ways to deal with them. Also, the NCI booklets *Radiation Therapy and You*, *Chemotherapy and You*, and *Eating Hints* have helpful information about cancer treatment and coping with side effects.

Followup Care

Regular followup exams are very important for any man who has had prostate cancer. If the cancer was confined to the prostate, the doctor will examine the patient regularly to be sure that the disease has not returned. If the cancer had spread beyond the prostate, the doctor will check the patient to decide what other medical care may be needed. Followup exams may include x-rays, scans, blood and urine tests, and other laboratory tests.

Living With Cancer

The diagnosis of prostate cancer can change the lives of patients and the people who care about them. These changes can be hard to handle. Patients and their families and friends may have many different and sometimes confusing emotions.

At times, patients and those close to them may be frightened, angry, or depressed. These are normal reactions when people face a serious health problem. Most people handle their thoughts and feelings best when they share them with their loved ones. Sharing can help everyone be more at ease and can open the way for others to show their concern and offer their support.

It is natural for a man and his partner to be concerned about the effects of prostate cancer and its treatment on their sexual relationship. They may want to talk with the doctor about possible side effects and whether they are likely to be temporary or permanent. Whatever the outlook, it is helpful if patients and their partners can talk about their concerns and help one another find ways to express their love during and after treatment.

Worries about tests, treatments, hospital stays, and medical bills are common. Doctors, nurses, social workers, and other members of the health care team can help calm fears and ease confusion. They also can provide information and suggest other resources.

Most patients and their families are concerned about what the future holds. Sometimes they use statistics to try to figure out whether the patient will be cured or how long he will live. It is important to remember, however, that statistics are averages based on large numbers of patients. They can't be used to predict what will happen to a certain patient because no two cancer patients are alike. The doctor who takes care of the patient and knows his medical history is in the best position to discuss the person's outlook (prognosis).

Patients should feel free to ask the doctor about their prognosis, but not even the doctor knows for sure what will happen. When doctors talk about surviving cancer, they may use the term remission rather than cure. Even though many prostate cancer patients recover completely, doctors use this term because the disease can recur.

Support for Cancer Patients

Living with a serious disease is hard for patients and those who care about them. Everyone involved faces problems and challenges. Finding the strength to cope with these difficulties is easier when people have helpful information and support services.

The doctor can explain the disease and give advice about treatment, working, or other activities. If patients and their loved ones want to discuss concerns about the future, family relationships, sexual activity, or finances, it also may help to talk with a nurse, social worker, counselor, or member of the clergy.

Friends and relatives who have had personal experiences with cancer can be very supportive. Also, it helps many patients to meet and talk with others who are facing problems like theirs. Cancer patients often get together in support groups, where they can share what they have learned about cancer, its treatment, and coping with the disease. It is important to keep in mind, however, that each patient is different. Treatments and ways of dealing with cancer that work for one person may not be right for another-even if they both have the same kind of cancer. It is always a good idea to discuss the advice of friends and family members with the doctor.

Often, a social worker at the hospital or clinic can suggest local and national groups that can provide emotional support, financial aid, transportation, home care, or other services. The American Cancer Society is one such group. This nonprofit organization has many services for patients and their families and offers a free booklet on sexuality and cancer. Other groups also can provide information about sexuality or the loss of bladder control. More information about these resources can be found later in this chapter.

Information about programs and services for cancer patients is also available through the Cancer Information Service. The toll-free number is 1-800-4-CANCER.

The public library is a good place to find books and articles on living with cancer. Cancer patients and their families can also find helpful suggestions in the NCI booklets listed at the end of this chapter.

Research To Understand Prostate Cancer

Prostate cancer is the most common type of cancer in men in the United States. It accounts for nearly one of every four cancers among American men. Researchers are doing studies to learn more about the causes and early detection of this common disease.

Causes

The causes of prostate cancer are not known. Researchers are trying to solve this problem. The more they can find out about the causes of this disease, the better the chance of finding ways to prevent it.

Studies in the United States show that prostate cancer is found mainly in men over age 55; the average age of patients at the time of diagnosis is 70. This disease is more common in black men than in white. In fact, black men in the United States have the highest rate of prostate cancer in the world. Still, doctors cannot explain why one man gets prostate cancer and another does not. They do know, however, that no one can "catch" prostate cancer from another person. Cancer is not contagious.

Scientists are studying the effects of diet. Some evidence suggests that a diet high in fat increases the risk of prostate cancer, but this link has not been proven.

Other studies show that men exposed to the metal cadmium during welding, electroplating, or making batteries may have an increased risk of getting the disease. Workers in the rubber industry also appear to develop prostate cancer more often than expected. More research is needed to confirm these results.

Scientists are also doing studies to find out whether benign prostatic hyperplasia, sexually transmitted viruses, or vasectomy increases the risk. At this time, we do not have clear evidence that these factors increase the chance of developing prostate cancer.

Men who think they may be at risk for prostate cancer should discuss their concerns with their doctor, who can suggest an appropriate schedule of checkups.

Detection

Researchers are doing studies to learn more about screening men for prostate cancer (checking for the disease in men who have no symptoms). They are studying the usefulness of the following screening methods alone and in combination: digital rectal examination, transrectal ultrasonography, and measurement of the prostate-specific antigen level in the blood.

The results of this research may change the way men are screened for prostate cancer. At present, NCI encourages doctors to do a yearly rectal exam for all men over 40 to increase the chance of detecting prostate cancer early. Men should talk with their doctor about prostate cancer, the symptoms to watch for, and an appropriate schedule of checkups. The doctor's advice will be based on the man's age, medical history, and other factors.

Medical Terms

Abdomen (AB-do-men): The part of the body located below the waist and between the hips.

Adenocarcinoma (AD-e-no-kar-si-NO-ma): A cancer that develops in the glandular lining of an organ. More than 95 percent of prostate cancers are adenocarcinomas.

Adrenal glands (ah-DREE-nal): Two glands located above the kidneys (one above each kidney). They produce several kinds of hormones, including a small amount of sex hormones.

Androgens (AN-dro-jenz): Male sex hormones produced by the testicles and, in small amounts, by the adrenal glands.

Antiandrogen (an-tee-AN-dro-jen): A drug that blocks the action of male sex hormones.

Anus (AY-nus): The opening at the lower end of the rectum through which solid waste is eliminated.

Benign (bee-NINE): Not cancerous; does not spread to other parts of the body.

Benign prostatic hyperplasia (hy-per-PLAY-zha): A noncancerous condition in which an overgrowth of prostate tissue pushes against the urethra and the bladder, blocking the flow of urine. Also called benign prostatic hypertrophy or BPH.

Biological therapy (by-o-LOJ-i-kal): Treatment with substances called biological response modifiers that can stimulate the immune system to fight disease more effectively. Also called immunotherapy.

Biopsy (BY-op-see): The removal of a sample of tissue for examination under a microscope to check for cancer cells.

Bladder: The hollow organ that stores urine.

Bone scan: Pictures of the bones that can show areas of rapid growth that may be a sign of cancer. To create these pictures, a radioactive substance is injected into the bloodstream. The substance collects in any areas of rapid growth. A scanner can pinpoint these areas.

Medical Terms (continued)

Cancer: A general term for more than 100 diseases in which abnormal cells multiply without control. Cancer cells can spread through the bloodstream and lymphatic system to other parts of the body.

Carcinoma (kar-sin-O-ma): Cancer that begins in the lining or covering of an organ.

Chemotherapy (kee-mo-THER-a-pee): Treatment with anticancer drugs.

Clinical trials: Studies conducted with cancer patients, usually to evaluate a promising new treatment. Each study is designed to answer scientific questions and to find better ways to treat patients.

CT or CAT scan: A series of detailed pictures of areas inside the body produced by a computer linked to an x-ray machine. Also called computed tomography scan or computed axial tomography scan.

Cystoscope (SIST-o-skope): A lighted instrument used to look at the inside of the bladder.

Dry orgasm: The experience of the height of pleasure during sexual activity without the release of semen.

Ejaculation: The release of semen through the penis during orgasm.

Estrogen (ES-tro-jin): A female sex hormone.

Genitourinary system (GEN-i-toe-YOO- rin-air-ee): The parts of the body that play a role in reproduction, in getting rid of waste products in the form of urine, or in both.

Hair follicle (FOL-i-kul): A sac in the skin from which a hair grows.

Hormone: A chemical substance that is formed in one part of the body, travels through the blood, and affects the function of cells elsewhere in the body.

Hormone therapy: Treatment that prevents cancer cells from getting the hormones they need to grow. Hormone therapy for prostate cancer keeps the cancer cells from getting male hormones. Treatment may involve removing the testicles or giving female hormones or other drugs to prevent the production of male hormones or to block their effect on cancer cells.

Medical Terms (continued)

Impotence (IM-po-tens): Inability to have an erection.

Incision (in-SI-zhun): A cut made during surgery.

Incontinence (in-KON-ti-nens): Inability to control the flow of urine from the bladder.

Intravenouspyelogram(in-tra-VEE-nus PY-uh-lo-gram): X-rays of the kidneys, ureters, and bladder taken after a dye is injected into a vein. Also called IVP. Local therapy: Treatment that affects a tumor and the tissue near it.

Luteinizing hormone-releasing hormone (LHRH) agonist (LOO-tin-eye-zing AG-o-nist): A substance that closely resembles LHRH, which controls the production of sex hormones. However, LHRH agonists affect the body differently than does LHRH. LHRH agonists keep the testicles from producing hormones.

Lymph (limf): The almost colorless fluid that travels through the lymphatic system and carries cells that help fight infection.

Lymph nodes (limf): Small, bean-shaped organs located along the channels of the lymphatic system. The lymph nodes store special cells that can trap bacteria or cancer cells traveling through the body in lymph. Also called lymph glands.

Lymphatic system(lim-FAT-ik): The tissues and organs that produce, store, and carry cells that fight infection and disease. This system includes the bone marrow, spleen, thymus, lymph nodes, and channels that carry lymph.

MRI: A procedure in which a magnet linked to a computer is used to create pictures of areas inside the body. Also called magnetic resonance imaging.

Malignant (ma-LIG-nant): Cancerous; can spread to other parts of the body.

Metastasis (meh-TAS-ta-sis): The spread of cancer from one part of the body to another. Cells in the metastatic (secondary) tumor are like those in the original (primary) tumor.

Oncologist (on-KOL-o-jist): A doctor who specializes in treating cancer. Some oncologists specialize in a particular type of cancer treatment. For example, a radiation oncologist treats cancer with radiation.

Orchiectomy (or-kee-EK-to-mee): Surgery to remove the testicles.

Medical Terms (continued)

Pathologist (path-OL-o-jist): A doctor who identifies diseases by studying cells and tissues under a microscope.

Pelvic: Referring to the area of the body located below the waist and surrounded by the hip and pubic bones.

Perineal prostatectomy (pe-ri-NEE-al): Surgery to remove the prostate through an incision made between the scrotum and the anus.

Prognosis (prog-NO-sis): The probable outcome or course of a disease; the chance of recovery.

Prostate: A male sex gland; it produces a fluid that forms part of semen.

Prostatectomy (pros-ta-TEK-to-mee): An operation to remove part or all of the prostate.

Prostate-specific antigen: A protein whose level in the blood goes up in some men who have prostate cancer or benign prostatic hyperplasia. Also called PSA.

Prostatic acid phosphatase (FOS-fa-tase): An enzyme produced by the prostate. Its level in the blood goes up in some men who have prostate cancer. Also called PAP.

Radiation therapy (ray-dee-AY-shun): Treatment with high-energy rays from x-rays or other sources to damage cancer cells. The radiation may come from a machine (external radiation therapy) or from radioactive materials placed inside the body as close as possible to the cancer (internal radiation therapy).

Radical prostatectomy: Surgery to remove the entire prostate. The two types of radical prostatectomy are retropubic prostatectomy and perineal prostatectomy.

Rectal exam: A procedure in which a doctor inserts a gloved, lubricated finger into the rectum and feels the prostate through the wall of the rectum to check the prostate for hard or lumpy areas.

Rectum: The last 5 to 6 inches of the large intestine leading to the outside of the body.

Remission (ree-MISH-un): Disappearance of the signs and symptoms of cancer. When this happens, the disease is said to be "in remission." Remission can be temporary or permanent.

Medical Terms (continued)

Retropubic prostatectomy (re-tro-PYOO-bik): Surgical removal of the prostate through an incision in the abdomen.

Scrotum (SKRO-tum): The external pouch of skin that contains the testicles.

Semen: The fluid that is released through the penis during orgasm. Semen is made up of sperm from the testicles and fluid from the prostate and other sex glands.

Staging: Doing exams or tests to learn the extent of a cancer, especially whether it has spread from its original site to other parts of the body.

Surgery: An operation.

Systemic therapy (sis-TEM-ik): Treatment that affects cancer cells throughout the body.

Testicles (TES-ti-kuls): The two egg-shaped glands that produce sperm and male hormones.

Testosterone (tes-TOS-ter-own): A male sex hormone.

Transurethral resection of the prostate (trans-yoo-REE-thral): The use of an instrument inserted through the penis to remove tissue from the prostate. Also called TUR or TURP.

Tumor: An abnormal mass of tissue.

Ultrasonography: A technique that uses sound waves that can't be heard by humans to produce pictures of areas inside the body. The pictures are created by a computer that analyzes the echoes produced by the waves as they bounce off tissues.

Urethra (yoo-REETH-ra): The tube that carries urine or semen to the outside of the body.

Urologist (yoo-ROL-o-jist): A doctor who specializes in diseases of the urinary organs in females and the urinary and sex organs in males.

Vasectomy (vas-EK-to-mee): An operation to cut or tie off the two tubes that carry sperm out of the testicles.

Resources

Information about prostate cancer is available from the sources listed below. You may wish to check for additional information at your local library or bookstore or from support groups in your community.

Cancer Information Service (CIS)
1-800-4-CANCER
The Cancer Information Service (CIS), a program of the National Cancer Institute, provides a nationwide telephone service for cancer patients and their families and friends, the public, and health care professionals. The staff can answer questions and can send booklets about cancer. They also may know about local resources and services. One toll-free number, 800-4-CANCER (800-422-6237), connects callers with the office that serves their area. Spanish speaking staff members are available.

American Cancer Society (ACS)
1599 Clifton Road, N.E., Atlanta, GA 30329; 1-800-ACS-2345
The American Cancer Society is a voluntary organization with a national office (at the above address) and local units all over the country. It supports research, conducts educational programs, and offers many services to patients and their families. It provides free booklets on prostate cancer, sexuality, and home care. Information about services and activities in local areas can be obtained by calling the Society's toll-free number, 1-800-ACS-2345 (1-800-227-2345), or the number listed under "American Cancer Society" in the white pages of the telephone book.

National Institute on Aging Information Center
Post Office Box 8057, Gaithersburg, MD 20898-8057; 1-800-222-2225
The National Institute on Aging, an agency of the Federal government, is concerned with the health problems of older Americans. The Information Center can send free printed material, including fact sheets about going to the hospital and about prostate problems, sexuality, and urinary incontinence.

National Kidney and Urologic Diseases Information Clearinghouse
Box NKUDIC, 9000 Rockville Pike, Bethesda, MD 20892; 301-468-6345
This Clearinghouse is a service of the Federal government's National Institute of Diabetes and Digestive and Kidney Diseases. It can supply free information about benign prostate enlargement and other noncancerous urinary tract problems.

For More Information

Cancer patients, their families and friends, and others may find the following booklets useful. They are available free of charge from the National Cancer Institute. You may request them by calling 1-800-4-CANCER.

Booklets About Cancer Treatment
- *Radiation Therapy and You: A Guide to Self-Help During Treatment*
- *Eating Hints: Recipes and Tips for Better Nutrition During Cancer Treatment*
- *Questions and Answers About Pain Control* (also available from the American Cancer Society)
- *Chemotherapy and You: A Guide to Self-Help During Treatment*
- *What Are Clinical Trials All About?*

Booklets About Living With Cancer
- *Taking Time: Support for People With Cancer and the People Who Care About Them*
- *Facing Forward: A Guide for Cancer Survivors*
- *When Cancer Recurs: Meeting the Challenge Again*
- *Advanced Cancer: Living Each Day*

Prostate Problems*

The prostate is a small organ about the size of a walnut. It lies below the bladder (where urine is stored) and surrounds the urethra (the tube that carries urine from the bladder). The prostate makes a fluid that becomes part of semen. Semen is the white fluid that contains sperm.

Prostate problems are common in men 50 and older. Most can be treated successfully without harming sexual function. A urologist (a specialist in diseases of the urinary system) is the kind of doctor most qualified to diagnose and treat many prostate problems.

Noncancerous Prostate Problems

Acute prostatitis is a bacterial infection of the prostate. It can occur in men at any age. Symptoms include fever, chills, and pain in the lower back and between the legs. This problem also can make it hard or painful to urinate. Doctors prescribe antibiotics for acute prostatitis and recommend that the patient drink more liquids. Treatment is usually successful.

Chronic prostatitis is a prostate infection that comes back again and again. The symptoms are similar to those of acute prostatitis except that there is usually no fever. Also, the symptoms are usually milder in chronic prostatitis. However, they can last a long time.

Chronic prostatitis is hard to treat. Antibiotics often work when the infection is caused by bacteria. But sometimes no disease-causing bacteria can be found. In some cases, it helps to massage the prostate to release fluids. Warm baths also may bring relief. Chronic prostatitis clears up by itself in many cases.

---

* Source: *Age Page*, National Institute on Aging, U.S. Department of Health and Human Services, Public Health Service, National Institutes of Health, Gaithersburg, MD 20898; 800-222-2225.

Benign prostatic hypertrophy (BPH) is enlargement of the prostate. This condition is common in older men. More than half of men in their 60's have BPH. Among men in their 70's and 80's, the figure may go as high as 90 percent.

An enlarged prostate may eventually block the urethra and make it hard to urinate. Other common symptoms are dribbling after urination and the urge to urinate often, especially at night. In rare cases, the patient is unable to urinate.

A doctor usually can detect an enlarged prostate by rectal exam. The doctor also may examine the urethra, prostate, and bladder using a cystoscope, an instrument that is inserted through the penis.

BPH Treatment Choices. There are several different ways to treat BPH:

- *Watchful waiting* is often chosen by men who are not bothered by symptoms of BPH. They have no treatment but get regular checkups and wait to see whether or not the condition gets worse.

- *Alpha blockers* are drugs that help relax muscles near the prostate and may relieve symptoms. Side effects can include headaches. Also, these medicines sometimes make people feel dizzy, lightheaded, or tired. Alpha blockers are new drugs, so doctors do not know their long-term effects. Some common alpha blockers are doxazosin (Cardura), prazosin (Minipress), and terazosin (Hytrin).

- *Finasteride* (Proscar) is a drug that inhibits the action of the male hormone testosterone. It can shrink the prostate. Side effects of finasteride include declining interest in sex, problems getting an erection, and problems with ejaculation. Again, because it is new, doctors do not know its long-term effects.

- *Surgery* is the treatment most likely to relieve BPH symptoms. However, it also has the most complications. Doctors use three kinds of surgery for BPH:

  - Transurethral resection of the prostate (TURP) is the most common. After the patient is given anesthesia, the doctor inserts a special instrument into the urethra through the penis. With the instrument, the doctor then removes part of the prostate to lessen its obstruction.
  - Transurethral incision of the prostate (TUIP) may be used when the prostate is not too enlarged. In this procedure, the doctor passes an instrument through the urethra to make one or two small cuts in the prostate.
  - Open surgery is used when the prostate is very enlarged. In open surgery, the surgeon makes an incision in the abdomen or between the scrotum and the anus to remove prostate tissue.

Men should carefully weight the risks and benefits of each of these options. The Agency for Health Care Policy and Research has designed a booklet to help in choosing a treatment; call 800-358-9295 and ask for their free patient guide on prostate enlargement.

Prostate Cancer

Prostate cancer is one of the most common forms of cancer among American men. About 80 percent of all cases occur in men over 65. For unknown reasons, prostate cancer is more common among African American men than white men.

In the early stages of prostate cancer, the disease stays in the prostate and is not life threatening. But without treatment, cancer can spread to other parts of the body and eventually cause death. Some 40,000 men die every year from prostate cancer that has spread.

Diagnosis. To find the cause of prostate symptoms, the doctor takes a careful medical history and performs a physical exam. The physical includes a digital rectal exam, in which the doctor feels the prostate through the rectum. Hard or lumpy areas may mean that cancer is present.

Some doctors also recommend a blood test for a substance called prostate specific antigen (PSA). PSA levels may be high in men who have prostate cancer or BPH. However, the test is not always accurate. Researchers are studying changes in PSA levels over time to learn whether the test may someday be useful for early diagnosis of prostate cancer.

If a doctor suspects prostate cancer, he or she may recommend a biopsy. This is a simple surgical procedure in which a small piece of prostate tissue is removed with a needle and examined under a microscope. If the biopsy shows prostate cancer, other tests are done to determine the type of treatment needed.

Prostate Cancer Treatment. Doctors have several ways to treat prostate cancer. The choice depends on many factors, such as whether or not the cancer has spread beyond the prostate, the patient's age and general health, and how the patient feels about the treatment options and their side effects. Approaches to treatment include:

- *Watchful waiting.* Some men decide not to have treatment immediately if the cancer is growing slowly and not causing symptoms. Instead, they have regular checkups so they can be closely monitored by their doctor. Men who are older or have another serious illness may choose this option.

- *Surgery* usually removes the entire prostate and surrounding tissues. This operation is called a radical prostatectomy. In the past, impotence was a side effect for nearly all men undergoing radical prostatectomy. But now, doctors can preserve the nerves going to the penis so that men can have erections after prostate removal.

Incontinence, the inability to hold urine, is common for a time after radical surgery for cancer. Most men regain urinary control within several weeks. A few continue to have problems that require them to wear a device to collect urine.

- Another kind of surgery is a *transurethral resection,* which cuts cancer from the prostate but does not take out the entire prostate. This operation is sometimes done to relieve symptoms caused by the tumor before other treatment or in men who cannot have a radical prostatectomy.

- *Radiation therapy* uses high-energy rays to kill cancer cells and shrink tumors. It is often used when cancer cells are found in more than one area. Impotence may occur in men treated with radiation therapy.

- *Hormone therapy* uses various hormones to stop cancer cells from growing. It is used for prostate cancer that has spread to distant parts of the body. Growth of breast tissue is a common side effect of hormone therapy.

More detailed information on the pros and cons of these treatment options is available from the Cancer Information Service at 800-422-6237; ask for the prostate cancer "PDQ for Patients."

Protecting Yourself

The best protection against prostate problems is to have regular medical checkups that include a careful prostate exam. See a doctor promptly if symptoms occur such as:

- a frequent urge to urinate,
- difficulty in urinating, or
- dribbling of urine.

Regular checkups are important even for men who have had surgery for BPH. BPH surgery does not protect against prostate cancer because only part of the prostate is removed. In all cases, the sooner a doctor finds a problem, the better the chances that treatment will work.

Resources

Agency for Health Care Policy and Research (AHCPR) Publications Clearinghouse, P.O. Box 8547, Silver Spring, MD 20907; 800-358-9295.
Ask for the free booklet called *Treating Your Enlarged Prostate*. It contains detailed information on the pros and cons of different treatments for BPH.

Cancer Information Service (CIS), National Cancer Institute, Building 31, Room 10A24, Bethesda, MD 20892; 800-4-CANCER.
CIS staff can answer questions and mail free booklets about prostate cancer. The prostate cancer "PDQ for Patients" contains detailed information on diagnosis and treatment. Spanish-speaking CIS staff are available during daytime hours.

National Kidney and Urologic Diseases Information Clearinghouse, Box NKUDIC, Bethesda, MD 20892; 301-468-6345.
Ask for free materials on BPH.

American Cancer Society, 1599 Clifton Road, NE, Atlanta, GA 30329; 800-227-2345.
Ask about their materials on prostate cancer.

Prostate Health Council, The American Foundation for Urologic Disease, Inc., 300 West Pratt Street, Suite 401, Baltimore, MD 21202; 800-242-2483.
Ask for free brochures in English and Spanish on prostate disease and prostate cancer.

For more information about health and aging, contact **National Institute on Aging Information Center**, P.O. Box 8057, Gaithersburg, MD 20898-8057; 800-222-2225, 800-222-4225 (TTY).
The NIA distributes free *Age Pages* on a number of topics, including *Cancer Facts for People Over 50, Urinary Incontinence*, and *Considering Surgery*.

Health Quackery[*]

Quacks — people who sell unproven remedies — have been around for years. You may remember the "snake oil" salesman who traveled from town to town making amazing claims about his "fabulous" product. Today's quack is only a little more slick. Sometimes only money is wasted, but it can be a serious problem if quackery prevents you from seeking professional medical care.

Who Are the Victims?

To the quack, people of all ages are fair game, but older people form the largest group of victims. In fact, a government study found that 60 percent of all victims of health-care fraud are older people.

Most people who are taken in by a quack's worthless and often dangerous "treatments" are desperate for some offer of hope. Because older people as a group have more chronic illnesses than younger people, they are likely targets for fraud.

What Do Quacks Promise?

Anti-Aging. The normal processes of aging are a rich territory for medical quackery. In a youth-oriented society, quacks find it easy to promote a wide variety of products. They simply say their products can stop or reverse aging processes or relieve conditions associated with old age. While there are products that may reduce wrinkles or reverse baldness for some people, these products cannot slow the body's aging process. However, not smoking, eating a healthy diet, and getting regular exercise may help prevent some diseases that occur more often as people age.

---

[*] Source: *Age Page*, National Institute on Aging, U.S. Department of Health and Human Services, Public Health Service, National Institutes of Health, Gaithersburg, MD 20898; 800-222-2225.

Arthritis Remedies. Arthritis "remedies" are especially easy to fall for because symptoms of arthritis tend to come and go. People with arthritis easily associate the remedy they are using with relief from symptoms. Arthritis sufferers have paid for bottled seawater, "extracts" from New Zealand green-lipped mussels, and Chinese herbal medicines (which have no herbs but may contain drugs that are dangerous).

There is no cure for most forms of arthritis, but treatments that can help reduce pain and enable greater movement are available. These include drugs, heat treatments, a balance of rest and exercise, and in some cases, surgery.

Cancer Cures. Quacks prey on the older person's fear of cancer by offering "treatments" that have no proven value — for example, a diet dangerously low in protein or drugs such as Laetrile. By using unproven methods, patients may lose valuable time and the chance to receive proven, effective therapy. This can reduce the chance for controlling or curing the disease.

How to Protect Yourself

One way to protect yourself is to question carefully what you see or hear in ads. Although there are exceptions, the editors of newspapers, magazines, radio, and TV do not regularly screen their ads for truth or accuracy.

Find out about a product before you buy it. Check out products sold door-to-door through an agency such as the Better Business Bureau.

The following are common ploys used by dishonest promoters:

- promising a quick or painless cure,
- promoting a product made from a "special" or "secret" formula, usually available through the mail and from only one company,

- presenting testimonials or case histories from satisfied patients,
- advertising a product as effective for a wide variety of ailments, or
- claiming to have the cure for a disease (such as arthritis or cancer) that is not yet understood by medical science.

Remember if it seems "too good to be true," it probably is.

Resources

If you have questions about a product, talk to your doctor or contact one of the following agencies:

Food and Drug Administration, HFE-88, 5600 Fishers Lane, Rockville, MD 20857. The Food and Drug Administration answers questions about medical devices, medicines, and food supplements that are mislabeled, misrepresented, or in some way harmful.

U.S. Postal Service, Office of Criminal Investigation, Washington, DC 20260-2166. The U.S. Postal Service monitors quack products purchased by mail.

Council of Better Business Bureaus, 4200 Wilson Boulevard, 8th Floor, Arlington, VA 22203. The Council of Better Business Bureaus offers publications and advice on products.

Federal Trade Commission, Room 421, 6th Street and Pennsylvania Ave., NW, Washington, DC 20580. The Federal Trade Commission looks into charges of false advertising in publications or on the radio and TV.

The Cancer Information Service (CIS), 800-4-CANCER. The CIS, funded by the National Cancer Institute, can answer questions about a broad range of cancer-related issues, including foods and products.

National Institute of Arthritis and Musculoskeletal and Skin Diseases (NIAMS) Information Clearinghouse, Box AMS, 9000 Rockville Pike, Bethesda, MD 20892; 301-495-4484. The NIAMS Information Clearinghouse answers questions about issues and products related to arthritis.

National Institute on Aging (NIA), P.O. Box 8057, Gaithersburg, MD 20898-8057; 800-222-2225, 800-222-4225 (TTY). The NIA offers a variety of information on health and aging.

Be Sensible About Salt[*]

Salt is naturally present in most foods. It is added to canned, packaged, and frozen foods in order to flavor and preserve them. We add it during cooking. We sprinkle it on our meal at the table. It makes food taste good. And it is good for us — in limited amounts.

Salt is a necessary part of life, not only because it flavors and protects foods. Our bodies need sodium, which is present in table salt. It helps to maintain blood volume, regulate water balance, transmit nerve impulses, and perform other vital functions.

But many people consume far too much salt. Salt consists of 40 percent sodium and 50 percent chloride. One teaspoon has 2 grams of sodium. The Food and Nutrition Board of the National Academy of Sciences believes that an adequate and safe level of sodium each day is 1.1 to 3.3 grams. Americans now consume between 2.3 and 6.9 grams daily.

High Blood Pressure

Older people in particular should be cautious about using too much salt. The main reason for caution is that overuse of sodium is one factor that is associated with high blood pressure (HBP). Having a family history of HBP and being overweight are major factors too. HBP in turn can lead to heart disease, stroke, and kidney failure. Blood pressure rises with age, and all of these disorders are much more common among older people.

Restricting the amount of sodium in the diet can control HBP in many people who already have the disease. It also can increase the effectiveness of drug treatment, making a lower dose possible.

---

[*] Source: *Age Page*, National Institute on Aging, U.S. Department of Health and Human Services, Public Health Service, National Institutes of Health, Gaithersburg, MD 20898; 800-222-2225.

Expert Health Advice

How to Cut Back

As people grow older their sensitivity to flavors and smells often decreases. Because of this, there may be a desire for more salt to combat the flat taste of foods.

If your doctor has suggested that you cut back on salt, there are several steps you can take. It is easy to change a few dietary habits that will reduce the level of sodium without greatly changing the diet.

First, learn which foods in general contain less sodium. Fresh foods usually have less sodium than processed ones. Fresh meat is lower in sodium than lunch meat, bacon, hot dogs, sausage, and ham — all of which have sodium added to flavor and preserve them.

Likewise, most fresh vegetables are naturally low in sodium. Canned vegetables and vegetable juices usually have salt added, but some new lines are canned without it. Plain frozen vegetables without sauces are generally lower in sodium. Fresh, frozen, and canned fruit and fruit juices are usually low in sodium. Check the ingredient or nutrient labels for salt content.

Commercially prepared foods such as soups, frozen dinners, and other "fast food" items have salt added in their preparation. Some of these are available with substantially less sodium, so check the labels.

Snacks — such as potato chips, pretzels, corn chips, popcorn, crackers, and nuts — normally have a great deal of salt added and are best eaten sparingly.

When grocery shopping, look for low-sodium and sodium-free items. Many food manufacturers list the sodium content of their products on the labels. (Foods labeled "salt-free," "sodium-free," "low-salt," or "low-sodium" must have this information.) If sodium is one of the first three ingredients listed, the product is high in sodium.

When cooking meals at home, try to reduce gradually the amount of salt you use each day and remember that adding salt is not the only way to flavor foods. You can also use lemon, pepper, herbs, spices, onion and garlic powders (not salts), powdered mustard, small amounts of sugar, finely chopped garlic, and fresh grated horseradish. Experiment with flavorings you haven't used before.

At the table, taste the food before adding salt. If you think the food needs salt, add only a small amount.

Ketchup, mustard, relish, salad dressings, sauces, brines, and dips contain sodium. As your use of salt goes down, it may be tempting to use more of these. But go easy on them. Pickles and olives are also prepared with a good amount of salt.

If food tastes more bland than it used to, try chewing it more thoroughly. Chewing breaks down food, allowing more molecules to interact with taste receptors in the mouth. It may also help to alternate bites of different foods. When you eat several bites of the same food, the flavor is stronger in the first bite than in the following ones.

Before using a salt substitute ask your doctor about it. These preparations usually contain potassium and can be harmful to people with some medical conditions.

Many books on the subject of cooking with less salt are now available in libraries and stores. Newspapers and magazines often offer low-salt recipes.

When eating out, choose items that are less likely to have large amounts of salt added. Some restaurants will prepare low-sodium meals if asked to do so.

Resources

For further information, contact the high Blood Pressure Information Center. They can send you a single free copy of *Questions About Weight, Salt, and High Blood Pressure*. Write to 120-80, National Institutes of Health, Box AP, Bethesda, MD 20205.

The Consumer Information Center has single free copies of *Sodium: Think About It* (529L) and *A Word About Low Sodium Diets* (527W). Write to the CIC at P.O. Box 100, Pueblo, CO 81009.

The National Institute on Aging (NIA) offers information on health and aging. For a list of available publications, write to the NIA Information Center, P.O. Box 8057, Gaithersburg, MD 20898-8057; 800-222-2225, 800-222-4225 (TTY).

Sexuality in Later Life[*]

Most older people want and are able to enjoy an active, satisfying sex life. Regular sexual activity helps maintain sexual ability. However, over time everyone may notice a slowing of response. This is part of the normal aging process.

Normal Changes With Age

Women may notice changes in the shape and flexibility of the vagina. These changes may not cause a serious loss in the ability to enjoy sex. Most women will have a decrease in vaginal lubrication that affects sexual pleasure. A pharmacist can suggest over-the-counter vaginal lubricants.

Men often notice more distinct changes. It may take longer to get an erection or the erection may not be as firm or large as in earlier years. The feeling that an ejaculation is about to happen may be shorter. The loss of erection after orgasm may be more rapid or it may take longer before an erection is again possible. Some men may find they need more manual stimulation.

As men get older, impotence seems to increase, especially in men with heart disease, hypertension, and diabetes. Impotence is the loss of ability to achieve and maintain an erection hard enough for sexual intercourse. Talk to your doctor. For many men impotence can be managed and perhaps even reversed.

Effects of Illness or Disability

Although illness or disability can affect sexuality, even the most serious conditions shouldn't stop you from having a satisfying sex life.

---

[*] Source: *Age Page*, National Institute on Aging, U.S. Department of Health and Human Services, Public Health Service, National Institutes of Health, Gaithersburg, MD 20898; 800-222-2225.

Heart disease. Many people who have had a heart attack are afraid that having sex will cause another attack. The risk of this is very low. Follow your doctor's advice. Most people can start having sex again 12 to 16 weeks after an attack.

Diabetes. Most men with diabetes do not have problems, but it is one of the few illnesses that can cause impotence. In most cases medical treatment can help.

Stroke. Sexual function is rarely damaged by a stroke and it is unlikely that sexual exertion will cause another stroke. Using different positions or medical devices can help make up for any weakness or paralysis.

Arthritis. Joint pain due to arthritis can limit sexual activity. Surgery and drugs may relieve this pain. In some cases drugs can decrease sexual desire. Exercise, rest, warm baths, and changing the position or timing of sexual activity can be helpful.

Surgery

Most people worry about having any kind of surgery — it is especially troubling when the sex organs are involved. The good news is that most people do return to the kind of sex life they enjoyed before having surgery.

Hysterectomy is the surgical removal of the womb. Performed correctly, a hysterectomy does not hurt sexual functioning. If a hysterectomy seems to take away from your ability to enjoy sex, a counselor can be helpful. Men who feel their partners are "less feminine" after a hysterectomy can also be helped by counseling.

Mastectomy is the surgical removal of all or part of a woman's breast. Although her body is as capable of sexual response as ever, a woman may lose her sexual desire or her sense of being desired. Sometimes it is useful to talk with other women who have had a mastectomy. Programs like the American Cancer Society's (ACS)

"Reach to Recovery" can be helpful for both women and men. Check your phone book for the local ACS listing.

Prostatectomy is the surgical removal of all or part of the prostate. Sometimes a prostatectomy needs to be done because of an enlarged prostate. This procedure rarely causes impotence. If a radical prostatectomy (removal of prostate gland) is needed, new surgical techniques can save the nerves going to the penis and an erection may still be possible. If your sexuality is important to you, talk to your doctor before surgery to make sure you will be able to lead a fully satisfying sex life.

Other Issues

Alcohol. Too much alcohol can reduce potency in men and delay orgasm in women.

Medicines. Antidepressants, tranquilizers, and certain high blood pressure drugs can cause impotence. Some drugs can make it difficult for men to ejaculate. Some drugs reduce a woman's sexual desire. Check with your doctor. She or he can often prescribe a drug without this side effect.

Masturbation. This sexual activity can help unmarried, widowed, or divorced people and those whose partners are ill or away.

AIDS. Anyone who is sexually active can be at risk for being infected with HIV, the virus that causes AIDS. Having safe sex is important for people at every age. Talk with your doctor about ways to protect yourself from AIDS and other sexually transmitted diseases. You are never too old to be at risk.

Emotional Concerns

Sexuality is often a delicate balance of emotional and physical issues. How we feel may affect what we are able to do. For example, men may fear impotence will become a more frequent problem as they age. But, if you are too worried about impotence, you can create enough stress to cause it. As a woman ages, she may become more anxious about her appearance. This emphasis on youthful physical beauty can interfere with a woman's ability to enjoy sex.

Older couples may have the same problems that affect people of any age. They may also have the added concerns of age, retirement and other lifestyle changes, and illness. These problems can cause sexual difficulties. Talk openly with your doctor or see a therapist. These health professionals can often help.

For More Information

For a list of publications from the National Institute on Aging (NIA), including an *Age Page* called "AIDS, HIV, and Older Adults," contact the NIA Information Center, P.O. Box 8057, Gaithersburg, MD 20898-8057; 800-222-2225, 800-222-4225 (TTY).

Shots for Safety[*]

Shots, or immunizations, are not just for infants and children. Adults also need to be vaccinated from time to time to be protected against serious infectious diseases. In fact, some shots are more important for adults than for children. Every year, thousands of older people die needlessly because they have not received the proper vaccinations.

The Public Health Service strongly encourages older adults to be immunized against influenza, pneumococcal diseases (especially pneumonia), tetanus, and diphtheria.

Influenza

Usually called the flu, influenza is a highly contagious disease that causes a variety of symptoms, including fever, aches and pains, sore throat, runny nose, and chills. When older people get the flu, they are more likely to get pneumonia, lose water (dehydration), or lose weight.

A new flu vaccine is made each year because the influenza virus tends to change each flu season. For this reason, it is necessary to get a yearly flu shot. To give your body time to build the proper defense, it is important to get a flu shot by mid-November, before the flu season usually starts.

Although side effects from flu shots are slight for most people, there may be a brief, low-grade fever and some minor aches and pains. According to the Centers for Disease Control and Prevention, recent flu vaccines have not caused serious side effects.

In addition to the flu shot, two anti-viral drugs — amantadine and rimantadine — can prevent or lessen infection by certain flu strains.

---

[*] Source: *Age Page*, National Institute on Aging, U.S. Department of Health and Human Services, Public Health Service, National Institutes of Health, Gaithersburg, MD 20898; 800-222-2225.

These drugs can be used by people who never had the flu vaccine or as extra protection by those who have been immunized. They can be taken soon after the early signs of flu are felt. While they don't actually prevent infection, they can reduce fever and other flu symptoms.

Pneumococcal Disease

Pneumococcal bacteria can cause a number of infections, including those affecting the lungs (pneumonia), the blood (bacteremia), or the covering of the brain (meningitis). Older people are two to three times more likely than younger people to suffer from pneumococcal disease. It can be much more severe in older adults.

At this time, medical experts agree that the pneumonia shot is needed only once. This one-time shot protects against most kinds of bacteria that cause pneumococcal disease. The Public Health Service recommends the pneumonia shot for all people age 65 and older, and for others who are at risk due to chronic diseases or weakened immune systems. Side effects (low-grade fever and local soreness) are minor and go away quickly. The pneumonia shot can be given at any time of the year. In fact, it can be given at the same time as the flu shot.

Tetanus and Diphtheria

Most people have been immunized against tetanus (sometimes called lockjaw) and diphtheria (a bacterial disease affecting the throat and windpipe). A booster shot is needed every 10 years to keep you protected from these rare but dangerous illnesses. During everyday activities (such as gardening or outside recreation), the tetanus bacteria can enter a break in the skin and cause infection. It is important to have a booster shot if you have a severe cut or puncture wound.

In most cases, the tetanus shot also includes the diphtheria vaccine. The immunity for diphtheria also lasts 10 years. The side effects of this shot are minor (soreness and a slight fever). The Centers for

Disease Control and Prevention suggests the use of mid-decade (e.g., 45, 55, etc.) birthdays as regular dates to review adult immunizations.

Other Immunizations

The Public Health Service also recommends certain people at risk be vaccinated against measles, mumps, rubella, and hepatitis B. Adults at risk include those who work on college campuses, at vocational training centers, and in the health care field. Ask your doctor or local health department if you need to have these shots.

If you are planning to travel abroad, check with your doctor or local health department about shots that may be required or highly recommended. Since some immunizations involve a series of shots, it is best to arrange to get them within 6 months of your trip.

Keeping a Shot Record

It is helpful to keep a personal immunization record with the types and dates of shots you have received, as well as any side effects or problems that you had. The medical record in your doctor's office should also be kept up-to-date.

Widespread use of vaccines can reduce the risk of developing a number of contagious diseases that seriously affect older people. You can protect yourself against these illnesses by including vaccinations as part of your regular health care.

Resources

For a free copy of the booklet *Immunization of Adults: A Call to Action*, contact **Centers for Disease Control and Prevention, National Immunization Program**, 1600 Clifton Road, Atlanta, GA 30333; 404-639-8225.

For a free copy of the booklet *Flu*, contact **National Institute of Allergy and Infectious Diseases**, 9000 Rockville Pike, Bethesda, MD 20892; 301-496-5717.

For more information about health and aging, contact **National Institute on Aging Information Center**, P.O. Box 8057, Gaithersburg, MD 20898-8057; 800-222-2225, 800-222-4225 (TTY).

What You Need To Know
About Skin Cancer[*]

The Skin

The skin is the body's outer covering. It protects us against heat and light, injury, and infection. It regulates body temperature and stores water, fat, and vitamin D. Weighing about six pounds, the skin is the body's largest organ. It is made up of two main layers: the outer epidermis and the inner dermis.

The epidermis (outer layer of the skin) is mostly made up of flat, scale-like cells called squamous cells. Under the squamous cells are round cells called basal cells. The deepest part of the epidermis also contains melanocytes. These cells produce melanin, which gives the skin its color.

The dermis (inner layer of skin) contains blood and lymph vessels, hair follicles, and glands. These glands produce sweat, which helps regulate body temperature, and sebum, an oily substance that helps keep the skin from drying out. Sweat and sebum reach the skin's surface through tiny openings called pores.

What Is Cancer?

Cancer is a group of more than 100 diseases. Although each type of cancer differs from the others in many ways, every cancer is a disease of some of the body's cells.

Healthy cells that make up the body's tissues grow, divide, and replace themselves in an orderly way. This process keeps the body in good repair. Sometimes, however, normal cells lose their ability to limit and direct their growth. They divide too rapidly and grow without any order. Too much tissue is produced, and tumors begin to form. Tumors can be benign or malignant.

---

[*] Source: National Cancer Institute, U.S. Department of Health and Human Services, 31 Center Drive, MSC 2580, Bethesda, MD 20892-2580; 800-4-CANCER.

- Benign tumors are not cancer. They do not spread to other parts of the body and are seldom a threat to life. Often, benign tumors can be removed by surgery, and they are not likely to return.

- Malignant tumors are cancer. They can invade and destroy nearby healthy tissues and organs. Cancer cells also can spread, or metastasize, to other parts of the body and form new tumors.

Types of Skin Cancer

The two most common kinds of skin cancer are basal cell carcinoma and squamous cell carcinoma. (Carcinoma is cancer that begins in the cells that cover or line an organ.) Basal cell carcinoma accounts for more than 90 percent of all skin cancers in the United States. It is a slow-growing cancer that seldom spreads to other parts of the body. Squamous cell carcinoma also rarely spreads, but it does so more often than basal cell carcinoma. However, it is important that skin cancers be found and treated early because they can invade and destroy nearby tissue.
Basal cell carcinoma and squamous cell carcinoma are sometimes called nonmelanoma skin cancer. Another type of cancer that occurs in the skin is melanoma, which begins in the melanocytes. More information about this disease can be found in the booklet *What You Need To Know About Melanoma.*

Cause and Prevention

Skin cancer is the most common type of cancer in the United States. According to current estimates, 40 to 50 percent of Americans who live to age 65 will have skin cancer at least once. Although anyone can get skin cancer, the risk is greatest for people who have fair skin that freckles easily — often those with red or blond hair and blue or light-colored eyes.

Ultraviolet (UV) radiation from the sun is the main cause of skin cancer. (Two types of ultraviolet radiation — UVA and UVB —

are explained later in this chapter.) Artificial sources of UV radiation, such as sunlamps and tanning booths, can also cause skin cancer.

The risk of developing skin cancer is affected by where a person lives. People who live in areas that get high levels of UV radiation from the sun are more likely to get skin cancer. In the United States, for example, skin cancer is more common in Texas than it is in Minnesota, where the sun is not as strong. Worldwide, the highest rates of skin cancer are found in South Africa and Australia, areas that receive high amounts of UV radiation.

In addition, skin cancer is related to lifetime exposure to UV radiation. Most skin cancers appear after age 50, but the sun's damaging effects begin at an early age. Therefore, protection should start in childhood to prevent skin cancer later in life.

Whenever possible, people should avoid exposure to the midday sun (from 10 a.m. to 2 p.m. standard time, or from 11 a.m. to 3 p.m. daylight saving time). Keep in mind that protective clothing, such as sun hats and long sleeves, can block out the sun's harmful rays. Also, lotions that contain sunscreens can protect the skin. Sunscreens are rated in strength according to a sun protection factor (SPF), which ranges from 2 to 30 or higher. Those rated 15 to 30 block most of the sun's harmful rays.

Research is underway to try to find new ways to prevent skin cancer. This research involves people who have a high risk of developing skin cancer — those who have already had the disease and those who have certain other rare skin diseases that increase their risk of skin cancer.

Symptoms

The most common warning sign of skin cancer is a change on the skin, especially a new growth or a sore that doesn't heal. Skin cancers don't all look the same. For example, the cancer may start as a small, smooth, shiny, pale, or waxy lump. Or it can appear as a firm red lump. Sometimes, the lump bleeds or develops a crust. Skin cancer can also start as a flat, red spot that is rough, dry, or scaly.

Both basal and squamous cell cancers are found mainly on areas of the skin that are exposed to the sun — the head, face, neck, hands, and arms. However, skin cancer can occur anywhere.

Actinic keratosis, which appears as rough, red or brown, scaly patches on the skin, is known as a precancerous condition because it sometimes develops into squamous cell cancer. Like skin cancer, it usually appears on sun-exposed areas but can be found elsewhere.

Changes in the skin are not sure signs of cancer; however, it is important to see a doctor if any symptom lasts longer than two weeks. Don't wait for the area to hurt — skin cancers seldom cause pain.

Detection and Diagnosis

Detection
The cure rate for skin cancer could be 100 percent if all skin cancers were brought to a doctor's attention before they had a chance to spread. Therefore, people should check themselves regularly for new growths or other changes in the skin. Any new, colored growths or any changes in growths that are already present should be reported to the doctor without delay. (A simple guide on how to do a skin self-exam is given later in this chapter.)

Doctors should also look at the skin during routine physical exams. People who have already had skin cancer should be sure to have regular exams so that the doctor can check the skin — both the treated areas and other places where cancer may develop.

Diagnosis
Basal cell carcinoma and squamous cell carcinoma are generally diagnosed and treated in the same way. When an area of skin does

How To Do a Skin Self-Exam

You can improve your chances of finding skin cancer promptly by performing a simple skin self-exam regularly.

The best time to do this self-exam is after a shower or bath. You should check your skin in a well-lighted room using a full-length mirror and a hand-held mirror. It's best to begin by learning where your birthmarks, moles, and blemishes are and what they usually look like. Check for anything new-a change in the size, texture, or color of a mole, or a sore that does not heal.

Check *all* areas, including the back, the scalp, between the buttocks, and the genital area.

1   Look at the front and back of your body in the mirror, then raise your arms and look at the left and right sides.

2   Bend your elbows and look carefully at the palms, the forearms, including the undersides, and the upper arms.

3   Examine the back and front of the legs. Also look between the buttocks and around the genital area.

4   Sit and closely examine the feet, including the soles and the spaces between the toes.

5   Look at your face, neck, and scalp. You may want to use a comb or a blow dryer to move hair so that you can see better.

By checking your skin regularly, you will become familiar with what is normal. If you find anything unusual, see your doctor right away. Remember, the earlier skin cancer is found, the better the chance for cure.

not look normal, the doctor may remove all or part of the growth. This is called a biopsy. To check for cancer cells, the tissue is examined under a microscope by a pathologist or a dermatologist. A biopsy is the only sure way to tell if the problem is cancer.

Doctors generally divide skin cancer into two stages: local (affecting only the skin) or metastatic (spreading beyond the skin). Because skin cancer rarely spreads, a biopsy often is the only test needed to determine the stage. In cases where the growth is very large or has been present for a long time, the doctor will carefully check the lymph nodes in the area. In addition, the patient may need to have additional tests, such as special x-rays, to find out whether the cancer has spread to other parts of the body. Knowing the stage of a skin cancer helps the doctor plan the best treatment.

Treatment Planning

In treating skin cancer, the doctor's main goal is to remove or destroy the cancer completely with as small a scar as possible. To plan the best treatment for each patient, the doctor considers the location and size of the cancer, the risk of scarring, and the person's age, general health, and medical history.

It is sometimes helpful to have the advice of more than one doctor before starting treatment. It may take a week or two to arrange for a second opinion, but this short delay will not reduce the chance that treatment will be successful. There are a number of ways to find a doctor for a second opinion:

- The patient's doctor may be able to suggest a doctor, such as a dermatologist or a plastic surgeon, who has a special interest in skin cancer.

- The Cancer Information Service, at 1-800-4-CANCER, can tell callers about treatment facilities, including cancer centers and other programs that are supported by the National Cancer Institute.

- Patients can get the names of doctors from local and national medical societies, a nearby hospital, or a medical school.

- The Directory of Medical Specialists lists doctors' names and gives their background. It is available in most public libraries.

Treating Skin Cancer

Treatment for skin cancer usually involves some type of surgery. In some cases, doctors suggest radiation therapy or chemotherapy. Sometimes a combination of these methods is used.

Surgery
Many skin cancers can be cut from the skin quickly and easily. In fact, the cancer is sometimes completely removed at the time of the biopsy, and no further treatment is needed.

Curettage and Electrodesiccation
Doctors commonly use a type of surgery called curettage. After a local anesthetic numbs the area, the cancer is scooped out with a curette, an instrument with a sharp, spoon-shaped end. The area is also treated by electrodesiccation. An electric current from a special machine is used to control bleeding and kill any cancer cells remaining around the edge of the wound. Most patients develop a flat, white scar.

Mohs' Surgery
Mohs' technique is a special type of surgery used for skin cancer. Its purpose is to remove all of the cancerous tissue and as little of the healthy tissue as possible. It is especially helpful when the doctor is not sure of the shape and depth of the tumor. In addition, this method is used to remove large tumors, those in hard-to-treat places, and cancers that have recurred. The patient is given a local anesthetic, and the cancer is shaved off one thin layer at a time. Each layer is checked under a microscope until the entire tumor is removed. The degree of scarring depends on the location and size of the treated area. This method should be used only by doctors who are specially trained in this type of surgery.

Cryosurgery

Extreme cold may be used to treat precancerous skin conditions, such as actinic keratosis, as well as certain small skin cancers. In cryosurgery, liquid nitrogen is applied to the growth to freeze and kill the abnormal cells. After the area thaws, the dead tissue falls off. More than one freezing may be needed to remove the growth completely. Cryosurgery usually does not hurt, but patients may have pain and swelling after the area thaws. A white scar may form in the treated area.

Laser Therapy

Laser therapy uses a narrow beam of light to remove or destroy cancer cells. This approach is sometimes used for cancers that involve only the outer layer of skin.

Grafting

Sometimes, especially when a large cancer is removed, a skin graft is needed to close the wound and reduce the amount of scarring. For this procedure, the doctor takes a piece of healthy skin from another part of the body to replace the skin that was removed.

Radiation

Skin cancer responds well to radiation therapy (also called radiotherapy), which uses high-energy rays to damage cancer cells and stop them from growing. Doctors often use this treatment for cancers that occur in areas that are hard to treat with surgery. For example, radiation therapy might be used for cancers of the eyelid, the tip of the nose, or the ear. Several treatments may be needed to destroy all of the cancer cells. Radiation therapy may cause a rash or make the skin in the area dry or red. Changes in skin color and/or texture may develop after the treatment is over and may become more noticeable many years later.

Topical Chemotherapy

Topical chemotherapy is the use of anticancer drugs in a cream or lotion applied to the skin. Actinic keratosis can be treated effectively with the anticancer drug, fluorouracil (also called 5-FU).

This treatment is also useful for cancers limited to the top layer of skin. The 5-FU is applied daily for several weeks. Intense inflammation is common during treatment, but scars usually do not occur.

Clinical Trials
In clinical trials (research studies with cancer patients), doctors are studying new treatments for skin cancer. For example, they are exploring photodynamic therapy, a treatment that destroys cancer cells with a combination of laser light and drugs that make the cells sensitive to light. Biological therapy (also called immunotherapy) is a form of treatment to improve the body's natural ability to fight cancer. Interferon and tumor necrosis factor are types of biological therapy under study for skin cancer.

Followup Care
Even though most skin cancers are cured, the disease can recur in the same place. Also, people who have been treated for skin cancer have a higher-than-average risk of developing a new cancer elsewhere on the skin. That's why it is so important for them to continue to examine themselves regularly, to visit their doctor for regular checkups, and to follow the doctor's instructions on how to reduce the risk of developing skin cancer again.

Questions To Ask the Doctor

Skin cancer has a better prognosis, or outcome, than most other types of cancer. Although skin cancer is the most common type of cancer in this country, it accounts for much less than one percent of all cancer deaths. It is cured in 85 to 95 percent of all cases. Still, any diagnosis of cancer can be frightening, and it's natural to have concerns about medical tests, treatments, and doctors' bills.

Patients have many important questions to ask about cancer, and their doctor is the best person to provide answers. Most people want to know exactly what kind of cancer they have, how it can be treated, and how successful the treatment is likely to be. The following are some other questions that patients might want to ask their doctor:

- What types of treatment are available?
- Are there any risks or side effects of treatment?
- Will there be a scar?
- Will I have to change my normal activities?
- How can I protect myself from getting skin cancer again?
- How often will I need a checkup?

Some patients become concerned that treatment may change their appearance, especially if the skin cancer is on their face. Patients should discuss this important concern with their doctor. And they may want to have a second opinion before treatment. (See "Treatment Planning," discussed earlier in this chapter.)

Skin Cancer Research

Scientists at hospitals and research centers are studying the causes of skin cancer and looking for new ways to prevent the disease. They are also exploring ways to improve treatment.

When laboratory research shows that a new prevention or treatment method has promise, doctors use it with people in clinical trials. These trials are designed to answer scientific questions and to find out whether the new approach is both safe and effective.

People who take part in clinical trials make an important contribution to medical science and may have the first chance to benefit from improved methods. People interested in taking part in a trial should discuss this option with their doctor. *What Are Clinical Trials All About?* is a National Cancer Institute booklet that explains some of the possible benefits and risks of such studies. The Institute's toll free number is listed at the end of this chapter.

One way to learn about clinical trials is through PDQ, a computerized resource developed by the National Cancer Institute.

This resource contains information about cancer treatment and about clinical trials in progress all over the country. The Cancer Information Service can provide PDQ information to patients and the public.

Medical Terms

Actinic keratosis (ak-TIN-ik ker-a-TO-sis): A precancerous condition of thick, scaly patches of skin; also called solar or senile keratosis.

Anesthetic (an-es-THET-ik): A drug that causes loss of sensation or feeling in a part (local) or all (general) of the body.

Basal cell carcinoma (BAY-sal sel kar-si-NO-ma): A type of skin cancer in which the cancer cells resemble the basal cells of the epidermis.

Basal cells: Small, round cells found in the lower part, or base, of the epidermis.

Benign (be-NINE): Not cancerous; does not invade nearby tissue or spread to other parts of the body.

Biological therapy (by-o-LOJ-i-kul): Treatment to stimulate or restore the ability of the immune system to fight disease. Also called immunotherapy.

Biopsy (BY-op-see): The removal of a sample of tissue that is then examined under a microscope to check for cancer cells.

Cancer: A general term for the more than 100 diseases in which cells grow and divide abnormally. Cancer cells can spread through the blood or lymphatic system to other parts of the body.

Carcinogen (kar-SIN-o-jin): Any agent that is known to cause cancer.

Carcinoma (kar-si-NO-ma): A type of cancer that begins in the lining or covering tissues of an organ.

Chemotherapy (kee-mo-THER-a-pee): Treatment with anticancer drugs.

Clinical trials: Studies conducted with people. Each study is designed to answer scientific questions and to find better ways to prevent or treat cancer.

Cryosurgery (kry-o-SIR-je-ree): Destruction of tissue by applying extreme cold.

Medical Terms (continued)

Curettage (kyoo-re-TAHZH): Removal of tissue with a curette.

Curette (kyoo-RET): A spoon-shaped instrument with a sharp edge.

Dermatologist (der-ma-TOL-o-jist): A doctor who specializes in the diagnosis and treatment of skin problems.

Dermis (DER-mis): The lower layer of skin.

Electrodesiccation (e-LEK-tro-des-i-KAY-shun): Use of an electric current to destroy cancerous tissue and control bleeding.

Epidermis (ep-i-DER-mis): The surface layer of skin.

Fluorouracil (floo-ro-YOOR-a-sil): An anticancer drug. Its chemical name is 5-fluorouracil, commonly called 5-FU.

Follicles (FAHL-i-kuls): Shafts through which hair grows.

Interferon (in-ter-FEER-on): A type of biological response modifier (a substance that can improve the body's natural response to disease). It slows the rate of growth and division of cancer cells, causing them to become sluggish and die.

Kaposi's sarcoma (KAP-o-seez sar-KO-ma): A relatively rare type of cancer that develops on the skin of some elderly persons or those with a weak immune system, including those with acquired immune deficiency syndrome (AIDS).

Lymph (limf): The almost colorless fluid that travels through the lymphatic system and carries cells that help fight infection and disease.

Lymph nodes: Small, bean-shaped structures in the lymphatic system. The lymph nodes store special cells that can trap cancer cells or bacteria traveling through the body in lymph.

Lymphatic system (lim-FAT-ik): The tissues and organs that produce, carry, and store cells that fight infection and disease. This system includes the bone marrow, spleen, thymus, lymph vessels, and lymph nodes.

Malignant (ma-LIG-nant): Cancerous (see Cancer).

Melanin (MEL-a-nin): The pigment of the skin. The amount of this substance accounts for variations in skin color in different people and different races.

Medical Terms (continued)

Melanocytes (me-LAN-o-sites): Cells that form and contain a pigment called melanin.

Melanoma (mel-a-NO-ma): Cancer that begins in the melanocytes. Melanoma usually starts in the skin, often in a dark mole. Unlike the more common skin cancers, melanoma tends to spread to internal organs.

Metastasize (me-TAS-ta-size): To spread from one part of the body to another. When cancer cells metastasize and form secondary tumors, the cells in the metastatic tumor are like those in the original (primary) tumor.

Mycosis fungoides (my-KO-sis fun-GOY-deez): A cancer of the body's immune, or defense system. This cancer, also called T-cell lymphoma, first appears on the skin.

Nonmelanoma skin cancer: Skin cancer that does not involve melanocytes. Basal cell cancer and squamous cell cancer are nonmelanoma skin cancers.

Pathologist (pa-THOL-o-jist): A doctor who studies cells and tissues removed from the body, then makes a diagnosis based on changes that diseases cause in these cells.

Photodynamic therapy (FO-to-die-NAM-ik): Treatment that destroys cancer cells with lasers and drugs that become active when exposed to light.

Plastic surgeon: A surgeon who specializes in minimizing scarring or disfigurement that may occur as a result of disease (such as skin cancer), accidents, or birth defects.

Precancerous (pre-KAN-ser-us): A term used to describe a condition that may or is likely to become cancer.

Prognosis (prog-NO-sis): The probable outcome of a disease; the prospect of recovery.

Radiation therapy (ray-dee-AY-shun): The use of high-energy rays to treat disease. Sources of radiation include x-ray, cobalt, and radium.

Risk factor: A substance or condition that increases an individual's chance of getting a particular type of cancer.

Sebum (SEE-bum): An oily substance produced by the skin.

Medical Terms (continued)

Skin graft: Skin that is moved from one part of the body to another.

Squamous cell carcinoma (SKWAY-mus sel kar-si-NO-ma): A type of skin cancer in which the cancer cells resemble the squamous cells of the epidermis.

Squamous cells: Flat cells that look like fish scales and make up most of the epidermis.

Stage: The extent of disease.

Sun protection factor (SPF): A number on a scale (from 2 upwards) for rating sunscreens. Sunscreens with an SPF of 15 to 30 protect the skin from most of the sun's harmful rays.

Sunscreen: A substance that blocks the effect of the sun's harmful rays. Using lotions that contain sunscreens can reduce the risk of skin cancer.

Surgery: An operation.

T-cell lymphoma (lim-FO-ma): A cancer of the immune system that appears in the skin; also called mycosis fungoides.

Topical chemotherapy (kee-mo-THER-a-pee): Treatment with anticancer drugs in a lotion or cream.

Tumor: An abnormal mass of tissue that results from excess cell division. Tumors perform no useful body function. They may be either benign or malignant.

Tumor necrosis factor (ne-KRO-sis): A type of biological response modifier (a substance that can improve the body's natural response to disease). Scientists are still learning how this substance causes cancer cells to die.

Ultraviolet (UV) radiation (ul-tra-VI-o-let ray-dee-AY-shun): Invisible rays that are part of the energy that comes from the sun. UV radiation can burn the skin and can cause skin cancer. UV radiation that reaches the earth's surface is made up of two types of rays, called UVA and UVB rays. UVB rays are more likely than UVA rays to cause sunburn, but UVA rays pass further into the skin. Scientists have long thought that UVB radiation can cause skin cancer. They now think that UVA radiation also may add to skin damage that can lead to cancer. For this reason, skin specialists recommend that people use sunscreens that block both kinds of UV radiation.

Resources

Information about skin cancer is available from the sources listed below. You may wish to check for additional information at your local library or bookstore and from support groups in your community.

Cancer Information Service (CIS)
The Cancer Information Service, a program of the National Cancer Institute, provides a nationwide telephone service for cancer patients and their families and friends, the public, and health care professionals. The staff can answer questions (in English or Spanish) and can send free National Cancer Institute booklets about cancer. They also know about local resources and services. One toll-free number, 1-800-4-CANCER (1-800-422-6237), connects callers all over the country with the office that serves their area.

American Cancer Society (ACS)
The American Cancer Society is a national voluntary organization with units all over the country. It supports research, conducts educational programs, and offers many services to patients and their families. To obtain information about services and activities in local areas, call the Society's toll-free number, 1-800-ACS-2345 (1-800-227-2345), or the number listed under "American Cancer Society" in the white pages of the telephone book.

Skin Cancer Foundation
245 Fifth Avenue, Suite 2402, New York, NY 10016; 212-725-5176
This nonprofit organization provides publications and audiovisual materials on the prevention, early detection, and treatment of skin cancer. The Foundation also publishes *Sun and Skin News* and *The Skin Cancer Foundation Journal*, which have non-technical articles on skin cancer. Send a stamped, self-addressed envelope to receive free printed information.

For Further Information

The National Cancer Institute booklets listed below are available free of charge by calling 1-800-4-CANCER.

- *Facing Forward: A Guide For Cancer Survivors*
- *Radiation Therapy and You: A Guide to Self-Help During Treatment*
- *Taking Time: Support for People With Cancer and the People Who Care About Them*
- *What Are Clinical Trials All About?*
- *What You Need To Know About Melanoma*
- *What You Need To Know About Moles and Dysplastic Nevi*
- *When Cancer Recurs: Meeting the Challenge Again*

A Good Night's Sleep[*]

Few things in life are as eagerly anticipated as a good night's sleep. Yet many older people find that bedtime is the hardest part of the day. Although sleep patterns change as we age, sleep that is disturbed and unrefreshing is not an inevitable part of aging. In fact, troubled sleep may be a sign of emotional or physical disorders and should be carefully evaluated by a doctor or sleep specialist.

Sleep and Aging

The normal sleep cycle consists of two different kinds of sleep — REM (rapid eye movement or dreaming sleep) and non-REM (quiet sleep). Everyone has about four to five cycles of REM and non-REM sleep a night. For older persons, the amount of time spent in the deepest stages of non-REM sleep decreases. This may explain why older people are thought of as light sleepers.

Although the amount of sleep each person needs varies widely, the range usually falls between seven and eight hours a night. While these individual requirements remain fairly constant throughout adulthood, aging does reduce the amount of sleep you can expect to get at any one time. By age 75, for a variety of reasons, some people may find they are waking up several times each night. However, no matter what your age, talk to a doctor if your sleep patterns change.

Common Sleep Disorders

At any age *insomnia* is the most common sleep complaint. Insomnia means taking a long time to fall asleep (more than 30 to 45 minutes), waking up many times each night, or waking up early and being unable to get back to sleep. With rare exceptions, insomnia is a symptom of a problem, not the problem itself.

---

[*] Source: *Age Page*, National Institute on Aging, U.S. Department of Health and Human Services, Public Health Service, National Institutes of Health, Gaithersburg, MD 20898; 800-222-2225.

Insomnia can be coupled with other sleep disorders. *Sleep apnea* is a common problem that causes breathing to stop for periods of up to 2 minutes, many times each night. *Central sleep apnea* happens when the respiratory muscles do not function as they should; *obstructive sleep apnea* happens when something blocks the flow of air through the neck passage. In either case the sleeper is totally unaware of his or her struggle to breathe. Daytime sleepiness coupled with loud snoring are clues that sleep apnea may be a problem. A doctor specializing in sleep disorders can make a definite diagnosis and recommend treatment. A wide range of treatments are available, including gadgets that help you stay off your back when sleeping, medication, and surgery.

Another common problem for older people is *nocturnal myoclonus*, unusual leg movements during sleep. One or both legs may twitch causing the sleeper to wake either completely or for a few seconds. The cause of these leg movements is not known and there is no cure. Medication can sometimes bring relief; mild cases may be helped by leg exercises.

Suggestions for a Good Night's Sleep

Getting a good night's sleep can make a big difference in your quality of life.

- Follow a regular schedule — go to sleep and get up at the same time each day.
- Try to exercise at regular times each day. Moderate physical activity 2 to 4 hours before bedtime may improve your sleep.
- To adjust your internal sleep clock, try to get some exposure to the natural light in the afternoon each day.
- Be aware of what you eat. Avoid drinking caffeinated beverages late in the day. As a stimulant caffeine can keep you awake. MSG (monosodium glutamate), a seasoning used in some Chinese cooking, can have the same effect. If you like a snack before bed, a glass of warm milk may help.

- Don't drink alcohol or smoke cigarettes to help you sleep. Drinking even small amounts of alcohol can make it harder to stay asleep. Smoking is not only dangerous (the hazard of falling asleep with a lit cigarette), but nicotine is a stimulant.

- Create a safe and comfortable sleeping environment. Make sure there are locks on all doors and smoke alarms on each floor. A lamp that's easy to turn on and a telephone by your bedside may be helpful. In addition, the room should be dark, well ventilated, and have all nonessential sounds blocked out.

- Develop a bedtime routine. Do the same things each night to tell your body that it's time to wind down. Some people watch the evening news, read a book, or soak in a warm bath.

- Use your bedroom only for sleeping. After turning off the light, give yourself about 15 minutes of trying to fall asleep. If you are still awake or if you lose your drowsiness, get up and go into another room until you feel sleepy again.

- Try not to worry about your sleep. Some people find that playing mental games is helpful. For example, think black — a black cat on a black velvet pillow on a black corduroy sofa, etc.; or tell yourself it's five minutes before you have to get up and you're just trying to get a few extra winks.

Additional Information Sources

If you are so tired during the day that you cannot function normally and if this fatigue lasts for more than 2 or 3 weeks, you should see your family doctor or a sleep disorders specialist for a complete evaluation.

For general information about sleep, contact the Better Sleep Council, P.O. Box 13, Washington, DC 20044; 703-683-8371. They publish the *A to Zzzz Guide to Better Sleep*. For information on sleep disorders, contact the Association of Professional Sleep Societies, 604 Second Street, SW, Rochester, MN 55902.

Two books may be helpful. The Wakefulness-Sleep Education and Research Foundation publishes *101 Questions About Sleep and Dreams* ($5). Contact the publisher at W-SERF, 4820 Rancho Viejo Drive, Del Mar, CA 92014. The American Association of Retired Persons (AARP) publishes *The Sleep Book: Understanding and Preventing Sleep Problems in People Over 50* ($10.95/discounts for members). Contact AARP at 1909 K Street, NW, Washington, DC 20049.

The National Institute on Aging (NIA) offers a variety of resources on aging. Contact the NIA Information Center, P.O. Box 8057, Gaithersburg, MD 20898-8057; 800-222-2225, 800-222-4225 (TTY).

Smoking: It's Never Too Late To Stop[*]

"I've smoked two packs of cigarettes a day for 40 years — what's the use of quitting now?"

At any age there are many reasons to stop smoking. Some of the benefits for older people include:

- Reduced risk of cancer and lung disease
- Healthier heart and lungs
- Improved blood circulation
- Better health for nonsmoking family members, particularly children

Smoking doesn't just cut a few years off the end of each smoker's life — it prematurely kills 390,000 people each year and seriously disables millions of others.

What Smoking Does

Cigarette smoke affects a smoker's lungs and air passages, causing irritation, inflammation, and excess production of mucus. These smoking effects can result in a chronic cough and, in more severe cases, the lung disease known as chronic bronchitis. Long-term lung damage can lead to emphysema, which prevents normal breathing.

Smoking, high blood pressure (HBP), and high blood cholesterol (a fatty substance in the blood) are major factors that contribute to coronary heart disease. A person with HBP or high cholesterol who also smokes has a much greater risk of heart attack than a person who has only one of these risk factors.

When a person stops smoking, the benefits to the heart and circulatory system begin right away. The risk of heart attack,

---

[*] Source: *Age Page*, National Institute on Aging, U.S. Department of Health and Human Services, Public Health Service, National Institutes of Health, Gaithersburg, MD 20898; 800-222-2225.

stroke, and other circulatory diseases drops. Circulation of blood to the hands and feet improves. Although quitting smoking won't reverse chronic lung damage, it may slow the disease and help retain existing lung function.

Smoking causes several types of cancer, including those of the lungs, mouth, larynx, and esophagus. It also plays a role in cancers of the pancreas, kidney, and bladder. A smoker's risk of cancer depends in part on the number of cigarettes smoked, the number of years of smoking, and how deeply the smoke is inhaled. After a smoker quits, the risk of smoking-related cancer begins to decline and within a decade the risk is reduced to that of a nonsmoker.

Smokers have a higher risk than nonsmokers of getting influenza, pneumonia, and other respiratory conditions such as colds. Influenza and pneumonia can be life-threatening in older people.

One woman in four over age 60 develops osteoporosis, a bone-thinning disorder that leads to fractures. There is evidence that cigarette smoking may increase the risk of developing this disabling condition.

Passive Smoking

There is growing evidence about the harmful effects of secondhand tobacco smoke on the health of nonsmokers. This should be an especially important concern if the husband or wife of a smoker has asthma, another lung condition, or heart disease. In addition, smoke in the home poses a health hazard for babies and young children. Passive smoking (exposure to another's smoke) by nonsmokers has been linked to a higher incidence of bronchitis, pneumonia, asthma, and inner ear infections in children. This is a good reason for a parent or grandparent to consider quitting or to avoid smoking while in the presence of young children and infants. New studies report that passive smoking increases the nonsmoker's risk for cancer.

How to Stop Smoking

Over 30 million Americans have been able to quit smoking, and recent surveys suggest that this decline in smoking is continuing. By giving up cigarettes, you can be healthier and feel healthier, regardless of how many years or how many cigarettes you have smoked.

There are many ways to stop smoking. No single method works for everyone, so each person must try to find what works best. Many people can stop on their own, but others need help from doctors, clinics, or organized groups. Some studies have found that older people who take part in programs to stop smoking have higher success rates than younger ones do.

Withdrawal symptoms reported by some people who quit smoking include anxiety, restlessness, drowsiness, difficulty concentrating, and digestive problems. Some people have no withdrawal symptoms at all.

Nicotine chewing gum is now available without a prescription to help people who are dependent on nicotine (a substance present in tobacco) overcome withdrawal symptoms. Many doctors also recommend joining an organized support group or using self-help materials to assist in quitting smoking. Nicotine chewing gum is not recommended for people who have certain forms of heart disease. Denture wearers may find it difficult to chew.

Where To Get Help

Organizations, doctors, and clinics offering stop-smoking programs are listed in telephone books under "Smokers' Treatment and Information Centers." Further information can be obtained from organizations such as the American Cancer Society, 1599 Clifton Road, Atlanta, GA 30329; the American Heart Association, 7320 Greenville Avenue, Dallas, TX 75231; and the American Lung Association, 1740 Broadway, P.O. Box 596, New York, NY 10019-4374. For all three organizations, consult your local telephone directory for listings of local chapters.

The Office on Smoking and Health collects and distributes information on health risks associated with smoking and methods for quitting. Write to the OSH at 5600 Fishers Lane, Park Building, Room 1-10, Rockville, MD 20857.

You may also contact the Office of Cancer Communications, National Cancer Institute, Bethesda, MD 20892. Or call the Cancer Information Service at 800-4-CANCER.

The National Institute on Aging offers a variety of information on health and aging. Write to the NIA Information Center, P.O. Box 8057, Gaithersburg, MD 20898-8057; 800-222-2225, 800-222-4225 (TTY).

Recovering After a Stroke[*]

What Is a Stroke?

A stroke is a type of brain injury. Symptoms depend on the part of the brain that is affected. People who survive a stroke often have weakness on one side of the body or trouble with moving, talking, or thinking.

Most strokes are ischemic (is-KEE-mic) strokes. These are caused by reduced blood flow to the brain when blood vessels are blocked by a clot or become too narrow for blood to get through. Brain cells in the area die from lack of oxygen. In another type of stroke, called hemorrhagic (hem-or-AJ-ic) stroke, the blood vessel isn't blocked; it bursts, and blood leaks into the brain, causing damage.

Strokes are more common in older people. Almost three-fourths of all strokes occur in people 65 years of age or over. However, a person of any age can have a stroke.

A person may also have a transient ischemic attack (TIA). This has the same symptoms as a stroke, but only lasts for a few hours or a day and does not cause permanent brain damage. A TIA is not a stroke but it is an important warning signal. The person needs treatment to help prevent an actual stroke in the future.

Purpose of This Chapter

This chapter is about stroke rehabilitation. Its goal is to help the person who has had a stroke achieve the best possible recovery. Its purpose is to help people who have had strokes and their families get the most out of rehabilitation.

Note that this chapter sometimes uses the terms "stroke survivor" and "person" instead of "patient" to refer to someone who has had

---

[*] Source: U.S. Department of Health and Human Services, Public Health Service, Agency for Health Care Policy and Research, Executive Office Center, Suite 501, 2101 East Jefferson St., Rockville, MD 20852; 800-358-9295.

a stroke. This is because people who have had a stroke are patients for only a short time, first in the acute care hospital and then perhaps in a rehabilitation program. For the rest of their lives, they are people

> A stroke may be frightening to both the patient and family. It helps to remember that stroke survivors usually have at least some spontaneous recovery or natural healing and often recover further with rehabilitation.

who happen to have had a stroke. The chapter also uses the word "family" to include those people who are closest to the stroke survivor, whether or not they are relatives.

Rehabilitation works best when stroke survivors and their families work together as a team. For this reason, both stroke survivors and family members are encouraged to read all parts of this chapter.

Recovering From Stroke

The process of recovering from a stroke usually includes treatment, spontaneous recovery, rehabilitation, and the return to community living. Because stroke survivors often have complex rehabilitation needs, progress and recovery are different for each person.

Treatment for stroke begins in a hospital with "acute care." This first step includes helping the patient survive, preventing another stroke, and taking care of any other medical problems.

Spontaneous recovery happens naturally to most people. Soon after the stroke, some abilities that have been lost usually start to come back. This process is quickest during the first few weeks, but it sometimes continues for a long time.

Rehabilitation is another part of treatment. It helps the person keep abilities and gain back lost abilities to become more independent. It usually begins while the patient is still in acute care. For many patients, it continues afterward, either as a formal rehabilitation *program* or as individual rehabilitation *services*. Many decisions about rehabilitation are made by the patient, family, and hospital staff before discharge from acute care.

The last stage in stroke recovery begins with the person's return to **community living** after acute care or rehabilitation. This stage can last for a lifetime as the stroke survivor and family learn to live with the effects of the stroke. This may include doing common tasks in new ways or making up for damage to or limits of one part of the body by greater activity of another. For example, a stroke survivor can wear shoes with velcro closures instead of laces or may learn to write with the opposite hand.

How Stroke Affects People

Effects on the Body, Mind, and Feelings
Each stroke is different depending on the part of the brain injured, how bad the injury is, and the person's general health. Some of the effects of stroke are:

- **Weakness (hemiparesis—hem-ee-par-EE-sis) or paralysis (hemiplegia—hem-ee-PLEE-ja) on one side of the body.** This may affect the whole side or just the arm or the leg. The weakness or paralysis is on the side of the body opposite the side of the brain injured by the stroke. For example, if the stroke injured the left side of the brain, the weakness or paralysis will be on the right side of the body.

- **Problems with balance or coordination.** These can make it hard for the person to sit, stand, or walk, even if muscles are strong enough.

- **Problems using language (aphasia and dysarthria).** A person with aphasia (a-FAY-zha) may have trouble understanding speech or writing. Or, the person may understand but may not be able to think of the words to speak or write. A person with dysarthria (dis-AR-three-a) knows the right words but has trouble saying them clearly.

- **Being unaware of or ignoring things on one side of the body (bodily neglect or inattention).** Often, the person will not turn to look toward the weaker side or even eat food from the half of the plate on that side.

- **Pain, numbness, or odd sensations.** These can make it hard for the person to relax and feel comfortable.

- **Problems with memory, thinking, attention, or learning (cognitive problems).** A person may have trouble with many mental activities or just a few. For example, the person may have trouble following directions, may get confused if something in a room is moved, or may not be able to keep track of the date or time.

- **Being unaware of the effects of the stroke.** The person may show poor judgment by trying to do things that are unsafe as a result of the stroke.

- **Trouble swallowing (dysphagia—dis-FAY-ja).** This can make it hard for the person to get enough food. Also, care must sometimes be taken to prevent the person from breathing in food (aspiration—as-per-AY-shun) while trying to swallow it.

- **Problems with bowel or bladder control.** These problems can be helped with the use of portable urinals, bedpans, and other toileting devices.

- **Getting tired very quickly.** Becoming tired very quickly may limit the person's participation and performance in a rehabilitation program.

- **Sudden bursts of emotion, such as laughing, crying, or anger.** These emotions may indicate that the person needs help, understanding, and support in adjusting to the effects of the stroke.

- **Depression.** This is common in people who have had strokes. It can begin soon after the stroke or many weeks later, and family members often notice it first.

Depression After Stroke

It is normal for a stroke survivor to feel sad over the problems caused by stroke. However, some people experience a major depressive disorder, which should be diagnosed and treated as soon as possible. A person with a major depressive disorder has a number of symptoms nearly every day, all day, for at least two weeks. These always include at least one of the following:

- Feeling sad, blue, or down in the dumps.
- Loss of interest in things that the person used to enjoy.

A person may also have other physical or psychological symptoms, including:

- Feeling slowed down or restless and unable to sit still.
- Feeling worthless or guilty.
- Increase or decrease in appetite or weight.
- Problems concentration, thinking, remembering, or making decisions.
- Trouble sleeping or sleeping too much.
- Loss of energy or feeling tired all of the time.
- Headaches.
- Other aches and pains.
- Digestive problems.
- Sexual problems.
- Feeling pessimistic or hopeless.
- Being anxious or worried.
- Thoughts of death or suicide.

If a stroke survivor has symptoms of depression, *especially thoughts of death or suicide,* professional help is needed right away. Once the depression is properly treated, these thoughts should go away. Depression can be treated with medication, psychotherapy, or both. If it is not treated, it can cause needless suffering and also makes it harder to recover from the stroke.

Disabilities After Stroke

A "disability" is difficulty doing something that is a normal part of daily life. People who have had a stroke may have trouble with many activities that were easy before, such as walking, talking, and taking care of "activities of daily living" (ADLs). These include basic tasks such as bathing, dressing, eating, and using the toilet, as well as more complex tasks called "instrumental activities of daily living" (IADLs), such as housekeeping, using the telephone, driving, and writing checks.

Some disabilities are obvious right after the stroke. Others may not be noticed until the person is back home and is trying to do something for the first time since the stroke.

What Happens During Acute Care?

The main purposes of acute care are to:

- Make sure the patient's condition is caused by a stroke and not by some other medical problem.

> Stroke survivors and family members may find the hospital experience confusing. Hospital staff are there to help, and it is important to ask questions and talk about concerns.

- Determine the type and location of the stroke and how serious it is.
- Prevent or treat complications such as bowel or bladder problems or pressure ulcers (bed sores).
- Prevent another stroke.
- Encourage the patient to move and perform self-care tasks, such as eating and getting out of bed, as early as medically possible. This is the first step in rehabilitation.

Before acute care ends, the patient and family with the hospital staff decide what the next step will be. For many patients, the next step will be to continue rehabilitation.

Preventing Another Stroke

People who have had a stroke have an increased risk of another stroke, especially during the first year after the original stroke. The risk of another stroke goes up with older age, high blood pressure (hypertension), high cholesterol, diabetes, obesity, having had a transient ischemic attack (TIA), heart disease, cigarette smoking, heavy alcohol use, and drug abuse. While some risk factors for stroke (such as age) cannot be changed, the risk factors for the others can be reduced through use of medicines or changes in lifestyle.

Patients and families should ask for guidance from their doctor or nurse about preventing another stroke. They need to work together to make healthy changes in the patient's lifestyle. Patients and families should also learn the warning signs of a TIA (such as weakness on one side of the body and slurred speech) and see a doctor **immediately** if these occur.

Deciding About Rehabilitation

Some people do not need rehabilitation after a stroke because the stroke was mild or they have fully recovered. Others may be too disabled to participate. However, many patients can be helped by rehabilitation. Hospital staff will help the patient and family decide about rehabilitation and choose the right services or program.

Types of Rehabilitation Programs
There are several kinds or rehabilitation programs:

- **Hospital programs.** These programs can be provided by special rehabilitation hospitals or by rehabilitation units in acute care hospitals. Complete rehabilitation services are available. The patient stays in the hospital during rehabilitation. An organized team of specially trained professionals provides the therapy. Hospital programs are usually more intense than other programs and require more effort from the patient.

- **Nursing facility (nursing home) programs.** As in hospital programs, the person stays at the facility during rehabilitation. Nursing facility programs are very different from each other, so it is important to get specific information about each one. Some provide a complete range of rehabilitation services; others provide only limited services.

- **Outpatient programs.** Outpatient programs allow a patient who lives at home to get a full range of services by visiting a hospital outpatient department, outpatient rehabilitation facility, or day hospital program.

- **Home-based programs.** The patient can live at home and receive rehabilitation services from visiting professionals. An important advantage of home programs is that patients learn skills in the same place where they will use them.

Individual Rehabilitation Services

Many stroke survivors do not need a complete range of rehabilitation services. Instead, they may need an individual type of service, such as regular physical therapy or speech therapy. These services are available from outpatient and home care programs.

Paying for Rehabilitation

Medicare and many health insurance policies will help pay for rehabilitation. Medicare is the federal health insurance program for Americans 65 years of age or over and for certain Americans with disabilities. It has two parts: hospital insurance (known as Part A) and supplementary medical insurance (known as Part B). Part A helps pay for home health care, hospice care, inpatient hospital care, and inpatient care in a skilled nursing facility. Part B helps pay for doctors' services, outpatient hospital services, durable medical equipment, and a number of other medical services and supplies not covered by Part A. Social Security Administration offices across the country take applications for Medicare and provide general information about the program.

In some cases, Medicare will help pay for outpatient services from a Medicare-participating comprehensive outpatient rehabilitation facility. Covered services include physicians' services; physical, speech, occupational, and respiratory therapies; counseling; and other related services. A stroke survivor must be referred by a physician who certifies that skilled rehabilitation services are needed.

Medicaid is a federal program that is operated by the states, and each state decides who is eligible and the scope of health services offered. Medicaid provides health care coverage for some low-income people who cannot afford it. This includes people who are eligible because they are older, blind, or disabled, or certain people in families with dependent children.

These programs have certain restrictions and limitations, and coverage may stop as soon as the patient stops making progress. Therefore, it is important for patients and families to find out exactly what their insurance will cover. The hospital's social service department can answer questions about insurance coverage and can help with financial planning.

Choosing a Rehabilitation Program

The doctor and other hospital staff will provide information and advice about rehabilitation programs, but the patient and family make the final choice. Hospital staff know the patient's disabilities and medical condition. They should also be familiar with the rehabilitation programs in the community and should be able to answer questions about them. The patient and family may have a preference about whether the patient lives at home or at a rehabilitation facility. They may have reasons for preferring one program over another. Their concerns are important and should be discussed with hospital staff.

Things to Consider When Choosing a Rehabilitation Program

- Does the program provide the service the patient needs?
- Does it match the patient's abilities or is it too demanding or not demanding enough?
- What kind of standing does it have in the community for the quality of the program?
- Is it certified and does its staff have good credentials?
- Is it located where family members can easily visit?
- Does it actively involve the patient and family members in rehabilitation decisions?
- Does it encourage family members to participate in some rehabilitation sessions and practice with the patient?
- How well are its costs covered by insurance or Medicare?
- If it is an outpatient or home program, is there someone living at home who can provide care?
- If it is an outpatient program, is transportation available?

A person may start rehabilitation in one program and later transfer to another. For example, some patients who get tired quickly may start out in a less intense rehabilitation program. After they build up their strength, they are able to transfer to a more intense program.

When Rehabilitation Is Not Recommended

Some families and patients may be disappointed if the doctor does not recommend rehabilitation. However, a person may be unconscious or too disabled to benefit. For example, a person who is unable to learn may be better helped by maintenance care at home or in a nursing facility. A person who is, at first, too weak for rehabilitation may benefit from a gradual recovery period at home or in a nursing facility. This person can consider rehabilitation at a later time. It is important to remember that:

- Hospital staff are responsible for helping plan the best way to care for the patient after discharge from acute care. They can also provide or arrange for needed social services and family education.

- This is not the only chance to participate in rehabilitation. People who are too disabled at first may recover enough to enter rehabilitation later.

What Happens During Rehabilitation

In hospital or nursing facility rehabilitation programs, the patient may spend several hours a day in activities such as physical therapy, occupational therapy, speech therapy, recreational therapy, group activities, and patient and family education. It is important to maintain skills that help recovery. Part of the time is spent relearning skills (such as walking and speaking) that the person had before the stroke. Part of it is spent learning new ways to do things that can no longer be done the old way (for example, using one hand for tasks that usually need both hands).

Setting Rehabilitation Goals
The goals of rehabilitation depend on the effects of the stroke, what the patient was able to do before the stroke, and the patient's wishes. Working together, goals are set by the patient, family, and rehabilitation program staff. Sometimes, a person may need to repeat steps in striving to reach goals.

If goals are too high, the patient will not be able to reach them. If they are too low, the patient may not get all the services that would help. If they do not match the patient's interests, the patient may not want to work at them. Therefore, it is important for goals to be realistic. To help achieve realistic goals, the patient and family should tell program staff about things that the patient wants to be able to do.

Rehabilitation Goals
- Being able to walk, at least with a walker or cane, is a realistic goal for most stroke survivors.
- Being able to take care of oneself with some special equipment is a realistic goal for most.
- Being able to drive a car is a realistic goal for some.

- Having a job can be a realistic goal for some people who were working before the stroke. For some, the old job may not be possible but another job or a volunteer activity may be.

Reaching treatment goals does not mean the end of recovery. It just means that the stroke survivor and family are ready to continue recovery on their own.

Rehabilitation Specialists

Because every stroke is different, treatment will be different for each person. Rehabilitation is provided by several types of specially trained professionals. A person may work with any or all of these:

- **Physician.** All patients in stroke rehabilitation have a physician in charge of their care. Several kinds of doctors with rehabilitation experience may have this role. These include family physicians and internists (primary care doctors), geriatricians (specialists in working with older patients), neurologists (specialists in the brain and nervous system), and physiatrists (specialists in physical medicine and rehabilitation).

- **Rehabilitation nurse.** Rehabilitation nurses specialize in nursing care for people with disabilities. They provide direct care, educate patients and families, and help the doctor to coordinate care.

- **Physical therapist.** Physical therapists evaluate and treat problems with moving, balance, and coordination. They provide training and exercises to improve walking, getting in and out of a bed or chair, and moving around without losing balance. They teach family members how to help with exercises for the patient and how to help the patient move or walk, if needed.

- **Occupational therapist.** Occupational therapists provide exercises and practice to help patients do things they could do before the stroke such as eating, bathing, dressing, writing, or cooking. The old way of doing an activity sometimes is no longer possible, so the therapist teaches a new technique.

- **Speech-language pathologist.** Speech-language pathologists help patients get back language skills and learn other ways to communicate. Teaching families how to improve communication is very important. Speech-language pathologists also work with patients who have swallowing problems (dysphagia).

- **Social worker.** Social workers help patients and families make decisions about rehabilitation and plan the return to the home or a new living place. They help the family answer questions about insurance and other financial issues and can arrange for a variety of support services. They may also provide or arrange for patient and family counseling to help cope with any emotional problems.

- **Psychologist.** Psychologists are concerned with the mental and emotional health of patients. They use interviews and tests to identify and understand problems. They may also treat thinking or memory problems or may provide advice to other professionals about patients with these problems.

- **Therapeutic recreation specialist.** These therapists help patients return to activities that they enjoyed before the stroke such as playing cards, gardening, bowling, or community activities. Recreational therapy helps the rehabilitation process and encourages the patient to practice skills.

- **Other professionals.** Other professionals may also help with the patient's treatment. An orthotist may make special braces to support weak ankles and feet. A urologist may help with bladder problems. Other physician specialists may help with medical or emotional problems. Dietitians make sure that the patient has a healthy diet during rehabilitation. They also educate the family about proper diet after the patient leaves the program. Vocational counselors may help patients go back to work or school.

Rehabilitation Team

In many programs, a special rehabilitation team with a team leader is organized for each patient. The patient, family, and rehabilitation professionals are all members. The team

> Rehabilitation professionals, the patient, and the family are vitally important partners in rehabilitation. They must all work together for rehabilitation to succeed.

has regular meetings to discuss the progress of treatment. Using a team approach often helps everyone work together to meet goals.

Getting the Most Out of Rehabilitation

What the Patient Can Do

If you are a stroke survivor in rehabilitation, keep in mind that you are the most important person in your treatment. You should have a major say in decisions about your care. This is hard for many stroke patients. You may sometimes feel tempted to sit back and let the program staff take charge. If you need extra time to think or have trouble talking, you may find that others are going ahead and making decisions without waiting. Try not to let this happen.

- Make sure others understand that you want to help make decisions about your care.
- Bring your questions and concerns to program staff.
- State your wishes and opinions on matters that affect you.
- Speak up if you feel that anyone is "talking down" to you; or, if people start talking about you as if you are not there.
- Remember that you have the right to see your medical records.

To be a partner in your care, you need to be well informed about your treatment and how well you are doing. It may help to record important information about your treatment and progress and write down any questions you have.

If you have speech problems, making your wishes known is hard. The speech-language pathologist can help you to communicate with other staff members, and family members may also help to communicate your ideas and needs.

Most patients find that rehabilitation is hard work. They need to maintain abilities at the same time they are working to regain abilities. It is normal to feel tired and discouraged at times because things that used to be easy before the stroke are now difficult. The important thing is to notice the progress you make and take pride in each achievement.

How the Family Can Help
If you are a family member of a stroke survivor, here are some things you can do:

- Support the patient's efforts to participate in rehabilitation decisions.
- Visit and talk with the patient. You can relax together while playing cards, watching television, listening to the radio, or playing a board game.
- If the patient has trouble communicating (aphasia), ask the speech-language pathologist how you can help.
- Participate in education offered for stroke survivors and their families. Learn as much as you can and how you can help.
- Ask to attend some of the rehabilitation sessions. This is a good way to learn how rehabilitation works and how to help.
- Encourage and help the patient to practice skills learned in rehabilitation.
- Make sure that the program staff suggests activities that fit the patient's needs and interests.

- Find out what the patient can do alone, what the patient can do with help, and what the patient can't do. Then avoid doing things for the patient that the patient is able to do. Each time the patient does them, his or her ability and confidence will grow.
- Take care of yourself by eating well, getting enough rest, and taking time to do things that you enjoy.

To gain more control over the rehabilitation process, keep important information where you can find it. One suggestion is to keep a notebook with the patient. Some things to include are provided in the sample later in this chapter.

Discharge Planning

Discharge planning begins early during rehabilitation. It involves the patient, family, and rehabilitation staff. The purpose of discharge planning is to help maintain the benefits of rehabilitation after the patient has been discharged from the program. Patients are usually discharged from rehabilitation soon after their goals have been reached.

Some of the things discharge planning can include are to:
- Make sure that the stroke survivor has a safe place to live after discharge.
- Decide what care, assistance, or special equipment will be needed.
- Arrange for more rehabilitation services or for other services in the home (such as visits by a home health aide).
- Choose the health care provider who will monitor the person's health and medical needs.
- Determine the caregivers who will work as a partner with the patient to provide daily care and assistance at home, and teach them the skills they will need.
- Help the stroke survivor explore employment opportunities, volunteer activities, and driving a car (if able and interested).

- Discuss any sexual concerns the stroke survivor or husband/wife may have. Many people who have had strokes enjoy active sex lives.

Preparing a Living Place

Many stroke survivors can return to their own homes after rehabilitation. Others need to live in a place with professional staff such as a nursing home or assisted living facility. An assisted living facility can provide residential living with a full range of services and staff. The choice usually depends on the person's needs for care and whether caregivers are available in the home. The stroke survivor needs a living place that supports continuing recovery.

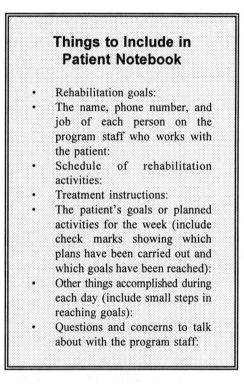

Things to Include in Patient Notebook

- Rehabilitation goals:
- The name, phone number, and job of each person on the program staff who works with the patient:
- Schedule of rehabilitation activities:
- Treatment instructions:
- The patient's goals or planned activities for the week (include check marks showing which plans have been carried out and which goals have been reached):
- Other things accomplished during each day (include small steps in reaching goals):
- Questions and concerns to talk about with the program staff:

It is important to choose a living place that is safe. If the person needs a new place to live, a social worker can help find the best place.

During discharge planning, program staff will ask about the home and may also visit it. They may suggest changes to make it safer. These might include changing rooms around so that a stroke survivor can stay on one floor, moving scatter rugs or small pieces of furniture that could cause falls, and putting grab bars and seats in tubs and showers.

It is a good idea for the stroke survivor to go home for a trial visit before discharge. This will help identify problems that need to be discussed or corrected before the patient returns.

Deciding About Special Equipment

Even after rehabilitation, some stroke survivors have trouble walking, balancing, or performing certain activities of daily living. Special equipment can sometimes help. Here are some examples:

- **Cane.** Many people who have had strokes use a cane when walking. For people with balancing problems, special canes with three or four "feet" are available.
- **Walker.** A walker provides more support than a cane. Several designs are available for people who can only use one hand and for different problems with walking or balance.
- **Ankle-foot orthotic devices (braces).** Braces help a person to walk by keeping the ankle and foot in the correct position and providing support for the knee.
- **Wheelchair.** Some people will need a wheelchair. Wheelchairs come in many different designs. They can be customized to fit the user's needs and abilities. Find out which features are most important for the stroke survivor.
- **Aids for bathing, dressing, and eating.** Some of these are safety devices such as grab bars and nonskid rub and floor mats. Others make it easier to do things with one hand. Examples are velcro fasteners on clothes and placemats that won't slide on the table.
- **Communication aids.** These range from small computers to homemade communication boards. The stroke survivor, family, and rehabilitation program staff should decide together what special equipment is needed. Program staff can help in making the best choices. Medicare or health insurance will often help pay for the equipment.

Preparing Caregivers

Caregivers who help stroke survivors at home are usually family members such as a husband or wife or an adult son or daughter. They may also be friends or even professional home health aides. usually one person is the main caregiver, while others help from time to time. An important part of discharge planning is to make sure that caregivers understand the safety, physical, and emotional needs of the stroke survivor, and that they will be available to provide needed care.

Since every stroke is different, people have different needs for help from caregivers. Here are some of the things caregivers may do:

- Keep notes on discharge plans and instructions and ask about anything that is not clear.
- Help to make sure that the stroke survivor takes all prescribed medicines and follows suggestions from program staff about diet, exercise, rest, and other health practices.
- Encourage and help the person to practice skills learned in rehabilitation.
- Help the person solve problems and discover new ways to do things.
- Help the person with activities performed before the stroke. These could include using tools, buttoning a shirt, household tasks, and leisure or social activities.
- Help with personal care, if the person cannot manage alone.
- Help with communication, if the person has speech problems. Include the stroke survivor in conversations even when the person cannot actively participate.
- Arrange for needed community services.
- Stand up for the rights of the stroke survivor.

If you expect to be a caregiver, think carefully about this role ahead of time. Are you prepared to work with the patient on stroke recovery? Talk it over with other people who will share the caregiving job with you. What are the stroke survivor's needs? Who can best help meet each of them? Who will be the main caregiver? Does caregiving need to be scheduled around the caregivers' jobs or other activities? There is time during discharge planning to talk with program staff about caregiving and to develop a workable plan.

Going Home

Adjusting to the Change

Going home to the old home or a new one is a big adjustment. For the stroke survivor, it may be hard to transfer the skills learned during rehabilitation to a new location. Also, more problems caused by the stroke may appear as the person tries to go back to old activities. During this time, the stroke survivor and family learn how the stroke will affect daily life and can make the necessary adjustments.

These adjustments are a physical and emotional challenge for the main caregiver as well as the stroke survivor. The caregiver has many new responsibilities and may not have time for some favorite activities. The caregiver needs support, understanding, and some time to rest. Caregiving that falls too heavily on one person can be very stressful. Even when family members and friends are nearby and willing to help, conflicts over caregiving can cause stress.

> A stroke is always stressful for the family, but it is especially hard if one family member is the only caregiver. Much time may be required to meet the needs of the stroke survivor. Therefore, the caregiver needs as much support as possible from others. Working together eases the stress on everyone.

Tips for Reducing Stress

The following tips for reducing stress are for both caregivers and stroke survivors.

- Take stroke recovery and caregiving one day at time and be hopeful.
- Remember that adjusting to the effects of stroke takes time. Appreciate each small gain as you discover better ways to doing things.
- Caregiving is learned. Expect that knowledge and skills will grow with experience.

- Experiment. Until you find what works for you, try new ways of doing activities of daily living, communicating with each other, scheduling the day, and organizing your social life.
- Plan for "breaks" so that you are not together all the time. This is a good way for family and friends to help on occasion. You can also plan activities that get both of you out of the house.
- Ask family members and friends to help in specific ways and commit to certain times to help. This gives others a chance to help in useful ways.
- Read about the experiences of other people in similar situations. Your public library has life stories by people who have had a stroke as well as books for caregivers.
- Join or start a support group for stroke survivors or caregivers. You can work on problems together and develop new friendships.
- Be kind to each other. If you sometimes feel irritated, this is natural and you don't need to blame yourself. But don't "take it out" on the other person. It often helps to talk about these feelings with a friend, rehabilitation professional, or support group.
- Plan and enjoy new experiences and don't look back. Avoid comparing life as it is now with how it was before the stroke.

Followup Appointments

After a stroke survivor returns to the community, regular followup appointments are usually scheduled with the doctor and sometimes with rehabilitation professionals. The purpose of followup is to check on the stroke survivor's medical condition and ability to use the skills learned in rehabilitation. It is also important to check on how well the stroke survivor and family are adjusting. The stroke survivor and caregiver can be prepared for these visits with a list of questions or concerns.

Where To Get Help

Many kinds of help are available for people who have had strokes and their families and caregivers. Some of the most important are:

- **Information about stroke.** A good place to start is with the books and pamphlets available from national organizations that provide information on this subject. Many of their materials are available free of charge. A list of these organizations follows.
- **Local stroke clubs or other support groups.** These are groups where stroke survivors and family members can share their experiences, help each other solve problems, and expand their social lives.
- **Home health services.** These are available from the Visiting Nurses Association (VNA), public health departments, hospital home care departments, and private home health agencies. Services may include nursing care, rehabilitation therapies, personal care (for example, help with bathing or dressing), respite care (staying with the stroke survivor so that the caregiver can take a vacation or short break), homemaker services, and other kinds of help.
- **Meals on Wheels.** Hot meals are delivered to the homes of people who cannot easily shop and cook.
- **Adult day care.** People who cannot be completely independent sometimes spend the day at an adult day care center. There they get meals, participate in social activities, and may also get some health care and rehabilitation services.
- **Friendly Visitor (or other companion services).** A paid or volunteer companion makes regular visits or phone calls to a person with disabilities.
- **Transportation services.** Most public transportation systems have buses that a person in a wheelchair can board. Some organizations and communities provide vans to take wheelchair users and others on errands such as shopping or doctor's visits.

Many communities have service organizations that can help. Some free services may be available or fees may be on a "sliding scale" based on income. It takes some work to find out what services and payment arrangements are available. A good way to start is to ask the social workers in the hospital or rehabilitation program where the stroke survivor was treated. Also, talk to the local United Way or places of worship. Another good place to look is the Yellow Pages of the telephone book under "Health Services," "Home Health Care," "Senior Citizen Services," or "Social Service Organizations." Just asking friends may turn up useful information. The more you ask, the more you will learn.

Additional Resources

ACTION, 1100 Vermont Ave., NW, Washington, DC 20525; 202-606-4855 (call for telephone number of regional office).
Sponsors older American volunteer programs.

Administration on Aging, 330 Independence Ave., SW, Washington, DC 20201; 800-677-1116 (call for list of community services for older Americans in your area).

AHA Stroke Connection (formerly the Courage Stroke Network), American Heart Association, 7272 Greenville Ave., Dallas, TX 75231; 800-553-6321 (or check telephone book for local AHA office).
Provides prevention, diagnosis, treatment, and rehabilitation information to stroke survivors and their families.

American Dietetic Association/National Center for Nutrition and Dietetics, 216 W. Jackson Blvd., Chicago, Il 60606; 800-366-1655 (Consumer Nutrition Hotline).
Consumers may speak to a registered dietitian for answers to nutrition questions, or obtain a referral to a local registered dietitian.

American Self-Help Clearinghouse, St. Clares-Riverside Medical Center, Denville, NJ 07834; 201-625-7101 (call for name and telephone number of state or local clearinghouse).
Provides information and assistance on local self-help groups.

Additional Resources (continued)

National Aphasia Association, P.O. Box 1887, Murray Hill Station, New York, NY 10156; Toll-free 800-922-4622.
Provides information on the partial or total loss of the ability to speak or comprehend speech, resulting from stroke or other causes.

National Easter Seal Society, 230 West Monroe St., Suite 1800, Chicago, IL 60606; 312-726-6200 (or check telephone book for local Easter Seal Society).
Provides information and services to help people with disabilities.

National Stroke Association, 8480 East Orchard Rd., Suite 1000, Englewood, CO 80111; 303-771-1700, Toll-free 800-STROKES (787-6537.
Serves as an information referral clearinghouse on stroke. Offers guidance on forming stroke support groups and clubs.

Rosalynn Carter Institute, Georgia Southwestern College, 600 Simmons St., Americus, GA 31709.
Provides information on caregiving. Reading lists, video products, and other caregiver resources are available by writing to the address listed above.

Stroke Clubs International, 805 12th St., Galveston, TX 77550; 409-762-1022 (call for the name of a stroke club located in your area).
Maintains list of over 800 stroke clubs throughout the United States.

The Well Spouse Foundation
P.O. Box 801, New York, NY 10023; 212-724-7209, Toll-free 800-838-0879.
Provides support for the husbands, wives, and partners of people who are chronically ill or disabled.

Medicare Information
Consumer Information Center, Department 59, Pueblo, CO 81009.
By writing to this address, you can receive a free copy of *The Medicare Handbook* (updated and published annually). This handbook provides information about Medicare benefits, health insurance to supplement Medicare, and limits to Medicare coverage. It is also available in Spanish.

For Further Information

Information in this booklet is based on *Post-Stroke Rehabilitation. Clinical Practice Guideline, Number 16.* It was developed by a non-federal panel sponsored by the Agency for Health Care Policy and Research (AHCPR), an agency for the Public Health Service. Other guidelines on common health problems are available, and more are being developed.

Four other patient guides are available from AHCPR that may be of interest to stroke survivors and their caregivers:

Preventing Pressure Ulcers: Patient Guide gives detailed information about how to prevent pressure sores (AHCPR Publication No. 92-0048).

Treating Pressure Sores: Patient Guide gives detailed information about treating pressure sores (AHCPR Publication No. 95-0654).

Urinary Incontinence in Adults: Patient Guide describes why people lose urine when they don't want to and how that can be treated (AHCPR Publication No. 92-0040).

Depression Is a Treatable Illness: Patient Guide discusses major depressive disorder, which most often can be successfully treated with the help of a health professional (AHCPR Publication No. 93-0053).

For more information about these and other guidelines, or to get more copies of this booklet, call toll-free: 800-358-9295, or write to Agency for Health Care Policy and Research, Publications Clearinghouse, P.O. Box 8547, Silver Spring, MD 20907.

Considering Surgery[*]

Deciding whether or not to have an operation is difficult for everyone. Most people for whom elective (nonemergency) surgery is recommended are given time to think the matter over and review other options. Often it's a good idea to get a second opinion.

Many people are uneasy about asking their doctor for another opinion. However, getting a second opinion is a good way to get additional expert advice from another doctor who knows a lot about treating your medical problem. In addition, a second opinion can reassure you that the decision to have surgery is the right one.

Choosing a Doctor for Another Opinion

The following suggestions apply to anyone who is considering surgery:

- Begin by asking your family doctor to explain your illness and treatment choices. An internist, general practitioner, or family practitioner is likely to give equal attention to surgical and nonsurgical treatments. Consult a surgeon once you and your doctor have decided that surgery is a promising method of treatment.

- When choosing a surgeon, it is useful to find out if he or she has been certified by a surgical board (such as the American Board of Orthopaedic Surgery or the American Board of Colon and Rectal Surgery). Surgeons who are board-certified have had a number of years of training in dealing with certain diseases and have passed exams for their specialty. Don't hesitate to call the doctor's office and ask for this information. Your state or local medical society and the hospital where the surgeon operates should also be able to verify his or her qualifications.

---

[*] Source: *Age Page*, National Institute on Aging, U.S. Department of Health and Human Services, Public Health Service, National Institutes of Health, Gaithersburg, MD 20898; 800-222-2225.

Another way of checking a surgeon's qualifications is to see if he or she is a Fellow of the American College of Surgeons. The letters F.A.C.S. after the surgeon's name indicate that he or she has passed an evaluation of surgical training and skills as well as ethical fitness.

- Try to choose an experienced surgeon who operates on a regular basis (several times a week) and who has treated a problem like yours before.

- If time permits, seek the advice of another qualified doctor. Getting a second opinion is a common medical practice that most doctors encourage. Don't be afraid to tell your surgeon that you want another opinion and would like your medical records forwarded to the second doctor. This can save time, money, and possible discomfort since tests you have already had may not need to be repeated if the second doctor has the results.

Getting a Second Opinion

Medicare and many private health insurance companies will help pay for a second opinion in the same way they pay for other services. Most Medicaid programs also pay for a second opinion.

When getting another opinion, tell the second doctor your symptoms, the type of surgery that has been recommended, and any tests you have already had. Ask the second doctor the same questions you asked the first one about the benefits and the risks of surgery.

If the second doctor agrees that surgery is needed, he or she usually will refer you back to the first doctor for the operation. If the second doctor disagrees with the first, you may feel you have enough information to decide what to do, you may wish to talk again with the first surgeon, or you may wish to see a third doctor. Your family doctor also may be able to help you decide what to do.

Asking the Right Questions

Before undergoing surgery, you will be asked to sign a statement giving consent for the operation. It is important to discuss all of your concerns about your condition and the operation with your surgeon before you sign this statement. In most cases, the surgeon will volunteer a great deal of information, but don't hesitate to ask any questions you still have. The following list might be helpful:

- What is the problem?
- What operation does the doctor plan?
- What are the chances of survival without the operation?
- How will the operation affect your health and lifestyle? Are there any activities you will not be able to do after surgery?
- Are there other forms of treatment that could be tried before surgery?
- What are the risks of surgery?
- How long is the recovery period and what is involved?
- How much will the operation cost? Will your insurance cover all of the costs, including special tests?
- How much experience has the surgeon had with this kind of operation?
- What percent of the operations were successful?
- Who will administer the anesthesia? A doctor or nurse-anesthetist who has experience treating older people?

Above all, be sure an operation is necessary and that the benefits outweigh the risks before you agree to undergo surgery.

For More Information

For information on when and why you should consider getting a second opinion write to the Health Care Financing Administration for the brochure *Thinking of Having Surgery?* The address is Surgery, HHS, Washington, DC 20201.

To find a specialist in your area who can give you a second opinion, ask your doctor or call the Second Surgical Opinion Hotline at 800-638-6833. In Maryland, call 800-492-6603.

For a free series of pamphlets called *When You Need an Operation*, write to the American College of Surgeons, Office of Public Information, 55 East Erie Street, Chicago, IL 60611.

For more information about health and aging, write to the National Institute on Aging Information Center, P.O. Box 8057, Gaithersburg, MD 20898-8057. The NIA distributes a number of free *Age Pages*, including "Hospital Hints," "Finding Good Medical Care," and "Who's Who in Health Care."

Taking Care of Your Teeth and Mouth*

A healthy smile is a bonus at any age. Too often older people — especially those who wear false teeth (or dentures) — feel they no longer need dental checkups. If you haven't learned the basics of oral health care, it is not too late to start. And even if you have, it's a good time to review.

Tooth Decay (Cavities)

Tooth decay is not just a children's disease; it can happen as long as natural teeth are in the mouth. Tooth decay is caused by bacteria that normally live in the mouth. The bacteria cling to teeth and form a sticky, colorless film called dental plaque. The bacteria in plaque live on sugars and produce decay-causing acids that dissolve minerals on tooth surfaces. Tooth decay can also develop on the exposed roots of the teeth if you have gum disease or receding gums (where gums pull away from the teeth, exposing the roots).

Just as with children, fluoride is important for adult teeth. Research has shown that adding fluoride to the water supply is the best and least costly way to prevent tooth decay. In addition, using fluoride toothpastes and mouthrinses can add protection. Daily fluoride rinses can be bought at most drug stores without a prescription. If you have a problem with cavities, your dentist or dental hygienist may give you a fluoride treatment during the office visit. The dentists may prescribe a fluoride gel or mouthrinse for you to use at home.

Gum (Periodontal) Disease

A common cause of tooth loss after age 35 is gum (periodontal) disease. These are infections of the gum and bone that hold the teeth in place. Gum diseases are also caused by dental plaque. The

---

* Source: *Age Page*, National Institute on Aging, U.S. Department of Health and Human Services, Public Health Service, National Institutes of Health, Gaithersburg, MD 20898; 800-222-2225.

bacteria in plaque causes the gums to become inflamed and bleed easily. If left untreated, the disease gets worse as pockets of infection form between the teeth and gums. This causes receding gums and loss of supporting bone. You may lose enough bone to cause your teeth to become loose and fall out.

You can prevent gum disease by removing plaque. Thoroughly brush and floss your teeth each day. Carefully check your mouth for early signs of disease such as red, swollen, or bleeding gums. See your dentist regularly — every 6-12 months — or at once if these signs are present.

Cleaning Your Teeth and Gums

An important part of good oral health is knowing how to brush and floss correctly. Thorough brushing each day removes plaque. Gently brush the teeth on all sides with a soft-bristle brush using fluoride toothpaste. Circular and short back-and-forth strokes work best. Take the time to brush carefully along the gum line. Lightly brushing your tongue also helps to remove plaque and food debris and makes your mouth feel fresh.

In addition to brushing, using dental floss is necessary to keep the gums healthy. Proper flossing is important because it removes plaque and leftover food that a toothbrush cannot reach. Your dentist or dental hygienist can show you the best way to brush and floss your teeth. If brushing or flossing results in bleeding gums, pain, or irritation, see your dentist at once.

An antibacterial mouthrinse, approved for the control of plaque and swollen gums, may be prescribed by your dentist. The mouthrinse is used in addition to carefully daily brushing and flossing.

Some people (with arthritis or other conditions that limit motion) may find it hard to hold a toothbrush. To overcome this, the toothbrush handle can be attached to the hand with a wide elastic band or may be enlarged by attaching it to a sponge, styrofoam ball, or similar object. People with limited shoulder movement may find brushing easier if the handle of the brush is lengthened by attaching a long piece of wood or plastic. Electric toothbrushes are helpful to many.

Other Conditions of the Mouth

Dry mouth (xerostomia) is common in many adults and may make it hard to eat, swallow, taste, and speak. This condition happens when salivary glands fail to work properly as a result of various diseases or medical treatments, such as chemotherapy or radiation therapy to the head and neck area. Dry mouth is also a side effect of more than 400 commonly used medicines, including drugs for high blood pressure, antidepressants, and antihistamines. Dry mouth can affect oral health by adding to tooth decay and infection.

Until recently, dry mouth was regarded as a normal part of aging. We now know that healthy older adults produce as much saliva as younger adults. So if you think you have dry mouth, talk with your dentist or doctor. To relieve the dryness, drink extra water and avoid sugary snacks, beverages with caffeine, tobacco, and alcohol — all of which increase dryness in the mouth.

Cancer therapies, such as radiation to the head and neck or chemotherapy, can cause oral problems, including dry mouth, tooth decay, painful mouth sores, and cracked and peeling lips. Before starting cancer treatment, it is important to see a dentist and take care of any necessary dental work. Your dentist will also show you how to care for your teeth and mouth before, during, and after your cancer treatment to prevent or reduce the oral problems that can occur.

Oral cancer (mouth cancer) most often occurs in people over age 40. The disease frequently goes unnoticed in its early, curable stages. This is true in part because many older people, particularly those wearing dentures, do not visit their dentists often enough and because pain is usually not an early symptom of the disease. People who smoke cigarettes, use other tobacco products, or drink excessive amounts of alcohol are at increased risk for oral cancer.

It is important to spot oral cancer as early as possible, since treatment works best before the disease has spread. If you notice any red or white patches on the gums or tongue, sores that do not heal within two weeks, or if you have difficulty chewing or swallowing, be sure to see a dentist.

A head and neck exam, which should be a part of every dental checkup, will allow your dentist to detect early signs of oral cancer.

Dentures

If you wear false teeth (dentures), keep them clean and free from food that can cause stains, bad breath, and gum irritation. Once a day, brush all surfaces of the dentures with a denture-care product. Remove your dentures from your mouth and place them in water or a denture-cleansing liquid while you sleep. It is also helpful to rinse your mouth with a warm salt-water solution in the morning, after meals, and at bedtime.

Partial dentures should be cared for in the same way as full dentures. Because bacteria tend to collect under the clasps of partial dentures, it is especially important to clean this area.

Dentures will seem awkward at first. When learning to eat with false teeth, select soft nonsticky food, cut food into small pieces, and chew slowly using both sides of the mouth. Dentures may make your mouth less sensitive to hot foods and liquids, and lower your ability to detect harmful objects such as bones. If problems in eating, talking, or simply wearing dentures continue after the first few weeks, see your dentist about making adjustments.

In time, dentures need to be replaced or readjusted because of changes in the tissues of your mouth. Do not try to repair dentures at home since this may damage the dentures which in turn may further hurt your mouth.

Dental Implants

Dental implants are anchors that permanently hold replacement teeth. There are several different types of implants, but the most popular are metal screws surgically placed into the jaw bones. If there isn't enough bone, a separate surgical procedure to add bone may be needed. Because bone heals slowly, treatment with implants can often take longer (4 months to 1 year or more) than bridges or dentures. If you are considering dental implants, it is important to select an experienced dentist with whom you can discuss your concerns frankly beforehand to be certain the procedure is right for you.

Professional Care

In addition to practicing good oral hygiene, it is important to have regular checkups by the dentist whether you have natural teeth or dentures. It is also important to follow through with any special treatments that are necessary to ensure good oral health. For instance, if you have sensitive teeth caused by receding gums, your dentist may suggest using a special toothpaste for a few months. Teeth are meant to last a lifetime. By taking good care of your teeth and gums, you can protect them for years to come.

Additional Dental Health Information

More information about general dental care is available from:

National Institute of Dental Research (NIDR), Building 31, Room 2C35, 31 Center Dr., MSC 2290, Bethesda, MD 20892-2290; 301-496-4261.
NIDR publishes information on oral research and general dental care. Some publications available are:
Fever Blisters and Canker Sores
Fluoride to Protect the Teeth of Adults
Rx for Sound Teeth
What You Need to Know About Periodontal (Gum) Disease

National Oral Health Information Clearinghouse, 1 NOHIC Way, Bethesda, MD 20892-3500; 301-402-7364.
NIDR also offers publications on oral health for special care patients through the National Oral Health Information Clearinghouse. Special care patients are people whose medical conditions or treatments affect oral health. Publications available include:
Dry Mouth (Xerostomia)
Chemotherapy and Oral Health
Periodontal Disease and Diabetes — A Guide
    for Patients
Radiation Therapy and Oral Health
TMD (Temporomandibular Disorders)
What You Need to Know About Oral Cancer

American Dental Association (ADA), 211 East Chicago Avenue, Chicago, IL 60611; 800-621-8099.
ADA distributes educational materials on dental health and sponsors the National Senior Smile Week.

National Agricultural Library, Food and Nutrition Information Center, Room 304, 10301 Baltimore Blvd., Beltsville, MD 20705-2351; 301-504-5719.
The Food and Nutrition Center offers the bibliography *Nutri-Topics Series: Nutrition and Dental Health.* This bibliography lists information available to consumers.

National Institute on Aging (NIA) Information Center, P.O. Box 8057, Gaithersburg, MD 20898-8057; 800-222-2225, 800-222-4225 (TTY).
NIA publishes fact sheets on various health-related topics of interest to older people and their families. For a complete listing of publications, call or write to the above address.

Safe Use of Tranquilizers[*]

Everyone is worried, tense, or nervous at one time or another. Most people have concerns that can cause them to feel uneasy or anxious, and older people are no exception. Sometimes these feelings of anxiety are accompanied by physical symptoms such as a tightness in the chest, trembling, choking, or rapid heart beat. Since a wide range of problems can produce these feelings, it is very important to have a thorough checkup if your symptoms continue.

There are many ways such symptoms can be managed. Sometimes physical activities or support from family or friends can make a difference. Sometimes professional assistance (individual, group, or family counseling) can be considered. And, sometimes, medications are helpful. "Minor" tranquilizers, or anti-anxiety drugs, recommended by a therapist and prescribed by a doctor, might be used at these times.

Ideally, tranquilizers are used in combination with counseling. The goal is usually to limit the dosage and length of an individual's tranquilizer use. This is especially important for older people because age-related changes often cause the body to use medications differently in later life. As a result, older people should pay close attention to side effects and safety considerations when taking tranquilizers.

Effects of Tranquilizers

Tranquilizers are central nervous system (CNS) depressants. That is, they slow down the nervous system and can cause drowsiness. Some individuals, particularly older people, may become sleepy, dizzy, unsteady on their feet, and confused when taking these drugs. If the medication is taken at night, these side effects may

---

[*] Source: *Age Page*, National Institute on Aging, U.S. Department of Health and Human Services, Public Health Service, National Institutes of Health, Gaithersburg, MD 20898; 800-222-2225.

occur the next day. As a result, when taking tranquilizers you should not drive, operate machinery, or do jobs that require you to be alert.

The effects of tranquilizers are greatly increased if they are taken at the same time as other CNS depressants such as antihistamines (medicines for allergies or colds), sleeping pills, prescription pain relievers, or muscle relaxants. It is also important to avoid alcohol when taking tranquilizers because it too is a powerful CNS depressant. Mixing large amounts of drugs and alcohol can cause unconsciousness and even death.

Some drugs, such as the ulcer drug cimetidine, may affect the body's use of tranquilizers. A doctor or pharmacist can tell you which drugs are safe to take with tranquilizers. Always tell the doctor what prescription and over-the-counter medications you are taking whenever he or she is considering a new medication for you.

Once you begin taking a tranquilizer, do not stop taking it suddenly. This can cause withdrawal symptoms including convulsions, muscle cramps, sweating, and vomiting. When it is time to stop your medication, the doctor will probably reduce the dose slowly to prevent these symptoms.

Sometimes people taking tranquilizers are afraid they will not be able to handle their problems without the medication. They may insist that their doctors prescribe tranquilizers for a longer period of time than is recommended. Since people who take tranquilizers for a long period of time may become dependent on them, it is very important to take this medication only under the careful supervision of a doctor.

Taking Tranquilizers Safely

When taking a tranquilizer you should observe the following safety tips:

- Make sure the doctor knows about all your current medications (prescription and over-the-counter) before you begin taking tranquilizers.
- Ask the doctor to explain any possible side effects of the tranquilizer he or she has prescribed.
- Follow the doctor's instructions exactly.
- Take only the amount of tranquilizer the doctor specifies — no more, no less.
- Take the tranquilizer only as often as prescribed — not more or less frequently.
- If you forget one dose of medicine, do not double the next dose.
- Let the doctor know if you feel unusually chilly while taking tranquilizers. Sometimes they can cause a change in body temperature.
- Try to avoid caffeine (found in coffee, tea, cola drinks, and chocolate) while taking tranquilizers — it can counteract the effects of the tranquilizer.
- If you think you may have taken too many tranquilizers, get emergency help right away.

For More Information

Tranquilizers can help many people manage the symptoms of anxiety. However, for these medicines to work safely and effectively, they must be taken as directed. Learning more about the medications the doctor prescribes will increase your health, safety, and well-being. For more information on the safe use of medications contact the following organizations:

The Elder Health Program provides patient information and service programs in geriatrics and gerontology. Contact University of Maryland, School of Pharmacy, 20 North Pine Street, Baltimore, MD 21201; 301-328-3243.

The AARP Pharmacy Service provides prescription drug information for older persons. Contact AARP Pharmacy Service, 1 Prince Street, Alexandria, VA 22314; 703-684-0244.

The Food and Drug Administration provides information about drugs and their side effects. Contact the Center for Drug Evaluation and Research, Consumer and Professional Affairs (HFD-365), 5600 Fishers Lane, Rockville, MD 20857; 301-295-8012.

The National Institute on Aging provides information about health and aging. Contact the Information Office, Federal Building, Room 6C12, Bethesda, MD 20892; 301-496-1752.

Stomach and Duodenal Ulcers*

What Is an Ulcer?

During normal digestion, food moves from the mouth down the esophagus into the stomach. The stomach produces hydrochloric acid and an enzyme called pepsin to digest the food. From the stomach, food passes into the upper part of the small intestine, called the duodenum, where digestion and nutrient absorption continue.

An ulcer is a sore or lesion that forms in the lining of the stomach or duodenum where acid and pepsin are present. Ulcers in the stomach are galled gastric or stomach ulcers. Those in the duodenum are called duodenal ulcers. In general, ulcers in the stomach and duodenum are referred to as peptic ulcers. Ulcers rarely occur in the esophagus or in the first portion of the duodenum, the duodenal bulb.

Who Has Ulcers?

About 20 million Americans develop at least one ulcer during their lifetime. Each year:

- Ulcers affect about 4 million people.
- More than 40,000 people have surgery because of persistent symptoms or problems from ulcers.
- About 6,000 people die of ulcer-related complications.

Ulcers can develop at any age, but they are rare among teenagers and even more uncommon in children. Duodenal ulcers occur for the first time usually between the ages of 30 and 50. Stomach ulcers are more likely to develop in people over age 60. Duodenal ulcers occur more frequently in men than women; stomach ulcers develop more often in women than men.

---

* Source: National Institute of Diabetes and Digestive and Kidney Diseases, U.S. Department of Health and Human Services, Public Health Service, National Institutes of Health, 2 Information Way, Bethesda, MD 20892; 301-654-3810.

What Causes Ulcers?

For almost a century, doctors believed lifestyle factors such as stress and diet caused ulcers. Later, researchers discovered that an imbalance between digestive fluids (hydrochloric acid and pepsin) and the stomach's ability to defend itself against these powerful substances resulted in ulcers.

Today, research shows that most ulcers develop as a result of infection with bacteria called Helicobacter pylori (H. pylori). While all three of these factors — lifestyle, acid and pepsin, and H. pylori — play a role in ulcer development, H pylori is now considered the primary cause.

Lifestyle
While scientific evidence refutes the old belief that stress and diet cause ulcers, several lifestyle factors continue to be suspected of playing a role. These factors include cigarettes, foods and beverages containing caffeine, alcohol, and physical stress.

Smoking
Studies show that cigarette smoking increases one's chances of getting an ulcer. Smoking slows the healing of existing ulcers and also contributes to ulcer recurrence.

Caffeine
Coffee, tea, colas, and foods that contain caffeine seem to stimulate acid secretion in the stomach, aggravating the pain of an existing ulcer. However, the amount of acid secretion that occurs after drinking decaffeinated coffee is the same as that produced after drinking regular coffee. Thus, the stimulation of stomach acid cannot be attributed solely to caffeine.

Alcohol
Research has not found a link between alcohol consumption and peptic ulcers. However, ulcers are more common in people who have cirrhosis of the liver, a disease often linked to heavy alcohol consumption.

Stress

Although emotional stress is no longer thought to be a cause of ulcers, people with ulcers often report that emotional stress increases ulcer pain. Physical stress, however, increases the risk of developing ulcers particularly in the stomach. For example, people with injuries such as severe burns and people undergoing major surgery often require rigorous treatment to prevent ulcers and ulcer complications.

Acid and pepsin

Researchers believe that the stomach's inability to defend itself against the powerful digestive fluids, acid and pepsin, contributes to ulcer formation. The stomach defends itself from these fluids in several ways. One way is by producing mucus, a lubricant-like coating that shields stomach tissues. Another way is by producing a chemical called bicarbonate. This chemical neutralizes and breaks down digestive fluids into substances less harmful to stomach tissue. Finally, blood circulation to the stomach lining, cell renewal, and cell repair also help protect the stomach.

Nonsteroidal anti-inflammatory drugs (NSAIDS) make the stomach vulnerable to the harmful effects of acid and pepsin. NSAIDs such as aspirin, ibuprofen, and naproxen sodium are present in many non-prescription medications used to treat fever, headaches, and minor aches and pains. These, as well as prescription NSAIDs used to treat a variety of arthritic conditions, interfere with the stomach's ability to produce mucus and bicarbonate and affect blood flow to the stomach and cell repair. They can all cause the stomach's defense mechanisms to fail, resulting in an increased chance of developing stomach ulcers. In most cases, these ulcers disappear once the person stops taking NSAIDS.

Helicobacter pylori

H. pylori is a spiral-shaped bacterium found in the stomach. Research shows that the bacteria (along with acid secretion) damage stomach and duodenal tissue, causing inflammation and ulcers. Scientists believe this damage occurs because of H. pylori's shape and characteristics.

H. pylori survives in the stomach because it produces the enzyme urease. Urease generates substances that neutralize the stomach's acid, enabling the bacteria to survive. Because of their shape and the way they move, the bacteria can penetrate the stomach's protective mucous lining. Here, they can produce substances that weaken the stomach's protective mucus and make the stomach cells more susceptible to the damaging effects of acid and pepsin.

The bacteria can also attach to stomach cells further weakening the stomach's defensive mechanisms and producing local inflammation. For reasons not completely

The History of Helicobacter pylori

In 1982, Australian researchers Barry Marshall and Robin Warren discovered spiral-shaped bacteria in the stomach, later named Helicobacter pylori (H. pylori). After closely studying H. pylori's effect on the stomach, they proposed that the bacteria were the underlying cause of gastritis and peptic ulcers.

Marshall and Warren came to this conclusion because in their studies all patients with duodenal ulcers and 80 percent of patients with stomach ulcers had the bacteria. The 20 percent of patients with stomach ulcers who did not have H. pylon were those who had taken NSAIDs such as aspirin and ibuprofen, which are a common cause of stomach ulcers.

Although their findings seem conclusive, Marshall and Warren's theory was hotly debated and remained in dispute. The debate continued even after Marshall and a colleague performed an experiment in which they infected themselves with H. pylon and developed gastritis.

Evidence linking H. pylori to ulcers mounted over the next 10 years as numerous studies from around the world confirmed its presence in most people with ulcers. Moreover, researchers from the United States and Europe proved that using antibiotics to eliminate H. pylon healed ulcers and prevented recurrence in about 90 percent of cases.

To further investigate these findings, the National Institutes of Health (NIH) established a panel to closely review the link between H. pylori and peptic ulcer disease. At the February 1994 Consensus Development Conference, the panel concluded that H. pylori plays a significant role in the development of ulcers and that antibiotics with other medicines can cure peptic ulcer disease.

understood, H pylori can also stimulate the stomach to produce more acid.

Excess stomach acid and other irritating factors can cause inflammation of the upper end of the duodenum, the duodenal bulb. In some people, over long periods of time, this inflammation results in production of stomach-like cells called duodenal gastric metaplasia. H. pylori then attacks these cells causing further tissue damage and inflammation, which may result in ulcer.

Within weeks of infection with H pylori, most people develop gastritis — an inflammation of the stomach lining. However, most people will never have symptoms or problems related to the infection. Scientists do not yet know what is different in those people who develop H pylori-related symptoms or ulcers. Perhaps, hereditary or environmental factors yet to be discovered cause some individuals to develop problems. Alternatively, symptoms and ulcers may result from infection with more virulent strains of bacteria. These unanswered questions are the subject of intensive scientific research.

Studies show that H pylori infection in the United States varies with age, ethnic group, and socioeconomic class. The bacteria are more common in older adults, African Americans, Hispanics, and lower socio-economic groups. The organism appears to spread through the fecal-oral route (when infected stool comes into contact with hands, food, or water). Most individuals seem to be infected during childhood, and their infection lasts a lifetime.

What Are the Symptoms of Ulcers?

The most common ulcer symptom is a gnawing or burning pain in the abdomen between the breastbone and the naval. The pain often occurs between meals and in the early hours of the morning. It may last from a few minutes to a few hours and may be relieved by eating or by taking antacids.

Less common ulcer symptoms include nausea, vomiting, and loss of appetite and weight. Bleeding from ulcers may occur in the stomach and duodenum. Sometimes people are unaware that they have a bleeding ulcer, because blood loss is slow and blood may not be obvious in the stool. These people may feel tired and weak. If the bleeding is heavy, blood will appear in vomit or stool. Stool containing blood appears tarry or black.

How Are Ulcers Diagnosed?

The NIH Consensus Panel emphasized the importance of adequately diagnosing ulcer disease and H pylori before starting treatment. If the person has an NSAID-induced ulcer, treatment is quite different from the treatment for a person with an H pylori-related ulcer. Also, a person's pain may be the result of nonulcer dyspepsia (persistent pain or discomfort in the upper abdomen including burning, nausea, and bloating), and not at all related to ulcer disease. Currently, doctors have a number of options available for diagnosing ulcers, such as performing endoscopic and x-ray examinations, and for testing for H. pylori.

Locating and monitoring ulcers

Doctors may perform an upper GI series to diagnose ulcers. An upper GI series involves taking an x-ray of the esophagus, stomach, and duodenum to locate an ulcer. To make the ulcer visible on the x-ray image, the patient swallows a chalky liquid called barium. An alternative diagnostic test is called an endoscopy. During this test, the patient is lightly sedated and the doctor inserts a small flexible instrument with a camera on the end through the mouth into the esophagus, stomach, and duodenum. With this procedure, the entire upper GI tract can be viewed. Ulcers or other conditions can be diagnosed and photographed, and tissue can be taken for biopsy, if necessary. Once an ulcer is diagnosed and treatment begins, the doctor will usually monitor clinical progress. In the case of a stomach ulcer, the doctor may wish to document healing with repeat x-rays or endoscopy. Continued monitoring of a stomach ulcer is important because of the small chance that the ulcer may be cancerous.

Testing for H. pylori

Confirming the presence of H. pylori is important once the doctor has diagnosed an ulcer because elimination of the bacteria is likely to cure ulcer disease. Blood, breath, and stomach tissue tests may be performed to detect the presence of H pylori. While some of the tests for H. pylori are not approved by the U.S. Food and Drug Administration (FDA), research shows these tests are highly accurate in detecting the bacteria. However, blood tests on occasion give false positive results, and the other tests may give false negative results in people who have recently taken antibiotics, omeprazole (Prilosec), or bismuth (Pepto-Bismol).

Blood tests

Blood tests such as the enzyme-linked immunosorbent assay (ELISA) and quick office-based tests identify and measure H pylori antibodies. The body produces antibodies against H pylori in an attempt to fight the bacteria. The advantages of blood tests are their low cost and availability to doctors. The disadvantage is the possibility of false positive results in patients previously treated for ulcers since the levels of H pylori antibodies fall slowly. Several blood tests have FDA approval.

Breath tests

Breath tests measure carbon dioxide in exhaled breath. Patients are given a substance called urea with carbon to drink. Bacteria break down this urea and the carbon is absorbed into the blood stream and lungs and exhaled in the breath. By collecting the breath, doctors can measure this carbon and determine whether H. pylori is present or absent. Urea breath tests are at least 90 percent accurate for diagnosing the bacteria and are particularly suitable to follow-up treatment to see if bacteria have been eradicated. These tests are awaiting FDA approval.

Tissue tests

If the doctor performs an endoscopy to diagnose an ulcer, tissue samples of the stomach can be obtained. The doctor may then perform one of several tests on the tissue. A rapid urease test detects the bacteria's enzyme urease. Histology involves visualizing the bacteria under the microscope. Culture involves specially processing the tissue and watching it for growth of H. pylori organisms.

How Are Ulcers Treated?

Lifestyle changes
In the past, doctors advised people with ulcers to avoid spicy, fatty, or acidic foods. However, a bland diet is now known to be ineffective for treating or avoiding ulcers. No particular diet is helpful for most ulcer patients. People who find that certain foods cause irritation should discuss this problem with their doctor. Smoking has been shown to delay ulcer healing and has been linked to ulcer recurrence; therefore, persons with ulcers should not smoke.

Medicines
Doctors treat stomach and duodenal ulcers with several types of medicines including H_2-blockers, acid pump inhibitors, and mucosal protective agents. When treating H. pylori, these medications are used in combination with antibiotics.

H_2 -blockers
Currently, most doctors treat ulcers with acid-suppressing drugs known as H_2-blockers. These drugs reduce the amount of acid the stomach produces by blocking histamine, a powerful stimulant of acid secretion.

H_2-blockers reduce pain significantly after several weeks. For the first few days of treatment, doctors often recommend taking an antacid to relieve pain.

Initially, treatment with H_2-blockers lasts 6 to 8 weeks. However, because ulcers recur in 50 to 80 percent of cases, many people must continue maintenance therapy for years. This may no longer be the case if H. pylori infection is treated. Most ulcers do not recur following successful eradication. Nizatidine (Axid) is approved for treatment of duodenal ulcers but is not yet approved for treatment of stomach ulcers. H_2-blockers that are approved to treat both stomach and duodenal ulcers are:

- Cimetidine (Tagamet)
- Ranitidine (Zantac)
- Famotidine (Pepcid).

Acid pump inhibitors
Like H_2-blockers, acid pump inhibitors modify the stomach's production of acid. However, acid pump inhibitors more completely block stomach acid production by stopping the stomach's acid pump — the final step of acid secretion. The FDA has approved use of omeprazolt for short-term treatment of ulcer disease. Similar drugs, including lansoprazole, are currently being studied.

Mucosal protective medications
Mucosal protective medications protect the stomach's mucous lining from acid. Unlike H_2-blockers and acid pump inhibitors, protective agents do not inhibit the release of acid. These medications shield the stomach's mucous lining from the damage of acid. Two commonly prescribed protective agents are:

- *Sucralfate (Carafate)*. This medication adheres to the ulcer, providing a protective barrier that allows the ulcer to heal and inhibits further damage by stomach acid. Sucralfate is approved for short-term treatment of duodenal ulcers and for maintenance treatment.

- *Misoprostol (Cytotec)*. This synthetic prostaglandin, a substance naturally produced by the body, protects the stomach lining by increasing mucus and bicarbonate production and by enhancing blood flow to the stomach. It is approved only for the prevention of NSAID-induced ulcers.

Two common non-prescription protective medications are:

- *Antacids.* Antacids can offer temporary relief from ulcer pain by neutralizing stomach acid. They may also have a mucosal protective role. Many brands of antacids are available without prescription.

- *Bismuth Subsalicylate.* Bismuth subsalicylate has both a protective effect and an antibacterial effect against H. pylori.

Antibiotics

The discovery of the link between ulcers and H. pylori has resulted in a new treatment option. Now, in addition to treatment aimed at decreasing the production of stomach acid, doctors may prescribe antibiotics for patients with H. pylori. This treatment is a dramatic medical advance because eliminating H pylori means the ulcer may now heal and most likely will not come back.

The most effective therapy, according to the NIH Panel, is a two-week, triple therapy. This regimen eradicates the bacteria and reduces the risk of ulcer recurrence in 90 percent of people with duodenal ulcers. People with stomach ulcers that are not associated with NSAIDs also benefit from bacterial eradication. While triple therapy is effective, it is sometimes difficult to follow because the patient must take three different medications four times each day for two weeks.

Typical 2-week, triple therapy

- Metronidazole 4 times a day
- Tetracycline (or amoxicillin) 4 times a day
- Bismuth subsalicylate 4 times a day

Typical 2-week, dual therapy

- Amoxicillin 2 to 4 times a day, or clarithromycin 3 times a day
- Omeprazole 2 times a day

In addition, the treatment commonly causes side effects such as yeast infection in women, stomach upset, nausea, vomiting, bad taste, loose or dark bowel movements, and dizziness. The two-week, triple therapy combines two antibiotics, tetracycline (e.g., Achromycin or Sumycin) and metronidazole (e.g., Flagyl) with bismuth subsalicylate (Pepto-Bismol). Some doctors may add an acid-suppressing drug to relieve ulcer pain and promote ulcer healing. In some cases, doctors may substitute amoxicillin (e.g., Amoxil or Trimox) for tetracycline or if they expect bacterial resistance to metronidazole, other antibiotics such as clarithromycin (Biaxin).

As an alternative to triple therapy, several two-week, dual therapies are about 80 percent effective. Dual therapy is simpler for patients to follow and causes fewer side effects. A dual therapy might include an antibiotic, such as amoxicillin or clarithromycin, with omeprazole, a drug that stops the production of acid.

Again, an accurate diagnosis is important. Accurate diagnosis and appropriate treatment prevent people without ulcers from needless exposure to the side effects of antibiotics and should lessen the risk of bacteria developing resistance to antibiotics.

Although all of the above antibiotics are sold in the United States, the FDA has not yet approved the use of antibiotics for treatment of H. pylori or ulcers. Doctors may choose to prescribe antibiotics to their ulcer patients as "off label" prescriptions as they do for many conditions.

When Is Surgery Needed?

In most cases, anti-ulcer medicines heal ulcers quickly and effectively. Eradication of H. pylori prevents most ulcers from recurring. However, people who do not respond to medication or who develop complications may require surgery. While surgery is usually successful in healing ulcers and preventing their recurrence and future complications, problems can sometimes result.

At present, standard open surgery is performed to treat ulcers. In the future, surgeons may use laparoscopic methods. A laparoscope is a long tube-like instrument with a camera that allows the surgeon to operate through small incisions while watching a video monitor. The common types of surgery for ulcers — vagotomy, pyloroplasty, and antrectomy — are described below:

Vagotomy
A vagotomy involves cutting the vagus nerve, a nerve that transmits messages from the brain to the stomach. Interrupting the messages sent through the vagus nerve reduces acid secretion. However, the surgery may also interfere with stomach emptying. The newest variation of the surgery involves cutting only parts of the nerve that control the acid-secreting cells of the stomach, thereby avoiding the parts that influence stomach emptying.

Antrectomy
Another surgical procedure is the antrectomy. This operation removes the lower part of the stomach (antrum), which produces a hormone that stimulates the stomach to secrete digestive juices. Sometimes a surgeon may also remove an adjacent part of the stomach that secretes pepsin and acid. A vagotomy is usually done in conjunction with an antrectomy.

Pyloroplasty
Pyloroplasty is another surgical procedure that may be performed along with a vagotomy. Pyloroplasty enlarges the opening into the duodenum and small intestine (pylorus), enabling contents to pass more freely from the stomach.

What Are the Complications of Ulcers?

People with ulcers may experience serious complications if they do not get treatment. The most common problems include bleeding, perforation of the organ walls, and narrowing and obstruction of digestive tract passages.

Bleeding

As an ulcer eats into the muscles of the stomach or duodenal wall, blood vessels may also be damaged, which causes bleeding. If the affected blood vessels are small, the blood may slowly seep into the digestive tract. Over a long period of time, a person may become anemic and feel weak, dizzy, or tired.

If a damaged blood vessel is large, bleeding is dangerous and requires prompt medical attention. Symptoms include feeling weak and dizzy when standing, vomiting blood, or fainting. The stool may become a tarry black color from the blood.

Most bleeding ulcers can be treated endoscopically — the ulcer is located and the blood vessel is cauterized with a heating device or injected with material to stop bleeding. If endoscopic treatment is unsuccessful, surgery may be required.

Perforation

Sometimes an ulcer eats a hole in the wall of the stomach or duodenum. Bacteria and partially digested food can spill through the opening into the sterile abdominal cavity (peritoneum). This causes peritonitis, an inflammation of the abdominal cavity and wall. A perforated ulcer that can cause sudden, sharp, severe pain usually requires immediate hospitalization and surgery.

Narrowing and obstruction

Ulcers located at the end of the stomach where the duodenum is attached, can cause swelling and scarring, which can narrow or close the intestinal opening. This obstruction can prevent food from leaving the stomach and entering the small intestine. As a result, a person may vomit the contents of the stomach. Endoscopic balloon dilation, a procedure that uses a balloon to force open a narrow passage, may be performed. If the dilation does not relieve the problem, then surgery may be necessary.

Points to Remember

- An ulcer is a sore or lesion that forms in the lining of the stomach or duodenum where the digestive fluids acid and pepsin are present.

- Recent research shows that most ulcers develop as a result of infection with bacteria called Helicobacter pylori (H. pylori). The bacteria produce substances that weaken the stomach's protective mucus and make the stomach more susceptible to damaging effects of acid and pepsin. H. pylori can also cause the stomach to produce more acid. Although acid and pepsin and lifestyle factors such as stress and smoking cigarettes play a role in ulcer formation, H. pylori is now considered the primary cause.

- Nonsteroidal anti-inflammatory drugs such as aspirin make the stomach vulnerable to the harmful effects of acid and pepsin, leading to an increased chance of stomach ulcers.

- Ulcers do not always cause symptoms. When they do, the most common symptom is a gnawing or burning pain in the abdomen between the breastbone and naval. Some people have nausea, vomiting, and loss of appetite and weight.

- Bleeding from an ulcer may occur in the stomach and duodenum. Symptoms may include weakness and stool that appears tarry or black. However, sometimes people are not aware they have a bleeding ulcer because blood may not be obvious in the stool.

- Ulcers are diagnosed with x-ray or endoscopy. The presence of H pylori may be diagnosed with a blood test, breath test, or tissue test. Once an ulcer is diagnosed and treatment begins, the doctor will usually monitor progress.

- Doctors treat ulcers with several types of medicines aimed at reducing acid production, including H_2-blockers, acid pump inhibitors, and mucosal protective drugs. When treating H. pylori, these medications are used in combination with antibiotics.

- According to an NIH panel, the most effective treatment for H. pylori is a two-week, triple therapy of metronidazole, tetracycline or amoxicillin, and bismuth subsalicylate.

- Surgery may be necessary if an ulcer recurs or fails to heal or if complications such as bleeding, perforation, or obstruction develop.

Conclusion

Although ulcers may cause discomfort, rarely are they life threatening. With an understanding of the causes and proper treatment, most people find relief. Eradication of H. pylori infection is a major medical advance that can permanently cure most peptic ulcer disease.

Additional Reading

DeCross AJ, Peura DA. Role of H. Pylori in peptic ulcer disease. *Contemporary Gastroenterology*, 1992; 5(4): 18-28.

Fedotin MS. Helicobacter pylori and peptic ulcer disease: Reexamining the therapeutic approach. *Postgraduate Medicine*, 1993; 94(3): 38-45.

Gilbert G, Chan CH, Thomas E. Peptic ulcer disease: How to treat it now. *Postgraduate Medicine*, 1991; 89(4): 91-98.

Larson DE, Editor-in-Chief. *Mayo Clinic Family Health Book*. New York: William Morrow and Company, Inc., 1990. General medical guide with sections on stomach problems and ulcers.

National Digestive Diseases Information Clearinghouse
2 Information Way
Bethesda, MD 20892-3570
(301) 654-3810
The National Digestive Diseases Information Clearinghouse (NDDIC) is a service of the National Institute of Diabetes and Digestive and Kidney Diseases, part of the National Institutes of Health, under the U.S. Public Health Service. The clearinghouse, authorized by Congress in 1980, provides information about digestive diseases and health to people with digestive diseases and their families, health care professionals, and the public. The NDDIC answers inquiries; develops, reviews, and distributes publications; and works closely with professional and patient organizations and government agencies to coordinate resources about digestive diseases. Publications produced by the clearinghouse are reviewed carefully for scientific accuracy, content, and readability. Publications produced by other sources are also reviewed for scientific accuracy and are used, along with clearinghouse publications, to answer requests.

Urinary Incontinence[*]

Loss of urine control, or urinary incontinence (in-CON-ti-nents), occurs in people of all ages, but is particularly common in older people. At least 1 in 10 persons age 65 or older suffers from incontinence. This condition can range from the discomfort of slight losses of urine to the disability and shame of severe, frequent wetting.

Persons with incontinence often withdraw from social life and try to hide the problem from their family, friends, and even their doctor. The relatives of a person with incontinence often do not know about the choices of treatment and may believe that nursing home care is the only option.

These reactions are unfortunate because in many cases incontinence can be treated and controlled, if not cured. Incontinence is not an inevitable result of aging. It is caused by specific changes in body function that often result from diseases or use of medications. If untreated, incontinence can increase the chance of skin irritation and might raise the risk of developing bedsores.

Persons who have problems controlling urine should seek prompt medical care to determine the cause and lessen the chance of other problems. Even when incontinence cannot be completely cured, modern products and ways of managing the condition can ease the discomfort and inconvenience it causes.

Incontinence may be brought on by an illness accompanied by fatigue, confusion, or hospital admission. Incontinence is sometimes the first and only symptom of a urinary tract infection. Curing the illness usually will relieve or clear up the incontinence.

---

[*] Source: *Age Page*, National Institute on Aging, U.S. Department of Health and Human Services, Public Health Service, National Institutes of Health, Gaithersburg, MD 20898; 800-222-2225.

Types of Incontinence

The most common forms of urinary incontinence are listed below.

- **Stress incontinence** is the leakage of urine during exercise, coughing, sneezing, laughing, lifting heavy objects, or other body movements that put pressure on the bladder. It occurs most often in women.

- **Urge incontinence** is the inability to hold urine long enough to reach a toilet. It is often found in people who have conditions such as stroke, dementia, Parkinson's disease, and multiple sclerosis, but it can occur in otherwise healthy persons.

- **Overflow incontinence** is the leakage of small amounts of urine from a bladder that is always full. In older men, this type of incontinence occurs when an enlarged prostate blocks the flow of urine from the bladder. Another cause is loss of normal bladder contractions in some people with diabetes.

- **Functional incontinence** occurs in many older people who have normal urine control but who have difficulty reaching a toilet in time because of arthritis or other crippling disorders.

Diagnosis

The first and most important step in treating incontinence is to see a doctor for a complete medical examination. This generally involves giving a detailed history of health and related problems, as well as undergoing a physical examination that focuses on the urinary and nervous systems and reproductive organs. The doctor will probably also want to check urine samples. In many cases, patients will then be referred to a urologist, a doctor who specializes in diseases of the urinary tract.

Treatment

Treatment of urinary incontinence should be tailored to each patient's needs. As a general rule, the last dangerous procedures should be tried first. The many options include:

- Certain behavioral techniques — including scheduled voiding, pelvic muscle exercises, and biofeedback — have been shown in recent studies to be very effective in reducing episodes of stress and urge incontinence.

- A number of medications can be used to treat incontinence. However, these drugs may cause side effects such as a dry mouth, eye problems, and buildup of urine; therefore, they must be used carefully under a doctor's supervision.

- Several types of surgery can improve or even cure incontinence that is related to a structural problem such as an abnormally positioned bladder or blockage due to an enlarged prostate. Artificial devices that replace or aid the muscles controlling urine flow have been tried in persons with incontinence. Many of these devices require surgical implantation.

Management

Sometimes incontinence cannot be cured, but it can be managed in several ways.

- Specially designed absorbent underclothing is available. Many of these garments are no more bulky than normal underwear, can be worn easily under everyday clothing, and free a person from the discomfort and embarrassment of incontinence.

- Incontinence may be managed by inserting a flexible tube known as a catheter into the urethra and collecting the urine into a container. However, long-term catheterization —

although sometimes necessary — creates many problems, including urinary infections. In men, an alternative to the indwelling catheter is an external collecting device. This is fitted over the penis and connected to a drainage bag.

It is important to remember that incontinence can be treated and often cured. Even incurable problems can be managed to reduce complications, anxiety, and stress. When treatment is not completely successful, management plans can help many persons with incontinence.

Resources

For more information about incontinence, contact the following: Help for Incontinent People, P.O. Box 544A, Union, SC 29379; the Simon Foundation for Continence, P.O. Box 835, Wilmette, IL 60091; and the National Kidney and Urologic Diseases Information Clearinghouse, P.O. Box NKUDIC, Bethesda, MD 20892.

For more information about health and aging, write to the National Institute on Aging Information Center, P.O. Box 8057, Gaithersburg, MD 20898-8057. The NIA distributes free *Age Pages* on a number of topics.

Who? What? Where? Resources for Women's Health and Aging[*]

It's true and every woman knows it. Some biological changes do occur with age. It gets harder to keep weight off; skin wrinkles; hair changes color. There are also some changes that are not visible. Bones may weaken and veins may stiffen.

It is not true that these changes result in women becoming frail, lonely, miserable, and unproductive. How successfully a woman ages depends to some degree on how she has lived. Diet, exercise, and lifestyle all play an important part in the process.

One goal of the National Institute on Aging (NIA) is to learn more about the health needs of older women and to communicate these research findings to the public. According to the U.S. Bureau of the Census, in 1990 there were over 18 million women over the age of 65; by 2030 that number will grow to over 37 million. Clearly, NIA has a special interest in studies of older women.

Who? What? Where? is a compilation of resources to help women of all ages plan for and cope with aging. It can help younger women establish the foundations for a healthy lifestyle; prepare middle age women for the changes their bodies are going through; and provide older women with information to improve the quality of their lives. NIA is one of the National Institutes of Health, the principal agency for biomedical research within the U.S. Department of Health and Human Services.

This chapter offers an overview of the major health and lifestyle issues affecting women today. Readers should contact the specific organizations mentioned for more details on each of the topics.

---

[*] Source: National Institute on Aging, U.S. Department of Health and Human Services, Public Health Service, National Institutes of Health, Gaithersburg, MD 20898; 800-222-2225.

Age Changes and Health Promotion

Accident Prevention

Older women need to be especially careful to avoid accidental mishaps. Accidents become more frequent and accidental injuries can be more serious in later life. Falling and automobile accidents are the most common causes of fatal injury in older people.

Several factors make older people prone to accidents: poorer eyesight and hearing can decrease awareness of hazards; arthritis, neurological diseases, and impaired coordination and balance can cause unsteadiness; illness or use of some medicines or alcohol can cause drowsiness; or preoccupation with personal problems can distract individuals from potential hazards. Many accidents can be prevented by staying in good mental and physical health and by improving safety habits.

Each year, falling causes serious fractures in about 210,000 older persons, 20 percent of whom die within the first year after their injury. In addition, a fall can result in months of pain and confinement or in the fear of falling again; for some older persons, it leads to institutionalization. Older women with osteoporosis have an increased chance of a fracture when they fall. (See section on osteoporosis.)

Age-related changes such as impaired vision and slower reaction time can cause automobile accidents. Many of these accidents could be prevented, however, by avoiding driving at night, by limiting the number of hours on the road, and by using extra caution when driving during rush hours and in winter weather.

It's also especially important for older people to avoid prolonged exposure to extreme heat or cold. Accidental hypothermia (abnormally low body temperature) can be avoided by wearing several layers of clothing and keeping the head covered. When older people live alone, they should arrange to have someone check on them daily when outside temperatures are very low. Overexposure to heat or to the sun can result in hyperthermia (heat stroke), a serious and potentially fatal condition. Older people, especially those with chronic diseases, can avoid hyperthermia by remaining in shady areas outside or in cool rooms during hot weather.

Tips for Preventing Accidental Falls

Taking measures to prevent accidents becomes especially important later in life. You can begin by maintaining good physical and mental health and by developing good safety habits. The likelihood of falling can be further reduced by taking precautionary measures, for example:

- Avoid becoming dizzy when standing up - rise slowly from a sitting or lying position.

- Provide plenty of lighting throughout your home, especially next to bedside tables, in halls, and on stairways.

- Install and use hand rails along both sides of a stairway.
- Mark the first and last steps with a bright, contrasting tape.

- Cover slippery surfaces with carpets or rugs that are in good repair and firmly anchored to the floor; attach nonskid rubber backing to area rugs.

- Check that floor surfaces throughout the home are flat and free of clutter.

- Use a nonskid floor wax on linoleum floors.

- Use nonskid adhesive strips or plastic mats in bathtubs.

- Install grab bars on bathroom walls.

- Arrange furniture so that the pieces don't create obstacles.

Organizations
American Association of Retired Persons (AARP)
55 Alive/Mature Driving Program
Traffic and Driver Safety Program
601 E Street, NW
Washington, DC 20049
(202) 434-2277, (800) 434-2277
This program is an 8-hour classroom, driver education refresher course for persons age 50 or older, taught by instructors who are 50 or older. In some states, a certificate of completion entitles the driver to a discount on automobile insurance.

American Automobile Association (AAA)
Check the telephone directory for your local AAA club.
The Mature Operator Program is offered by local AAA clubs. It is an 8-hour classroom course for persons age 55 and over to enhance driving knowledge and awareness of new techniques and information about safe driving.

The National Safety Council
444 North Michigan Avenue
Chicago, IL 60611
(312) 527-4848, (800) 621-7619
This is a nonprofit public service organization whose goal is to prevent accidents and improve the health of Americans. It maintains an extensive library on health and safety subjects.

Readings
Available from the National Institute on Aging Information Center, P.O. Box 8057, Gaithersburg, MD 20898-8057:

"Accident Prevention." *Age Page*

Accidental Hypothermia: A Winter Hazard for Older People

"Heat, Cold, and Being Old." *Age Page*

Hyperthermia: A Hot Weather Hazard for Older People

"Preventing Falls and Fractures." *Age Page*

"Safety Belt Sense." *Age Page*

Other Publications
Prevention of Injury to Older Adults: A Selected Bibliography. Prepared by the Centers for Disease Control (CDC), this publication includes abstracts covering topics such as driving, use of alcohol, and home safety. Write to the CDC, 1600 Clifton Road, Atlanta, GA 30333.

Safety for Older Consumers: Home Safety Checklist. Prepared by the U.S. Consumer Product Safety Commission, 1985. Available from the Consumer Information Center, P.O. Box 100, Pueblo, CO 81009 (Stock No. 424R, $.50).

Menopause

Menopause is a natural part of the life cycle. Although it signals the end of the childbearing years, for many women it also signals a time of life when the day-to-day responsibilities of child care lessen. Many women see menopause as a milestone, a time for new activities and new interests; some find it sexually liberating. Sadly, some still think of menopause in negative terms. Despite the stereotypes, research shows that women can be as healthy during menopause as during other times in life. Each woman's early health is the best predictor of her health during menopause and later years.

Menopause is the time when menstruation stops and the ability to have children ends. This "change of life" marks the time when ovaries stop producing eggs, and levels of the female hormones, estrogen, and progesterone decrease. Menopause generally occurs at around age 50, but this varies widely among women.

Most women experience some symptoms during menopause. These may include changes in the menstrual cycle (such as lighter bleeding or irregularity in the time menstruation occurs each month), hot flashes or flushes (short episodes of heat that spread over the upper body, at times accompanied by sweats), and vaginal changes (dryness or itching and burning that may result in painful intercourse). Some women report headaches, sleep disturbances, and mild depression or irritability.

For most women, the symptoms associated with menopause are mild and require no medical treatment. For women who have relatively more severe problems, treatments are available that can relieve discomfort. A doctor may suggest hormone replacement therapy (HRT) to relieve the symptoms of menopause. HRT also slows the age-related bone loss that can lead to osteoporosis and protects against heart disease. (See sections on heart disease and osteoporosis.) However, as with most medications, there are risks as well as benefits associated with HRT. A woman beginning menopause should discuss the potential benefits and risks of HRT with her doctor.

Most women continue to function normally during the years following menopause. Sexuality can remain an important part of life, and older women experience few changes in their physical capacity for sex. Vaginal discomfort related to hormonal changes can be successfully relieved or eliminated through treatment.

Organizations
American College of Obstetricians and Gynecologists (ACOG)
409 12th Street, SW
Washington, DC 20024
(202) 638-5577
ACOG offers patient education pamphlets entitled *The Menopause Years*, *Estrogen Use*, and *Preventing Osteoporosis*.

National Women's Health Network
1325 G Street, NW

Washington, DC 20005
(202) 347-1140
This national organization serves as a clearinghouse for information
on women's health issues. It also publishes a newsletter that reports
on health issues.

Readings
Available from the National Institute on Aging Information Center,
P.O. Box 8057, Gaithersburg, MD 20898-8057:

The Menopause Time of Life

"Should You Take Estrogen?" *Age Page*

Other Publications
Change of Life: The Menopause Handbook, by Susan Flamholtz
Trien. New York: Fawcett, 1986.

Estrogen: The Facts Can Change Your Life, by Lila Nachtigall,
M.D. and Joan Rattner Heilman. New York: Harper & Row, 1986.

Hot Flashes: Newsletter for Midlife and Older Women. Prepared by
The School of Allied Health Professionals, SUNY at Stony Brook,
New York 11794.

The Menopause Manual, by Wolf H. Utian and Ruth S. Jacobowitz.
New York: Prentice Hall Press, 1990.

Nutrition and Physical Fitness

Most older women will get the nutrients they need by eating a
variety of nutritious foods each day. A well-balanced daily diet
includes at least two servings of dairy products such as low fat or
skim milk, and reduced-fat cheese, cottage cheese, or yogurt; two
servings of a protein such as poultry, fish, beans, nuts, or lean
meat; four to five servings of fruits and vegetables including a

citrus fruit or juice and a dark green leafy vegetable; and four servings of breads and cereal products (preferably made with whole grain or enriched flours), rice, or pasta. Limiting the amount of fat, eating enough fiber, and decreasing excess salt are also good eating habits. Following a doctor's advice about eating is best, especially if an illness requires changes in what or how much is eaten. Some prescription drugs interact with foods; others affect the appetite or change the body's nutritional needs.

Maintaining a healthy weight remains important but may become more difficult for older women. Activity levels may decrease, especially if a woman leaves an active job for a relatively slower-paced life as a retiree. To avoid becoming overweight, women should reduce the number of calories consumed daily. However, the body's need for protein, carbohydrates, minerals, and vitamins remains the same. Thus, it becomes especially important to eat high quality foods — fruits, vegetables, and natural grains — and to avoid some processed foods which frequently are high in calories, fat, sodium, and refined sugar.

Very little research has been done to define how aging changes the body's use of various nutrients. Some studies show that aging may affect the need for certain vitamins and minerals. For example, the body's ability to absorb calcium and vitamin D decreases with age. This may be a factor in the increasing risk of osteoporosis and bone fractures in the older population. Although recommended dietary allowances (RDAs) for infants, children, and adults have been published, guidelines on specific nutritional needs of older people are scarce. Research studies are attempting to show how these needs change with age and whether healthy changes in eating habits may prevent or delay age-dependent diseases. The results of these studies ultimately may make it possible to establish RDAs for persons over age 65.

A healthy diet is as important for preventing disease as it is for maintaining health. Well-balanced diets that are high in fiber and low in saturated fat appear to have a role in preventing cancer, high blood pressure, and coronary artery disease and in controlling diabetes. Adequate calcium intake is important to prevent osteoporosis.

Good health also depends on staying physically active in later years. Although it may be necessary for an older woman to gradually modify the type and duration of her exercise sessions, maintaining a regular fitness program is important. Even a woman who has never exercised can improve her health by adopting a program of regular aerobic exercise. As little as 30 minutes of exercise three times a week can improve energy levels and mental outlook. Walking, swimming, dancing, and bicycling are good exercises for older women because they put relatively little stress on bones and joints. It's a good idea to check with a doctor before beginning a new exercise program.

Current evidence from research studies shows that exercise strengthens the heart and lungs, lowers blood pressure, reduces the risk of diabetes, lowers the level of certain fats in the blood, and strengthens the bones.

Women who exercise regularly — even into their 90s — report they have more energy, endurance, and flexibility. Their legs are stronger and they move around more easily. In addition, they find that they sleep better, experience less anxiety, and have improved family relations. Regular exercise classes also provide an opportunity for interacting with others. Senior citizens' centers, community centers, adult education programs, and local chapters of the YWCA are good sources of information about exercise programs for older women.

Organizations
American Dietetic Association (ADA)
216 West Jackson Boulevard, Suite 800
Chicago, IL 60606
(312) 899-0040
The ADA works to improve the dietary habits of all people and to

advance the science of dietetics and nutrition, as well as to promote education in these areas. A newsletter and publications are available.

National Dairy Council
6300 North River Road
Rosemont, IL 60018
(708) 696-1020
The National Dairy Council offers a range of educational materials for the general public on nutrition, weight control, and osteoporosis.

National Digestive Disease Information Clearinghouse
9000 Rockville Pike, Box NDDIC
Bethesda, MD 20892
(301) 468-6344
Established by the National Institute of Diabetes and Digestive and Kidney Diseases, one of the National Institutes of Health, this clearinghouse offers referrals and resources on digestive diseases and nutrition.

President's Council on Physical Fitness and Sports
701 Pennsylvania Avenue, NW, Suite 250
Washington, DC 20004
(202) 272-3421
This organization provides information to the public on the importance of physical fitness. The Council trains professionals to carry out health and fitness demonstration programs for older people and provides brochures, books, posters, films, and a speakers bureau.

Readings
Available from the National Institute on Aging Information Center, P.O. Box 8057, Gaithersburg, MD 20898-8057:

"Be Sensible About Salt." *Age Page*

"Dietary Supplements: More Is Not Always Better." *Age Page*

"Don't Take It Easy - Exercise!" *Age Page*

"Hints for Shopping, Cooking, and Enjoying Meals." *Age Page*

"Nutrition: A Lifelong Concern." *Age Page*

Available from the Consumer Information Center, P.O. Box 100, Pueblo, CO 81009:

Nutrition and the Elderly. Prepared by the Food and Drug Administration (Stock No. FDA91-2243, free).

Nutrition and Your Health: Dietary Guidelines for Americans. Prepared by the Department of Agriculture, 1990 (Stock No. 519R, free).

Thrifty Meals for Two. Prepared by the Department of Agriculture, 1985 (Stock No. 116R, $2.50).

Other Publications
Exercise: How to Get Started. Prepared by the National Heart, Lung, and Blood Institute (NHLBI), 9000 Rockville Pike, Building 31, Room 4A-21, Bethesda, MD 20892.

Jane Brody's Nutrition Book, by Jane Brody. New York: Bantam Books, 1987.

Sexuality in Later Life

Older women have observed major changes in society's attitudes toward sexuality. As a result of these changes, there is now recognition that people remain sexually active throughout their life. Women can remain physiologically responsive in later life. Some women even say that after menopause, when the fear of pregnancy and the distractions of midlife have passed, they become especially responsive sexually.

Certain physical changes do occur in a woman's genitals - the tissues of her vulva and vagina become thinner, and she takes longer to become aroused and to lubricate sufficiently for penetration — but these changes usually do not interfere with a woman's sexual pleasure. When vaginal changes do make intercourse uncomfortable, lubricating creams or hormone replacement therapy often can help. One study found that women who had intercourse three times a month were less likely to suffer from vaginal atrophy then those who had intercourse less than 10 times a year.

One difficulty with a woman's sexuality in her later years is not her unwillingness or her inability to participate in sex; it is the lack of suitable partners. Because women outlive men by 7 or 8 years, and because women tend to marry men a few years older than they are, most married women eventually are widowed.

As more women lose their partners, many will find satisfaction by relating to people not in typically "sexy" ways at all, but through touch and human contact with individuals of all ages. As women age, they can benefit — both physically and psychologically - by expressing their sexuality and need for human warmth and companionship.

Although illness and disability in later life can affect sexuality, even the most serious diseases rarely warrant stopping sexual activity. For example, joint pain due to rheumatoid arthritis responds to medicines and surgery. Exercise, rest, warm baths, and changes in position and timing of sexual activity — such as avoiding the time of day when discomfort is worst — can help restore sexual enjoyment.

Excessive use of alcohol, which delays orgasm, is probably the most widespread drug-related cause of sexual problems.

Tranquilizers, antidepressants, and certain high blood pressure drugs also can reduce sexual desire. This effect is reversed when the medication is stopped. A doctor often can prescribe a drug with fewer side effects.

Public acceptance of sexuality in later life is growing. We can expect that, for succeeding generations, the special aspects of sexuality associated with aging will become better understood, and the diagnosis and treatment of sexual problems can be refined to a much greater extent.

Organizations
American Association of Sex Educators, Counselors and Therapists (AASECT)
435 N. Michigan Avenue, Suite 1717
Chicago, IL 60611
AASECT publishes the National Register of Certified Sex Educators and Sex Therapists, a list that can help you locate a reputable sex therapist, educator, or counselor in your community ($2.00).

Sex Information and Education Council of the U.S. (SIECUS)
130 West 42nd Street, Suite 2500
New York, NY 10036
(212) 819-9770
The goals of SIECUS are to support and examine scientific research on human sexuality. It provides education, training, and leadership programs in the field of human sexuality.

Readings
Available from the National Institute on Aging Information Center, P.O. Box 8057, Gaithersburg, MD 20898-8057:

"Sexuality in Later Life." *Age Page*

Other Publications
Love and Sex After 60, Revised Edition, by Robert N. Butler, M.D. and Myrna 1. Lewis, A.C.S.W. New York: Harper & Row, 1988.

Sex Over 40. A practical, authoritative newsletter directed to the sexual concerns of the mature adult. For subscription information, write to PPA, Inc., P.O. Box 1600, Chapel Hill, NC 27515, or call (919) 929-2148.

"Sexuality in the Second Half of Life," by Aurelia Jones Goodwin with Lynn Scott. In *Ourselves, Growing Older,* by Paula Brown Doress, Diana Laskin Siegal, and The Midlife and Older Women Book Project. New York: Simon and Schuster, 1987.

"Still Sexy at Sixty," in *How A Woman Ages,* by Robin Marantz Henig. New York: Ballantine, 1985.

Skin

Changes in the appearance of the skin are a natural part of growing older. Laugh lines and crinkles at the corners of the eyes may give character and expression to an older woman's face. Despite the claims of numerous cosmetics, little can be done to prevent or erase wrinkles. Exposure to the sun while young, cigarette smoking, and heredity are the most important factors in how a woman's skin ages.

Skin is the largest organ of the body. It contains blood vessels, oil and sweat glands, hair follicles, and nerve endings. The skin protects internal organs from the outside environment. It senses temperature, pressure, and pain. It regulates body temperature to keep heat inside during cold weather and to release heat during warm weather. And it warns of internal disease, drug reactions, or allergies.

The skin's aging process takes place in a similar manner for everyone. It is a normal process that involves a slow decline in the skin's structure and function. Some major changes that take place as a result of physical aging include:

- Elasticity in skin decreases and the underlying support structure changes gradually, producing wrinkles and sagging.
- Skin cells reproduce more slowly and have a shorter lifespan, so injuries take longer to heal.
- Skin color becomes less even.
- The skin becomes less effective as a barrier; its ability to protect against sunlight, substances that cause allergic reactions, detergents, and other harmful elements is reduced.
- Fewer sweat glands and decreasing activity of oil glands cause more dry skin and itching problems.

Sun exposure is an important cause of premature aging in skin. Wrinkles, sagging skin, discoloration, and brown "age spots" can all result from sun-related damage. Women spend millions of dollars each year on wrinkle creams, skin bleaches, dry skin lotions, and other products in an attempt to keep their skin looking smooth, healthy, and younger. The best protection for skin is to limit sun exposure beginning early in life. Women who protect themselves (by using clothing and sunscreens when going outdoors, and by avoiding unnecessary sun exposure) rarely show marked signs of skin aging until after 50 and even then aging progresses at a slower rate.

Sun damage causes not only premature aging but skin cancer as well. The chance of developing skin cancer increases with advancing age, especially among people who live in sunny regions of the country or who have jobs requiring them to work outside. When detected early and treated promptly, most cases of skin cancer can be cured. The best defense against skin cancer is learning to notice the warning signs. These include the growth of a new spot or changes in a mole such as a difference in color, size, shape, or in the appearance of its surface (scaliness, oozing, crusting, or bleeding).

Organizations
American Academy of Dermatology
930 N. Meacham Road
Schaumburg, IL 60173-4965
(708) 330-9830
The Academy represents dermatologists and provides pamphlets and referrals to the public.

The American Academy of Facial Plastic and Reconstructive Surgery
1110 Vermont Avenue, NW, Suite 220
Washington, DC 20005-3522
(202) 842-4500
This organization offers educational brochures about various types of cosmetic surgery.

The Skin Cancer Foundation
245 Fifth Avenue, Suite 2402
New York, NY 10016
(212) 725-5176
The Foundation works to promote public awareness of the importance of early detection and treatment of skin cancer and offers a variety of health education materials. Requests for publications should indicate a specific topic and include a self-addressed stamped envelope.

Readings
Available from the National Institute on Aging Information Center, P.O. Box 8057, Gaithersburg, MD 20898-8057:

"Skin Care and Aging." *Age Page*

Other Publications
Skin Secrets: A Dermatologist's Prescription for Beautiful Skin at Any Age, by Joseph Bark. New York: McGraw-Hill, 1988.

Use of Medicines

Older women use more medicines than any other segment of the population. They also have the highest rate of chronic or long-term illness (such as arthritis, diabetes, high blood pressure, and heart disease), which means it is common for them to take many different drugs at the same time and for long periods of time.

Drugs taken by older people act differently from the way they do in younger people, probably because of normal changes in body makeup that occur with age. Such changes can affect the length of time a drug remains in the body and the amount of the drug absorbed by body tissues.

There are precautions that can be taken to reduce the risks associated with drug use. For example:

- Take the exact dosage prescribed by the doctor.
- Ask the doctor or pharmacist any questions.
- Never take medicine prescribed for someone else.
- Tell the doctor about all other medicines being taken.
- Report any problems with specific medications to the doctor.
- Keep a daily record of all medications — include both prescription and over-the-counter drugs.
- Call the doctor if unusual reactions occur.

A chemical agent strong enough to cure an ailment is also strong enough to cause harm if not used wisely. If a prescribed drug seems to be doing more harm than good, do not hesitate to call the doctor. Another medicine can often be substituted that will be effective.

Organizations
AARP Pharmacy Service
500 Montgomery Street
Alexandria, VA 22314

(703) 684-0244, (800) 456-2277

This service provides information on common prescription drugs, their side effects, and cost differences between brand name and generic drugs. It publishes a series of leaflets, called "Medication Information Leaflets for Seniors," which discuss 350 prescription drugs. The service also operates 12 pharmacies throughout the country for members of AARP.

Food and Drug Administration Center for Drug Evaluation and Research
CDER - Executive Secretariat (HFD-8)
5600 Fishers Lane
Rockville, MD 20857
(301) 295-8012

This federal office can answer questions about the drug approval process, drug reactions, and other issues concerning new or approved medications.

Readings
Available from the National Institute on Aging Information Center, P.O. Box 8057, Gaithersburg, MD 20898-8057:

"Safe Use of Medicines by Older People." *Age Page*

"Safe Use of Tranquilizers." *Age Page*

Other Publications
About Your Medicines. Prepared annually by the U.S. Pharmacopeial Convention, Inc., this book provides information on several hundred of the most common over-the-counter and prescription drugs. For copies, write to Drug Information Division, 12601 Twinbrook Parkway, Rockville, MD 20852.

Complete Guide to Prescription and Non-Prescription Drugs, by H. Winter Griffith, M.D. East Rutherford, NJ: Putnam Publishing Group, 1990.

Elder-Ed: Using Your Medicines Wisely. Prepared by the National Institute on Drug Abuse. Available from the Government Printing Office, 710 North Capitol Street, NW, Washington, DC 20402 (Stock No. 00017002400969-5, $4.75).

Worst Pills, Best Pills: The Older Adult's Guide to Avoiding Drug-Induced Death or Illness, by Sidney M. Wolfe, M.D. et al. Washington, DC: Public Citizen Health Research Group, 1988.

Common Disorders of Later Life

Alzheimer's Disease and Other Cognitive Changes

It is not unusual for a woman to forget the name of someone she recently met, misplace her keys or glasses, or overlook an item or two at the grocery store. This is normal behavior. However, severe mental decline is by no means a normal part of growing older. Signs of cognitive decline in an older person may include significant memory loss, bizarre behavior or personality deterioration, confusion, or extreme combativeness. These symptoms may indicate a condition that can be treated and cured. However, they are also the signs of other disorders which can be treated but not cured.

Two forms of incurable mental impairment that occur in old age are Alzheimer's disease and multi-infarct dementia. Alzheimer's disease affects nerve cells in the outer layer of the brain (cerebral cortex) causing a large number of brain cells to die. Nearly 4 million older Americans have this disease. Alzheimer's disease affects more women than men because women live longer. Multi-infarct dementia results from a series of small strokes. This condition accounts for about 20 percent of all irreversible cases of mental impairment; Alzheimer's disease accounts for 50 to 60 percent of such cases.

A thorough medical, psychiatric, and neurological evaluation should be done when a person shows symptoms of mental impairment. This is especially important since many reversible conditions mimic irreversible disorders. The patient's medical history contains information on previous illnesses and use of medicines, psychological tests evaluate orientation and memory, and neurological tests detect anatomical changes in the brain.

What may appear to be profound mental impairment may be a condition that can be corrected. Common causes of reversible impairment are poor nutrition, adverse drug reactions, infection, high fever, and minor head injuries. Emotional problems frequently cause reversible symptoms as well. Anxiety, boredom, loneliness, and depression can all appear as mental impairment.

Organizations

Alzheimer's Association
919 N. Michigan Avenue, Suite 1000
Chicago, IL 60611
(312) 335-8700, (800) 272-3900
The Alzheimer's Association serves as a clearinghouse for all aspects of Alzheimer's disease - including medical, psychosocial, research, legal, political, fund raising, and family support.

Alzheimer's Disease Education and Referral Center (ADEAR)
P.O. Box 8250
Silver Spring, MD 20907-8250
(301) 495-3311
Established by NIA, the ADEAR Center distributes information to health professionals, patients and their families, and the general public on Alzheimer's disease, current research activities, and available services.

National Institute of Neurological Disorders and Stroke (NINDS)
P.O. Box 5801
Bethesda, MD 20824
(301) 496-5751

NINDS, one of the National Institutes of Health, offers information and publications on disorders such as dementia, stroke, brain tumors, and Parkinson's disease.

Readings

Alzheimer's Disease, by William A. Check. New York: Chelsea House Publishers, 1989.

Alzheimer's Disease Information Packet. Available from ADEAR, P.O. Box 8250, Silver Spring, MD 20907-8250.

Alzheimer's Disease Information Packet. Available from NINDS, P.O. Box 5801, Bethesda, MD 20824.

Care of Alzheimer's Patients: A Manual for Nursing Home Staff, by Lisa P. Gwyther. Chicago, IL: Alzheimer's Disease and Related Disorders Association, 1986.

The Loss of Self: A Family Resource for the Care of Alzheimer's Disease and Related Disorders, by Drs. Donna Cohen and Carl Eisdorer. New York: Norton and Company, 1986.

The Myth of Senility: The Truth About the Brain and Aging, by Robin Marantz Henig. Glenview, IL: Scott, Foresman and Company, 1988.

Understanding Alzheimer's Disease: What It Is, How to Cope with It, Future Directions, edited by Miriam K. Aronson, Ed.D. New York: Macmillan Publishing Company, 1988.

Cancer

Cancer is a group of more than 100 diseases in which some of the body's cells multiply without control. The result is usually a malignant tumor which grows and invades nearby tissue. (Benign tumors are growths that do not spread.) Cancer cells can also spread to other parts of the body where they form new tumors. The incidence of cancer rises with increasing age. More than half of all cancer patients are over age 65. The most common types of cancer among women are breast cancer, lung cancer, and cancers of the colon and rectum. Older women also have a higher incidence of cancer of the uterus and ovaries.

The symptoms of cancer vary depending on where the tumor is located. Pain is rarely an early sign of cancer. However, a cough that lasts for more than two weeks, a lump or thickening in the breast, a persistent change in bowel habits, unusual bleeding or discharge, or a sore that doesn't heal are all symptoms that should be reported to a doctor. Tests can be done to determine whether they are signs of cancer or some other disorder.

Early detection of cancer is important because cancers that are found early can often be treated successfully. Modern cancer treatment includes surgery, radiation therapy, chemotherapy, hormone therapy, and biological therapy. For the best outlook, a person with cancer should be treated promptly by well-qualified doctors at the best available treatment facility.

Even if there are no symptoms, certain diagnostic tests should be done regularly. Starting at age 50, a woman should have a mammogram (an x-ray of the breast) every year. At the same time, her doctor should check her breasts for changes that could be a sign of breast cancer.

Monthly breast self-examination is also important. Other tests that should be done on a regular basis include a Pap smear to detect cancer of the cervix, a pelvic exam to detect cancer of the uterus or ovaries, a rectal exam to detect cancer of the rectum, and a fecal occult blood test to detect cancer of the colon or rectum. A physician can determine how often a woman should have these exams.

Although scientists do not yet know how to prevent cancer, there are several things a woman can do to reduce her risk of cancer.

These include not smoking, eating a diet low in fat and high in fiber, drinking alcohol only in moderation, and avoiding excess sunlight and unnecessary x-rays.

Organizations

Cancer Information Service
Office of Cancer Communications
Building 31, Room 1OA24
Bethesda, MD 20892
800-4-CANCER (800-422-6237)
The Cancer Information Service is a service of the National Cancer Institute, one of the National Institutes of Health. It provides information and free publications on cancer prevention, detection, causes, treatment, research, and rehabilitation.

American Cancer Society, Inc. (ACS)
National Headquarters
1599 Clifton Road, NE
Atlanta, GA 30329
800-ACS-2345, (800-227-2345)
The ACS is a nonprofit organization that offers a variety of services to cancer patients and their families. Local ACS chapters are listed in the telephone book.

The National Coalition for Cancer Survivorship (NCCS)
1010 Wayne Avenue, 5th Floor
Silver Spring, MD 20910
(301) 585-2616
NCCS helps cancer survivors and their families start local support groups or contact existing ones, sponsors a clearinghouse of national resources for support and information on life after cancer diagnosis, provides advice to reduce cancer-based discrimination, and serves as a unified voice of cancer survivors.

Readings

Available from the National Institute on Aging Information Center, P.O. Box 8057, Gaithersburg, MD 20898-8057:

"Cancer Facts for People Over 50." *Age Page*

"Smoking: It's Never Too Late To Stop." *Age Page*

Other Publications

The American Cancer Society Cancer Book, by Arthur Holleb, M.D. Garden City, NY: Doubleday & Company, 1986.

Choices: Realistic Alternatives in Cancer Treatment, Revised Edition, by Marion Morra and Eve Potts. New York: Avon Books, 1987.

What You Need to Know About Cancer. Available from the Cancer Information Service, 800-4-CANCER (800-422-6237).

Depression

Many women feel "blue" now and then. But when feelings of sadness or being "down in the dumps" continue for some time without a letup, the depressed mood may have become a serious illness that doctors call clinical depression. At that point, it's important to find help. Depression can be treated very successfully and there is no reason for suffering.

Depressive disorders are more prevalent in older women than in older men. Because women live longer than men, they are particularly vulnerable to life events such as loss of a spouse, poverty, and chronic illnesses that can lead to depressive symptoms. Serious depression can take many forms. It can be characterized by feelings of emptiness, persistent sadness, or anxiety; tiredness and decreased energy; loss of interest or pleasure in ordinary activities; restlessness and irritability; aches and pains that just won't go away; difficulty concentrating, remembering, or making decisions; or, at worst, thoughts of death or suicide. If several of these symptoms continue for two weeks or more, a physical examination and psychological evaluation are advised.

It is important to seek professional help because depression in older people is tricky to diagnose, and its symptoms are often dismissed as a natural part of aging. Often, depression is a side effect of drugs commonly taken by older people for problems such as arthritis, hypertension, and heart conditions. Confusion or forgetfulness could be either depression or a symptom of Alzheimer's disease.

Depression can also hide behind a smiling face. For depressed people who live alone, constant feelings of isolation and loneliness can change with an outing to the doctor or when someone comes to visit. Rather than sharing troubling feelings, the person is buoyed by contact with the outside world and, for the moment, the symptoms of depression go away.

Researchers have made a lot of progress in recognizing the problem of depression in older people. Studies show that 60 to 80 percent of depressed older people can be successfully treated outside a hospital with psychotherapy alone or in combination with special drugs to combat the illness. In recent years, short-term "talk therapy" has been shown to be effective.

Getting help doesn't have to be difficult. The first step is to overcome attitudes that may stand in the way, such as the feeling that a depressed person can simply "snap out of it" or that getting help is a sign of weakness. That kind of thinking is unfortunate because proper treatment could make a great difference in an older person's life. A family physician, a clinic, or health maintenance organization should be able to provide a referral to a mental health expert for appropriate evaluation and treatment. Some people avoid seeking help because they are afraid of how expensive treatment might be. Often, the problem can be solved within weeks — not months or years of therapy or medications. Also, some organizations, such as community mental health centers, offer treatment based on a patient's ability to pay.

Organizations

DEPRESSION Awareness, Recognition, and Treatment (D/ART) Program
National Institute of Mental Health
D/ART Public Inquiries
5600 Fishers Lane, Room 15C-05
Rockville, MD 20857
(301) 443-4513
The D/ART Program offers several publications on depression, including one especially written for older people called, *If You're Over 65 and Feeling Depressed ... Treatment Brings New Hope.*

National Alliance for the Mentally Ill (NAMI)
2101 Wilson Boulevard, Suite 302
Arlington, VA 22201
(703) 524-7600, (800) 950-NAMI (800-950-6264)
The Alliance's Medical Information Series includes brochures that provide families and patients with information on a variety of mental illnesses and their treatments, including one publication entitled *Mood Disorders, Depression and Manic Depression.* Affiliate groups in several states provide emotional support and information about mental illness and how to find appropriate local services.

National Depressive and Manic-Depressive Association
P.O. Box 1939
Chicago, IL 60690
(312) 642-0049
The Association has over 200 chapters across the U.S. and Canada which offer support to people with depressive illnesses and their families. It sponsors education and research programs and distributes numerous brochures, videotapes, and audio programs.

National Mental Health Association (NMHA)
Information Center
1021 Prince Street
Alexandria, VA 22314-2971

(703) 684-7722, (800) 969-6642
NMHA has groups across the U.S. that provide information, referrals, and support. It publishes information on various mental health issues including depression and it's treatment.

Readings
Getting Up When You're Feeling Down: A Woman's Guide to Overcoming and Preventing Depression, By Harriet B. Braiker. New York: G.P. Putnam's Sons, 1988

The Good News About Depression: Cures and Treatments in the New Age of Psychiatry, by Mark S. Gold. New York: Villard Books, 1986.

To Be Old and Sad: Understanding Depression in the Elderly, by Nathan Billig. Lexington, MA: Lexington Books, 1987.

Heart Disease

Heart disease is traditionally considered to be a man's disease. However, once women pass through menopause, the risk of heart disease increases dramatically as circulating estrogen diminishes. Estrogen seems to protect women against heart disease during the childbearing years. One in nine women between the ages of 45 and 64 has some form of cardiovascular disease, a category that includes coronary heart disease, hypertension, angina, and stroke. The incidence rises to one in three for women age 65 and older. Yet recent studies have shown that doctors may be treating women with heart disease less aggressively than they treat men.

Medical researchers theorize that the amount of estrogen is associated with the level of high density lipoproteins (HDL). HDLs help to remove cholesterol from the tissues and reduce death from heart disease. Although many factors come into play, there are indications that postmenopausal estrogen replacement therapy may be helpful in reducing the risk of heart disease.

The statistics on heart disease and women are staggering. Heart attack is the number one killer of American women, although men are more likely than women to have heart attacks during the middle-age years. Women who have heart attacks are twice as likely as men to die within the first few weeks; women are two to three times more likely than men to suffer a second heart attack within 5 years of the first; and 39 percent of women die within a year after a heart attack compared with 31 percent of men. Women also may be less likely to benefit from bypass surgery, a riskier procedure for women because they have smaller blood vessels than men and are more likely to have more advanced disease at the time of surgery.

In addition, an older woman's risk of high blood pressure is greater than a man's. High blood pressure, or hypertension, becomes more common with advancing age, and after the age of 65, a higher proportion of women than men have hypertension. A healthy blood pressure is 120 (systolic pressure) over 80 (diastolic pressure), written 120/80. A reading over 140/90 is considered high.

One form of hypertension — isolated systolic hypertension (ISH) — is particularly common in older people. ISH occurs when the systolic pressure is elevated and the diastolic pressure remains within the normal range. Older African American women have twice the rate of ISH as White women and African American or Caucasian men. Research has recently demonstrated a low-cost drug treatment that can prevent strokes, heart attacks, and other cardiac problems resulting from ISH.

Hypertension has been called "the silent killer" because it damages the kidneys, eyes, blood vessels, and heart without necessarily causing any symptoms. Eventually, this damage may lead to kidney failure, blindness, stroke, and heart attack. A person with high blood pressure is three times more likely than someone with normal blood pressure to develop congestive heart failure and eight times more likely to have a stroke. Although most cases of hypertension cannot be cured, they can be controlled with weight loss, exercise, changes in diet, and medication.

Women also are more likely than men to have high levels of cholesterol in their blood. High cholesterol levels are associated with cardiovascular disease. An inherited tendency to accumulate blood fats and a diet high in saturated fats and cholesterol can cause high cholesterol levels. About half the women over 55 have high blood cholesterol (over 240 mg) compared to one-third of men the same age. And women have a much higher rate of strokes, which occur when a blood clot clogs an artery that supplies blood to the brain.

How can women lower their risk of heart disease? They can stop smoking, control high blood pressure, start an exercise program with the approval of their physician, avoid obesity, and limit their intake of fat and cholesterol from eggs, organ meats, high-fat dairy products, deep fried foods, red meats, and most snack foods.

Organizations
American Heart Association (AHA)
7320 Greenville Avenue
Dallas, TX 75231
(214) 373-6300
AHA supports research, education, and community service programs with the objective of reducing premature death and disability from cardiovascular diseases and stroke. Local chapters are found in many communities.

Mended Hearts
c/o American Heart Association
7320 Greenville Avenue
Dallas, TX 75231
(214) 706-1442
Mended Hearts provides information, encouragement, and services to heart disease patients and their families.

National Heart, Lung, and Blood Institute (NHLBI)
9000 Rockville Pike
Bethesda, MD 20892
(301) 496-4236

NHLBI, one of the National Institutes of Health, provides leadership for a national program of research and education on causes, prevention, diagnosis, and treatment of diseases of the heart, blood vessels, blood, and lungs, and on the use of blood and the management of blood resources.

Readings
Available from the National Institute on Aging Information Center, P.O. Box 8057, Gaithersburg, MD 20898-8057:

"High Blood Pressure: A Common But Controllable Disorder..." *Age Page*

"Stroke Prevention and Treatment." *Age Page*

Other Publications
Coronary Risk Factor Statement for the American Public. Available from AHA, 7320 Greenville Avenue, Dallas, TX 75231.

Eat Well, But Wisely: To Reduce Your Risk of Heart Attack. Available from AHA, 7320 Greenville Avenue, Dallas, TX 75231.

Heart Attack and Stroke: Signals and Action. Available from AHA, 7320 Greenville Avenue, Dallas, TX 75231.

Heart Attacks. Available from NHLBI, 9000 Rockville Pike, Bethesda, MD 20892. NIH Publication No. 86-2700.

Heart Attacks, Hypertension and Heart Drugs, by M. Gabriel Khan. Emmaus, PA: Rodale Press, 1986.

Heartbeat: A Complete Guide to Understanding and Preventing Heart Disease, by Emmanuel Horovitz. Los Angeles, CA: Health Trend Publications, 1988.

How to Make Your Heart Last a Lifetime. Available from AHA, 7320 Greenville Avenue, Dallas, TX 75231.

Osteoarthritis

Osteoarthritis (OA) — one of the most common forms of arthritis — is caused by degeneration of the cartilage that cushions bones where they move against one another in joints. OA develops in almost everyone by age 65. Only half of affected people experience symptoms such as pain and stiffness in the fingers or in weight-bearing joints (knees, hips, and spine). Joint inflammation is rare in OA. As in most forms of arthritis, OA is a chronic condition.

Although the exact cause of OA is still unknown and it cannot be cured, symptoms can usually be reduced and the more serious physical handicaps prevented. The form of treatment recommended by a doctor depends on how severe the symptoms are and which joints are affected. General approaches to treatment are to control pain with heat and medications such as aspirin and ibuprofen; to reduce stress on joints with rest and braces; and to pre- vent and reduce stiffness and strengthen muscles supporting the joints by regular exercise. Joint replacement surgery is an option for severe problems.

Organizations

Arthritis Foundation
1314 Spring Street, NW
Atlanta, GA 30309
(800) 283-7800
The Foundation is committed to determining the causes and cures for arthritis and to improving treatments for people with arthritis. Services offered include public information and education about arthritis, referrals to specialists and community resources such as arthritis clinics, rehabilitation, and home care.

National Arthritis and Musculoskeletal and Skin Diseases Information Clearinghouse
Box AMS
9000 Rockville Pike

Bethesda, MD 20892
(301) 495-4484
Established by the National Institute on Arthritis, Musculoskeletal and Skin Diseases, one of the National Institutes of Health, this clearinghouse offers referrals and resources on osteoporosis, arthritis, and other musculoskeletal and skin diseases.

Readings
Available from the National Institute on Aging Information Center, P.O. Box 8057, Gaithersburg, MD 20898-8057:

"Arthritis Advice." *Age Page*

"Arthritis Medicines." *Age Page*

Other Publications
Guide to Independent Living for People with Arthritis. Atlanta, GA: The Arthritis Foundation, 1988.

Total Hip Joint Replacement. An NIH Consensus Development Conference Summary, Vol. 4, No. 4, 1982. Single copies available from the NIH Office of Medical Applications of Research, Building 1, Room 216, Bethesda, MD 20892.

Osteoporosis

Osteoporosis is a condition in which decreasing bone mass results in thinner, more porous bone that fractures easily. Some degree of bone loss is normal in both men and women with advancing age, but in women the sharp decrease in estrogen following menopause accelerates the rate of bone loss. In some women, this bone loss is so severe it results in osteoporosis, the major cause of bone fractures in women over age 50. It is estimated that osteoporosis currently affects 24 million American women.

Osteoporosis is sometimes called a "silent disease" because it has no symptoms during its early stages. Unfortunately the condition is usually not recognized until it reaches an advanced stage when fractures occur — most often in the spine, wrists, and hips. Ordinary x-rays do not show bone loss until about 30 percent of the bone density has been lost. However, a number of medical tests are available for diagnosing osteoporosis. These include the single and dual-photon absorptiometry, dual-energy x-ray absorptiometry, and computerized tomography (or CT scan). The reason for choosing one test over another depends on the area of the body to be examined, available equipment, and insurance coverage. Many doctors feel that routine testing to predict a woman's chance of having osteoporosis-related bone fractures is not warranted. However, a woman who is at high risk for osteoporosis may want to ask her doctor about a bone density measurement. Risk factors include an early menopause (either naturally or from a hysterectomy), low body weight, physical inactivity, being Caucasian, or having a relative with osteoporosis.

Estrogen replacement therapy (ERT) may be prescribed for postmenopausal women to protect them from disease. It is often prescribed for women with osteoporosis or for those who are at high risk of developing it. ERT supplements the decreasing amounts of estrogen produced by the body. Estrogen slows bone loss and improves the body's absorption and retention of calcium helping to prevent osteoporosis-related bone fractures. A woman considering ERT should discuss its benefits and risks with her doctor. For postmenopausal women who cannot take estrogen, the drug calcitonin is now being used to slow bone breakdown and reduce the pain associated with osteoporosis.

Current recommendations to prevent osteoporosis involve regular weight-bearing exercise (e.g., walking, dancing, jogging) and consuming adequate amounts of calcium and vitamin D throughout fife. Experts suggest that before menopause, women should have 1,000 mg of calcium each day; after menopause, women need 1,500 mg of calcium daily. Calcium-rich foods include low-fat milk, cheese, and yogurt. The recommended dietary allowance for vitamin D — which is needed by the body to absorb calcium — is

200 I.U. each day which can be obtained from 15 minutes of sunshine or from fortified milk.

Organizations

American Academy of Orthopedic Surgeons
222 South Prospect Avenue
Park Ridge, IL 60068
(708) 823-7186
This is a professional association of orthopedic surgeons. The Academy offers an educational brochure to the public called Osteoporosis.

National Arthritis and Musculoskeletal and Skin Diseases Information Clearinghouse
Box AMS
9000 Rockville Pike
Bethesda, MD 20892
(301) 495-4484
Established by the National Institute on Arthritis, Musculoskeletal and Skin Diseases (NIAMS), one of the National Institutes of Health, this clearinghouse offers referrals and resources on osteoporosis, arthritis, and other musculoskeletal and skin diseases.

National Osteoporosis Foundation (NOF)
2100 M Street, NW, Suite 602
Washington, DC 20037
(202) 223-2226
This voluntary organization offers programs nationwide to educate professionals and the public about osteoporosis and related research.

Readings

Available from the National Institute on Aging Information Center, P.O. Box 8057, Gaithersburg, MD 20898-8057:

"Osteoporosis: The Bone Thinner." *Age Page*

"Should You Take Estrogen?" *Age Page*

Other Publications

Boning Up on Osteoporosis. Available from NOF/Aging, 2100 M Street, NW, Suite 602, Washington, DC 20037.

The Older Person's Guide to Osteoporosis. Available from NOF/Aging, 2100 M Street, NW, Suite 602, Washington, DC 20037.

Osteoporosis. A Medicine for the Layman publication. Available from Clinical Center Communications, National Institutes of Health, 9000 Rockville Pike, Building 10, Room 1C255, Bethesda, MD 20892 or call (301) 496-2563.

Osteoporosis. Scientific Workshop: Research Directions in Osteoporosis, 1987. Single copies available from the NIAMS Information Clearinghouse, Box AMS, Bethesda, MD 20892.

Osteoporosis: Cause, Treatment, Prevention. Prepared by NIAMS, 1986 (Stock No. 417R, $.50).

Osteoporosis: The Silent Thief, by William A. Peck and Louis V. Avioli. Glenview, IL: Scott Foresman, 1988.

Preventing Osteoporosis: Dr. Kenneth H. Cooper's Preventive Medicine Program, by Kenneth H. Cooper. M D. New York: Bantam Books, 1989.

Urinary Incontinence

Urinary incontinence, the involuntary loss of urine, affects almost 40 percent of women who are 60 years of age and older. Incontinence ranges from the slight loss of urine to severe and frequent wetting. Because those affected often isolate themselves, refusing to leave home or see other people for fear of an "accident," incontinence can be both a medical and a social problem.

Two common types of incontinence in older women are urge incontinence, in which the person has a strong urge to urinate and is unable to hold urine long enough to reach a toilet, and stress incontinence, in which leakage occurs during physical exertion or when sneezing or coughing. Stress incontinence also occurs in younger women.

Incontinence can be treated or controlled in many cases. It is not an inevitable result of aging but is caused by specific changes in body function — for example, it may result from a disease or the use of certain medicines. If left untreated, incontinence can cause skin irritation and increase the chance of developing bedsores in nursing home residents.

Several treatment methods can be used to relieve incontinence. They include behavioral techniques and exercises, medications, and surgery. Kegel exercises, which strengthen the muscles around the vagina that help support the bladder, are often used to treat stress incontinence and can improve urine retention. Bladder training, a program of scheduled voiding, is an effective treatment for many women with incontinence. It is based on principles of behavior modification and consists of patient education and urination at specific time intervals. Several different medications can be prescribed for incontinence, although because they sometimes cause side effects (such as eye problems, dry mouth, or a buildup of urine) their use must be supervised carefully by a doctor. In addition, surgery has been used successfully to improve or even cure structural problems such as abnormalities in the position of the bladder.

Women who have incontinence are sometimes reluctant to discuss this problem with their doctor. Because there are so many treatment options, women who have trouble controlling urine should seek prompt medical attention to determine the cause. Even when incontinence cannot be completely controlled, new products and ways of managing the condition can ease discomfort and inconvenience.

Organizations
Alliance for Aging Research
2021 K Street, NW, Suite 305
Washington, DC 20006
(202) 293-2856
The Alliance serves as a clearinghouse for information about aging research and conducts a variety of educational programs. The Alliance has developed an easy-to-read brochure called, *Incontinence: Everything You Wanted to Know But Were Afraid to Ask.*

Continence Restored
785 Park Avenue
New York, NY 10021
(212) 879-3131
This self help organization provides information and support with the assistance of medically trained leaders.

HIP (Help for Incontinent People)
P.O. Box 544
Union, SC 29379
(803) 579-7900, (800) BLADDER (800-252-3337)
HIP is a self-help and patient advocacy group that offers encouragement, information, and resource listings for incontinent individuals. It also publishes the *Resource Guide of Continence Products and Services* and a quarterly newsletter *The HIP Report.*

National Kidney and Urologic Diseases Information Clearinghouse
P.O. Box NKUDIC
9000 Rockville Pike
Bethesda, MD 20892
(301) 468-6345
Established by the National Institute of Diabetes and Digestive and Kidney Diseases, one of the National Institutes of Health, this clearinghouse offers referrals and resources on kidney and urologic diseases and their causes and treatments.

The Simon Foundation for Continence
Box 835
Wilmette, IL 60091
(800) 237-4666
The Foundation is a nonprofit educational group and serves as a source of information on incontinence. It publishes books, tapes, and a newsletter *The Informer*.

Readings
Available from the National Institute on Aging Information Center, P.O. Box 8057, Gaithersburg, MD 20898-8057:

"Urinary Incontinence." *Age Page*

Controlling Urinary Incontinence.

Other Publications
Managing Incontinence: A Guide to Living With the Loss of Urinary Control, by Cheryle B. Gartley. Ottawa, IL: Jameson Books, 1985.

Staying Dry: A Practical Guide to Bladder Control, by Kathryn L. Burgio, K. Lynette Pearce, and Angelo J. Lucco. Baltimore, MD: Johns Hopkins University Press, 1989.

Taking Charge

Caregiving

Caregiving presents a special challenge to adult children of older parents. With older people living well into their eighties and nineties, it's no longer unusual for a woman in her sixties to be the primary caregiver for a parent, an aging spouse, a friend, or even a grandchild. Caregiving may often be stressful, but it is not always a burden. It usually means helping with meals, shopping, and other daily activities. In a recent survey, individuals considered "caregivers" were those helping an older person with one or more daily functions such as eating, bathing, dressing, or using the bathroom.

Caregiving is also a critical issue in our country today. The number of people over age 85 — those in greatest need of daily help — is increasing rapidly and is expected to more than double within the next 15 years. This rapid growth, combined with a declining birth rate and an increasing number of women in the work force, has resulted in more diverse groups taking on the responsibility for caregiving. Many groups are developing new ways of enabling families to share in partnership with other types of support systems, although the nature of such partnerships and the proper division of responsibility remain complex issues and are subject to much debate. As our population ages, more of us will face responsibilities for older relatives and friends.

A Caregiver's Checklist
People providing care, particularly for an older parent or a spouse, may find the following strategies helpful:

- Give reassurance to the person being cared for by expressing support and by showing that you can be depended upon to help solve problems.
- Become informed about areas relating to the older person's situation. This may include familiarity with legal matters (wills and property ownership),financial arrangements, health care resources, support services, housing and recreation resources, and knowledge about aging processes.
- Obtain a professional assessment of the older person's problems. Seek out health professionals. trained in caring for older persons by calling your local medical society, hospital, or medical school. A lawyer or a financial advisor may also be of assistance.
- Help the person retain control of his or her affairs as much as possible. Limits often have to be placed on autonomy due to illness, finances, or for other reasons, but the older

person's participation in making decisions is still almost always possible.

- Share caregiving responsibilities with family, friends, professionals, and paid helpers. Do not try to do everything alone.
- Brainstorm with family and friends about ways to help an older family member remain active.
- When making a change, start with the smallest step possible. This will help you avoid becoming overwhelmed if many difficult decisions have to be made; they may not all have to be made at one time.
- Seek professional counseling if a situation or relationship with an older person becomes too demanding.
- Take time off for yourself. You also need recreation and time to pursue personal interests. Be honest with the older person about the limitations on your time and energy.

Organizations
Administration on Aging (AoA)
Department of Health and Human Services
330 Independence Avenue, SW
Washington, DC 20201
(202) 619-0724: general information
(202) 619-0641: publications
The AoA is a federal agency that provides information about social services, nutrition, education, senior centers, and other programs for older Americans. It offers *A Directory of State and Regional Agencies on Aging*, which lists local Area Agencies on Aging (also called Offices on Aging).

Children of Aging Parents
Woodbourne Office Campus
1609 Woodbourne Road, Suite 302A
Levittown, PA 19057
(215) 945-6900
This organization provides a variety of services, including starter information for those interested in becoming caregivers, and a

matching service for people starting a support group. They also offer workshops for the general public, printed materials, and a bimonthly newsletter.

Readings

Caregiving: Helping an Aging Loved One, by Jo Home. Glenview, IL: AARP Books, Scott Foresman and Company, 1987.

Caregiving and You: A Resource Guide for Long-Term Care, by George J. Pfeiffer and Joyce Ruddock. Reston, VA: The Center for Corporate Health, Inc., 1990.

Taking Care of Today and Tomorrow: A Resource Guide for Health, Aging and Long-Term Care. Reston, VA: The Center for Corporate Health, Inc., 1991.

You and Your Aging Parent: A Family Guide to Emotional, Physical and Financial Problems, 3rd edition, by Barbara Silverstone mid Helen K. Hyman. New York: Pantheon Press, 1989.

Finances

Many older women are able to enjoy their retirement years with enough money to meet their basic needs and enjoy some leisure activities. Others face poverty for the first time in old age. Retirement savings often must be used for expensive medical treatment; high inflation rates erode the fixed incomes or savings that many older persons depend on; and many older women simply outlive their assets.

Women generally earn lower salaries than men and this further limits retirement benefits. Benefits are calculated on average lifetime earnings, so time spent at home to rear children reduces both pensions and Social Security income in later life. Women are also more likely to work part time and to work for employers who do not offer pension benefits, such as in the service industry. Moreover, although Social Security is intended to supplement other forms of retirement income, for a majority of women over age 65 it is the only source of support.

A large group of older women do not receive the benefits they are eligible for, either because they do not know about them or how to get them, or because they are too proud to accept this assistance. Others, especially those for whom English is a second language, may not understand complicated paperwork necessary to initiate payments. Thus, only half of older persons eligible for Supplemental Security Income actually receive benefits.

Keeping Financial Records
Keeping a personal record of important information can help make financial planning more efficient. This written document should note the locations of valuable papers and property. The following are examples of what this record might include:

- Assets and sources of income (pension funds and interest income)
- Social Security information
- Investment income, savings, stocks, bonds, property
- Insurance numbers on policies for life, health, and property (home and car)
- Bank accounts (checking, savings, and credit union accounts)
- Income tax returns
- Liabilities, such as what is owed to whom and when payments are due
- Mortgages and debts
- Credit cards and charge accounts

Organizations
Social Security Administration (SSA)
Office of Public Inquiries
6401 Security Boulevard

Baltimore, MD 21235
(301) 965-1234, (800) 772-1213
SSA is the Federal agency that runs the national retirement system. It provides information about Social Security (coverage, earnings records, claims eligibility, and adjustments), Medicare, and Medicaid. Upon request, SSA can provide an estimate of your benefits. The Supplemental Security Income (SSI) program is also administered by SSA and provides additional payments to older persons already receiving public assistance. SSA branch offices are listed in local telephone directories.

Readings
Available from the National Institute on Aging Information Center, P.O. Box 8057, Gaithersburg, MD 20898-8057:

"Getting Your Affairs in Order." *Age Page*

Other Publications
Managing Your Personal Finances. Prepared by the Department of Agriculture, 1987, this 3-part series includes *The Principles of Managing Your Finances* (Stock No. 189R, $3.25), *Financial Tools Used in Money Management* (Stock No. 190R, $1.50), and *Coping With Change* (Stock No. 191R, $1.75).

Understanding Social Security, 1991. Prepared by the Social Security Administration. Available from the Consumer Information Center, P.O. Box 100, Pueblo, CO 81009.

Housing Options

In later years, changing circumstances often create the need for a new living arrangement. Costly maintenance and utility bills, the desire to move nearer to family, to live in a smaller home, or the need for regular nursing attention are just a few of the reasons older people may have to reconsider where they are living.

Today, many housing choices are available. Some people arrange "in-home" services for special needs (e.g., homemaker or home health aide services, home-delivered meals, escort or transportation services); others consider renting out a portion of their home. Additional choices include moving to a smaller home, moving in with family members, moving to a group home where older people share one residence, moving to an apartment house with communal dining facilities and on-call nursing assistance, or moving to a community designed especially for older people. Many types of housing offer support services, as in a continuing care community or a nursing home.

With so many housing alternatives available, it is important to take time to assess issues of cost, independence, availability of medical care, and other aspects of personal concern. This can be done by gathering facts about possible choices, borrowing books from the library, writing for information, and talking candidly with other people about their housing situations.

Organizations
American Association of Homes for the Aging (AAHA)
901 E Street, NW, Suite 500
Washington, DC 20004
(202) 783-2242
AAHA is a national organization whose members include nonprofit nursing homes, independent housing facilities, continuing care facilities, and homes for the aging. They offer a brochure called *The Continuing Care Retirement Community: A Guidebook for Consumers, 1991* ($4.00).

National Association for Home Care (NAHC)
519 C Street, NE
Stanton Park
Washington, DC 20002
(202) 547-7424
The NAHC monitors federal and state activities affecting home care and focuses on issues relating to home health care. They publish *Caring Magazine* on a bimonthly basis.

National Citizen's Coalition for Nursing Home Reform
1224 M Street, NW, Suite 301
Washington, DC 20005
(202) 393-2018
The Coalition serves as a voice enabling consumers to be heard on issues concerning the quality of care in long-term care facilities.

National Council of Senior Citizens
National Senior Citizens Education and Research Center
Nursing Home Information Service
1331 F Street, NW
Washington, DC 20004
(202) 347-8800
The Information Service is a referral center for consumers of long-term care services. They offer information on nursing homes and alternative community and health services and on how to select a nursing home.

Readings
Available from the National Institute on Aging Information Center, P.O. Box 8057, Gaithersburg, MD 20898-8057:

"When You Need a Nursing Home." *Age Page*

Other Publications
Choosing a Nursing Home, by Seth B. Goldsmith. New York: Prentice-Hall Press, 1990.

Eldercare: Choosing and Financing Long-Term Care, by Joseph Matthews. Berkeley, CA: Nolo Press, 1990.

The Nursing Home Handbook: A Guide for Families, by Jo Horne. Glenview, IL: AARP Books, Scott, Foresman and Company, 1990.

Your Home, Your Choice: A Workbook for Older People and Their Families. Prepared by AARP and the Federal Trade Commission. Available from AARP at 601 E Street, NW, Washington, DC 20049 (free).

Widowhood

The average age of widowhood in the United States is 56. As a result, half of all women over age 65 live as widows. This high rate of widowhood occurs because women tend to marry men older than themselves and because life expectancy from birth is seven or eight years longer for women than for men.

Becoming a widow often means that a relationship lasting most of a lifetime has ended; it can cause profound grief. Recovery is often painful and takes time. The period of most intense grief can last from a few months to a year or more. During this time, it is normal for a women to feel despair or depression, irritability, and even anger toward the person who died. Crying or talking a great deal about him is also normal until the death is accepted. After this grieving process, a woman is usually able to increase her range of independence and find new friends and activities to enrich life. Some women need special help with the social and psychological problems associated with being widowed.

Loneliness is also common during this period. It sometimes takes an extra effort to find social activities and friends, but many resources are available. Many women make new friendships through a variety of affiliations with religious, civic, or volunteer organizations, and through community and social activities.

Women who find themselves alone as a result of being widowed may need to develop new skills for a changing role. For example, some must learn to manage financial matters for the first time - such as paying bills, balancing a checkbook, and handling insurance benefits. To help them, a growing number of national and local organizations provide support.

Organizations
ACTION
1100 Vermont Avenue, NW
Washington, DC 20525

(202) 606-4902, (800) 424-8867
A federal agency, ACTION administers domestic volunteer programs, including Retired Senior Volunteer Program, Foster Grandparent Program, Senior Companion Program, and others.

National Displaced Homemaker Network
1625 K Street, NW, Suite 300
Washington, DC 20006
(202) 467-6346
The agency fosters the development of programs across the U.S. with services to help displaced homemakers, including individual counseling, support groups, employment/training seminars, vocational testing, and a job club.

Widowed Persons Service
American Association of Retired Persons (AARP)
601 E Street, NW
Washington, DC 20049
(202) 434-2277
A service of AARP, this organization provides group sessions, publications about legal matters, volunteer opportunities, and other resources for newly widowed persons.

Readings
Consumer Guide to the FTC Funeral Rule. Prepared by the Federal Trade Commission, 1984. Available from the Consumer Information Center, P.O. Box 100, Pueblo, CO 81009 (Stock No. 438R, $.50).

A Second Start: A Widow's Guide to Financial Survival at a Time of Emotional Crisis, by Judith N. Brown and Christina Baldwin. New York: Simon & Schuster, 1986.

Suddenly Alone: A Woman's Guide to Widowhood, by Philomene Gates. New York: Harper & Row, 1990.

Widow to Widow, by Phyllis Silverman. New York: Springer Publishing Company, 1986.

The Widow's Handbook: A Guide for Living, by Charlotte Foehner and Carol Cozart. Golden, CO: Fulcrum, Inc., 1988.

Research

Research on Women's Health

The health and well-being of older women is a major focus of research at the National Institute on Aging (NIA). Studies have helped scientists understand how and why women age and have shown that while some aspects of aging are similar in men and women, distinct differences do occur. An important conclusion of NIA research is that different organs, different systems, and different individuals age at different rates. Physical and mental decline with age is not inevitable.

NIA conducts and supports a wide range of studies. Some research projects focus primarily on issues of women's health, such as osteoporosis and hip fractures, hormonal changes with age, urinary incontinence, and the psychological health of older women. Other projects examine the effects of menopause and the role of women as caregivers. Aspects of aging that are relevant to both sexes are also investigated. These include Alzheimer's disease, cancer, changes in the function of the heart with age, resistance to disease, and the development of frailty.

NIA conducts a major research study of human aging, the Baltimore Longitudinal Study of Aging (BLSA), which was begun in 1958. The study of more than 1,100 women and men, age 20 to 97, is helping scientists learn more about older people's health and well-being across the lifespan. One of the central questions addressed by the BLSA is how the differences between men and women interact to cause (or prevent) disease or disability.

The BLSA is also documenting similarities. For example, men and women are alike when it comes to age-related adaptations in cardiac structure and function; both men and women maintain their distinctive personality characteristics as they age, and patterns of forgetting verbal material are similar for men and women with advancing years.

BLSA findings have enormous practical significance. For both women and men, they suggest ways to delay, reduce, or even reverse increasing vulnerability to disease and frailty with age. Some studies may lead to better ways to predict heart disease among healthy women. In the area of disease prevention, the finding that nearly all women over age 55 have no immunity to tetanus may mean that routine immunization guidelines need to be revised.

The quality of life for older women is as important as their length of life. As knowledge increases about aging processes and with studies focusing on the special health issues of women, NIA research will make significant contributions to the health and independence of older women.

Additional Resources

Organizations
The following organizations can also provide information helpful to older women.

American Association of Retired Persons (AARP)
Women's Initiative
601 E Street, NW
Washington, DC 20049
(202) 434-2277
Members of AARP include more than 15 million people over age 50 (not all are retired). The Association offers information and services related to retirement and insurance and promotes general policies that benefit older persons.

Additional Resources (continued)

Organizations (continued)

American Association of University Women (AAUW)
1111 16th Street, NW
Washington, DC 20036
(202) 785-7700
AAUW, a membership organization, is the nation's leading advocate for educational equity for women and girls. It offers Career Development Grants to women reentering the work force, making a career change, or advancing their current career.

American Diabetes Association (ADA)
1660 Duke Street
Alexandria, VA 22314
(703) 549-1500, (800) 232-3472
Members of ADA include physicians, research scientists, and dietitians, as well as people with diabetes and their families. The Association sponsors educational lectures, film presentations, diabetes screening clinics, and raises funds for diabetes research.

Commission on Legal Problems of the Elderly
1800 M Street, NW, 2nd Floor, South Lobby
Washington, DC 20036
(202) 331-2297
The Commission works to improve the quality and quantity of legal services for older citizens. It refers requests for services to appropriate agencies or groups.

Elderhostel, Inc.
75 Federal Street
Boston, MA 02110
(617) 426-7788
Elderhostel is a nonprofit educational program for adults age 60 and over. The program consists of one week courses taught in residence at various college campuses; the courses offer a range of liberal arts subjects presented at an introductory level. Free catalogs are available on request.

Gray Panthers
1424 16th Street, NW, Suite 602
Washington, DC 20036
(202) 387-3111
This coalition of activists works to promote the concerns of older people through newsletters and publications.

Additional Resources (continued)

Organizations (continued)

National Council on Alcoholism and Drug Dependence, Inc.
12 West 21st Street
New York, NY 10010
(212) 206-6770 / (800) 475-HOPE (800-475-4673)
This nonprofit organization informs the public about alcoholism and drug abuse and promotes programs for prevention.

National Council on the Aging (NCOA)
409 Third Street, SW, Second Floor
Washington, DC 20024
(202) 479-1200 / (800) 424-9046
NCOA helps to promote concerns of interest to older persons by conducting seminars on wellness, offering a range of publications (public policy/advocacy, education, and training), and providing resources for public education.

National Health Information Center
P.O. Box 1133
Washington, DC 20013
(800) 336-4797
The Center will help locate resources pertaining to health information; specific questions about health are referred to appropriate organizations, experts, or federal agencies.

National Organization for Women (NOW)
1000 16th Street, NW, Suite 700
Washington, DC 20036
(202) 331-0066
NOW is an advocacy group that monitors local and national legislation affecting American women. Through local chapters, members participate in activities concerned with women's rights issues.

National Senior Citizens Law Center
1815 H Street, NW, Suite 700
Washington, DC 20006
(202) 887-5280
The Center is a public interest law firm with attorneys who specialize in areas of federal law having the greatest impact on the older poor.

Additional Resources (continued)

Organizations (continued)

National Women's Health Network
1325 G Street, NW
Washington, DC 20005
(202) 347-1140
This national organization serves as a clearinghouse for information on women's health issues. It also publishes a newsletter on health and lobbying efforts.

National Women's Health Resource Center (NWHRC)
2440 M Street, NW, Suite 201
Washington, DC 20037
(202) 293-6045
NWHRC is an information clearinghouse on issues of women's health in the areas of public education, advocacy, clinical services, and research. The organization's newsletter, National Women's Health Report, is available by subscription.

Older Women's League (OWL)
666 11th Street, NW, Suite 700
Washington, DC 20001
(202) 783-6686
OWL's national membership is committed to helping meet various special needs of middle-aged and older women, especially in areas such as Social Security, pension rights, health insurance, and caregiver support services. OWL uses volunteers to help with mailings, to maintain a referral resource file, and to answer letters from women writing in from across the country with questions.

Wider Opportunities for Women (WOW)
National Commission on Working Women
Lower Level, 1325 G Street, NW
Washington, DC 20005
(202) 638-3143
The Commission is a private organization that focuses on the concerns of women working in service industries, clerical occupations, retail stores, and factories.

Additional Resources (continued)

Readings

The following listing is a brief sample of the many publications that are available on health concerns of older women. A local library or bookstore is a good source of additional information.

After 65: Resources for Self-Reliance, edited by Theodore Irwin. New York: Public Affairs Pamphlet No. 501A, 1982.

Aging Well: A Guide for Successful Seniors, by James F. Fries. Reading, MA: Addison-Wesley, 1989.

Aging with Style and Savvy, by Denise Perry Donavin. Chicago, IL: American Library Association, 1990.

Forum. A newsletter for older women. Prepared by the School of Allied Health Professionals, Health Sciences Center, SUNY at Stony Book, New York 11794.

Growing Older, Getting Better: A Handbook for the Second Half of Life, by Jane Porcino, Ph.D. New York: Continuum, 1991.

Looking Forward, by Isador Rossman, M.D. New York: E.P. Dutton, 1989.

Paying the Price of Catastrophic Illness: From Accidents to Alzheimer's. A report by the Subcommittee on Health and Long-Term Care, House Select Committee on Aging, 1986. For copies, write to the Subcommittee at the House Office Building, Annex 2, Room 377, Washington, DC 20515.

Pocket Guide to Federal Help for the Disabled Person. Prepared by the Department of Education, 1985 (Stock, No. 113R, $1.00).

"Report of the Public Health Service Task Force on Women's Health Issues: Health Concerns of Older Women," Volume 1, in *Public Health Reports*, Vol. 100, No. 1, January-February 1985, p. 92.

Women's Health: Report of the Public Health Service Task Force on Women's Health Issues, Volume II. Prepared by the Public Health Service, 1985. For copies, write to Dr. Agnes H. Donahue, Executive Secretary, PHS Coordinating Committee on Women's Health Issues, National Institutes of Health, Westwood Building, Room 949, Bethesda, MD 20892.

Who's Who in Health Care*

In many cases, the family doctor is no longer the sole provider of medical care and advice for older Americans. Older people are treated not only by doctors and nurses, but by technicians, medical assistants, and therapists. With this variety of health providers, it is important to understand which professional can offer the best and least costly care for a specific problem and which services normally will be paid by Medicare.

The following definitions cover some, but not all, of the medical practitioners frequently seen by older people:

Doctors of medicine (M.D.) use all accepted methods of medical care. They treat diseases and injuries, provide preventive care, do routine checkups, prescribe drugs, and do some surgery. M.D.'s complete medical school plus 3 to 7 years of graduate medical education. They must be licensed by the state in which they practice.

Doctors of osteopathic medicine (D.O.) provide general health care to individuals and families. The training osteopaths receive is similar to that of an M.D. In addition to treating patients with drugs, surgery, and other treatments, a D.O. may emphasize movement in treating problems of muscles, bones, and joints.

Family practitioners are M.D.'s or D.O.'s who specialize in providing comprehensive, continuous health care for all family members, regardless of age or sex.

Geriatricians are physicians with special training in the diagnosis, treatment, and prevention of disorders in older people. Geriatric medicine recognizes aging as a normal process, not a disease state.

---

* Source: *Age Page*, National Institute on Aging, U.S. Department of Health and Human Services, Public Health Service, National Institutes of Health, Gaithersburg, MD 20898; 800-222-2225.

Internists (M.D. or D.O.) specialize in the diagnosis and medical treatment of diseases in adults. Internists do not deliver babies.

Surgeons treat diseases, injuries, and deformities by operating on the body. A general surgeon is qualified to perform many common operations, but many specialize in one area of the body. For example, neurosurgeons treat disorders relating to the nervous system, spinal cord, and brain; orthopedic surgeons treat disorders of the bones, joints, muscles, ligaments, and tendons; and thoracic surgeons treat disorders to the chest.

The above physicians may refer patients to the following specialists:

- Cardiologist — a heart specialist
- Dermatologist — a skin specialist
- Endocrinologist — a specialist in disorders of the glands of internal secretion, such as diabetes
- Gastroenterologist — a specialist in diseases of the digestive tract
- Gynecologist — a specialist in the female reproductive system
- Hematologist — a specialist in disorders of the blood
- Nephrologist — a specialist in the function and diseases of the kidneys
- Neurologist — a specialist in disorders of the nervous system
- Oncologist — a specialist in cancer
- Ophthalmologist — an eye specialist
- Otolaryngologist — a specialist in diseases of the ear, nose, and throat
- Physiatrist — a specialist in physical medicine and rehabilitation
- Psychiatrist — a specialist in mental, emotional, and behavioral disorders
- Pulmonary specialist — a physician who treats disorders of the lungs and chest

- Rheumatologist — a specialist in arthritis and rheumatism
- Urologist — a specialist in the urinary system in both sexes and the male reproductive system

Most of the services of M.D.'s and D.O.'s are covered by Medicare.

Dental Care

Dentists (D.D.S. or D.M.D.) treat oral conditions such as gum disease and tooth decay. They give regular checkups and routine dental and preventive care, fill cavities, remove teeth, provide dentures, and check for cancers in the mouth. Dentists can prescribe medication and perform oral surgery. A general dentist might refer patients to a specialist such as an **oral surgeon**, who does difficult tooth removals and surgery on the jaw; an **endodontist**, who is an expert on root canals; a **periodontist**, who is knowledgeable about gum diseases; or a dentist who specializes in geriatrics. Medicare will not pay for any dental care except for surgery on the jaw or facial bones.

Eye Care

Ophthalmologists (M.D. or D.O.) specialize in the diagnosis and treatment of eye diseases. They also prescribe eyeglasses and contact lenses. Ophthalmologists can prescribe drugs and perform surgery. They often treat older people who have glaucoma and cataracts. Medicare helps pay for all medically necessary surgery or treatment of eye diseases and for exams and eyeglasses to correct vision after cataract surgery. But it will not pay for a routine exam, eyeglasses, or contact lenses.

Optometrists (O.D.) generally have a bachelor's degree plus four years of graduate training in a school of optometry. They are trained to diagnose eye abnormalities and prescribe, supply, and adjust eyeglasses and contact lenses. In most states optometrists can use drugs to diagnose eye disorders. An optometrist may refer patients to an ophthalmologist or other medical specialist in cases requiring medication or surgery. Medicare pays for only a limited number of optometric services.

Opticians fit, supply, and adjust eyeglasses and contact lenses which have been prescribed by an ophthalmologist or optometrist. They cannot examine or test the eyes, or prescribe glasses or drugs. Opticians are licensed in 22 states and may have formal training. Traditionally, most opticians are trained on the job.

Mental Health Care

Psychiatrists (M.D. or D.O.) treat people with mental and emotional difficulties. They can prescribe medication and counsel patients, as well as perform diagnostic tests to determine if there are physical problems. Medicare will pay for a portion of both inpatient and outpatient psychiatric costs.

Psychologists (Ph.D., Psy.D., Ed.D., or M.A.) are health care professionals trained and licensed to assess, diagnose, and treat people with mental, emotional, or behavioral disorders. Psychologists counsel people through individual, group, or family therapy. Medicare will pay for a portion of psychologists' counseling services when performed in connection with the services of a psychiatrist or other physician.

Nursing Care

Registered nurses (R.N.) may have 2, 3, or 4 years of education in a nursing school. In addition to giving medicine, administering treatments, and educating patients, R.N.'s also work in doctors' offices, clinics, and community health agencies. Medicare does not cover private duty nursing. It helps pay for general nursing services by reimbursing hospitals, skilled nursing facilities, and home health agencies for part of the nurses' salaries.

Nurse practitioners (R.N. or N.P.) are registered nurses with training beyond basic nursing education. They perform physical examinations and diagnostic tests, counsel patients, and develop treatment programs. Nurse practitioners may work independently, such as in rural clinics, or may be staff members at hospitals and other health facilities. They are educated in a number of specialties, including gerontological nursing. Medicare will help pay for services performed under the supervision of a doctor.

Licensed practical nurses (L.P.N.) have from 12 to 18 months of training and are most frequently found in hospitals and long-term care facilities where they provide much of the routine patient care. They also assist physicians and registered nurses.

Rehabilitative Care

Occupational therapists (O.T.) assist those whose ability to function has been impaired by accident, illness, or other disability. They increase or restore independence in feeding, bathing, dressing, homemaking, and social experiences through specialized activities designed to improve function. Occupational therapy services are paid by Medicare if the patient is in a hospital or a skilled nursing facility or is receiving home health care. Coverage is also available for services provided in physicians' offices or to hospital outpatients. O.T.'s have either a bachelor's or master's degree with special training in occupational therapy.

Physical therapists (P.T.) help people whose strength, ability to move, or sensation is impaired. They may use exercise; heat, cold, or water therapy; or other treatments to control pain, strengthen muscles, and improve coordination. All P.T.'s complete a bachelor's degree and some receive further postgraduate training. Patients are usually referred to a physical therapist by a doctor, and Medicare pays some of the costs of outpatient treatments. Physical therapy performed in a hospital or skilled nursing facility is covered by Medicare.

Speech-language pathologists are concerned with speech and language problems. **Audiologists** are concerned with hearing disorders. Both specialists test and evaluate patients and provide treatment to restore as much normal function as possible. Many speech-language pathologists work with stroke victims, people who have had their vocal cords removed, or those who have developmental speech and language disorders. Audiologists work with people who have difficulty hearing. They recommend and sometimes dispense hearing aids. Speech-language pathologists and audiologists have at least a master's degree. Most are licensed by the state in which they practice. Medicare generally will cover the diagnostic services of speech-language pathologists and audiologists; it will not cover routine hearing evaluations or hearing aid services.

General Care

Pharmacists are knowledgeable about the chemical makeup and correct use of medicines — the names, ingredients, side effects, and uses in the treatment of medical problems. Pharmacists have legal authority to dispense drugs according to formal instructions issued by physicians, dentists, or podiatrists. They also can provide information on nonprescription products sold in pharmacies. Pharmacists must complete 5 to 6 years of college, fulfill a practical experience requirements, and pass a state licensing examination to practice.

Physician assistants (P.A.) usually work in hospitals or doctor's offices and do some of the tasks traditionally performed by doctors, such as taking medical histories and doing physical examinations. Education for a P.A. includes 2 to 4 years of college followed by a 2-year period of specialized training. P.A.'s must always be under the supervision of a doctor. Medicare will pay for the services provided by a P.A. only if they are performed in a hospital or doctor's office under the supervision of a physician.

Podiatrists (D.P.M.) diagnose, treat, and prevent diseases and injuries of the foot. They may do surgery, make devices to correct or prevent foot problems, provide toenail care, and prescribe certain drugs. A podiatrist completes four years of professional school and is licensed. Medicare will cover the cost of their services except routine foot care. (However, routine foot care is covered if it is necessary because of diabetic complications.)

Registered dietitians (R.D.) provide nutrition care services and dietary counseling in health and disease. Most work in hospitals, public health agencies, or doctors' offices, but some are in private practice. R.D.'s complete a bachelor's or a graduate degree with a program in dietetics/nutrition and complete an approved program in dietetic practice such as an internship. Medicare generally will not pay for dietitian services; however, it does reimburse hospitals and skilled nursing facilities for a portion of dietitian's salaries.

"Nutritionist" is a broad term. Currently, practitioners who wish to call themselves nutritionists need not fulfill a licensing or certification requirement. The title may be used by a wide range of people, including R.D.'s, those who take a correspondence or other short-term course in nutrition, or even people who are self-taught. Before seeking the advice of a health practitioner in nutrition, it is a good idea to ask what kind of training and practical experience the person has received.

Social workers in health care settings go after community services for patients, provide counseling when necessary, and help patients and their families handle problems related to physical and mental illness and disability. They frequently coordinate the multiple aspects of care related to illness, including discharge planning from hospitals. A social worker's education ranges from a bachelor's degree to a doctorate. Most have a master's degree (M.S.W.). Medicare covers services provided by social workers if they work in such settings as hospitals, home health care agencies, hospices, and health maintenance organizations.

These and other health professionals are especially important to older adults, some of whom require a great deal of medical attention. Ideally, all health professionals will work together to provide older people with care that is comprehensive, cost-effective, and compassionate.

Resources

For additional resources on health and aging, write to the National Institute on Aging Information Center, P.O. Box 8057, Gaithersburg, MD 20898-8057.

Getting Your Affairs in Order[*]

One thing each of us, young and old, can do to plan for the future is to get our financial and personal records in order. These records can be useful for budgeting income, for making investments, or for retirement and estate planning.

Older people sometimes need help from relatives and friends with managing their legal or financial affairs — either temporarily or by having these responsibilities gradually assumed. Because the person who provides care often has little knowledge of vital information and records, the task is much simpler if papers are already in order.

Each situation is different, but the following suggestions may help you to begin organizing your financial and personal records.

Personal Records

A personal records file should include the following information:

- Full legal name
- Social Security number
- Legal residence
- Date and place of birth
- Names and addresses of spouse and children (or location of death certificate if any are deceased)
- Location of will or trust
- Location of birth certificate and certificates of marriage, divorce, and citizenship
- List of employers and dates of employment
- Education and military records
- Religious affiliation, name of church or synagogue, and names of clergy
- Memberships in organizations and awards received

[*] Source: *Age Page*, National Institute on Aging, U.S. Department of Health and Human Services, Public Health Service, National Institutes of Health, Gaithersburg, MD 20898; 800-222-2225.

- Names and addresses of close friends, relatives, doctors, and lawyers or financial advisors
- Requests, preferences, or prearrangements for burial

A family member or friend should know the location of this personal records file and of all important papers and documents. It is not necessary to reveal the contents of wills or trusts.

Financial Records

A financial records file is a place to list information about insurance policies, bank accounts, deeds, investments, and other valuables. Here is a suggested outline:

- Sources of income and assets (pension funds, interest income, etc.)
- Social Security and Medicare information
- Investment income (stocks, bonds, property)
- Insurance information (life, health, and property) with policy numbers
- Bank accounts (checking, savings, and credit union)
- Location of safe deposit boxes
- Copy of most recent income tax return
- Liabilities — what is owed to whom and when payments are due
- Mortgages and debts — how and when paid
- Credit card and charge account names and numbers
- Property taxes
- Location of all personal items such as jewelry or family treasures

Having this information available can help you plan for any changes that might come up in the years ahead — such as retirement, a move, or a death in the family — by providing the needed details to make the best decisions.

An important consideration in financial planning is the cost of medical services and long-term care, although there is often no easy or simple way to determine how to meet these future needs. It is important to learn what is and is not covered by **Medicare**, the program under the Social Security Administration that provides medical care for older people. For example, Medicare does not cover most nursing home or home care. **Medicaid** is a program for people with limited income; it pays for some community services. New laws may change Medicare and Medicaid coverage; but meanwhile, you may wish to explore the developing long-term care insurance options. State laws vary, so it is important to check with your area office on aging, a lawyer, or financial planner for information related to estates, inheritance, taxes, insurance, Medicaid, or Medicare.

Caring for an older person or preparing for your own old age can be more successfully managed by making decisions and arrangements before a crisis develops. Three legal documents (power of attorney, durable power of attorney, and living will) can be helpful in assuming responsibility for another person's affairs. A standard power of attorney or durable power of attorney can be set up to give one person power to handle personal or financial matters for another. Because the standard power of attorney loses its effectiveness if the principal becomes legally incompetent, a durable power of attorney is better. A durable power of attorney continues even if a person becomes incapacitated. A living will provides written instructions concerning health care in the event of terminal illness. Living wills are recognized in most, but not all, states. The living will makes it easier for a person to know how to make difficult health care decisions on a relative's behalf and can help avoid family conflict.

Resources

Consult a lawyer before setting up a power of attorney, durable power of attorney, joint account, trust, or guardianship. Be sure to ask for the cost of a legal consultation before visiting a lawyer. For help in locating a lawyer, most libraries have legal directories or write to the American Bar Association's Lawyer Referral and Information Service at 750 North Lake Shore Drive, Chicago, IL 60611.

Free legal and financial services are often available to help older people and their families. For assistance, contact your local agency on aging or one of the following organizations: National Association of Area Agencies on Aging, 1112 Sixteenth Street, NW, Suite 100, Washington, DC 20036; the National Association of State Units of Aging, 2033 K Street, NW, Suite 304, Washington, DC 20006; or the Legal Counsel for the Elderly, 601 E Street, NW, 4th Floor, Washington, DC 20049.

The National Institute on Aging provides information on health and aging. Write to the NIA Information Center, P.O. Box 8057, Gaithersburg, MD 20898-8057.